PERSONALITY

FOURTEENTH EDITION

THEORY AND RESEARCH

Daniel Cervone
Professor of Psychology, University of Illinois at Chicago

Lawrence A. Pervin†
Professor Emeritus, Rutgers University

EDITORIAL DIRECTOR	Veronica Visentin
ASSISTANT EDITOR	Ethan Lipson
SENIOR EDITORIAL MANAGER	Leah Michael
EDITORIAL MANAGER	Judy Howarth
CONTENT MANAGEMENT DIRECTOR	Lisa Wojcik
CONTENT MANAGER	Nichole Urban
SENIOR CONTENT SPECIALIST	Nicole Repasky
PRODUCTION EDITOR	Umamaheswari Gnanamani
PHOTO RESEARCHER	Preethi Devaraj
COVER PHOTO CREDIT	PeopleImages/Getty Images

This book was set in 10/12 Times LT Std by SPi Global and printed and bound by Quad Graphics Versailles.

Founded in 1807, John Wiley & Sons, Inc. has been a valued source of knowledge and understanding for more than 200 years, helping people around the world meet their needs and fulfill their aspirations. Our company is built on a foundation of principles that include responsibility to the communities we serve and where we live and work.

Evaluation copies are provided to qualified academics and professionals for review purposes only, for use in their courses during the next academic year. These copies are licensed and may not be sold or transferred to a third party. Upon completion of the review period, please return the evaluation copy to Wiley. Return instructions and a free of charge return shipping label are available at: www.wiley.com/go/returnlabel. If you have chosen to adopt this textbook for use in your course, please accept this book as your complimentary desk copy. Outside of the United States, please contact your local sales representative.

ISBN: 9781119492061 (POD)
ISBN: 9781119492078 (EVAL)

Library of Congress Cataloging-in-Publication Data

Names: Cervone, Daniel, author. | Pervin, Lawrence A., author.
Title: Personality : theory and research / Daniel Cervone, Professor of
 Psychology, University of Illinois at Chicago, Lawrence A. Pervin,
 Professor Emeritus, Rutgers University.
Description: Fourteenth edition. | Hoboken, NJ : John Wiley & Sons, Inc.,
 [2019] | Includes bibliographical references and index. |
Identifiers: LCCN 2018031126 (print) | LCCN 2018033452 (ebook) | ISBN
 9781119492047 (Adobe PDF) | ISBN 9781119492016 (ePub) | ISBN 9781119492061
 (pbk.)
Subjects: LCSH: Personality.
Classification: LCC BF698 (ebook) | LCC BF698 .P375 2019 (print) | DDC
 155.2—dc23
LC record available at https://lccn.loc.gov/2018031126

The inside back cover will contain printing identification and country of origin if omitted from this page. In addition, if the ISBN on the back cover differs from the ISBN on this page, the one on the back cover is correct.

V10017939_031120

To the memory of Lawrence A. Pervin

PREFACE

The 14th edition of *Personality: Theory and Research* begins with sad news. Professor Lawrence A. Pervin passed away on June 23, 2016. The present revision was prepared independently.

Professor Pervin's contributions to personality science are simultaneously appreciated and underappreciated. What is appreciated is his independent scholarly work: research, theory, and especially integrative analyses and critiques of the discipline's research programs and conceptual models. Across the decades, Larry Pervin challenged the field to be better than it was. He tutored us on how to improve.

What likely is underappreciated is the reverberating impact of his professional efforts. For example, readers of the current 29th volume of *Psychological Inquiry* recognize the Journal as a uniquely valuable forum for the development and exchange of ideas in personality and social psychology. But what percentage of readers knows that this entire intellectual exchange, across the decades, owes its existence to the efforts of Larry Pervin, the Journal's founding editor? I also note his efforts in organizing an edited volume of extraordinarily strength, namely, the first edition of the *Handbook of Personality* (Pervin, 1990). Its diverse contributions compelled the reader to explore the challenges that contributing authors posed for one another and the harmonies that could be heard amidst the many voices (Cervone, 1991).

With regard to the present text, Professor Pervin not only is the founding author. He also remains an indelible intellectual presence. His original conception – to combine, for the benefit of the student, coverage of personality theory, personality research, and clinical case examples – continues to provide the book's structure. His impact can be felt throughout the pages of 14e.

To Students and Instructors

It is now well more than four decades since the first edition of this text. The field has developed and the book has changed to keep pace. As described below, *Personality: Theory and Research* contains a major new feature that is designed to keep pace with these developments. But before discussing changes, let's consider what remains the same.

The Aims Remain the Same

The volume's basic aims remain the same as they were when Larry Pervin crafted the first edition:

1. *Present the major theoretical perspectives on personality.* The field's *major* theoretical perspectives are covered in depth. Some textbooks cover numerous theories, including minor perspectives with little relevance to the contemporary scientific field. That strategy bears a cost: When many theories are reviewed, the more influential ones may not be covered in sufficient depth. We strive to provide intellectually deep coverage of each of the field's main theoretical perspectives. Note that by "perspectives" we mean that we cover not only the work of the classic theorists (e.g., Freud, Rogers) but also theoretical and empirical advances by other investigators who embraced the general perspectives developed originally by those theorists.

2. *Achieve balance.* We strive to present unbiased coverage of the theories of personality. This does not mean that our coverage is not critical. We discuss both the strengths and limits of each theory. Our evaluations, however, are not designed to persuade students of the merits of a particular approach but to broaden their understanding and enhance their own critical thinking skills.

3. *Integrate theory and research.* We aim to show the student how theory and research inform one another. Theoretical developments spur research, and research contributes to the development, modification, and evaluation of personality theories.

4. *Integrate case material with theory.* By necessity, theory and research deal with abstractions and generalizations, rather than with specific and unique individuals. To bridge the gap between the general and the specific, we present case study material that illustrates how each theory assesses and interprets the individual. We follow one case throughout the book to show how the various theories relate to the same person. Thus, the student can ask, "Are the pictures of a person gained through the lens of each theory completely different from each other, or do they represent complementary perspectives?" Our inclusion of case material also enables the student who is interested in clinical psychology to see connections between personality psychology and clinical practice.

5. *Provide the basis for comparison of the theories.* Coverage of each of the theoretical perspectives is consistent. We present each theory's treatment of personality structures, processes or dynamics, personality development, and clinical applications. Subsequent to this coverage, we evaluate the theories at the conclusions of chapters. Through the given chapter, students are provided the opportunity to make their own comparisons and begin to come to their own conclusions concerning the merits of each.

6. *Present the field in an accessible manner, while respecting its complexity.* We strive to teach students about the field of personality psychology as it really exists—including some of its nuances and complexities. Yet we strive to make this presentation accessible, including using a writing style that addresses students' interests and questions and provides necessary background content.

New to 14e

Although the goals of the text have remained the same, the content clearly has changed over time, in keeping with changes in the field. Along with deleting or abbreviating coverage of the theories that no longer seemed as important to the field as they once were, we have expanded coverage of others, often in response to feedback from reviewers. As a scientific enterprise, the study of personality is not unlike the unfolding of personality itself, reflecting both continuity and at times dramatic shifts. We have attempted to present both in each new edition of the text. Finally, in accord with the view that sometimes "less is more," in many places we have been more concise and focused in our discussion.

The book's writing style has shifted over the years too; it increasingly features a "conversational" tone. The style is purposeful; the goal is to engage the reader directly in ways that prompt critical thinking. Students probably have more intuitions—often good, solid intuitions—about the material in this course than about any other class in the college curriculum. The textbook author, and classroom instructor, can capitalize on these intuitions to encourage students to think critically about personality science—and science in general.

In addition to these incremental changes, 14e contains a major new feature. Substantial *Contemporary Developments* sections appear within five chapters of the text. Four of these sections are devoted to a topic that receives scant coverage in other texts: *Contemporary Developments in Personality Theory*. The intellectual activity that is personality theory did not cease at the close of the millennium. Investigators continue to pursue the challenges that motived the Grand Theorists of the 20th century. Four such developments are found in within coverage of the four theoretical perspectives that receive multi-chapter coverage in the text: psychodynamic theory, phenomenological theory, trait theory, and social-cognitive theory. The four 21st-century theories that are included were selected not only "on their own merits" but also because each addresses limitations in 20th-century theorizing in a particularly direct manner. The *Contemporary Developments in Personality Theory* material thus is another opportunity for students to think critically. Readers are encouraged to consider limitations in prior theorizing as a prelude to the coverage of new developments.

In addition, Chapter 2 (*The Scientific Study of People*) contains a section on *Contemporary Developments in Personality Research*. Readers learn about computerized text analysis methods through which researchers infer personality characteristics by analyzing spontaneous language use in social media.

Finally, material that previously appeared in print in Chapter 15, *Assessing Personality Theory and Research*, has been moved to the online Instructor Companion Site at www.wiley.com/go/cervone/personality14e. Because that material is a reflection on prior chapters and the state of the professional field, it is not absolutely necessary for understanding the personality theory and research covered in Chapters 1–14. Nonetheless, highly engaged students may wish to revisit topics, contemplate the field, and consider ways in which they themselves can advance it by reading Chapter 15 online.

Professor Pervin and I always hoped that *Personality: Theory and Research* will enable students to appreciate the scientific and practical value of systematic theorizing about the individual, to understand how evidence from case studies and empirical research informs the development of personality theories, and to discover a particular theory of personality that makes personal sense to them and is useful in their own lives.

ACKNOWLEDGMENTS

I thank the Psychology staff at John Wiley & Sons not only for their continued support but also for their suggestions that have strengthened the text. I am also grateful to many students and instructors who have sent me questions and suggestions for future coverage; feel free to keep sending them to dcervone@uic.edu.

I also thank Dr. Walter D. Scott, of Washington State University, for giving permission to include the case study that appears in Chapter 14. Dr. Scott was the therapist for the case, whose assessment tools and case report were prepared collaboratively by Dr. Scott and the author.

I am particularly grateful to Professor Tracy L. Caldwell of Dominican University. Dr. Caldwell prepared the extensive set of supplementary material available at the book's Instructor Companion Site at www.wiley.com/go/cervone/personality14e, suggested the "toolkit" metaphor that appears in Chapter 1, and has provided invaluable input on both science and pedagogy that has strengthened this text across multiple editions.

DANIEL CERVONE

Professor of Psychology, University of Illinois at Chicago

CONTENTS

7 Trait Theories of Personality: Allport, Eysenck, and Cattell   180

8 Trait Theory: The Five-Factor Model and Contemporary Developments   205

9 Biological Foundations of Personality   241

Personality Theory: From Everyday Observations to Systematic Theories

1

Chapter Focus

I can be selfish, but I believe it is because I try to be perfect. Perfect in the sense I want to be an "A" student, a good mother, a loving wife, an excellent employee, a nourishing friend. My significant other thinks I try too hard to be "Mother Teresa" at times—not that that is a bad thing. But I can drive myself insane at times. I have led a hard childhood and adulthood life; therefore I believe I am trying to make up for all the bad times. I want to be productive, good—make a difference in my world.

I'm a real jackass. I'm intelligent enough to do well in school and study genetics but have no idea when to shut up. I often am very offensive and use quite abrasive language, although I'm shy most of the time and talk to few people. I'm sarcastic, cruel, and pompous at times. Yet I've been told that I'm kind and sweet; this may be true, but only to those I deem worthy of speaking to with some frequency. I'm very fond of arguing and pretty much argue for fun.

I have always been described by others as cynical and/or as having integrity. I would describe myself as inquisitive, philosophical and justice-oriented. I craze organization, but my room is the messiest one I have seen thus far ... like the room of a toddler. I am introspective but I don't reach many conclusions about myself. I seem very passive and mellow – but I am just too tired to get fired up.

This person is shy at times. They tend to open up to some people. You never know when they're happy or sad. They never show their real feelings, and when they do it's so hard for them. They did have a trauma experience that closed them up—where they seem to be afraid to let their real self show. They are funny and do have a lot of fun and are fun to be around, but at times it's hard to know if they're really having a good time. The person is loved by a lot of people and is an extremely giving person but doesn't like "seriousness."

These sketches were written by people just like you: students beginning a course on the psychology of personality. When I teach the class, on Day 1, I ask people to describe their personality and that of a friend. Two things happen. First, students can answer the question; when asked to "describe your personality," they rarely say "I don't know how to do that; it's only the first day of personality class." Second, as you see here, their answers are often detailed, nuanced, and insightful—so much so that one is tempted to ask: Is the class filled with personality theorists?

In a sense, it is. We're all personality theorists. We ask about ourselves and others: "Why am I so shy?" "Why are my parents so weird?" "Am I so shy *because* my parents are so weird?" Even before taking a personality class, we devise answers that are sophisticated and often accurate. You already hold ideas about personality and put them to work to understand the events of your day, to anticipate the events of your next day, and to help yourself and your friends handle the stresses, bumps, and bruises of life.

"But"—you may be asking yourself—"if I already know so much about personality, what will I learn in this class? In other words, "What is the professional personality psychologist doing that I'm not doing already?" This chapter addresses this question by introducing the scientific goals and methods of psychologists who study personality. But first, we will define our key term and comment on the status of this scientific field.

Questions to be Addressed in this Chapter

1. How do scientific theories of personality differ from the ideas about persons that you develop in your daily life?

2. Why is there more than one personality theory and in what general ways do the theories differ?

3. What are personality psychologists trying to accomplish; in other words, what aspects of persons and individual differences are they trying to understand and what factors are so important that they must be addressed in any personality theory?

Defining Personality

Personality psychology is concerned with the dynamics of intra-individual functioning and the coherence and thematic unity of particular lives.

Block (1992, p. xiii)

You already have an intuitive understanding of "personality." Is a formal definition even necessary? It is because—as so often happens with words—different people use the word "personality" in different ways. The differences can create confusion in both an introductory course and the professional field (Cervone, 2005). Let us therefore examine some ways in which the word "personality" is used. We then will provide a formal definition of the term.

In one common usage, people say, for example, that "Ellen DeGeneres has a lot of personality" or "My psych professor has no personality." Personality here means "charisma". This is *not* the way that personality psychologists use the word; this book is most definitely *not* about "Charisma: Theory and Research".

Professional psychologists use the word "personality" in two ways. Specifically, they propose two types of personality variables, that is, two types of concepts for understanding people and how they differ.

1. **Dispositions.**   One type of variable is *personality dispositions*. In general, in the sciences, dispositions are descriptions; dispositional terms describe what a person or thing tends to do. A glass vase tends to break if you bump into it. "Fragile" is a dispositional term that describes this tendency. Some types of turtles tend to live very long lives. "Longevity" describes this tendency (turtles are "high in longevity" compared to many other species). In the study of personality, psychologists try to identify the personality dispositions that best describe individuals and the major ways that people differ from one another.

   People have a lot of tendencies: sleeping when tired, eating when hungry, bored when reading a textbook. Which count as *personality* dispositions? You can figure this out for yourself. Think about how you use the word "personality," and you will quickly realize that you employ the word to describe psychological characteristics with two qualities: "personality" tendencies are (a) *enduring* and (b) *distinctive*.

   - By "enduring," we mean that personality characteristics are at least somewhat consistent across time and place. If one day you find yourself acting a little strange—maybe because you are stressed about something—you likely would not say that your "personality has changed" on that day. You use the word "personality" to describe characteristics that endure for long periods of time: months and years and perhaps your entire life.
   - By "distinctive," we mean that personality characteristics differentiate people from one another. If asked to describe your personality, you would not say, "I tend to feel sad when bad things happen but happy when good things happen." *Everybody* feels sad/happy when bad/good things happen. These tendencies are not distinctive. But if, like one of our opening sketches, someone is *"shy most of the time … sarcastic, cruel, and pompous at times … yet kind and sweet to those deemed worthy of speaking to,"* then *that* is a distinctive—and is therefore a (rather complex) personality disposition.

2. **Inner Mental Life.**   A second set of concepts refers to inner mental life. Personality psychologists study the beliefs, emotions, and motivations that comprise the mental life of the individual. Conflicts between alternative desires; memories that spring to mind and fill you with emotion; emotions that interfere with your ability to think; long-term goals that

make otherwise mundane tasks meaningful; self-doubts that undermine efforts to achieve these goals—these and more are the features of mental life targeted by the personality psychologist.

A technical term—used in the quote above, from the personality psychologist Jack Block—for this scientific target is "intraindividual functioning". Personality psychology is not only concerned with differences between people or *inter*individual differences. Personality psychologists are fundamentally concerned with the interplay of thoughts and emotions within the mind or *intra*individual mental functioning.

Many branches of psychology study mental life. What's unique about personality psychology? One distinctive feature is the field's concern with how multiple aspects of mental life are connected to one another or "cohere" (Block, 1992; Cervone & Shoda, 1999). Compare this interest to the primary interests in other branches of psychology. A cognitive psychologist may study memory. A social psychologist may study self-concept. An educational psychologist might address perfectionistic tendencies at school. But the personality psychologist is concerned with how these distinct systems cohere in the life of an individual. You just saw such personality coherence in the opening quote above; the person's memory (of a hard life) was connected to her self-concept (being a productive person who makes a difference to the world), which, in turn, explained her perfectionism ("striving to be perfect").

A useful concept to describe these connections is "system". A **system** is any connected set of interacting parts that comprise whole. Personality can be thought of as a system. Distinct psychological qualities—beliefs, values, emotions, goals, skills, memories—influence one another and comprise the person as a whole (Mischel & Shoda, 1995; Nowak, Vallacher, & Zochowski, 2005)

We now are in a position to define personality. In psychology, **personality** refers to *psychological systems that contribute to an individual's enduring and distinctive patterns of experience and behavior.* As you can see, the definition combines the two meanings above. Ideally, the personality psychologist will be able to identify psychological systems (aspects of inner mental life) that help to explain people's distinctive experiences and actions (their dispositions).

Why Study Personality?

Why take a course in personality? One way to answer this question is to compare the material in this course with other courses in psychology. Consider intro psych—the typical Psych 101. Students are sometimes disappointed with its content. The course does not seem to be about whole, intact people. Instead, one learns about parts of people (e.g., the visual system, the autonomic nervous system, long-term memory, etc.) and some of the things people do (learning, problem-solving, decision-making, etc.). "Where in psychology," one reasonably might ask, "does one learn about the whole, intact person?" The answer is here, in personality psychology. Personality theorists address the total person, trying to understand how different aspects of an individual's psychological life are related to each other and relate also to the society and culture in which the person lives (Magnusson, 2012). One reason for studying personality psychology, then, is that it addresses psychology's most complex and interesting topic: the whole, integrated, coherent, unique individual.

Another reason is the impact of personality psychology on the wider intellectual world. Personality theories have been influential not only within scientific psychology. They also have influenced society at large. In fact, they have been so influential that they probably have affected your thinking even before you enrolled in this course. Have you ever said that someone has a big "ego"? Or called a friend an "introvert"? Or asked whether a slip-of-the-tongue reveals something about the hidden beliefs of the speaker? If so, you were already using terms and ideas that come from personality psychology.

Here are three indications of the influence of personality psychology:

- At the end of the 20th century, scholars (Haggbloom et al., 2002) identified the most influential scientific psychologists of the 20th century. Who made the list? In the top 25, the *majority* were investigators who contributed to the psychology of personality.

- The end of the century was also the end of the millennium. A television network polled historians and others to determine the 100 most influential people—of any sort—of the past 1000 years. The only psychologist to make the list—and easily, at #12—was a personality theorist: the psychodynamic theorist, Sigmund Freud (A & E's Biography: 100 Most Influential People of the Millennium https://wmich.edu/mus-gened/mus150/biography100.html).

- In 2007, a statistical analysis identified the highest-impact book authors in the humanities or social sciences (fields including not only psychology, but also political science, philosophy, linguistics, literary criticism, sociology, and cultural studies). The singularly most-cited living author was a personality theorist: the social cognitive theorist Albert Bandura (https://www.timeshighereducation.com/news/most-cited-authors-of-books-in-the-humanities-2007/405956.article).

Here, in personality theory and research, you will find the most influential ideas in the history of the psychological sciences.

Three Goals for the Personality Theorist

Now let's return to an earlier question: What is the professional personality psychologist doing that you, the reader, are not?

Consider what you do. You interact—in person and electronically—with friends and family. You observe people not only in person, but also in movies and videos, and (through writing) in books, magazines, and blogs. You think about yourself: your strengths and weaknesses, hopes and plans, and responsibilities to others. And you learn how others do these same things, when they tell you about themselves, *their* friends and families, and *their* hopes and dreams. Somehow, from this everyday observations, you develop thoughts about human nature and the main ways that people differ from one another.

For most people, that is plenty of thinking about personality. But personality psychologists are not "most people." Psychologists who study personality pursue three goals that distinguish their activities from the nonprofessional who is interested in persons.

1. Scientific Observation

Personality psychologists do not observe people casually. Instead, they pursue *scientific* observation. The features that make observations "scientific" vary from one science to another. In personality psychology, three stand out:

1. **Study diverse groups of people.** Psychologists cannot base personality theories merely on observations of people they happen to run into in daily life. They must observe diverse groups of individuals, to ensure that conclusions about personality represent the lives the world's citizens. This need is particularly critical because people from different nations and cultures may differ in ways that become apparent only once they are studied within their specific life contexts (Cheng, Wang, & Golden, 2011). Not only nations and cultures, but

also subcultures—associated with ethnicity, spiritual beliefs, or economic circumstances—may display distinctive psychological characteristics (Oyserman, 2017).

In today's personality science, researchers often succeed admirably in reaching such diverse participants group. For example, one research team summarized self-descriptions of personality from participants in 56 nations (Schmitt et al., 2007). Another studied personality tendencies across regions of the globe and found that more mild climates foster more outgoing (sociable, open-minded) personality styles. The ability to study global populations is made easier by a technological advance. By analyzing "big data"—large bodies of information acquired by recording computer users' preferences and statements on social media and other internet sites (Bleidorn, Hopwood, & Wright, 2017)—researchers can get information about people throughout the world.

These trends, however, are recent. Before the 21st century, the majority of participants in psychological research were from Europe and North America—which contain less than 20% of the world's population, combined. This is significant in that all of the major theories of personality developed prior to the present century.

2. **Ensure that observations of people are objective.** A second requirement is "objectivity". Information that is *not* influenced by the subjective personal opinions and desires of the person getting the information is called "objective". If you step on a scale and it tells you your weight, the scale is "objective": It is not influenced by your own subjective desires for a different weight. Psychologists strive for scientific methods that provide information about personality that is objective.

Objective methods promote a key goal of science: replicability. Whenever one scientist reports a finding, others should be able to replicate it; in other words, they should be able to repeat the procedures and get the same result. Using an example above, if one team of researchers found that mild climates predict outgoing personality styles, you should be able to repeat their procedures and find the same thing.

It turns out that replicability is difficult to achieve—so much so that psychology recently has experienced a "replication crisis" (Shrout & Rodgers, 2017). Researchers have sometimes found it hard to replicate well-known findings. Although these difficulties primarily have occurred in branches of the field other than personality psychology, the overall question of replicability is significant in our field—particularly so because one valuable source of evidence in personality psychology cannot, even in principle, be replicated: case studies. Case studies are in-depth examinations of a particular individual (see Chapter 2). For example, a therapist might report a case study of a client in therapy. As a general rule, case studies cannot be replicated; if you read a clinical case study, you cannot contact the client and repeat the study.

3. **Use specialized tools to study thinking, emotion, and neurobiological systems.** Psychologists observe people, just as you do. But they also make observations using specialized tools. These tools often are designed to overcome specific obstacles to obtaining scientific information. Here are two examples. Suppose that you want to learn about the personality characteristics of large numbers of people. An obstacle is the sheer cost and difficulty of contacting people and having them complete personality tests. A specialized tool researchers use to overcome this obstacle is computer software that assesses personality characteristics by analyzing the language use in social media (Park et al., 2014). A second example is that, if you try to study people's feelings—their moods and emotions—by asking them how they feel, some people are reluctant to discuss their feelings openly. Researchers have developed tools to assess moods and emotions without ever explicitly asking people to talk about themselves (Quirin, Kazén, & Kuhl, 2009). For example, if research participants are asked to describe the emotion expressed in an abstract image, their descriptions reveal their own emotional state (Bartoszek & Cervone, 2017).

2. Scientific Theory

The fundamental goal of science is to *explain* events (Salmon, 1989). Scientists develop explanatory frameworks—that is, theories—to explain their scientific observations.

What exactly is a scientific theory? The word "theory" can be used in different ways. For example, you might say that you "have a theory that my friend Liliana is anxious because she's really attracted to some guy and hasn't told him." Even if you are right, your idea about Liliana is not, in and of itself, a scientific theory of Liliana's personality. Scientific theories of personality have three distinctive qualities; they are *systematic*, *testable*, and *comprehensive*.

1. **Systematic.**   As we have noted, you already have developed lots of different ideas about different people. But you probably have not gone to the trouble of relating all of them to one another. Suppose that on one you say "Liliana is anxious because she's really attracted to some guy and hasn't told him" and on another you say "My mother gets anxious all the time; she must have inherited it." If so, you usually do not have to relate the statements to each other; people don't force you to explain why one case had an interpersonal cause (relationship breakup) and another had a biological cause (inherited tendencies). But personality psychologists must relate all their ideas to one another, to create a systematically organized theory.

2. **Testable.**   If you tell a friend "My parents are weird," your friend is not likely to say "Prove it!" But the scientific community says "Prove it!" any time a scientist says anything. The personality psychologist must develop theoretical ideas that can be tested by objective scientific evidence. This is true of any science, of course. But in personality psychology, attaining the goal of a testable theory can be particularly difficult. This is because the field's subject matter includes features of mental life—goals, dreams, wishes, impulses, conflicts, emotions, unconscious mental defenses—that are enormously complex and inherently difficult to study scientifically.

3. **Comprehensive.**   Suppose that you have just rented an apartment and are considering inviting in a roommate to share rent costs. When deciding who to invite, you might ask yourself questions about their personalities: Are they fun loving? Conscientious? Open-minded? And so forth. Yet there also are a lot of other questions that you do not have to ask: If they are fun loving, is it primarily because they inherited this quality or learned it? If they are conscientious now, are they likely to be more or less conscientious 20 years from now? When thinking about persons, you can be selective, asking some questions and ignoring others. But a personality theory must be comprehensive, addressing all significant questions about personality functioning, development, and individual differences. This is what distinguishes personality theory from theorizing in most other branches of psychology. The personality theorist cannot be satisfied with studying "parts" of persons. The personality theorist is charged with comprehensively understanding the person as a whole.

3. Applications: From Observation and Theory to Practice

As the quotes from students that open this chapter make clear, people formulate insightful ideas about personality prior to studying personality psychology. Yet, in everyday life, people rarely convert their personal insights into systematic applications. You may recognize that one friend's problem is a lack of self-confidence and that another's is an inability to open up emotionally. Yet, after realizing this, you probably don't design therapies to boost people's confidence in themselves or enable them to open up. Personality psychologists, however, do this. They aim not only to develop testable, systematic theory but also to convert their theoretical ideas into beneficial applications.

In fact, many of the personality theorists you will learn about in this book did not start out in personality psychology. Instead, they often first worked as counselors, clinical psychologists, or physicians. Their personality theories were efforts to understand why their clients were experiencing psychological distress and how that distress could be reduced.

In summary, personality psychologists aim to (1) to observe people scientifically, (2) develop theories that are systematic, testable, and comprehensive, and (3) to turn their research findings and theoretical conceptions into practical applications. It is these goals that distinguish the work of the personality psychologist from that of the poet, the playwright, the pop psychologist—or the student writing personality sketches on the first day of class. Lots of people develop insightful ideas about the human condition. But the personality psychologist is uniquely charged with organizing theoretical ideas into comprehensive, testable, and practical theories.

Throughout this book, we evaluate the personality theories by judging how well they achieve these goals. This book's final chapter, a commentary on the current state of the field that can be found on the text's companion website www.wiley.com/college/cervone, judges how successful the field of personality psychology as a whole has been in achieving these five aims.

Answering Questions about Persons Scientifically: Understanding Structures, Processes, Development, and Therapeutic Change

Personality psychologist addresses four distinct topics; in other words, there are four issues that every personality theory must address. We can introduce them with a simple "mental experiment".

Think of someone you know well, for example, a good friend or family member. Two things you know for sure are:

1. Whatever the individual's personality is like today, it likely was similar last month and last year, and likely will be similar next month and next year. You might say that personality is "stable" over time.

2. Despite this stability in personality, the individual's thoughts, feelings, and actions also change. Sometimes they are happy and other times sad. Sometimes they are in control of their emotions and sometimes they "fly off the handle."

Two things you do not know absolutely for sure, but that probably think are correct, are:

3. If you saw the person when they were a toddler or a grade schooler, their personality would not be the same as it is now. Their personality likely has changed, or "developed," over time.

4. If the person suddenly experiences a period of psychological distress—for example, a period of depression or anxiety—they probably could "bounce back" from this. In fact, there might be something you could do to improve the person's psychological well-being.

These four points correspond directly to the topics addressed by personality psychologists. The psychologist introduces formal scientific terms to describe the topics, but the topics themselves are fundamentally the same. They are: (1) personality *structure*—the enduring "building blocks" of personality; (2) personality *process*—dynamic changes in thinking, emotion, and motivation that can occur from one moment to the next; (3) *growth and development*—how we develop into the unique person each of us is, and (4) *psychopathology and behavior change*—how people change and why they sometimes resist change or are unable to change. We introduce these topics now. You will see them again, over and over, in later chapters.

Structure

People possess psychological qualities that endure from day to day and from year to year. The enduring qualities that distinguish individuals from one another are referred to as personality **structures**.

Structural concepts in personality psychology are similar to structural concepts you are familiar with from other fields. For example, from study of human biology, you already know that there are enduring biological structures including individual organs (the heart, the lungs) and organ systems (the circulatory system, the digestive system). Analogously, personality theorists hope to identify enduring psychological structures. These structures may involve emotion (e.g., a biological structure that contributes to good or bad mood), motivation (e.g., a desire to achieve succeed or to be accepted by others), cognition (e.g., a negative belief about oneself that contributes to states of depression, Beck, 1991), or skills (e.g., a high or low level of "social intelligence," Cantor & Kihlstrom, 1987).

You will see throughout this textbook that the different personality theories provide different conceptions of personality structure. A more technical way of saying this is that the theories adopt different **units of analysis** when analyzing personality structure (Little, Lecci, & Watkinson, 1992). The "units of analysis" idea is important, so we will illustrate it.

As you read this textbook, you may be sitting in a chair. If we ask you to describe it, the chair, you may say that it "weighs about 15 pounds," or that it "is made of wood," or that it "is unattractive". Weight, physical substance (the wood), and attractiveness are different units of analysis for describing the chair. Although the units may be related in some way (e.g., wood chairs may be heavier than plastic ones), they plainly are distinct.

The general idea is that virtually anything can be described in more than one way—that is, through more than one unit of analysis. Personality is no exception. The different theories of personality you will learn about in this book use different units of analysis to analyze personality structure. The resulting analyses may each be correct, in their own way. Yet each may provide different types of information about personality.

We will illustrate this point with an example: a difference between "trait" and "type" units of analysis.

One popular unit of analysis is that of a personality **trait**. The word *trait* generally refers to a consistent style of emotion or behavior that a person displays across a variety of situations. Someone who consistently acts in a way that we call "conscientious" might be said to have the trait of "conscientiousness". A term that is essentially synonymous with *trait* is *disposition;* traits describe what a person tends to do or is predisposed to do. You probably already use trait terms to describe people. If you say that a friend is "outgoing," "honest," or "disagreeable," you are using trait terms. There is something implicit—something that "goes without saying"—when you use these terms. If you say that a friend is, for example, "outgoing," the term implies two things: (1) the person tends to be outgoing *on average* in his/her own daily behavior (even if, on occasion, he/she does not act this way), and (2) the person tends to be outgoing *compared to others*. If you use trait terms this way, then you are using them in the same way as most personality psychologists do.

Traits usually are thought of as continuous dimensions. Like the biological traits of height and weight, people have more or less of a given trait, with most people being in the middle of the dimension.

A different unit of analysis is **type**. A personality "type" is a clustering of many different traits. For example, some researchers have explored combinations of personality traits and suggested that there are three types of persons: (1) people who respond in an adaptive, resilient manner to psychological stress; (2) people who respond in a manner that is socially inhibited or emotionally overcontrolled; and (3) people who respond in an uninhibited or undercontrolled manner (Asendorpf, Caspi, & Hofstee, 2002).

Types, unlike traits, may be thought of as distinct categories. In other words, people of one versus another type do not simply have more or less of a given characteristic but have categorically different characteristics.

"I'm neither a good cop nor a bad cop, Jerome. Like yourself, I'm a complex amalgam of positive and negative personality traits that emerge or not, depending on circumstances."

Process

Just as theories can be compared in terms of how they treat personality structure, one can compare their treatment of personality processes. In any scientific field, a "process" is something that changes over time; as the philosopher Wittgenstein put it, we use the word "process" to refer to psychological phenomena that "have duration and a course" (Wittgenstein, 1980, §836). A personality **process** thus is a psychological activity (involving thoughts, feelings, or actions) that may change over relatively brief periods of time.

Even though you are the same person from one day to the next, you experience rapidly changing personality processes all the time. One moment you are studying. The next, you are distracted by thoughts of a friend. Next, you're hungry and getting a snack. Then you're feeling guilty about not studying. Next, you're feeling guilty about overeating. This rapidly changing flow of motivation, emotion, and action is what personality psychologists attempt to explain when studying personality processes.

Personality processes are often referred to by a more technical name: personality "dynamics". When using this term, psychologists are borrowing a word from a different field of study: physics. In physics, "dynamics" refers to the ways in which physical objects move across some period of time (e.g., how an object moves toward Earth if you drop it). In personality, "dynamics" refer to psychological processes (involving thinking, emotion, or motivation) that change over time (Cervone & Little, 2017).

Study of personality processes, or dynamics, is where the contemporary science of personality started. European psychologists of the late 19th century became interested in how different parts of mental life—for example, memory of past events and conscious experiences in the present—become connected to one another in the self-concept of an individual person (Lombardo & Foschi, 2003). Throughout the first two-thirds of the 20th century, dynamic processes remained a centerpiece of personality theory. In the late 20th century, personality psychology's focus of attention shifted somewhat, with more researchers studying the stable differences between people rather than the personality dynamics of the individual. But in the current field, the study of personality dynamics is, in a sense, "making a comeback" (Rauthmann, in press). Researchers increasingly explore dynamic changes in personality dynamics that occur across the diverse circumstances of an individual's life.

Just as in the study of personality structure, one finds that, in the study of personality processes, different theorists employ different units of analysis. The differences commonly involve different approaches to the study of motivation. Personality theorists emphasize different motivational processes. Some highlight basic biological drives. Other theorists argue that people's anticipations of future events are more important to human motivation than are biological drive states experienced in the present. Some theorists emphasize the role of conscious thinking processes in motivation. Others believe that most important motivational processes are unconscious. To some, the motivation to enhance and improve oneself is most central to human motivation. To others, such an emphasis on "self-processes" underestimates the degree to which, in some cultures of the world, self-enhancement is less important to motivation than is a desire to enhance one's family, community, and wider world. In their explorations of motivational processes, the personality theorists you will read about in this book are attempting to bring contemporary scientific evidence to bear on classic questions about human nature that have been discussed and debated in the world's intellectual traditions for more than two millennia.

Growth and Development

Personality theorists try to understand not only what individuals are like in the here and now, but how they got this way. They strive, in other words, to understand personality development (Mroczek & Little, 2006; Specht, 2017).

The overall study of personality development encompasses two challenges that are relatively distinct. One is to characterize patterns of development that are experienced by most, if not all, persons. A theorist might, for example, posit that all individuals develop through a distinct series of stages, or that certain motives or emotional experiences are more common at one versus another age for most persons. A second challenge is to understand developmental factors that contribute to individual differences. What factors cause individuals to develop one versus another personality style?

In the study of individual differences, a classic division of possible causes separates "nature" from "nurture". We may be who we are because of our biological nature, that is, because of biological features that we inherited. Alternatively, our personality may reflect our nurturing, that is, our experiences in our family and in society. In a joking manner, we might say, "If you don't like your personality, who should you blame: Your parents, because of the way they nurtured you? Or your parents, because of the genes they passed on to you that shaped your biological nature?"

At different points in its history, psychological research has tended to highlight either nature or nurture as causal factor. In the middle parts of the 20th century, theorists focused heavily on environmental causes of behavior and devoted relatively little attention to genetic influences. Starting in the 1970s, investigators began systematic studies of similarity in the personalities of twins. These studies provided unambiguous evidence that inherited factors contribute to personality.

In recent years, there has been a third trend. Researchers have identified interactions between genetic and environmental factors. A critical finding is that environmental experiences activate genetic mechanisms, essentially "switching" genes on and off (Champagne, 2018). Since genes code for proteins that become the structural material of the body, this means that certain types of experiences can alter the biology of the organism (Gottlieb, 1998; Rutter, 2012). This finding, in turn, implies that the traditional notion of nature *versus* nurture hardly makes sense. Nature and nurture—experience and biology—are not competing forces; instead, they work together, shaping the organism across its life span (Lewontin, 2000; Meaney, 2010).

You might already be asking yourself: What aspects of personality are affected by what types of biological and environmental influences? This is a big question whose answers are considered throughout this textbook. For now, though, we will provide a quick preview of some of the factors highlighted by contemporary findings in personality psychology.

Genetic Determinants

Genetic factors contribute strongly to personality and individual differences (Kim, 2009). Contemporary advances enable the personality psychologist to pinpoint specific paths through which genes affect personality. One main path is through **temperament**, a term that refers to biologically based emotional and behavioral tendencies that are evident in early childhood (Strelau, 1998).

Temperament characteristics that have been studied in depth are fear reactions and inhibited behavior (Fox, Henderson, Marshall, Nichols, & Ghera, 2005). People differ considerably in the degree to which they respond fearfully, especially when encountering unfamiliar, novel situations (e.g., a social setting with many strangers). Genes contribute to individual differences in brain systems that are involved in this fear response. These biological differences, in turn, produce psychological differences in behavior and emotion (Fox & Reeb-Sutherland, 2010). Since genetic factors contribute to the development of the brain, in this work, the psychologist can identify a precise link from genes to biological systems to temperament, as expressed in emotion and behavior. An interesting feature of this work is that it points to the impact not only of genes, but also of the environment. Some evidence indicates that temperamentally shy children change, becoming less shy, when they experience day care in which they encounter large numbers of other children every day (Schmidt & Fox, 2002), though data on this point are somewhat mixed (Kagan, 2011).

Genetic bases of personality also are explored by evolutionary psychologists, that is, psychologists who study the evolutionary basis of psychological characteristics (Buss & Hawley, 2011). Evolutionary psychologists propose that contemporary humans possess psychological tendencies that are a product of our evolutionary past. People are predisposed to engage in certain types of behavior because those behaviors contributed to survival and reproductive success over the course of human evolution. An evolutionary analysis of genetic influences differs fundamentally from the analyses reviewed in the two preceding paragraphs. In an evolutionary analysis, investigators are not interested in genetic bases of individual *differences*. Instead, they are searching for the genetic basis of human *universals,* that is, psychological features that all people have in common. Most of our genes are shared. Even so-called racial differences involve merely superficial differences in features such as skin tone; the basic structure of the human brain is universal (Cavalli-Sforza & Cavalli-Sforza, 1995). The evolutionary psychologist suggests, then, that we all inherit psychological mechanisms that predispose us to respond to the environment in ways that proved successful over the course of evolution. For example, some scientists who study emotion suggest that a number of basic emotions (e.g., anger, sadness, joy, disgust, fear) are products of evolution (Ekman, 1993, 1994; Izard, 1994; Panksepp, 2011).

Environmental Determinants

Even the most biologically oriented of psychologists recognizes that personality is shaped, to a significant degree, by the environment. If we did not grow up in a society with other people, we would not even be *persons* in the way in which that term commonly is understood. Our concept of self, our goals in life, and the values that guide us develop in a social world. Some environmental determinants make people similar to one another, whereas others contribute to individual differences and individual uniqueness. The environmental determinants that have proven to be important in the study of personality development include culture, social class, family, and peers.

Culture   Significant among the environmental determinants of personality are experiences individuals have as a result of membership in a particular culture: "Culture is a key determinant of what it means to be a person" (Benet-Martinez & Oishi, 2008, p. 543). Each culture has its own institutionalized and sanctioned patterns of learned behaviors, rituals, and beliefs. These cultural practices, which in turn often reflect long-standing religious and philosophical beliefs, provide people with answers to significant questions about the nature of the self, one's role in one's community, and the values and principles that are most important in life. As a result, members of a culture may share personality characteristics.

Interestingly, people often may be unaware of shared cultural tendencies because they take them for granted. For example, if you live in North America or western Europe, you may underestimate the extent to which your conception of yourself and your goals in life are shaped by a culture that strongly values individual rights, in which individuals compete in an economic marketplace, and in which the society as a whole is marked by high levels of financial inequality (Stephens, Markus, & Phillips, 2014). Since everyone in these regions of the world experiences these cultural features, we take them for granted and may assume that they are universal. Yet much evidence indicates that people in other regions of the world experience different cultural features. Asian cultures appear to place a greater value on a person's contribution to his or her community rather than on individualism and personal gain (Nisbett, Peng, Choi, & Norenzayan, 2001). In fact, even within the Western world, cultural beliefs about the individual's role in society have changed from one historical period to another. The idea that individuals compete against one another in an economic marketplace in order to improve their position in life is a feature of contemporary Western societies, but it was not evident in these same societies in the Middle Ages (Heilbroner, 1986).

Culture, then, may exert an influence on personality that is subtle yet pervasive. The culture we live in defines our needs and our means of satisfying them, our experiences of different emotions and how we express what we are feeling, our relationships with others and with ourselves, what we think is funny or sad, how we cope with life and death, and what we view as healthy or sick (Markus & Kitayama, 2011).

Social Class   Although certain patterns of behavior develop as a result of membership in a culture, others may develop as a result of membership in a particular social class within a given culture. Many aspects of an individual's personality can only be understood by reference to the group to which that person belongs. One's social group—whether lower class or upper class, working class or professional—is of particular importance. Research indicates that socioeconomic status influences the cognitive and emotional development of the individual (Bradley & Corwyn, 2002). Social class factors affect not only educational opportunities, job prospects, and access to social resources. They may also indirectly affect social experiences, such as the experience of small or large networks of friends and family, and psychological qualities such as the tendency to focus, or not, on one's long-term future (Markus & Stevens, 2017).

Family   Another environmental factor of profound importance is the influence of the family (Park, 2004; Pomerantz & Thompson, 2008). Parents may be warm and loving or hostile and rejecting, overprotective and possessive, or aware of their children's need for freedom and autonomy. Each pattern of parental behavior affects the personality development of the child. Parents influence their children's behavior in at least three important ways:

1. Through their own behavior, parents present situations that elicit certain behavior in children (e.g., frustration leads to aggression).

2. Parents serve as role models for identification.

3. Parents selectively reward behaviors.

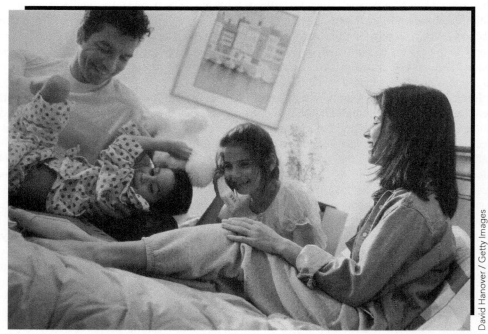

Experiences in a family can create both similarities and differences among family members.

David Hanover / Getty Images

At first, we may think of family practices as an influence that makes family members similar to one another. Yet family practices also can create within-family differences. Consider differences between male and female family members. Historically, in many societies, male children have received family privileges and opportunities that were unavailable to female children. These differences in how families have treated boys and girls surely did not make boys and girls similar to one another; rather, they contributed to differences in male and female development. In addition to gender, other family practices that may produce differences between family members involve birth order. Parents sometimes express subtle preferences toward firstborn children (Keller & Zach, 2002), who tend to be more achievement-oriented and conscientious than later-born siblings (Paulhus, Trapnell, & Chen, 1999).

Peers   What environmental features outside of family life are important to personality development? The child's experiences with members of his or her peer group are one feature. Personality development is influenced by peer groups as a whole—who socialize the individual into rules and norms for behavior—and by one-on-one relationships within peer groups, which can shape people's perceptions of themselves (Reitz, Zimmermann, Hutteman, Specht, & Neyer, 2014). Some psychologists view peer influences as more important to personality development than family experiences (Harris, 1995). Perhaps "the answer to the question 'Why are children from the same family so different from one another?' (Plomin & Daniels, 1987) is, because they have different experiences outside the home and because their experiences inside the home do not make them more alike" (Harris, 1995, p. 481). Peer groups. These experiences may affect personality in an enduring manner. For example, children who experience low-quality friendships that involve a lot of arguing and conflict tend to develop disagreeable, antagonistic styles of behavior (Berndt, 2002).

Psychopathology and Behavior Change

Constructing a personality theory may strike you as an ivory tower activity, that is, an abstract intellectual exercise that fails to relate to the important concerns of everyday life. Yet personality theories are potentially of great practical importance. People often face complicated psychological problems: They are depressed and lonely, a close friend is addicted to drugs, they are anxious about sexual relations, frequent arguments threaten the stability of a romantic relationship. To solve such problems, one requires some sort of conceptual framework that specifies causes of the problem and factors that might bring about change. In other words, one needs a personality theory.

Historically, the practical problems that have been most important to the development of personality theories have involved psychopathology. Many of the theorists discussed in this book were also therapists. They began their careers by trying to solve practical problems they faced when trying to help their clients. Their theories were, in part, an attempt to systematize the lessons about human nature that they learned by working on practical problems in therapy.

Although not all personality theories had clinical origins, for any theory, a crucial bottom line for evaluating the theoretical approach is to ask whether its ideas are of practical benefit to individuals and to society at large.

Important Issues in Personality Theory

We have just reviewed four topic areas in the study of personality: (1) personality structure, (2) personality processes, (3) personality development, and (4) psychopathology and behavior change. Next, we will consider a series of conceptual issues that are central to the field. By "conceptual issues," we mean a set of questions about personality that are so fundamental that they may arise no matter what topic one is addressing and that one must address regardless of one's theoretical perspective.

Philosophical View of the Person

No theory can be adequately understood without some knowledge of the cultural and personal soil from which it springs.

Rogers (1959, p. 185)

Personality theorists do not confine themselves to narrow questions about human behavior. Instead, they boldly tackle the big, broad question: What is the basic nature of human nature? Personality theorists, in other words, provide philosophical views about the basic nature of human beings. One critical consideration when evaluating a theory, then, is the overall view of the person that it provides.

Personality theories embrace strikingly different views of the essential qualities of human nature. Some view people as rational actors—beings who reason about the world, weigh the costs and benefits of alternative courses of action, and behave based on these rational calculations. To others, human nature is animalistic, with people primarily driven by irrational forces.

Where did the difference among theories come from? Philosophical views arise in sociohistorical contexts. In other words, the historical circumstances of the psychologist influence the theory that he or she develops. In the late 19th century, scientists explored the physics of energy—and Sigmund Freud proposed an energy-based model of mind (Chapter 3). The crisis of World War II prompted a broad intellectual movement that confronted issues of personal responsibility and freedom of choice, and this movement, in turn, informed the humanistic and phenomenological personality theories (Chapters 5 and 6) that developed in the 1950s (Fulton, 1999). At around the same time, mathematicians and engineers developed machines that seemed to think – computers—and psychologists adopted the metaphor that the mind is like a computer. In our current era, scientists in multiple fields explore the nature of complex systems (Holland, 2014; a complex system is one that contains large numbers of highly interacting parts)—and personality theorists adopt "systems" perspectives on personality structure and dynamics (Kuhl, Quirin, & Koole, 2015; Mayer, 2015; Mischel & Shoda, 1995). If Freud had been born in 1956 instead of 1856, he would not have developed the theory that he did.

Internal and External Determinants of Behavior

Is human behavior and experience determined by processes inside the person or causes external to the person? If you are a hardworking student, is it because of your confidence and personal goals (an internal cause) or your parents and schooling (an external cause). If you are disappointed in yourself, is it because of your perfectionistic thinking (an internal cause) or because social forces provided less support and fewer opportunities to people of your nationality, ethnic group, or gender (an external cause)?

All theories of personality recognize that both external and internal factors are influential. Nonetheless, they differ considerably in the emphasis they give to one or the other. Consider the differences between the most influential psychologists of the 20th century: Sigmund Freud and B. F. Skinner. According to Freud, we are controlled by internal forces: unconscious impulses and emotions that are buried deep in our unconscious minds. According to Skinner, we are controlled by external forces: environmental rewards and punishments that govern our actions. "A person does not act upon the world, the world acts upon him," Skinner writes (1971, p. 211).

Freud's and Skinner's views are extreme in the light of contemporary scientific knowledge. Virtually all personality psychologists today acknowledge both external and internal determinants of human action. Nonetheless, contemporary theories continue to differ markedly in the degree to which they emphasize one versus the other factor. These differences become apparent when one examines the basic variables—or, as we called them earlier, the basic units of analysis—of a given theory. Consider two perspectives you will read about in later chapters. In trait theories of personality, the basic units of analysis refer to structures in the person that purportedly are inherited and produce highly generalized patterns of behavior (McCrae & Costa, 2008). In social cognitive theories of personality, the basic units of analysis are knowledge structures and thinking processes that are acquired through interaction with the social and cultural environment

(Bandura, 1999; Mischel & Shoda, 2008). As you can infer from their basic units, these theories differentially emphasize internal and external determinants of personality.

Consistency Across Situations and Over Time

How consistent is personality from situation to situation? To what extent are you "the same person" when with friends as you are with your parents? Or when you are at a party versus present during a classroom discussion? And how consistent is personality across time? How similar is your personality now to what it was when you were a child? And how similar will it be 20 years from now?

Answering these questions is more difficult than it may appear. In part, this is because one has to decide on what counts as an example of personality consistency versus inconsistency. Consider a simple example. Suppose that you have two supervisors at a job, one male and one female, and that you tend to act in an agreeable manner toward one supervisor and disagreeably toward the other. Are you being inconsistent in your personality? If one thinks that a basic feature of personality is agreeableness, then the answer is yes. But suppose this situation were analyzed by a psychologist who adheres to psychoanalytic theory, which suggests that (1) people you encounter in your adult life may symbolically represent parental figures and (2) a basic personality dynamic involves attraction toward one's opposite-sex parent and rivalry toward the same-sex parent—something called an "Oedipal complex". From this view, you may be acting in a very *consistent* manner. The different job supervisors may symbolically represent different parental figures, and you may be consistently reenacting Oedipal motives that cause you to act in a different manner toward one versus the other person.

Even if people agree on what counts as consistency, they may disagree about the factors that cause personality to be consistent. Consider consistency over time. It unquestionably is the case that individual differences are stable, to a significant degree, over long periods of time (Fraley, 2002; Roberts & Del Vecchio, 2000). If you are more extraverted than your friends today, you are quite likely to be more extraverted than these same people 20 years from now. But why? One possibility is that the core structures of personality are inherited and that they change little across the course of life. Another possibility, however, is that the environment plays a critical role in fostering consistency. Exposure to the same family members, friends, educational systems, and social circumstances over long periods of time may contribute to personality consistency over time (Lewis, 2002).

No personality theorist thinks that you will fall asleep an introvert and wake up the next morning an extravert. Yet the field's theoretical frameworks do provide different views on the nature of personality consistency and change and on people's capacity to vary their personality functioning across time and place. To some theorists, variation in behavior is a sign of inconsistency in personality. To others, it may reflect a consistent personal capacity to adapt one's behavior to the different requirements of different social situations (Mischel, 2004).

The Unity of Experience and Action and the Concept of Self

Our psychological experiences generally have an integrated, or coherent, quality to them (Cervone & Shoda, 1999b). Our actions are patterned and organized, rather than random and chaotic. As we move from place to place, we retain a stable sense of ourselves, our past, and our goals for the future. There is a unity to our experiences and action.

Although we take it for granted that our experiences are unified, in some sense this fact is quite surprising. The brain contains a large number of information-processing systems, many of which function at the same time, in partial isolation from one another (Pinker, 1997). If we examine the contents of our own conscious experiences, we will find that most of our thoughts are fleeting. It is hard to keep any one idea in mind for long periods. Seemingly random ideas pop into our heads. Nonetheless, we rarely experience the world as chaotic or our lives as disjointed. Why?

A major challenge for personality science is to understand how people developed a consist, unified sense of self.

There are two types of answers to this question. One is that the multiple components of the mind function as a complex system. The parts are interconnected, and the patterns of interconnection enable the multipart system to function in a smooth, coherent manner. Computer simulations of personality functioning (Nowak, Vallacher, & Zochowski, 2002), as well as neuroscientific investigations of the reciprocal links among brain regions (Sporns, 2010; Tononi & Edelman, 1998), are beginning to shed light on how the mind manages to produce coherence in experience and action.

The second type of answer involves the concept of the self. Although we may experience a potentially bewildering diversity of life events, we do experience them from a consistent perspective, that of ourselves (Harré, 1998). People construct coherent autobiographical memories, which contribute to coherence in our understanding of who we are (Conway & Pleydell-Pearce, 2000). The concept of the self, then, has proven valuable in accounting for the unity of experience (Baumeister, 1999; Robins, Norem, & Cheek, 1999; Robins, Tracy, & Trzesniewski, 2008).

Varying States of Awareness and the Concept of the Unconscious

Are we aware of the contents of our mental life? Or do most mental activities occur outside of awareness or unconsciously?

On the one hand, much of the brain's activities unquestionably occur outside of awareness. Consider what is happening as you read this book. Your brain is engaging in large numbers of functions ranging from the monitoring of your internal physiological state to the deciphering of the marks of ink that constitute the words on this page. All this occurs without your conscious attention. You do not consciously have to think to yourself "I wonder if these squiggles of ink form words" or "Maybe I should check to see if sufficient amounts of oxygen are getting to my bodily organs." These functions are executed automatically. But these functions are not the ones of main interest to the personality psychologist.

Personality scientists ask whether significant aspects of personality functioning—motivation, emotions—occur outside of awareness. If there is evidence that they do, the personality scientist tries to conceptualize the mental systems that give rise to conscious and unconscious processes (Kihlstrom, 2008; Pervin, 2003). The fact that *some* brain functions occur outside of awareness does not imply that the most significant personality processes occur without our awareness. People engage in much self-reflection. They are particularly likely to reflect on themselves when they face life circumstances of great importance, where the decisions that are made (e.g., whether and where to attend college, whether to marry a certain person, whether to have children, what profession to pursue) have major long-term consequences. In these critical circumstances, conscious processes are influential. Thus, many personality psychologists study conscious self-reflection, even while recognizing that numerous aspects of mental life occur outside of awareness.

The Influence of the Past, Present, and Future on Behavior

Are we prisoners of our past? Or is our personality shaped by present events and personal aspirations for the future? Theorists agree that behavior can be influenced only by factors operating in the present; a basic principle of causality is that presently active processes are the causes of events. In this sense, only the present is important in understanding behavior. But the present can be influenced by experiences in the remote past or in the recent past. Similarly, what one is thinking about in the present can be influenced by thoughts about the immediate future or the distant future. People vary in the extent to which they worry about the past and the future. And personality theorists differ in their concern with the past and the future as determinants of behavior in the present. As you will see in the chapters ahead, some theorists suggest that we are primarily prisoners of our past. Psychoanalytic theory posits that personality structures are formed through experiences in childhood and that the personality dynamics established then persist throughout the life course. Others are harshly critical of this psychoanalytic conclusion. Personality construct theory (Chapter 11) and social-cognitive theory (Chapters 12–13) suggest that people have the capacity to change their own personal capabilities and tendencies and to explore the social and psychological systems that give people this lifelong capacity for personal agency (Bandura, 2006).

Meaning and Reasons for Action

If you observe some people and want to describe what they are doing, how would you do it? It sounds simple at first: Just count their behaviors. You might count the number of times a person talks, or smiles, or frowns, or checks social media. But is this sufficient? Are any two people who have the same "counts"—for example, 6 talks, 5 smiles, 2 frowns, and 29 social media checks in an hour—the same, in a psychologically significant way?

The problem with "just counting" is that the counts overlook people's reasons for action. One person might be smiling because she's happy. Another might smile as a way of putting other people in a good mood. Yet others might smile to make a good impression or as a strategy to control their anxiety. The existence of different reasons means that people who are doing the same thing behaviorally are not the same psychologically. Reasons for action may vary widely from one person to the next. When one research team asked people why they had sex, participants identified more than a dozen different reasons: stress reduction, attaining social status, expressing love and commitment to someone, sheer physical pleasure, feelings of obligation, and more (Meston & Buss, 2007).

The implication is that, in personality theory and research, one often must pay attention to subjective *meaning* rather than merely to observable behavior. People do not respond merely to physical stimuli in the environment. They respond to social circumstances that have personal meaning to them.

Although this point is obvious once stated, you will see that personality theories differ in the degree to which they pay attention to subjective meaning and people's reasons for action. Some theorists do count behaviors (Chapter 8) or study the influence of physical stimuli (Chapter 10) without deeply exploring people's reasons for action. However, most of the personality theorists are centrally concerned with the way in which people make sense of—or "assign meaning to"— the situations, events, and relationships that make up their lives.

Can We have a Science of Personality? What kind of a Science can it be?

A final issue of importance concerns the type of theory of personality that one reasonably can pursue. We have taken it for granted thus far that one can craft a *science* of personality, in other words, that the methods of science can inform the nature of persons. This assumption seems to be a safe one. People are objects in a physical universe. They consist of biological systems comprised of physical and chemical parts. Science thus should be able to tell us something about them.

Nonetheless, one can reasonably question the forms of scientific analysis that can be applied to the understanding of persons. Much of the progress of science has involved analyses that are reductionistic. A system is understood by reducing a complex whole to its simpler parts and showing how the parts give rise to the functioning of the whole.

lubilub / Getty Images

One challenge is building a theory of personality is cultural variation; the nature of personality and individual differences may vary from one culture to another. For example, in India, people recognize three main personality traits, the trigunas, which are characteristics first identified centuries ago in Hindu philosophy (Singh, Misra, & De Raad, 2013). These traits generally are not found in studies conducted in Western cultures, such as the United States.

Such analyses work wonderfully when applied to physical systems. A biological system, for example, can be understood in terms of the biochemistry of its parts. The chemistry, in turn, can be understood in terms of the underlying physics of the chemical components. But personality is not merely a physical system. As just noted, people respond to meaning. There is no guarantee that the traditional scientific procedures of breaking a system into constituent parts will be sufficient to understand processes of meaning construction. Numerous scholars have suggested that importing the methods of the physical sciences into the study of human meaning systems is a mistake (e.g., Geertz, 2000). To such commentators, the idea that people have "parts" is "at best a metaphor" (Harré, 1998, p. 15). The risk of adopting this metaphor is that, to use a cliche, "the whole may be greater than the sum of the parts."

By analogy, consider an analysis of a great work of art. In principle, one could analyze its parts: There's paint of one color over here, paint of some other color there, and so on. But this sort of analysis will not enable one to understand the greatness of the painting. This requires viewing the work as a whole and understanding the historical context in which it was made. By analogy, a listing of the psychological parts of an actual person may, in principle, fail to portray the whole individual and the developmental processes that contributed to his or her uniqueness. A question to ask yourself when reading this textbook, then, is whether the personality theorists are as successful as was da Vinci at providing holistic psychological portraits of complex individuals.

Evaluating Personality Theories

As we have noted, a unique feature of the scientific field of personality psychology is that it contains more than one guiding theory. Multiple theories of personality inform us about human nature and individual differences. A natural question, then, is how to evaluate the theories, one versus the other. How can one judge the strengths and limitations of the various theories? What criteria should be used to evaluate them?

To evaluate something, one generally asks what it is supposed to do. One then can judge how well it is doing it. A more formal way to say this is that one asks about the *functions* that the entity is supposed to serve. One then can evaluate the degree to which it is carrying out those functions. Like all scientific theories, theories of personality can serve three key functions: They can (1) organize existing information, (2) generate new knowledge about important issues, and (3) identify entirely new issues that are deserving of study.

The first of these functions is obvious. Research provides an array of facts about personality, personality development, and individual differences. Rather than merely listing these facts in an unordered manner, it would be useful to organize them systematically. A logical, systematic ordering of facts would enable one to keep track of what scientists know about personality. This can make it easier to put that knowledge to use.

The second function is somewhat less obvious. In any field of study, there are issues—involving both basic science questions and applications of scientific knowledge—that everyone in the field recognizes as important. A good theory fosters new knowledge about these issues. It is generative. The theory helps people to generate new knowledge about the topics they recognize as important to their field. In biology, Darwin's theory of natural selection was useful not only because it organized known facts about the world's flora and fauna. Its additional value is that it opened new pathways of knowledge about biology. In personality psychology, some theories have proven to be highly generative. They have prompted researchers who are familiar with the theory to use its ideas to generate new knowledge about personality.

The third function is of particular interest to both the personality scientist and the public at large. A personality theory may identity entirely new areas of study—areas that people might never have known about were it not for the theory. Psychodynamic theory opened the door to psychological issues that were utterly novel to most people: the possibility that our most important thoughts and emotions are unconscious, the possibility that events early in childhood determine our adult personality characteristics. Other theories also have this quality. Evolutionary psychology (reviewed in Chapter 9) makes the novel suggestion that contemporary patterns of thought and behavior are not learned in contemporary society but, instead, are inherited from our ancestral past. Behaviorism (Chapter 10) raises the possibility that actions that we attribute to our free choice, or free will, are ultimately caused by the environment. These theories' fascinating and sometimes radical hypotheses about human nature have prompted much valuable new investigation into human nature.

In sum, you can evaluate the theories you will learn about in this textbook by gauging their success in (1) organizing information, (2) generating knowledge, and (3) identifying important issues to study.

The Personality Theories: An Introduction

We have now reviewed a series of points: topics that must be addressed by a personality theory, important issues that arise as one confronts these topics, and criteria that can be used to evaluate a theory of personality. Now, in the final section of this chapter, we turn to the theories themselves.

The Challenge of Constructing a Personality Theory

By this point in our chapter, it is clear that constructing a comprehensive theory of personality is extremely difficult. Theorists must pursue a challenging set of scientific goals that go beyond one's intuitive thinking about personality. They must address a broad set of *what, how,* and *why* questions about personality structure, processes, development, and change. They must consider determinants of personality ranging from the molecular to the sociocultural and conceptual issues ranging from the philosophical view of persons that is embedded in their theory to the question of whether one can have a scientific theory of persons in the first place.

Does any one person do this ideally? Is there a single theory that is so comprehensive in its scope, so consistent with scientific evidence, and so uniquely able to foster new knowledge that it is accepted universally? The answer, quite simply, is no. There exist different theoretical frameworks. Each has its strengths, and each its limitations. More important, each has its unique virtues; in other words, each of a variety of theories provides some unique insights into human nature. It is for this reason that this textbook is organized around personality theories—plural.

The Personality Theories: A Preliminary Sketch

What theoretical frameworks have had the biggest impact on the field? This book will introduce you to six theoretical approaches. We provide a brief sketch of these approaches here, so that you can get a sense of the terrain ahead.

We begin with psychodynamic theory (Chapters 3 and 4), the approach pioneered by Freud. Psychodynamic theory views the mind as an energy system; the basic biological energies of the body reside, in part, in the mind. Mental energies, then, are directed to the service of basic bodily needs. However, people generally cannot gratify sexual and other bodily desires whenever they wish. Instead, the drive to gratify bodily needs often conflicts with the dictates of society. Behavior, then, reflects a conflict between biological desires on the one hand and social constraints on the other. In psychoanalysis, the mind is said to contain different systems that serve different functions: satisfying bodily needs, representing social norms and rules, and striking a strategic balancing between biological drives and social constraints. An additional defining feature of psychodynamic theory is that much of this mental activity is said to occur outside of one's conscious awareness. We are not aware of the drives that underlie our emotions and behavior; they are unconscious.

Phenomenological theories, reviewed next (Chapters 5 and 6), contrast starkly with the psychodynamic view. Phenomenological theories are less concerned with unconscious process and more concerned with people's conscious experience of the world around them, that is, their phenomenological experience. Phenomenological theorists recognize that people have biologically based motives, yet they believe that people also possess "higher" motives involving personal growth and self-fulfillment and that these motives are more important to personal well-being than are the animalistic drives highlighted by Freud. Finally, compared to psychodynamic approaches, phenomenological theory places much greater emphasis on the self. The development of a stable and coherent understanding of oneself is seen as key to psychological health.

Trait approaches to personality, reviewed in Chapters 7 and 8, differ strikingly from both of the previous formulations. The differences reflect not only different views about the nature of personality, but also different scientific beliefs about the best way of building a personality theory. Most trait theorists believe that, to construct a theory of personality, one must begin by solving two scientific problems: (1) determining which individual differences are most important to measure and (2) developing a reliable measure of these individual differences. Once these problems are solved, one would be able to measure the most important individual differences in personality, and these measurements could serve as a basis for constructing a comprehensive theory of persons. A main development in the late-20th-century history of the field is that many personality psychologists came to conclude that these problems had, in fact, been solved. Much consensus has been achieved on the question of what individual differences are most important and on how they can be measured.

Chapter 9 addresses one of the most exciting aspects of contemporary personality science, namely, research on the biological foundations of personality. This includes findings regarding the genetic bases of personality traits, as well as work revealing the brain systems that underlie individual differences. In this chapter, we devote coverage not only to trait theories but also to evolutionary psychology. Evolutionary psychologists explain contemporary patterns of social behavior in terms of mental mechanisms that are a product of our evolutionary past.

Chapter 10 introduces the ideas of behaviorism, which represent a learning approach to personality. In behavioral theories, behavior is seen as an adaptation to rewards and punishments experienced in the environment. Since different people experience different patterns of reward in different settings, they naturally developed different styles of behavior. Basic learning processes, then, are said to account for the stylistic variations in behavior that we call "personality." Behaviorism presents a profound challenge to the theories presented previously. To the behaviorist, the units of analysis of the previous theories—the psychodynamic theorist's "unconscious forces," the "self" of phenomenological theories, personality "traits"—are not causes of behavior. They merely are descriptions of patterns of thinking, emotion, and behavior that ultimately are caused by the environment that, according to the behaviorist, shapes our behavior.

Chapter 11 introduces a markedly different theoretical approach, that of personal construct theory. Personal construct theory addresses people's capacity to interpret the world. Unlike the behaviorist, who is most concerned with how the environment determines our experiences, the personal construct theorist studies the subjective ideas, or constructs, that people use to interpret the environment. One person may view the college environment as challenging, another as boring; one person may view dating circumstances as romantic, another as sexually threatening. Personal construct theorists explore the possibility that most individual differences in personality functioning stem from the different constructs that people use to interpret their world.

The final theoretical perspective is that of social-cognitive theory (Chapters 12 and 13). In some respect, social-cognitive theory is similar to the personal construct approach; social-cognitive theorists study personality by analyzing the thinking processes that come into play as people interpret their world. However, the social-cognitive perspective expands upon personal construct theory in at least two important ways. First, as suggested by its name, social-cognitive theory explores in detail the social settings in which people acquire knowledge, skills, and beliefs. Personality develops through back-and-forth influences, or *reciprocal interactions,* between people and the settings (i.e., the family, interpersonal, social, and cultural settings) of their lives. Second, social-cognitive theory devotes much attention to questions of *self-regulation,* which refers to the psychological processes through which people set goals for themselves, control their emotional impulses, and execute courses of action.

Chapter 14 considers personality in context. We explore contemporary research that illustrates the critical point that you often can learn much about people's personalities by studying the life contexts—the social situations, cultural settings, interpersonal relationships, and so on—that make up their life. This research heavily capitalizes on the social-cognitive perspective discussed in Chapters 12 and 13, while providing a broad portrait of contemporary psychological research on social settings and the individual. We end, in Chapter 15 (available at the book's website, www.wiley.com/go/cervone/personality14e), by critically evaluating the field of personality psychology as a whole.

The textbook takes advantage of contemporary knowledge in brain science. Today's personality psychologist has access to information about the brain that was unavailable in the past, when the primary personality theories were developed. This knowledge enables us to reevaluate the personality theories from a contemporary brain-science perspective. We'll do this throughout the book, in multiple chapters, in a feature called *Personality and the Brain.*

Finally, *Personality: Theory and Research* recognizes that theoretical innovation in this field did not cease at the end of the 20th century. *Contemporary Developments* sections, found in a number of chapters ahead, show you how current-day psychologists have built upon the foundations established by earlier theorists.

On the Existence of Multiple Theories: Theories as Toolkits

The fact that this book presents these multiple theories might at first seem odd. Courses in most other scientific disciplines (e.g., chemistry, physics) are not organized around a series of different theories. Knowledge is organized by one commonly accepted conceptual framework. In part, this reflects the maturity of these other fields, which have been around longer than the science of psychology. Yet even the "mature sciences" may harbor different views of the same phenomenon. Suppose that you were to ask a physicist about the nature of light. You might learn that physics has a theory that says that light is a wave. And you might learn that physics also has a theory that says that light is composed of individual particles. If you were to ask "Which theory is right?", you would be told "Neither". Light acts as a wave and as a particle. Both a wave theory and a particle theory capture important information about the nature of light.

The same is true for the personality theories. Each captures important information about human nature. As you read about them, you should not be asking yourself "Which theory was right, and which ones are wrong?" Instead, it is better to evaluate them by asking how useful they are in advancing basic knowledge and applications. Even a theory that gets some things wrong may have much value (Proctor & Capaldi, 2001).

As we were preparing a recent edition of this textbook, a colleague suggested to us a useful metaphor for thinking about personality theories. It is useful because it moves one away from simplistic right/wrong evaluations and toward a more sophisticated view. She suggested that theories are like toolkits. Each theory contains a set of "tools". Some of these tools are theoretical concepts. Others are research methods. Some are techniques for assessing personality. Yet others are methods for doing therapy. Each element of the theory is a tool in that each serves one or more functions; each, in other words, enables one to carry out one or more jobs. The jobs are things like describing individual differences, identifying basic human motivations, explaining the development of self-concept, identifying the causes of emotional reactions, predicting performance in work settings, or reducing psychological distress via therapy. These are jobs the psychologist wants to do. Each theory provides conceptual tools for doing them.

The toolkit metaphor has two benefits: It leads one (1) to ask good questions about personality theories and (2) to avoid asking bad ones. To see these benefits, imagine that you are evaluating actual physical toolkits. If you saw a plumber, an electrician, and an auto mechanic each carrying a toolkit of their profession, you would not go up to any of them and say "Your toolkit is wrong." The idea that a toolkit could be wrong hardly makes sense. A toolkit may be less good than another for doing a particular job. It may be less useful for a range of jobs than some other toolkit that contains more tools. It may be more practical than some other toolkit that contains more tools because the larger toolkit is unwieldy. You would evaluate toolkits by asking about what you can do with them and how they might be improved by adding, or sometimes removing, tools. You would not evaluate them by asking "Which one is correct?"

Similarly, when evaluating the different personality theories we present, we encourage you to ask questions such as "What can one do with the conceptual tools of this theory?" "What advantages do its conceptual tools have in relation to other theories?" or "What tools could be added to (or subtracted from) the theory to make it better?" These questions are better than asking "Which theory is right?"

The toolkit metaphor has a final implication. It suggests that the existence of multiple theories in contemporary personality psychology might not be such a bad thing. In the world of actual physical tools, when people have different toolkits they might learn new things from one another. They might add a tool from someone else's kit or be inspired to attempt someone else's job with the tools they have. In the long run, the diversity among toolkits may improve everyone's work. The same may be true in the world of theoretical tools. When multiple theories exist, investigators are more likely to face research findings and theoretical arguments that challenge their favored view. The challenges may prompt them to refine, extend, and ultimately improve their own thinking. Theoretical diversity thus can accelerate the overall progress of a discipline.

We hope you enjoy your tour through the erratic, but progressing, enterprise of personality theory and research.

MAJOR CONCEPTS

Personality	Structure	Temperament	Type
Process	System	Trait	Units of analysis

REVIEW

1. We all think about personality in our day-to-day lives. The work of personality theorists differs from this everyday thinking in that personality theories pursue five goals that are uncommon in everyday thinking about persons. They engage in (1) *scientific observations* that underlie theories that are (2) internally coherent and *systematic,* (3) *testable,* and (4) *comprehensive,* and that foster (5) useful *applications.*

2. Personality theories address *what, how,* and *why* questions about personality by developing theories that address four

distinct topics: (1) personality structure, (2) personality processes, (3) personality development, and (4) personality change (including via psychotherapy).

3. Personality theorists have confronted a range of issues throughout the history of the field. In developing theories that encompass these issues, the theorist hopes to develop a framework that serves three scientific functions: (1) organizing existing knowledge about personality, (2) fostering new knowledge on important issues, and (3) identifying new issues for study.

4. The existence of multiple theories in the field can be understood by thinking of theories as toolkits, each of which provides unique conceptual tools for doing the jobs of the personality psychologist.

The Scientific Study of People

2

Chapter Focus

Three students in a course on personality work together on a research project. They have been instructed to develop a research method for studying the effects of achievement motivation on academic performance. At their first meeting, they realize that they have drastically differing opinions about how to proceed. Alex is convinced that the best approach is to follow one student over the course of the semester, carefully recording all relevant information (grades, changes in motivation, feelings about courses, etc.) to obtain a complete and in-depth picture of a particular case. Sarah, however, thinks little of Alex's idea because his conclusions would apply only to that one person. She suggests that the group develop a set of motivation questions and give the questions to as many students as possible. She then would examine the correlation between questionnaire responses and performance in school. Yolanda thinks that neither of these approaches is good enough. She thinks that the best way to understand things scientifically is to run experiments. She suggests an experimental manipulation that causes some people to feel motivated and others to feel unmotivated, followed by a measure of test performance.

The students' views illustrate the three major methods in personality research: case studies, correlational studies using questionnaires, and laboratory experiments. This chapter introduces you to these three research methods. First, however, we review the different types of information, or data sources that might go into any study, as well as the general goals that investigators have when they conduct research on personality.

Questions to be Addressed in this Chapter

1. What kind of information is it important to obtain when studying personality?

2. What does it mean to say that scientific observations must be "reliable" and "valid"?

3. How should we go about studying people? Should we conduct research in the laboratory or in the natural environment? Through the use of self-reports or reports of others? Through study of many subjects or a single individual?

4. How much difference does it make to study people with one or another type of data? Or through one versus another approach to research? In other words, to what extent will the person "look the same" when studied from different vantage points or perspectives?

Chapter 1 suggested that, at an intuitive level, everyone is a personality theorist. We all think about people—what makes them "tick"; what affects their psychological development; how, and why, they differ. The personality psychologist's theorizing, however, differs from yours. As you learned, personality scientists must formulate their ideas very explicitly, so that they can be tested by objective scientific evidence.

Here in Chapter 2, we turn to personality research. In so doing, we find a similar theme. Everybody, at an intuitive level, is a personality researcher. We all observe differences among people, and distinctive patterns of behavior that make individuals unique. These observations constitute the "research evidence" we use to formulate our intuitive personality theories.

However, your intuitive "research" differs from that of the personality scientist. Scientists follow established procedures that are designed to yield to information that is objective and accurate. They report their methods and results in scientific journals, so other scientists can replicate their procedures and verify their findings. This chapter introduces you to the types of research personality psychologists conduct and report.

Although this chapter is devoted to research, not theory, the topics are interrelated. One cannot first conduct "theory-free" research and only later develop theories to explain the research results. This is impossible because there is no such thing as truly "theory-free" research. Research involves the systematic study of relationships among events. Generally, we need a theory to identify the events that are most important to study and the methods that are adequate for studying them. Here is an example to illustrate the point.

Suppose that you wanted to test this research hypothesis: Anxiety about dating relationships lowers college students' academic performance. To test it, you would have to measure people's level of anxiety. But how? It is impossible to proceed without making some theoretical assumptions. For example, if you ask people directly "Are you anxious about dating?," you are assuming that people (1) are aware of their level of anxiety, and thus capable of reporting it, and (2) will honestly tell, you, a researcher, about the degree of anxiety they experience. These assumptions could be wrong, and a personality theory might specify exactly how they are wrong. For example, psychodynamic theories (Chapters 3–4) suggest that people may be unaware of their emotions and therefore unable to report accurately about their emotional life. If this theory is right, then you need a different research method.

The Data of Personality Psychology

There is more than one way to get scientific information, or data, about persons. Consider the options. You could ask a person to tell you what she is like. Alternatively, you could observe her in her day-to-day activities to see for yourself. Or, since this would be rather time-consuming, you could ask other people who know this person well to report on her personality. A fourth possibility would be one that does not rely on anyone's subjective observations or judgments but instead looks at objective facts about the person's life (school records, job performance, etc.).

Lots of Data

Personality psychologists have recognized these options and have defined four categories of data that one might use in research (Block, 1993). They are (1) life record data (L-data), (2) observer data (O-data), (3) test data (T-data), and (4) self-report data (S-data). This yields a handy acronym: LOTS of data. Personality psychologists consider four data types because each one, individually, has unique strengths and limitations (Ozer, 1999).

L-data is information obtained from a person's life (L) history or life record. For example, researchers interested in the relation between personality factors and school performance obtain life record data: students' grades in school (Caprara, Vecchione, Alessandri, Gerbino, & Barbaranelli, 2011). To study the impact of psychological stress on long-term health outcomes, researchers obtain end-of-life L-data: health records indicating length of life, or longevity (Puterman et al., 2016). Researchers interested in the relation between personality and criminality do not have to ask "Have you committed any crimes?" and rely on the truthfulness of people's answers. Instead, they can access L-data: court and police records of arrests and convictions (Huesmann, Eron, & Dubow, 2002). For many purposes, however, other types of data are needed.

O-data is information provided by individuals who have observed (O) the individual whose personality is being assessed, who is referred to as the "target" individual. Generally, knowledgeable observers—for example, parents, friends, teachers, or coworkers—complete questionnaires or other rating forms in which they describe the qualities of the target person. O-data are particularly valuable when target persons may be unable to describe themselves accurately. Consider, for example, the challenge of assessing emotional intelligence (EI), which is a person's ability to identify and control emotions experienced by oneself and others. Can a researcher assess EI by asking people to describe their own level of EI? If the concept of EI is valid, they cannot. Consider an individual who is low in EI. That person, according to EI theory, lacks insight into his or her own emotions. Since they lack this insight, they would be expected to be *un*able to describe their emotional life accurately. Here is where O-data are useful; knowledgeable observers might be able to assess the target person's EI. In one study, researchers assessed EI among members of work teams by collecting O-data; participants rated the EI of their coworkers. They found that O-data were a better predictor of workplace behavior than were self-ratings of EI (Elfenbein, Barsade, & Eisenkraft, 2015).

T-data is information obtained from experimental procedures that measure people's performance on tasks (T). When performing the tasks, participants generally are unaware of the personal quality the task is designed to measure. Because of this, T-data tasks are often called **implicit measures** of personality; people are not explicitly asked to describe themselves (Gawronski & De Houwer, 2014). Personality psychologists first developed large numbers of T-data tasks in the middle of the 20th century. The personality trait psychologist Raymond Cattell and colleagues (see Chapter 7), for example, measured emotional reactions by recording people's tendency to fidget while sitting in a chair, or their facial expressions while experiencing mild electric shocks (Cattell & Gruen, 1955). Later in the century, researchers developed T-data procedures that capitalized on advances in related fields, such as cognitive psychology. In the study of cognition, individual differences in people's knowledge of a topic can be measured by recording response times, that is, the speed with which research participants can answer questions. People with more knowledge of a topic have shorter response times. In the study of personality, response-time tasks proved useful in research on self-concept. People commonly think about different personal qualities they possess and have more self-knowledge about some qualities than others. Response times that are collected when people answer questions about themselves can reveal the aspects of self that they think about the most (Markus, 1977). Other T-data procedures measure people's ability to perform a task that is difficult. For example, children's ability to control their impulses can be measured through the "Marshmallow Test" (Mischel, 2014), which requires children to wait calmly in order to receive a reward.

Finally, **S-data** is information that participants report about themselves (the "S" stands for "self"). By far the most common source of S-data is questionnaires. When completing a personality questionnaire, the test-taker is asked to play the role of observer of his or her own personality, making ratings about the self (e.g., "Are you a conscientious person?"). Personality questionnaires may be designed to measure a single personality characteristic or the entire domain of personality. In the latter case, the questionnaire generally contains a large number of test items, with subsets of items being designed to capture each of a series of distinct personal qualities (Tellegen & Waller, 2008). S-data have significant limitations. People may display a response bias in which they underreport personal qualities that are negative or overreport ones that are positive (McGee et al., 2016). Even if participants are trying to describe themselves accurately, the researcher may be interested in a psychological quality that people are not consciously aware of and thus cannot describe (see Chapters 3–4). If a self-report measure is used in different cultures, the test items may have different meaning, and thus assess different personal qualities, in one versus another cultural context (van de Vijver & He, 2017). Yet self-reports do have a big advantage: convenience. It is relatively easy to obtain self-report data either in person or over the Internet. Questionnaire-based S-data this is a very commonly used data source.

The LOTS categories are a useful simple system for thinking about alternative types of data. However, as the science of personality advances, new types of measurement have been developed. Additional categories may be necessary to capture the field's contemporary diversity of methods (Cervone & Caprara, 2001). For example, data about personality and the brain (reviewed below) do not easily fit the LOTS scheme.

Contemporary Developments in Personality Research: Social Media and Language-Based Assessments

Some research methods in personality psychology have been around for ages. For example, personality questionnaires (the most common type of S-data) have been with us for a century; they were first developed by the United States Army during World War I (Woodworth, 1918). Many of the T-data tasks used in research today were devised in the late-20th century.

Other research methods, however, are much newer. One particularly contemporary method combines two developments.

Language

The first development involves the analysis of language. When you think of "data" in psychology research, you probably first think of numbers rather than words. This is a reasonable thing to think; most of the scientific data in psychology is, in fact, numerical. Researchers use numerical scales to measure psychological qualities and responses that people make in experiments. Numerical data have a big advantage: They are easy to analyze. Specialized statistical software, and even general-purpose number-management tools such as Microsoft Excel, enable any researcher to quickly analyze large amounts of numerical information.

The recent development is the availability of software that analyzes language. **Computerized text analysis methods** are software tools that take, as their input, words and sentences (Tausczik & Pennebaker, 2010). When analyzing the text, the software can identify, and count the frequency of, any of a wide variety of linguistic features that may be of interest to a researcher. For example, a researcher might be interested in the use of first-person pronouns ("I," "my") that indicate when people are thinking about themselves, or emotion words ("overjoyed," "cried") that reveal people's feelings about events they are discussing.

Once words, phrases, or sentences are counted, researchers can relate these language-based measures to other outcomes of interest. For example, one psychological outcome of great interest to both personality and clinical psychologists is the experience of depression. It is known that depression causes people to focus on themselves and their personal concerns. This self-focus, in turn, should cause people's language use to contain more personal pronouns—words like "I" and "my." Computerized text analysis reveals that language use and depression are, in fact, related; people who use more personal pronouns are more likely to be depressed (Bernard, Baddeley, Rodriguez, & Burke, 2016).

Note an interesting implication of this finding: Language use can serve as an *assessment of* depression. In other words, you can find out who is and is not likely to be depressed merely by analyze the words people use. More generally, analyses of language use might detect individual differences in any of a wide variety of personal qualities.

Researchers of course were able to read text and count the frequency with which people use different types of words prior to the development of text-analysis software. Yet the computerized process has a big advantage. It enables researchers to analyze extremely large bodies of text without relying on the efforts of human readers.

Social Media

The second development is one with which you are already familiar: social media. Social media use today is widespread. In the United States, more than four out of five adults have a social media profile (https://www.statista.com/statistics/273476/percentage-of-us-population-with-a-social-network-profile/). Globally, the most popular social media site, Facebook, has nearly two billion users (https://www.google.com/search?q=how+many+facebook+users+are+there&oq=how+many+facebook+users+are+there&aqs=chrome..69i57j0l5.3747j0j7&sourceid=chrome&ie=UTF-8). This number is incredibly large in historical context; today's population of Facebook users exceeds the size of the entire human population of a century ago.

At this point in your reading, you may have just had an insight that personality researchers, too, have had. The two developments, computerized text analysis and social media, can be combined. Computerized text analysis can analyze people's language in social media—for example, what people write in posts on Facebook pages. If language can be used to assess personality, and if computerized text analysis can be done with Facebook posts, then one could assess personality characteristics in huge populations of people—and without going to the cost and effort of giving people formal personality questionnaires.

In an exemplary study using language-based assessments (Park et al., 2014), researchers aimed to assess individual differences in general tendencies to display one versus another type of behavior, for example, the tendencies to be social outgoing or "extraverted" or to be hardworking and reliable or "conscientious". Their work consisted of two distinct research steps:

- In the first step of their study, they obtained two pieces of information for each of thousands of research participants: (1) Facebook status messages and (2) scores on personality questionnaires (which were administered through an online website). Statistical analyses enabled the researchers to identify features of language—for example, individual words—that tended to be used most often by people with high and low scores on the questionnaires.

• In step 2, the goal was to determine whether features of language identified in step 1 could *predict* personality characteristics in a second group participants. The researchers obtained information about thousands of additional participants, analyzed their language use, and tried to predict both S-data (participants' descriptions of their own personality) and O-data (ratings of the personality characteristics of participants that were made by their friends, that is, by observers of the participant's personality).

Findings revealed the power of language-based assessments. Through their novel method of analyzing language on social media, the researchers were able to predict traditional S-data and O-data. There were substantial positive correlations between the language-based markers of personality and both (a) people's descriptions of their own personality (the S-data) and (b) observers' ratings of those people (the O-data). These positive correlations were found for each of five personality tendencies—the "Big Five": extraversion and conscientiousness, as noted, and also neuroticism, agreeableness, and openness to new experiences (see Chapter 8 for details on these Big Five traits).

What exactly were these language-based markers of personality? Figure 2.1 displays an example. In the figure, the size of each word indicates the degree to which use of that word was correlated with level of extraversions. As you can see, people whose Facebook posts included emotionally exuberant words ("Love!" "Amazing") and such as references to social settings and plans ("tonight" "party") were more likely to be extraverts. Knowledge of these language–personality links allows you to "read" an individual's personality in his or her Facebook posts!

How Do Data from Different Sources Relate to One Another?

Having introduced four categories of data, a question to ask is whether measures obtained from the different types of data agree with one another (Pervin, 1999). If a person rates herself as high on conscientiousness, will others (e.g., friends, teachers) rate her similarly? If an individual scores high on a questionnaire measuring depression, will ratings given by a professional interviewer lead to a similar score? If an individual rates himself as high on extraversion, will he score high on that trait in a laboratory-designed situation to measure that trait (e.g., participation in a group discussion)?

The seemingly simple question of whether different data sources relate to one another is more complicated than it sounds. Numerous factors influence the degree to which data sources are related. One is the question of which data sources one is talking about. Personality psychologists frequently have found that self-reports (S-data) are often discrepant from scores obtained from laboratory procedures (T-data). Self-report questionnaires tend to involve broad judgments that relate to a wide variety of situations (e.g., "I generally am pretty even tempered"), whereas experimental procedures measure personality characteristics in a very specific context. This difference often is critical, resulting in discrepancies between the two types of data.

Self-reports (S-data) and observer reports (O-data) tend to be related more closely. Personality psychologists commonly find significant levels of agreement when comparing self-ratings to observer ratings (Funder, Kolar, & Blackman, 1995; McCrae & Costa, 1987). Yet here, too, different types of research procedures can lead to different conclusions (John & Robins, 1994; Kenny, Albright, Malloy, & Kashy, 1994; Pervin, 1999). When the personality characteristic being rated is highly evaluative (e.g., stupid, warmhearted), self-perception biases enter the rating process, lowering agreement between self and observer ratings (John & Robins, 1993, 1994; Robins & John, 1997). Moreover, some personality characteristics are more observable

FIGURE 2.1 Words, phase, and topics with the strongest correlations to extraversion, as predicted by language (*N* = 4,824). Large central word clouds (red, blue, and gray) contain the 100 words and phrases with highest correlations with high and low predicted extraversion. Word size is proportional to correlation size; color indicates word frequency. Underscores (_) are used to connect words within phrases and do not occur in the original text. The smaller surrounding word clouds (green) are the six most highly correlated topics, or clusters of semantically related words. Within topics, word size and color indicate word prevalence. All correlations are significant (*p* < .001).
(Original or adapted from Park, 2014)

and easier to judge than others (e.g., sociability versus neuroticism), leading to greater agreement between self and observer ratings as well as to greater agreement among ratings obtained from different observers of the same person (Funder, 1995; John & Robins, 1993). Furthermore, some individuals appear to be easier to read or more "judgeable" than others (Colvin, 1993). In sum, a variety of factors—including the degree to which a personality characteristic is evaluative and observable, and the degree to which the person being rated is "judgeable"—affect the correspondence between data sources.

In general, the different sources of data about personality should be recognized as having their own advantages and disadvantages. Self-report questionnaires have a clear advantage: People know a lot about themselves, so if a psychologist wants to know people, maybe the best thing to do is to ask them about themselves (Allport, 1961; Kelly, 1955; Lucas & Diener, 2008). Yet, self-report methods have limits. People's descriptions of themselves on questionnaires can be influenced by irrelevant factors such as the phrasing of test items and the order in which items appear on a test (Schwarz, 1999). People also may lie or may unconsciously distort their questionnaire responses (Paulhus, Fridhandler, & Hayes, 1997), perhaps in an attempt to present themselves in a positive light.

For such reasons, some researchers feel that the best measure of an individual's personality is questionnaire ratings by *others* who know the person. Yet here, too, problems may arise; different raters may sometimes rate the same person in quite different ways (Hofstee, 1994; John & Robins, 1994; Kenny et al., 1994). As a result, some psychologists contend that the field should not rely so heavily on questionnaires—whether those questionnaires are self-reports or are reports by other people who are familiar with a given individual. Instead, objective measures of behavior and of biological systems underlying that behavior may be a more reliable source of evidence for building a science of personality (Kagan, 2003). Yet the personality psychologist is often interested in aspects of personal experience that do not have any simple behavioral or biological markers. If one wants to know about people's conscious perceptions of themselves and their beliefs about the world around them, then we're back where we started: The best thing to do is to ask them.

Fixed Versus Flexible Measures

Another way in which sources of data about personality can differ involves the question of whether measures are fixed or flexible. By "fixed," we mean procedures in which exactly the same measures (e.g., exactly the same test items) are administered to all the people in a psychological study, and scores for all the people are computed in exactly the same way. Such "fixed" procedures are, by far, the most commonly employed method in personality psychology. If psychologists want to know about people's characteristics, they generally give large groups of people precisely the same test items and compute scores for everyone in a common manner.

Fixed procedures have clear advantages: They are objective and simple. Yet they have two limitations as well. One is that some of the test items that the psychologist asks may be irrelevant to some of the individuals taking the test. If you have ever taken a personality questionnaire, you may have felt that some of the questions were good ones, tapping into an important feature of your personality, whereas others were not good ones, in that they asked about topics irrelevant to you. A fixed testing procedure does not differentiate between the two types of items; it simply adds up all of your responses and computes for you a total score on a test. The second limitation is that some features of your personality may not be included in a fixed test. You may possess some idiosyncratic psychological quality—an important past experience, a unique skill, a guiding religious or moral value, a long-term goal in life—that is not mentioned in any of the psychologist's test items.

These limitations can, in principle, be overcome by adopting flexible testing procedures—in other words, procedures that do something other than give all people a common set of questions. Various options are available (Cervone & Shadel, 2003; Cervone, Shadel, & Jencius, 2001; Huprich & Meyer, 2011). For example, one is to administer a fixed set of test items, but to allow them to indicate which items are more or less relevant to them (Markus, 1977). Another is to give people unstructured personality tests, that is, tests in which the items allow people to describe themselves in their own words, rather than forcing them to respond to descriptions worded entirely by the experimenter. A question such as "True or false: I like going to large parties" would be a structured item, whereas the question "What activities do you enjoy on the weekends?" would be unstructured. Unstructured methods have proven to be quite valuable in assessing the self-concept. These methods include asking people to list words or phrases that describe important aspects of their personality (Higgins, King, & Mavin, 1982) or to tell stories that relate their memories of important life experiences that they have had (McAdams, 2011; Woike & Polo, 2001).

Personality psychologists have a technical vocabulary to describe these fixed versus flexible measures. Fixed measures, which are applied in the same manner to all persons, are referred to as **nomothetic.** The term comes from the Greek for "law," *nomos,* and refers here to the search for scientific laws that apply, in a fixed manner, to everyone. Flexible assessment techniques tailored to the particular individual being studied are referred to as **idiographic,** a term deriving from the Greek *idios,* referring to personal, private, and distinct characteristics (as in "idiosyncratic"). In general, then, nomothetic techniques describe a population of persons in terms of a fixed set of personality variables, using a fixed set of items to measure them. Idiographic techniques, in contrast, have the primary goal of obtaining a portrait of the potentially unique, idiosyncratic individual. As you will see in later chapters, the personality theories differ in the degree to which they rely on fixed versus flexible (nomothetic versus idiographic) testing procedures.

[handwritten margin note: nomo = fixed / idio = flexible]

Personality and Brain Data

The four types of data discussed above—the "LOTS" data types—are psychological. That is, these data sources inform researchers about people's psychological responses: their behavior, thoughts, and emotional reactions.

In addition to the psychology, personality psychologists are interested in biology. They want to identify biological mechanisms that contribute to people's enduring and distinctive patterns of feeling, thinking, and behaving—that is, to their personality. (Recall our definition of *personality* from Chapter 1.) The primarily biological mechanisms are found, of course, in the brain. Personality psychologists thus need brain data to complement their psychological "LOTS" data.

Two types of evidence about brain functioning have proven particularly valuable to personality psychology. We'll describe them briefly here, and you'll see them again in the chapters ahead.

The first source of brain data capitalizes upon the brain's electrical properties. **Electroencephalography (EEG)** is a method for recording electrical activity in the brain. The recordings are made through electrodes placed on the scalp. These electrodes record the electrical activity of the brain's individual cells, or *neurons*; the biochemical activity of neurons inside the brain generates electrical activity that is so powerful that it can be detected by electrodes outside the brain, on the scalp. EEG recordings generally are made in laboratories; however, portable, wearable technologies have recently been developed that enable recordings to be made outside of laboratory settings (Casson et al., 2010).

In EEG research, numerous electrodes are placed on different regions of the scalp. Each electrode is most sensitive to brain activity in regions of the brain closest to it. By analyzing activity in multiple electrodes, then, researchers can determine which areas of the brain are most active at any given time. By simultaneously monitoring participants' (a) psychological state (e.g., experience of different emotions) and (b) EEG activity (specifically, activity in each of the electrodes), researchers can relate psychological activity to brain activity and thus identify regions of the brain that may underpin specific psychological states and functions.

The second source of evidence about the brain is **functional magnetic resonance imaging (fMRI)**, a method for depicting (or "imaging") brain activity while a person carries out different tasks (or psychological "functions"). fMRI draws upon the fact that blood flow to different areas of the brain fluctuates as those brain areas become active during task performance. Just as additional blood flows to a muscle in your arm if you use it to lift a weight, additional blood flows to an area of your brain if you use it to, for example, solve a problem, remember a past event, or form a mental image. fMRI technology detects these variations in blood flow and produces a picture of the brain that shows its most highly active regions, and thus "functional" regions—that is, the regions that contributed directly to the task being performed (Ulmer & Jansen, 2010).

In fMRI research, participants are placed in a specialized device called a brain scanner. The scanner contains a powerful magnet that detects variations in blood flow (which are detectable thanks to the magnetic properties of blood cells). While in the scanner, participants see task instructions, pictures, and other stimuli on video screens and perform tasks in response to these stimuli. The brain scans are taken while participants perform these tasks.

As noted, EEG and fMRI provide information about biological functions, not psychological experiences. However, by combining the biological methods with the psychological LOTS data described above, researchers can link biology to psychology and discover the biological bases of personality processes and structures.

Personality Theory and Assessment

One of the jobs that a personality psychologist must accomplish is assessment. A *personality assessment* is any standardized procedure—that is, a procedure with a well-specified set of steps—for learning about an individual's personality or for measuring differences in personality among people in a population. (A *population* is any large group of individuals of interest to a given researcher.) Personality assessment procedures yield the basic data that psychologists use to accomplish their main professional goals, such as predicting people's behavior, conducting experimental research on basic personality processes, and, in clinical applications, understanding psychological problems and formulating therapy strategies.

When selecting a source of data to use in personality assessment, the psychologist has a lot of options: four different sources of psychological data; idiographic versus nomothetic strategies for collecting data through those sources; and different methods for obtaining evidence about the brain, as discussed above. How is one to choose?

Theory commonly guides the choice. Theories of personality dictate targets of assessments, that is, the aspects of personality that are most important to study. The choice of an assessment target may dictate the source of data one pursues. Let's briefly consider four targets of assessment in personality psychology.

- *Average Behavior:*   Some personality theories target for study people's typical, average behavior. Average behavioral tendencies are thought to reveal inner personality structure. Assessments, then, are designed to measure what people do on average—their average tendency to be calm (vs. anxious), outgoing (vs. socially withdrawn), honest (vs. deceptive), and so forth (Van der Linden, Tsaousis, & Petrides, 2012).

- *Variability in Behavior:*   Other theories suggest that assessing average tendencies in behavior is insufficient. One also must explore *variations* in behavior across social settings. Patterns of variability—for example, warm relationships with one parent and hostile relationships with another; or anxious behavior in some situations and calm, confident behavior in others—are thought to be revealing of personality structure (Mendoza-Denton & Ayduk, 2012).

- *Conscious Thought:*   A third target for assessment is conscious experience, that is, a person's flow of conscious thoughts, feelings, and emotions. In a study of personality and conscious experience, a researcher might, for example, ask people to describe their beliefs about themselves, their personal goals in life, or their feelings (of excitement or boredom, worry or calm concentration) as they go about the events of their day (Nakamura & Csikszentmihalyi, 2009).

- *Unconscious Mental Events:*   A fourth target for assessment is thoughts and feelings that are *not* conscious. Some personality theories highlight *unconscious* mental events, that is, mental events (e.g., thoughts, motives) of which people are not aware. Researchers whose work is guided by these theories must, then, devise methods for uncovering unconscious mental contents (McClelland, Koestner, & Weinberger, 1989).

The relations among theory, targets of assessment, and choice of data source will be illustrated again and again in the chapters ahead. For now, note that these relations underscore a theme from Chapter 1: One can't study personality by first collecting a lot of data and then creating a theory. One first needs a theory to decide what to measure and how to measure it.

Goals of Research: Reliability, Validity, Ethical Behavior

No matter what question one is studying, and no matter what method one chooses, a research project cannot succeed unless its procedures possess two qualities: Measures of personality (1) must be replicable (if the study is run twice, it should turn out the same way both times) and (2) must truly measure the theoretical concept of interest in a given study. In the language of research, measures must be (1) reliable and (2) *valid*.

Reliability

The concept of **reliability** refers to the extent to which observations can be replicated. The question is whether measures are dependable or stable. If we give people a personality measure, and then give it to them again a short time later, we expect that the measure will reveal similar personality characteristics at the two time points. If it does not, it is said to be unreliable.

Various factors may affect the reliability of a psychological test. Some involve the psychological state of the people who are being observed; people's responses may be affected by transient factors such as their mood at the time that they are observed. For example, suppose that you take a personality test on two different days and on one, but not the other, you're in a particularly grouchy mood. Your mood might alter your responses on that day, causing you to get a different test score across the two occasions. Other factors involve the test itself. For example, ambiguities in test items can lower reliability. Carelessness in scoring a test or ambiguous rules for interpreting scores can also lead to a lack of agreement, or lack of reliability, among testers.

Reliability commonly is measured in two different ways, with the different techniques providing answers to different questions about a test (West & Finch, 1997). One method gauges internal consistency: Do the different items on the test correlate with one another, as one would expect if each item is a reflection of a common psychological construct? The second measures test–retest reliability: If people take the test at two different points in time, do they get the same, or highly similar, test scores? The differences between the types of reliability are made plain by a simple example. Suppose that one added a few intelligence test items to a test of extraversion. The test–retest reliability of measure would remain high (since people would probably have similar performance on the intelligence test items at different points in time). But the internal consistency of the test would be lowered (since responses on extraversion and intelligence test items probably would not be correlated).

Validity

In addition to being reliable, observations must be valid. **Validity** is the extent to which observations actually reflect the phenomena of interest in a given study. The concept of validity is best illustrated by an example in which a measure is not valid: One could assess people's intelligence by asking them trivia questions about the winners of TV talent shows. The measure could turn out to be reliable. But it would not be valid because these trivia questions are not indicators of the mental capabilities that we call "intelligence".

For a test to be useful in the development and testing of personality theory, it must have *construct validity*: It must be a valid measure of the psychological variable, or construct, that it purports to measure (Cronbach & Meehl, 1955; Ozer, 1999). To establish that a test possesses construct validity, personality psychologists generally try to show that the test relates systematically to some external criterion, that is, to some measure that is independent of (i.e., external to) the test itself. Theoretical considerations guide the choice of an external criterion. For example, if one were to develop a test of the tendency to experience anxiety and wanted to establish its construct validity, one would use theoretical ideas about anxiety to choose external criteria (e.g., physiological indices of anxious arousal) that the test should predict. One generally would establish validity by showing that the test correlates with the external criterion. However, in addition to correlational data, tests of validity might involve comparisons of two groups of people who are theoretically relevant to the test. A group of people who have been diagnosed by clinical psychologists as suffering from an anxiety disorder, for example, should get higher scores on the purported anxiety test than people who have not been so diagnosed; otherwise, one obviously would not have a valid test of anxiety.

There are other aspects of validity (Ozer, 1999; West & Finch, 1997). For example, if one is proposing a new personality test, one should be able to demonstrate that the test has *discriminant* validity: It should be distinct, empirically, from other tests that already exist. If, hypothetically, one proposes a new test of "worrying tendencies" and finds that it correlates extremely highly with existing tests of neuroticism, then the new test is of little value because it lacks discriminant validity.

In sum, reliability concerns the questions of whether a test provides a stable, replicable measure, and validity concerns the questions of whether a measure actually taps, and is influenced by, the psychological quality it is supposed to be measuring.

The Ethics of Research and Public Policy

Research in psychology is laden with ethical concerns. Ethical issues pervade both the conduct of research and the reporting of research results (Smith, 2003). These concerns are long-standing. A half-century ago, in a famed line research, participants in the role of "teachers" were instructed to teach other participants ("learners") a list of paired associate words and to punish them with an electric shock when they made errors on the word list (Milgram, 1965). Although actual shock was not used, the "teachers" believed it was. In another study, participants in a simulated prison environment were given the roles of guards or prisoners (Zimbardo, 1973). "Guards" verbally and physically abused the "prisoners," who allowed themselves to be treated in a dehumanized way. In both studies, people experienced such severe stress that one must question whether the gains to science outweighed the costs to participants.

In today's field, psychologists' activities are guided by a long-standing set of ethical policies adopted by the American Psychological Association (1981). Their essence is that "the psychologist carries out the investigation with respect and concern for the dignity and welfare of the people who participate." This includes evaluating the ethical acceptability of the research, determining whether subjects in the study will be at risk in any way and establishing a clear and fair agreement with research participants concerning the obligations and responsibilities of each. Although deception is recognized as necessary in some cases, it must be minimized. Researchers always bear a responsibility to minimize participants' physical and mental discomfort and harm. In addition to the APA guidelines, similar federal guidelines (that is, within the United States, guidelines formulated by a branch of the U.S. federal government) guide research. All research projects in psychology must be reviewed and approved by an ethics board that evaluates whether the research adheres to these guidelines.

As noted, ethical principles also apply to the reporting of research results. A long-standing concern is "the spreading stain of fraud" (*APA Monitor,* 1982)—that is, the possibility that the researcher's reporting of results is not accurate but, instead, has been distorted by his or her personal motives. In the 1970s, statistical analyses indicated that Sir Cyril Burt, a once prominent British psychologist, intentionally misrepresented data when reporting research on the inheritance of intelligence (Kamin, 1974). Early in the 20th century, a researcher was forced to retract from the scientific literature a previously published study because it did not accurately report valid research results (Ruggiero & Marx, 2001). More recently, a psychologist resigned from his job after admitting that data in multiple studies of his were entirely fabricated (*New York Times,* November 2, 2011). In response to such events, the field has adopted improved standards for making research procedures and data open to the public, who can check on the veracity of published findings (Hesse, 2018).

Much more subtle than fraud are personal and social biases that affect how scientific questions are developed and what kinds of data are accepted as evidence (Pervin, 2003). In the study of sex differences, for example, researchers might pose questions in a manner that is gender-biased (e.g., asking whether "women are as skillful as men" on a task) or accept the validity of research results that fit their preexisting expectations about men and women. Although scientists strive to remain objective, they—just like anyone else—may sometimes fail to recognize how their personal opinions and expectations affect their judgments and conclusions.

The ethical reporting of research in personality psychology is important not only to advances in science, but also to society at large. Personality research is applied in numerous domains: clinical treatments for psychotherapy; educational policies to motivate students; tests to select among applicants for jobs; and so forth. These applications heighten the research psychologist's responsibility to report research accurately and comprehensively.

Three General Strategies of Research

All personality scientists hope to obtain research results that are reliable and valid, as you learned above. They differ, however, in the strategies through which they try to achieve that goal. Three overarching research strategies predominate in the field: (1) Case Studies; (2) Correlational Studies; and (3) Experiments. Let's introduce these three strategies now. You'll see them again and again in later chapters.

Case Studies

One strategy is to study individual persons in great detail. Many psychologists feel that in-depth analyses of individual cases, or **case studies**, are the best way to capture the complexities of human personality.

In a case study, a psychologist interacts extensively with the individual who is the target of the study. In these interactions, the psychologist tries to develop an understanding of the psychological structures and processes that are most important to that individual's personality. Using a term introduced previously, case studies inherently are *idiographic* methods in that the goal is to obtain a psychological portrait of the particular individual under study.

Case studies may be conducted purely for purposes of research. Historically, however, most case studies have been conducted as part of clinical treatment. Clinical psychologists, of course, must gain an understanding of the unique qualities of their clients in order to craft an intervention, so the clinical setting inherently provides case studies of personality. Case studies by clinicians have played an important role in the development of some major theories of personality. In fact, many of the theorists we will discuss in this book were trained as clinical psychologists, counseling psychologists, or psychiatrists. They initially tried to solve the problems of their patients and then used the insights obtained in this clinical setting to develop their theories of personality.

Case Studies: An Example

To illustrate the insights that can be gained by a systematic case study, we will consider work by the Dutch personality psychologist Hubert Hermans (2001). Hermans is interested in the fact that people's thoughts about themselves—or their self-concept—are generally multifaceted. People think of themselves as having a variety of psychological characteristics. These concepts about the self develop as individuals interact with other people. Since each of us interacts with many different people, different aspects of our self-concept might often be relevant to different situations that feature different individuals. You might see yourself as being serious and articulate when interacting with professors, fun loving and confident when hanging out with friends, and romantic yet anxious when on a date. To understand someone's personality, then, it might be necessary to study how different aspects of the self come into play as people think about their life from different viewpoints that involve individuals who play different roles in their life. Hermans (2001) refers to these different viewpoints as different "positions" one can take in viewing oneself.

This view of the self-concept raises a major challenge for most forms of research. Correlational and experimental studies generally provide a small amount of information about each of a large number of persons. But to understand the complexity of self-concept as Hermans describes, it requires a large amount of information about a person and the individuals and social circumstances that make up that person's life. When this level of detail about the individual is required, personality psychologists turn to the technique of case studies.

Hermans (2001) reports a case study that reveals the complexity of personality in our modern day and age, in which people from different cultures come in contact with one another much more frequently than in the past, due to the migration of individuals from one part of the world to another for purposes of education or employment. In this case study, Hermans employs a systematic research method that can be used in the study of a single individual. The method is one in which an individual is asked to list characteristics that describe his or her own attributes, as well as to list people and situations that are important to him or her. The individual is then asked to indicate the degree to which each personal characteristic is important, or prominent, in each of the situations. Using these ratings, Hermans provides a depiction of the organization of the individual's beliefs (Figure 2.2).

Consider the case of Ali, a 45-year-old man living in the Netherlands, who grew up in Algeria and then for more than 20 years lived in northern Europe, worked for a Dutch company, and was married to a Dutch woman. Ali views his life as having distinct components, and he exhibits different personality characteristics in these different life settings. One component of his self-concept involved family members, on both his own side of the family and his wife's. These people tended to be very accepting of him. When he was with these people, Ali was happy and outgoing, and was willing to make sacrifices for other individuals. Yet, Ali's view of himself and his social world contained a second component. As is readily understandable for someone who has moved to a new culture that may not always be accepting of immigrants, Ali recognized that some people discriminated against him or held political views with which he disagreed. With these people, he felt vulnerable and disillusioned. Interestingly, he also felt this way with his sister, whom both he and his wife viewed as "the witch of the family" (Hermans, 2001, p. 359). The detailed information provided by this case study, then, provides insight into the textures of this individual's life that is generally unavailable through other research methods.

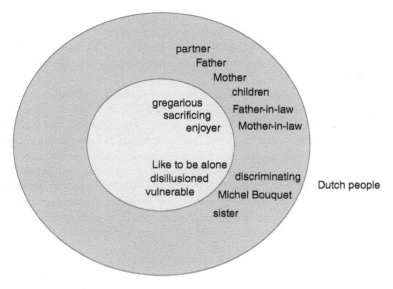

FIGURE 2.2 Case-Study Representation of Self-Concept: The image represents the multifaceted self-concept of an Algerian living in the Netherlands and married to a Dutch woman.
Adapted from Hermans (2001).

Correlational Studies

Personality tests and questionnaires are used where the intensive study of individuals is not possible or desirable and where it is not possible to conduct laboratory experiments. Beyond this, the advantage of personality questionnaires is that a great deal of information can be gathered on many people at one time. Although no one individual is studied as intensively as with the case study approach, the investigator can study many different personality characteristics in relation to many different research participants.

The use of personality tests and questionnaires has tended to be associated with an interest in the study of individual differences. Many personality psychologists believe that the critical first step in understanding human nature is to chart the differences among people. Personality questionnaires often are designed to measure these individual differences. For example, personality psychologists might have an interest in using questionnaires to measure individual differences in anxiety, self-consciousness, friendliness, the tendency to take risks, or other psychological qualities.

In addition to measuring these personality variables, the psychologist generally wishes to know how they go together. Are anxious people more friendly than less anxious people? Or less friendly? Do self-conscious people take fewer risks? Are risk-taking people friendlier? Such questions are addressed in **correlational research**. This term comes from the statistic used to gauge the degree to which two variables go together: the **correlation coefficient**. A correlation coefficient is a number that reflects the degree to which two measures are linearly related. If people who have higher scores on one variable tend also to have higher scores on the other one, then the variables are said to be *positively* correlated. (Anxiety and self-consciousness would tend to be correlated in this way.) If people who have higher scores on one variable tend to have *lower* scores on the other one, then the variables are said to be *negatively* correlated. (Anxiety and self-confidence might be correlated this way, since people who express low self-confidence are likely to report being relatively more anxious.) Finally, if two variables do not go together in any systematic linear manner, they are said to be uncorrelated. (Anxiety and friendliness may be uncorrelated, since both anxious and nonanxious people may be either friendly or unfriendly.) The correlation coefficient is computed in such a way that a perfect positive correlation—that is, a correlation in which the point falls exactly on a single line—is a correlation of 1.0. A perfect negative correlation is one of –1.0. A correlation of zero indicates that there is no linear relation between two measures.

Note that the term *correlational research* refers to a research *strategy,* not merely to a particular statistical measure (the correlation). The strategy is one in which researchers examine the relation among variables in a large population of people, where none of the variables is experimentally manipulated. In some circumstances, researchers may not compute a simple correlation coefficient to examine the relation between two variables; they may, for instance, use more complex statistical procedures that determine whether two variables are related, even after controlling for the influence of some other variables. (For example, one might ask whether intelligence test scores are related to personal income after controlling for other variables, such as the income level of one's parents.) Even if such alternative approaches to analyzing data are used, one will still have a correlational research strategy if one is looking at the relation among variables without manipulating these variables experimentally.

Correlational Research: An Example

A compelling example of the power of correlational research to answer questions that cannot be answered through any other technique is found in a study relating personality characteristics to longevity (Danner, Snowdon, & Friesen, 2001). The question being asked in this research is whether the tendency to experience positive emotions is related to how long people live. Prior work had established that people's emotional life can influence their physical well-being. For example, emotions are associated with activation of the autonomic nervous system (ANS); ANS activity, in turn, influences the cardiovascular system (Krantz & Manuck, 1984), which is critical to health. The implication of this prior work is that if one could identify people who differ in their tendencies to experience positive and negative emotions, and could follow these people for a long enough period of time, one might find that people who tended to experience high degrees of positive emotion will live longer. Note that this is a question that can *only* be answered through correlational research. A case study is not convincing because, even if one does identify a case in which someone experiences a lot of positive emotions and lives for many years, it is impossible to know if the single case is typical of people in general. An experimental study is impossible, both because one cannot easily manipulate people's general tendency to experience emotional states and because it would be unethical to manipulate a variable that might lower people's length of life. Correlational research on this topic could be conducted thanks to a project known as the "nun study" (Danner et al., 2001). This is a study of a large number of Catholic nuns living in the United States. The nuns in the study were all born before the year 1917. In 1930, an administrative official of the Catholic Church had asked them to write an autobiography. The researchers, with the permission of the nuns, read these autobiographies and coded them according to the amount of positive emotions expressed in the writing. Some autobiographies contained relatively little positive emotional content (e.g., "I intend to do the best for our order, for the spread of religion and for my personal sanctification"), whereas others indicated that the writer experienced high degrees of positive emotion ("the past year … has been a very happy one. Now I look forward with eager joy"; Danner et al., 2001, p. 806).

During the 1990s and the year 2000, approximately 40% of the nuns, who at the time ranged in age from 75 to 95 years, died. The researchers could relate the experience of positive emotions, as indicated in the biographies of 1930, to length of life at the end of the century.

This study revealed a strikingly large relationship between emotional experience and length of life. Nuns who experienced more positive emotions in the 1930s lived longer. The relation between emotional experience and longevity can be represented by counting the number of

Jerry Gay/Getty Images

Personality research employing a correlational research strategy indicates that individuals who experience a relatively high level of positive emotions tend to live longer.

positive emotion words that were used in the autobiographies and dividing the population into quartiles (i.e., four groupings, each representing approximately one-fourth of the population) ranging from low to high amounts of emotion words (Table 2.1). Of the nuns who had expressed a high amount of positive emotions, only about one-fifth died during the observation period. Of the nuns who expressed low amounts of positive emotion, more than half died! This is true even though the high and low groups were of the same age at the beginning of the observation period.

Experiments

One of the great achievements of science is not a research finding but a research method: the controlled experiment. The key feature of a controlled experiment is that participants are assigned at *random* to an experimental condition. The overall experiment contains a number of different

Table 2.1   **Relation Between Expression of Positive Emotions in Writing as Measured Early in Life and Longevity**

Positive Emotion Words	Age	Died (%)
Quartile I (low)	79.9	55
Quartile II	81.1	59
Quartile III	79.7	33
Quartile IV (high)	79.0	21

Source: Danner, D. D., Snowdon, D. A., & Friesen, W. V. (2001). Positive emotions in early life and longevity: Findings from the nun study. *Journal of Personality & Social Psychology, 80*, 804–813.

conditions that manipulate one or more variables of interest. If people in one condition respond differently than people in another, then one can conclude that the variable that was manipulated causally influenced their responses. This conclusion is valid precisely because people are assigned to conditions randomly. Random assignment assures that there is no systematic relationship between the experimental conditions and people's preexperimental psychological tendencies. If people in different conditions act differently after the experimental manipulation, despite being the same before it occurred, then the manipulation was the cause of the differences in response. This research strategy, in which variables are manipulated through the random assignment of persons to different conditions, is the hallmark of **experimental research**.

Experimental Research: An Example

A powerful example of experimental research is the work of Claude Steele (1997) and colleagues on a phenomenon known as "stereotype threat". Stereotype threat can occur when people are trying to perform a task well (e.g., they are taking an exam) and there exists a stereotype concerning the abilities of their social, ethnic, or gender group. For example, there may be a stereotype that women are less good at math then men, or that people of different ethnic backgrounds differ in intelligence. If an individual who belongs to a stereotypes group thinks about the stereotype, a psychological threat arises: The individual knows that he or she may confirm the stereotype. This stereotype threat can interfere with performance. For example, if you are taking a difficult exam and become distracted by thoughts that you might confirm a stereotype associated with a group of which you are a member, then this distraction might, like any distraction, cause you to perform less well.

In principle, one could study stereotype threat processes through case studies or correlational studies. However, as we have noted, these approaches would not provide convincing evidence that stereotype threat causally influences performance. To explore this potential causal influence, Steele and colleagues have studied stereotype threat experimentally (Steele, 1997). For example, they have examined the performance of African-American and European-American college students on verbal test items of the sort that might be included on an intelligence test; a negative stereotype about intelligence is one of various stereotypes about African-Americans that persist in U.S. culture. The experiment featured two conditions. In one, all participants first completed a demographic questionnaire in which they were asked to indicate their race. In the other, the demographic questionnaire was omitted. Black and white students were assigned at random to one or the other condition. The results of the study revealed that completing the demographic questionnaire lowered the subsequent test performance of black students—stereotype threat processes caused them to perform less well than whites. This was not the case where there was no race prime; that is, where stereotype threat processes were not activated. Although we review this study for the purpose of illustrating the experimental method, one, of course, should also note its social implications. By asking about racial background on demographic questionnaires, one may inadvertently produce differences in intelligence test scores. Thus, if a group of black students were to obtain lower intelligence test scores than white students, this would not necessarily mean that they possess less intelligence; instead, they could be suffering from stereotype-threat processes that cause the test scores to underestimate their actual intellectual capabilities.

Stereotype-threat processes can occur in other settings and with members of other groups. For example, women may be subject to negative stereotypes with regard to performance in mathematics. The threat of confirming these stereotypes may contribute to male–female differences in mathematics test performance. Consistent with this idea, gender differences in which men outperform women in mathematics have been shown to be eliminated when stereotype threat is reduced (Spencer, Steele, & Quinn, 1999). Experimental research on stereotype threat thus illuminates a general psychological process that contributes to important life outcomes.

Table 2.2 **Summary of Potential Strengths and Limitations of Alternative Research Methods**

Potential Strengths	Potential Limitations
CASE STUDIES AND CLINICAL RESEARCH	
1. Avoid the artificiality of laboratory	1. Lead to unsystematic observation
2. Study the full complexity of person–environment relationships	2. Encourage subjective interpretation of data
3. Lead to in-depth study of individuals	3. Do not establish causal relationships
QUESTIONNAIRES AND CORRELATION RESEARCH	
1. Study a wide range of variables	1. Establish relationships that are associational rather than causal
2. Study relationships among many variables	2. Problems of reliability and validity of self-report questionnaires
3. Large samples easily obtained	3. Individuals not studied in depth
LABORATORY STUDIES AND EXPERIMENTAL RESEARCH	
1. Manipulate specific variables	1. Exclude phenomena that cannot be studied in the laboratory
2. Record data objectively	2. Create an artificial setting that limits the generality of findings
3. Establish cause–effect relationships	3. Foster demand characteristics and experimenter expectancy effects

Evaluating Alternative Research Approaches

Having now reviewed the three major research strategies, we are in a position to evaluate them in detail. As we already have noted, each has strengths and limitations (Table 2.2).

Case Studies and Clinical Research: Strengths and Limitations

A major advantage of case studies, particularly as they are conducted in clinical settings, is that they overcome the potential superficiality and artificiality of correlational and experimental methods. In a case study, the investigator learns about deeply important aspects of an individual's life, which may not occur in a brief experiment or a survey questionnaire. Clinicians conducting case studies directly observe how the client thinks and feels about events. One examines the behavior of interest directly and does not have to extrapolate from a somewhat artificial setting to the real world.

A further advantage is that clinical research may be the only feasible way of studying some phenomena. When one needs to study the full complexity of personality processes, individual environment relationships, and the within-person organization of personality, in-depth case studies may be the only option.

The in-depth study of select individuals differs in two main ways from research on groups (Pervin, 1983). First, relationships established for a group as a whole may not reflect the way any individual within the group behaves; group statistics inherently do not inform one about individuals in the group. The second difference follows from the first: An analysis of group data may obscure interesting relationships that can be found only by studying individual cases. Early in the field's history, Henry Murray advanced this argument. A group statistic, he noted, "leaves unexplained the uncommon (exhibited-by-the-minority) response … Averages obliterate the 'individual characters of individual organisms' and so fail to reveal the complex interaction of forces which determine each concrete event" (1938, p. viii).

Yet case studies have three major drawbacks. (1) Findings from one case study may not generalize to another. It thus is hard to establish generalizable scientific principles through case studies. (2) The case study method cannot demonstrate causality. An example demonstrates this limitation. Imagine a clinical case study that describes improvements in a person's well-being across a year of therapy. You cannot conclude that the therapy was the cause of the improvement; other events in the person's life may have been responsible. (3) Case studies commonly employ sources of data that are "subjective," in other words, that rely in part on the personal beliefs and opinions of the research. A therapist's subjective beliefs about her client, or about the value of her preferred therapy method, may inadvertently bias the presentation in a case study. This limitation is usually overcome in correlational and experimental studies thanks to their use of objective measurement procedures.

The Use of Verbal Reports   Clinical research in personality generally relies on what people say about themselves, or "verbal reports". Verbal reports present a number of difficulties. First and foremost, people's statements about themselves may be inaccurate. As you will learn in Chapters 3 and 4, psychodynamic psychologists argue that people systematically distort their statements in order to defend their self-image and avoid anxiety. Second, even when people do want to describe themselves accurately, they often cannot because many mental events occur outside of consciousness. For example, when asked why they made a particular decision, people may answer inaccurately because they are not consciously aware of subtle situational factor that influenced their choice (Nisbett & Wilson, 1977; Wilson, Hull, & Johnson, 1981). Whether for defensive reasons or due to the inaccessibility of cognitive and emotional processes, verbal self-reports are questionable sources of reliable and valid data (West & Finch, 1997; Wilson, 1994).

Yet one should not push this argument too far. For certain purposes, with certain types of data-gathering methods, verbal reports can provide valuable data (Ericsson & Simon, 1993). Which kinds of verbal responses are most useful and trustworthy? If you want to learn about personality dynamics—mental events that change over the course of time (Cervone & Little, 2017)—a guideline for selecting research methods is to recall that people can only report about things to which they have paid attention. If a researcher asks participants about subtle situational factor that they never noticed in the first places, the participants' answers plainly will lack validity (White, 1980). If you ask people to report, for example, why they purchased one product over another in the supermarket when they were not attending to this decision at the time, they will give you an inference or a hypothesis rather than an account of what occurred.

What research strategies, using verbal reports, are valid indicators of a person's flow of thoughts? One valuable strategy is simply to ask people to think out loud when they are performing a task (Ericsson & Simon, 1993). For example, in research on educational achievement and the impact of anxiety and helpless feelings on educational progress, one research team (Elliott & Dweck, 1988) ask children to think aloud when trying to solve a series of logic problems. Children who were concerned about the possibility that observers would find out that they lack ability on the task spontaneously made negative statements (e.g., "my stomach hurts"). Similarly, in sport psychology, researchers have used think-aloud methods to understand the flow of thoughts that occur as people are playing golf (Whitehead, Taylor, & Polman, 2015) and engaged in distance running (Samson, Simpson, Kamphoff, & Langlier, 2017). As these researchers know, think-aloud methods are superior to retrospective methods in which researchers asks people, after the fact, what they earlier had been thinking. Memory errors inevitably may create errors in retrospective reports.

Correlational Research and Questionnaires: Strengths and Limitations

A main advantage of correlational studies using questionnaires is sample size. It often is possible to study large numbers of people. As noted earlier, by conducting research through the Internet, psychologists can obtain extremely large and diverse samples of participants (Fraley, 2007).

Another advantage of the correlational approach concerns reliability. Many questionnaires provide extremely reliable indices of the psychological constructs they are designed to measure.

This is important because tests must be reliable in order to detect important features of personality that might be overlooked otherwise. For example, researchers find that individual differences in personality traits are highly stable over time; people who differ in extraversion or conscientiousness in young adulthood will probably differ in middle and later adulthood as well (e.g., Costa & McCrae, 2002). One could not detect this fact unless the measures of the personality traits were highly reliable.

Correlational studies have been enormously popular among personality psychologists. Yet it is important to be aware of three limitations of this research strategy. The first limitation is one that differentiates correlational studies from case studies. Case studies provide richly detailed information about an individual. In contrast, correlational studies provide relatively superficial information about individual persons. A correlational study will provide information about an individual's scores on the various personality tests that happen to have been used in the research. But if there are some other variables that are important to an individual person, a correlational study generally will not reveal them.

The second limitation is one that case studies and correlational studies share. As in a case study, in a correlational study, it is difficult to draw firm conclusions about causality. The fact that two variables are correlated does not mean that one variable necessarily caused the other. A "third variable" could have influenced both of the variables in one's study and caused those variables to be correlated. For example, in the nun study, it is possible that some psychological, biological, or environmental factor that was not measured in the study caused some nuns to experience fewer positive emotions *and* to live less long. As a hypothetical example, if one conducted a study akin to the nun study with college students, one might find that positive emotionality would predict longevity. But that would not necessarily mean that the tendency to experience positive emotions during college caused people to live longer. For example, levels of academic success could function as a third variable. Students who are doing extremely well in college might experience more positive emotions as a result of their academic success. They also might obtain more lucrative jobs after graduation, again as a result of their academic success. Their high-paying jobs might enable them to pay for superior health care, which in turn could lengthen their life whether or not they continue to experience frequent position emotions. In this hypothetical example, emotions and length of life would be correlated, but not because of any direct causal connection between the two.

A third limitation concerns the widespread reliance on self-report questionnaires. When people are describing themselves on a questionnaire, they may be biased to answer items in a way that has nothing to do with the exact content of the items or the psychological construct that the psychologist is trying to assess. These biases are called **response styles**. Two illustrative response-style problems can be considered. The first is called *acquiescence*. It involves the tendency to agree consistently (or disagree consistently) with items regardless of their content. For example, a test-taker may prefer to say "Yes" or "I agree" when asked questions, rather than saying "No" or "I disagree". The second response style is called *social desirability*. Instead of responding to the intended psychological meaning of a test item, a subject may respond to the fact that different types of responses are more or less desirable. If, hypothetically, a test item asks "Have you ever stolen anything from a store?," the answer "No" is clearly a more socially desirable response than "Yes". If people are biased to answer questions in a socially desirable manner, then their test scores may not accurately reflect their true psychological characteristics.

A research report that highlights the problem of distortion of questionnaire responses, while also emphasizing the potential value of clinical judgment, is that of Shedler, Mayman, and Manis (1993). In this research conducted by psychologists with a psychoanalytic orientation who were skeptical of accepting self-report data at face value, individuals who "looked good" on mental health questionnaire scales were evaluated by a psychodynamically oriented clinician. On the basis of his clinical judgments, two subgroups were distinguished: one defined as being genuinely psychologically healthy in agreement with the questionnaire scales and a second defined as consisting of individuals who were psychologically distressed but who maintained an illusion of mental health through defensive denial of their difficulties. Individuals in the two groups were found to differ significantly in their responses to stress. Subjects in the illusory mental health group were found to show much higher levels of coronary reactivity to stress than subjects in the genuinely healthy group. Indeed, the former subjects were found to show even greater levels of coronary reactivity to stress than subjects who reported their distress on the mental health questionnaire scales. The differences in reactivity to stress between the genuinely healthy subjects and the "illusory" healthy subjects were considered not only to be statistically significant but medically significant as well. Thus, it was concluded that "for some people, mental health scales appear to be legitimate measures of mental health. For other people, these scales appear to measure defensive denial. There seems to be no way to know from the test score alone what is being measured in any given respondent" (Shedler et al., 1993, p. 1128).

Those who defend the use of questionnaires note that such problems often can be eliminated through careful test construction and interpretation. Psychologists can reduce or eliminate the effects of acquiescence by varying the wording of items on a test so that consistent "yes" responses do not give one a higher overall test score. They can employ questionnaires that are specifically designed to measure the degree to which a given person tends to endorse socially desirable responses. Comprehensive personality questionnaires commonly include test items or scales to measure whether subjects are faking or trying to present themselves in a particularly favorable or socially desirable way. Including such scales in a research project, however, often is inconvenient or costly, and thus, such scales often are lacking in particular studies.

Laboratory, Experimental Research: Strengths and Limitations

In many ways, our ideal image of scientific investigation is laboratory research. Ask people for their description of a scientist, and they are likely to conjure up an image of someone in a sterile lab. As we have already seen, this image is too limited; personality psychologists employ a range of scientific methods, and laboratory research is but one of them. Yet it is an important one. The experimental approach, as we have noted, has the unique ability to manipulate variables of interest and thereby to establish cause–effect relationships. In the experiment that is properly designed and carried out, every step is carefully planned to limit effects to the variables of interest. Few variables are studied, so that the problem of disentangling complex relationships does not exist. Systematic relationships between changes in some variables and consequences for other variables are established so that the experimenter can say "If X, then Y." Full details of the experimental procedure are reported so that the results can be replicated by investigators in other laboratories.

Psychologists who are critical of laboratory research suggest that too often such research is artificial and has limited relevance to other contexts. The suggestion is that what works in the laboratory may not work elsewhere. Furthermore, although relationships between isolated variables may be established, such relationships may not hold when the complexity of actual human behavior is considered. Also, since laboratory research tends to involve relatively brief exposures to stimuli, such research may miss important processes that occur over time. As you read about personality research in the subsequent chapters of this book, a question to ask yourself is how successful the different theories are in establishing experimental findings that generalize to real-world situations.

As a human enterprise, experimental research with humans lends itself to influences that are part of everyday interpersonal behavior. The investigation of such influences might be called the social psychology of research. Let us consider two important illustrations. First, some factors influencing the behavior of human subjects may not be part of the experimental design. Among such factors may be cues implicit in the experimental setting that suggest to the subject that the experimenter has a certain hypothesis and, "in the interest of science," the subject behaves in a way that will confirm it. Such effects are known as **demand characteristics** and suggest that the psychological experiment is a form of social interaction in which subjects give purpose and meaning to things (Orne, 1962; Weber & Cook, 1972). The purpose and meaning given to the research may vary from subject to subject in ways that are not part of the experimental design and thereby serve to reduce both reliability and validity.

Complementing these sources of error or bias in the subject are unintended sources of influence or error in the experimenter. Without realizing it, experimenters may either make errors in recording and analyzing data or emit cues to the subjects and thus influence their behavior in a particular way. Such unintended **experimenter expectancy effects** may lead subjects to behave in accordance with the hypothesis (Rosenthal, 1994; Rosenthal & Rubin, 1978). For example, consider the classic case of Clever Hans (Pfungst, 1911). Hans was a horse that by tapping his foot could add, subtract, multiply, and divide. A mathematical problem would be presented to the horse and, incredibly, he was able to come up with the answer. In attempting to discover the secret of Hans's talents, a variety of situational factors were manipulated. If Hans could not see the questioner or if the questioner did not know the answer, Hans was unable to provide the correct answer. On the other hand, if the questioner knew the answer and was visible, Hans could tap out the answer with his foot. Apparently the questioner unknowingly signaled Hans when to start and stop tapping his hoof: The tapping would start when the questioner inclined his head forward, increase in speed when the questioner bent forward more, and stop when the questioner straightened up. As can be seen, experimenter expectancy effects can be quite subtle and neither the researcher nor subject may be aware of their existence.

It should be noted that demand characteristics and expectancy effects can occur as sources of error in all three forms of research. However, they have been considered and studied most often in relation to experimental research. In addition, as noted, experimental research often is seen as most closely approximating the scientific ideal. Therefore, such sources of error are all the more noteworthy in relation to this form of research.

Many of the criticisms of experimental research have been attacked by experimental psychologists. In defending laboratory experiments, the following statements are made: (1) Such research is the proper basis for testing causal hypotheses. The generality of the established relationship is then a subject for further investigation. (2) Some phenomena would never be discovered outside of the laboratory. (3) Some phenomena can be studied in the laboratory that would be difficult to study elsewhere (e.g., subjects are given permission to be aggressive in contrast with the often quite strong restraints in natural social settings). (4) There is little empirical support for the contention that subjects typically try to confirm the experimenter's hypothesis or for the significance of experimental artifacts more generally. Indeed, many subjects are more negativistic than conforming (Berkowitz & Donnerstein, 1982).

Even if one accepts these four points, there remains one criticism of laboratory research that is difficult, if not impossible, to overcome. It is that some phenomena simply cannot be produced in the laboratory. A personality theory may make predictions about people's emotional reactions to extreme levels of stress or their thoughts about highly personal matters. For such questions, laboratory methods may not work. It would be unethical to create extremely high levels of stress in the lab. In a brief laboratory encounter, people are unlikely to reveal any thoughts about matters that are highly personal. The personality scientist sometimes is not afforded the luxury of the simple laboratory study.

Summary of Strengths and Limitations

In assessing these alternative approaches to research, we must recognize that we are considering potential, rather than necessary, strengths and limitations (Table 2.2). In fact, findings from one approach generally coincide with those from another approach (Anderson, Lindsay, & Bushman, 1999). What it comes down to is that each research effort must be evaluated on its own merits and for its own potential in advancing understanding rather than on some preconceived basis. Alternative research procedures can be used in conjunction with one another in any research enterprise. In addition, data from alternative research procedures can be integrated in the pursuit of a more comprehensive theory.

Personality Theory and Personality Research

In Chapter 1, we considered the nature of personality theory: psychologists' efforts to systematize what is known about personality and to point research in directions that yield new knowledge. In this chapter, we have considered the nature of personality research: psychologists' efforts to bring objective scientific evidence to bear on their theories. We reviewed the kinds of data obtained by personality psychologists and then the strengths and limits of three traditional types of personality research (case studies, correlational research, and laboratory experiments).

As we already have noted, personality theory and personality research are not two separate, unrelated enterprises; they are inherently intertwined. Theory and research are related for two reasons, one of which we already have noted: Theoretical conceptions suggest avenues for exploration and specify the types of data that qualify as "evidence" about personality. Personality researchers are interested in a person's physiological reactions and are uninterested in their astrological signs because personality theories contain ideas that relate physiology to psychological functioning, while leaving no room for the influence of astrological forces.

Theory and research tend to be related in another way. Theorists have preferences and biases concerning how research should be conducted. The father of American behaviorism, John B. Watson, emphasized the use of animals in research in part because of his discomfort in working with humans. Sigmund Freud, founder of psychoanalytic theory, was a therapist who did not believe that important psychoanalytic phenomena could be studied in any manner other than in therapy. Hans Eysenck and Raymond Cattell, two trait theorists of historic importance, were trained, early in their careers, in sophisticated statistical methods involving correlation, and these methods fundamentally shaped their theoretical ideas.

Historically, personality researchers have tended to fall on one or the other side of three issues associated with the three approaches to research: (1) "making things happen" in research (experimental) versus "studying what has occurred" (correlational), (2) all persons (experimental) versus the single individual (clinical), and (3) one aspect or few aspects of the person versus the total individual. In other words, there are preferences or biases toward clinical, experimental, and correlational research.

Despite the objectivity of science, research is a human enterprise and such preferences are part of research as a human enterprise. All researchers attempt to be as objective as possible in the conduct of their research, and generally they give "objective" reasons for following a particular approach to research. That is, the particular strengths of the research approach followed are emphasized relative to the strengths and limitations of alternative approaches. Beyond this, however, a personal element enters. Just as psychologists feel more comfortable with one or another kind of data, they feel more comfortable with one or another approach to research.

Further, different theories of personality are linked with different research strategies and thereby with different kinds of data. In other words, the links among theory, data, and research are such that the observations associated with one theory of personality often are of a fundamentally different type than those associated with another theory. The phenomena of interest to one theory of personality are not as easily studied by the research procedures useful in the study of phenomena emphasized by another theory of personality. One personality theory leads us to obtain one kind of data and follow one approach to research, whereas another theory leads us to collect different kinds of data and follow another approach to research. It is not that one or another is better but rather that they are different, and these differences must be appreciated in considering each approach to theory and research. This has been true historically and remains true in the current scientific discipline (Cervone, 1991). Since the remaining chapters in this textbook are organized around the major theoretical approaches to personality, it is important to keep such linkages and differences in mind in comparing one theory with another.

Personality Assessment and the Case of Jim

As we have seen, personality research involves the effort to measure individuals on a personality characteristic assumed to be of theoretical importance. The term *assessment* generally is used to refer to efforts to measure personality aspects of individuals in order to make an applied or practical decision: Will this person be a good candidate for this job? Will this person profit from one or another kind of treatment? Is this person a good candidate for this training program? In addition, the term *assessment* often is used to refer to the effort to arrive at a comprehensive understanding of individuals by obtaining a wide variety of information about them. In this sense, assessment of a person involves administering a variety of personality tests or measures in the pursuit of a comprehensive understanding of his or her personality.

As noted, such an effort also provides for a comparison of results from different sources of information. This book assumes that each technique of assessment gives a glimpse of human behavior and that no one test gives, or can hope to give, a picture of the total personality of an individual. People are complex, and our efforts to assess personality must reflect this complexity. In the chapters that follow, we will consider a number of theories of personality and approaches to personality assessment. In addition, we will consider the assessment of an individual, Jim, from the standpoint of each theory and approach to assessment. Through this approach, we will be able to see the relation between theory and assessment and also to consider the extent to which different approaches result in similar pictures of the person.

Before we describe Jim, here are some details concerning the assessment project. Jim was a college student when, in the late 1960s, he volunteered to serve as a subject for a project involving the intensive study of college students. He participated in the project mainly because of his interest in psychology but also because he hoped to gain a better understanding of himself. At the time, various tests were administered to him. These tests represented a sampling of the tests then available. Obviously, theories of personality and associated tests that had not been developed at the time could not be administered. However, Jim agreed to report on his life experiences and to take some additional tests 5, 20, and 25 years later. At those times, an effort was made to administer tests developed in association with emerging theories of personality.

Thus, we do not have the opportunity to consider all the tests at the same point in time. However, we are able to consider the personality of an individual over an extended period of time and, thereby, examine how the theories—and the tests—relate to what occurred earlier in life and what followed later. Let us begin with a brief sketch derived from Jim's autobiography and follow him throughout the text as we consider the various approaches to personality.

Autobiographical Sketch of Jim

In his autobiography, Jim reported that he was born in New York City after the end of World War II and received considerable attention and affection as a child. His father is a college graduate who owns an automobile sales business; his mother is a housewife who also does volunteer reading for the blind. Jim described himself as having a good relationship with his father and described his mother as having "great feelings for other people—she is a totally loving woman". He is the oldest of four children, with a sister four years younger and two brothers, one five years younger and one seven years younger. The main themes in his autobiography concern his inability to become involved with women in a satisfying way, his need for success and his relative failure since high school, and his uncertainty about whether to go on to graduate school in business administration or in clinical psychology. Overall he felt that people had a high estimate of him because they used superficial criteria but that inwardly he was troubled.

We have here the bare outline of a person. The details will be filled in as he is considered from the standpoint of different personality theories. Hopefully, by the end of the book, a complete picture of Jim will emerge.

MAJOR CONCEPTS

Case studies
Computerized text analysis
  methods
Correlation coefficient
Correlational research
Demand characteristics

Electroencephalography
  (EEG)
Experimental research
Experimenter expectancy
  effects
Functional magnetic resonance
  imaging (fMRI)

Idiographic (strategies)
Implicit Measures
L-data
Nomothetic (strategies)
O-data
Reliability

Response style
S-data
T-data
Validity

REVIEW

1. Research involves the systematic study of relationships among phenomena or events. Four types of data are obtained in personality research: L-data, O-data, T-data, and S-data (LOTS). Three approaches to personality research are clinical research, laboratory experimentation, and correlational research using questionnaires.

2. A contemporary development in research methods is the availability of computerized text analysis methods, which are software tools that take, as their input, words and sentences. The words people use (e.g., in social media) may be revealing of their personality.

3. All research shares the goals of reliability and validity—of obtaining observations that can be replicated and for which there is evidence of a relation to the concepts of interest. As a human enterprise, research involves ethical questions concerning the treatment of subjects and the reporting of data.

4. Clinical research involves the intensive study of individuals. This research method was illustrated by a case study involving the self-concept of an individual as he confronted the different social situations of his life.

5. In correlational research, the investigator measures two or more variables and determines the degree to which they are associated with each other. Questionnaire measures are particularly important in correlational research. This research method was illustrated with research in which personality factors were found to predict longevity.

6. Experimental research involves the manipulation of one or more variables to determine their causal impact on outcomes of interest. This approach to research was illustrated by the manipulation of variables related to the phenomenon of stereotype threat.

7. Each of three approaches to research can be viewed as having its own set of potential strengths and limitations (Table 2.2). Thus, each research strategy has the potential to produce particular insights as well as its own pitfalls.

8. Theories of personality differ in their preferences for types of data and approaches to research. In other words, there tend to be linkages among theory, type of data, and method of research. It is important to keep such linkages in mind as the major theories of personality are considered in the chapters that follow. A single case studied from the standpoint of each theoretical perspective also will be presented for illustrative and comparative purposes.

A Psychodynamic Theory: Freud's Psychoanalytic Theory of Personality

3

Questions to be Addressed in this Chapter

Sigmund Freud (1856–1939):
   A View of the Theorist

Freud's View of the Person

Freud's View of the Science of Personality

Freud's Psychoanalytic Theory of Personality

Major Concepts

Review

Chapter Focus

The number one player on the tennis team is getting ready to play for the state title. She has never met her opponent before, so she decides to introduce herself before the match. She strolls onto the court where her opponent is warming up and says. "Hi, I'm Amy. Glad to beat you." You can imagine how embarrassed Amy was! Flustered, she corrected her innocent mistake and walked over to her side of the court to warm up. "Wow," Amy thought, "where did that come from?"

Was Amy's verbal slip so innocent? Freud wouldn't have thought so. In his view, Amy's silly mistake was actually a very revealing display of unconscious aggressive drives. Freud's psychoanalytic theory is illustrative of a psychodynamic and clinical approach to personality. Behavior is interpreted as a result of the dynamic interplay among motives, drives, needs, and conflicts. The research consists mainly of clinical investigations as shown in an emphasis on the individual, in the attention given to individual differences, and in attempts to assess and understand the total individual. Contemporary researchers, however, devote much attention to the challenge of studying psychodynamic processes in the experimental laboratory.

Questions to be Addressed in this Chapter

1. How did Freud develop his theory, and how did historical and personal events shape this development?

2. What are the key features of Freud's theoretical model of the human mind?

3. How do people protect themselves against experiences of anxiety, and in what ways (according to Freud) are these anxiety-reduction strategies a centerpiece of personality dynamics?

4. How important is early childhood experience for later personality development?

Sigmund Freud (1856–1939): A View of the Theorist

Sigmund Freud was born in Moravia (in what is now the city of Fribor of the Czech Republic) in 1856. His family soon moved to Vienna, where he spent most of his life. Freud was the first child of his parents, but his father, 20 years older than his mother, had two sons by a previous marriage. His parents then had seven more children after his birth. Within this large group of family members, the intellectually precocious Sigmund was his mother's favorite—and he knew it. Later in life, Freud famously commented, from experience, that a man who has been the indisputable favorite of his mother "keeps for life the feeling of a conqueror, that confidence of success that often induces real success" (Freud, 1900, p. 26).

As a boy, Freud had big dreams. He wanted to become a great general or government official. But anti-Semitism limited the possibility for advancement in these fields for Freud, who was Jewish. He thus pursued a career in medicine instead.

ullstein bild / Contributor / Getty Images

Sigmund Freud and his daughter Anna Freud. Both contributed to the development of psychodynamic conceptions of personality.

Freud's medical training, at the University of Vienna, profoundly shaped his later theorizing about personality. A key figure in this training was a professor of physiology named Ernst Brücke, who took part in an intellectual movement known as **mechanism**. The mechanist movement addressed questions about the nature and possibilities of the science of biology. It is best understood by contrasting it with an opposing movement, "vitalism." Vitalists argued that biological science could *not* fully explain biological life because life arose from nonmaterial forces (like a soul, or spirit, that animates an otherwise lifeless body). Mechanists argued that the principles of natural science could, in fact, provide comprehensive explanation. Basic physical and chemical factors could fully explain the functioning of organisms, including life itself (Gay, 1998). The mechanist position, which is taken for granted today, opened the door for a complete natural science of persons. Brücke's rejection of vitalism and embrace of the scientific principles of mechanism provide a foundation for the dynamic view of personality Freud developed later in life (Sulloway, 1979).

After earning his medical degree, Freud worked in the field of neurology. Some of his early research involved a comparison of adult and fetal brains. He concluded that the earliest structures persist throughout life—a view that was a precursor to his later views of personality development. However, for financial reasons, including the need to support a family, Freud abandoned his research career and became a practicing physician.

In 1897, the year following his father's death, Freud was plagued by periods of depression and anxiety. To understand his problems, Freud began an activity that proved utterly fundamental to the development of psychoanalysis: a *self*-analysis. Freud analyzed the contents of his own experiences, concentrating in particular on his dreams, which he thought would reveal unconscious thoughts and desires. He continued this self-analysis throughout his life, devoting the last half hour of each workday to it.

In his therapeutic work, Freud tried various techniques to uncover psychological causes of his patient's problems. One was hypnosis, which he learned about from the renowned French psychiatrist Jean Charcot. But finding that not all patients could be hypnotized, he explored other methods. The one that proved crucial to his work was **free association**. In the free-association technique, the person being analyzed allows all of his or her thoughts to come forth without inhibition or falsification of any kind. By letting thoughts flow freely, one may discover hidden associations among ideas. For Freud, the free-association technique was both a therapy and a scientific method; it provided the primary evidence for his theory of personality.

In 1900, Freud published his most significant work, *The Interpretation of Dreams*. Here, Freud no longer was concerned merely with treating patients. He was developing a theory of mind—a conceptual model of the mind's basic structures and working principles. The book, though brilliant, was slow to catch on; in its first eight years of publication, *The Interpretation of Dreams* sold only 600 copies. Freud's views about the psychology of childhood (which you'll learn below) were ridiculed. Medical institutions that taught Freud's views were boycotted. An early follower, Ernest Jones, was forced to resign a neurological appointment for inquiring into the sexual life of his patients, in the manner that Freud's theory suggested. At a personal level, during World War I, Freud lost his financial savings and feared for the lives of two sons in the war. In 1920, a daughter, age 26, died. This historical context may have partly contributed to Freud's development, at age 64, of a theory of the death instinct—a wish to die, in opposition to the life instinct or a wish for survival.

Yet Freud persevered and gradually achieved widespread recognition. Lectures in the United States in 1909 greatly enhanced his profile outside of Europe. An International Psychoanalytic Association was founded in 1910. During these and subsequent years, Freud published prolifically, had a waiting list of patients, and achieved increasing fame. Thanks to his efforts and those of his followers, by the time of his death in London on September 23, 1939 (he had fled Vienna a year earlier to escape the Nazis), he was an international celebrity. Today, Freud's ideas and his psychoanalytic terminology are known even to people who never have read a word of his writing or taken a single psychology course. Among 20th-century figures, Freud's contributions to Western intellectual life are exceeded perhaps only by those of Einstein.

Many glorify Freud as a compassionate, courageous genius. Others, noting his battles and breaks with colleagues, see him as an authoritarian, intolerant figure (Fromm, 1959). Whatever one's view of his personality, Freud unquestionably pursued his work with great courage. He bravely presented personal details of his own life to illustrate his theory. He withstood the criticism of colleagues and the scorn of society at large. He did this, as he wrote to an associate, "in the service" of "a dominating passion … a tyrant [that] has come my way … it is psychology" (Gay, 1998, p. 74).

Freud's View of the Person

Throughout this book, when we introduce a theory of personality, we first will review the life of the theorist (as above for Freud). Then, prior to detailing the given theory's treatment of personality structures and processes, we will present its overall view of the person. Each major theory of personality contains a broad conception of human nature, or a view of the person. We present these conceptions at the outset for two reasons: (1) They provide a foundation for understanding. You quickly will gain knowledge of the most important ideas of a given theory—knowledge you can build upon when reading subsequent material. (2) These "View of the Person" sections answer a question you might be asking yourself: "Why should I bother to learn about this personality theory?" The answer is that, in all cases in this book, the given personality theory addresses big ideas: the nature of mind, human nature, and society. These "big picture" ideas are summarized in the *View of the Person* sections of the text.

The Mind as an Energy System

Freud's theory of personality is fundamentally a theory of mind—a scientific model of the overall architecture of mental structures and processes. In formulating a model of mind, Freud explicitly "[considers] mental life from a *biological* point of view" (Freud, 1915/1970, p. 328). He recognizes the mind as part of the body, asks what the body is like, and derives principles of mental functioning from overall principles of physiological functioning.

As we noted, to Freud, the body is a mechanistic **energy system**. It follows, then, that the mind, being part of the body, also is a mechanistic energy system. The mind gets mental energies from the overall physical energies of the body.

An energy-system view of mind contrasts with alternative perspectives one could adopt. For example, instead, one could view the mind as an information system. In an information system, material is merely stored somewhere and drawn upon when needed. Information on the hard drive of your computer, or information written into a book on the shelf of a library, is like this—it merely sits there inertly, in storage, to be accessed as needed. In Freud's energy model, however, mental contents do not merely sit in storage inertly. Mental contents *do* things. The mind contains instinctual drives that are "piece[s] of activity" that exert "pressure … [an] amount of force" (Freud, 1915/1970, p. 328) on the overall psychic apparatus. The overall mind, then, is a system that contains and directs these energetic forces.

If one takes this view, then the major scientific problem is to explain what happens to mental energy: how it flows, gets sidetracked, or becomes dammed up. Freud's view of mental energy includes three core ideas. One is that there is a limited amount of energy. If much energy is used in one way, less is available for other purposes. Energy used for cultural purposes, for example, is no longer available for sexual purposes, and vice versa. A second idea is that energy can be blocked from one channel of expression and, if it is blocked, the energy does not "just go away." Instead, it gets expressed in some other manner, along a path of least resistance.

Finally, fundamental to Freud's energy model is the idea that the mind functions to achieve a state of quiescence (Greenberg & Mitchell, 1983). Bodily needs create a state of tension, and the person is driven to reduce that tension to return to a quiet internal state. A simple example is that if you are lacking food, you experience the state of tension we call hunger, and this drives you to seek some object in the environment that satisfies your hunger, eliminating the tension and returning you to a state of quiescence. (Of course, Freud explores examples of dramatically greater complexity than this one, as you will see.) The goal of all behavior, then, is the pleasure that results from the reduction of tension or the release of energy. The personality theory of Freud that you will learn about in this chapter is basically a detailed model of the personality structures and processes that are responsible for this dynamic flow of mental energy.

Why the assumption that the mind is an energy system? It derives from developments in physics in Freud's time. The 19th-century physicist Hermann von Helmholtz had presented the principle of conservation of energy: Matter and energy can be transformed but not destroyed. Not only physicists but also members of other disciplines were studying the laws of energy changes in systems. Freud's medical training included the idea that human physiology could be understood in terms of physical forces that adhere to the principle of conservation of energy. The age of energy and dynamics provided scientists with a new conception of humans: "that man is an energy system and that he obeys the same physical laws which regulate the soap bubble and the movement of the planets" (Hall, 1954, pp. 12–13). Freud developed this general view into a well-specified theory of personality.

In psychoanalysis, then, ideas have mental energy that remains stored in the mind; that is, the energy is conserved within the mind. However, under special circumstances, the energy associated with an idea can be released. The question of how this occurs is central to psychoanalytic theory. Interestingly, the answer to this question did not first come from Freud but from an associate of his, the Viennese physician Joseph Breuer.

In the summer of 1882, in an event of incalculably great importance to the development of psychoanalytic thought, Breuer told Freud about a patient of his named Anna O. Anna O. suffered from a bizarre collection of symptoms whose biological causes could not be determined: partial paralysis, blurred vision, persistent cough, and difficulty conversing in her native language, German, despite being able to speak fluently in her second language, English. Symptoms of this sort are known as *hysterical* symptoms, that is, symptoms of the disorder *hysteria*. Since the days of ancient Greek medicine, the term *hysteria* has been used to refer to a disorder in which people experience physical symptoms (especially involving disturbed motor movement or perceptual experience) that are caused by emotional problems rather than by ordinary physical disease or disability (Owens & Dein, 2006). In contemporary psychology and psychiatry, hysteria is known as conversion disorder, because an emotional problem is transformed, or converted, into a psychological problem involving motor movement or perception. (Conversion disorder is also known as a type of "somatic" disorder because psychological content affects the functioning of the body, or soma.)

Anna O. herself stumbled upon a treatment for her hysterical symptoms. She found that she would experience relief from a symptom if she could trace it to a traumatic event in her past. If she managed to become aware of a long-forgotten event that was the original cause of the symptom, and if she relived the original emotional trauma associated with that event, the symptom would then either be reduced in severity or completely go away.

Breuer, and then Freud, referred to this psychological experience as a **catharsis**. Catharsis refers to a release and freeing of emotions by talking about one's problems. (In colloquial terms, we might say that in catharsis, the person gets an experience "off his chest" or gets it "out of his system.") By reexperiencing a traumatic event that she had stored away in her memory, Anna O. experienced a cathartic release of the pent-up mental energy that was causing her symptoms. Freud applied the cathartic method of treating hysterical symptoms to his own patients and reported great success.

The notion of catharsis has two implications for understanding the human mind. One is that, to Freud, it further confirms his view that the mind is an energy system. It is the release of the energy associated with long-forgotten memories that allows for the patient's improvement. The second implication is the following. Before a cathartic experience, Freud's patients appeared totally unaware that their symptoms were caused by the contents of their mind. The traumatic events that originally caused their symptoms seemingly were completely forgotten. Yet the symptoms continued. This means that mental contents *of which people were unaware* were continuously active within their own minds. The mind, then, appears to have more than one part. It not only has a region of ideas of which people are consciously aware but also a more mysterious, hidden region of ideas that lie outside of awareness. Freud refers to these ideas as *unconscious*. Freud's notion (which we review in detail below) that our day-to-day psychological life is governed by ideas that are unconscious revolutionized people's understanding of human nature.

Personality and the Brain
Hysteria (Conversion Disorder)

When you first learn about hysteria, it probably sounds kind of weird. People experience disruptions in movement or perception—paralysis; blurred vision—that are caused by emotional problems. Could this be true?

One reason it might not be true is that people are faking. Maybe they really have emotional problems, but, if nobody is paying attention to their problems, they feign injury or illness to attract more attention from others. When Freud first started studying hysteria, some of his peers in fact thought that hysterics were fakers.

How could you find out if hysterical symptoms are real or fake? One possibility is to turn to contemporary evidence on personality and the brain.

Researchers (Voon Brezing, Gallea, & Hallet 2010) have used brain-imaging techniques to study patients with conversion disorder (the contemporary term for hysteria; Owens & Dein, 2006). They studied 16 people diagnosed with the disorder. These individuals exhibited unexplained motor-movement symptoms such as tremors, tics, or abnormal movements when walking. The researchers compared this group of patients to a group of 16 psychologically and biologically healthy volunteers.

Individuals from both groups had their brains scanned using fMRI (see Chapter 2) as they viewed pictures of faces that were displayed on a video screen. The faces displayed varying emotions: happiness, fear, or neutral (i.e., an emotionally neutral facial expression). With this research procedure, the researchers could determine whether brain activity in patients and healthy volunteers differed in response to emotional stimuli.

There are, logically, two types of results. One possibility is that the brains of the two groups of people (patients and healthy volunteers) would not differ. The other, of course, is that their brains *would* differ, and perhaps in a way that revealed a biological basis for the connection hypothesized by Freud: a connection between emotional distress and symptoms of hysteria.

And differ they did. Brain activation among conversion disorder patients differed from brain activation in healthy volunteers when emotional faces were displayed (Voon et al., 2010). The nature of the difference is fascinating. Within the brains of patients, there were stronger connections between regions of the brain associated with emotion and those associated with motor movement—exactly what Freud might have expected! As the researchers explain, these connections could generate the symptoms of the disorder. Among conversion disorder patients, emotional arousal would connect to, and disrupt, the normal functioning of those parts of the brain that produce motor movements. Subsequent research results similarly led to the conclusion that, in conversion disorder, regions of the brain involved in emotional response may "hijack" (Voon et al., 2011, p. 2402) the brain's normal systems for controlling movements of the body.

This research employed a technology unimaginable in Freud's day. But it revealed exactly the sort of connection between emotion and bodily movement that he had in mind all along.

The Individual in Society

A second major aspect of Freud's view of the person concerns the relation between the individual and society. Freud's view contrasts with an alternative perspective that had been central to Western culture. The alternative sees people as essentially good. Society, however, corrupts them. People are born innocent but experience a world of temptations and fall from grace. This is the story of the Old Testament: Adam and Eve, created in God's image, are born with inherent innocence and goodness but are corrupted through the temptation of Satan. This view also is prominent is Western philosophy. The great French philosopher Rousseau argued that, prior to the development of contemporary civilization, people were relatively content and experienced primarily feelings of compassion toward others. Civilization, he thought, changed things for the worse by creating competition for resources that, in turn, fostered feelings of jealousy and suspicion.

soberve / Getty Images

Freud's ideas were radical. In his time, people commonly thought that human development followed a path "from good to evil": people were born innocent but corrupted by society - a lesson illustrated by the Biblical story of Adam and Eve. But Freud proposed that people were born with sexual and aggressive drives and that the role of society was to constrain these basic instincts.

Freud turned this conception on its head. In psychoanalysis, sexual and aggressive drives are an inborn part of human nature. Individuals, functioning according to a *pleasure principle*, seek the pleasurable gratification of those drives. The role of society is to curb these biologically natural tendencies. A major function of "civilization [is] to restrict sexual life" (Freud, 1930/1949, p. 51). Society teaches the child that biologically natural drives are socially unacceptable, and society maintains social norms and taboos that drive this lesson home. Civilized society, then, does not cause innocent children to "fall from grace." Children are far from grace when born; they possess erotic desires and aggressive drives that society takes steps to restrict. The response of civilization to these sexual drives of the individual is akin to the response of a politically dominant segment of society trying to maintain its power against a suppressed underclass: "Fear of a revolt by the suppressed elements drives it to stricter precautionary measures" (Freud, 1930/1949, p. 51).

Freud's overall theory, then, includes not only a radical view of the mind but also this equally radical rethinking of the relation between the individual and society.

Freud's View of the Science of Personality

Freud's view of science, within the study of personality, is complex. On the one hand, he was completely committed to a natural science of persons. Physics was his model. Freud was "passionately committed to a scientific model that would mirror physics, the paragon of the natural sciences" (Tauber, 2010, p. 27). This commitment caused Freud to appreciate the relationship between theory and research and the need for theoretical concepts that are sharply defined.

Yet, in the conduct of his work, Freud proceeded in ways that you might not expect for someone so thoroughly committed to a scientific worldview. Scientists often construct theories carefully and only after accumulating great bodies of evidence. Freud, however, theorized boldly. He created a theory of enormous breadth, based on a body of evidence—his encounters with his patients—that was relatively narrow. Freud looked forward to scientific advances, in his lifetime and beyond, that might confirm his core insights.

A second way in which Freud's work violates one's expectations about a scientific worldview concerns the type of data that he did, and did not, draw upon. Unlike all the other personality theorists you will learn about in this book, Freud neither ran experiments in a laboratory nor created or used standard psychological tests. He placed faith in only one of the three forms of evidence you learned about in Chapter 2: case study evidence. Freud analyzed case studies via the method of free association. This evidence, he felt, was necessary and sufficient for building a scientific theory of personality.

The free-association method pursued by Freud and his followers provided a wealth of information about individual clients. Probably no other method in psychology even approximates the information about the individual that is yielded in a psychoanalytic case study. Yet contemporary scientists generally doubt that the evidence it yields is sufficient for theory building. They particularly question Freud's lack of interest in laboratory research. "Instead of training scientists," one scholar writes, "Freud ended up training practitioners in a relatively fixed system of ideas" (Sulloway, 1991, p. 275). Only after Freud's lifetime did large numbers of research psychologists investigate the psychoanalytic phenomena through experimental methods; you'll see their findings later in our coverage of psychoanalytic theory.

Freud's Psychoanalytic Theory of Personality

Chapter 1 explained that personality theories address personality (1) structures, (2) processes, and (3) development. Let's see how Freud's theory addresses these three topics now.

Structure

Freud's goal in analyzing personality structure was to provide a conceptual model for understanding the human mind. He asked, "What are the basic structures of the mind, and what do they do?" The highly original answers he provided are complex. Freud provided not one but two conceptual models of the mind; the models complemented one another. One model addressed levels of consciousness: Are the contents of mind something that we are aware of (conscious) or not (unconscious)? The other concerns functional systems in the mind: What does a given mental system do? We review these models in turn.

Levels of Consciousness and the Concept of the Unconscious

What's going on in your mind? What thoughts are in your head? We generally answer this question by paying attention to our flow of thinking; for example, right now, you may be thinking about the material in this chapter or about things you would prefer to be doing if you didn't have

CURRENT QUESTIONS

What Price the Suppression of Exciting Thoughts?

Freud suggested that the price of progress in civilization is increased inhibition of the pleasure principle and a heightened sense of guilt. Does civilization require such an inhibition? What are the costs to the individual of efforts to suppress wishes and inhibit "unbridled gratification" of desires?

Research by Daniel Wegner and his associates suggests that the suppression of exciting thoughts may be involved in the production of negative emotional responses and the development of psychological symptoms such as phobias (irrational fears) and obsessions (preoccupation with uncontrollable thoughts). In this research, subjects were told not to think about sex. Trying not to think about sex produced emotional arousal, just as it did in subjects given permission to think about sex. Although arousal decreased after a few minutes in both

groups, what followed differed for subjects in the two groups. In the first group, the effort to suppress exciting thoughts led to the intrusion of these thoughts into consciousness and the reintroduction of surges of emotion. This was not found when subjects were given the opportunity to think about sex.

The researchers suggest that the suppression of exciting thoughts can promote excitement; that is, the very act of suppression may make these thoughts even more stimulating than when we purposefully dwell on them. In sum, such efforts at suppression may not serve us well either emotionally or psychologically.

Source: Petrie Booth, & Pennebaker (1998), Wegner (1992, 1994), Wegner et al. (1990).

to read this chapter for class. This flow of thoughts—the mental contents that you are aware of just by paying attention to your own thinking—are called "conscious" thoughts. One of Freud's great insights is that the flow of conscious thoughts is *not* a complete answer to the question, What's going on in your mind? Far from it. To Freud, conscious thoughts are just a fragment of mental contents—a tip of the iceberg.

According to psychoanalytic theory, there are substantial variations in the degree to which we are aware of mental phenomena. Freud proposed three levels of awareness. The **conscious** level, as noted, includes thoughts of which we are aware at any given moment. A **preconscious** level contains mental contents of which we easily could become aware if we attended to them. For example, before reading the present sentence, you probably were not thinking about your phone number; it was not part of your consciousness. But you easily could think of your phone number (indeed, you may be doing so right now!); it is a simple matter to attend to information that is in the preconscious and to bring it to consciousness. The third level is the **unconscious**. Unconscious mental contents are parts of the mind of which we are unaware and *cannot become aware* except under special circumstances. Why not? According to Freud, it is because they are anxiety provoking. We possess thoughts and desires that are so traumatic or socially unacceptable that consciously thinking about them provokes anxiety. "The reason why such ideas cannot become conscious is that a certain force opposes them" (Freud, 1923, p. 4). Our desire to protect ourselves from the anxiety these thoughts elicit forces them to reside outside of conscious awareness, in the unconscious.

Freud was not the first person to recognize that parts of mental life are unconscious. He was, however, the first to explore qualities of unconscious life in scientific detail and to explain a range of everyday behavior in terms of unconscious mental forces. How did he do this? Freud attempted to understand the properties of the unconscious by analyzing a variety of psychological phenomena: slips of the tongue, neuroses, psychoses, works of art, rituals. Of particular importance was his analysis of dreams.

Dreams The content of dreams vividly reveals that the mind contains unconscious contents that differ dramatically from conscious thinking. In psychoanalytic theory, dreams have two levels of content: a manifest content, which is the storyline of a dream, and a latent content, which consists of the unconscious ideas, emotions, and drives that are manifested in the dream's storyline. What Freud found in analyzing dreams is that unconscious life can be utterly bizarre. The unconscious is alogical (opposites can stand for the same thing). It disregards time (events of different periods may coexist). It disregards space (size and distance relationships are neglected so that large things fit into small things and distant places are brought together). It deals in a world of symbols, where many ideas may be telescoped into a single word and where a part of any object may stand for many things. Through processes of symbolization, a penis can be represented by a snake or nose; a woman by a church, chapel, or boat; and an engulfing mother by an octopus. An everyday action such as writing may symbolize a sexual act: The pen is the male organ and the paper is the woman who receives the ink (the semen) that flows out in the quick up-and-down movements of the pen (See Groddeck, 1923/1961).

Freud's theory of dreams had a second component. In addition to positing two levels of dreams—their manifest and latent content—Freud proposed a particular relation between the two levels. The latent content consists of unconscious wishes. The manifest content is a wish fulfillment; the storyline of the dream (the manifest content) symbolically represents the fulfillment of unconscious wishes that it may be impossible to fulfill in everyday waking life. In the dream, the person can satisfy a hostile or sexual wish in a disguised and therefore safe way. A vengeful unconscious desire to kill someone, for example, may be expressed in a dream of a battle in which a particular figure is killed. In *The Interpretation of Dreams*, Freud analyzes a large number of dreams in the style of a detective, with each element of the dream treated as a clue to the underlying wish that the dream represents, but in disguised form.

The Motivated Unconscious
Although Freud believed the unconscious to be a region of mind that stores mental contents, it is critical to recognize that the nature of the storage is very different than, for example, the storage of books in a library. In a library, books are assigned their place based on logical grounds (a library classification system). Once on the shelf, the books just sit there doing nothing (until someone takes one off the shelf). The unconscious is nothing like this. It is not purely logical. And the material does not "just sit there". The unconscious is highly motivated.

Motivational principles come into play in two respects. First, mental contents enter the unconscious for motivated reasons. The unconscious stores ideas that are so traumatic that, if they were to remain in conscious awareness, they would cause psychological pain. These thoughts might include, for example, memories of traumatic life experiences; feelings of envy, hostility, or sexual desire directed toward a forbidden person; or a desire to harm a loved one. In keeping with our basic desire to pursue pleasure and avoid pain, we are motivated to banish such thoughts from awareness. Second, thoughts in the unconscious influence ongoing conscious experience. Indeed, that statement may be the best one-line summary of Freud's fundamental message to the world. Our ongoing psychological experiences—our conscious thoughts, feelings, and actions—are, according to Freud, fundamentally determined by mental contents of which we are unaware, the contents of the unconscious. Why did we have a strange slip of the tongue? A dream that seems to make no sense? A sudden experience of anxiety when nothing anxiety provoking seemed to be happening? Strong feelings of attraction toward, or repulsion from, someone we just met? Feelings of guilt that seem irrational because we can't figure out anything that we did wrong? All such cases, to Freud, are motivated by unconscious mental forces.

Relevant Psychoanalytic Research
The unconscious is never observed directly. What evidence, then, supports the idea of an unconscious part of the mind? Let us review the range of evidence that might be considered supportive of the concept of the unconscious, beginning with Freud's clinical observations. Freud realized the importance of the unconscious after observing hypnotic phenomena. As is well known, people under hypnosis can recall things they previously could not. Furthermore, they perform actions under posthypnotic suggestion without consciously knowing that they are behaving in accordance with that suggestion; that is, they fully believe that what they are doing is voluntary and independent of any suggestion by another person. When Freud discarded the technique of hypnosis and continued with his therapeutic work, he found that often

patients became aware of memories and wishes previously buried. Frequently, such discoveries were associated with painful emotion. It is indeed a powerful clinical observation to see a patient suddenly experience tremendous anxiety, sob hysterically, or break into a rage as he or she recalls a forgotten event or gets in touch with a forbidden feeling. Thus, it was clinical observations such as these that suggested to Freud that the unconscious includes memories and wishes that not only are not currently part of our consciousness but are "deliberately buried" in our unconscious.

What of experimental evidence? In the 1960s and 1970s, experimental research focused on unconscious perception or what was called **perception without awareness**. Can the person "know" something without knowing that he or she knows it? For example, can the person hear or perceive stimuli, and be influenced by these perceptions, without being aware of these perceptions? Currently, this is known as *subliminal perception*, or the registration of stimuli at a level below that required for awareness. For example, in some early research, one group of subjects was shown a picture with a duck image shaped by the branches of a tree. Another was shown a similar picture but without the duck image. For both groups, the picture was presented at a rapid speed so that it was barely visible. This was done using a tachistoscope, an apparatus that allows the experimenter to show stimuli to subjects at very fast speeds, so that they cannot be consciously perceived. The subjects then were asked to close their eyes, imagine a nature scene, draw the scene, and label the parts. Would the two groups differ, that is, would subjects in the group "seeing" the picture with the duck image draw different pictures than would subjects in the other group? And, if so, would such a difference be associated with differential recall as to what was perceived? What was found was that more of the subjects viewing the duck picture had significantly more duck-related images (e.g., "duck," "water," "birds," "feathers") in their drawings than did subjects in the other group. However, these subjects did not report seeing the duck during the experiment, and the majority even had trouble finding it when they were asked to look for it. In other words, the stimuli that were not consciously perceived still influenced the imagery and thoughts of the subjects (Eagle, Wolitzky, & Klein, 1966).

Research by Weinberger (Siegel & Weinberger, 2009; Weinberger & Siegel, 2011) suggests that exposure to feared stimuli, outside of awareness, can be of therapeutic value. In this research, subjects with a fear of spiders were exposed to pictures of spiders below the level of awareness. They then were engaged in a test of how close they would come to being willing to touch an actual tarantula. Relative to subjects exposed to neutral outdoor scenes, again below the level of awareness, those exposed to the pictures of spiders were significantly more able to make approach behaviors toward the feared object.

Note that the mere fact that people can perceive and be influenced by stimuli of which they are unaware does not suggest that psychodynamic or motivational forces are involved. Is there evidence that such is or can be the case? Two relevant lines of research can be noted. The first, called **perceptual defense**, involves a process by which the individual defends against the anxiety that accompanies actual recognition of a threatening stimulus. In a relevant early experiment, subjects were shown two types of words in a tachistoscope: neutral words such as apple, dance, and child and emotionally toned words such as rape, whore, and penis. The words were shown first at very fast speeds and then at progressively slower speeds. A record was made of the point at which the subjects were able to identify each of the words and their sweat gland activity (a measure of tension) in response to each word. These records indicated that subjects took longer to recognize the emotionally toned words than the neutral words and showed signs of emotional response to the emotionally toned words before they were verbally identified (McGinnies, 1949). Despite criticism of such research (e.g., Did subjects identify the emotionally toned words earlier but were reluctant to verbalize them to the experimenter?), there appears to be considerable evidence that people can, outside of awareness, selectively respond to and reject specific emotional stimuli (Erdelyi, 1985).

Another line of research has examined a phenomenon called **subliminal psychodynamic activation** (Silverman, 1976, 1982; Weinberger, 1992). In this work, researchers attempt to stimulate unconscious wishes without making them conscious. This generally is done by presenting material that is related to either threatening or anxiety-alleviating unconscious wishes and then observing participants' subsequent reactions. The material is shown for extremely brief periods of time, in theory, long enough to activate the unconscious wish but short enough so that it is not recognized consciously. In the case of threatening wishes, the material is expected to stir up unconscious conflict and thus to increase psychological disturbance. In the case of an anxiety-alleviating wish, the material is expected to diminish unconscious conflict and thus to decrease psychological disturbance. For example, the content "I Am Losing Mommy" might be upsetting to some subjects, whereas the content "Mommy and I Are One" might be reassuring.

In a series of studies, Silverman and colleagues produced such subliminal psychodynamic activation effects. In one study, this method was used to present conflict-intensifying material ("Loving Daddy Is Wrong") and conflict-reducing material ("Loving Daddy Is OK") to female undergraduates. For subjects prone to conflict over sexual urges, the conflict-intensifying material, presented outside of awareness, was found to disrupt memory for passages presented after the subliminal activation of the conflict. This was not true for the conflict-reducing material or for subjects not prone to conflict over sexual urges (Geisler, 1986). The key point here is that the content that is upsetting or relieving to various groups of subjects is predicted beforehand on the basis of psychoanalytic theory and that the effects occur only when the stimuli are perceived subliminally or unconsciously.

Another interesting use of the subliminal psychodynamic activation model involves the study of eating disorders. In the first study in this area, healthy college-age women and women with signs of eating disorders were compared in terms of how many crackers they would eat following subliminal presentation of three messages: "Mama Is Leaving Me," "Mama Is Loaning It," "Mona Is Loaning It" (Patton, 1992). Based on psychoanalytic theory, the hypothesis tested was that subjects with an eating disorder struggle with feelings of loss and abandonment in relation to nurturance and therefore would seek substitute gratification in the form of eating the crackers once the conflict was activated subliminally through the message "Mama Is Leaving Me." Indeed, the eating disorder subjects who received the abandonment stimulus ("Mama Is Leaving Me") below threshold showed significantly more cracker eating than subjects without an eating disorder or subjects with an eating disorder exposed to the abandonment stimulus above threshold.

This study was replicated with the additional use of pictorial stimuli—a picture of a sobbing baby and a woman walking away along with the "Mommy Is Leaving Me" message and a picture of a woman walking along with the neutral stimulus, in this case "Mommy Is Walking." Once more, significantly more crackers were eaten by the women with eating disorders subliminally exposed to the abandonment phrase and picture than by the women with eating disorders exposed to these stimuli above threshold or by the women without an eating disorder exposed to the stimuli above or below threshold (Gerard, Kupper, & Nguyen, 1993).

Some view the research on perceptual defense and subliminal psychodynamic activation as conclusive experimental evidence of the importance of psychodynamic, motivational factors in determining what is "deposited into" and "kept in" the unconscious (Weinberger, 1992). However, the experiments have frequently been criticized on methodological grounds, and at times some of the effects have been difficult to replicate or reproduce in other laboratories (Balay & Shevrin, 1988, 1989; Holender, 1986).

Current Status of the Concept of the Unconscious   The concept of a motivated unconscious is central to psychoanalytic theory. But how is this idea viewed more generally by psychologists in the field? At this point, almost all psychologists, whether psychoanalytic or otherwise, would agree that many mental events occur outside of conscious awareness and that unconscious processes influence what we attend to and how we feel. A leading researcher who is not a follower of psychoanalytic theory concluded that "unconscious influences are ubiquitous. It is clear that people sometimes consciously plan and act. More often than not, however, behavior is influenced by unconscious processes; that is, we act and then, if questioned, make our excuses" (Jacoby, Lindsay, & Toth, 1992, p. 82).

CURRENT APPLICATIONS

Motivated Unconscious Processes in Political Judgments

When you think about candidates for political office, *how do you think*? Are your thoughts analytical, rational, and calm—free from emotions and motivations that might color your conclusions?

Freud's theory of personality suggests that our thinking is never free from emotional and motivational biases. Just as we psychologically defend against information threatening to ourselves, we may defend against information threatening to our favored candidates. Evidence of this comes from research conducted during a U.S. presidential election (Westen, Blagov, Havenski, Kilts, & Hamann, 2006). Researchers presented to participants information threatening to one of three target persons: (1) a political candidate they favored, (2) the opposing candidate, or (3) a well-known but neutral figure (e.g., a famous athlete). While they were exposed to, and made judgments about, this information, participants' brain activity was recorded using fMRI.

Participants' psychological and biological responses differed depending on whether the threatening information related to their favored candidate. First, consider the psychology. When thinking about information threatening to their favored candidate, participants were defensive. They judged that such information cast a bad light on the opposing candidate but that it did not have the same negative implications for their favored candidate. And what about the biology? When participants were making judgments about information threatening to their preferred candidate, regions of the brain associated with emotional response were particularly active. Emotional reactions, then, appeared to drive defensive information processing.

Another study provides evidence not only that motivated reasoning about political candidates can occur but that it can occur unconsciously (Weinberger & Westen, 2008). This research built on earlier evidence that stimuli presented subliminally (outside of awareness) can affect the likability ratings of a target presented afterward in awareness. The research was inspired by an actual 2000 Bush campaign advertisement, which subliminally presented (perhaps accidentally) the word RATS in association with Democrats. Could such a subliminal (unconscious) presentation affect one's political views?

In this research, conducted over the Internet, subjects completed an information page and then were presented with one of four subliminal stimuli: RATS, STAR (rats spelled backward), ARAB, or XXXX, followed by a photograph of a young man above perceptual threshold. Next, subjects were asked to evaluate the young man, presented as a political candidate, on a number of characteristics (e.g., honesty, competence, appeal as a candidate). Would the subliminal presentation of the four stimuli lead to different judgments concerning the supposed candidate? First, the investigators checked whether the participants could perceive the subliminal stimulus and threw out the data for the few for whom this was the case. In other words, the results pertained only to those subjects for whom the subliminal stimuli of interest were indeed perceived outside of awareness. Would the four subliminal stimuli affect ratings of the "candidate"? Would the effect be the same? As predicted, subliminal presentation of the RATS stimulus led to a more negative evaluation of the hypothetical candidate than did any of the other stimuli. In other words, there could be unconscious processing of information that affected subsequent judgments.

In sum, the two experiments together supported the psychoanalytic view of motivated unconscious processing of information.

So does this mean that most contemporary psychologists are Freudians? Not at all. Research does indicate that much of mental life occurs outside of consciousness. But, as many writers emphasize (Kihlstrom, 2002), this fact does not necessarily support Sigmund Freud's *particular conception of* the unconscious—a conception based on an energy model of mind and in which two primary forms of unconscious mental energy drive a spectrum of psychological processes.

The Psychoanalytic Unconscious and the Cognitive Unconscious   Many research studies of unconscious processes demonstrate nonconscious influences on behavior, as Freud would have predicted. On the other hand, the content of the unconscious material in these studies have little, if anything, to do with the material studied by Freud. The findings from these studies, then, indicate the existence of unconscious influences, but these are unconscious influences that may have little to do with the psychological experiences discussed by Freud. This distinction—between the traumatic sexual and aggressive unconscious content of interest to Freud, and the relatively mundane unconscious content studied by many contemporary researchers in personality and social psychology—suggests that one should distinguish between the psychoanalytic unconscious and what has been called the cognitive unconscious (Kihlstrom, 2008; Pervin, 2003).

As we have seen, the psychoanalytic view of the unconscious emphasizes the irrational, illogical nature of unconscious functioning. In addition, analysts presume that the contents of the unconscious mainly involve sexual and aggressive thoughts, feelings, and motives. Finally, analysts emphasize that what is in the unconscious is there for motivated reasons, and these contents exert a motivational influence on daily behavior. In contrast to this perspective, according to the cognitive view of the unconscious, there is no fundamental difference in quality between unconscious and conscious processes. According to this view, unconscious processes can be as intelligent, logical, and rational as conscious processes. Second, the cognitive view of the unconscious emphasizes the variety of contents that may be unconscious, with no special significance associated with sexual and aggressive contents. Third, related to this perspective, the cognitive view of the unconscious does not emphasize motivational factors. According to the cognitive view, cognitions are unconscious because they cannot be processed at the conscious level, because they never reached consciousness, or because they have become overly routinized and automatic. For example, tying one's shoe is so automatic that we no longer are aware of just how we do it. We act similarly with typing and where letters are on the keyboard. Many of our cultural beliefs were learned in such subtle ways that we cannot even spell them out as beliefs. As noted in Chapter 1, we are not even aware of them until we meet members of a different culture. However, such unconscious contents are not kept there for motivated reasons. Nor do they necessarily exert a motivational influence on our behavior, although such an influence is possible. Indeed, there is a growing literature on what are called *implicit motives*, that is, motives that operate outside of awareness, as distinguished from *explicit motives* that operate within awareness. It is interesting that measures of conscious, explicit motives and measures of unconscious, implicit motives have little relation to one another and predict different kinds of behavior (Schultheiss, 2008). Finally, there is evidence that subliminal stimuli can affect our thoughts and feelings, but these stimuli need not be of special psychodynamic significance such as a threatening wish (Klinger & Greenwald, 1995; Nash, 1999) (Table 3.1).

Many of these contrasting views are captured in the following statement by J. F. Kihlstrom, a leading proponent of the cognitive view of the unconscious:

> *The psychological unconscious documented by latter-day psychology is quite different from what Sigmund Freud and his psychoanalytic colleagues had in mind in Vienna. Their unconscious was hot and wet; it seethed with lust and anger; it was hallucinatory, primitive, and irrational. The unconscious of contemporary psychology is kinder and gentler than that and more readily bound and rational, even if it is not entirely cold and dry.*

Source: Kihlstrom, Barnhardt, and Tataryn (1992, p. 788).

Table 3.1   Comparison of Two Views of the Unconscious: Psychoanalytic and Cognitive

Psychoanalytic View

1. Emphasis on illogical, irrational unconscious processes
2. Content emphasis on motives and wishes
3. Emphasis on motivated aspects of unconscious functioning

Cognitive View

1. Absence of fundamental difference between conscious and unconscious processes
2. Content emphasis on thoughts
3. Focus on nonmotivated aspects of unconscious functioning

Although efforts have been made to integrate the psychoanalytic and cognitive views of the unconscious (Bornstein & Masling, 1998; Epstein, 1994; Westen & Gabbard, 1999), differences remain. In sum, although the importance of unconscious phenomena is recognized and the investigation of such phenomena has become a major area of research, the uniquely psychoanalytic view of the unconscious remains questionable for many, perhaps most, nonpsychoanalytic investigators.

Concurrent with these differing views, research on the brain by neuroscientists (Chapter 9) has come upon findings of interest to both psychoanalysts and cognitive scientists. First, there is evidence that events of early childhood may leave an emotional memory that influences later functioning without the person having a conscious memory of the event. This is because a part of the brain, the amygdala, is involved at that point in time but prior to the development of more mature brain structures involved in memory, such as the hippocampus (Nadel, 2005). Beyond this, there is evidence of neural systems that are capable of keeping unwanted memories out of awareness, the kind of motivated forgetting emphasized by psychoanalysts (Anderson et al., 2004). Findings such as these will help to clarify just which parts of the psychoanalytic and cognitive views of the unconscious make most scientific sense.

Id, Ego, and Superego

In 1923, Freud significantly augmented his theorizing by presenting a second model of mind. He did not abandon his prior distinctions among conscious, preconscious, and unconscious regions of mind, yet he judged that "these distinctions have proved to be inadequate" (Freud, 1923, p. 7). The inadequacy was the following. For Freud, there seemed to exist a psychological agency (the ego, see below) that had two important qualities. On the one hand, it was unitary in its functioning. It did a single type of thing in a coherent, consistent manner. Yet, on the other hand, it *varied* in its degree of consciousness. Sometimes its functioning involved conscious processes, but sometimes it functioned unconsciously. This clearly was a problem for psychoanalytic theory. Freud needed to capture the unitary quality of this psychological agency, and the distinction among levels of consciousness did not do it. Freud needed another conceptual tool. The one he forged proved to be among the most enduringly important features of psychoanalytic theory: the distinction among the id, the ego, and the superego. Each is a distinct mental system that carries out a particular type of psychological function.

The **id** is the original source of all drive energy—the "great reservoir" (Freud, 1923, p. 20) of mental energies. The psychological functions toward which the id directs these energies are very simple. The id seeks the release of excitation or tension. It carries out a mental function described previously: the reduction of tension in order to return to a quiet internal state.

In carrying out this function, the id operates according to the **pleasure principle**, which is particularly simple to define: The id pursues pleasure and avoids pain. The point is that the id does not do anything else. It does not devise plans and strategies for obtaining pleasure or wait patiently for a particularly pleasing object to appear. It does not concern itself with social norms and rules; "it is totally non-moral" (Freud, 1923, p. 40). The id seeks immediate release of tension, no matter what. The id cannot tolerate frustration. It is free of inhibitions. It has qualities of a spoiled child: It wants what it wants when it wants it.

The id seeks satisfaction in either of two ways: through action or merely through imagining that it has gotten what it wants. To the id, the fantasy of gratification is as good as the actual gratification. In terms of the regions of mind outlined previously by Freud, the id functions entirely outside of conscious awareness. It is "unknown and unconscious" (Freud, 1923, p. 14).

In marked contrast to the id is the **superego**. The functions of the superego involve the moral aspects of social behavior. The superego contains ideals for which we strive, as well as ethical standards that will cause us to feel guilt if we violate them. The superego, then, is an internal representation of the moral rules of the external, social world. It functions to control behavior in accord with these rules, offering rewards (pride, self-love) for "good" behavior and punishments (guilt, feelings of inferiority) for "bad" behavior. The superego may function on a very primitive level, being relatively incapable of reality testing—that is, of modifying its action depending on circumstances. In such cases, the person is unable to distinguish between thought and action, feeling guilty for thinking something even if it did not lead to action. Furthermore, the individual is bound by black–white, all–none judgments, and by the pursuit of perfection. Excessive use of words such as *good*, *bad*, *judgment*, and *trial* express a strict superego. But the superego can also be understanding and flexible. For example, people may be able to forgive themselves or someone else if it is clear that something was an accident or done under severe stress. In the course of development, children learn to make such important distinctions and to see things not only in all-or-none, but also right-or-wrong, black-or-white terms.

The third psychoanalytic structure is the **ego**. Whereas the id seeks pleasure and the superego seeks perfection, the ego seeks reality. The ego's function is to express and satisfy the desires of the id in accordance with two things: opportunities and constraints that exist in the real world and the demands of the superego.

Whereas the id operates according to the pleasure principle, the ego operates according to the **reality principle**: Gratification of the instincts is delayed until a time when something in reality enables one to obtain maximum pleasure with the least pain or negative consequences. As a simple example, sexual drives in the id may impel you to make a sexual advance toward someone you find attractive. But the ego may stop you from acting impulsively; the ego would monitor reality, judging whether there is any chance that you might actually succeed and delaying action until it develops a strategy that might bring success. According to the reality principle, the energy of the id may be blocked, diverted, or released gradually, all in accordance with the demands of reality and the superego. Such an operation does not contradict the pleasure principle but, rather, represents a temporary suspension of it.

Imagezoo / Getty Images

In Freud's psychoanalytic theory, personality structures conflict. The ego tries to satisfy the desired of the id, while also attending to constraints established by the superego.

The ego has capabilities that the id does not. The ego can distinguish fantasy from reality. It can tolerate tension and create compromises through rational thought. Unlike the id, it changes over time, with more complex ego functions developing over the course of childhood.

Although the ego may sound like the decision-making "chief executive" of personality, Freud thought that the ego was weaker than the metaphor of an "executive" implies. The ego instead is "like a man on horseback, who has to hold in check the superior strength of the horse" (Freud, 1923, p. 15). It is the horse (the id) who provides all the energy. The rider tries to direct it, but, ultimately, the more powerful beast may end up going wherever it wants.

In sum, Freud's ego is logical, rational, and tolerant of tension. In its actions, it must conform to the dictates of three masters: the id, the superego, and the world of reality.

The concepts of conscious, unconscious, id, ego, and superego are highly abstract. Freud knew this. He did not intend to imply that there are three gremlin-like beings running around in your head. Instead, he judged that mental life involves the execution of three distinct psychological functions, and he posited an abstract mental system that executes each of the functions. The nature of these structures becomes clearer and less abstract when one also considers the psychological processes through which their functions are carried out. We turn to these processes now.

Process

The process aspects of personality theory are, as we have noted, concerned with motivational dynamics. Freud's view of mental (psychic) energy is thoroughly biological. In psychoanalytic theory, the source of all psychic energy lies in states of excitation within the body. These states seek expression and tension reduction. These states are called *instincts*, or *drives*. Though both words have been used when Freud's writing has been translated into English, the term *drive* captures Freud's idea better than does the term *instinct*. The word *instinct* commonly is used to describe a fixed pattern of action (e.g., a bird instinctually builds a nest). In contrast, a drive is a source of energy that can motivate any of a variety of specific actions depending on the opportunities and constraints that are presented in a given environment. This idea, of drives, is what Freud had in mind when discussing personality processes.

Within this framework, two questions naturally arise: (1) How many basic human instinctual drives are there, and what are they? (2) What happens to the energy associated with these drives? In other words, how is it expressed in everyday experience and action? Freud answers the first question by presenting a theory of life and death instincts. He answers the second by analyzing the dynamics of functioning and mechanisms of defense.

Life and Death Instincts

Daily life consists of a wide array of activities: work, time with friends, education, time with romantic partners, sports, arts, music, and so forth. Since most people engage in each of these activities, one might suppose that there is a basic human instinct for each one (an instinct to work, to have friends, to become educated, etc.). But this sort of "multi-instinct model" is *not* the sort of theory that Freud pursued. Instead, throughout his career, Freud tried to explain the diversity of human activity in terms of a very small number of instincts. He tried to achieve theoretical parsimony (as we discussed in Chapter 1), with the diverse complexities of human behavior being understood through a relatively simple theoretical formulation.

Freud's thoughts about the exact nature of mental drives changed during his career. In an earlier view, he proposed ego instincts, relating to tendencies toward self-preservation, and sexual instincts, relating to tendencies toward preservation of the species. In a later view—which stands as the final, classic psychoanalytic model—there were still two instincts, but they were the **life instinct** and **death instinct**.

The life instinct includes drives associated previously with both the earlier ego and sexual instincts; in other words, the life instinct impels people toward the preservation and reproduction of the organism. Freud gave a name to the energy of the life instinct: **libido**. The death instinct is the very opposite of the life instinct. It involves the aim of the organism to die or return to an inorganic state.

At an intuitive level, it may immediately strike you that the notion of a "death instinct" is unusual, if not implausible. Why would people have an instinct to die? Such intuitions would match those of many psychologists, including many psychoanalysts; the death instinct remains one of the most controversial and least accepted parts of psychoanalytic theory. Yet the idea of a death instinct was consistent with some ideas of 19th-century biology with which Freud was familiar (Sulloway, 1979); it reflected Freud's idea that a basic tendency of the organism is to seek a state of calmness. It also is consistent with observations of the human condition. Sadly, many people escape psychological problems through suicide, which can be understood as a manifestation of a drive to die. Furthermore, Freud felt that the death instinct was often turned away from oneself and directed toward others in acts of aggression. This occurs so commonly that some analysts refer to the instinct as an aggressive instinct.

This model of motivation processes is highly integrated with Freud's model of psychoanalytic structures. The sexual and aggressive drives are parts of one of the psychoanalytic structures, namely, the id. The id, as you will recall, is the first of the personality structures, that is, the one with which we are born. An implication, then, is that sexual and aggressive drives are part of the basic human nature with which we are born. We do not have to learn to have sexual and aggressive drives; we are born with them. To Freud, our psychological lives are essentially powered by these two basic drives.

The Dynamics of Functioning

If one posits only two instinctual drives, one faces an intellectual puzzle: How can one account for the diversity of motivated human activities, many of which do not seem obviously related to sex or aggression? Freud's creative solution to this problem was to posit that a given instinctual drive could be expressed in a wide variety of ways. Mechanisms of the mind, can redirect the energy to diverse activities.

In the dynamics of functioning, what exactly can happen to one's instincts? They can, at least temporarily, be blocked from expression, expressed in a modified way, or expressed without modification. For example, affection may be a modified expression of the sexual instinct, and sarcasm a modified expression of the aggressive instinct. It is also possible for the object of gratification of the instinct to be changed or displaced from the original object to another object. Thus, the love of one's mother may be displaced to the wife, children, or dog. Each instinct may be transformed or modified, and the instincts can combine with one another. Football, for example, can gratify both sexual and aggressive instincts; in surgery there can be the fusion of love and destruction. It should already be clear how psychoanalytic theory is able to account for so much behavior on the basis of only two instincts. It is the fluid, mobile, changing qualities of the instincts and their many alternative kinds of gratification that allow such variability in behavior. In essence, the same instinct can be gratified in a number of ways, and the same behavior can have different causes in different people.

Virtually every process in psychoanalytic theory can be described in terms of the expenditure of energy in an object or in terms of a force inhibiting the expenditure of energy, that is, inhibiting gratification of an instinct. Because inhibition involves an expenditure of energy, people who direct much of their efforts toward it end up feeling tired and bored. The interplay between expression and inhibition of instincts forms the foundation of the dynamic aspects of psychoanalytic theory. The key to this theory is the concept of **anxiety**. In psychoanalytic theory, anxiety is a painful emotional experience representing a threat or danger to the person. In a state of "free-floating" anxiety, individuals are unable to relate their state of tension to a specific danger; in contrast, in a state of fear, the source of threat is known. According to the theory, anxiety represents a painful emotion that acts as a signal of impending danger to the ego; that is, anxiety, an ego function, alerts the ego to danger so that it can act.

The psychoanalytic theory of anxiety states that at some point, the person experiences a trauma, an incident of harm or injury. Anxiety represents a repetition of the earlier traumatic experience but in miniature form. Anxiety in the present, then, is related to an earlier danger. For example, a child may be severely punished for some sexual or aggressive act. Later in life, this person may experience anxiety in association with the inclination to perform the same sexual or aggressive act. The earlier punishment (trauma) may or may not be remembered. In structural terms, what is suggested is that anxiety develops out of a conflict between the push of the id instincts and the threat of punishment by the superego. That is, it is as if the id says, "I want it," the superego says, "How terrible," and the ego says, "I'm afraid."

Anxiety, Mechanisms of Defense, and Contemporary Research on Defensive Processes

Anxiety is such a painful state that we are incapable of tolerating it for very long. How are we to deal with such a state? If, as Freud suggests, our minds harbor sexual and aggressive instincts that are socially unacceptable, then how do we manage not to be anxious all the time? Freud's answer to this question constitutes one of the most enduring aspects of his theory of personality. He proposed that we mentally defend ourselves against anxiety-provoking thoughts. People develop **defense mechanisms** against anxiety. We develop ways to distort reality and exclude feelings from awareness so that we do not feel anxious. These defense mechanisms are functions carried out by the ego; they are a strategic effort by the ego to cope with the socially unacceptable impulses of the id.

> *Some things are too terrible to be true.*
>
> *Source:* Bob Dylan.

Denial   Freud distinguished among a number of distinct defense mechanisms. Some of them are relatively simple, or psychologically primitive, whereas others are more complex. A particularly simple defense mechanism is **denial**. People may, in their conscious thoughts, deny the existence of a traumatic or otherwise socially unacceptable fact; the fact is so "terrible" that they deny that it is "true," as Dylan's lyric suggests. People may begin using the defense mechanism of denial in childhood. There may be denial of reality, as in a boy, who, in fantasy, denies a lack of power, or denial of an internal impulse, as when an irate person protests, "I do not feel angry." The saying that someone "doth protest too much" specifically references this defense. Denial of reality is commonly seen where people attempt to avoid recognizing the extent of a threat. The expression "Oh, no!" upon hearing of the death of a close friend represents the reflex action of denial. Children have been known to deny the death of a loved animal and long afterward to behave as if it were still alive.

When Edwin Meese, former attorney general in the Reagan administration, was asked how much he owed in legal bills, he replied, "I really don't know. It scares me to look at it, so I haven't looked at it." The mother of former U.S. President Bill Clinton was quoted as saying, "When bad things happen, I brainwash myself to put them out of my mind. Inside my head, I construct an airtight box. I keep inside it what I want to think about and everything else stays behind the walls. Inside is white, outside is black. The only gray I trust is the streak in my hair." A friend of one of the authors organizes her mail into three "in boxes" on her desk that are labeled "Unimportant Stuff," "Important Stuff," and "Stuff I'm Afraid to Look At." Initially, such avoidance may be conscious, but later it becomes automatic and unconscious, so that the person is not even aware of "not looking."

Denial of reality is also evident when people say or assume that "it can't happen to me" in spite of clear evidence of impending doom. This defense was seen in Jews who were victims of the Nazis. A book (Steiner, 1966) about the Nazi concentration camp Treblinka describes how the population acted as if death did not exist, in spite of clear evidence to the contrary. The extermination of a whole people was so unimaginable that individuals could not accept it. They preferred to accept lies rather than to bear the terrible trauma of the truth.

Is denial necessarily a bad thing? Should we always avoid self-deception? Psychoanalysts generally assume that although the mechanisms of defense can be useful in reducing anxiety, they also are maladaptive by turning the person away from reality. Thus, psychoanalysts view "reality orientation" as fundamental to emotional health and doubt that distortions about oneself and others can have value for adaptive functions (Colvin & Block, 1994; Robins & John, 1996). Yet, some psychologists suggest that positive illusions and self-deceptions can be adaptive. Positive illusions about one's self, about one's ability to control events, and about the future can be good, perhaps essential, for mental health (Taylor & Brown, 1994; Taylor et al., 2000). The answer to these differing views appears to depend on the extent of distortion, how pervasive it is, and the circumstances under which it occurs. For example, it may be helpful to have positive illusions about oneself as long as they are not too extreme. And denial and self-deception may provide temporary relief from emotional trauma and help the person avoid becoming overwhelmed by anxiety or depression. Denial may be adaptive where action is impossible, as when a person is in a situation that cannot be altered (e.g., a fatal illness) but is maladaptive when it prevents one from taking constructive action to alter a situation that can be changed.

Projection   Another relatively primitive defense mechanism is **projection**. In projection, what is internal and unacceptable is projected out and seen as external. People defend against the recognition of their own negative qualities by projecting them onto others. For example, rather than recognize hostility in the self, an individual sees others as being hostile. Much laboratory research has been devoted to the study of projection. At first, researchers found it difficult to demonstrate the phenomenon in the lab (Halpern, 1977; Holmes, 1981). However, in more recent years, investigators have documented that, in fact, people tend to project their undesired psychological qualities onto others.

Newman and colleagues have studied projection by analyzing specific thinking processes that might lead people to project their undesired qualities onto others (Newman, Duff, & Baumeister, 1997). The basic idea is that people tend to dwell on those features of themselves that they do not like. Whenever one dwells on a topic, the topic comes to mind easily—in the language of this research, the topic becomes "chronically accessible" (Higgins & King, 1981). So if you think that you are lazy, and you dwell on this feature of self, then the concept of laziness might come to mind relatively quickly and frequently for you. This reasoning puts one just one step away from the phenomenon of projection. This final step is that, whenever one interprets the actions of other people, one does so by using concepts in one's own mind. If one interprets others' actions using ideas that also are negative features of one's own self-concept, then one ends up projecting these negative features onto others. To return to our example, if "laziness" comes to mind quickly for you, and you see a person sitting on a beach in the middle of a workday, you might conclude that this is a lazy person. Someone else, in contrast, might merely conclude that the person is relaxing, rather than being lazy. But note that central to the psychoanalytic view of projection is that the key personality feature is both projected onto others and denied as part of the self; that is, it is the other person that is lazy, not me.

Experimental findings support this interpretation of projection (Newman et al., 1997). In this research, participants were exposed to bogus negative feedback on two personality attributes. They then were asked to try to suppress thoughts about one of the two attributes while they discussed the other one; such thought-suppression instructions often backfire, causing people subsequently to think about the personal quality that they were trying to suppress. Later in the experimental session, participants viewed a videotape that depicted a somewhat anxious-looking individual. Participants were asked to rate this person on a series of personality trait dimensions. Findings revealed that participants projected their suppressed negative quality onto others. In other words, they judged that the *other* person possessed the negative personality attribute that they themselves had been trying not to think about earlier in the experiment. Although these findings fit with psychoanalytic thought, the authors rely on explanatory principles that are based on principles of social cognitive psychology (discussed in Chapters 12 and 13) rather than on principles of psychoanalysis.

Isolation, Reaction Formation, and Sublimation   In addition to denial and projection, another way to deal with anxiety and threat is to isolate events in memory or to isolate emotion from the content of a memory or impulse. In **isolation**, the impulse, thought, or act is not denied access to consciousness, but it is denied the normal accompanying emotion. For example, a woman may experience the thought or fantasy of strangling her child without any associated feelings of anger. The result of using the mechanism of isolation is intellectualization, an emphasis on thought over emotion and feeling, and the development of logic-tight compartments. In such cases, the feelings that do exist may be split, as in the case where a man separates women into two categories—one with whom there is love but no sex and the other with whom there is sex but no love (Madonna–whore complex).

People who use the defense mechanism of isolation also often use the mechanism of **undoing**. Here, the individual magically undoes one act or wish with another. "It is a kind of negative magic in which the individual's second act abrogates or nullifies the first, in such a manner that it is as though neither had taken place, whereas in reality both have done so" (A. Freud, 1936, p. 33). This mechanism is seen in compulsions in which the person has an irresistible impulse to perform some act (e.g., the person undoes a suicide or homicide fantasy by compulsively turning off the gas jets at home), in religious rituals, and in children's sayings such as "Don't step on the crack or you'll break your mother's back."

In **reaction formation**, the individual defends against expression of an unacceptable impulse by only recognizing and expressing its opposite. This defense is evident in socially desirable behavior that is rigid, exaggerated, and inappropriate. The person who uses reaction formation cannot admit to other feelings, such as overprotective mothers who cannot allow any conscious hostility toward their children. Reaction formation is most clearly observable when the defense breaks down, as when the man who "wouldn't hurt a fly" goes on a killing rampage.

A defense mechanism that you may recognize in yourself is **rationalization**. Rationalization is a more complex, mature defense mechanism than a process such as denial in that in rationalization people do not simply deny that a thought or action occurred. In rationalization, people recognize the existence of an action but distort its underlying motive. Behavior is reinterpreted so that it appears reasonable and acceptable. The ego, in other words, constructs a rational motive to explain an unacceptable action that is actually caused by the irrational impulses of the id. Particularly interesting is that with rationalization the individual can express the dangerous impulse, seemingly without disapproval by the superego. Some of the greatest atrocities of humankind have been committed in the name of love. Through the defense of rationalization, we can be hostile while professing love, immoral in the pursuit of morality. Of course, to be truly effective as a defense mechanism, one must not be aware of this. Thus, you might use rationalization but be unaware of doing so. One might even say "Oh, I'm just rationalizing." but not really mean it.

According to the psychologist Dan Ariely (2012), most people lie on occasion or at some point commit a dishonest act. Yet, almost all consider themselves to be honest, moral individuals. How can this be? According to Ariely, people rationalize such acts through rationalizations such as "Everyone does it.", "It was just a white lie.", or "It was just a minor act—hardly constituting theft or cheating."

Another device used to express an impulse of the id in a manner that is free of anxiety is **sublimation**. In this relatively complex defense mechanism, the original object of gratification is replaced by a higher cultural goal that is far removed from a direct expression of the instinct. Whereas the other defense mechanisms meet the instincts head on and, by and large, prevent discharge, in sublimation, the instinct is turned into a new and useful channel. In contrast to the other defense mechanisms, here, the ego does not have to maintain a constant energy output to prevent discharge. Freud interpreted da Vinci's Madonna as a sublimation of his longing for his mother. Becoming a surgeon, butcher, or boxer can represent sublimations, to a greater or lesser degree, of aggressive impulses. Being a psychiatrist can represent a sublimation of 'Peeping Tom' tendencies. In all, Freud felt that the essence of civilization is contained in a person's ability to sublimate sexual and aggressive energies.

Fred Matos / Getty Images

Michelangelo worked on the Pietá for almost two years. Where did he get the energy? Freudian theory would suggest that, through the defense mechanism of sublimation, Michelangelo transformed sexual energy that was originally directed toward his mother into the artistic energy required to sculpt Jesus and Mary.

Repression   Finally, we come to the major defense mechanism of psychoanalytic theory: **repression**. In repression, a thought, idea, or wish is dismissed from consciousness. It is so traumatic and threatening to the self that it is buried in the unconscious, stored away in the depths of the mind. Repression is viewed as playing a part in all the other defense mechanisms and, like these other defenses, requires a constant expenditure of energy to keep that which is dangerous outside of consciousness.

Freud first recognized the defense mechanism of repression in his therapeutic work. After many weeks or months of therapy, patients would remember traumatic events from their past (and experience a catharsis). Prior to recalling the event, the idea of the event, of course, was in the person's mind. But it was outside of the person's conscious awareness. Freud reasoned that the person first experienced the event consciously but that the experience was so traumatic that the individual repressed it.

To Freud, these therapeutic experiences were sufficient evidence to establish the reality of repression. However, other investigators over the years have studied repression experimentally. An early study was done by Rosenzweig (1941). He varied the level of personal involvement in a task and then studied research participants' (in this case, college undergraduates) recall of their success or failure on the activity. When participants were personally involved with the experiment, they recalled a larger proportion of tasks that they had been able to complete successfully than tasks they had been unable to complete; they presumably repressed the experiences of failure. When the students did not feel threatened, they remembered more of the uncompleted tasks.

In similar research conducted years later, women high in sex guilt and women low in sex guilt were exposed to an erotic videotape and asked to report their level of sexual arousal. At the same time, their level of physiological response was recorded. Women high in sex guilt were found to report less arousal than those low in sex guilt but to show greater physiological arousal. Presumably, the guilt associated with sexual arousal led to repression or blocking of awareness of the physiological arousal (Morokoff, 1985).

Research supports the view that some individuals may be characterized as having a repressive style (Weinberger, 1990). They rarely report that they experience anxiety or other negative emotions; outwardly, they appear calm. However, their calmness appears to be bought at a price. Repressors react more to stress than do nonrepressors and are more prone to develop a variety of illnesses (Contrada, Czarnecki, & Pan, 1997; Derakshan & Eysenck, 1997). The cheerfulness of repressors sometimes masks high blood pressure and high pulse rates, which puts people at risk for illnesses such as heart disease and cancer (Denollet, Martens, Nyklicek, Conraads, & de Gelder, 2008). This fits with other evidence suggesting that a lack of emotional expressiveness is associated with increased risk of illness (Cox & MacKay, 1982; Levy, 1991; Temoshok, 1985, 1991).

In sum, contemporary research has firmly established that people are sometimes motivated to banish from their conscious experience thoughts that are threatening or painful. As Freud would have expected, some people who consciously report that they are free from psychological distress harbor anxiety-related thoughts and emotions of which they appear to be unaware. On the other hand, it is not clear that contemporary experimental research supports the exact conception of defenses put forth by Freud. In particular, it is hard to demonstrate in laboratory experiments that a defensive function is being served, that is, that the person is being protected from anxiety by the process being studied. Thus, for example, whereas practicing psychoanalysts find the evidence in support of the concept of repression compelling, experimental researchers find the evidence to be inconclusive.

Growth and Development

In Chapter 1, we noted that the study of personality development encompasses two distinct challenges: identifying (1) general patterns that characterize the development of most or all people and (2) factors that contribute to the development of differences among people. In his psychoanalytic theory, Freud combined these two concerns in a manner that was extraordinarily original. He proposed that all persons develop through a series of stages. He then proposed that events that occur at these stages are responsible for personality styles and differences among individuals in personality styles, which are evident throughout life. Early life experiences, and the particular stage at which these experiences occur, are said to have a permanent effect on personality; indeed, a strong psychoanalytic position would suggest that the most significant aspects of later personality are entirely determined by the end of the first five years of life.

The Development of the Instincts and Stages of Development

By now, you should be able to figure out the primary question that Freud would ask in studying development. If one embraces an energy model of mind in which behavior is in the service of instinctual drives, then major questions involve the development of instincts: What is the nature of the instincts that the individual experiences, and must cope with, during the course of development?

Once again, Freud's answer is thoroughly biological. He theorized, first, that instinctual drives tend to center on particular regions of the body, which he called **erogenous zones**. He then suggested that the particular erogenous zone that is most important to biological gratification at a given point in time changes systematically across the course of development. At different points in development, in other words, one versus another part of the body is the primary focus of gratification. The resulting set of ideas is a theory of *psychosexual stages* of development. Development occurs in a series of distinct steps, or stages. And each stage is characterized by a bodily source of gratification. Freud's use of the word *sexual* in the phrase "psychosexual stages" corresponds more closely to our word *sensual*; each stage, then, is characterized by a distinct region of sensual gratification. Within that basic framework, the question is the number, and nature, of the stages.

Freud proposed that the first stage of development is one in which sensual gratification centers on the mouth. He called this the **oral stage** of development. Early oral gratification occurs in feeding, thumb-sucking, and other mouth movements characteristic of infants. In adult life, traces of orality are seen in chewing gum, eating, smoking, and kissing. In the early oral stage, the child is passive and receptive. In the late oral stage, with the development of teeth, there can be a fusion of sexual and aggressive pleasures. In children, such a fusion of instinctual gratification is seen in the eating of animal crackers. In later life, we see traces of orality in various spheres. For example, academic pursuits can have oral associations within the unconscious: One is given "food for thought," asked to "incorporate" material in reading, and told to "regurgitate" what has been learned on exams.

CURRENT QUESTIONS

Recovered Memories or False Memories?

Psychoanalysts suggest that through the defense mechanism of repression, people bury memories of traumatic experiences of childhood in the unconscious. They also suggest that under some conditions, such as psychotherapy, individuals can recall their forgotten experiences. On the other hand, others question the accuracy of adult recall of childhood experiences. The issue has reached headline proportions as individuals report recalling experiences of childhood sexual abuse and initiate lawsuits against individuals now recalled to be the perpetrators of the abuse. Although some professionals are convinced of the authenticity of these memories of sexual abuse, and suggest that a disservice is done to the person when we do not treat them as real, others question their authenticity and refer to them as part of a "false memory syndrome." While some view the recovery of these memories as beneficial to those who previously repressed the trauma of abuse, others suggest that the "memories" are induced by the probing questions of therapists convinced that such abuse has taken place.

An article in a professional psychological journal asks: "What scientific basis is there for the authenticity of memories of sexual abuse that were 'repressed' but then 'remembered' with the help of a therapist? How are scientists, jurists, and distressed individuals themselves to distinguish true memories from false ones?" Answering these questions is difficult. On the one hand, we know that people can forget events that subsequently are remembered. This is obvious from one's own experiences in remembering events from one's past. Yet there is an alternative possibility that is intriguing—indeed, somewhat disturbing. It is that we might sometimes "recall" events that never occurred in the first place. We might sometimes have "false memories."

Research documents that it is possible for people to experience false memories, that is, recollections of events that did not, in fact, occur. For example, Mazzoni and Memon (2003) conducted a study involving three experimental sessions that were each separated in time by one week. In the first session, adult research participants completed a survey in which they reported the likelihood that they had experienced each of a large series of life events in their childhood. In session two, the experimenters conducted an experimental manipulation involving two of the events from the survey. The two events were minor medical procedures: a tooth extraction and the removal of a skin sample from one's small finger. For one of the events, participants merely were exposed to a paragraph of information about the type of event. For the other event, participants were asked to imagine the event occurring. In the third session, participants completed the survey again and reported any memories they had of the two target events. The hypothesis was that imagining the events (i.e., forming a mental imagine of the event occurring in one's life years earlier) could cause people to believe that the event, in fact, had occurred.

This is what happened. Whether they had imagined the tooth extraction or the removal of a skin sample, participants were more likely to believe that the event had occurred and to imagine some aspects of the event if they merely had been asked to imagine it a week earlier. A critical aspect of this particular study is that one of the events, the skin sample removal, surely had never occurred to the participants; medical records in the area that the study was conducted indicated that physicians never employed the procedure. Thus,

the findings showed that participants ended up remembering information (e.g., aspects of the physical setting, the medical personnel involved) about an event that never had occurred.

This sort of study does not resolve the question of whether the memories of a particular client in therapy are accurate or false. In individual cases, this issue surely will remain controversial. Psychologists have no reliable method of distinguishing between "recovered memories" and "false memories" in each individual case. However, the research does demonstrate that it is at least possible for people to "remember" events that demonstrably had not occurred.

Source: Loftus (1997), Mazzoni and Memon (2003), Williams (1994).

In the second stage of development, the **anal stage** (ages two and three), there is excitation in the anus and in the movement of feces through the anal passageway. The expulsion of the feces is believed to bring relief from tension and pleasure in the stimulation of the mucous membranes in that region. The pleasure related to this erogenous zone involves the organism in conflict. There is conflict between elimination and retention, between the pleasure in release and the pleasure in retention, and between the wish for pleasure in evacuation and the demands of the external world for delay. This last-named conflict represents the first crucial conflict between the individual and society. Here, the environment requires the child to violate the pleasure principle or be punished. The child may retaliate against such demands by intentional soiling. Psychologically, the child may associate having bowel movements with losing something important, which leads to depression, or may associate bowel movements with giving a prize or gift to others, which may create feelings of power and control.

In the **phallic stage** (ages four and five), excitation and tension are focused on the genitals. The biological differentiation between the sexes leads to psychological differentiation. The male child develops erections, and the new excitations in this area lead to increased interest in the genitals and the realization that the female lacks the penis. This leads to the fear that he may lose his penis—**castration anxiety**. The father becomes a rival for the affections of the mother, as suggested in the song "I Want a Girl Just Like the Girl That Married Dear Old Dad." The boy's hostility toward the father is projected onto the father, with the consequent fear of retaliation. This leads to what is known as the **Oedipus complex**. According to the Oedipus complex, every boy is fated in fantasy to kill his father and marry his mother. The complex can be heightened by actual seductiveness on the part of the mother. Castration anxiety can be heightened by actual threats from the father to cut off the penis. These threats occur in a surprising number of cases.

An interesting experimental illustration of the Oedipus complex is found in the subliminal psychodynamic activation studies we reviewed previously. As you read, in this research, stimuli are presented to subjects subliminally in a tachistoscope. Particular stimuli presumably activate unconscious conflicts. In one study, researchers included stimuli designed to activate Oedipal conflicts. They then examined the effects of Oedipal activation on males' performance in a competitive situation (Silverman, Ross, Adler, & Lustig, 1978). The stimuli chosen to intensify versus reduce Oedipal conflict were "Beating Dad Is Wrong" and "Beating Dad Is OK." In addition, neutral stimuli (e.g., "People Are Walking") were presented. These stimuli were presented tachistoscopically after participants engaged in a dart-throwing competition. Participants were tested again for dart-throwing performance following subliminal exposure to each type of stimulus.

As expected, the two Oedipal stimuli had clear-cut effects and in different directions: The "Beating Dad Is OK" stimulus produced higher scores than the neutral stimulus, whereas the "Beating Dad Is Wrong" stimulus produced lower scores.

It is important to note that these results were not obtained when the stimuli were presented above threshold. The psychodynamic activation effects appear to operate at the unconscious level rather than at the conscious level. In addition, since these subliminal effects are not always found in psychological research, it is noteworthy that the authors emphasized that the experimental stimuli used and the responses measured must be relevant to the motivational state of the research participants. To ensure this in their work, participants were first primed with picture and story material containing Oedipal content.

Developmental processes during the phallic stage differ for females versus males. According to Freud, females realize they lack a penis and blame the mother, the original love object. In developing **penis envy**, the female child chooses the father as the love object and imagines that the lost organ will be restored by having a child by the father.[1] Whereas the Oedipus complex is abandoned in the boy because of castration anxiety, in the female, it is started because of penis envy. As with the male, conflict during this period is in some cases accentuated by the father's seductiveness toward the female child. And, as with the male, the female child resolves the conflict by keeping the father as a love object but gaining him through identification with the mother.

Do children actually display Oedipal behaviors, or are these all distorted memories of adults, in particular of patients in psychoanalytic treatment? A study investigated this question through the use of parents' reports of parent–child interactions, as well as through the analysis of children's responses to stories involving parent–child interaction. It was found that at around age four, children show increased preference for the parent of the opposite sex and an increased antagonism toward the parent of the same sex. These behaviors diminish at around the age of five or six. What is interesting in this study is that although the researchers came from a differing theoretical orientation, they concluded that the reported Oedipal behaviors coincided with the psychoanalytic view of Oedipal relations between mothers and sons and between fathers and daughters (Watson & Getz, 1990).

As part of the resolution of the Oedipus complex, the child identifies with the parent of the same sex. The child now gains the parent of the opposite sex through **identification** with, rather than defeat of, the parent of the same sex. The development of an identification with the parent of the same sex is a critical issue during the phallic stage and, more generally, is a critical concept in developmental psychology. In identification, individuals take on themselves the qualities of another person and integrate them into their functioning. In identifying with their parents, children assume many of the same values and morals. It is in this sense that the superego has been called the heir to the resolution of the Oedipus complex.

According to Freud, all major aspects of our personality character develop during the oral, anal, and phallic stages of development. After the phallic stage, the child enters a **latency stage** during which, according to Freud, the child experiences a decrease in sexual urges and interest. The onset of puberty, with the reawakening of the sexual urges and Oedipal feelings, marks the beginning of the **genital stage**. Dependency feelings and Oedipal strivings that were not fully resolved during the pregenital stages of development now come back to rear their ugly heads. The turmoil of adolescence is partly attributable to these factors. According to Freud, successful progression through the stages of development leads to the psychologically healthy person—one who can love and work.

---

[1] Psychoanalytic theory has been criticized by feminists on a variety of grounds. Perhaps more than any other concept, the concept of penis envy is seen as expressing a chauvinistic, hostile view toward women. This issue will be addressed in Chapter 4 in the Critical Evaluation section.

asiseeit / Getty Images

Identification: In Freud's analysis of psychosexual development, the child eventually identifies with the same-sex parent, taking on that parent's interests and values.

major contribution

Erikson's Psychosocial Stages of Development   Freud devoted little attention to development after the early years of life. All "the action" in personality development, Freud thought, occurred by the end of the phallic stage. Other psychologists who were deeply sympathetic to Freud's overall model of personality thought he had underestimated the importance of personality development later in life. They tried, then, to understand later life development within a psychodynamic perspective. The most important of these theorists was Erik Erikson (1902–1994).

Erikson believed that development was not merely psychosexual but also psycho*social*. Stages of development include social concerns (Table 3.2). To Erikson, the first stage of personality development is significant not just because of the localization of pleasure in the mouth but because in the feeding situation a relationship of trust or mistrust is developed between the infant and the mother. Similarly, the anal stage is significant not only for the change in the nature of the major erogenous zone but also because toilet training is a significant social situation in which the child may develop a sense of autonomy or succumb to shame and self-doubt. In the phallic stage, the child must struggle with the issue of taking pleasure in, as opposed to feeling guilty about, being assertive, competitive, and successful.

For Erikson (1950), the latency and genital stages are periods when the individual develops a sense of industry and success or a sense of inferiority and, perhaps most important of all, a sense of identity or a sense of role diffusion. The crucial task of adolescence, according to Erikson, is the establishment of a sense of ego identity, an accrued confidence that the way one views oneself has a continuity with one's past and is matched by the perceptions of others. In contrast to people who develop a sense of identity, people with role diffusion experience the feeling of not really knowing who they are, of not knowing whether what they think they are matches what others think of them, and of not knowing how they have developed in this way or where they are heading in the future. During late adolescence and the college years, this struggle with a sense of identity may lead to joining a variety of groups and to considerable anguish about the choice of a career. If these issues are not resolved during this time, the individual is, in later life, filled with a sense of despair: Life is too short, and it is too late to start all over again.

Table 3.2   Erikson's Eight Psychosocial Stages of Development and Their Implications for Personality

Psychosocial Stage	Age	Positive Outcomes	Negative Outcomes
Basic trust vs. mistrust	1 year	Feelings of inner goodness, trust in oneself and others, optimism	Sense of badness, mistrust of self and others, pessimism
Autonomy vs. shame and doubt	2–3 years	Exercise of will, self-control, able to make choices	Rigid, excessive conscience, doubtful, self-conscious shame
Initiative vs. guilt	4–5 years	Pleasure in accomplishments, activity, direction, and purpose	Guilt over goals contemplated and achievements initiated
Industry vs. inferiority	Latency	Able to be absorbed in productive work, pride in completed product	Sense of inadequacy and inferiority, unable to complete work
Identity vs. role diffusion	Adolescence	Confidence of inner sameness and continuity, promise of a career	Ill at ease in roles, no set standards, sense of artificiality
Intimacy vs. isolation	Early adulthood	Mutuality, sharing of thoughts, work, feelings	Avoidance of intimacy, superficial relations
Generativity vs. stagnation	Adulthood	Ability to lose oneself in work and relationships	Loss of interest in work, impoverished relations
Integrity vs. despair	Later years	Sense of order and meaning, content with self and one's accomplishments	Fear of death, bitter about life, and what one got from it or what did not happen

Ted Streshinsky / Corbis/Getty Images

Erik H. Erikson.

In his research on identity formation, Marcia (1994) has identified four identity statuses.

- In identity achievement, the individual has established a sense of identity following exploration. Such individuals function at a high psychological level, being capable of independent thought, intimacy in interpersonal relations, complex moral reasoning, and resistance to group demands for conformity or group manipulation of their sense of self-esteem.

- In identity moratorium, the individual is in the midst of an identity crisis. Such individuals are capable of high levels of psychological functioning, but are still struggling to answer the question of who they are, and thus are less prepared than the identity achievers to make commitments.

- In identity foreclosure, the individual is committed to an identity without having gone through a process of exploration. Such individuals tend to be rigid, highly responsive to group demands for conformity, and sensitive to manipulation of their self-esteem.

- In identity diffusion, the individual lacks any strong sense of identity or commitment. Such individuals are very vulnerable to blows to their self-esteem, often are disorganized in their thinking, and have problems with intimacy. In sum, Marcia suggests that individuals differ in how they go about handling the process of identity formation, with such differences being reflected in their sense of self, thought processes, and interpersonal relations. Although not necessarily establishing fixed patterns for later life, how the process of identity formation is handled is seen as having important implications for later personality development.

Continuing with his description of the later stages of life and the accompanying psychological issues, Erikson suggests that some people develop a sense of intimacy, an acceptance of life's successes and disappointments, and a sense of continuity throughout the life cycle, whereas other people remain isolated from family and friends, appear to survive on a fixed daily routine, and focus on both past disappointments and future death. Although the ways in which people do and do not resolve these critical issues of adulthood may have their roots in childhood conflict, Erikson suggests that this is not always the case and that they have a significance of their own (Erikson, 1982).

In sum, Erikson's contributions are noteworthy in three ways: (1) He has emphasized the psychosocial as well as the instinctual basis for personality development, (2) he has extended the stages of development to include the entire life cycle and has articulated the major psychological issues to be faced in these later stages, and (3) he has recognized that people look to the future as well as to the past and that how they construe their future may be as significant a part of their personality as how they construe their past.

The Importance of Early Experience   Psychoanalytic theory emphasizes the role of early life events for later personality development. Evidence of the importance of parenting practices when children are in need of psychological resources fits with this perspective (Pomerantz & Thompson, 2008). Many researchers, however, suggest a much greater potential for development and change in personality across the entire life span. Although the issue is complex, with no uniform consensus, many scholars highlight the fact that, to a degree not fully appreciated by Freud, changes in an individual's environment that occur later in life can bring about changes in personality (Kagan, 1998; Lewis, 2002). Indeed, in contrast to the themes established by Freud, a major trend in contemporary psychology is the study of personality dynamics across the entire course of life, from childhood to older adulthood (Baltes, Staudinger, & Lindenberger, 1999).

The complexities of the issue can be illustrated with two studies. The first, conducted by a psychoanalyst (Gaensbauer, 1982), involved the study of affect development in infancy. The infant, Jenny, was first studied systematically when she was almost four months old. Prior to this time, at the age of three months, she had been physically abused by her father. At that time she was brought to the hospital with a broken arm and a skull fracture. She was described by hospital personnel as being a "lovable baby"—happy, cute, sociable—but also as not cuddling when held and as being "jittery" when approached by a male. Following this history of abuse, Jenny was placed in a foster home, where she received adequate physical care but minimal social interaction. This was very much in contrast with her earlier experience with her natural mother, who spent considerable time with her and breast-fed her "at the drop of a hat." The first systematic observation occurred almost a month after placement in the foster home. At this time, Jenny's behavior was judged to be completely consistent with a diagnosis of depression—lethargic, apathetic, disinterested, collapsed posture. A systematic analysis of her facial expressions indicated five discrete affects, each meaningfully related to her unique history. Sadness was noted when she was with her natural mother. Fearfulness and anger were noted when she was approached by a male stranger but not when approached by a female stranger. Joy was noted as a transient affect during brief play sequences. Finally, interest-curiosity was noted when she interacted with female strangers.

After she was visited in her foster home, Jenny was placed in a different foster home where she received warm attention. Following two weeks in this environment, she was again brought to the hospital for further evaluation, this time by her second foster mother. This time, she generally appeared to be a normally responsive infant. She showed no evidence of distress and even smiled at a male stranger. After an additional month at this foster home, she was brought to the hospital by her natural mother for a third evaluation. Generally, she was animated and happy. However, when the mother left the room, she cried intensely. This continued following the mother's return despite repeated attempts to soothe her. Apparently, separation from her natural mother continued to lead to a serious distress response. In addition, sadness and anger were frequently noted.

At eight months old, Jenny was returned to her natural mother, who left her husband and received counseling. At the age of 20 months, she was described as appearing to be normal and having an excellent relation with her mother. However, there continued to be the problem of anger and distress associated with separation from her mother.

These suggest that there was evidence of both continuity and discontinuity between Jenny's early emotional experiences and later emotional reactions. In general, she was doing well, and her emotional responses were within the normal range for infants of her age. At the same time, the anger reactions in response to separations and frustration appeared to be a link to the past. The psychoanalyst conducting the study suggested that perhaps isolated traumatic events are less important than the repeated experiences of a less dramatic but more persistent nature. In other words, the early years are important but more in terms of patterns of interpersonal relationships than in terms of isolated events.

The second study, conducted by a group of developmental psychologists, assessed the relationship between early emotional relationships with the mother and later psychopathology (Lewis, Feiring, McGuffog, & Jaskir, 1984). In this study, the attachment behavior of boys and girls one year of age toward their mothers was observed. The observation involved a standardized procedure consisting of a period of play with the mother in an unstructured situation, followed by the departure of the mother and a period when the child was alone in the playroom, and then by the return of the mother and a second free play period. The behavior of the children was scored systematically and assigned to one of three attachment categories: avoidant, secure, or ambivalent. The avoidant and ambivalent categories suggested difficulties in this area. Then at six years of age, the competence of these children was assessed through the mothers' completion of a Child Behavior Profile. The ratings of the mothers were also checked against teacher ratings. On the basis of the Child Behavior Profile, the children were classified into a normal group, an at-risk group, and a clinically disturbed group.

What was the relation between early attachment behavior and later pathology? Two aspects of the results are particularly noteworthy. First, the relations for boys and girls differed. For boys, attachment classification at one year of age was significantly related to later pathology. Insecurely attached boys showed more pathology at age six than did securely attached boys. For girls, there was no relationship between attachment and later pathology. Second, the authors noted a difference between trying to predict pathology from the early data (prospective) as opposed to trying to understand later pathology in terms of earlier attachment difficulties (retrospective). If one starts with the boys who at age six were identified as being at risk or clinically disturbed, 80% would be found to have been assigned to the avoidant- or ambivalent-attachment category at age one—a very strong statistical relationship. But, if one took all boys classified as insecurely attached (avoidant or ambivalent) at age one and predicted them to be at risk or clinically disturbed at age six, one would be right in only 40% of the cases. The reason for this is that far more of the boys were classified as insecurely attached than were later diagnosed as at risk or disturbed. Thus, the clinician viewing later pathology would have a clear basis for suggesting a strong relationship between pathology and early attachment difficulties. On the other hand, focusing on the data in terms of prediction would suggest a much more tenuous relationship and the importance of other variables. As Freud himself recognized, when we observe later pathology, it is all too easy to understand how it developed. On the other hand, when we look at these phenomena prospectively, we are made aware of the varied paths that development can follow.

The Development of Thinking Processes

The most prominent aspect of Freud's work on development is his theory of psychosexual stages (see Growth and Development in this chapter). In addition to the development of instinctual drives, however, Freud also addressed the development of thinking processes. Here, his work rests on a theoretical distinction between two different modes, or processes, of thinking; he called them primary and secondary process thought. Before defining these terms, we note that Freud, with this distinction, addressed an issue of enormously broad significance. It is, in essence, the question of how the mind works—the processes through which the mind deals with information. We might think that the human mind, like a computer, processes information in one basic way. Your personal computer processes information the same way whether the computer is new or old, and whether the information being processed is emotionally exciting or boring. No matter what, information is processed digitally in the machine's central processing unit. Maybe the human mind is like this, too. Then again, maybe it isn't—and Freud suggested it isn't. He concluded that the mind processes information in two distinctly different ways.

In psychoanalytic theory, **primary process** thinking is the language of the unconscious. Primary process thought is illogical and irrational. In primary process thinking, reality and fantasy are indistinguishable. These features of primary process thought—an absence of logic, a confusion of appearance and reality—may seem so odd at first that you may reject this aspect of Freudian theory. Yet consider some examples. As you grew up, you only gradually developed the capacity for logical, rational thought. Very young children do not have the capacity to formulate logical arguments. Yet they clearly are thinking! This means that they must be thinking in a manner that lacks adult rationality and logic. To Freud, they are thinking via primary process thought. Consider dreams. Sometimes you wake up when having a nightmare. Your heart may be racing, and you may be in a cold sweat. If so, this means that your body was reacting to the contents of the dream, preparing its physiological systems to respond. But, of course, there is nothing to respond to: It's just a dream. This means that you were reacting to a fantasy as if it were real; in the dream, fantasy and reality are confused.

Secondary process thinking is the language of consciousness, reality testing, and logic. It develops only after the child first has the capacity for primary process thought and thus is secondary. The development of this capacity parallels the development of the ego. With the development of the ego, the individual becomes more differentiated, as a self, from the rest of the world, and self-preoccupation decreases.

Contemporary psychologists have recognized, as did Freud, that the mind works according to more than one thinking process. Epstein (1994) has distinguished between experiential thinking and rational thinking. *Experiential thinking*, analogous to primary process thinking, is viewed as occurring earlier in evolutionary development and is characterized by being holistic, concrete, and heavily influenced by emotion. Often, it is used in interpersonal situations to be empathic or intuitive. *Rational thinking*, analogous to secondary process thinking, is viewed as occurring later in evolutionary development and is characterized as being more abstract, analytical, and following the rules of logic and evidence. For example, rational thinking would be used in solving mathematical problems.

The potential conflict between the two systems of thought can be seen in an experiment in which subjects were asked to choose between drawing a winning red jelly bean from a bowl that contained 1 out of 10 red jelly beans and a bowl that contained 8 out of 100 red jelly beans (Denes-Raj & Epstein, 1994). Having been told the proportion of red jelly beans in the two bowls, subjects knew that the rational thing to do was to select the bowl with the higher proportion—1 out of 10. Yet, despite this, many subjects felt that their chances were better with the bowl that contained more red jelly beans, despite the poorer odds. This conflict between what they felt and what they knew expressed the conflict between the experiential and rational thought systems. According to Epstein (1994), the two systems are parallel and can act in conjunction with one another as well as in conflict with one another. Other psychologists have suggested other, related, two-part distinctions. Many contemporary psychologists, then, feel that Freud was fundamentally correct in positing more than one form of thought; they tend to differ from Freud in the details, that is, in their specific beliefs about the nature of the two aspects of thinking. The study of primary versus secondary process thought, then, is one in which Freud's ideas remarkably anticipated future developments in the field.

This chapter has considered Freud's approach to three of the four topics addressed in a personality theory: structure, processes, and development. In our next chapter, we consider the fourth: psychopathology and clinical applications designed to improve people's lives. We also review alternative psychodynamic models developed throughout the 20th century and there in the 21st.

MAJOR CONCEPTS

Anal stage	Free association	Penis envy	Repression
Anxiety	Genital stage	Perception without awareness	Secondary process
Castration anxiety	Id	Perceptual defense	Sublimation
Catharsis	Identification	Phallic stage	Subliminal psychodynamic
Conscious	Isolation	Pleasure principle	activation
Death instinct	Latency stage	Preconscious	Superego
Defense mechanisms	Libido	Primary process	Unconscious
Denial	Life instinct	Projection	Undoing
Ego	Mechanism	Rationalization	
Energy system	Oedipus complex	Reaction formation	
Erogenous zones	Oral stage	Reality principle	

REVIEW

1. Psychoanalytic theory illustrates a psychodynamic, clinical approach to personality. The psychodynamic emphasis is expressed in the interpretation of behavior as a result of the interplay among motives or drives. The clinical approach is expressed in the emphasis on material observed during intensive treatment of individuals.

2. Freud posited a mechanistic, deterministic, energy-based model of the mind. This model directly reflected the 19th-century scientific and medical training Freud received.

3. Freud built his theory on case study evidence. In his view, the in-depth analysis of clinical cases was the only valid method for uncovering the dynamics of the conscious and unconscious mind.

4. The core of Freud's theory is an integrated analysis of both personality structures and personality processes. The structures are three mental systems—the id, ego, and superego—which function according to different operating principles that inherently conflict with one another. The processes involve mental energy whose origin is in the id but whose expression is channeled, blocked, or distorted by the actions of the ego, working within constraints represented in the superego.

5. Personality dynamics in psychoanalytic theory involve conflict. Impulsive drives in the id seek immediate expression, which conflicts with both the ego's desire to delay impulses to meet the constraints of reality and the superego's desire for actions that adhere to moral standards. Any given action, then, is a compromise among these competing desires of the different psychic agencies. Defense mechanisms are strategies employed by the ego to defend against the anxiety aroused by the unacceptable drives and desires of the id.

6. In the psychoanalytic theory of personality development, the individual progresses through a series of developmental stages. Each stage involves a distinct region of the body that serves as a primary focus of sensual gratification. These stages of development occur early in life, in childhood. To a greater extent than any other theory, Freud's psychoanalytic theory suggests that the experiences of early childhood have an enduring, immutable influence on the personality characteristics of the individual.

7. The psychoanalyst Erik Erikson attempted to broaden and extend psychoanalytic theory through an emphasis on the psychosocial stages of development.

Freud's Psychoanalytic Theory: Applications, Related Theoretical Conceptions, and Contemporary Research

4

Questions to be Addressed in this Chapter

Psychodynamic Personality Assessment: Projective Tests

Psychopathology

Psychological Change

The Case of Jim

Related Theoretical Conceptions

Contemporary Developments in Personality Theory: Neuropsychoanalysis

Critical Evaluation

Major Concepts

Review

Chapter Focus

When you were a kid, did you ever play the cloud game? It had to be a day when there were big white fluffy clouds against the blue background of the sky. You would lie on your back in the grass with a friend and stare at the clouds until you "saw" something. If you tried long and hard enough, you could find all kinds of interesting things: animals, dragons, the face of an old man. Quite often, pointing out your discoveries to your friend was impossible. Exactly what you saw could only be seen by you. Why did you see the things you saw? It must have been something about you that you "projected" onto the cloud in the sky.

This is the basic idea behind projective tests such as the Rorschach Inkblot Test and the Thematic Apperception Test (TAT). In this chapter, we focus on these tests because they are techniques of personality assessment associated with psychodynamic theory. Projective tests use ambiguous stimuli to elicit highly individualistic responses, which can then be interpreted by the clinician. This chapter also considers Freud's attempts to understand and explain the symptoms presented by his patients and his efforts to develop a systematic method of treatment. After considering more recent developments in psychoanalytic theory, including challenges to Freud's ideas from other psychodynamic theorists, we turn to a critical evaluation and summary.

Questions to be Addressed in this Chapter

1. How can one assess personality from a psychodynamic perspective?

2. What, according to psychoanalysis, are the causes of psychopathology and the best methods for treating psychologically distressed persons?

3. Why did some of Freud's early followers break with his approach, and what novel theoretical ideas did they advance?

4. What recent developments in personality psychology are inspired by Freud's work, and what does contemporary scientific evidence say about Freud's original psychoanalytical enterprise?

In the previous chapter, you learned the ideas that define Freud's psychoanalytic theory of personality. In this chapter, you will see what one can do with these ideas. This chapter discusses how the theoretical ideas of psychoanalysis can be applied to practical questions of personality assessment and psychological change in therapy.

You will also see "what one can do with" Freud's ideas in a second sense of this phrase. Throughout the 20th century, a series of psychologists judged that, rather than apply Freud's ideas, it would be better to change them. These theorists retained some key features of Freud's thinking—especially the study of internal mental dynamics, or "psychodynamics"—but significantly modified and extended other aspects of his original theory. A second goal of this chapter is to review these post-Freudian psychodynamic theories. Our coverage includes a contemporary theoretical development known as "neuropsychoanalysis."

A third goal of this chapter concerns contemporary research. More than was the case in Chapter 3, here we examine contemporary research on psychodynamic processes. At the end of the chapter, we evaluate Freud's psychoanalytic perspective from the perspective of current research findings.

Psychodynamic Personality Assessment: Projective Tests

We begin with a challenge that is central to both personality theory and clinical practice, namely, psychological assessment. The challenge, specifically, is to develop methods that shed light on the nature of an individual's personality, including causes of any psychological distress. Ideally, these methods would have two features. The first is obvious: They should be accurate, or valid (recall our discussion of validity in Chapter 2). The second is a bit more subtle. Assessment procedures should be quick and efficient. The clinician may need quickly to gain some insight into a client's personality in order to make preliminary treatment decisions.

Consider for a moment the difficulties from a psychoanalytic perspective. If you want to assess someone's personality, what would you do? You obviously could not "just ask" someone about psychoanalytic content. Direct questions—for example, "How often do you think about killing one of your parents so you can have sex with the other one?"—are absurd for at least two reasons: (1) The person being tested *can't* answer the question (the relevant material is unconscious, and its mere mention activates defense mechanisms that protect the material from reaching consciousness), and (2) even if the person could answer them, he or she probably wouldn't want to; that is, most people would not want to reveal such aspects of their personality to others.

Freud addressed this challenge by using, as his tool of assessment, the free-association technique. However, even if one were to assume its validity—a big "if"—the free-association method clearly does not meet the goal of efficiency. It may take weeks or months to develop a client–therapist relationship that is sufficiently strong that the client will reveal deep-seated conflicts in free associations. Recognizing this reality, investigators inspired by Freud's theory sought new assessment methods. The most influential of these is a set of procedures known as **projective tests**.

The Logic of Projective Tests

The defining feature of projective tests is that the test items are ambiguous. The person being assessed is asked to respond to each of a series of ambiguous test items. In order to respond to the item, the person must interpret it; that is, he or she must figure out what the test item looks like or means. The fundamental logic behind the projective tests is that the person's interpretations will be revealing of his or her personality. It is thought, in other words, that the individual will "project" aspects of his or her own personality onto the test item when interpreting it (hence the name *projective tests*).

This use of ambiguous test items is unlike other, more typical psychological questionnaires or surveys. When writing test items for a questionnaire, psychologists usually strive for clarity. A questionnaire item such as "Do you like things?" would usually be seen as a terrible test item because it is so ambiguous; "What things are you talking about?" the test-taker might ask. But in projective assessment, this ambiguity is the very point of the test. The psychologist is interested in how the test-taker constructs meaning out of the vague stimulus.

The psychologist of course is not interested in responses to test items per se. Responses to the test items are interesting only because they might be revealing of the individual's *typical* style of thinking, which in turn is interesting because it may be revealing of underlying, unconscious psychodynamics. A key assumption in the use of projective tests, then, is that the individual's interpretation of test items during a testing session with the psychologist will be indicative of how the person interprets typically ambiguous circumstances in his or her daily life.

Two projective tests have received particularly widespread use: the Rorschach Inkblot Test and the Thematic Apperception Test (TAT). Although these tests were not developed by Freud, they are related closely to psychoanalytic theory in three ways:

1. Psychoanalytic theory emphasizes the complex organization of personality functioning. The theory views personality as a dynamic system through which the individual organizes and structures external stimuli. Projective testing procedures allow people to respond in complex ways as they interpret test stimuli. People don't just say "yes" or "no" in response to test items; instead, they formulate their own responses. The assessor thus can observe complex patterns of thinking, as required from a psychodynamic perspective.

2. Psychoanalytic theory emphasizes the importance of the unconscious and defense mechanisms. In projective tests, the purpose of the test and the way it will be interpreted are hidden from the subject. The test thus may get behind the defenses of the test-taker.

3. Psychoanalytic theory emphasizes a holistic understanding of personality. The theorist is interested in the relations among parts of the person. Projective tests facilitate a holistic interpretation of the individual. The test is scored according to an overall patterning and organization of test responses rather than by interpreting any single response as an index of a particular personality characteristic.

The Rorschach Inkblot Test

Although inkblots had been used earlier, Hermann Rorschach, a Swiss psychiatrist, first fully grasped their potential for personality assessment. He put ink on paper and folded the paper so that symmetrical but ill-defined forms were produced. He then showed these images to hospitalized patients. Through a process of trial and error, he identified inkblots that elicited different responses from different psychiatric groups. Rorschach settled on 10 such cards; the test, then, consists of 10 cards containing these inkblots.

When conducting the Rorschach test, the assessor only presents enough information to enable the person to complete the task. The test is presented as "just one of many ways used nowadays to try to understand people." People are asked to look at each card and tell the assessor what they see represented on the card. They are free to focus on the whole image or any part of the inkblot. After asks people to explain why they felt that a given test item represented what they said it did. All responses are recorded.

In interpreting these responses, one is interested in how the response, or percept, is formed, the reasons for the response, and its content. Percepts that match the structure of the inkblot suggest a good level of psychological functioning that is well oriented toward reality. On the other hand, poorly formed responses that do not fit the structure of the inkblot suggest unrealistic fantasies or bizarre behavior. The content of subjects' responses (whether they see mostly animate or inanimate objects, humans or animals, and content expressing affection or hostility) makes a great deal of difference in interpreting the subjects' personalities. For example, the assessor would make different interpretations of two sets of responses—one where animals are seen repeatedly as fighting and a second where humans are seen as sharing and involved in cooperative efforts.

Content may be interpreted symbolically. An explosion may symbolize intense hostility; a pig, gluttonous tendencies; a fox, a tendency toward being crafty and aggressive; spiders, witches, and octopuses, negative images of a dominating mother; gorillas and giants, negative attitudes toward a dominating father; and an ostrich, an attempt to hide from conflicts (Schafer, 1954).

When interpreting test responses, each response is used to suggest hypotheses or possible interpretations about the individual's personality, and the hypotheses are checked against other responses by the individual. The examiner also notes any unusual behavior and uses this as a source of data for further interpretation. For example, a subject who constantly asks for guidance

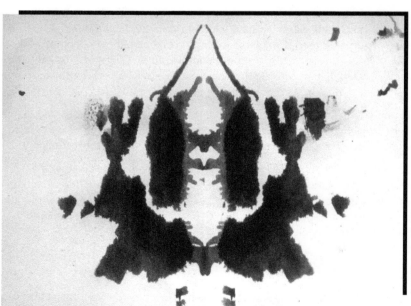

Lambert/Getty Images, Inc.

An imagine similar to that used in the Rorschach inkblot test.

Rorschach inkblot test: The Rorschach interpreter assumes that the subject's personality is projected onto unstructured stimuli such as inkblots.

may be interpreted as dependent. A subject who seems tense, asks questions in a subtle way, and looks at the back of the cards may be interpreted as suspicious and possibly paranoid.

The Thematic Apperception Test (TAT)

A second widely used projective test is the Thematic Apperception Test (TAT), developed by Henry Murray and Christina Morgan. The TAT consists of cards with scenes on them. Most scenes depict one or two people, though some are more abstract. The assessor presents these ambiguous scenes one after the other and, for each, asks the person to make up a story based on the scene. The story includes what is going on, the thoughts and feelings of the people in the scene, what led up to the scene, and the outcome.

Since the scenes are ambiguous, the individual's personality may be projected onto the stimulus as he or she interprets it and may be revealed in the stories told. "The test is based on the well-recognized fact that when a person interprets an ambiguous social situation he is apt to expose his own personality as much as the phenomenon to which he is attending" (Murray, 1938, p. 530). The assumption is that people are not aware they are talking about themselves when weaving stories about the pictures. Their defenses thus can be bypassed. TAT responses can be scored systematically according to a scheme developed by Murray, or on a more impressionistic basis.

The TAT has been used not only clinically but in experimental research, particularly in the area of human motivation. Research by the psychologist David McClelland and colleagues (McClelland, Koestner, & Weinberger, 1989) indicates that individual differences in motives, such as the motive to achieve, are uniquely revealed in the themes of stories created by research participants in response to TAT pictures. Motives measured by stimuli such as the TAT (implicit motives) result in different scores and predict different behaviors than motives measured by self-report questionnaires (explicit motives) (Schultheiss, 2008).

Projective Tests: Do They Work?

Projective tests have been widely used by personality and clinical psychologists during the past half-century. They have been administered to literally millions of persons (Lilienfeld, Wood, & Garb, 2000). Given their widespread use over the years, the natural question to ask is "Do they work?"

By "work," in the context of psychological testing, one generally means "Do they predict important life outcomes?" In the terminology we introduced in Chapter 2, the question is whether the tests are valid. This question is more complicated than it sounds. There are at least two complications. The first is the possibility that projective tests predict some types of outcomes but not others. It might be impossible to give a simple yes or no answer to the question "Do projective tests work?" because they might work, or be valid, for predicting only some types of outcomes. A second complication is that there are different ways of scoring projective tests. Over the years, different psychologists have developed different schemes for interpreting and classifying people's responses to projective test items (Exner, 1986; Westen, 1990). It is possible, then, that some scoring systems might work well, whereas others might not.

These complications suggest that one cannot answer the question of whether projective tests work by considering only one or two isolated studies. Instead, what is required are comprehensive reviews of the various scoring schemes and the range of outcomes that the psychologist might wish to predict. A particularly extensive review of this sort was completed by Lilienfeld and colleagues (2000). These authors were attentive to the complexities involved in assessing the validity of projective tests. They reviewed research on a variety of projective methods, including the Rorschach and TAT, and on a variety of methods for scoring responses on these tests.

What did they find? On the one hand, their review indicated that some scoring methods are valid for some purposes. For example, when TAT stories are scored for the presence of themes related to achievement motivation, as suggested by psychologists such as David McClelland (McClelland, Koestner, & Weinberger, 1989), there is evidence that the TAT responses are correlated with measures of motivated behavior. However, such positive results proved to be exceptions. The review by Lilienfeld and colleagues (2000) indicated that projective tests commonly do not work. For example, although there may be a variety of ways to score Rorschach responses, the choice of scoring scheme seems not to make much difference; "the overwhelming majority of Rorschach indexes" (Lilienfeld et al., 2000, p. 54) were not consistently related to outcomes of interest. And although there may be some validity to methods for scoring achievement themes in TAT responses, "most TAT scoring systems" (p. 54), like the Rorschach systems, also lack validity.

These negative conclusions about the validity of projective tests are congruent with those of many other scholars (Dawes, 1994; Rorer, 1990) who have taken an objective look at research on projective tests and have found that they simply do not work well enough to be used in clinical practice. Indeed, the Lilienfeld group (2000) recommends that students of psychology no longer should obtain extensive training in the use of these tests and notes that a committee of the American Psychological Association has concurred that projective tests should not be a component of 21st-century training in psychology.

Why don't projective tests work very well? That is, why is it that they rarely enable psychologists to predict life outcomes with high levels of accuracy? There are many possible reasons, but two stand out. The first concerns inter-judge reliability: If two psychologists (two "judges") score a person's responses to a projective test, will they agree with one another (will the judgments be reliable)? When using standard questionnaires, the reliability of scoring can be taken for granted; for example, if you take a multiple-choice test, a person or a machine-scoring system can score the test with perfect accuracy. But with projective tests, psychologists are not dealing with simple multiple-choice responses but rather with complex verbal statements that must be interpreted. The psychologist's interpretations may reflect not only the thoughts of the person taking the test but also those of the psychologist who does the scoring. The thoughts, feelings, and interpretive biases of the psychologist may influence the scoring of the test. If different psychologists have different interpretive biases, then interjudge reliability will be low. Research indicates that projective tests often do suffer from this problem. The interjudge reliability of scoring is not sufficiently high. Even when using the most well-developed of the Rorschach scoring systems, "only about half" of the Rorschach variables reach a "minimum acceptable threshold" of reliability (Lilienfeld et al., 2000, p. 33). If different psychologists do not even agree on how to score a person's test responses, then the scores that they compute are, of course, unlikely to yield accurate predictions of the person's behavior.

A second limitation is that the content of the projective test items commonly has nothing to do with the content of the test-taker's day-to-day life. It might be that an individual exhibits a distinctive style of thinking when contemplating, for example, relations with members of the opposite sex to which he or she is attracted. A psychological test that contained stimuli representing members of the opposite sex might pick up on this thinking style. But there is no guarantee that the person's thinking style will manifest itself when he or she is confronted with abstract blotches of ink. The few projective tests that are successful tend to use "stimuli that are especially relevant to the construct being assessed" (Lilienfeld et al., 2000, p. 55). For example, researchers interested in people's thoughts about interpersonal relations might use TAT cards that feature interpersonal themes (Westen, 1991). But this commonly is not done; instead, context commonly has been disregarded, and a generic set of stimulus materials (e.g., the set of Rorschach cards) is used to predict an individual's thoughts and feelings in a wide variety of contexts. And here the predictions commonly fail. As you will see in subsequent chapters, other personality theories employ psychological testing procedures that are much more sensitive to these issues of social context than are the projective tests of psychodynamic theory.

What do the limitations of projective testing say about Freud's psychoanalytic theory of personality? Some might argue that they say very little. In evaluating Freud, it is important to recall that he himself did not develop or use projective tests. He relied entirely on the free-association method in clinical interviews. So Freud's theory might be fine, even if the testing procedures developed by followers of Freud are flawed. However, one goal for a personality theorist is to provide guidelines that might inspire the construction of psychological testing procedures with high levels of reliability and validity. Whatever its other strengths, psychoanalysis generally has failed to achieve this goal. Although future developments may improve the validity of testing methods and thus respond to the criticisms that have been raised (Lilienfeld et al., 2000), psychological testing and prediction unquestionably do not constitute a strength of the psychodynamic tradition.

Psychopathology

Freud spent most of his professional time treating patients with neurotic disorders. He concluded that the psychological processes of his neurotic patients were basically similar to the psychological processes of people who were not suffering from neuroses and seeking therapy. Neuroses could be found, to one degree or another and in one form or another, in all people. Thus, Freud's analyses of pathology—its development, primary psychological dynamics, and treatment—are integral to his general theory of personality.

Personality Types

One aspect of Freud's analysis of pathology was developmental. Here, he addressed the questions of why an individual would develop pathology and why it would be a pathology of a particular type. This analysis is closely related to an idea you already have learned about, namely, Freud's theory of psychosexual stages of developmental (see Chapter 3). At any given developmental stage, the individual may experience a failure in the development of the instincts. Such failures are called **fixations**. If individuals receive so little gratification during a stage of development that they are afraid to go to the next stage, or if they receive so much gratification that there is no motivation to move on, a fixation will occur. If it does, later in life the individual will try to obtain the same type of satisfaction that was appropriate at the earlier stage (i.e., the one at which the fixation occurred). For example, an individual fixated at the oral stage may, as an adult, seek oral gratification in eating, smoking, or drinking.

A developmental phenomenon related to that of fixation is **regression**. In regression, the individual seeks to return to an earlier mode of satisfaction, an earlier point of fixation. Regression often occurs under conditions of stress, so that many people overeat, smoke, or drink too much alcohol only during periods of frustration and anxiety.

Since there are three distinct stages of early childhood development—oral, anal, and phallic— three personality styles may result from fixations (Table 4.1).

The characteristics of the **oral personality** type, which results from fixation at the oral stage of development, involve themes of taking things into, toward, and for oneself. Oral personalities are narcissistic, that is, interested only in themselves. They do not have a clear recognition of others as separate and valuable entities. Other people are seen only in terms of what they can give (feed). Oral personalities are always asking for something, either in terms of a modest, pleading request or an aggressive demand.

Image Source / Getty Images

Why the cigar? Freud's theory suggests that a fixation at the oral stage of development can create a life-long pattern of taking things into, toward, and for oneself.

Table 4.1   **Personality Characteristics Associated with Psychoanalytic Personality Types**

Personality Type	Personality Characteristics
Oral	Demanding, impatient, envious, covetous, jealous, rageful, depressed (feels empty), mistrustful, pessimistic
Anal	Rigid, striving for power and control, concerned with shoulds and oughts, pleasure and possessions, anxiety over waste and loss of control, concern with whether to submit or rebel
Phallic	*Male*: exhibitionistic, competitive, striving for success, emphasis on being masculine—macho—potent
	Female: naive, seductive, exhibitionistic, flirtatious

The **anal personality**, which stems from fixation at the anal stage of development, reflects a transformation of gratifications of anal impulses in the childhood years. In general, the traits of the anal character relate to anal-stage processes that have not been completely relinquished. The important processes at that stage are bodily processes (accumulation and release of fecal material) and interpersonal relations (the struggle of wills over toilet training). Tying the two together, the anal person sees excretion as symbolic of enormous power. That such a view persists is shown in many everyday expressions, such as the reference to the toilet as "the throne." The change from the oral to the anal character is one from "give me" to "do what I tell you," or from "I have to give you" to "I must obey you". The anal character is known by a triad of traits, called the anal triad: orderliness and cleanliness, parsimony and stinginess, and obstinacy. The emphasis on cleanliness is expressed in the saying "Cleanliness is next to godliness". The anal-compulsive personality has a need to keep everything clean and in order, representing a reaction formation against an interest in things that are disorderly and unclean. The second trait of the triad, parsimony/stinginess, relates to the anal-compulsive's interest in holding onto things, an interest dating back to a wish to retain the powerful and important feces. The third trait in the triad, obstinacy, relates to the anal character's infantile defiance against parting with stools, particularly on command by others. Dating back to toilet training and the struggle of wills, anal personalities often seek to be in control of things and have power or dominance over others.

Just as the oral and anal character types reflect partial fixations at the first two stages of development, the **phallic personality** character results from fixation at the phallic stage, during the Oedipus complex. Fixation here has different implications for men and women, and particular attention has been given to the results of partial fixation for males. Whereas success for the oral person means "I get," and success for the anal person means "I control," success for the phallic male means "I am a man". The phallic male must deny all possible suggestions that he has been castrated. For him, success means that he is "big" in the eyes of others. He must at all times assert his masculinity and potency, an attitude exemplified by Theodore Roosevelt's saying, "Speak softly but carry a big stick." The excessive, exhibitionist quality to the behavior of these people is expressive of the underlying anxiety concerning castration.

The female counterpart of the male phallic character is known as the hysterical personality. As a defense against Oedipal wishes, the little girl identifies to an excessive extent with her mother and femininity. She uses seductive and flirtatious behavior to maintain the interest of her father but denies its sexual intent. The pattern of behavior then is carried over into adulthood, where she may attract men with flirtatious behavior but deny sexual intent and generally appear to be somewhat naive. Hysterical women idealize life, their partners, and romantic love, often finding themselves surprised by life's uglier moments.

Conflict and Defense

Psychoanalytic theory proposes that psychopathology results from individuals' efforts to gratify instincts that were fixated at an earlier stage of development. The individual still seeks sexual and aggressive gratification in infantile forms. The problem for the person is that this potential gratification is associated with past trauma, such as the trauma of not having been able to express Oedipal desires. Expression of a wish thus may signal danger to the ego. This creates anxiety. There is, then, a conflict: A given desire and potential behavior are associated with both pleasure and pain. You may wish to indulge in sexual behavior but find that your desires are blocked by feelings of guilt or fear of punishment. You may wish to retaliate against powerful others (who symbolically represent the parents) but find your desire for revenge to be inhibited by anxieties about retaliation from powerful others (who again represent the parents). In all such cases, there is intrapsychic conflict between a wish and anxiety. The result often is that the individual can't say "no," can't be assertive, or otherwise feels blocked and unhappy (Table 4.2).

To reduce the painful experience of anxiety, defense mechanisms (see Chapter 3) are deployed. A person may, for example, deny sexual and aggressive feelings or project them onto others. If the defense is successful, the person no longer recognizes the feelings as his or her own and thus experiences less anxiety. If less successful, the energy associated with the unconscious sexual or aggressive drives may express itself in pathological **symptoms**. A symptom—such as a tic, psychological paralysis, or a compulsion—is a disguised expression of a repressed impulse. The meaning of the symptom, the nature of the dangerous instinct, and the nature of the defense all remain unconscious. A mother's obsession with the thought that something bad will happen to her child may, unknown to the mother, be caused by her own underlying rage at her child and anxiety about harm that she herself may do to it. A hand-washing compulsion may express both the wish to be dirty or do "dirty" things, and the defense against the wish is expressed in excessive cleanliness. Again, the person may be unaware of the wish or the defense and be troubled only by the symptom.

To summarize the psychoanalytic theory of psychopathology, in psychopathology there is a conflict between a drive or wish (instinct) and the ego's sense (anxiety) that danger will ensue if the wish is expressed (discharged). The wishes date back to childhood: Wishes and fears that were part of a specific time period in childhood are carried over into adolescence and adulthood. The person attempts to handle the painful anxiety that results from intrapsychic conflict via defense mechanisms. If the conflict is too great, the use of defense mechanisms can lead to neurotic symptoms or psychotic withdrawal from reality. Symptoms express the unconscious conflict between the wish or drive and anxiety. Each case of abnormal behavior, then, arises from an underlying

Table 4.2   **Psychoanalytic Theory of Psychopathology**

Illustrative Conflicts		Behavior Consequences of Defense Mechanisms
WISH	ANXIETY	DEFENSE
I would like to have sex with that person.	Such feelings are bad and will be punished.	Denial of all sexual behavior, obsessive preoccupation with the sexual behavior of others.
I would like to strike out at all those people who make me feel inferior.	If I am hostile, they will retaliate and really hurt me.	Denial of wish or fear: "I never feel angry," "I'm never afraid of anyone or anything."
I would like to get close to people and have them feed me or take care of me.	If I do, they will smother me or leave me.	Excessive independence and avoidance of getting close to people or fluctuations between approaching people and moving away from them; excessive need to take care of others.

conflict between a wish and a fear that dates back to an earlier period in childhood. Problems of adulthood, then, are a repetition of aspects of childhood. There continue to be childlike parts of us that, under stress and some other conditions, may become more active and troublesome.

Psychological Change

How does psychological change come about? Once a person has established a way of thinking about and responding to situations, through what process does a change in personality take place? The psychoanalytic theory of growth suggests that there is a normal course of human personality development, one that occurs because of an optimum degree of frustration. Where there has been too little or too much frustration at a particular stage of growth, personality does not develop normally and a fixation takes place. When this occurs, the individual repeats patterns of behavior regardless of other changes in situations. Given the development of such a neurotic pattern, how is it possible to break the cycle and move forward?

Insights into the Unconscious: Free Association and Dream Interpretation

In therapy, the first challenge is to gain insight into the problematic psychodynamics of the patient. As you learned in Chapter 3, Freud's method for accomplishing this was the **free-association** technique. The patient is asked to report to the analyst every thought that comes to mind, to delay reporting nothing, to withhold nothing, to bar nothing from coming to consciousness. Freud was interested in free associations to material that occurred not only in normal daily experiences but also in dreams. Dreams, as we discussed in the previous chapter, provide insight into unconscious desires. Through the free-association method, the analyst and patient are able to

In the free-association method, patients may experience transference: a development of attitudes toward the analyst that are based on attitudes held earlier toward parental figures.

Unilux / Getty Images

go beyond the manifest content of the dream to the latent content, the hidden unconscious wish that the storyline of the dream expresses.

At first, Freud thought that making the unconscious conscious was sufficient to effect change and cure. This was in keeping with his original belief that repressed memories were a basis for pathology. However, Freud gradually realized that more than a simple recovery of memories was required. Patients needed to acquire emotional insight into their wishes and conflicts. The process of therapeutic change in psychoanalysis, then, involves coming to grips with emotions and wishes that were previously unconscious and struggling with these painful experiences in a relatively safe environment. If psychopathology involves fixation at an early stage of development, then in psychoanalysis individuals become free to resume their normal psychological development. If psychopathology involves damming up the instincts and using energy for defensive purposes, then psychoanalysis involves a redistribution of energy so that more energy is available for mature, guiltless, less rigid, and more gratifying activities. If psychopathology involves conflict and defense mechanisms, then psychoanalysis involves reducing conflict and freeing the patient from the limitations of the defensive processes. If psychopathology involves an individual dominated by the unconscious and the tyranny of the id, then psychoanalysis involves making conscious what was unconscious and putting under control of the ego what was formerly under the domination of the id or superego.

The Therapeutic Process: Transference

We have seen that psychoanalysis views therapy as a learning process in which the individual resumes and completes psychological growth that was interrupted earlier in life, when their neurosis began. The key process is that the patient is reexposed to earlier emotional situations that they could not handle in the past, but can now handle with the aid of the therapist. This reexposure is affected by a psychological dynamic known as **transference**.

Transference is the development of attitudes toward an individual that are based on attitudes held earlier in life toward significant others (especially parents). Transference can occur in everyday life; for example, research shows that people's mental images of past significant others shape their interpretations of new interpersonal relationships (Andersen & Chen, 2002). However, it is particularly significant to psychoanalytic therapy.

In therapeutic transference, patients express attitudes toward the analyst that duplicate attitudes they expressed earlier in life toward significant figures. For example, a patients who thought that an analyst's note taking may lead them to be exploited by the analyst could be duplicating concerns about exploitation that they first experienced with family figures earlier in life. Or oral characters, for example, may express concerns about "feeding" the analyst and getting enough from the analyst in return that repeat earlier parental encounters.

Transference can occur within any type of therapy. Psychoanalysis, however, distinctively exploits it as a force for behavior change. Many formal qualities of the analytic situation are structured to enhance the development of transference. The patient lying on the couch supports the development of a dependent relationship. The scheduling of frequent meetings (up to five or six times a week) strengthens the emotional importance of the analytic relationship to the patient's daily existence. Finally, the fact that patients become so tied to their analysts, while knowing so little about them as people, means that their responses are almost completely determined by their neurotic conflicts. The analyst remains a mirror or blank screen on which the individual projects wishes and anxieties.

These analytic features promote the development of a transference neurosis. It is here that patients play out, full blown, their old conflicts. They display wishes and anxieties as if they are trying to gain from the analyst what had been lacking in childhood. Rather than seeking a way out of competitive relationships, the patients may only seek to castrate the analyst; rather than seeking to become less dependent on others, they may seek to have the analyst gratify all their dependency needs. Once these experiences occur, patient and analyst can examine the instinctual and defensive components of the original infantile conflict. Change occurs when insight has been gained, with patients comprehending—intellectually and emotionally—the nature of their conflicts. They thereby gain freedom to perceive the world anew and to gratify their instincts in a mature, conflict-free way.

Why do these psychological gains occur specifically in the analytic setting when they did not occur previously in the patient's life? There are three key therapeutic factors. First, in analysis the conflict is less intense than it was in the original situation. Second, the analyst assumes an attitude that is different from that of the parents. Finally, patients in analysis are older and more mature; they thus are more able to use parts of their ego that were under-developed earlier in life. These three factors provide the basis for what Alexander and French (1946) call the "corrective emotional experience". Psychoanalytic theory suggests that through insight into old conflicts, through an understanding of the needs for infantile gratifications and recognition of the potential for mature gratification, and through an understanding of old anxieties and a recognition of their lack of relevance to current realities, patients may progress toward maximum instinctual gratification within the limits set by reality and their own moral convictions.

A Case Example || Little Hans

A deep appreciation of Freud's analysis of personality can be gained through his case studies. Freud reported in detail on a small number of cases. Although these case reports often were written early in his career and thus do not fully reflect his final structural model of personality, they nonetheless reveal his general approach to the complex conflicts and anxieties of the mind. We summarize one such case here, the case of Little Hans (published in 1909).

Little Hans was a five-year-old boy who suffered from an extreme fear, or a phobia. He feared that a horse would bite him and, therefore, refused to leave the house. Freud's report of the case is unusual in that it did not involve a treatment by Freud himself; the boy was treated by his father. However, the father kept detailed notes on Hans's treatment and frequently discussed Hans's progress with Freud. Freud's interpretation of the case is highly illustrative of his psychoanalytic principles, particularly his theories of infantile sexuality, the Oedipus complex and castration anxiety, the dynamics of symptom formation, and the process of behavior change.

Events Leading Up to Development of the Phobia

Our account of events in the life of Little Hans begins at age three. At this point Hans had a lively interest in his penis, which he called his "widdler." He derived much pleasure in touching his own penis and was preoccupied with "widdlers" in others. The interest in touching his penis, however, led to threats by his mother. "If you do that, I shall send you to Dr. A. to cut off your widdler. And then what will you widdle with?" Thus, there was a direct castration threat. Freud pinpointed this as the beginning of Hans's castration complex.

Hans's interest in widdlers extended to noting the large size of the widdlers of horses on the street and lions at the zoo and analyzing the differences between animate and inanimate objects (animals have widdlers, unlike tables and chairs). Hans was curious about many things, but Freud related this child's general thirst for knowledge to sexual curiosity. Hans continued to be interested in whether his mother had a widdler and said to her, "I thought you were so big you'd have a widdler like a horse." When he was three and a half, a sister was born, who also became a focus for his widdler concerns. "But her widdler's still quite small. When she grows up, it'll get bigger all right." According to Freud, Hans could not admit what he really saw, namely, that there was no widdler there. To do so would mean that he would have to face his own castration anxieties. These anxieties occurred at a time when he was experiencing pleasure in the organ, as witnessed in his comments to his mother while she dried and powdered him after his bath.

Hans: Why don't you put your finger there?
Mother: Because that'd be piggish.
Hans: What's that? Piggish? Why? (laughing) But it's great fun.

(Continued)

A Case Example | Little Hans (*continued*)

Thus Hans, now more than four years old and preoccupied with his penis, began some seduction of his mother. It was at this point that his nervous disorders became apparent. The father, attributing the difficulties to sexual overexcitation due to his mother's tenderness, wrote Freud that Hans was "afraid that a horse will bite him in the street" and that this fear seemed somehow to be connected with his having been frightened by seeing a large penis. (Recall that Hans, at a very early age, noticed what large penises horses have and inferred that his large mother must "have a widdler like a horse.") Hans was afraid of going into the street and was depressed in the evenings. He had bad dreams and was frequently taken into his mother's bed. While walking in the street with his nurse, he became extremely frightened and sought to return home to be with his mother. The fear that a horse would bite him became a fear that the horse would come into his room. He had developed a full-blown phobia, an irrational dread or fear of an object.

Interpretation of the Symptom

The father attempted to deal with his son's fear of horses by offering him an interpretation. Hans was told that the fear of horses was nonsense, that the truth was that he (Hans) was fond of his mother and that the fear of horses had to do with an interest in their "widdlers." On Freud's suggestion, the father explained to Hans that women do not have "widdlers." Apparently this provided some relief, but Hans continued to be bothered by an obsessive wish to look at horses, though he was then frightened by them. At this point, his tonsils were taken out, and his phobia worsened. He was afraid that a white horse would bite him. He continued to be interested in "widdlers" in females. At the zoo, he was afraid of all the large animals and was entertained by the smaller ones. Among the birds, he was afraid of the pelican. In spite of his father's truthful explanation, Hans sought to reassure himself. "And everyone has a widdler. And my widdler will get bigger as I get bigger, because it does grow on me." According to Freud, Hans had been making comparisons among the sizes of widdlers and was dissatisfied with his own. Big animals reminded him of this defect and were disagreeable to him. The father's explanation heightened his castration anxiety, as expressed in the words "it does grow on me," as if it could be cut off. For this reason he resisted the information, and thus it had no therapeutic results. About this Freud mused, "Could it be that living beings really did exist which did not possess widdlers? If so, it would no longer be so incredible that they could take his own widdler away, and, as it were, make him into a woman."

At around this time, Hans reported the following dream. "In the night there was a big giraffe in the room and a crumpled one; and the big one called out because I took the crumpled one away from it. Then it stopped calling out; and then I sat down on top of the crumpled one." The father's interpretation was that he, the father, was the big giraffe, with the big penis, and the mother was the crumpled giraffe, missing the genital organ. The dream was a reproduction of a morning scene in which the mother took Hans into bed with her. The father warned her against this practice ("The big one called out because I'd taken the crumpled one away from it"), but the mother continued to encourage it. The mother encouraged and reinforced the Oedipal wishes. Hans stayed with her and, in the wish fulfillment of the dream, he took possession of her ("Then the big giraffe stopped calling out; and then I sat down on top of the crumpled one").

Freud's strategy in understanding Hans's phobia was to suspend judgment and to give his impartial attention to everything there was to observe. He learned that prior to the development of the phobia, Hans had been alone with his mother at a summer place. There, two significant events occurred. First, he heard the father of one of his friends tell her that a white horse there bit people and that she was not to hold her finger up to its mouth. Second, while pretending to be horses, a friend who rivaled Hans for the affection of the little girls fell down, hit his foot, and bled. In an interview with Hans, Freud learned that Hans was bothered by the blinders on horses and the black band around their mouths. The phobia became extended to include a fear that horses dragging a heavy van would fall down and kick their feet. It was then discovered that the exciting cause of his phobia—the event that capitalized on a psychological readiness for the formation of a phobia—was that Hans had witnessed a horse falling down. While walking outside with his mother one day, Hans had seen a horse pulling a van fall down and begin to kick its feet.

The central feature in this case was the phobia about the horse. What is fascinating in this regard is how often associations concerning a horse came up in relation to the father, the mother, and Hans himself. We have already noticed Hans's interest in his mother's "widdler" in relation to that of a horse. To his father, he said at one point: "Daddy, don't trot away from me." Could the father, who wore a mustache and eyeglasses, be the horse that Hans was afraid of, the horse that would come into his room at night and bite him? Or could Hans himself be the horse? Hans was known to play horse in his room, to trot about, fall down, kick about with his feet, and neigh. He repeatedly ran up to his father and bit him, just as he feared the horse would do to him. Hans was overfed. Could this relate to his concerns about large, fat horses? Finally, Hans was known to have called himself a young horse and to have a tendency to stamp his feet on the ground when angry, similar to what the horse did when it fell down. To return to the mother, could the heavily laden carts symbolize the pregnant mother and the horse falling down the birth or delivery of a child? Are such associations coincidental, or can they play a significant role in our understanding of the phobia?

According to Freud, the major cause of Hans's phobia was his Oedipus conflict. Hans felt more affection for his mother than he could handle during the phallic stage of his development. Although he had deep affection for his father, he also considered him a rival for his mother's affections. When he and his mother stayed at the summer cottage and his father was away, he was able to get into bed with his mother and keep her for himself. This heightened his attraction for his mother and his hostility toward his father. For Freud, "Hans was really a little Oedipus who wanted to have his father 'out of the way,' to get rid of him, so that he might be alone with his handsome mother and sleep with her. This wish had originated during his summer holidays, when the alternating presence and absence of his father had drawn Hans's attention to the condition upon which depended the intimacy with his mother which he longed for." The fall and injury to his friend and rival during one of those holidays were significant in symbolizing for Hans the defeat of his rival.

The Solution to the Oedipal Conflict

When he returned home from the summer holidays, Hans's resentment toward his father increased. He tried to suppress the resentment with exaggerated affection. He arrived at an ingenious solution to the Oedipal conflict. He and his mother would be parents to children, and the father could be the granddaddy. Thus, as Freud notes, "The little Oedipus had found a happier solution than that prescribed by destiny. Instead of putting his father out of the way, he had granted him the same happiness that he desired himself: He made him a grandfather and let him too marry his own mother." But such a fantasy could not be a satisfactory solution, and Hans was left with considerable hostility toward his father. The exciting cause of the phobia was the horse falling down. At that moment, Hans perceived a wish that his father might similarly fall down and die. The hostility toward his father was projected onto the father and was symbolized in the horse, because he himself nourished jealous and hostile wishes against him. He feared the horse would bite him because of his wish that his father would fall down, and fears that the horse would come into his room occurred at night when he was most tempted by Oedipal fantasies. In his own play as a horse and in his biting of his father, he expressed an identification with his father. The phobia expressed the wish and the anxiety and, in a secondary way, accomplished the objective of leaving Hans home to be with his mother.

In sum, both his fear that a horse would bite him and his fear that horses would fall down represented the father who was going to punish Hans for the evil wishes he was harboring against him. Hans was able to get over the phobia, and, according to a later report by Freud, he appeared to be functioning well. What factors allowed the change? First, there was the sexual enlightenment by the father. Although Hans was reluctant to accept this, and it at first heightened his castration anxiety, it did serve as a useful piece of reality to hold onto. Second, the analysis provided by his father and by Freud was useful in making conscious for Hans what had formerly been unconscious. Finally, the father's interest in and permissive attitude toward Hans's expression of his feelings allowed a resolution of the Oedipus conflict in favor of an identification with the father, diminishing both the wish to rival the father and the castration anxiety, and thereby decreasing the potential for symptom development. To the contemporary personality scientist, the case of Little Hans is very limited if viewed as a scientific investigation. The father's interviewing was not systematic, his close adherence to Freud's thinking may have biased his observations and interpretations, and Freud was primarily dependent on secondhand reports. Though aware of these limitations, Freud nonetheless was impressed with the data on Hans. Whereas before he had based his theory on the childhood memories of adult patients, now, in the case of Little Hans, he began to observe the sexual life of children.

The case of Little Hans simultaneously gives us an appreciation of the wealth of information available to the analyst and the problems inherent in interpreting such data. This one case alone yields information relevant to multiple theoretical ideas: infantile sexuality, fantasies of children, functioning of the unconscious, the process of conflict development and conflict resolution, the process of symptom formation, symbolization, and the dream process. We see Freud's courage and boldness in trying to discover secrets of human functioning in spite of limitations in his observations. Yet we also see Freud interpreting data that most contemporary psychologists would reject; most 21st-century psychology scientists would see the data this case provides as so unsystematic, and so potentially biased, that it could not serve as a foundation for scientific theorizing.

The Case of Jim

Rorschach and Thematic Apperception Test (TAT) Data

The Rorschach Inkblot Test and the Thematic Apperception Test (TAT) were administered to Jim by a professional clinical psychologist. On the Rorschach, Jim gave relatively few responses—22 in all. This is surprising in view of other evidence of his intelligence and creative potential. It may be interesting to follow his responses to the first two cards and to consider the interpretations formulated by the psychologist, who also is a practicing psychoanalyst.

CARD 1

Jim:	The first thing that comes to mind is a butterfly.
Interpretation:	Initially cautious and acts conventionally in a novel situation.
Jim:	This reminds me of a frog. Not a whole frog, like a frog's eyes. Really just reminds me of a frog.
Interpretation:	He becomes more circumspect, almost picky, and yet tends to overgeneralize while feeling inadequate about it.
Jim:	Could be a bat. More spooky than the butterfly because there is no color. Dark and ominous.
Interpretation:	Phobic, worried, depressed, and pessimistic.

CARD 2

Jim:	Could be two headless people with their arms touching. Looks like they are wearing heavy dresses. Could be one touching her hand against a mirror. If they're women, their figures are not good. Look heavy.
Interpretation:	Alert to people. Concern or confusion about sexual role. Anal-compulsive features. Disparaging of women and hostile to them—headless and figures not good. Narcissism expressed in mirror image.
Jim:	This looks like two faces facing each other. Masks, profiles—more masks than faces—not full, more of a façade, like one with a smile and one with a frown. He presents a façade, can smile or frown, but doesn't feel genuine. Despite façade of poise, feels tense with people. Repeated several times that he was not imaginative. Is he worried about his productivity and importance?

A number of interesting responses occurred on other cards. On the third card Jim perceived women trying to lift weights. Here again was a suggestion of conflict about his sexual role and about a passive as opposed to an active orientation. On the following card he commented that "somehow they all have an Alfred Hitchcock look of spooky animals," again suggesting a possible phobic quality to his behavior and a tendency to project dangers into the environment. His occasional references to symmetry and details suggested the use of compulsive defenses and intellectualization while experiencing threat. Disturbed and conflicted references to women come up in a number of places. On Card 7, he perceived two women from mythology who would be good if they were mythological but bad if they were fat. On the next to last card he perceived "some sort of a Count, Count Dracula. Eyes, ears, cape. Ready to grab, suck blood. Ready to go out and strangle some woman." The reference to sucking blood suggested tendencies toward oral sadism, something that also appeared in another percept of vampires that suck blood. Jim followed the percept of Count Dracula with one of pink cotton candy. The tester interpreted this response as suggesting a yearning for nurturance and contact behind the oral sadism; that is, the subject uses oral aggressive tendencies (e.g., sarcasm, verbal attacks) to defend against more passive oral wishes (e.g., to be fed, to be taken care of, and to be dependent).

The examiner concluded that the Rorschach suggested a neurotic structure in which intellectu-alization, compulsivity, and hysterical operations (irrational fears, preoccupation with his body) are used to defend against anxiety. However, it was suggested that Jim continues to feel anxious and uncomfortable with others, particularly authority figures. The report from the Rorschach concluded: "He is conflicted about his sexual role. While he yearns for nurturance and contact from the motherly female, he feels very guilty about the cravings and his intense hostility toward women. He assumes a passive orientation, a continual role playing and, behind a facade of tact, he continues his rage, sorrow, and ambition."

What kinds of stories did Jim tell on the TAT? Most striking about these stories were the sadness and hostility involved in all interpersonal relationships. In one story a boy is dominated by his mother, in another an insensitive gangster is capable of gross inhumanity, and in a third a husband is upset to learn that his wife is not a virgin. In particular, the relationships between men and women constantly involve one putting down the other. Consider this story.

Looks like two older people. The woman is sincere, sensitive, and dependent on the man. There is something about the man's expression that bespeaks of insensitivity—the way he looks at her, as if he conquered her. There is not the same compassion and security in her presence that she feels in his. In the end, the woman gets very hurt and is left to fend for herself. Normally I would think that they were married but in this case I don't because two older people who are married would be happy with one another.

In this story we have a man being sadistic to a woman. We also see the use of the defensive mechanism of denial in Jim's suggestion that these two people cannot be married since older married people are always happy with one another. In the story that followed the aforementioned one, there is again the theme of hostile mistreatment of a woman. In this story there is a more open expression of the sexual theme, along with evidence of some sexual role confusion.

This picture brings up a gross thought. I think of Candy. The same guy who took advantage of Candy. He's praying over her. Not the last rites, but he has convinced her that he is some powerful person and she's looking for him to bestow his good graces upon her. His knee is on the bed, he's unsuccessful, she's naive. He goes to bed with her for mystical purposes. [Blushes] She goes on being naive and continues to be susceptible to that kind of thing. She has a very, very sweet compassionate look. Could it possibly be that this is supposed to be a guy wearing a tie? I'll stick with the former.

The psychologist interpreting these stories observed that Jim appeared to be immature, naive, and characterized by a gross denial of all that is unpleasant or dirty, the latter for him including both sexuality and marital strife. The report continued: "He is vacillating between expressing sadistic urges and experiencing a sense of victimization. Probably he combines both, often in indirect expressions of hostility while feeling unjustly treated or accused. He is confused about what meaningful relationships two people can have. He is ambivalently idealistic and pessimistic about his own chances for a stable relationship.

Since he sees sex as dirty and as a mode for using or being used by his partner, he fears involvement. At the same time he craves attention, needs to be recognized, and is often preoc-cupied with sexual urges."

Across the Rorschach and TAT, a number of themes emerge:

1. Involves a lack of warmth in interpersonal relationships, including a disparaging and some-times sadistic orientation toward women.

2. The experience of tension and anxiety behind a facade of poise.

3. Conflict and confusion about his sexual identity. Although there is evidence of intelligence and creative potential, there also is evidence of rigidity and inhibition in relation to the unstructured nature of the projective tests. Compulsive defenses, intellectualization, and denial are only partially successful in helping him deal with his anxieties.

Comments on the Data

These data about Jim highlight the most attractive feature of projective tests. Their disguise enables one to penetrate the façade of someone's personality (in psychoanalytic terms, his or her defenses) in order to view the person's underlying needs, motives, or drives. Information presented in Jim's autobiography (Chapter 2) did not indicate the psychological themes evident in his projective test responses. At the same time, the interpretations from the projective tests fit with and elaborate upon themes in his autobiography such as his hiding his tension behind a façade of poise and his conflicted relationship with women.

As we not only examine psychoanalytic theory but also look forward to other theories to come, an interesting point arises. It is difficult to see how other theories of personality could make as much use of this data about Jim as psychoanalytic theory can. The assessment practices associated with other theories are unlikely to reveal this sort of information. It is only on the Rorschach that we obtain content such as "women trying to lift weights," "Count Dracula ready to grab, suck blood. Ready to go out and strangle some woman," and "pink cotton candy." The TAT is unique in revealing references to themes of sadness and hostility in interpersonal relationships. These responses allow for the psychodynamic interpretations. An important part of Jim's personality functioning appears to involve a defense against sadistic urges. The references to sucking blood and to cotton candy, together with the rest of his responses, allow for the interpretation that he is partially fixated at the oral stage. In relation to this, it is interesting to observe that Jim has an ulcer, which involves the digestive tract, and that he had to drink milk (a treatment of choice at one time) to manage this condition.

As Freud's fame grew, he attracted followers. As may be inevitable with any person of fame and the followers he or she attracts, some followed closely in his footsteps, whereas others rejected one or more aspects of his thinking and embarked in new directions—directions they may never have considered were it not for Freud, yet that he himself would not have taken. In the remainder of this chapter, we review this post-Freudian psychodynamic tradition.

Related Theoretical Conceptions

Two Early Challenges to Freud: Adler and Jung

Among the many early analysts who broke with Freud and developed their own schools of thought were Alfred Adler and Carl G. Jung. Both were early and important followers of Freud, Adler having been president of the Vienna Psychoanalytic Society and Jung president of the International Psychoanalytic Society. Both split with Freud over what they felt was an excessive emphasis on the sexual instincts.

Alfred Adler (1870–1937)

For approximately a decade, Alfred Adler was an active member of the Vienna Psychoanalytic Society. However, in 1911, when he presented his views to the other members of this group, the response was so hostile that he left it to form his own school of Individual Psychology. What ideas could have been considered so unacceptable to psychoanalysts?

Perhaps most significant in Adler's split from Freud was his greater emphasis on social urges and conscious thoughts than on instinctual sexual urges and unconscious processes. Early in his career Adler became interested in bodily inferiorities and how people compensate for them. A person with a weak bodily organ may attempt to compensate for this weakness by making special efforts to strengthen that organ or to develop other organs. Someone who stutters as a child may attempt to become a great speaker. A person with an auditory impairment may attempt to develop special listening or musical sensitivities. Adler gradually realized that there was a general principle here. People consciously experience feelings of inferiority and are motivated to compensate for these painful inferiorities. To Adler, "it is the feeling of inferiority, inadequacy, insecurity, which determines the goal of an individual's existence" (Adler, 1927, p. 72).

Adlerian thinking reformulates traditional Freudian interpretations. To take an historical example, U.S. president Theodore Roosevelt emphasized toughness by saying that one should "carry a big stick." To Freud, such statements are a defense against castration anxiety. An Adlerian might instead see this as expressing compensatory strivings against feelings of inferiority. As another example, Freudians might see an extremely aggressive woman as expressing penis envy, whereas Adlerians might see such persons as expressing a masculine protest or rejection of the stereotyped feminine role of weakness and inferiority. According to Adler, how a person attempts to cope with such feelings becomes a part of his or her style of life—a distinctive aspect of his or her personality functioning.

The principle of striving to compensate for inferiority does not apply merely to select individuals who suffer from a physical limitation. It applies to everyone. This is because everyone, in childhood, experiences inferiority. "One must remember that every child occupies an inferior position in life" (Adler, 1927, pp. 69–70). All young children see that they are less able to cope

Adler's theory proposes that people are motivated to compensate for feelings of inferiority. These compensatory strivings can shape the development of a person's life. The motives explored by Adler sometimes are evident in the life stories of highly successful persons. This photo depicts Brian Wilson, founder of the Beach Boys, one of the most popular groups in the history of contemporary music. What was the origin of Wilson's success? His official Web site reports that "After years of abuse by his father, he was left nearly deaf in one ear, depressed and lacking self-esteem. 'I overcompensated,' he said. 'I felt inferior because I only had one good ear. I compensated for that inferiority, and made some superior music.'"

Xavi Torrent / Contributor / Getty Images

with objects and events than are adults or older children whom they encounter. Everyone, then, experiences the motivating force of inferiority feelings.

These Adlerian concepts are more socially oriented than are Freud's. To Adler, compensatory strivings reflect will to power, that is, the individual's efforts to be a powerful, effective social being by coping with inferiorities and feelings of helplessness. In neurotic form, strivings for superiority may be expressed in efforts to exert power and control over others. In healthier form, a person experiences an "upward drive" toward unity and perfection. In the healthy person the striving for superiority is expressed in social feeling and cooperation as well as in assertiveness and competition. From the beginning people have a social interest, that is, an innate interest in relating to people and an innate potential for cooperation. Adler also emphasized people's feelings about the self, how they respond to goals that direct their behavior toward the future, and how the order of birth among siblings can influence their psychological development. Consistent with Adler's views, later research indicated that first-borns are somewhat more conscientious and conservative, preserving their "first-place" status in the (Paulhus, Trapnell, & Chen, 1999; Sulloway, 1996). Also consistent with Adler's ideas contemporary researchers have become explored power as a fundamental determinant of human behavior (Keltner, Gruenfeld, & Anderson, 2003). However, Adler's school of individual psychology itself has not had a major direct impact on 21st century personality theory and research.

Carl G. Jung (1875–1961)

Carl Jung's role in the history of psychodynamic theory is utterly unique. Early in his career as a physician, the Swiss scholar read the writings of Freud, was deeply impressed, and established a correspondence with the Vienna psychoanalyst. When Freud and Jung eventually met, they deeply impressed one another. They developed a relationship that was both professional and personal; their written correspondence suggests that they related as much in the style of father and son as professional colleagues. Freud came to view Jung as his "crown prince"—the person who would carry on Freud's psychoanalytic tradition after Freud's death. But this isn't what happened. Their relationship began to deteriorate beginning in 1909, due to a mixture of professional and personal conflicts (Gay, 1998). In 1914, Jung resigned his position as president of the International Psychoanalytic Association.

Why the split between Freud and Jung? From Jung's perspective, it was because he felt that Freud had overemphasized sexuality. Jung viewed the libido not as a sexual instinct but as a generalized life energy. Although sexuality is a part of this basic energy, the libido also includes strivings for pleasure and creativity. To Jung, this reinterpretation of the libido was the primary reason for his break with Freud. (Freud, in contrast, viewed their breakup in psychoanalytic terms, with Jung expressing Oedipal feelings toward his professional father, Freud.)

Bettmann / Contributor / Getty Images

Carl Jung.

This reinterpretation of libidinal energy is just one feature that differentiates Jung's analytic psychology from Freud's psychoanalysis. Jung felt that Freud overemphasized the idea that our current behavior is a mere repetition of the past, with instinctual urges and psychological repressions of childhood being repeated in adult life. Instead, Jung believed that personality development also has a forward-moving directional tendency. People try to acquire a meaningful personal identity and a sense of meaning in self. Indeed, people are so forward looking that they commonly devote efforts to religious practices that prepare them for a life after death.

A particularly distinguishing feature of Jung's psychology is his emphasis on the evolutionary foundations of the human mind. Jung accepted Freud's emphasis on the unconscious as a storehouse of repressed experiences from one's life. But he added to this idea the concept of the **collective unconscious**. According to Jung, people have stored within their collective unconscious the cumulative experiences of past generations. The collective unconscious, as opposed to the personal unconscious, is universal. It is shared by all humans as a result of their common ancestry. It is part of our human as well as our animal heritage, and thus it is our link with the collective wisdom of millions of years of past experience: "This psychic life is the mind of our ancient ancestors, the way in which they thought and felt, the way in which they conceived of life and the world, of gods and human beings. The existence of these historical layers is presumably the source of belief in reincarnation and in memories of past lives" (Jung, 1939, p. 24).

The collective unconscious contains universal images or symbols, known as *archetypes*. Archetypes, such as the Mother archetype, are seen in fairy tales, dreams, myths, and some psychotic thoughts. Jung was struck with similar images that keep appearing, in slightly different forms, in different cultures that are distant from one another. For example, the Mother archetype might be expressed in different cultures in a variety of positive or negative forms: as life giver, as all giving and nurturant, as the witch or threatening punisher ("Don't fool with Mother Nature"), and as the seductive female. Archetypes may be represented in our images of persons, demons, animals, natural forces, or objects. The evidence in all cases for their being a part of our collective unconscious is their universality among members of different cultures from past and current time periods.

Another important aspect of Jung's theory is his emphasis on how people struggle with opposing forces within them. For example, there is the struggle between the face or mask we present to others, represented in the archetype of the persona, and the private or personal self. If people emphasize the persona too much, there may be a loss of sense of self and a doubting about who they are. On the other hand, the persona, as expressed in social roles and customs, is a necessary part of living in society. Similarly, there is the struggle between the masculine and feminine parts of ourselves. Every male has a feminine part (the archetype of the anima) and every female has a masculine part (the archetype of the animus) to their personality. If a man rejects his feminine part, he may emphasize mastery and strength to an excessive degree, appearing cold and insensitive to the feelings of others. If a woman rejects her masculine part, she may be excessively absorbed in motherhood. Psychologists currently interested in stereotyped sex roles would probably applaud Jung's emphasis on these dual aspects in everyone's personality, although they might question his characterizing some as specifically masculine and others as feminine. An interesting yet controversial feature of Jung's analysis is the contention that gender-role stereotypes are not a product of an individual's social experience but of the experiences of one's ancestors over the course of evolution. A similar idea is found in contemporary evolutionary psychology (Chapter 9).

Jung emphasizes that all individuals face a fundamental personal task: finding unity in the self. The task is to bring into harmony, or integrate, the various opposing forces of the psyche. The person is motivated and guided along the path to personal knowledge and integration by the most important of all Jungian archetypes: the self. In Jungian psychology "the self" does not refer to one's conscious beliefs about one's personal qualities. Instead, the self is an unconscious force, specifically, an aspect of the collective unconscious that functions as an "organizing center" (Jung and Collaborators, 1964, p. 161) of the person's entire psychological system. Jung believed that the self often is represented symbolically in circular figures—the circle representing a sense of wholeness that can be achieved through self-knowledge. Mandalas, which are circular symbols that contain pathways toward a centerpoint, serve as vivid symbols of the struggle for knowledge of our true selves. Since the self is an archetype of the collective unconscious, and the collective unconscious is a universal aspect of human personality, according to Jungian theory one should expect to find similar symbolic representations of the self across diverse human cultures. And one does. Symbols found in human cultures separated widely in time and place often contain remarkably similar imagery that, according to Jung, represents the universal unconscious motive to grow in self-knowledge.

To Jung, the search for the self is a never-ending quest. "Personality as a complete realization of the fullness of our being is an unattainable ideal. But unattainability is no counter argument against an ideal, for ideals are only signposts, never goals" (Jung, 1939, p. 287). The struggle described here can become a particularly important aspect of life once people have passed the age of 40 and defined themselves to the outside world in a variety of ways.

Another contrast in Jung's theory is that between introversion and extraversion. Everyone relates to the world primarily in one of two directions, though the other direction always remains a part of the person. In the case of introversion, the person's basic orientation is inward, toward the self. The introverted type is hesitant, reflective, and cautious. In the case of extraversion the person's basic orientation is outward, toward the outside world. The extraverted type is socially engaging, active, and adventuresome.

As with Adler, we have considered only some of the highlights of Jung's theory. Jung is considered by many to be one of the great creative thinkers of the 20th century. His theory has influenced intellectual trends in many fields outside of psychology. Jungian centers for clinical training continue to exist in many countries. Yet, Jung's work has had little impact within scientific psychology. To a large degree, this reflects the fact that Jung often did not state his ideas in a manner that could be tested according to standard scientific methods. His imaginative theorizing commonly was more speculative than that of other personality theorists—so speculative that elements of this theorizing are difficult, if not impossible, to support or to disprove through objective scientific methods.

The Cultural and Interpersonal Emphasis: Horney and Sullivan

Reinterpreting Motivational Forces

In the middle of the 20th century, a group of psychoanalytic theorists began a deep rethinking of basic psychoanalytic principles. These writers felt that, to a greater degree than Freud had appreciated, personality develops through interpersonal interactions. These interpersonal actions inherently occur within social and cultural contexts. Their work thus constitutes a cultural and interpersonal emphasis within the psychoanalytic tradition.

As Greenberg and Mitchell (1983) have explained, there are two different ways of emphasizing interpersonal factors from a psychodynamic perspective. One adheres to traditional Freudian principles. In this classic psychoanalytic view, the motivational forces in the development of the individual are biological drives (the id's drives toward pleasure). The central features of personality development are the individual's efforts to manage these biologically based desires, which often conflict with social norms. Once personality structures are developed in this manner, they in turn influence social life. The instinctual drives, then, are primary: They are the initial forces driving development and are responsible for the formation of personality structure. Social relationships—for example, with peers and friends—are of secondary importance. Social relationships do not determine personality structure in this traditional Freudian account. They are *determined by* personality structures whose development is an outgrowth of the biologically based desires of the id.

The ideas of interpersonal psychodynamic theorists differed strikingly from this Freudian tradition. The interpersonal view sees social relations as primary, not secondary. Personality structures are thought to develop through (i.e., as a result of) interactions with others. Other people display emotional styles that influence one's own emotional life. They provide evaluations that influence one's own self-concept. Acceptance by others becomes a basic motivational force.

Although many writers contributed to this interpersonal tradition, two figures of particular historical importance are Karen Horney and Harry Stack Sullivan.

Karen Horney (1885–1952)

Karen Horney was trained as a traditional analyst in Germany. She then came to the United States, in 1932. Shortly thereafter she split with traditional psychoanalytic thought and developed her own theoretical orientation and psychoanalytic training program.

A major difference between Horney's work and traditional psychoanalytic thinking involved the question of universal biological influences as opposed to cultural influences: "When we realize the great import of cultural conditions on neuroses, the biological and physiological conditions, which are considered by Freud to be their root, recede into the background" (1937, p. viii). Three considerations led her to this conclusion. The first was the role of culture in the development of gender identity. The influence of cultural factors on "ideas of what constitutes masculinity or femininity was obvious, and it became just as obvious to me that Freud had arrived at certain conclusions because he failed to take them into account" (1945, p. 11). Second was her association with another psychoanalyst, Erich Fromm, who drew her attention to social and cultural influences. Third, when moving from European culture to the United States, Horney judged that she observed differences in personality structure between European and U.S. patients. Beyond this, these observations led her to conclude that interpersonal relationships are at the core of all healthy and disturbed personality functioning.

Horney's emphasis in neurotic functioning is on how individuals attempt to cope with basic anxiety—the feeling a child has of being isolated and helpless in a potentially hostile world. According to her theory of neurosis, in the neurotic person there is conflict among three ways of responding to this basic anxiety. These three patterns, or neurotic trends, are known as moving toward, moving against, and moving away. All three are characterized by rigidity and the lack of fulfillment of individual potential, the essence of any neurosis. In moving toward, a person attempts to deal with anxiety by an excessive interest in being accepted, needed, and approved of. Such a person accepts a dependent role in relation to others and, except for the unlimited desire for affection, becomes unselfish, undemanding, and self-sacrificing. In moving against, a person assumes that everyone is hostile and that life is a struggle against all. All functioning is directed toward denying a need for others and toward appearing tough. In moving away, the third component of the conflict, the person shrinks away from others into neurotic detachment. Such people often look at themselves and others with emotional detachment, as a way of not getting emotionally involved with others. Although each neurotic person shows one or another trend as a special aspect of their personality, the problem is really that there is conflict among the three trends in the effort to deal with basic anxiety.

Before leaving Horney, we should consider her views concerning women. These views date back to her early work within traditional psychoanalytic thought and are reflected in a series of papers collected in *Feminine Psychology* (1973). As noted from the start, Horney had trouble accepting Freud's views of women. She felt that the concept of penis envy might be the result of a male bias in psychoanalysts who treat neurotic women in a particular social context: "Unfortunately, little or nothing is known of psychologically healthy women, or of women under different cultural conditions" (1973, p. 216). She suggested that women are not biologically disposed toward masochistic attitudes of being weak, dependent, submissive, and self-sacrificing. Instead, these attitudes indicated the powerful influence of social forces.

Bettmann/Getty Images

Karen Horney.

In sum, both in her views of women and in her general theoretical orientation, Horney rejected Freud's biological emphasis in favor of a social, interpersonal approach. Partly as a result of this difference, she held a much more optimistic view concerning people's capacity for change and self-fulfillment.

Harry Stack Sullivan (1892–1949)

Of the theorists considered in this section, Sullivan, an American, most emphasized the role of social, interpersonal forces in human development. His theory has been known as the Interpersonal Theory of Psychiatry (Sullivan, 1953), and his followers created a Sullivan school of interpersonal relations.

In Sullivan's view, emotional experiences are not based in biological drives, as Freud posited, but in relations with others. This is true even in the early stages of life. For example, anxiety may be communicated by the mother in her earliest interaction with the infant; thus, from the start, anxiety is interpersonal in character rather than purely biological. The self, a critical concept in Sullivan's thinking, similarly is social in origin. The self develops out of feelings experienced while in contact with others and from reflected appraisals or perceptions by a child as to how he or she is valued or appraised by others. Experiences of anxiety as opposed to security in interpersonal relations contribute to the development of different parts of the self. The "good me" is associated with pleasurable experiences; the "bad me" with pain and threats to security; and the "not me"—a part of the self that is rejected—is associated with intolerable anxiety.

Sullivan's emphasis on social influences is seen in his views on the development of the person. Like Erikson (Chapter 3), Sullivan judged that the developmental period beyond the time of the Oedipus complex contributed significantly to the overall development of the person. He particularly emphasized the juvenile era and preadolescence. During the juvenile stage—roughly the grammar school years—a child's experiences with friends and teachers begin to rival the influence of his or her parents. Social acceptance becomes important, and the child's reputation with others becomes an important source of self-esteem or anxiety. During preadolescence, a relationship with a close friend of the same sex becomes particularly important. This relationship of close friendship, of love, forms the basis for the development of a love relationship with a person of the opposite sex during adolescence. In later years, child psychologists highlighted the importance of early relationships with peers that were anticipated, years earlier, by Sullivan (Lewis, 2002).

Object Relations, Self Psychology, and Attachment Theory

Object Relations Theory

The interpersonal approach of Sullivan represented a significant break with the psychoanalytic tradition established by Freud. As noted, Sullivan's interpersonal approach placed greater emphasis on developmental experiences that occur after the Oedipal period (e.g., during preadolescence). We now consider schools of thought that moved in a different direction. A group of psychodynamic thinkers known as object relations theorists were, like Sullivan, interested in interpersonal relations. However, they presented ideas that "are essentially developmental theories that examine developmental processes and relationships *prior to* the Oedipal period" (St. Clair, 1986, p. 15).

You, the student, face an immediate potential obstacle in understanding object relations theory. It is the meaning of the word *object*. In psychodynamic theory, the word takes on a definition that differs from its typical use. We usually use the word *object* to refer to something that isn't human: a chair, a lamp, a box, and so forth. In object relations theory, however, the word *object* generally refers to a person. Psychoanalysts beginning with Freud posited that people have drives that are directed toward the thing that can satisfy the drive by reducing tension. This thing toward which the drive is directed is an object. Since the need to reduce tension generally is satisfied by a person (the hungry infant seeks the mother's breast, the adult is sexually attracted to another person), significant objects are persons.

In studying objects then, object relations theorists are interested in the world of interpersonal relations (Greenberg & Mitchell, 1983; Westen & Gabbard, 1999). They are concerned with how experiences with important people in the past are represented as parts or aspects of the self and then, in turn, affect one's relationships with others in the present. In some respects, this theorizing is close to Freud's original psychoanalytic model. Yet there is a difference. Object relations theorists do not explain all aspects of personality development, and later personality functioning, in terms of conflicts between biological drives and social constraints, as Freud did. Instead, they focus on mental representations of relationships with objects (i.e., others). Relationships experienced in early childhood determine the nature of the mental models, or mental representations, of others that one forms. Once formed, these mental representations remain in the mind. Later in life, the mental representations formed in childhood influence one's experiences in new relationships: "residues of past experiences … shape [later] perceptions of individuals and relationships" (St. Clair, 1986).

Self Psychology and Narcissism

A theoretical development that is closely related to object relations theory is the set of ideas known, in psychodynamic theorizing, as self psychology. (Note that many psychologists who are *not* psychodynamic in their orientation also are interested in the self, and sometimes refer to their work as a "self psychology." In this section we specifically are addressing the self psychology that developed within the overall psychodynamic tradition.)

A particular focus of self psychology is a phenomenon known as *narcissism*. Although the exact meaning of narcissism varies slightly from one psychodynamic theorist to another, the term generally refers to an investment of mental energy in the self. In healthy, mature personality development, people can respond to their own needs while also being responsive to the needs of others. The narcissistic need to display features of the self may even display itself in socially positive ways, such as in creative products that display an artist's inner being (St. Clair, 1986). However, if developmental experiences result in less maturity, a person may display a narcissistic personality; that is, their narcissism may become a predominant feature of their personality, with negative implications for their relationships with others. In the narcissistic personality, the person has a grandiose sense of self-importance and is preoccupied with fantasies of unlimited success and power. Narcissists (i.e., individuals who develop a predominantly narcissistic personality) have an exaggerated feeling of being entitled to things from others, of deserving the admiration and love of others, and of being special or unique. Because so much mental energy is self-directed, narcissists lack empathy with the feelings and needs of others.

Although narcissists display positive self views, they also are vulnerable to blows to self-esteem. They need admiration from others. They at times idealize others around them, yet at

Encyclopaedia Britannica / Contributor / Getty Images

The contemporary concept of narcissism can be dated back to ancient Greek mythology. Narcissus was so taken with his own beauty that he could do nothing other than stare at his image, which eventually led to his death.

other times devalue others; in therapy it is not unusual for the narcissistic individual to idealize the therapist as extremely insightful at one moment and to berate the same therapist as stupid and incompetent at the next moment.

Narcissism has been the focus of much systematic research for many years. One goal in the study of narcissism is the development of assessment instruments that can distinguish narcissists from others. Henry Murray, who developed the TAT, also developed an early narcissism questionnaire (Figure 4.1). More recently, a Narcissistic Personality Inventory (NPI) (Raskin & Hall, 1979, 1981) has been developed (Figure 4.1). Individuals scoring high on the NPI have been found to use many more self-references (e.g., I, me, mine) than those scoring low (Raskin & Shaw, 1987). In another study, a relationship was found between high scores on the NPI and being described by others as exhibitionistic, assertive, controlling, and critical-evaluative (Raskin & Terry, 1987). Individuals scoring high on narcissism have been found to evaluate their performance more positively than it is evaluated by peers or staff, demonstrating a significant self-enhancement bias relative to individuals scoring low on narcissism (John & Robins, 1994;

Murray's Narcissism Scale (1938, p. 181)

I often think about how I look and what impression I am making upon others.

My feelings are easily hurt by ridicule or by the slighting remarks of others.

I talk a good deal about myself, my experiences, my feelings, and my ideas.

Narcissism Personality Inventory (Raskin & Hall, 1979)

I really like to be the center of attention.

I think I am a special person.

I expect a great deal from other people.

I am envious of other people's good fortune.

I will never be satisfied until I get all that I deserve.

FIGURE 4.1

Illustrative items from questionnaire measures of narcissism.

Robins & John, 1997). Moreover, whereas most people feel uncomfortable and self-conscious when they see themselves in a mirror or on videotape, this is not the case for narcissistic individuals. Just like the mythical Narcissus, who admired his own reflection in a pond, narcissistic individuals spend more time looking at themselves in mirrors, prefer to watch themselves rather than another person on videotape, and indeed receive an "ego boost" from watching themselves on videotape (Robins & John, 1997).

Researchers also have focused on the thinking processes and interpersonal tendencies of narcissistic individuals (Morf & Rhodewalt, 2001; Rhodewalt & Sorrow, 2002). Narcissistic persons are found to have not only a self-aggrandizing attributional style but also fairly simple self-concepts and a cynical mistrust of others (Rhodewalt & Morf, 1995). These findings are consistent with the picture of the narcissist as a person preoccupied with the maintenance of his or her exaggerated self-esteem. In relation to this, it is not surprising that narcissistic individuals seek romantic partners who will be admiring of them, in contrast with non-narcissistic individuals who seek caring partners (Campbell, 1999).

Much of the research on narcissism has used correlational methods. Investigators commonly relate NPI scores to scores on other questionnaires or to observations of behavior (e.g., self-references, looking at self in the mirror). However, investigators increasingly have employed experimental methods. For example, building on clinical observations that narcissists respond to criticism or threat to self-esteem with feelings of rage, shame, or humiliation, Rhodewalt and Morf (1998) exposed individuals with high and with low narcissism scores (NPI) to experiences of success and failure on two tests described as measures of intelligence. Since the items on the measures were moderately difficult, subjects would be uncertain about the accuracy of their responses, and feedback concerning accuracy could be manipulated by the experimenters. To observe the effects of failure following success as opposed to preceding success, half the subjects received success feedback for the first test and failure feedback for the second test, and the other half the reverse order of feedback. Following each test, subjects were asked to respond to questions concerning their emotions and to indicate their attributions for their performance. As predicted, individuals high on narcissism (NPI) reacted to failure with greater anger than did individuals scoring low on narcissism, particularly when the failure followed success. This result was consistent with the view that narcissistic anger is a response to perceived threats to the narcissist's grandiose self-image. In addition, individuals scoring high on narcissism were found to be particularly vulnerable to swings in self-esteem as a consequence of receiving positive and negative feedback about the self. Feelings of happiness were similarly greatly affected by such feedback. Finally, narcissists were found to be more self-aggrandizing in attributing success to their own ability, and more blaming of others in accounting for failure, than were less narcissistic subjects. In sum, the experimental findings supported the clinical observations concerning the vulnerability of narcissists to blows to their self-esteem and their response to such blows with anger.

Attachment Theory

The last theoretical development we will discuss in this review of post-Freudian psychodynamic theories is attachment theory. Attachment theory is of particular relevance to the contemporary science of personality. Some writers believe that current research on attachment processes has resurrected psychodynamic theory within the scientific field (Shaver & Mikulincer, 2005, 2012), as Freud's theories had been severely criticized over the years.

Attachment theory originated in theoretical work by a British psychoanalyst, John Bowlby, and was significantly advanced by the developmental psychologist Mary Ainsworth (Ainsworth & Bowlby, 1991; Bretherton, 1992; Rothbard & Shaver, 1994). Bowlby was interested in the effects of early separation from parents on personality development—a major problem in England during World War II when many children were sent to the countryside, far from their parents, to be safe from enemy bombing of the cities. In a traditional Freudian approach to this issue, one would inquire into how separation from the parents affected the development of instinctual drives (involving sex and aggression) during the Oedipal period. But here is where Bowlby's work differed from that of Freud. Based on his knowledge of ethology (a branch of biology focusing on the study of animals in their natural environment), Bowlby suggested that there exists a psychological system that is specifically dedicated to parent–child relationships. He called this the **attachment behavioral system (ABS)**.

According to Bowlby, the ABS is innate; that is, all persons have such a system as a result of their biological endowment. The ABS has motivational significance; it is a system that motivates the infant to be close to (i.e., to seek physical proximity to) caregivers, especially when there is a threat in the environment. A young child clinging to adults for comfort and security, then, would be an example of a behavior motivated by the ABS. During development, as the infant gains a greater sense of security in its relations with adults, the proximity of adult attachment figures provides a "secure base" for explorations of the environment.

Attachment theory predicts that the effects of developmental processes involving attachment are long lasting. The prediction is based on the following rationale. Child–parent relations create, in the child, symbolic mental representations involving the self and caregivers. These mental representations, called **internal working models**, contain abstract beliefs and expectations about significant others. Once formed, internal working models endure; they are long-lasting personality structures.

Bowlby's attachment theory recognizes individual differences in attachment. Different infants may experience different types of interactions with caregivers, since parents differ in how responsive they are to infants' needs. These parental differences create different internal working models in the child. These mental representations, in turn, can contribute to differences in children's behavior and emotion in interactions with significant others.

These theoretical ideas received a major boost from research involving a novel methodology: the "Strange Situation" procedure developed by Mary Ainsworth (Ainsworth, Bleher, Waters, & Wall, 1978). This procedure is designed to identify individual differences in attachment styles via direct observation of parent–child interactions. (Direct observation of parents is more convincing than, for example, merely asking parents to report their interactions with children, since parents' reports might be inaccurate.) In the Strange Situation procedure, psychologists observe infants' responses to the departure (separation) and return (reuniting) of the mother or other caregiver in a structured laboratory setting. Based on these observations, Ainsworth and her colleagues classified infants into different attachment types. About 70% of infants were classified as being of a *secure* attachment type; these infants were those who were sensitive to the departure of the mother but greeted her upon being reunited, were readily comforted, and were then able to return to exploration and play. About 20% of infants displayed an attachment style that was labeled *anxious-avoidant*. This style was marked by little protest over separation from the mother and, upon her return, avoidance in terms of turning, looking, or moving away from the mother. Finally, about 10% of infants were classified as *anxious-ambivalent;* these infants had difficulty separating from the mother and reuniting with her upon her return. Their behavior mixed pleas to be picked up with squirming and insistence on being let down.

The Strange Situation paradigm provides an objective procedure for studying psychodynamic processes that can be used to explore a variety of research questions. For example, if one wants to know whether attachment patterns are similar across cultures, one can employ the standardized Strange Situation paradigm in different cultural contexts. Results of such research (Van Ijzendoorn & Kroonenberg, 1988) document between-culture difference in the prevalence of different attachment styles (as well as differences between groups within a given cultural setting). For example, a study in Korea found a very low rate of avoidance attachment among Korean infants, which may reflect parental styles distinctive to that culture (Jin, Jacobvitz, Hazen, & Jung, 2012).

Attachment Styles in Adulthood   In more recent years, psychologists have used the attachment framework to understand not only parent–child relationships but also romantic relationships in adulthood. Individual differences in emotional bonds in infancy may be related to individual differences in the way emotional bonds are established later in life. To study this possibility, Hazan and Shaver (1987) had research participants complete a newspaper survey or "love quiz." As a measure of attachment style, the newspaper readers described themselves as fitting one of three categories in terms of their relationships with others. These three categories were descriptive of the three attachment styles. As a measure of their current style of romantic love, subjects were asked to respond to questions listed under a banner headline in the newspaper: "Tell Us about the Love of Your Life." Responses to the questions concerning the most important love relationship they ever had formed the basis for scores on 12 love experience scales. Additional questions were asked concerning each person's view of romantic love over time and recollections of childhood relationships with parents and between parents.

Did the different types of respondents (*secure, avoidant, anxious-ambivalent*) also differ in the way they experienced their most important love relationships? This appears to be the case. Secure attachment styles were associated with experiences of happiness, friendship, and trust; avoidant styles with fears of closeness, emotional highs and lows, and jealousy; and anxious-ambivalent styles with obsessive preoccupation with the loved person, a desire for union, extreme sexual attraction, emotional extremes, and jealousy. In addition, the three groups differed in their views or mental models of romantic relationships: *Secure* lovers viewed romantic feelings as being somewhat stable but also waxing and waning, and they discounted the kind of head-over-heels romantic love often depicted in novels and movies; *avoidant* lovers were skeptical of the lasting quality of romantic love and felt that it was rare to find a person one can really fall in love with; *anxious-ambivalent* lovers felt that it was easy to fall in love but rare to find true love. Finally, *secure* subjects, in comparison with subjects in the other two groups, reported warmer relationships with both parents, as well as between their two parents.

Subsequent research has extended these findings. For example, attachment style is found to be related not only to interpersonal relationships, but to orientations toward work. Secure persons approach their work with confidence, are relatively unburdened by fears of failure, and do not allow work to interfere with personal relationships; *anxious-ambivalent* subjects are very much influenced by praise and fear of rejection at work and allow love concerns to interfere with work performance; *avoidant* subjects use work to avoid social interaction and, although they do well financially, are less satisfied with their jobs than secure subjects (Hazan & Shaver, 1990). Other work relates attachment style to psychopathology. Attachment tends to predict psychopathology in interaction with other factors. For example, if people encounter highly stressful life events (e.g., experiences with crime, war, or terrorism), those individuals with an avoidant attachment style undergo greater psychological distress than others (Mikulincer & Shaver, 2012).

Many studies of attachment style in adulthood have relied on self-report data. However, a clever study by Fraley and Shaver (1998) examined the relation between attachment style and separation behavior in couples through naturalistic observation. The behavior of couples temporarily separating from each other was observed in an airport. Researchers approached couples waiting in an airport lobby and asked them to complete a questionnaire on "The Effects of Modern Travel on Close Relationships." The individuals in the couples independently filled out the questionnaire, which included a measure of attachment style. Another member of the research team took a seat within viewing distance of the couple and took notes on their interactions while they awaited flight departure. These behaviors were coded into attachment behavior categories such as *Contact Seeking* (e.g., kissing, watching from window after partner has boarded), *Contact Maintenance* (e.g., hugging, unwillingness to let go), *Avoidance* (e.g., looking elsewhere, breaking off contact), and *Resistance* (e.g., wanting to be held but also resisting contact, signs of anger or annoyance). Among women (but not men), individuals differing in

Personality and the Brain
Attachment

Twentieth-century pioneers in the study of attachment, such as Bowlby and Ainsworth, did not have data on brain systems that underlie attachment. Twenty-first century advances, however, have opened the door to research on attachment processes and the brain.

Since the door has been opened only recently, the exact brain systems underlying attachment processes are not yet fully understood. A review of research (Coan, 2010), however, does already point to some general principles. One is that the brain does not contain a single "attachment mechanism" within one particular brain region. Instead, multiple brain systems contribute to the development and maintenance of attachment processes, and they generally are systems that take part in a number of psychological functions in addition to attachment. A second principle is that the brain systems that play the key roles in attachment are likely to be the same ones that are key to human emotions. Attachment processes are fundamentally emotional. Parents respond to emotional displays by their infants (e.g., a smile or cry), and infants desire the warm emotional response of the parent. Brain systems that enable the infant to experience and display emotional reactions, then, are certain to take part in attachment processes.

With regard to the question of exactly which brain mechanisms are involved, you should remember that the brain contains two kinds of material. One is cellular. The brain contains a massive number of individual cells, called *neurons*, which are organized into the various substructures that make up the overall anatomy of the brain. The other kind is molecular. Neurons communicate with one another by sending *neurotransmitters*—molecules that travel from one neuron to another and affect the activity of the neuron to which they travel. Let's first look at attachment processes and neurotransmitters.

One neurotransmitter implicated in attachment processes is *oxytocin*, which is active in numerous parts of the brain involved in emotional response. The effects of oxytocin can be evaluated experimentally. In different experimental conditions, researchers give participants a nasal spray containing either oxytocin or an inert placebo chemical, and then evaluate the effects of oxytocin on subsequent attachment-related responses. In one study (Buchheim et al., 2009), participants with insecure attachment styles were given oxytocin or a placebo, and then were shown drawings with attachment-related themes (e.g., a small girl, by herself, looking out the window of a home). For each picture, participants were asked to judge the degree to which different phrases (e.g., "This girl seems to be desperate, maybe deserted by someone," or "She is ill and has to stay inside ... her mother comes in and embraces here") fit the picture. The researchers found that, after receiving the oxytocin spray, participants were more likely to judge that security-related phrases (e.g., the one including the text "her mother ... embraces her") fit the pictures (Buchheim et al., 2009). The result suggests, then, that oxytocin directly affects attachment feelings and thoughts.

What about attachment processes and brain anatomy? Research implicates two regions of the brain; one is not surprising, but the other is. The unsurprising region is a set of neural circuits known to be involved in emotional responses and simple forms of motivation (basic desires to approach and avoid rewards and punishments; see Coan, 2010). These neural circuits are found primarily in a lower region of the brain known as the limbic system.

The surprising region is a structure in the lower rear of the brain known as the cerebellum. The cerebellum is primarily involved in the control of motor movement, which would seem to make it an unlikely candidate to participate in attachment processes. But recent research shows that the cerebellum also is involved in the experience of emotion and attempts to control emotional reactions (Schutter & van Honk, 2009), including attachment-related emotions. In one study, conducted with a set of individuals with a history of psychological distress, researchers used brain scans to measure the volume of neural matter in the cerebellum. They did so among individuals who had experienced varying degrees of interpersonal loss (e.g., loss, through death, of a loved one) and varying attachment styles. People with different attachment styles differed in cerebellar anatomy. The differences were most apparent when examining the relation between experiences of loss and the cerebellum. Among people with an avoidant attachment style, the experience of a higher number of interpersonal losses was associated with lower cerebellar volume. Among people with a less avoidant, more secure, style, the experience of a higher number of interpersonal losses was associated with *higher* cerebellar volume. The psychological variable, attachment style, and the neural variable, volume of neural matter in the cerebellum, thus were strongly linked.

More research is needed to determine the exact role of the cerebellum in attachment processes and, more generally, to identify the brain mechanisms involved in the development of different attachment styles early in life. But current findings already provide significant clues to this scientific puzzle.

attachment style displayed different behavior. Compared to *nonavoidant* women, highly *avoidant* women were less likely to seek and maintain contact with their partners and to provide care and support to their partners, and they were more likely to show withdrawal behavior such as pulling away and not making eye contact. Interestingly, the behavior of *avoidant* women was quite different when they were accompanying their partner in travel as opposed to separating from them. Whereas the listed behaviors were true of *avoidant* women during separation, when they were to be flying with their partner (a setting that poses no threat of abandonment), they were more likely to seek care from and contact with their partners. In sum, at least for women, the attachment dynamics originally found in studies of children also applied in the context of adult romantic relationships.

Attachment Types or Dimensions?   As we noted, Ainsworth suggested that individual differences in attachment style could be understood in terms of three attachment types. In other words, she proposed what we called (back in Chapter 1) units of analysis involving type variables. The idea was that different attachment types are qualitatively distinct.

Although the idea of distinct categorical types is attractive to many, categorical variables are rare. Most observable psychological qualities—variations in behavior, emotions, and so forth—are affected by a large number of factors. When many factors are at play, outcomes usually varies dimensionally, not categorically. As attachment an exception, with true categorical differences?

Evidence suggests "no." Fraley and Spieker (2003) examined data from a very large number of 15-month-old children who had participated in the Strange Situation paradigm. Rather than merely asking how many children fell into one versus another attachment category, they asked a logically prior question: Are there attachment categories in the first place? Or might the differences among children actually involve simple dimensions? This question can be addressed through somewhat complex, yet highly informative, statistical procedures that ask whether different psychological characteristics go together so consistently that they form distinct categories (Meehl, 1992). The results indicated that, for attachment styles, this was not the case. Instead, variations in attachment involved continuous dimensions.

These findings raise the question of exactly what dimensions might best capture individual differences in attachment style. One possibility involves a theoretical model of individual differences in internal working models of the self and others (Bartholomew & Horowitz, 1991; Griffin & Bartholomew, 1994). Following Bowlby, according to this model attachment patterns can be defined in terms of two dimensions, reflecting the internal working model of the self and the internal working model of others (Figure 4.2). Each dimension involves a positive end and a negative end. Illustrative of the positive self end would be a sense of self-worth and expectations that others will respond positively. Illustrative of the positive other end would be expectations that others will be available and supportive, lending themselves to closeness. As show in Figure 4.2, this model leads to the addition of a fourth attachment style, that of *dismissing*. Individuals with

```
┌─────────────────────────────────────────────────────────────────────────┐
│                              Positive Other                               │
│              Secure                               Preoccupied             │
│   (Comfortable with intimacy and autonomy)  (Preoccupied with relationships)│
│  Positive Self                                           Negative Self     │
│             Dismissing                              Fearful                │
│  (Dismissing of intimacy; counter-dependent)  (Fearful of intimacy; socially avoidant)│
│                              Negative Other                               │
└─────────────────────────────────────────────────────────────────────────┘
```

FIGURE 4.2 Bartholomew's dimensions of self and other internal working models and associated attachment patterns.
Bartholomew & Horowitz (1991); Griffin and Bartholomew (1994). Copyright © 1994 by the American Psychological Association. Reprinted by permission.

this attachment pattern are not comfortable with close relationships and prefer not to depend on others but still retain a positive self-image.

The research presented here just scratches the surface of what has become an important area of investigation. Attachment styles have been associated with partner selection and stability of love relationships (Kirkpatrick & Davis, 1994), with the development of adult depression and difficulties in interpersonal relationships (Bartholomew & Horowitz, 1991; Carnelley, Pietromonaco, & Jaffe, 1994; Roberts, Gotlib, & Kassel, 1996), with movement toward becoming more religious (Kirkpatrick, 1998), and with how individuals cope with crises (Mikulciner, Florian, & Weller, 1993). In addition, one study suggests that attachment style develops out of family experiences shared by siblings, rather than being strongly determined by genetic factors (Waller & Shaver, 1994). Thus, an impressive research record is beginning to develop (Fraley & Shaver, 2008).

Yet it is important to note a number of points. First, despite suggestive evidence of continuity of attachment style, there also is evidence that these styles are not fixed in stone. At this point the amount of continuity over time of attachment style, and the reasons for greater or lesser continuity, remain issues of considerable debate. Second, these studies tend to look at attachment patterns as if each person had just one attachment style. Yet, there is evidence that the same individual can have multiple attachment patterns, perhaps one in relationships with males and another with females, or one for some contexts and another for different contexts (Baldwin, 1999; Sperling & Berman, 1994). Finally, it is important to recognize that much of this research involves the use of self-reports and the recall of experiences in childhood. In other words, we need more evidence about the actual behavior of individuals with different adult attachment patterns and research that follows individuals from infancy through adulthood. In sum, research to date supports Bowlby's view of the importance of early experience for the development of internal working models that have powerful effects on personal relationships. At the same time, further research is needed to define the experiences in childhood that determine these models, the relative stability of such models, and the limits of their influence in adulthood.

Contemporary Developments in Personality Theory: Neuropsychoanalysis

At heart, Freud was a neuroscientist—a "biologist of the mind," as the author Frank Sulloway phrased it (Sulloway, 1979). Early in his career, Freud hoped to identify brain mechanisms that could explain basic psychological abilities such as memory and attention, as well as the more complex personality dynamics that later became the focus of psychoanalytic theory. He devoted much of his work to this challenge in the early 1890's. These efforts culminated in a book, known as the *Project for a Scientific Psychology* (Freud, 1895), in which Freud suggested ways in which the activities of neurons (the cells of the brain) might give rise to psychological abilities, primary and secondary thinking processes (see Chapter 3), and consciously felt experience.

In historical retrospect, Freud's *Project* was remarkable. He anticipated results from research conducted many decades later, such as the finding that experiences create changes in neuronal systems that, in turn, are the basis of memory for those experiences (Centonze, Siracusano, Calabresi, & Bernardi, 2004; Pribram, 2005). Yet Freud became discouraged about the *Project*. After spending substantial time on it, he recognized a limitation in his own work: It was too speculative. This speculative quality is something he could not avoid. In Freud's day, knowledge about the workings of the brain was quite limited. This base of knowledge could barely support an analysis of simple processes of learning and memory. As Freud realized, it was entirely insufficient to support a detailed theory of how the brain contributes to the complex motivations, emotions, and defense mechanisms that were his true interest. After expending enormous effort on the *Project*, he concluded that his own work has a mistake; he wrote to a colleague that, "I no longer understand the state of mind in which I concocted the psychology" [i.e., the *Project for a Scientific Psychology*] (quoted in Nagy, 1991 p. 120).

Freud thus changed directions (Northoff, 2012). Starting with his next major work, *The Interpretation of Dreams*, Freud devoted himself exclusively to *psychological* analyses of personality structure and dynamics. His overall orientation remained that of a biologist (Sulloway, 1979). But he analyzed the workings of the mind without also trying to identify the brain systems underlying mental events. That, he knew, was a challenge that could only be met in the future.

Has the future arrived? Does contemporary neuroscience provide the brain-level explanation of psychodynamic processes that Freud lacked? Investigators who take part in the enterprise known as **neuropsychoanalysis** think so.

Neuropsychoanalysis

Neuropsychoanalysis is a movement. It is not the work of any one theorist but, instead, is an enterprise in which a number of psychologists and neuroscientists take part. It also is not a unique theory of personality. Instead—exactly as the name suggests—neuropsychoanalysis is an effort to determine whether 21st-century neuroscience can provide what Freud's 19th-century neuroscience could not: a brain-based understanding of psychoanalytic structures and processes.

Because numerous people contribute to the neuropsychoanalytic enterprise, it is not possible briefly to summarize the full range of ideas and findings. However, a valuable summary of key contributions of neuropsychoanalysis is provided by two writers who have themselves been significant to the neuropsychoanalytic effort: the late Jaak Panksepp, a neuroscientist from Estonia who spent much of his academic career in the United States (Panksepp passed away in 2017), and Mark Solms, a psychoanalyst and neuropsychologist from South Africa who coined the term "neuropsychoanalysis" (Johnson & Mosri, 2016).

Neuropsychoanalysis: Four Key Contributions

Panksepp and Solms (2012) outline four key contributions of neuropsychoanalysis. In each case, the contribution rests on neuroscience methods and findings that were unavailable to Freud or his followers in the early decades of the 20th century. We will introduce each one by relating it to one of the aspects of Freud's theory that you learned about in Chapter 3.

Animalistic Drive and Animal Models in Human Emotion

In psychoanalytic theory, the id houses a small set of instinctual drives that are "animalistic" in nature. The unconscious forces impel people toward self-preservation and sexual reproduction (the life instincts) and can power acts of aggression (the death instinct). In light of this theory, ask yourself: What would you expect to find when studying the brain through contemporary research methods?

There is a two-part answer to this question. One is that there should be specific subsystems of the brain that generate basic instinctual drives. The other is that you would expect to find these systems in the brains of both humans and nonhuman animals; the "animalistic" nature of Freudian drives suggests that the brains of a wide range of mammalian species should have basic-drive systems that resemble those of humans.

Contemporary neuroscientific findings are consistent with this expectation. Neuroscientists have, in fact, identified neural systems that are similar in structure and function in human and nonhuman animals, and they directly contribute to the experience of feeling states. In a key type of research that supports this conclusion, researchers stimulate specific brain regions electrically. Electrical stimulation of different brain areas of animals' brains produce different emotions, including fear, rage (anger), lust (sexual desire), and seeking (motivation to pursue a reward; Panksepp (2011). The key brain regions are subcortical, that is, they are in lower regions of the brain whose anatomy is similar in numerous animal species.

Self-Deception and the Neuroscience of "Confabulation"

When Freud listened to his patients, he did not take their statements "at face value". He knew that anything patients said about themselves could be self-deceptions; the defensive strategies of the ego could repress some of the patient's memories, distort other memories, and result in statements by the patient that—unbeknownst to the patient—were disconnected from reality. Patients would think they were telling the truth about their past, but their mind would be deceiving them.

Despite Freud's painstaking clinical efforts, there were two inherent limits to his analysis of self-deception. One is purely psychological. Whenever patients make statements that are not accurate, it is difficult to distinguish between two possibilities: (1) the patients unconsciously are deceiving themselves; (2) the patients *consciously* are deceiving *their therapist*; for example, individuals may not feel comfortable enough with their therapist to reveal the truth about painful personal events, or may wish to make up stories about themselves to impress the therapist. The second involves the connection between the psychological and the biological. Once Freud abandoned the *Project*, he also abandoned hope of identifying brain regions that might underlie self-deceptive thoughts.

A second contribution of neuropsychoanalysis is the identification of these brain regions (Panksepp and Solms, 2012). Key research is conducted with people who engage in "confabulation". Confabulation is a form of false memory, that is, of the apparent memory of experiences and information that is unquestionably not accurate (Schneider, 2003). Confabulation may be observed in cases of brain damage (e.g., that might result from a brain tumor), with patients making statements that that unquestionably seem to believe, yet that are plainly incorrect. For example, a patient hospitalized in Switzerland was certain that he was in Bordeaux, France; it is reported that when he looked out a window, he acknowledged that his environment looked nothing like France yet insisted that "I am not crazy, I know that I am in Bordeaux!" (Schneider, 2003, p. 663). Another patient, after an operation to treat a brain tumor, told his doctor (who were fully aware of the surgery) that he merely had hit his head while playing sports and that he then consulted a sports psychologist who told him that he was fine (Solms, https://www.futurelearn.com/courses/what-is-a-mind/0/steps/9266).

Contemporary research on confabulation overcomes both of the limitations encountered by Freud. First, in cases of confabulation, there is no question that patients' statement are genuine cases of self-deception. Some confabulations are so obviously wrong—so disconnected from reality—that no one would ever believe them except the patient making the statement. This could not be a strategy for making a good impression on a therapist. Solms (https://www.futurelearn.com/courses/what-is-a-mind/0/steps/9266) interprets such statements as a motivated self-deception that is an "inadequate attempt" to deal with extreme stress in which patients engage in "an overly emotionally colored, distorted, overly wishful … use of [false] memory Solms ().

Why are the patients' attempts to deal with stress so inadequate? In many cases, it is because brain damage has reduced their ability to make plans and decisions. Research findings indicate that many patients who confabulate have experienced damage to the frontal lobes of the brain, which are required for "executive functioning," that is, the control of logical flows of thought and action that match up to requirements in the environment (Schneider, 2003; Turner, Cipolotti, Yousry, & Shallice, 2008). Such findings address the second limitation experienced by Freud; they identify a neural basis of self-deceptive thinking of the sort that Freud hoped to identify when working on the *Project*.

Dreaming and the Brain

To appreciate the third contribution of neuropsychoanalysis, think back to two facts you likely learned in introductory psychology. One is that there are stages of sleep, one of which is rapid eye movement (REM) sleep. A distinctive feature of REM sleep is that if you wake someone during this sleep stage, that usually report that they had been dreaming. A second fact is that the brain region from which signals are sent that control activity during REM sleep is the pons, a structure in the brain stem (the lowest region of the brain, which sits just above the spinal cord).

What does this have to do with psychoanalysis? Recall that, to Freud, dreaming was a highly complex mental process in which dream content reflected the life—the desires, memories, and defensive strategies—of the dreamer. The pons, a simple low-level brain mechanism, could never generate such complex mental activity.

Contemporary neuroscientific evidence shows that it does not have to. Solms (2000) reviews evidence showing that dreaming and REM sleep are distinct; specifically, different brain mechanisms control one versus the other activity. Unlike REM sleep, dreaming is influenced by relatively *high*-level brain mechanisms. The high-level brain mechanisms that produce the imagery of dreams are connected to a range of additional brain systems involved in thinking and memory. Importantly, this means that dream imagery can be "actively constructed through complex cognitive processes" (Solms, 2000, p. 846)—precisely as Freudian theory would expect.

From Neural Mechanisms to Therapy Methods

The fourth contribution of neuropsychoanalysis identified by Panksepp and Solms concerns the treatment of psychological disorders. Once Freud abandoned his *Project* for a neuroscience of psychological processes, he also abandoned any hope of identifying neuroscience-based treatments for mental disorders. As you have learned, the focus of Freud's therapy method was entirely psychological—the free association method and the dynamics of the associated therapist—patient relationship—not biological. But neuropsychoanalysis opens the door to the use of both psychological and biological interventions.

Specifically, neuropsychoanalysts suggest that animal models can inform therapy for humans. In other words, research conducted with nonhuman animals on neural systems and emotion and provides clues to effective treatment of human psychological disorders—including highly prevalent disorders such as anxiety or depression. "By understanding the neurobiological nature of relevant brain emotional systems, optimally studied in detail in animal models, novel ways to envision and treat human depression should emerge" (Panksepp et al., 2014, p. 473).

An advantage of animal-model research is that it provides knowledge of specific neural systems involved in the production of emotional states. With that knowledge, therapists can, in principle target those neural systems directly. Directly influencing a biological system that generates distressful emotion could reduce patients' distress. One such therapy strategy uses deep brain stimulation (DBS).

Deep brain stimulation is a surgical procedure. In the surgery, an extremely small electrical device is implanted in a specific region of the brain. The device sends out electrical signals that influence levels of brain activity in that region. Research using animal models provides information about the specific brain region that should be targeted to treat a given disorder (Panksepp et al., 2014). One disorder for which DBS has been employed is depression. DBS has been shown not only to reduce the emotional and behavioral symptoms of depression (Mayberg et al., 2005), but also to reduce negative thinking patterns that contribute to the disorder. For example, one team of therapists treated seven depressed patients whose depression was not relieved by traditional forms of therapy (Hilimire et al., 2015). In the DBS treatment, over a four-week period electrical stimulation was applied to an area of the limbic system of the brain that was known, from prior research, to be involved in depressed emotional states. DBS affected the way in which patients thought about themselves; specifically, it reduced "negative self-bias," which is the tendency to have negative thoughts and feelings about one's own personal qualities. Compared to their experiences before treatment, after DBS therapy the patients were less likely to describe their personal qualities in negative terms; their negative self-bias was reduced.

Implications for Psychoanalytic Theory

The general implications of neuropsychoanalysis for Freud's psychoanalytic theory are clear. Contemporary neuroscience research has generated some findings that are entirely consistent with Freudian theory. Freud's psychological model depicted a mind that contained basic animalistic drives (in the id) and a mental system (the ego) that defended against anxiety through defensive strategies that could result in people deceiving themselves about their own past. The brain does, in fact, contain biological systems that correspond to these psychological functions.

There is a second implication that was not mentioned above, but that you might be able to figure out if you compare our discussion of neuropsychoanalysis with what you learned earlier about psychoanalytic theory. Consider these facts one at a time:

- Neuropsychoanalysis uses animal models to identify brain systems that produce basic emotional states such as fear and rage.

- These emotional states appear to correspond to the instinctual drive states discussed in Freud's psychoanalytic theory.

- In psychoanalytic theory, instincts are part of the id.

- In psychoanalytic theory, the id is part of the unconscious; it functions outside of conscious awareness.

- But emotional states such as fear and rage are felt *consciously*. People *feel* afraid and angry, and these feeling states are a defining feature of consciousness.

The implication is spelled out vividly by Solms (2013): "The conclusion is inescapable: *consciousness is generated in the id*" (p. 12). Rather than being a hidden unconscious force, id impulses are "the fount of all consciousness" (p. 16). As Solms notes, this conclusion "has massive implications for psychoanalysis" (p. 16). It forces a rethinking of fundamental psychoanalytic processes since, in Freud's view, those processes dealt with drive states that were *un*conscious.

Limitations?

Neuropsychoanalysis is a major theoretical advance. Neuropsychoanalysts' ability to identify brain mechanisms that contribute to psychoanalytic phenomena, to apply that knowledge to clinical treatment, and to revisit core issues of psychoanalytic theory accomplishes many of the goals that Freud himself could not achieve in the 1890's. Yet one does have to keep this advance in perspective.

Neuropsychoanalysts tend to highlight ways contemporary evidence about the brain that is consistent with elements of psychoanalytic theory. Yet there also are elements of psychoanalytic theory that plainly are *in*consistent with current knowledge of the brain. For example, Freud posited a death instinct. Contemporary neuroscientists have not found a neural mechanism corresponding to the death instinct, and it is safe to assume that they are not going to do so; if one applies the logic of Darwinian theory, it is difficult to see how a death instinct could ever have evolved (since it appears not to have advantages for adaptation). Freud proposed that early life experiences have a fixed effect on personality, with few if any substantial changes in personality structure occurring after the start of the latency period. Again, it is extremely difficult to reconcile this theoretical position with contemporary brain science. Current-day evidence show that brain systems change—or are highly "plastic" (see Chapter 9)— even after the early years of childhood. This brain plasticity plainly is not consistent with the Freudian view that early life experiences entirely determine the later-like structure of the mind.

A second concern is that neuropsychoanalysts' focus on animal models—and therefore on the similarity between humans and nonhuman animals—may cause them to give insufficient attention to differences between humans and nonhuman animals. Consider recent findings about neurotransmitters, the biochemicals that are responsible for communication between brain cells. Although the same neurotransmitters are found in multiple species, this does not mean that the different species are psychologically similar. Researchers recently compared neurotransmitter function in humans and other primates. When focusing on the striatum (a system within the limbic system that is involved in responses to rewarding stimuli), they found that our species has a "unique profile" (Raghanti, 2018, p. 5 early ed) of neurotransmitter activity. The unique biochemical makes us *differ from* other species. Specifically, the uniquely human biochemical profile causes our species to be distinctively attentive to social cues, less aggressive, and more knowledgeable of environmental factors that may influence our behavior.

A similar concern comes from research in which brain-imaging methods are used to identify the brain systems involved in human emotional experience. When a large team of researchers reviewed evidence from more than 150 imaging studies (Kober et al., 2008), they found that emotion is generated by a complex network of brain structures. Some of these were limbic-system structures that humans share with nonhuman animals. But others were higher-level structures in the brain's cortex—a brain region that is developed to a unique degree in humans. A challenge for neuropsychoanalysts is not merely to identify contemporary findings about the brain that are consistent with the theorizing of Freud, but also to grapple to additional discoveries about the brain that challenge the psychoanalytic—and neuropsychoanalytic—perspective.

Critical Evaluation

Throughout our text, we not only will present theories of personality but also will evaluate them. We will do so by considering the five criteria we presented in Chapter 1, each of which is a goal to be achieved in a formal scientific theory of personality. As we discussed, the five criteria are the degree to which (1) the theory is based on good scientific observations, specifically, observations that are diverse in nature, are objective, and illuminate specific cognitive, affective, and biological systems of personality; whether the theory itself is (2) systematic, (3) testable, and (4) comprehensive; and whether the theory (5) yields valuable applications. After reviewing these five points, we will summarize the major contributions of the given theory.

Scientific Observation: The Database

One of the most distinctive features of psychoanalysis is its database. Freud developed a novel form of scientific observation: the free-association method. He based his theory almost entirely on the information yielded by this method.

Most contemporary personality scientists judge that Freud's exclusive reliance on the free-association technique is a major drawback. Clinical observations of patients can provide a useful starting point for theorizing, but for Freud it was both a starting point and an ending point! He never pursued the sort of standardized, objective, replicable observations that are the hallmark of science. Instead, he relied on a free-association database that is limited in at least two respects. It is not at all diverse. Freud's clients were a relatively small number of fairly well-educated persons living in one particular city in central Europe. It is exceptionally risky to generalize from these observations to the psychological life of all persons. Second, there is no guarantee of objectivity in data collection. The person who is observing and interpreting the data—Freud—is the same person who developed the theory. One cannot know whether Freud's interpretation of his cases was biased by his own desire to find evidence that supported his theorizing.

Freud's clinical observations, then, are inadequate as a foundation for developing and testing a scientific theory, as many have noted (Edelson, 1984; Grunbaum, 1984, 1993). Rather than constituting unbiased observations of experiences and recollections by patients, many critics suggest that Freud often biased his observations by using suggestive procedures and by inferring that memories existed at the unconscious level (Crews, 1993; Esterson, 1993; Powell & Boer, 1994). Eysenck, a frequent and passionate critic of psychoanalysis, whose views we will consider later in this textbook, suggests that "we can no more test Freudian hypotheses on the couch than we can adjudicate between the rival hypotheses of Newton and Einstein by going to sleep under the apple tree" (1953, p. 229).

Theory: Systematic?

A second criterion for evaluating a personality theory is whether the theory is systematic. The theory should not be a disconnected set of statements about persons. Instead, its ideas should relate to one another in a logical, coherent manner.

On this score, Freud excels. The very different elements of the theory are interrelated in an exceptionally coherent manner. The process and structure aspects of the theory are related in a clear manner, with the id, ego, and superego (the psychological structures) playing different roles in the gratification of mental energy within the constraints of reality (the central personality processes, or dynamics). Freud's analyses of development in childhood, of psychological change in therapy, and of the role of society in civilizing the individual all follow logically from his analyses of personality structure and processes. Freud was an exceptional theorist, and his skill is clearly evident in the well-specified interrelations among the disparate elements of his theory. At the same time, it is important to recognize that as time has passed differing views have evolved concerning various elements of psychoanalytic theory. Thus, there are less unity and dogma in psychoanalysis and greater flux (Westen, Gabbard, & Ortigo, 2008).

Theory: Testable?

Although Freud systematically related the different elements of his theory to one another, this does not imply that the overall theory is testable in an unambiguous manner. A theory could be systematic and yet still have features that make it difficult to test. Unfortunately, such is the case for psychoanalysis. It commonly is difficult to determine how, exactly, one could prove a theoretical prediction in psychoanalysis to be wrong.

The problem is that psychoanalysts can account for almost any outcome. Even opposite outcomes can be fit within the psychoanalytic explanatory system. Suppose a Freudian thinks that an instinctual drive will give rise to a certain form of behavior. If the behavior appears, the theory is confirmed. If the behavior does not appear, the psychoanalyst may conclude that the instinctual drive was so strong that defense mechanisms became active and prevented the behavior. Again the theory is confirmed. If some unanticipated form of behavior appears, the psychoanalyst could interpret it as a compromise between the instinct and a defense mechanism—again with no negative consequences for the theory as a whole.

Psychoanalysts are not unaware that their theoretical framework has this limitation. Some might even think that it is not a big problem; it is possible to construe psychoanalysis as a framework for interpreting events rather than as a scientific theory that makes specific testable predictions (Ricoeur, 1970). Most contemporary psychologists, however, feel that Freud's work should be assessed using the standard criteria for evaluating a scientific theory. These criteria include whether the theory is testable. A limitation of psychoanalysis, then, is that it is so flexible that—like a ruler made of pliable rubber that can be bent, twisted, pushed, and pulled to yield any of a variety of measurements of a given object—it fails to make hard-and-fast predictions that could be proven wrong. The "infinite pliability of defense mechanisms [is] the Freudian's insurance against ever encountering uninterpretable material" (Crews, 1998, p. xxv). In sum, even strong supporters of the psychoanalytic model are critical of its excessive reliance on case study material: "That psychoanalysts seriously shot themselves in the foot by never evolving from case study methods as their primary mode of hypothesis testing is beyond doubt" (Westen, Gabbard, & Ortigo, 2008, p. 95).

Theory: Comprehensive?

Another question to ask about a personality theory is whether it is comprehensive. Does the theorist cover all aspects of personality or merely concentrate on those aspects that are most easily addressed by his or her theoretical system?

Both friend and foe of psychoanalysis must recognize that Freud's theory of personality is extraordinarily comprehensive. Freud addresses an exceptionally wide range of issues: the nature of mind, the relation between persons and society, dreams, sexuality, symbolism, the nature of human development, therapies for psychological change—the list goes on and on. Freud provides the most comprehensive of all the major personality theories. As you will see in subsequent chapters, many theories developed subsequent to Freud's say little or nothing about major aspects of the human experience that he addressed in depth.

Applications

In many respects, applications are a strength of psychoanalytic theory. This should not be surprising. Psychoanalysis at first *was* an application; that is, Freud began his psychological work by addressing applied questions involving the treatment of hysteria. He only subsequently developed his work into a general theory of personality. Freud thus gave great effort to the challenge of applying psychological theory to the improvement of individual lives.

This effort was not in vain. In the decades since Freud first developed his therapy and theory, a great many studies have evaluated the question of whether psychoanalytic therapy is effective. Because this is a textbook of personality theory and research, not of clinical applications, we will not review this work in detail. We merely raise two points. On the one hand, psychoanalysis unquestionably "works" (Galatzer-Levy, Bachrach, Skolnikoff, & Waldron, 2000). That is, if one asks whether people who enter into psychoanalytic therapy are better off than people who did not obtain therapy, and if one answers this question by reviewing the many therapy outcome studies that have been done over the years, one finds that psychoanalysis often benefits clients significantly. In addition, there is evidence of the efficacy of brief psychodynamically oriented psychotherapy (Shedler, 2010).

A second point, however, is that other therapies benefit clients, too. Other theories of personality have fostered alternative forms of treatment that often are of great benefit to clients, as you will see in the subsequent chapters of this book. These alternative treatments quite commonly do not feature the core elements of psychoanalysis (such as a search for conflictual unconscious contents that are the underlying cause of current problems), yet they still do work. Many psychologists see this as a major strike against psychoanalytic theory. Freud provided a specific theory of the origins of psychological distress and the steps needed for relieving it. To the extent that nonpsychoanalytic therapies work, too, they raise questions about the fundamental premises of Freud's theory.

Major Contributions and Summary

Even the harshest critic must recognize that Freud made major contributions to psychology. In closing our discussion of psychodynamic theories, we note contributions of two types.

Freud at a Glance					
Structure	Process	Growth and Development	Pathology	Change	Illustrative Case
Id, ego, superego; unconscious, preconscious, conscious	Sexual and aggressive instincts; anxiety and the mechanisms of defense	Erogenous zones; oral, anal, phallic stages of development; Oedipus complex	Infantile sexuality; fixation and regression; conflict; symptoms	Transference; conflict resolution; "Where id was, ego shall be"	Little Hans

By closely observing the working of the mind, Freud identified important phenomena that previously had been overlooked by psychologists. Even if one does not agree with Freud's *explanations* of all these phenomena, he must be credited with identifying, as important targets of psychological study, phenomena of enormous significance: unconscious motivational and emotional processes; defensive strategies for coping with psychological threat; the sexually charged nature of childhood. If personality psychology had lacked Freud's insights into these phenomena, its history would have been much less rich.

A second contribution was his formulating a theory of sufficient complexity. By "sufficient" we mean that his ideas were complex enough to do justice to the complexities of human development and individuality. By obtaining richly detailed observations of persons and by willing to forge ahead with his theorizing, Freud provided a theory that accounts—rightly or wrongly—for almost all aspects of human behavior. No other theory of personality comes close to psychoanalysis in its comprehensiveness. Few others give comparable attention to the functioning of the

Table 4.3   **Summary of Strengths and Limitations of Psychoanalytic Theory**

Strengths	Limitations
1. Provides for the discovery and investigation of many interesting phenomena	1. Fails to define all its concepts clearly and distinctly
2. Develops techniques for research and therapy (free association, dream interpretation, transference analysis)	2. Makes empirical testing difficult, at times impossible
	3. Endorses the questionable view of the person as an energy system
3. Recognizes the complexity of human behavior	4. Tolerates resistance by parts of the profession to empirical research and change in the theory
4. Encompasses a broad range of phenomena	

individual as a whole. Even if one were to presume that multiple aspects of Freud's work were fundamentally wrong, in its structure his psychoanalytic theory provides a model of what a truly comprehensive theory would look like.

Today, views concerning Freud's works and contributions range from the judgment that it is of little relevance to contemporary science to the view, emblazoned across the front of a major U.S. magazine on the occasion of the 150th anniversary of Freud's birth, that "Freud is *NOT* Dead" (*Newsweek* Magazine, 2006). Whereas some are critical of psychoanalytic errors made in the treatment of certain disorders (e.g., schizophrenia; Dolnick, 1998) and of limited evidence supportive of psychoanalysis's major hypotheses, others are more supportive of its treatment methods and cite its enduring contributions to empirical research. Indeed, it has been suggested that many psychoanalytic views (e.g., motives, unconscious mental representations) now are part of traditional personality and social psychology (Westen, Gabbard, & Ortigo, 2008). We end by summarizing some of the strengths and limits of psychoanalytic theory (Table 4.3). Whatever the limits of his work, psychology has benefited from the contributions of Freud, whose genius in observing human behavior has rarely been equaled.

MAJOR CONCEPTS

Anal personality	Fixation	Oral personality	Regression
Attachment behavioral system (ABS)	Free association	Phallic personality	Symptom
Collective unconscious	Internal working model	Projective test	Transference

REVIEW

1. Projective tests, such as the Rorschach Inkblot Test and Thematic Apperception Test (TAT), have been used by psychodynamically oriented investigators to assess personality. They are valuable in that they provide disguised methods for tapping an individual's unique interpretations of the world, including the person's complex organization of individual perceptions. However, they also present problems of reliability and validity of interpretation.

2. The psychoanalytic theory of psychopathology emphasizes the importance of fixations, or failures in development, and regression, or the return to earlier modes of satisfaction. The oral, anal, and phallic character types express personality patterns resulting from partial fixations at earlier stages of development.

Psychopathology is seen to involve conflict between instinctual wishes for gratification and the anxiety associated with these wishes. Defense mechanisms represent ways to reduce anxiety but can result in the development of symptoms. The case of Little Hans illustrates how a symptom, such as a phobia, can result from conflicts associated with the Oedipus complex.

3. Psychoanalysis is a therapeutic process in which the individual gains insight into and resolves conflicts dating back to childhood. The methods of free association and dream interpretation are used to gain insight into unconscious conflicts. Therapeutic use is also made of the transference situation, in which patients develop attitudes and feelings toward their therapist that relate to experiences with earlier parental figures.

4. A number of analysts broke with Freud and developed their own schools of thought. Alfred Adler emphasized social concepts more than biological concepts, and Carl Jung emphasized a generalized life energy and the collective unconscious. Analysts such as Karen Horney and Harry Stack Sullivan emphasized the importance of cultural factors and interpersonal relations, and were part of the group known as neo-Freudians.

5. Recent clinical developments in psychoanalysis have focused on problems of self-definition and self-esteem. Psychoanalysts in this group, known as object relations theorists, emphasize the importance of relationship seeking as opposed to the expression of sexual and aggressive instincts. The concepts of narcissism and the narcissistic personality have gained particular attention. Bowlby's attachment model and related research illustrate the importance of early experiences for later personal relationships, as well as other aspects of personality functioning.

6. An evaluation of psychoanalysis suggests its tremendous contribution in calling attention to many important phenomena and developing techniques for research and therapy. At the same time, the theory suffers from ambiguous, poorly defined concepts and problems in testing specific hypotheses.

A Phenomenological Theory: The Personality Theory of Rogers

5

Questions to be Addressed in this Chapter

Carl R. Rogers (1902–1987): A View of the Theorist

Rogers's View of the Person

Rogers's View of the Science of Personality

The Personality Theory of Carl Rogers

Major Concepts

Review

Chapter Focus

You are really nervous before a first date, so your mother gives you some advice: "Just be yourself. Your true self." But that advice doesn't seem too helpful. Well intentioned though she may be, Mom raises two problems. First, you want to impress your date and get him or her to like you. What if your date does not like your "true self"? Even if you do like Mom's plan, there is a second problem: What exactly is your "true" self?

The nature of the self, and the tension between being yourself versus wanting to be liked by other people, are central concerns in the personality theory developed by Carl Rogers. Rogers first addressed these concerns in his work as a clinical psychologist. He combined his clinical insights with systematic empirical research to develop a theory of the totality of the individual that highlighted the person's efforts to develop a meaningful sense of self.

In addition to being a self-theory, Rogers's work also can be categorized as a *phenomenological* theory. A phenomenological theory is one that emphasizes the individual's subjective experience of his or her world—in other words, his or her phenomenological experience. As a therapist, Rogers's overarching goal was to understand the client's phenomenological experience of the self and the world in order to assist the client in personal growth. As a theorist, his overarching goal was to develop a framework to explain the nature and development of the self as the core element of personality.

Rogers's phenomenological self-theory can also be described by another term: *humanistic*. Rogers's work is part of a humanistic movement in psychology whose core feature was to emphasize people's inherent potential for growth.

This chapter, then, introduces you to the theory—the phenomenological, humanistic, self-theory—that is the enduring legacy of one of the great American psychologists of the 20th century, Carl Rogers.

Questions to be Addressed in this Chapter

1. What is the self, and why might one not act in a manner consistent with one's true self?

2. Freud viewed motivation in terms of tension reduction, the pursuit of pleasure, and intrapsychic conflict. Is it possible to view human motivation, instead, in terms of personal growth, self-actualization, and feelings of congruence?

3. How important is it for us to have a stable self-concept? How important is it for our internal feelings to match our self-concept? What do we do when feelings are in conflict with our self-beliefs?

4. What are the childhood conditions that produce a positive sense of self-worth?

In the previous chapters, you learned about Freud's psychoanalytic theory of personality and related psychodynamic positions. We now introduce a second, entirely different perspective. It is that of the American psychologist Carl Rogers. His work exemplifies a phenomenological approach to the study of persons.

At the outset, you should consider how these conceptions, Freud's and Rogers's, are related. Rogers did not disagree with everything Freud said about persons. He recognized that Freud provided some insights about the workings of the mind that are of enduring value. Also, Rogers worked in a style that was similar in some ways to that of Freud. Rogers, like Freud, began his career as a therapist and based his general theory of personality primarily on his therapeutic experiences. However, these affinities are less important than are some deep differences. Rogers disagreed sharply with major emphases of Freudian theory: its depiction of humans as controlled by unconscious forces; its assertion that personality is determined, in a fixed manner, by experiences early in life; its associated belief that adult psychological experience is a repeating of the repressed conflicts of the past. To Rogers, these psychodynamic views did not adequately portray human existence or human potential. Rogers thus provided a new theory of the person. It emphasized conscious perceptions of the present rather than merely unconscious residues of the past, interpersonal experiences encountered across the course of life rather than merely parental relations in childhood, and people's capacity to grow toward psychological maturity rather than merely their tendency to repeat childhood conflicts.

Rogers expands our conception of human nature, and in a very positive direction. To many contemporary psychologists, his positive conception of the person, developed during the mid-20th century, is of enduring importance. "Half a century on from when Rogers first developed his theory, it still has profound consequences for the person and their ability to maintain and enhance themselves" (McMillan, 2004, p. ix).

Carl R. Rogers (1902–1987): A View of the Theorist

"I speak as a person, from a context of personal experience and personal learning." This is how Rogers describes himself, in a chapter entitled "This Is Me," in his 1961 book *On Becoming a Person*. The chapter is a personal, very moving account by Rogers of the development of his professional thinking and personal philosophy. Rogers states what he does and how he feels about it:

> This book is about the suffering and the hope, the anxiety and the satisfaction, with which each therapist's counseling room is filled. . . It is about me as I try to perceive his (the client's) experience, and the meaning and the feeling and the taste and flavor that it has for him. It is about me as I rejoice at the privilege of being a midwife to a new personality as I stand by with awe at the emergence of a self, a person, as I see a birth process in which I have had an important and facilitating part.
>
> *Source:* Rogers (1961, pp. 4–5).

Carl R. Rogers was born on January 8, 1902, in Oak Park, Illinois. He was reared in a strict and uncompromising religious and ethical atmosphere. His parents had the welfare of their children constantly in mind and inculcated in them a worship of hard work. Rogers's description of his early life reveals two main trends that are reflected in his later work. The first is the concern with moral and ethical matters. The second is the respect for the methods of science. The latter appears to have developed out of exposure to his father's efforts to operate their farm on a scientific basis and Rogers's own reading of books on scientific agriculture.

Rogers started his college education at the University of Wisconsin, majoring in agriculture, but after two years, he changed his professional goals and decided to enter the ministry. During a trip to Asia in 1922, he had a chance to observe commitments to other religious doctrines as well as the bitter mutual hatreds of French and German people, who otherwise seemed to be likable individuals. Experiences like these influenced his decision to go to a liberal theological seminary, the Union Theological Seminary in New York. Although he was concerned about questions regarding the meaning of life for individuals, Rogers had doubts about specific religious doctrines. Therefore, he chose to leave the seminary, to work in the field of child guidance, and to think of himself as a clinical psychologist.

Michael Rougier / Time & Life / Getty Images

Carl R. Rogers.

Rogers obtained his graduate training at Teachers College, Columbia University, receiving his Ph.D. in 1931. His education included exposure to both the dynamic views of Freud and the rigorous experimental methods then prevalent at Teachers College. Again, there were the pulls in different directions, the development of two somewhat divergent trends. In his later life, Rogers attempted to bring these trends into harmony. Indeed, these later years represent an effort to integrate the religious with the scientific, the intuitive with the objective, and the clinical with the statistical. Throughout his career, Rogers tried continually to apply the objective methods of science to what is most basically human.

In 1968, Rogers and his more humanistically oriented colleagues formed the Center for the Studies of the Person. The development of the center expressed a number of shifts in emphasis in Rogers's studies from work within a formal academic structure to work with a collection of individuals who shared a perspective, from work with disturbed individuals to work with normal individuals, from individual therapy to intensive group workshops, and from conventional empirical research to the phenomenological study of people. Rogers believed that most of psychology was sterile and generally felt alienated from the field. Yet the field continued to value his contributions. He was president of the American Psychological Association in 1946–1947, was one of the first three psychologists to receive the Distinguished Scientific Contribution Award (1956) from the profession, and in 1972 was the recipient of the Distinguished Professional Contribution Award.

With Rogers, the theory, the man, and the life are interwoven. In his chapter "This Is Me," Rogers lists 14 principles that he learned from thousands of hours of therapy and research. Here are some illustrations:

1. In my relationships with persons I have found that it does not help, in the long run, to act as though I were something that I am not.

2. Experience is, for me, the highest authority.

3. It has been my experience that persons have a basically positive direction.

Source: Rogers (1961a, pp. 16–17).

Rogers's View of the Person

The Subjectivity of Experience

Rogers's theory is built on a deeply significant insight into the human condition. In our daily living, we believe we experience an objective world of reality. When we see something occur, we believe it exists as we saw it. When we tell people about the events of our day, we believe we are telling them what really happened. We are so confident in our objective knowledge of an objective reality that we rarely question it. But Rogers does. He explains: "I do not react to some absolute reality, but to *my perception of* this reality" (Rogers, 1951, 1977, p. 206, emphasis added). The "reality" we observe is really a "private world of experience . . . , the phenomenal field" (Rogers, 1951, 1977, p. 206).

This **phenomenal field**—the space of perceptions that makes up our experience—is a *subjective* construction. The individual constructs this inner world of experience, and the construction reflects not only the outer world of reality but also the inner world of personal needs, goals, and beliefs. Inner psychological needs shape the subjective experiences that we interpret as objectively real.

Consider some simple examples. If a child sees an angry look from its mother, or you detect a disappointed look from a dating partner, these emotions—anger, disappointment—are the reality that is experienced. But this so-called reality could be wrong. Personal needs (to be accepted by the mother, to be attractive to the dating partner) may contribute to our perceiving the other as angry or disappointed. Yet people commonly fail to recognize this influence of inner needs on perceptions of the outer world. Failing to recognize this, the individual "perceives his *experience* as reality. His *experience* is his reality" (Rogers, 1959, 1977, p. 207). We are sure things really exist as we saw them. Yet our seeing is not an objective recording of the world of reality but a subjective construction that reflects our personal needs.

Feelings of Authenticity

Two additional aspects of Rogers's analysis of the subjectivity of experience define his core view of the person. The first is that people are prone to a distinctive form of psychological distress. It is a feeling of alienation or detachment—the feeling that one's experiences and daily activities do not stem from one's true, authentic self. Why do these feelings arise? Because we need the approval of others, we tell ourselves that *their* desires and values are our own. The child tries to convince himself that it really is bad to hit his baby sister, just as his parents say, even though it feels good to do so. The adult tries to convince herself that it really is good to settle down into a traditional career and family lifestyle, as valued relatives instruct, even though she really prefers a life of independence. When this happens, the individual *thinks* but does not *feel* an attachment to his or her own values. "Primary sensory and visceral reactions are ignored" and "the individual begins on a pathway that he later describes as 'I really don't know myself'" (Rogers, 1951, 1977, p. 213). Rogers relates the case of a client who described her experiences as follows: "I've always tried to be what the others thought I should be, but now I'm wondering whether I shouldn't just see that I am what I am" (Rogers, 1951, 1977, p. 218).

Maybe you've got the wrong job? Rogers's theory of personality stressed that people can get caught up in activities that do not feel right, or "authentic," for them. A lack of authenticity creates distress.

Note how Rogers's conception of the deliberate/thoughtful and the instinctive/visceral aspects of the organism differs from Freud's. To Freud, visceral reactions were animalistic impulses that needed to be curbed by the civilized ego and superego. Distorting and denying these impulses was part of normal, healthy personality functioning. But to Rogers, these instinctive visceral reactions are a potential source of wisdom. Individuals who openly experience the full range of their emotions, who are "accepting and assimilating [of] all the sensory evidence experienced by the organism" (Rogers, 1951, 1977, p. 219), are psychologically well adjusted.

Conflict between instinctive and rational elements of mind thus is not an immutable feature of the human condition in Rogers's view. Rather than conflict, persons can experience congruence. They can realize a state in which their conscious experiences and goals are consistent with their inner, viscerally felt values.

The Positivity of Human Motivation

The final key aspect of Rogers's view of persons is his conception of human motivation. Rogers's clinical experiences convinced him that the core of our nature is essentially positive. Our most fundamental motivation is toward positive growth. Rogers recognized that some institutions may teach us otherwise. Some religions, for example, teach that we are basically sinful. The institution of psychoanalysis teaches that our basic instincts are sexual and aggressive. Rogers did recognize that people can, and often do, act in ways that are destructive and evil. But his basic contention is that, when we are functioning freely, we are able to move toward our potential as positive, mature beings.

To those who called him a naive optimist, Rogers was quick to point out that his conclusions were based on decades of experience in psychotherapy:

> *I do not have a Pollyanna view of human nature . . . individuals can and do behave in ways which are incredibly . . . [yet I] work with such individuals . . . to discover the strongly positive directional tendencies which exist in them.*

> *Source*: Rogers (1961, p. 27).

Here is a profound respect for people, a respect that is reflected in Rogers's theory of personality and his person-centered approach to psychotherapy.

A Phenomenological Perspective

Rogers takes a *phenomenological* approach to the study of persons. Here at the outset of our coverage of his work, then, we should explain what is meant by this lengthy term.

In psychology or other disciplines, such as philosophy, a phenomenological approach is one that investigates people's conscious experiences. The investigation, in other words, does not try to characterize the world of reality as it exists independent of the human observer. Instead, one is interested in the experiences of the observer: how the person experiences the world.

A bit of reflection on the material of the previous two chapters should reveal why Rogers's position was so noteworthy within personality psychology. The psychodynamic tradition was *not* particularly interested in phenomenology. To Freud, conscious phenomenological experience is not the core of personality. Indeed, conscious experience may be related in only the most indirect ways to that core, which involves unconscious drives and defenses. As you will see in subsequent chapters, some other theories that initially were developed at around the same time as Rogers's (e.g., trait theory, behaviorism) devote relatively little attention to the textures and dynamics of everyday phenomenological experience. Rogers, then, was an important voice in promoting the psychological study of **phenomenology**.

Rogers's View of the Science of Personality

What does Rogers's concern with phenomenological experience have to do with his view of the science of personality? Are these two independent things: a phenomenological perspective on psychology on the one hand and a viewpoint on science on the other? Or might one have an implication for the other?

A bit of reflection suggests that a marriage between a traditional conception of science and a concern with phenomenological experience may be difficult. Science, as usually conceived, rests on clear-cut data: Laboratory instruments inform us about entities' objective physical features (size, mass, electrical charge, etc.). Rogers, however, argues that personality psychology must address subjective internal experiences. These experiences cannot be measured in the manner of objective physical qualities. Instead, they have a subjective quality; their meaning rests on the interpretations of the individual having the experience (the subject who is experiencing things).

Rogers's work can be understood as an attempt to draw on the best of two worlds, that of traditional science and that of the clinical understanding of subjective experience. In therapy, his main goal was not to classify his client within a scientific taxonomy or to identify some past causal factor that was a key determinant of his client's behavior. Instead, his goal was to gain a deep understanding of how his clients experienced their world. His efforts in this regard were similar to a reader's efforts to understand the world as experienced by the narrator of a first-person novel or the author of an autobiography. On the other hand, Rogers had great respect for the scientific method and felt that psychology could eventually establish itself as a lawful science. He was particularly careful to subject his ideas about the effective forms of therapy to scientific testing. Rogers made a valiant effort to wed the scientific and the human sides of personality science.

The Personality Theory of Carl Rogers

Having introduced Rogers, his overall view of human nature, and his conception of personality science, we now turn to the details: the specifics of Rogers's theory of personality.

Structure

The Self

In Chapter 1, we distinguished between the structure and process aspects of personality theories. This distinction, useful in understanding the work of Freud, is valuable again in learning about the theory of Carl Rogers. Let's first examine the structure aspects of Rogerian theory, whose key structural concept is the self.

According to Rogers, the self is an aspect of phenomenological experience. It is one aspect of our experience of the world, that is, one of the things that fill our conscious experience is our experience of ourselves, or of "a self." Phrased more formally, according to Rogers, the individual perceives external objects and experiences and attaches meanings to them. The total system of perceptions and meanings make up the individual's phenomenal field. That subset of the phenomenal field that is recognized by the individual as "me," or "I" is the self. The **self**, or **self-concept**, represents an organized and consistent pattern of perceptions. Although the self changes, it always retains this patterned, integrated, organized quality. Because the organized quality endures over time and characterizes the individual, the self is a personality structure. To Rogers, the self is not a little person inside of us. The self does not independently control behavior. Rather, the self is an organized set of perceptions possessed by the individual, who is ultimately responsible for his or her actions.

The pattern of experiences and perceptions known as the self is, in general, available to awareness. That is, people are consciously aware that it includes conscious self-perceptions. Although individuals do have experiences of which they are unaware, the self-concept is primarily conscious. (Note that Rogers's use of the term *self* differs from that of Carl Jung, whose views were discussed in the previous chapter. Jung thought of the self as an unconscious archetypal force, whereas Rogers uses the term *self* to refer to our conscious self-concept.)

Rogers did recognize two different aspects to the self: an actual self and an **ideal self**. Rogers recognized that people naturally think about not only themselves in the present but also their potential selves in the future. They thus generate an organized pattern of perceptions not only of their current self but also of an ideal self that they would like to be. The ideal self, then, is the self-concept that an individual would most like to possess. It includes the perceptions and meanings that potentially are relevant to the self and that are valued highly by the individual. Rogers thus recognizes that our views of ourselves contain two distinct components: the self that we believe we are now and the self that we ideally see ourselves becoming in the future.

Rogers maintained that he did not begin his theoretical work by deciding that it was important to study the self. In fact, he first thought that *self* was a vague, scientifically meaningless term. However, he listened carefully to his clients, who commonly expressed their psychological experience in terms of a self; clients would report that they "did not feel like themselves", "were disappointed in themselves", and so forth. It became clear to Rogers, then, that the self was a psychological structure through which people were interpreting their world.

Personality and the Brain
The Intuitive Self

There are different ways of thinking about oneself. Some require a lot of "figuring out"; that is, considerable thought is required to determine an answer to a question about yourself, even though the question involves a familiar topic: you. If someone asks you how you'd react if you were caught up in a natural disaster, how you'd differ if you were raised in a different culture, or what your personality will be like in old age, you don't know the answers for sure; you don't have firm "intuitions". You have to give the questions considerable thought to figure out answers.

The personality theorist Carl Rogers was particularly interested in cases in which people do have intuitions. He thought that people possess a core, true self that they can experience at a deep, intuitive level. Rogers's reasoning, combined with the cases of *non*intuitive thinking about the self (above), yields an interesting prediction about personality and the brain. If intuitive and nonintuitive thinking about the self differ, then different regions of the brain should be active during intuitive versus nonintuitive thinking about the self.

Brain-imaging methods have addressed this question. One study (Lieberman, Jarcho, & Satpute, 2004) was conducted with two groups of participants: 11 college soccer players and 11 improvisational actors. Members of both groups were shown words relevant either to (1) soccer (e.g., agile, fit) or to (2) acting (e.g., creative, quick-witted); the researchers reasoned that participants would think intuitively only about words relevant to their own group. When each word was presented, participants judged whether the word "describes me". Brain scans were taken while participants performed the task. By analyzing the resulting brain images, the researchers could determine if different parts of the brain are active during intuitive and nonintuitive thinking.

Indeed they are. Unlike what was found when participants were thinking nonintuitively (e.g., soccer players thinking about acting), when people were thinking intuitively about themselves, the active brain regions were ones that were "more affective at their core" (Lieberman et al., 2004, p. 431), that is, more connected to emotional life. These included the amygdala, a brain system central to emotional processing; an area in the temporal lobe (the large mass of brain matter on each side of the brain) that is thought to contribute to the rapid processing of information; and the posterior cingulate cortex, an area in the central, rear (i.e., toward the back of the head) portion of the brain.

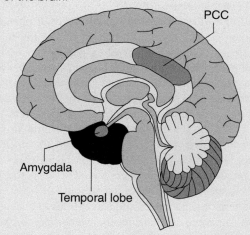

More recent neuroscience findings bear on another distinction drawn by Rogers, namely, the difference between the actual and ideal self. The actual self concerns the self in the present. The ideal self refers to possibilities that lie in the future. Rogers' psychological distinction between present- and future-oriented thinking about the self implies that different brain regions may be active during these different forms of thinking.

To explore this question, in one recent study researchers (D'Argembeau et al., 2010) showed participants a series of adjectives. In two different experimental conditions, participants judged whether the words described (1) their present, actual self, or (2) their future self, specifically, personality attributes they might possess five years from the present. Brain scans revealed different patterns of activation during these tasks. Specifically, an area near the front of the brain, the medial prefrontal cortex, was more active when people thought about their *present* self than their self in the future. The researchers suggest that this region in the prefrontal cortex is particularly active when people think about material to which they are psychologically "connected," and people naturally feel more connected to their present, actual self than to thoughts about themselves five years in the future. Consistent with this interpretation, the medial prefrontal cortex was also less active when

people thought about themselves as they were five years in the past (D'Argembeau et al., 2008, 2010).

Carl Rogers's theory of personality was psychological, not biological. He did not theorize about brain systems that underlie the capacity to think intuitively about the self, and to contemplate the self in the present and future. The results reviewed here thus cannot be viewed as directly supporting Rogers's theory (since, when it comes to the brain, he had no specific theory). Nonetheless, contemporary findings in neuroscience are consistent with Rogers's contention that intuitive, deeply felt conceptions of the self are a distinctive aspect of human mental life.

Measuring Self-Concept

The Q-Sort Technique   Once he recognized the centrality of self-concept, Rogers knew that he needed an objective way to measure it. To this end, he primarily used the **Q-sort technique**, which had been developed by Stephenson (1953).

In the Q-sort, the psychologist administering the test gives the test-taker a set of cards, each of which contains a statement describing a personality characteristic: "Makes friends easily", "Has trouble expressing anger", and so forth. Test-takers sort these cards according to the degree to which each statement is seen as descriptive of themselves. This is done on a scale labeled *Most characteristic of me* on one end and *Least characteristic of me* on the other. People are asked to sort the cards according to a forced distribution, with most of the cards going in the middle and relatively few being sorted at either extreme end; this ensures that the individual carefully considers the content of each personality attribute in comparison to the others.

Two features of the Q-sort are particularly noteworthy. One is that it strikes an interesting balance between fixed and flexible measures (see Chapter 2). The same statements are given to all test-takers; in this respect, the measure is fixed. But the tester does not merely give a person a score by adding up test responses in a fixed manner that is the same for all persons. Instead, the test is flexible in that test-takers indicate which subset of items is most characteristic of themselves, from their own point of view. Different subsets of items are characterized as "most like me" and "not like me" by different individuals. The test, then, yields a more flexible portrait of the individual than is obtained by other measures, whose content is entirely fixed (as you will see in subsequent chapters). Yet it is not entirely flexible. People must use statements provided by the experimenter, instead of their own self-descriptions, and must sort the statements in a manner prescribed by the psychologist rather than according to a distribution that makes the most sense to them.

The second feature is that the Q-sort can be administered to individuals more than once in order to assess both the actual self and the ideal self. In the latter assessment, people are asked to categorize the statements according to the degree to which they describe the self that they ideally would like to be. By comparing the two Q-sorts, ideal and actual self, one can obtain a quantitative measure of the difference, or discrepancy, between the two aspects of self-concept. As you will see in Chapter 6, these discrepancies are important to psychopathology and therapeutic change.

The Semantic Differential   A classic method for assessing self-concept is the semantic differential (Osgood, Suci, & Tannenbaum, 1957). In the semantic differential, the individual rates a concept on a number of seven-point scales defined by polar adjectives such as good–bad, strong–weak, or active–passive. Or example, a person may rate a concept "My Self" or "My Ideal Self" using these scales. A rating on any one scale would indicate whether the subject felt that one of the adjectives was very descriptive of the concept or somewhat descriptive or whether neither adjective was applicable to the concept. The ratings are made in terms of the meaning of the concept for the individual.

Like the Q-sort, the semantic differential incorporates a structure that is valuable for data analysis while also being flexible regarding the exact concepts and scales that are used. There is no single standardized semantic differential. A variety of scales can be used in relation to concepts such as father, mother, and doctor to determine the meanings of phenomena for the individual. For example, consider rating the concepts "My Self" and "My College" on scales such as liberal–conservative, scholarly–fun loving, and formal–informal. To what extent do you see yourself and your college as similar? How does this relate to your satisfaction as a student at this college? Research indicates that students who view themselves as dissimilar from their college environment are more likely to become dissatisfied with college life and to drop out (Pervin, 1967a, 1967b).

A classic illustration of how the semantic differential can be employed involves a case of multiple personality. In the 1950s, two psychiatrists, Corbett Thigpen and Harvey Cleckley, made famous the case of "the three faces of Eve". This was the case of a woman who possessed three personalities, each of which predominated for a period of time, with frequent shifts back and forth. The three personalities were called Eve White, Eve Black, and Jane. As part of a research endeavor, the psychiatrists were able to have each of the three personalities rate a variety of concepts on the semantic differential. The ratings were then analyzed both quantitatively and qualitatively by two psychologists (C. Osgood and Z. Luria) who did not know the subject. Their analysis included both descriptive comments and interpretations of the personalities that went beyond the objective data. For example, Eve White was described as being in contact with social reality but under great emotional stress, Eve Black was described as out of contact with social reality but quite self-assured, and Jane was described as superficially very healthy but quite restricted and undiversified. A more detailed, though still incomplete, description of the three personalities based on the semantic differential ratings is presented in Figure 5.1. The analysis on the basis of these ratings turned out to fit quite well with the descriptions offered by the two psychiatrists (Osgood & Luria, 1954).

Eve White	Perceives the world in an essentially normal fashion, is well socialized, but has an unsatisfactory attitude toward herself. The chief evidence of disturbance in the personality is the fact that ME (the self-concept) is considered a little bad, a little passive, and definitely weak.
Eve Black	Eve Black has achieved a violent kind of adjustment in which she perceives herself as literally perfect, but, to accomplish this break, her way of perceiving the world becomes completely disoriented from the norm. If Eve Black perceives herself as good, then she also has to accept HATRED and FRAUD as positive values.
Jane	Jane displays the most "healthy" meaning pattern, in which she accepts the usual evaluations of concepts by her society yet still maintains a satisfactory evaluation of herself. The self concept, ME, while not strong (but not weak, either) is nearer the good and active directions of the semantic space.

FIGURE 5.1 Brief personality descriptions, based on semantic differential ratings, in a case of multiple personality.
Adapted from Osgood and Luria (1954).

Process

As you have just seen, unlike Freud, Rogers did not present a highly elaborate model of personality structure, with personality divided into a number of parts. He instead presented a simple model that highlighted what he felt was the central structure in personality, namely, the self. A similar intellectual style is seen in his discussion of personality process. Rogers posited a single overarching motivational principle—one that, again, involves the self.

Self-Actualization

Rogers did not think that behavior was primarily determined by animalistic drive states, as did Freud. Rogers felt that, instead, the most fundamental personality process is a forward-looking tendency toward personality growth. He labeled this a tendency toward **self-actualization**. "The organism has one basic tendency and striving—to actualize, maintain, and enhance the experiencing organism" (Rogers, 1951, p. 487). In a poetic passage, Rogers described life as an active process, comparing it to the trunk of a tree on the shore of the ocean as it remains erect, tough, and resilient, maintaining and enhancing itself in the growth process: "Here in this palm-like seaweed was the tenacity of life, the forward thrust of life, the ability to push into an incredibly hostile environment and not only to hold its own, but to adapt, develop, become itself" (Rogers, 1963, p. 2).

CURRENT QUESTIONS

Self-Ideal Congruence: Gender Differences Over Time?

Rogers's notion of the ideal self, and the Q-sort method he espoused, influenced later research on self-concept. For example, Block and Robins (1993) examined change in self-esteem from adolescence into young adulthood. Has your self-esteem changed from your early teens to your early twenties? According to Block and Robins, the answer to this question may depend on your gender: On average, self-esteem increases for males and decreases for females over these formative years of life.

Level of self-esteem was defined as the degree of similarity between the perceived self and the ideal self. Both of these constructs were measured by an adjective Q-sort, which includes such self-descriptive items as "competitive," "affectionate," "responsible," and "creative". Subjects whose perceived self was highly similar to their ideal self were high in self-esteem. In contrast, subjects whose perceived self was highly dissimilar to their ideal self were low in self-esteem.

Between the ages of 14 and 23, males became more self-confident and females became less self-confident. Whereas at age 14 males scored similarly in self-esteem, by age 23 they scored much higher. Apparently, males and females differ in how they experience the adolescent years and how they negotiate the transition into adulthood. For men, the news is good: This phase of life is associated with coming closer to one's ideal. Unfortunately, the opposite is true for women: They move further away from their ideal as they enter adulthood.

What personality attributes characterize men and women with high self-esteem? Block and Robins used extensive interview data collected at age 23 and found that the high self-esteem women valued close relationships with others. High self-esteem men, in contrast, were more emotionally distant and controlled in their relationships with others. These sex differences in relationships reflect the very different expectations society holds for what it means to be a man or a woman. Not surprisingly, those young adults whose personalities fit these cultural expectations well are more likely to feel good about themselves and have a self-concept that is close to their ideal self.

Left unanswered by this study is a phenomenological question that would have been of interest to Rogers: What is the content of the ideal self? Do males and females differ in their perceptions of what constitutes the ideal? The ideal self seems particularly susceptible to external influence—what we perceive as valued in society. The content of the ideal self tells us something about the attributes a person values and thus uses to derive self-esteem. An interesting question for future research is how the content of the ideal self influences psychological adjustment. Does the person's ideal self capture characteristics of a self-actualized human being or society's definition of what constitutes the ideal man or woman?

Rogers proposed that people are motivated toward self-actualization - a motive toward personal growth, independence, and freedom of expression

The concept of actualization refers to an organism's tendency to grow from a simple entity to a complex one, to move from dependence toward independence, from fixity and rigidity to a process of change and freedom of expression. The concept includes the tendency of each person to reduce needs or tension, but it emphasizes the pleasures and satisfactions that are derived from activities that enhance the organism.

Rogers himself never developed a measure of the self-actualizing motive. Over the years, however, others have done so. One such effort involves a 15-item scale that measures the ability to act independently, self-acceptance or self-esteem, acceptance of one's emotional life, and trust in interpersonal relations (Figure 5.2). Scores on this questionnaire measure of self-actualization have been found to be related to other questionnaire measures of self-esteem and health, as well as to independent ratings of individuals as self-actualizing persons (Jones & Crandall, 1986).

Similarly, Ryff (1995; Ryff & Singer, 1998, 2000) has postulated a multifaceted conception of positive mental health that includes self-acceptance, positive relations with others, autonomy, environmental mastery, purpose in life, and personal growth. The personal growth component is conceptually close to Rogers's view of the growth process and self-actualization. Her questionnaire, the Personal Growth Scale, defines someone high on personal growth as someone who has

> It is always necessary that others approve of what I do. (F)
> I am bothered by fears of being inadequate. (F)
> I do not feel ashamed of any of my emotions. (T)
> I believe that people are essentially good and can be trusted. (T)

FIGURE 5.2 Illustrative items from an index of self-actualization.
Adapted from Jones and Crandall (1986).

a feeling of continued development, has a sense of realizing their potential, is open to new experiences, and is changing in ways that reflect more self-knowledge and effectiveness. In addition, there is evidence that people are happiest when they are pursuing goals congruent with the self (Little, 1999; McGregor & Little, 1998).

Self-Consistency and Congruence

The principle of self-actualization, by itself, clearly is not sufficient to account for the dynamics of personality functioning. Much of psychological life consists of conflicts, doubts, and psychological distress, rather than a continual march toward personal actualization. The theoretical challenge for Rogers, then, is to account for a more complete range of personality dynamics within his overall self-based theory of the person. One way Rogers accomplishes this is by positing that people seek self-consistency and a sense of congruence between their sense of self and their everyday experience. According to Rogers, the organism functions to maintain consistency (an absence of conflict) among self-perceptions and to achieve congruence between perceptions of the self and experiences: "Most of the ways of behaving which are adopted by the organism are those which are consistent with the concept of the self" (Rogers, 1951, p. 507).

The concept of **self-consistency** originally was developed by Lecky (1945). According to Lecky, the organism does not seek to gain pleasure and to avoid pain but, instead, seeks to maintain its own self-structure. The individual develops a value system, the center of which is the individual's valuation of the self. Individuals organize their values and functions to preserve the self-system. Individuals behave in ways that are consistent with their self-concept, even if this behavior is otherwise unrewarding to them. If you, for example, see yourself as a poor speller, you may try to behave in a manner consistent with this self-perception.

In addition to self-consistency, Rogers emphasized the importance to personality functioning of **congruence** between the self and experience, that is, between what people feel and how they view themselves. For example, if you view yourself as a kind person who expresses empathy toward others but have an experience in which you think you were cold and unempathic, you confront an **incongruence** between your sense of self and your experience. If you think of yourself as a quiet person but suddenly find yourself acting in a highly outgoing manner (e.g., at a party), you may experience a distressing sense of having acted in a way that is "not me".

States of Incongruence and Defensive Processes

Sometimes, people do experience an incongruence between self and experience that suggests a basic inconsistency in the self. When this occurs, what happens? Rogers posits that anxiety is the result of a discrepancy between experience and the perception of the self. The person who, for example, believes that he or she never hates anyone but suddenly experiences hateful feelings will be anxious after becoming aware of this incongruence. Once this happens, the person will be motivated to defend the self; he or she will engage in defensive processes. In this regard, Rogers's work is similar to Freud's. To Rogers, however, defensive processes are not centered on a defense against recognition of basic biological impulses in the id. They involve defense against a loss of a consistent, integrated sense of self.

To Rogers, then, when we perceive an experience as threatening because it conflicts with our self-concept, we may not allow the experience to be conscious. Through a process called **subception**, we can be aware of an experience that is discrepant with the self-concept before it reaches consciousness. The response to the threat presented by recognition of experiences that are in conflict with the self is that of defense. Thus, we react defensively and attempt to deny awareness to experiences that are dimly perceived to be incongruent with the self-structure.

Two defensive processes are **distortion** of the meaning of experience and **denial** of the existence of the experience. Denial serves to preserve the self-structure from threat by denying it conscious expression. Distortion, a more common phenomenon, allows the experience into awareness but in a form that makes it consistent with the self: "Thus, if the concept of self includes the characteristic 'I am a poor student', the experience of receiving a high grade can be easily distorted to make it congruent with the self by perceiving in it such meanings as, 'That professor is a fool'; 'It was just luck'" (Rogers, 1956, p. 205). What is striking about this last example is the emphasis it places on self-consistency. What is otherwise likely to be a positive experience, receiving a high grade, now becomes a source of anxiety and a stimulus for defensive processes to be set in operation. In other words, it is the relation of the experience to the self-concept that is key.

Research on Self-Consistency and Congruence

The emphasis on self-consistency might lead one to wonder whether it is healthier to see oneself as essentially the same person across situations or to see oneself as quite different in various social roles. In a relevant study, subjects were asked to rate themselves on various personality characteristics in various social roles (e.g., son or daughter, friend, student). Measures of variability (consistency) across the roles then were related to self-reports of psychological well-being. The results indicated that individuals with highly variable role identities were more likely to be anxious, depressed, and low in self-esteem (Donohue, Robins, Roberts, & John, 1993). In other words, in accord with Rogers, high variability in the self-concept can be bad for mental health because it can be indicative of an unintegrated "core" self.

Early research by followers of Rogers confirmed the hypothesis that individuals would be slower to perceive words that were personally threatening than they would be to perceive neutral words (Chodorkoff, 1954). This tendency was particularly characteristic of defensive, poorly adjusted individuals. Poorly adjusted individuals, in particular, attempt to deny awareness to threatening stimuli. Similar processes were found in the area of recall of stimuli that are consistent versus inconsistent with the self. Here, it was found that generally subjects were better able to recall adjectives they felt were descriptive of themselves than they were of adjectives they felt were most unlike themselves. Here too, poorly adjusted individuals, in particular, showed as greater difference in ability to recall adjectives consistent versus inconsistent with the self (Cartwright, 1956). In sum, the accuracy of perception and recall of self-related stimuli appears to be a function of the degree to which the stimuli are consistent with the self-concept.

The studies just discussed relate to perception and recall. What of overt behavior? Aronson and Mettee (1968) found results that were consistent with Rogers's view that individuals behave in ways that are congruent with their self-concepts. In a study of dishonest behavior, they reasoned that if people are tempted to cheat, they will be more likely to do so if their self-esteem is low than if it is high; that is, whereas cheating is not inconsistent with generally low self-esteem, it is inconsistent with generally high self-esteem. The data gathered indeed suggested that whether or not an individual cheats is influenced by the nature of the self-concept. People who have a high opinion of themselves are likely to behave in ways they can respect, whereas people with a low opinion of themselves are likely to behave in ways that are consistent with that self-image.

Other research supports the view that the self-concept influences behavior in varied ways (Markus, 1983). For example, people often behave in ways that lead others to confirm the perception they have of themselves—a self-fulfilling prophecy (Darley & Fazio, 1980; Swann, 1992). People who believe they are likable may behave in ways that lead others to like them, whereas those who believe they are unlikable may behave in ways that lead others to dislike them (Curtis & Miller, 1986). For better or for worse, your self-concept may be maintained by behaviors of others that were influenced in the first place by your own self-concept.

Similarly, people with low self-esteem are so prone to maintain a consistent self-concept that they sometimes fail to take even simple actions that might put them in a better mood.

They seem resigned to maintaining a poor self-image and the experience of negative emotions. Heimpel, Wood, Marshall, and Brown (2002) conducted a series of studies designed to test the hypothesis that people who report having low self-esteem are less motivated to change their negative moods, as compared to high self-esteem persons. In one study, an experimental mood induction was used to put people into a sad mood. Participants then chose a videotape to watch. The choices included a video of a comedy routine—which, as people knew, could put them into a better mood. You might expect that everyone would choose to watch a comedy routine. The large majority of high self-esteem persons do so. But only a minority of low self-esteem persons chose to watch it. Most of the low self-esteem persons, in other words, failed to make a choice that would change their negative mood. Their choice produced consistency—a consistent negative mood even when they could have made themselves feel better. The tendency to maintain consistency in psychological experience, then, may sometimes override a simple hedonistic tendency to feel better.

The Need for Positive Regard

> *Since those years, I have come to believe that in order to thrive, a child must have at least one adult in her life who shows her unconditional love, respect, and confidence.*
>
> *Source:* Supreme Court Justice Sotomayor (2013, p.16).

We have seen, then, that individuals commonly try to act in accordance with their self-concept and that experiences inconsistent with the self-concept are often ignored or denied. But why? Why, in Rogerian theory, would the individual be distressed by a rift between experience and self and, therefore, be in need of defense? Why couldn't people accept all experiences, good and bad, as steps toward self-actualization?

Rogers answered this question by proposing that all persons possess a basic psychological need. It is a **need for positive regard**. The idea is that people need not only the obvious biological facts of life—food, water, shelter, and so on—but also something psychological. They need to be accepted and respected by others, that is, to receive others' positive regard.

Rogers sees the need for positive regard as a powerful force in the workings of personality. Indeed, it is so powerful that it can draw one's attention away from experiences of personal value. "The expression of positive regard by a significant social other can become [so] compelling" that a person becomes more attuned to "the *positive regard* of such others than toward *experiences* which are of positive value in *actualizing* the organism" (Rogers, 1959, 1977, p. 225). People, then, can lose touch with their own true feelings and values in their pursuit of positive regard from others. This is how individuals can develop the feelings of detachment from their true self that we discussed at the outset of this chapter (see the subsection "Feelings of Authenticity"). In pursuing positive regard from others, people may disregard or distort their experiences of their own inner feelings and desires.

This need for positive regard is particularly central to child development. The infant needs the parents' love, affection, and protection. The parents, throughout childhood, provide information on what is good, that is, what is regarded positively. A primary question is whether parents give the child positive regard unconditionally—that is, whether they show that they respect and prize the child no matter what. An alternative possibility is that the parents will show greater respect and love for the child only if the child adheres to some forms of behavior and not others. This alternative Rogers describes as **conditions of worth**; the child is made to feel like a worthy individual only if he/she has some thoughts and feelings but not others.

If the child receives positive regard unconditionally, then there is no need to deny experiences. However, if children experience conditions of worth, then they need to balance their own natural tendencies with their need for positive regard from the parents. The child then may cope by denying an aspect of his or her own experience—essentially denying, or distorting, a feature of his or her true self. For example, suppose a male child shows interest in the arts but the parents discourage this interest, perhaps judging that their child should pursue activities that are more gender stereotypical for males (e.g., sports). To attain the parents' regard, the child then may deny an interest in the arts. In so doing, the parents have created an interpersonal setting that causes the child to deny, and lose touch with, an aspect of his own self.

To summarize, Rogers did not feel a need to use the concepts of motives and drives to account for the activity and goal-directedness of the organism. For him, the person is basically active and self-actualizing. As part of the self-actualizing process, we seek to maintain a congruence between self and experience. However, because of past experiences with conditional positive regard, we may deny or distort experiences that threaten the self-system.

Growth and Development

Early in his career, prior to writing a formal theory of personality, Rogers spent much time working with children. In the city of Rochester, New York, he worked as a clinical psychologist in an office of the Society for the Prevention of Cruelty to Children and then as director of a guidance center that oversaw social agencies that served children in the local community (Kirschenbaum, 1979). Although Rogers did not do formal scientific research on personality development, he did gain much firsthand experience with the development of children and wrote extensively on the psychological treatment of children and youth. These early career experiences are reflected in his later writings, which explore the development of personality from a phenomenological perspective.

To Rogers, development is not confined to the early years of life, as Freud suggested. People grow toward self-actualization throughout the life course, experiencing ever greater complexity, autonomy, socialization, and maturity. The self, after becoming a separate part of the phenomenal field early in life, continues to grow in complexity throughout life. Rogers's work suggested that developmental factors must be considered at two levels of analysis. At the level of parent–child interactions, the question is whether the parents provide an environment that is optimal for psychological growth; to Rogers, this would be an environment that provides unconditional positive regard. At the level of internal psychological structures, the question is whether individuals experience congruence between self and daily experience or, conversely, distort aspects of their experience in order to attain others' regard and a consistent self-concept.

The major developmental concern for Rogers, then, is whether the child is free to grow, to be self-actualizing, or whether conditions of worth cause the child to become defensive and operate out of a state of incongruence. Research associated with attachment theory (Chapter 4) supports the view that a parenting environment that provides for unconditional positive regard is associated with later secure attachment style and the characteristics of a fully functioning, self-actualizing person (Fraley & Shaver, 2008). Healthy development of the self takes place in a climate in which the child can experience fully, can accept him- or herself, and can be accepted by the parents, even if they disapprove of particular types of behavior. This point is emphasized by most child psychiatrists and psychologists. It is the difference between a parent saying to a child "I don't like what you are doing" and saying "I don't like you." In saying "I don't like what you are doing," the parent is accepting the child while not approving of the behavior. This contrasts with situations in which a parent tells a child, verbally or in more subtle ways, that his or her behavior is bad and that he or she is bad. The child then feels that recognition of certain feelings would be inconsistent with the picture of him- or herself as loved or lovable, leading to denial and distortion of these feelings.

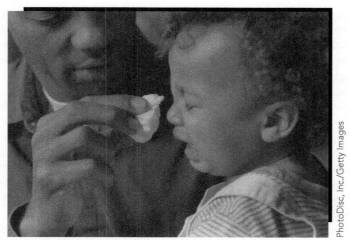

Positive Regard: Healthy personality development is fostered through the communication of unconditional positive regard to the child.

Research on Parent–Child Relationships

A variety of studies suggest that acceptant, democratic parental attitudes facilitate the most growth. Whereas children of parents with these attitudes show accelerated intellectual development, originality, emotional security, and control, the children of rejecting, authoritarian parents are unstable, rebellious, aggressive, and quarrelsome (Baldwin, 1949; Pomerantz & Thompson, 2008). Most critical are children's perceptions of their parents' appraisals. If they feel that these appraisals are positive, they will find pleasure in their bodies and in their selves. If they feel that these appraisals are negative, they will develop insecurity and negative appraisals of their bodies (Jourard & Remy, 1955). Apparently, the kinds of appraisals that parents make of their children largely reflect the parents' own degree of self-acceptance. Mothers who are self-accepting also tend to accept their children (Medinnus & Curtis, 1963).

A classic study of the origins of **self-esteem** by Coopersmith (1967) further supported the importance of the dimensions suggested by Rogers. Coopersmith defined self-esteem as the evaluation an individual typically makes with regard to the self. Self-esteem, then, is an enduring personal judgment of worthiness, not a momentary good or bad feeling resulting from a particular situation. Children in the study completed a simple self-report measure of self-esteem, with most items coming from scales previously used by Rogers. Some findings involved the relation of self-esteem to other personality characteristics. For example, compared to children low in self-esteem, those high in self-esteem were found to be more assertive, independent, and creative in solving problems.

A more important aspect of Coopersmith's study is that it provided evidence on the critical question, What are the origins of self-esteem? Coopersmith obtained not only child self-esteem scores, but information about the children's perceptions of their parents and information about parental child-rearing attitudes, practices, and lifestyles (obtained via interviews with mothers). Interestingly, indicators of social prestige that one might think would be influential—such as wealth, degree of education, job title—were *not* strongly related to children's self-esteem scores. Instead, children's self-esteem was related more strongly to interpersonal conditions in the home and the immediate environment. Children appeared to develop self-views through a process of reflected appraisal in which they used opinions of themselves that were expressed by others as a basis for their own self-judgments.

What specific parental attitudes and behaviors were important to the formation of self-esteem? Three were shown to be particularly influential. The first was the degree of acceptance, interest, affection, and warmth expressed by parents toward the child. Mothers who were more loving and developed closer relationships with their children had children with higher self-esteem. Children appeared to interpret the mother's interest as signifying that they were worthy persons deserving of others' attention and affection. The second important feature of parent–child interaction involved permissiveness and punishment. Parents of children with high self-esteem established, and firmly enforced, clear demands for appropriate behavior. They generally tried to affect behavior by using rewards. In contrast, the parents of low self-esteem children did not establish clear guidelines for behavior, were harsh and disrespectful toward children, tended to use punishment rather than reward, and stressed force and loss of love. The third feature was whether parent–child relations were democratic or dictatorial. Parents of children with high self-esteem had established and enforced extensive rules for conduct, yet, in so doing, they treated children fairly within these defined limits and recognized the rights and opinions of the child. Parents of children low in self-esteem set few and poorly defined limits and were autocratic, dictatorial, rejecting, and uncompromising in their methods of control.

Coopersmith summarized his findings as follows: "The most general statement about the origins of self-esteem can be given in terms of three conditions: total or nearly total acceptance of the children by their parents, clearly defined and enforced limits, and the respect and latitude for individual actions that exist within the defined limits" (1967, p. 236). Coopersmith further suggested that the important factor is the children's *perception of* the parents, not necessarily the specific actions the parents display. The total family climate influences the child's perception of the parents and their motives.

Another study further supports Rogers's contention that child-rearing conditions that provide children with psychological safety and psychological freedom will foster children's creative potential (Harrington, Block, & Block, 1987). Conditions of psychological safety are provided by parental expressions of unconditional positive regard for the child and empathic understanding. Psychological freedom is expressed in permission to engage in unrestrained expression of ideas. In a test of this view, child-rearing practices and parent–child interaction patterns were measured for children between the ages of three and five years (Figure 5.3). Remarkably, the researchers were able to obtain independent ratings (that is, ratings not made by the parent) of creative potential in the children not during early childhood but years later, in adolescence. They found a significant positive association between childhood (preschool) environmental conditions of psychological safety and freedom and creative potential assessed both in preschool and, years later, in adolescence. The degree to which parent–child interactions were "Rogerian", then, appeared to be an important environmental factor contributing to personality development. Finally, recent evidence of the influence of child reading on self-esteem comes from an exceptionally large-scale research project (Orth, 2018). The participants were a nationally representative (U.S.) sample of more than 8,000 people. They were studied longitudinally; specifically, beginning in 1979, they were studied as they grew from age 8 to age 27. Throughout this period, the researcher obtained measures not only of individuals' self-esteem, but also of the child-rearing environments that they experienced. These methods enabled the researcher to relate child-rearing practices to self-esteem development convincingly. The results? Environmental influences did, in fact, affect self-esteem. Specifically, children who grew up in a physically safe environment and whose parents were highly affectionate, interpersonally responsive, and not overly harsh and restrictive – in other words, who were "Rogerian" – developed high levels of self-esteem. Remarkably, good parenting affected self-esteem not only during the childhood and teenage years; the effects were evident even into adulthood. Other factors, such as maternal depression and the presence of the father in the home, also influenced self-esteem; however, these factors exerted their influence partly by affecting the quality of parenting that children experienced in the home (Orth, 2018).

Creativity-Fostering Environment

Parents respect the child's opinions and encourage expression of them.

Parents and child have warm, intimate time together.

Children are allowed to spend time with other children or families who have different ideas or values.

Parents are encouraging and supportive of the child.

Parents encourage the child to proceed independently.

The Creativity Personality

Tends to be proud of accomplishments.

Is resourceful in initiating activities; becomes strongly involved in activities.

Has a wide range of interests.

Is comfortable with uncertainties and complexities.

Perseveres in the face of adversity.

FIGURE 5.3 Illustrative characteristics of creativity-fostering environments and the creative personality. Adapted from Harrington, Block, & Block, 1987.

Despite such findings, some psychologists question whether the concept of self-esteem is sufficient for a science of personality. Critics generally think the term is too global. Most people experience times in their lives when they think well of themselves and others in which they are self-critical, and the self-esteem construct masks these cross-situational variations. Nonetheless, others feel that the concept of global self-esteem has merit and that self-esteem has implications for many aspects of psychological functioning (Dutton & Brown, 1997). This present chapter is devoted primarily to presentation of Rogers's theory. In our next chapter, we turn in more detail to contemporary research that bears on these questions about self-esteem processes and about the utility of the construct of self-esteem for personality science.

Social Relations, Self-Actualization, and Well-Being Later in Life

According to Rogerian theory, the relation between social acceptance and positive self-regard is important not only to child development but also to personality functioning throughout life. Research bears on this hypothesis.

Roberts and Chapman (2000) analyzed data from a long-term longitudinal study of the psychological development of adult women. In this data set, women were studied over a 30-year period extending from young adulthood into midlife. Although the study was not organized according to the personality theory of Carl Rogers, it did contain two measures that bear on Rogerian hypotheses. One was an index of psychological well-being; participants indicated their sense of well-being, including feelings of self-esteem, at four time points across the 30-year time period of the study. The second was an index of role quality, that is, whether people experienced supportive social relations in life roles including both marriage and work. Rogerian theory of course would predict that positive, supportive social relations would increase psychological well-being. The supportive relations should provide people with a sense of positive regard and make them less likely to engage in defensive processing that might contribute to psychological distress and a lower sense of self.

A key feature of this longitudinal research is that, by studying people at different points in their lives, the researchers could examine the impact of role quality on changes in well-being. These analyses generally were in accord with predictions that one would make from Rogerian theory. People who experienced a high degree of distress in their marriage and work roles experienced lower levels of well-being, whereas people who experienced more satisfying social roles showed positive changes in their well-being and personal maturity (Roberts & Chapman, 2000).

Although it is difficult to establish causality in this type of research (i.e., to determine whether social relations actually exerted a causal influence on well-being), the results are consistent with the Rogerian hypothesis that views of self and psychological well-being can change across the course of life and that the degree of positive regard one receives from significant individuals in one's life can contribute directly to these changes.

As you can see, Rogers's ideas continue to be of relevance to the contemporary field. In our next chapter, we look more closely at contemporary research that bears on Rogers's theorizing while also considering clinical applications of his principles and alternative theoretical conceptions that relate strongly to Rogers's phenomenological perspective.

MAJOR CONCEPTS

Conditions of worth	Ideal self	Phenomenology	Self-consistency
Congruence	Incongruence	Q-sort technique	Self-esteem
Denial	Need for positive regard	Self-actualization	Subception
Distortion	Phenomenal field	Self-concept (or the "Self")	

REVIEW

1. The phenomenological approach emphasizes an understanding of how people experience themselves and the world around them. The person-centered theory of Carl Rogers is illustrative of this approach.

2. Throughout his life, Rogers attempted to integrate the intuitive with the objective, combining a sensitivity to the nuances of experience with an appreciation for the rigors of science.

3. Rogers emphasized the positive, self-actualizing qualities of the person. In his research, he emphasized a disciplined effort to understand subjective experience, or the phenomenal field, of the person.

4. The key structural concept for Rogers was the self—the organization of perceptions and experiences associated with the "self," "me," or "I." Also important is the concept of the ideal self, or the self-concept the person would most like to possess. The Q-sort is one method used to study these concepts and the relation between them.

5. Rogers deemphasized the tension-reducing aspects of behavior and, instead, emphasized self-actualization as the central human motive. Self-actualization involves continuous openness

to experience and the ability to integrate experiences into an expanded, more differentiated sense of self.

6. Rogers also suggested that people function to perceive self-consistency and to maintain congruence between perceptions of the self and experience. However, experiences perceived as threatening to the self-concept may, through defensive processes such as distortion and denial, be prevented from reaching consciousness. A variety of studies support the view that people will behave in ways to maintain and confirm the perception they have of themselves.

7. People have a need for positive regard. Under conditions of unconditional positive regard, children and adults are able to grow within a state of congruence and be self-actualizing. On the other hand, where positive regard is conditional, people may screen experiences out of awareness and limit their potential for self-actualization.

8. Children are influenced in their self-judgments through the process of reflected appraisal. Parents of children with high self-esteem are warm and accepting but also are clear and consistent in their enforcement of demands and standards.

Rogers's Phenomenological Theory: Applications, Related Theoretical Conceptions, and Contemporary Research

6

Chapter Focus

A good friendship has qualities that are both wonderful and mysterious. If you're stressed out, if life is giving you too much to handle, talking to a friend—simply discussing your problems and having the person listen carefully—can make you feel better. It's hard to know why. Even if your friend doesn't have any specific advice, even if he or she doesn't offer any solutions to life's problems, the mere fact that the person is there for you, ready to listen, can make things feel better.

And what does your friend make you feel better about? School? Relationships? Maybe. But if you're lucky, your friend makes you feel better about that most important of things: you. By letting you explore and express your feelings, your friend somehow improves your sense of self. You end up accepting your limitations and appreciating your strengths.

Providing this type of relationship, and accomplishing this sort of change in self-concept, was Carl Rogers's goal in his client-centered therapy. His therapeutic approach, which was a foundation on which he built his theory of personality (Chapter 5), is one focus of this chapter. As you will learn, in therapy, Rogers tried to discover how his clients denied and distorted aspects of their everyday experience. He then created a therapeutic relationship—a kind of trusting friendship in a therapeutic setting—within which clients could abandon these distortions, explore their true self, and thereby experience personal growth.

In addition to learning about this clinical application of Rogers's theory of personality, a second goal of this chapter is to review theoretical conceptions that are closely related to that of Rogers. We consider three conceptions that address aspects of Rogers's thinking, namely, the: (1) the human potential movement; (2) the positive psychology movement; and (3) existentialism, a school of thought in philosophy. We also review, in detail, a comprehensive contemporary development in personality theory that addresses Rogers's concern with the integrative self: Personality Systems Interaction Theory.

Finally, this chapter devotes greater attention to questions of culture than did Chapter 5. As you will see, some cross-cultural studies question whether the psychological dynamics studied by Rogers in the United States are a universal feature of human psychological experience.

Questions to be Addressed in this Chapter

1. According to Rogers, how do psychological distress and pathology develop, and what factors are necessary to bring about psychological change in therapy?

2. How did writers in the human potential movement add to Rogers's understanding of human personality?

3. What does the contemporary positive psychology movement say about human personality and potentials?

4. What is existentialism, how do existentialist ideas relate to personality theory and research, and how do they relate, specifically, to Rogers's work?

5. What are the implications of contemporary research—including cross-cultural research on self-concept, motivation, and personality—for Rogers's phenomenological theory?

Clinical Applications

We begin this chapter where Rogers began his own professional career: in the psychological clinic, facing the challenges of psychopathology and personality change. These clinical applications were integral to Rogers's development of his personality theory and remained a major focus of Rogers's work throughout his career.

Rogers's work in therapy involved more than just a set of techniques; it included a worldview—that is, a broad perspective on the nature of the therapeutic setting. Rogers's thinking can be understood by contrasting it to Freud's. Freud, trained as a physician, treated his clients as patients. The client was a person with problems that had to be diagnosed and cured. The therapist was the person with diagnostic and curative expertise. Rogers, in contrast, emphasized the expertise and curative power of the client. In developing his therapeutic approach, "a person seeking help was not treated as a dependent patient but rather as a responsible client" (Rogers, 1977, p. 5). To Rogers, the client possesses an inherent drive toward psychological health. The therapist's task is merely to help the client to identify conditions that may interfere with personal growth, thereby allowing the person to overcome these obstacles and to move toward self-actualization.

Psychopathology

Self-Experience Discrepancy

Before we consider Rogers's approach to treating psychological distress, we should address a logically prior question: From where does psychological distress come? If people have such a strong capacity for self-actualization, then why are they experiencing psychological distress in the first place? The core elements of Rogers's answer to this question were introduced in the previous chapter. They involve the self and whether the person experiences a congruence between self and experience.

To Rogers, healthy persons are individuals who can assimilate experiences into their self-structure. They are open to experiencing rather than interpreting events in a defensive manner. It is such persons who experience a **congruence** between self and experience.

In contrast, the neurotic person's self-concept has become structured in ways that do not fit organismic experience. They deny awareness of significant sensory and emotional experiences. Experiences that are incongruent with the self-structure are subceived; that is, threatening events are detected below levels of conscious awareness and then are either denied or distorted. This distortion results in a discrepancy between actual psychological experiences and the self's awareness of experience, or a **self-experience discrepancy**. Such discrepancies involve a rigid defense of the self against experiences that might threaten the self-concept. Rogers (1961) gives the immediately recognizable example of "the intellectualizing person who talks about himself and his feelings in abstractions, leaving you wondering what is *actually* going on within him" (p. 64). Rogers's point, of course, is that you, the observer, are not the only person who is unaware of what is actually going on within. By distorting his experiences, the person has lost an accurate sense of his or her true self.

Consistent with his rejection of a medical model, Rogers did not differentiate among types of pathology. He did not want a diagnostic scheme within which individual persons were classified and then treated merely as examples of one versus another type of psychological disorder. He did, however, differentiate among forms of defensive behaviors. For example, one such defensive behavior is *rationalization*. In rationalization, a person distorts behavior in such a way as to make it consistent with the self. If you view yourself as a person who never makes mistakes and then a mistake seems to occur, you may rationalize it by blaming the error on another person. Another defensive behavior is *fantasy*. A man who defensively believes himself to be an adequate person may fantasize that he is a prince and that all women adore him, and he may deny any experiences that are inconsistent with this image. A third example of defense behavior is *projection*. Here, an individual expresses a need but in such a form that the need is denied to awareness and the behavior is viewed as consistent with the self. People whose self-concept involves no "bad" sexual thoughts may feel that others are making them have these thoughts.

The descriptions of these defensive behaviors are quite similar to the ones given by Freud. For Rogers, however, the important aspect of these behaviors is their handling of an incongruence between self and experience by denial in awareness or distortion of perception: "It should be noted that perceptions are excluded because they are contradictory, not because they are derogatory" (Rogers, 1951, p. 506). Furthermore, classification of the defenses is not as critical to Rogerian theory as it is to Freudian theory.

Psychological Change

In the preceding chapter, you learned about Rogers's most important contribution to personality science: his theory of personality. This theory, however, was not Rogers's own highest priority. His main professional focus was the process of psychotherapy. Rogers committed himself to understanding how personality *change* can come about. Thus, the process of change, or of becoming, was his greatest concern. His most enduring contribution to understanding change was work in which he outlined necessary conditions of therapy; he described, in other words, types of circumstances and events that need to occur in the relationship between client and therapist in order for personality change to occur. To many people, this therapeutic approach remains as vibrant and relevant today as it was when Rogers first formulated it a half-century ago (McMillan, 2004).

Therapeutic Conditions Necessary for Change

In his early work, Rogers emphasized the therapeutic technique of *reflection*. In this nondirective approach, therapists do not guide the flow of events in therapy. Instead, they merely summarize, or reflect back to, the client their understanding of what the client has just said. Reflection, though simple, is effective. It conveys to the client a feeling of having been thoroughly, deeply understood by the therapist.

Jose Luis Pelaez Inc / Getty Images

Rogerian therapists are attentive to their clients. By showing that they understand their client's feelings and support the client unconditionally, the Rogerian therapist provides a setting in which the client can experience personal growth.

Because some nondirective counselors were perceived as passive and uninterested, Rogers changed his focus to emphasize client-centeredness. In his **client-centered therapy**, the therapist not only uses the technique of reflection but also plays a more active role in understanding the experiences of the client. Ultimately, Rogers believed that the critical variable in client-centered therapy is the nature of the interpersonal encounter that develops between the therapist and client, or what is referred to as the therapeutic climate (Rogers, 1966). Rogers described the ideal therapeutic climate in terms of a set of conditions, three of which are core conditions that he saw as necessary for therapeutic change to occur (McMillan, 2004). If therapists provide these conditions in a way that is phenomenologically meaningful to the clients, then therapeutic change should occur.

Rogers hypothesized three conditions as critical to the therapeutic movement: congruence (or "genuineness"), unconditional positive regard, and empathic understanding.

The first of the three conditions is **congruence** or genuineness. Congruent or genuine therapists display to clients their true thoughts and feelings. The congruent therapist does not present a scientific or medical façade but instead is interpersonally open and transparent. He or she experiences events in the therapeutic encounter in a natural manner and shares with the client his or her genuine feelings—even when feelings toward the client are negative. "Even with such negative attitudes, which seem so potentially damaging but which all therapists have from time to time, I am suggesting that it is preferable for the therapist to be real than to put on a false posture of interest, concern, and liking that the client is likely to sense as false" (Rogers, 1966, p. 188). The client thus experiences a real interpersonal relationship with the therapist rather than the stilted, formal relationship that one might usually experience with a health care or mental health-care provider.

The second condition essential for therapeutic movement is **unconditional positive regard**. This means that the therapist communicates a deep and genuine caring for the client as a person. The client is prized in a total, unconditional way. The experience of respect and unconditional positive regard enables clients to explore their inner self with confidence.

Finally, the third therapeutic condition is **empathic understanding**. This refers to the therapist's ability to perceive the client's experiences as they are experienced by the client. The therapist strives to achieve empathy with the client during the moment-to-moment encounter of psychotherapy. The therapist, then, does not intellectually detach himself or herself from the encounter in order to provide a technical diagnosis of the client's problems. Nor does the client receive a reformulation of his or her life in technical psychological jargon. Instead, through active listening, the therapist strives to understand the meaning and subjective feeling of the events experienced by the client and to make it clear to the client that he or she is in fact being understood empathically by the therapist.

In Rogers's view, these three therapeutic conditions are of fundamental importance, independent of the theoretical orientation of the therapist. The theory behind client-centered therapy thus has an "if–then" quality: If certain therapeutic conditions exist, then processes inherently will occur that lead to personality change.

Outcomes of Client-Centered Therapy

What the hell is wrong with me?
I'm not who I want to be.

Source: The Clash.

Having presented the core elements of Rogers's therapeutic approach, we now ask, Does it work? Does client-centered therapy benefit the client?

To determine whether a therapy works, one must first determine what it means, in principle, for a therapy to "work." What is the core aspect of psychological distress that should be relieved by therapy? Rogers's answer to this question is the one suggested—in more blunt terms than Rogers's—by the British punk rock band The Clash. Deep psychological distress does not arise merely from objective events in the world. It results from an internal sense of personal inadequacy, from a sense that one is not "who I want to be"—or, in Rogerian terms, from a lack of congruence between one's actual self and ideal self. For therapy to "work," then, the client should achieve greater actual–ideal self-congruence.

Having said that, the research challenge is to devise scientifically objective and reliable methods of testing the hypothesis that one's therapy improves this core aspect of personality, the self-concept. Rogers contributed greatly to the development of research methods for meeting this challenge. He was part of a movement important to the profession of psychology, namely, the process of opening up the field of psychotherapy for systematic investigation. Rogers's main goal was to evaluate therapy through methods that were objective. He recognized that a big limitation in the methods of evaluating therapy provided by Freud and his followers was that their methods were too subjective. In psychoanalytic therapy, the only way for an outsider (i.e., someone other than the therapist and client) to evaluate the success of therapy was to read a case study written by the therapist. The problem here should be obvious to you. The case study may be biased. The therapist—the psychoanalyst whose professional success is supposed to be evaluated—is writing the case study that is the basis of the evaluation. In principle, the therapist might unwittingly overestimate the degree of beneficial therapeutic change that occurred when writing his or her case report. In his client-centered therapy, then, Rogers wanted a means of evaluating therapeutic success that was superior to the subjective reports of a therapist.

Rogers took a number of steps designed to allow the scientific community and the public at large to evaluate his therapeutic efforts. He allowed himself and his colleagues to be taped, and sometimes even filmed, while engaging in therapy. He and his colleagues employed objective measures of self-concept, such as the Q-sort (Chapter 5), so that therapy outcomes could be evaluated objectively. Such steps may seem obvious in retrospect—yet they were not taken by psychoanalysts.

A classic study that illustrates the efforts of Rogers and his students to meet the challenge of evaluating Rogerian therapy through objective procedures was conducted by Butler and Haigh (1954), two of Rogers's students. First consider their research hypothesis at a conceptual level: It was that Rogerian therapy would bring about, in clients, a greater congruence between the ideal and actual self. Now consider the challenge of moving from the abstract conceptual level to the concrete level of actually doing research. How would you test this idea about relations among different aspects of a person's self-concept? This is the hard part of personality psychology—moving smoothly and convincingly from the theoretical formulation to the research details. Butler and Haigh made this move by using the Q-sort. Specifically, they used it twice. They asked research participants to complete one Q-sort procedure in which they rated their actual self (i.e., participants sorted items according to how they currently see themselves) and a second one in which participants rated their ideal self (i.e., they sorted items according to whether the attributes described features they ideally would like to possess). With two measures, it is possible to compute a correlation, for any given person, between the actual and ideal self Q-sortings. This correlation is, then, a numerical index of the degree of congruence between the actual and ideal self; a higher positive correlation indicates a greater congruence between the actual and ideal self.

With this index of actual–ideal self congruence in hand, then, Butler and Haigh (1954) looked at the effects of Rogerian therapy. They examined a group of people both before and after the individuals experienced an average of 31 sessions of Rogerian therapy. What did they find? Before therapy, the relation between people's actual and ideal self was quite low: The average correlation was zero. But after therapy, the congruence between these two aspects of self increased significantly. The average post-therapy correlation between the actual and ideal self Q-sorts was +.34. Rogers's therapy worked, as evaluated by an objective measurement procedure, the Q-sort.

Having read that conclusion, you might ask yourself at least two other questions. First, were the effects of therapy long lasting? Fortunately, Butler and Haigh (1954) tested for this by conducting a follow-up measurement six months after therapy ended. At the time of follow-up, the actual–ideal correlation remained about the same, .31. This suggests that therapeutic changes indeed do last. A second question is, Are psychologically distressed people who experience therapy as well off, after therapy, as people who were never distressed in the first place? This question does not have quite as happy an answer. Butler and Haigh (1954) also asked a group of persons who were not seeking counseling to complete the Q-sort measures, and in this group the ideal–actual self correlation was .58; this group, in other words, displayed considerably higher congruence between the actual and ideal self than did the therapy group after counseling. Nonetheless, Rogerian therapy was shown to produce significant gains.

In the years since the pioneering work of Butler and Haigh (1954), much work has evaluated the popularity and effectiveness of Rogerian therapy. A recent appraisal of the status of client-centered therapy indicates that the approach flourished not only during Rogers's lifetime but also after his death. Therapeutic applications and scientific evaluations of the effectiveness of Rogerian therapy frequently were conducted in both the United States and Europe (Kirschenbaum & Jourdan, 2005). A clear majority of studies indicates that a combination of the three conditions identified by Rogers in fact do foster therapeutic change. Therapy changes include a decrease in defensiveness and an increase in openness to experience among clients, the development of a more positive and more congruent self, the promotion of more positive feelings toward others, and a shift away from using the values of others to asserting one's own evaluations. These results underscore the conclusion that Rogers's identification of conditions that foster success in psychotherapy is one of his most enduring contributions to psychology.

Presence

Rogers's view of the conditions necessary for therapeutic improvement changed relatively little over the years after he first formulated them. However, one addition is noteworthy. It is the notion of presence (see Bozarth, 1992; McMillan, 2004). Rogers gradually came to believe that "perhaps I have stressed too much the three basic conditions (congruence, unconditional positive regard, and empathic understanding)" (quoted in Bozarth, 1992) and that, in addition to these three relative objective features of the therapeutic setting, another feature was more elusive, difficult to describe, almost mystical, yet of much importance. "When I am intensely focused on a client," Rogers came to believe, "just my presence seems to be healing" (quoted in Bozarth, 1992). Rogers became aware that, in particularly successful therapeutic encounters, he himself experienced his own core self in interaction with his clients and responded to them in a deeply intuitive way that they sometimes were able to share with him. "I may behave in strange and impulsive ways in the relationship, ways which I cannot justify rationally . . . but these strange behaviors turn out to be *right* . . . my inner spirit has reached out and touched the inner spirit of the other" (Rogers, quoted in McMillan, 2004). To the client-centered therapist, these deeply intuitive, almost spiritual

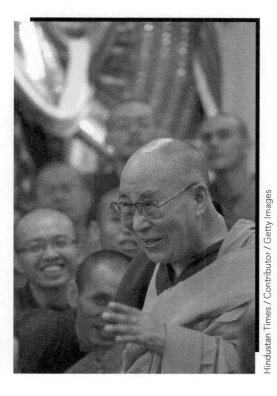

The Dalai Lama, spiritual leader of Tibet. The Dalai Lama's consistently empathic focus in interpersonal interaction creates a powerful psychological climate that contributes to his being called Kundun, which in Tibetan means "presence" (or "The Presence")—precisely the term that Rogers eventually came to use to capture the psychological effects of empathic focus that he observed occurring in his client-centered therapy.

Hindustan Times / Contributor / Getty Images

A Case Example ‖ Mrs. Oak

Statistical summaries of the overall effectiveness of Rogers's therapy, such as those cited, are critical to evaluating the effectiveness of Rogers's therapy. Yet, they fail to capture its spirit. The experience of a therapeutic encounter with Rogers is much better conveyed by a case study. Let us consider, then, one of Rogers's well-known cases, that of Mrs. Oak. This case is available to us because, as part of his process of opening up clinical psychology for objective investigation, Rogers (with this client's permission, of course) taped therapy sessions and made transcripts available to the public.

As Rogers described in a 1954 book, Mrs. Oak was a housewife in her late thirties when she came to the University of Chicago Counseling Center. She reported having great difficulty in her relationships with her husband and her adolescent daughter. Mrs. Oak blamed herself for her daughter's psychosomatic illness. Mrs. Oak was described by her therapist as a sensitive person who was eager to be honest with herself and deal with her problems. She had little formal education but was intelligent and had read widely. Mrs. Oak was interviewed 40 times over a period of five-and-one-half months, at which point she terminated treatment.

In early interviews, Mrs. Oak spent much of her time talking about specific problems she had with her daughter and her husband. Gradually, though, the conversation shifted. She increasingly talked about her feelings. At first, the therapist thought Mrs. Oak was a shy, almost nondescript person. He quickly sensed, however, that she was a sensitive and interesting person. His respect for her grew, and he described himself as experiencing a sense of respect for—and awe of—her capacity to struggle ahead through turmoil and pain. He did not try to direct or guide her; instead, he found satisfaction in trying to understand her, in trying to appreciate her world, in expressing the acceptance he felt toward her.

Given the supportive therapeutic climate, Mrs. Oak began to become aware of feelings she had previously denied to awareness. In the 24th interview, she became aware of conflicts with her daughter that related to her own adolescent development. She felt a sense of shock at becoming aware of her own competitiveness. In a later interview, she became aware of the deep sense of hurt inside of her. The therapist gently and supportively reflected back to Mrs. Oak her past efforts to cover up her hurt and her new efforts to absorb this hurt, describing it as a new discovery of the poem that was her self.

At first, this increased awareness led to a sense of disorganization. Mrs. Oak began to feel more troubled and neurotic, as if she were going to pieces. She also felt resentful that her therapist was not being very helpful and would not take responsibility for the sessions. She felt very strongly at times that the therapist didn't "add a damn thing." But in the course of therapy, she eventually developed exactly what Rogers was striving for in his client-centered approach: a sense of relationship with the therapist that, she came to recognize, was the basis of her therapeutic improvement. Although progress did not occur in all areas, by the end of therapy Mrs. Oak exhibited significant gains in many areas. She began to feel free to be her self, to listen to herself, and to make independent evaluations. She began to accept herself as a worthwhile human being. She decided that she could not continue in her marriage, arrived at a mutually agreeable divorce with her husband, and obtained and held a challenging job. Through the conditions created within the therapeutic environment, Mrs. Oak was able to break down defenses that had been maintaining a marked incongruence between her self and her experience. With this increase in self-awareness, she was able to make positive changes in her life and become a more self-actualized human being.

---

encounters can be highly transformative. Interpersonal experiences between client and therapist that seem "beyond words and logic" (McMillan, 2004, p. 65) are thought to foster deep psychological change.

The notion of presence, and its potential therapeutic benefits, has received little scientific attention. Yet, the concept of presence, as used by Rogerians, is recognized in other intellectual circles and other cultures, which suggests that it may have a reality that is deserving of scientific study. For example, Tibetans refer to their social and political leader, the Dalai Lama, as *Kundun*, which, in Tibetan, literally means "presence" (or "The Presence"). They use the term to refer to the same psychological qualities recognized by Rogers: the powerful feeling of interpersonal connection created by the exceptional awareness and emotional openness of their spiritual leader.

The Case of Jim

Semantic Differential: Phenomenological Theory

Jim completed ratings of the concepts self, ideal self, father, and mother using the semantic differential (Chapter 5), a simple rating scale. Although the semantic differential is not the exact measure recommended by Rogers, its results can be related to Rogerian theory since its procedures have a phenomenological quality and assess perceptions of self and ideal self.

First, consider how Jim perceives his self. Based on the semantic differential, Jim sees himself as intelligent, friendly, sincere, kind, and basically good—as a wise person who is humane and interested in people. At the same time, other ratings suggest that he does not feel free to be expressive and uninhibited. Thus, he rates himself as reserved, introverted, inhibited, tense, moral, and conforming. There is a curious mixture of perceptions: being involved, deep, sensitive, and kind while also being competitive, selfish, and disapproving. There is also the interesting combination of perceiving himself as being good and masculine but simultaneously weak and insecure. One gets the impression of an individual who would like to believe that he is basically good and capable of genuine interpersonal relationships at the same time that he is bothered by serious inhibitions and high standards for himself and others.

This impression comes into sharper focus when we consider the self-ratings in relation to those for the ideal self. In general, Jim did not see an extremely large gap between his self and his ideal self. However, large gaps did occur on a number of specific scale items. For example, Jim rated his actual self as low on a weak–strong scale and his ideal self as high on the same scale; in other words, Jim would like to be much stronger than he feels he is. Assessing his ratings on the other scales in a similar way, we find that Jim would like to be more of each of the following than he currently perceives himself to be: warm, active, egalitarian, flexible, lustful, approving, industrious, relaxed, friendly, and bold. Basically, two themes appear. One has to do with warmth: Jim is not as warm, relaxed, and friendly as he would like to be. The other theme has to do with strength: Jim is not as strong, active, and industrious as he would like to be.

Jim's ratings of his parents give some indication of where he sees them in relation to himself in general and to these qualities in particular. First, if we compare the way Jim perceives his self with his perception of his mother and father, he clearly perceives himself to be much more like his father than his mother. Also, he perceives his father to be closer to his ideal self than his mother, although he perceives himself to be closer to his ideal self than either his mother or his father. However, in the critical areas of warmth and strength, the parents tend to be closer to the ideal self than Jim is. Thus, his mother is perceived to be warmer, more approving, more relaxed, and friendlier than Jim, while his father is perceived to be stronger, more industrious, and more active than Jim. The mother is perceived as having an interesting combination of personality characteristics. On the one hand, she is perceived as affectionate, friendly, spontaneous, sensitive, and good. On the other, she is perceived as authoritarian, superficial, selfish, unintelligent, intolerant, and uncreative.

Comments on the Data

Compared to the earlier data, involving the Rorschach (Chapter 4), we begin here to get another picture of Jim. We learn of his popularity and success through high school and of his good relationship with his father. We find support for the suggestions from the projective tests of anxiety and difficulties with women. Indeed, we learn of Jim's fears of ejaculating too quickly and not being able to satisfy women. However, we also find an individual who believes himself to be basically good and interested in doing humane things. We become aware of an individual who has a view of his self and a view of his ideal self, and of an individual who is frustrated because of the feelings that leave a gap between the two.

Given the opportunity to talk about himself and what he would like to be, Jim talks about his desire to be warmer, more relaxed, and stronger. We feel no need here to disguise our purposes, for we are interested in Jim's perceptions, meanings, and experiences as he reports them. We are interested in what is real for Jim—in how he interprets phenomena within his own frame of reference. We want to know all about Jim, but all about Jim as he perceives himself and the world about him. When using the data from the semantic differential, we are not tempted to focus on drives, and we do not need to come to grips with the world of the irrational. In Rogers's terms, we see an individual who is struggling to move toward self-actualization, from dependence toward independence, from fixity and rigidity to freedom and spontaneity. We find an individual who has a gap between his intellectual and emotional estimates of himself. As Rogers would put it, we observe an individual who is without self-consistency, who lacks a sense of congruence between self and experience.

Related Conceptions: Human Potential, Positive Psychology, and Existentialism

You now have seen the fundamentals of Rogers's phenomenological theory of personality. The remainder of this chapter presents two related topics. First, we consider theoretical conceptions that are related to Rogers's work. Specifically, we will consider three of them: (1) the human potential movement, (2) the positive psychology movement, and (3) existentialism. Next, we present contemporary research that bears on Rogerian theory. This research often is conducted by people who may not call themselves "Rogerians," yet their work addresses topics that are at the heart of Rogers's conception of human nature.

The Human Potential Movement

Rogers is not the only theorist to have emphasized people's capacity for self-actualization. Others recognized that personality functioning involves more than a mere repetition of past motives and conflicts, as suggested by Freud. Instead people have potentialities; that is, a basic feature of personality functioning is that people have a capacity to move forward to realize their inherent potentials. This theme was developed in the middle of the 20th century by writers such as Gardner Murphy (1958), who placed the study of potentialities at the center of personality psychology, and Kurt Goldstein, who felt that, despite its merits, Freudian theory "fails to do justice to the positive aspect of life . . . to recognize that the basic phenomenon of life is an incessant process of coming to terms with the environment" (1939, p. 333). Such theoretical contributions to the **human potential movement** came to be known as a "third force" in psychology (Goble, 1970) because they offered an alternative to psychoanalysis (Chapter 3) and to behaviorism (Chapter 10). We will consider one major theorist in the human potential movement, Abraham H. Maslow.

Abraham H. Maslow (1908–1970)

Abraham Maslow (1968, 1971), like Rogers, emphasized the positive aspects of human experience. He proposed that people are basically good or neutral rather than evil, with everyone possessing an impulse toward growth and the fulfillment of potentials. Psychopathology results from a twisting and frustration of this essential nature of the human organism. To Maslow, social structures that restrict the individual from realizing his or her potential are a root cause of this frustration. Thanks in part to Maslow, the human potential movement became popular among individuals who felt excessively restricted and inhibited by their environment. Maslow speaks to these concerns and encourages the belief that things can be better if people are free to express themselves and be themselves.

Bettmann/Getty Images

Abraham H. Maslow.

In addition to this overall spirit, Maslow's views have been important in two ways. First, he suggested a view of human motivation that distinguishes between such biological needs as hunger, sleep, and thirst and such psychological needs as self-esteem, affection, and belonging. One cannot survive as a biological organism without food and water; likewise, one cannot develop fully as a psychological organism without the satisfaction of other needs as well. Thus, these needs can be arranged in a hierarchy from basic physiological needs to important psychological needs (Figure 6.1). Maslow suggested that, in their research and theorizing, psychologists have been overly concerned with basic biological needs, especially the organism's response to tension caused by biological deficits. While accepting that such motivation exists, Maslow highlighted higher-level motivational processes of the sort that are expressed when people are creative and are fulfilling their potential.

A second major contribution by Maslow (1954) was his intensive study of healthy, self-fulfilling, self-actualizing individuals. Maslow basically reasoned that, if one wants to learn about personality, there is no need to restrict one's study merely to either (1) everyday, normal personality functioning or (2) breakdowns in normal functioning that result in psychopathology. Instead, the psychologist should attend to the other end of the spectrum: people who are "abnormal" in that they are exceptionally positive, unusually highly functioning, self-actualized individuals.

Who are these people? Maslow considered individuals from history as well as from his own historical period (e.g., Abraham Lincoln, Albert Einstein, Eleanor Roosevelt; a more contemporary writer might consider figures such as Mother Teresa or Nelson Mandela). The point is that these exceptional figures possessed qualities that are informative to the personality psychologist because they tell us about human potentials. Maslow concluded that these people's features

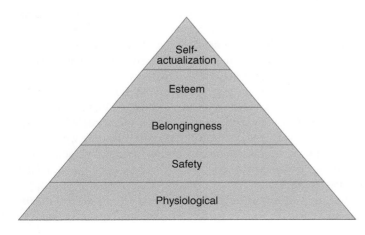

FIGURE 6.1 Schematic representation of Maslow's hierarchy of needs.

included the following characteristics: They accept themselves and others for what they are; they can be concerned with themselves but also are free to recognize the needs and desires of others; they are capable of responding to the uniqueness of people and situations rather than responding in mechanical or stereotyped ways; they can form intimate relationships with at least a few special people; they can be spontaneous and creative; and they can resist conformity and assert themselves while responding to the demands of reality. Maslow suggested that all of us have the potential to move increasingly in the direction of these qualities.

The Positive Psychology Movement

Maslow's focus on the positive aspects of human nature anticipated a contemporary movement in psychology. It is known as the positive psychology movement (Gable & Haidt, 2005; Seligman & Csikszentmihalyi, 2000) or sometimes called the human strengths movement (Aspinwall & Staudinger, 2002).

The writings of psychologists in the 21st-century positive psychology movement echo themes sounded a half-century earlier by Rogers and writers in the human potential movement. Contemporary positive psychologists believe that, in the past, human frailty and psychopathology have been overemphasized (i.e., except in the words of people such as Rogers and Maslow). Psychologists have tended to examine individuals suffering from distress, to use those experiences as their foundation for theorizing about people in general, and as a result to end up with theories that emphasize the negative. Recall what you have learned about Freud. He was trying to build a model of personality that applied to all persons. Yet his database for the theory—the experiences on which he built his conception of the individual—almost entirely involved persons who were suffering from high levels of psychological distress.

What is the cost of focusing on distress and pathology? The positive psychologist argues that this focus causes the psychologist to overlook human strengths. One ends up with a distorted picture of personality that underemphasizes the positive. In an effort to rectify this situation, contemporary psychologists have tried to portray the nature of human strengths and virtues. The psychologist Martin Seligman, who has been key in promoting the positive psychology movement, has contributed much to this work (Seligman & Peterson, 2003; Seligman, Rashid, & Parks, 2006).

Classifying Human Strengths

Seligman and colleagues (Seligman & Peterson, 2003) have tried to classify human strengths. In other words, they have attempted to bring the positive side of human nature to the attention of psychological scientists and thereby to foster systematic research, they have tried to take an initial step that often is critical to scientific progress: the development of a comprehensive classification scheme. This effort has two objectives: (1) to identify criteria that would cause a psychological characteristic to be called a strength and (2) to use these criteria to identify a list of strengths.

Seligman and colleagues identified a set of criteria that are defining of human strengths. They include the following. For a characteristic to be a strength, it should be an enduring characteristic of the person that is beneficial in a variety of life domains. (Thus, "creativity" would be classified as a strength, whereas a narrow-focused skill such as "good at poker" would not.) It should be something that both parents and the larger society try to foster in children and that is celebrated by one's community when it is developed. (Qualities such as perseverance and honesty, and institutions that try to foster these qualities such as Girl Scouts and Boy Scouts, illustrate what Seligman and colleagues have in mind.) Finally, these researchers suggest that a strength is something that is valued in all or almost all cultures of the world. This set of features, then, serves as the criteria for calling something a human strength.

What, then, are the qualities that meet these criteria? Seligman and Peterson (2003) provide a preliminary list that groups strengths into six categories: wisdom, courage, love, justice, temperance (e.g., forgiveness), and transcendence (e.g., appreciation of beauty). These are qualities that we, today, immediately recognize as positive features of the human personality. Importantly, they also are qualities that would be recognized as positive across cultures and across historical time periods. The point of listing these qualities—obvious as any such list may seem in retrospect—is that the process serves as a corrective to theories that emphasized the negative side of human experience. In psychoanalytic theory, many of these qualities would have been seen as secondary to human experience. They would be classified merely as products of the superego, which is ultimately weaker than the impulsive id. Positive psychology gives us a different view of the human condition. It suggests that these virtues are central to human experience and can be enhanced by parenting and by social institutions.

Seligman's early research was on learned helplessness and depression. Although he more recently switched to an interest in the positive aspects of personality functioning, he has retained an interest in the treatment of depression, developing a positive psychotherapy approach to lowering depression and raising well-being (Seligman, Rashid, & Parks, 2006). In contrast with standard approaches to the treatment of depression that target depressive symptoms, positive psychotherapy focuses on increasing positive emotion and meaning. Exercises such as listing one's strengths and how to apply them in daily life, each day writing down three good things that happened, and writing a letter to someone expressing gratitude illustrate the focus fundamental to positive psychotherapy. Seligman reports preliminary positive results, but the approach to treatment is in need of further independent research.

The Virtues of Positive Emotions

In addition to its identification of human virtues, another notable quality of research associated with the positive psychology movement is its study of positive emotions. Psychologists commonly have studied emotions such as fear, anxiety, and anger. However, they have devoted less attention to the role of positive emotions—pride, love, happiness—in personality development and functioning.

A very positive step toward understanding these emotions has been taken by the psychologist Barbara Fredrickson, who has proposed a *broaden-and-build theory* of positive emotions (Fredrickson, 2001, 2009). This theory posits that positive emotions have a specific effect on thoughts and action. Positive emotions broaden thought and action tendencies. They widen the range of ideas that come to mind and the range of actions that individuals pursue. The positive emotion of interest, for example, leads people to pursue novel activities. The emotion of pride motivates one to continue the creative or achievement activities that caused one to feel proud of oneself. In this way, positive emotions contribute directly to the further building of human competencies and achievements.

Research has supported the predictions of Fredrickson's broaden-and-build theory. For example, in one study (Tugade & Fredrickson, 2004), research participants were presented with a stressful experience; they were told they were to give a public speech that would be videotaped. (If you picture yourself suddenly being asked to give a videotaped speech in front of strangers, you'll recognize that this is a stressor for most persons.) The investigators measured three qualities of interest: (1) how resilient people were, that is, individual differences in people's general tendency to recover from stress and deal effectively with novel situations; (2) physiological indications of stress, such as heart rate, as people prepared their speech; and (3) positive emotions, that is, the extent to which people reported feeling positive emotions during the experiment, despite the fact that it was stressful.

As expected, people who scored high on resilience (i.e., people who generally tend to cope well with things) experienced lesser degrees of cardiovascular activity indicating stress. However, the key result of interest involved the third measure, positive emotions. People who experienced positive emotions during the study—people who were able to look on the bright side of things, remaining interested and amused during the experience of giving a speech—experienced less stress. This means that the primary reason that some people were resiliently calm is that they were able to experience positive emotions. As predicted by Fredrickson's theory, these people's positive emotions seemed to cancel out some of the effects of stress. They thus were able to remain in greater control of their thoughts and actions and to feel less stressful arousal than others. People who experience more positive emotions, then, could be said to be more resilient. Positive emotions act as "coping resources that help buffer (psychologically and physiologically) against negative emotional life experiences" (Tugade & Fredrickson, 2004, p. 331).

Flow

A third notable area of investigation in positive psychology is Mihaly Csikszentmihalyi's (1990) work on the concept of *flow*. Flow describes a feature of conscious experiences. It refers specifically to positive states of consciousness with the following characteristics: a perceived match between personal skills and environmental challenge, a high level of focused attention, involvement in an activity such that time seems to fly by and irrelevant thoughts and distractions do not enter into consciousness, a sense of intrinsic enjoyment in the activity, and a temporary loss of self-consciousness such that the self is not aware of functioning or regulating activity.

Flow experiences can take place in activities as diverse as work, hobbies, sports, dancing, and social interactions. It is expressed in statements such as "When I am involved, everything just seems to come to me. I just float along, feeling both excited and calm and want it to continue endlessly. It's not rewards that count but just the pleasure in the activity itself." Csikszentmihalyi's interest in the positive aspects of human functioning began with his observation during World War II that, although many people lost their decency, others expressed the best of what people can be. Subsequently, he was influenced by the work of Carl Rogers and Abraham Maslow, leading to an emphasis on the study of strength and virtue as opposed to weakness and pathology.

These three areas of study—Seligman's classification of human strengths, Fredrickson's broad-and-build theory of positive emotions, and Csikszentmihalyi's work on flow—illustrate the promise and achievements of the positive psychology movement. Yet more work remains. A primary challenge is not only to show that some people have superior virtues and relatively positive emotional experiences but also to show how these qualities can be developed in everybody. Commentators have noted that this remains a limitation of the field. Researchers have yet to identify social practices and community institutions that are best for building personal strengths (Gable & Haidt, 2005).

Existentialism

The approach known as **existentialism** is not new to psychology, but one could hardly say that it has an established or secure place in mainstream academic psychology. Existentialism is an approach that many people are deeply moved by, yet, there is no single representative figure, nor is there agreement about its basic theoretical concepts. There are religious existentialists, atheistic existentialists, and antireligion existentialists. There are those existentialists who emphasize hope and optimism, as well as those who emphasize despair and nothingness. There are those who emphasize the philosophical roots of existentialism and those who emphasize the phenomena of clinical cases.

Granted all this diversity, what is it that establishes a common ground among those who would define themselves as existentialists? What is it about this approach that captivates some and leads others to reject it? Perhaps the most defining element of existentialism is the concern with *existence*, the concern with the person in the human condition. The existentialist is concerned with phenomena that are inherent in the nature of being alive, human, existing. What constitutes the essence of existence varies for different existentialists; however, all agree that certain concerns are fundamental to the very nature of our being and cannot be ignored, dismissed, explained away, or trivialized. Perhaps most of all, for the existentialist, people and experience are to be taken seriously.

Another major aspect of the existential view is the significance of the individual. The existentialist sees the person as singular, unique, and irreplaceable. Related to this is an emphasis on freedom, consciousness, and self-reflection. Freedom distinguishes humans from other animals. Freedom also involves responsibility for choices, for action, for being authentic, or for acting in "bad faith" and being inauthentic. In addition, there is the existential concern with death, for it is here as nowhere else that the individual is alone and completely irreplaceable. Finally, there is an emphasis on phenomenology and an understanding of the unique experience of each person rather than in terms of some standardized definition or the confirmation of some hypothesis: "Existentialism works at the personal meaning in contrast to general theory" (Marino, 2004, p. xii).

In many ways Rogers represented an existential emphasis. For example, consider his discussion of loneliness (Rogers, 1980). What is it that constitutes the existential experience of loneliness? Rogers suggested a number of contributing factors: the impersonality of our culture, its transient quality, the fear of a close relationship. However, what most defines loneliness is the effort to share something very personal with someone and to find that it is not received or is rejected. In contrast, there is the feeling of being understood. Here the person has the sense that another individual can empathize in an understanding, accepting way. The feeling of being understood is associated with safety and relief from existential loneliness.

Another illustration involves the search for meaning in human existence. The existential psychiatrist Viktor Frankl (1955, 1958) struggled to find meaning while imprisoned in a concentration camp during World War II. Frankl suggests that the will to find meaning is the most human phenomenon of all, since other animals never worry about the meaning of their existence. Existential frustration and existential neurosis involve frustration and lack of fulfillment of the will to find meaning. Such a neurosis does not involve the instincts or biological drives but rather is spiritually rooted in the person's escape from freedom and responsibility. In such cases, the person blames destiny, childhood, the environment, or fate for what is. The treatment for such a condition, logotherapy, involves helping patients to become what they are capable of being, helping them to realize and accept the challenges of the opportunities that are open to them.

Contemporary Experimental Existentialism

Can one study issues raised by existentialists, such as fear of death, with experimental methods? A particularly compelling example of such research is work on people's awareness and fear of death. Existentialists have long conjectured that thoughts of death are a central feature of human experience. Experimental existential psychologists have advanced beyond the earlier philosophical analyses by taking this general idea—people's awareness of, and fear of, death—and turning it into specific, testable hypotheses. A significant step forward in this regard is *terror management theory* (Greenberg, Solomon, & Arndt, 2008; Solomon, Greenberg, & Pyszczynski, 2004). Terror management theory (TMT) examines the consequences of combining two factors: people's desire to live (which people share with all other animals) and people's awareness of the inevitability of death (an awareness that is uniquely human). TMT posits that people's awareness of death makes them vulnerable to being completely overwhelmed by terrifying death anxiety. The question that arises then is how people manage to avoid terror. How do people obtain meaning in life once they recognize that death is inevitable and (in principle) could occur at any time?

Terror management theorists suggest that part of the answer lies in social and cultural institutions or worldviews. These institutions and worldviews serve a psychological function: They buffer against the fear of death. The idea of TMT is that cultural institutions furnish meaning in life—even if one does dwell on the inevitability of death. How does this work? Well, the exact answer depends on where in the world you live; different cultures furnish different types of meaning systems. But two examples make the TMT point clear. In many cultures, religious institutions teach that there is an afterlife (e.g., a heaven and a hell). The belief in an afterlife buffers against the terror of death. Even if one starts to feel terrified at the prospect of the death of the body, one can find comfort in the belief in the afterlife of the soul. Other cultures emphasize that the individual is one component of a larger circle of persons: the family, the community, and so forth (see Chapter 14). Even though one may die as an individual, there is a sense in which one lives on in the life of one's offspring. The idea of TMT, then, is that these social practices are resources that help people to cope with the fear of death.

A specific hypothesis follows from TMT: Increasing death anxiety, what is known as *mortality salience*, should lead to greater commitment to one's cultural beliefs and greater rejection of cultural beliefs that might threaten one's worldview. Along similar lines, increased mortality salience should lead to greater agreement with and affection for those who share one's beliefs and greater hostility and disdain for those who do not share or challenge one's beliefs. To study this hypothesis experimentally, one must be able to manipulate mortality salience and observe the effects on commitment to one's own cultural beliefs relative to those of others.

Thomas Sherwood / EyeEm / Getty Images

Research on mortality salience indicates that a reminder of the inevitability of death, such as the sight of a cemetery, will increase people's sense of commitment to aspect of their own culture, such as their nation and its flag.

In various studies, mortality salience has been increased in the following ways: Subjects are asked to respond to tasks such as "Describe the emotions that the thought of your own death arouse in you" or "Write down what you think will happen to you as you physically die." Subjects view a film of a gory automobile accident; subjects respond to death anxiety scales; and subjects are exposed to subliminal death primes. In support of the hypothesis, such increases in mortality salience have been found to produce effects such as the following: greater fondness for members of one's own group and rejection of members of different groups; greater anxiety about a blasphemous attitude toward cultural icons such as the American flag or symbols of one's own religion; greater physical aggression toward those who attack one's political orientation; and increased donations to charities that benefit one's in group. Increasing mortality salience has also been found to decrease interest in sex when sex is viewed as more of an animal act but to increase interest in sex when sex is viewed as an act of human love. Finally, high self-esteem has been found to serve an anxiety-buffering effect in relation to death anxiety; that is, increased mortality salience has more of an effect on individuals low in self-esteem than on people high in self-esteem.

In summary, existentialism is a philosophical movement that is defined by its topics of primary interest. As we have seen, four features of existentialism stand out. First, existentialists are concerned with understanding existence—the person in the human condition. Second, existentialists are concerned with the individual. Rather than trying to understand human existence by searching for abstract theoretical principles, by studying broad political or social systems, or by engaging in metaphysical speculations about the universe and where it came from, the existentialist addresses the experiences of the individual person. Third, existentialists emphasize the human capacity for free choice, a capacity that comes from people's unique ability to reflect consciously on alternative possibilities. Finally, existentialists devote much attention to the phenomenological experiences of anguish and despair—the feelings of "existential crisis"—that result when people reflect on their alienation from the world, a loss of meaning in life, or the inevitability of death.

Developments in Research: The Self and Authenticity

Discrepancies among Parts of the Self

According to Rogers, then, psychological pathology results from discrepancies between self-concept and actual experience. Much contemporary research similarly focuses on the role of discrepancies in psychological distress. However, this work differs somewhat from that of Rogers. It tends to focus less on discrepancies between self and experience, and more on an internal psychological discrepancy: discrepancies between different parts of the self.

A particularly influential theory of discrepancies among parts of the self has been proposed by the psychologist Higgins (1999; Higgins & Scholer, 2008). Higgins's work addresses the relation between aspects of self-concept and emotional experience. His work extends Rogers's thinking by differentiating between two aspects of one's future self. In addition to the ideal self, which was recognized by Rogers, Higgins suggests that everyone possesses an ought self—that is, an aspect of self-concept that is concerned with duties, responsibilities, and obligations. The ideal self, in contrast, centers on personal hopes, ambitions, and desires.

According to Higgins's theory, discrepancies between actual self and ideal self lead to dejection-related emotions. For example, if someone has an ideal self of being an A student but receives a C in a class, he or she will likely feel disappointed, sad, or even depressed. In contrast, discrepancies between self and ought self should lead to agitation-related emotions. For example, if someone has an ought self of being an A student but receives a C, he or she will likely feel fearful, threatened, or anxious. Thus, the distinction between ideal self and ought self is important because it helps separate two kinds of self-relevant emotions: those related to dejection (e.g., disappointment, sadness, depression) and those related to agitation (e.g., fear, threat, anxiety).

In research related to this theory, people are asked to describe how they actually are (their actual self) and how they ideally would like to be (their ideal self). Researchers determine the degree to which these different descriptions are discrepant. (For example, if you say "I actually am lazy" and "Ideally, I would be hardworking," that is coded as a self-discrepancy.) It is predicted that people with larger self-discrepancies will be more vulnerable to negative emotional experiences. In a key piece of research, Higgins, Bond, Klein, and Strauman (1986) found that people with large discrepancies between the actual self and ideal self were more likely to be depressed, whereas people with actual–ought discrepancies were more likely to be anxious. Because Higgins's theory and research methods are closely related to a personality theory, you will learn about later in the text, social-cognitive theory, we will return to his work in Chapter 13.

More recent findings by other investigators suggest that the relation between self-discrepancies and emotional experience is not fixed but, instead, can vary. An important factor is the degree to which people are aware of their self-discrepancies at any given time. If some feature of the social environment causes people to dwell on themselves, then discrepancies among aspects of the self-concept may influence emotional experience more strongly. Phillips and Silvia (2005) tested this idea using a simple experimental manipulation employed frequently in research on the self: a mirror. Looking at a mirror has the effect of drawing one's attention to oneself. In their research, some people completed measures of self-concept and of emotional experience while sitting at a table that faced a large mirror. Other people, in a different experimental condition, could not see themselves in a mirror. (The experimenters simply turned the mirror around so that its nonreflective back side faced the research participants.) The researchers found that self-discrepancies were linked more strongly to emotional experience in conditions of high self-awareness, that is, when people faced the mirror (Phillips & Silvia, 2005). The results indicate that, to understand the role of self-concept in psychological experience, one must consider situational factors with the power to draw attention to features of the self.

Fluctuations in Self-Esteem and Contingencies of Worth

Rogers's ideas about the self-implied that people possess a relatively stable sense of self-worth, or self-esteem. To bring about changes in people's sense of self, it appeared that systematic efforts, such as client-centered therapy, were required. There is evidence that children as young as four years of age begin to develop a sense of self-worth and that between the ages of six and nine they develop a sense of global self-esteem (Robins, Tracy, & Trzesniewski, 2008). At the same time, some contemporary research suggests that self-esteem may fluctuate to a greater extent than Rogers had anticipated. Particularly informative work on this topic comes from Jennifer Crocker and colleagues (Crocker & Knight, 2005; Crocker & Wolfe, 2001).

Crocker and Wolfe (2001) are interested in "contingencies of self-worth." Their idea is that a person's self-esteem depends on—or is "contingent on"—positive and negative events. Self-esteem rises when we get an A1 in a class and falls when we get an F−. We feel better about ourselves when someone asks us out on a date and worse when we ask someone out and they laugh at us and hang up the phone. It is these successes and failures that are the **contingencies of self-worth** on which self-esteem depends. Although a person's typical, average level of self-esteem may be relatively stable, one's day-to-day sense of self-worth may fluctuate considerably as one experiences these positive and negative contingent events.

In addition to the possibility of fluctuations in self-esteem, Crocker and Wolfe's theoretical framework highlights another point: People may differ in the degree to which any given event is, for them, a contingency of self-worth. One person might not care much about his or her grades in classes because he or she is basically interested in getting dates. Another might not be concerned with acceptance/rejection by dating partners because his or her only big concern is academic grades. Such people should experience fluctuating self-esteem in different situations. "The impact of events" on one's self-esteem should depend "on the perceived relevance of those events to one's contingencies of self-worth" (Crocker & Wolfe, 2001, p. 594).

Crocker and colleagues have applied their theoretical ideas to a topic of particular relevance to those readers of this book who might be considering going to graduate school: fluctuations in self-esteem among college students as they receive acceptances and rejections from graduate programs (Crocker, Sommers, & Luhtanen, 2002). Participants in this study completed a measure of self-esteem, as well as measures of positive and negative effects, twice a week on a regular schedule, as well as on any days on which they received a notification of admission (or not) from a graduate program. This enabled the investigators to study fluctuations in self-esteem. At the outset of the study, the degree to which each participant's self-worth was contingent on academic success was measured; this was done by asking people to report the degree to which they get a self-esteem boost from events such as getting good grades. This procedure enabled the investigators to test the hypothesis that self-esteem would fluctuate as a result of acceptances/rejections, but only for students for whom academic success was an important contingency of self-worth. This hypothesis was confirmed. Among students who based their self-esteem on academic performance, self-esteem went up and down as a result of acceptances and rejections (respectively). However, among students for whom academic success was not a central element of self-worth, the same objective events—graduate school acceptances and rejections—had little impact on self-esteem.

The analyses of Crocker and colleagues are a valuable extension of Rogers's analyses of self-concept. They extend the work by identifying particular social contexts that contribute not only to typical, average levels of self-esteem but also to those day-to-day fluctuations in people's sense of self that are so much a part of everyday life.

Before leaving discussion of the concept of self-esteem, it is worthwhile to note that although high self-esteem would appear to be a good thing, surprisingly it is not necessarily related to measures of objective outcome. For example, self-reported self-esteem has not been found to be related to objective measures of outcome such as school achievement, social popularity, and job performance (Baumeister, Campbell, Krueger, & Vons, 2003). Rather than a global self-esteem that is related to all aspects of performance, self-esteem may have many components to it, each of which is related to a specific area.

Authenticity and Internally Motivated Goals

Another research trend that is in accord with Rogers's views is recent work on the concept of **authenticity**, defined as the extent to which people behave in accord with their self as opposed to behaving in terms of roles that foster false self-presentations (Ryan, 1993; Sheldon, Ryan, Rawsthorne, & Ilardi, 1997). A key idea in work on authenticity is that, to understand human experience, one cannot look merely at people's observable behaviors. One must explore inner feelings as well. Specifically, one must ask whether people feel that their activities are consistent with their true self—that is, are authentic—rather than being phony actions that express a false self.

Certainly, we all are aware of times when we have felt we were being more "authentic" and other times when we felt we were being "inauthentic" or "phony." Is the degree to which an individual feels authentic in situations in daily life related to measures of satisfaction and well-being? Indeed, this has been found to be the case. That is, in accord with the prior theorizing of humanistic and phenomenologically oriented psychologists, authenticity was found to be associated with being a more fully functioning person. In addition to this overall relationship with psychological being, it was found that the more genuine and self-expressive people feel they are in a specific situation, the more extraverted, agreeable, conscientious, and open to experience they are likely to be in that situation (Sheldon et al., 1997). In other words, individuals may vary in their behavior from situation to situation, but the critical question is whether they feel they are being authentic and true to their self overall as well as in specific situations.

Self-Determination Theory

Self-determination theory (Deci & Ryan, 2012a, b), suggests that all human beings have fundamental psychological needs to be *competent*, *autonomous*, and *related to others* (*CAR*). In other words, these are viewed as the basic, universal human needs. The need for competence refers to feeling effective in one's actions. The need to be autonomous refers to the need to act in autonomous, self-directed ways and to engage in tasks that are intrinsically motivated (motivated by intrinsic rewards) as opposed to engaging in tasks that are coerced, forced, or compelled (motivated by external rewards and punishments). The need for relatedness refers to feeling connected with others and having a sense of belonging in one's community. Satisfaction of these basic psychological needs is associated with healthy psychological functioning, just as Rogers would suggest. It is also associated with greater satisfaction in interpersonal relationships. In a spirit very much in tune with Rogers and existential psychologists, Ryan and Deci suggest that "existentially, what defines a person's life is the way in which it is experienced. Well-being, mental health, and a life well lived are all about experiencing love, freedom, efficacy, and meaningful goals and values" (2008, p. 654).

Of particular importance to self-determination theory is the emphasis on autonomous motivation as opposed to controlled motivation. There are at least two critical elements to this difference. First, there is the question of whether action is autonomous, or self-initiated, as opposed to controlled by others, or externally regulated. In addition, there is the question of whether action is freely chosen as opposed to compelled. Action conducted out of feelings of guilt and anxiety would emanate from within the person but would have a compelled as opposed to a freely chosen quality, and it would not qualify as self-determined action. In sum, self-determined action takes place because of its intrinsic interest to the person and its quality of being freely chosen.

Does it make a difference whether action is reflective of self-determined motivation? Recent research suggests that people show greater effort and persistence in relation to autonomous goals than in relation to goals that are pursued only because of external pushes or internal sanctions such as anxiety or guilt (Koestner, Lekes, Powers, & Chicoine, 2002; Sheldon & Elliot, 1999). In addition, there is evidence that the pursuit of self-determined, intrinsic, approach goals is associated with physical health and psychological well-being in contrast with the deleterious effects of the pursuit of forced, extrinsic, avoidance goals (Dykman, 1998; Elliot & Sheldon, 1998; Elliot, Sheldon, & Church, 1997; Kasser & Ryan, 1996). Thus, it is suggested that "to the extent that goal self-concepts do not represent or are not concordant with the true self, people may not be able to meet their psychological needs" (Sheldon & Elliot, 1999, p. 485). More generally, studies confirm the hypothesis that people make particularly good progress on personal goals when the goals are "self-concordant," that is, consistent with one's own personal values rather than being imposed by someone else (Koestner et al., 2002). Of particular interest to college students may be the finding that when students are intrinsically motivated to learn, their learning tends to be deeper and more conceptual, and remembered better than when it is extrinsically motivated by grades or rewards (Benware & Deci, 1984).

CURRENT QUESTIONS

What Is the Nature of Effective Motivation? Is Internal Motivation or External Motivation Better? What about a Combination of the Two?

In a study conducted independent of self-determination theory and the earlier discussion of authenticity, but that fits within these frameworks, investigators asked whether internal motives (intrinsic motives, internal rewards) or universal motives (extrinsic motives, external rewards) produce better outcomes, and whether a combination of the two might be best: What mix of motives—internal, instrumental, or both—is most conducive to success?

Over the course of nine classes, over ten thousand cadets at the West Point Military Academy rated how much each motive influenced their decision to attend the Academy. Illustrative contrasting motives were "A desire to be trained as a leader in the US Army" (internal) and "A desire to get a good job later in life." (instrumental). Scores for these motives were then related to later military performance. As expected, those with strong internal motives were more likely to graduate and to receive early promotion recommendations

relative to those with strong instrumental motives. However, what was unexpected was the finding that cadets with strong motives of both kinds performed worse than did those with strong internal motives but weak instrumental motives. In other words, the instrumental motives appeared to weaken the positive effects of the internal motives that are essential to success.

Drawing a parallel to the college world and consistent with Deci & Ryan, the authors suggest that motives to learn (internal) are much more conducive to success than are motives to get good grades (extrinsic). They concluded that holding instrumental (extrinsic) motives may damage persistence and performance in educational and occupational contexts over long periods of time.

Sources: Wrzesniewski and Schwartz (2014), Wrzesniewski, Schwartz, Cong, Kane, and Kolditz (2014).

From a humanistic standpoint, these results make perfectly good sense. Yet, two caveats are worthy of note. First, it is important to keep in mind that it is not the goal per se that is important but why the goal is being pursued. The same goal can be pursued for intrinsic or extrinsic reasons, suggesting that goals such as financial success and community involvement can express either motivation. This is important in reminding us that we cannot assume that we know the motivation for a goal just from awareness of the content of the goal.

The second caveat is the following: It is easy to assume that these principles of motivation apply to all people. However, recent research suggests that they may be culturally specific rather than universal features of human psychology. In this work, Anglo-American and Asian-American children were compared in terms of their relative intrinsic motivation when choices were (a) made for them versus (b) made by authority figures or peers. Anglo-American children showed more intrinsic motivation when they made their own choices. However, Asian-American children showed greater intrinsic motivation when their choices were made *for them* by trusted authority figures or peers (Iyengar & Lepper, 1999). Thus, the extent to which self-determination reflects a universal human need requires careful consideration and more research. More generally, the Rogerian emphasis on self-actualization may be most appropriate to understanding people who live in a Western culture in which Rogers formulated his theory.

A final note in relation to self-determination theory concerns its recent emphasis on how social contexts can facilitate or impair satisfaction of the basic psychological needs (Deci & Ryan, 2012a). In particular, there is an interest in how cultural values and economic systems promote or thwart autonomy. For example, capitalism is viewed as a complex system that can either support or thwart autonomy. In the former case, capitalism fosters autonomy that maximizes creativity and innovation. In the latter case, however, capitalism can thwart autonomous, intrinsic motivation by its focus on accumulation, personal gain, and recognition.

Cross-Cultural Research on the Self

The research on intrinsic motivation among Asian-American and Anglo-American children that we have just reviewed raises a general question. Carl Rogers was an American psychologist. He developed his theory on the basis of clinical experiences with Americans. Most of the psychological research on self processes conducted during Rogers's lifetime was conducted with citizens of the United States, Canada, or western Europe. The question that arises, then, is as follows: Does Rogers's work provides us with a general view of human nature or with a view that pertains primarily to people in the industrialized Western world? This is a deep and important question that has relevance far beyond the personality theory of Carl Rogers. All theoretical conceptions of human nature inevitably are constructed by people who live in a certain geographical location, in a certain culture, at a certain point in history. The question, then, is whether the theorist possibly can circumvent the limits of his or her circumstances to provide a theoretical framework that applies to all persons, in all cultures and all historical contexts.

Cultural Differences in the Self and the Need for Positive Self-Regard

The basic nature of the self, as well as the extent of the need for positive regard, may vary from culture to culture (Benet-Martinez, 2008; Heine, Lehman, Markus, & Kitayama, 1999; see Chapter 14). For example, one of the distinctive differences between Eastern and Western cultures is the degree to which the self is viewed as connected to others (Markus & Cross, 1990). In Eastern cultures, the self-concept consists of connections with others, and individual parts that cannot be understood when separated from the greater, collective whole. This cultural understanding of self stands in contrast to the dominant view of the self in Western civilization, which views the self as unique and separate from others. One of the authors of this book, while teaching a multiethnic group of students in Hawaii, was struck with the very different views of the self expressed by students from these two cultures. In fact, what was particularly striking was that at times those from one culture could not comprehend what was being expressed about the self by members of the other culture.

As we have reviewed, Rogers believed that all people have a need for positive self-regard. To Rogers, unconditional acceptance of the individual, whatever his or her faults may be, is the pathway to psychological health. Such unconditional regard builds the individual's sense that he

Personality and the Brain
Culture and the Self

Not long ago in the history of psychological science, "culture" and "brain" were explanations of behavior that competed. Some theorists explained behavior by referring to the beliefs and skills that people acquire by living in a culture. Others disagreed, saying that the proper explanation would refer to neural systems within the brain.

The debate between these competing camps of theorists has a happy conclusion: They were both right. The brain evolved, in part, to enable people to acquire the beliefs and skills of their culture. Cultural experience, in turn, shapes the "wiring" of the developing brain. An example of how this works comes from research on a central feature of personality, namely, the self.

People learn who they are—their roles in life; their rights and obligations; what it means to be a person—through interactions with the people and social practices of their culture. Neuroscience research shows how these cultural experiences are represented in the brain. A key strategy in this research is to compare brain activity among individuals from parts of the world whose cultures are known to differ.

Zhu, Ziang, Fan, and Han (2007) compared college students from Eastern (China) and Western (e.g., England and North America) cultures. They took brain images while participants performed the following task. As each of a series of personality trait adjectives (e.g., "brave," "childish") appeared on screen, participants judged whether the word accurately described (1) themselves or (2) their mother. The study employed a within-subjects experimental design, so each participant made a number of "self" judgments and "mother judgments." When analyzing the resulting brain images, the researchers

focused on a region in the front of the brain known as the medial prefrontal cortex (MPFC) because it had been shown, in prior research, to be a brain region that is highly active when people make judgments about themselves. Consistent with prior research in Western cultures, the researchers found that, among Western participants, the MPFC was highly active during judgments about the self but not during judgments about one's mother. However, Eastern participants were different. Among people from China, the MPFC was active during both self-judgments and mother judgments. As the researchers summarized, "the representation of Chinese mother cannot be distinguished from the representation of their selves, in terms of the MPFC Activity" (Zhu et al., 2007, p. 1314). Fascinatingly, this merger of self and other at a biological level of analysis parallels cultural findings at a psychological level of analysis, which show that self-concept in the East consists of closer psychological connections with others than in the West.

Subsequent work provides related evidence about culture and the brain. In a study with participants from the United States and Japan, variations in participants' cultural beliefs (specifically, their beliefs about the degree to which they are interconnected with others in their culture) predicted levels of MPFC activation that occurred while people made judgments about themselves (Chiao et al., 2009). Again, then, culturally based thinking and brain activity were linked.

Thanks to findings such as these, psychology's traditional debates about "culture versus biology" are being replaced by new understandings of how culture and biology work together in the shaping of personality.

or she is a valued, prized person. In the absence of such unconditional regard, the individual's need for a positive self-view may be unfulfilled, leading to psychological distress.

But is this how things work for all persons the world over? If psychological processes regarding the self are akin to biological processes, then the answer is yes. But psychological processes involving the self may not be like this. The very notion of self—of one's identity, one's role in family and society, one's goals, one's purpose in life—is acquired socially. People acquire a sense of self from interaction with the individuals who make up their family, community, and wider culture. It is possible, then, that some cultures in essence *teach* people to have a need for positive regard; a culture that values the individual and individual achievements may foster the belief that individuals should enhance their own well-being. In principle, other cultures may teach people a different way of life that does not involve a striving for positive self-regard.

Compelling evidence that there are, in fact, variations from culture to culture in the nature and functioning of self-esteem are found in the study of differences between Japanese and American culture. Heine, Lehman, Markus, and Kitayama (1999) review evidence that the basic patterns and functions of self-esteem seem to vary from one culture to another. In the United States, most people report having relatively high self-esteem; as Rogers might have predicted, people seem biased to maintain positive self-views. But in Japan, there is no sign whatsoever of this bias; as many people report low self-esteem as high self-esteem. In psychological studies conducted in the United States, people seem inevitably to engage in psychological strategies to maintain high self-esteem. For example, they compare themselves to others who are not doing well, they blame others for personal failure, and they lower the perceived importance of activities on which they cannot perform competently (reviewed in Brown, 1998). But Heine and colleagues (1999, p. 780) "are unable to find clear and consistent evidence of any self-esteem maintenance strategies within the Japanese psychological literature."

Rather than being prone to an enhancement of self-esteem, Heine and colleagues (1999; also see Kitayama & Markus, 1999; Kitayama Markus, Matsumoto, & Norasakkunkit, 1997) contend that Japanese culture makes one prone to self-criticism. In Japan, this self-criticism serves a valuable personal and social function. It motivates people toward self-improvement that can benefit the individual and his or her society. In Japan, then, self-criticism is not "bad." It is not a sign of being depressed or down on oneself. Instead, it is "good"—that is, it is a functional, valuable way for individuals to mesh with their surrounding culture. Consistent with this view, tendencies toward self-criticism and the experience of discrepancies between the actual and ideal self are predictive of depression in North America but are less strongly related to depression in Japan (Heine et al., 1999).

In summary, it appears that the cultures of the United States and of Japan teach people different ways of evaluating the self. If you, the reader, are a citizen of North America, then you may be particularly prone to engage in psychological strategies that maintain a positive view of self. If your professor gives you a bad grade on a paper, you may conclude that there is something wrong with the professor. If a romantic partner dumps you, you may conclude that the relationship wasn't all that important anyway. If you didn't get into the college of your choice, you may conclude that it was because you didn't take your application seriously enough. These conclusions are functional in the cultural system of the United States; they enable you to maintain a high sense of self-esteem in a culture that values high self-esteem. But if you are a citizen of Japan, you may be much more likely to draw other conclusions that are more self-critical; in so doing, you would be fitting in with a culture that values continual personal improvement. These variations in the nature and functioning of self-evaluation and self-esteem are understandable in light of contemporary research on culture and personality; however, these variations were not well anticipated by Carl Rogers when he formulated his theory of personality and self.

Contemporary Developments in Personality Theory: Personality Systems Interaction Theory and the Integrated Self

A distinctive feature of Rogers's theory of personality is that it is holistic. Most other theories dissect personality into a set of distinct parts (e.g., the id/ego/superego structural variables of Freud's psychoanalytic theory, or the personality trait variables you will see in Chapters 7 and 8). Rogers, by contrast, believed that personality cannot be dissected into parts; the core of personality, the self, is an organized, integrated whole. Just as you cannot understand a whole painting by breaking the image into little parts and studying them one piece at a time, you cannot understand a person as a whole, in Rogers's view, by dividing the individual into a set of variables that are analyzed one-at-a-time.

A Limitation of Rogerian Theory: What Exactly Is the "Integrated Self"?

A strength of Roger's approach, as you have seen, is that it captures people's experience of themselves, or their "phenomenology". People commonly experience themselves as whole, unified persons, not as collections of personality variables. Consider your own experience when making a significant life decision such as choosing what college to attend or deciding whether to maintain or break up a relationship. When deciding, you rely on intuitions about what is right for you; for example, you might conclude that one school "just doesn't fit my personality" but that another "really does feel like a good place for me." Now consider these feelings. They concern yourself as a whole; your intuitions do not center on one "part" of your personality but, instead, on your whole self. This experience of a unified, integrated, whole self that can guide your intuitive decision-making aligns with Rogers's theory.

But what exactly is this whole, integrated self? A limitation of Rogers's theory is that he does not answer this question in a precise way. When it comes to the analysis of the self, Rogers's theory is more descriptive than explanatory; he vividly described the psychological experiences that compel one to propose an integrated self as the core of personality, but never explained where this integrated self comes from.

Consider what needs to be explained. When one analyzes the workings of the mind, it is immediately obvious that mental processes are highly diverse. People hold a wide variety of beliefs and possess a near-infinity of memories. Everyone experiences a diverse range of emotions, which sometimes conflict with one another and often change rapidly from one moment to the next. Furthermore, a variety of motives, values, and rules for social behavior guide everyday actions. At a biological level of analysis, these diverse psychological processes are possible because people possess brains that contain large numbers of distinct neural subsystems. The diversity and complexity of psychological and neural processes is so great that one cannot help but ask whether the idea of a singular, "integrated" self is more fiction than fact. What needs to be explained is how a whole, integrated self emerges out of this psychological and biological diversity. Rogers did not accomplish this; he never identified the psychological or neural systems that enabled people to experience an integrated, unified sense of self.

In historical retrospect, it is hard to blame him. Contemporary scientific understanding of mental processes and associated brain systems developed almost entirely *after* Rogers penned his theory of personality in the middle of the 20th century. However, thanks to these developments, today's personality scientists can advance beyond the understanding of self that was provided by Rogers. One major advance is the *Personality Systems Interaction (PSI) Theory* of the German psychologist Julius Kuhl and his colleagues (Kuhl, 2000, 2010; Kuhl & Koole, 2004).

Personality Systems Interaction Theory

The first step in learning about Personality Systems Interaction theory is to understand what *type* of theory it is. Many psychological theories concern mental content, where "content" refers to the type of information that the mind contains. For example, Rogers's distinction between the *actual* and the *ideal* self is based on content. The content of the actual self is information about a person's current psychological qualities, whereas the content of the ideal self is information about desired qualities that one might not currently possess. PSI theory, by contrast, identifies different types of mental systems with different *functional* properties; in other words, the systems work (or "function") differently, no matter what content goes into them.

The following analogy helps to clarify the distinction between function and content. Your smart phone stores music on a solid-state flash memory device. Decades ago, people stored music exclusively on vinyl records. Current-day flash memory and old-fashioned vinyl work differently no matter what music you put on them; they have different physical properties and therefore function differently, no matter what the musical content. Similarly, it is possible to identify mental systems whose functioning differs from one another, no matter what content—that is, no matter what beliefs and feelings about the self—goes into them.

Four Functionally Distinct Personality Systems

PSI theory identifies four personality systems that each has distinct functional properties. The second of the four is key to the theory's analysis of the holistic, integrated self[1]:

1. **Analytical Thinking System:** The analytical thinking system is a mental system that processes material in a logical, step-by-step manner. You commonly are consciously aware of this step-by-step analytic thinking when you "talk to yourself" about your day. For example, if you tell yourself things like "Today, I have to start writing a paper for my psych class. And I also need to get to work by 7," these consciously accessible thoughts about your goals and intentions are produced by the analytic thinking system.

2. **Holistic Thinking-and-Feeling System.** The Holistic Thinking-and-Feeling System is not a step-by-step thinking system. Instead, it is a *parallel-processing* system. A parallel processing system is one in which large numbers of psychological processes occur at the same time, or "in parallel". Cognitive psychologists have recognized since the 1980s that parallel processing is a central feature of the human mind (Rumelhart &McClelland, 1986). The brain, with its billions upon billions of neurons, inherently engages in large numbers of activities at the same time.

   PSI theory recognizes that two features of parallel processing systems are of great importance to personality. One is that parallel processes occur outside of consciousness. Conscious awareness is limited; in other words, it is impossible to be aware of a large number of things at the same time. It is therefore inevitable that, if many mental activities occur at the same time, they will occur outside of conscious awareness. A simple illustration of this point is that sometimes ideas "pop into your head" for no apparent reason. Before they popped into your head, there had to have been some mental activities—but you were unaware of them.

   A second feature of parallel processing systems is that different processes often are interconnected. Although your brain may be engaged in multiple thinking processes at the same

---

[1] The present summary is not a complete presentation of all aspects of PSI theory. It focuses specifically on the theory's treatment of the regulation of behavior by cognitive systems that interact with emotional states. Also note that the terminology used to reference the systems varies slightly from the terminology employed by Kuhl (2004), in order to obtain a relatively simpler introductory presentation of the ideas.

time, the interconnections among these processes allow information to be combined. For example, if you are near someone who lights a fire (e.g., a fireplace or campfire), your brain engages in a number of different perceptual processes: your visual system sees the light, your auditory system hears the crackling of the fire, and your haptic system (or sense of "touch") perceives warmth. But what is your conscious experience? You do not consciously experience three distinct streams of information involving light, sound, and temperature. Instead, these information streams are connected to one another, and you are consciously aware of a single, integrated, whole object: the fire.

PSI theory argues that interconnections among mental processes that occur in parallel are key to the integrated sense of self-described by Rogers. Parallel-processing connections enable the mind to automatically combine multiple thoughts and feelings about the self into an integrated whole. "The integrated self [is] based on parallel processing that integrates cognitive, emotional, motivational, and volitional processes within the person" (Kuhl, Quirin, & Koole, 2015, p. 119). Once these thoughts, feelings, and motives are combined, you are consciously aware of a single, whole self.

PSI theory even identifies a brain basis of this integrated self-system. As you know, the brain has two hemispheres, the left and the right. The right hemisphere is known to be more strongly involved in parallel processing, and thus is a neural basis for the integrated self (Kuhl et al., 2015).

3. **Intuitive Behavior Control System.** A third PSI system is called the Intuitive Behavior Control System. This is a mental system that allows you to engage in behavior without have to pay attention to each step you are taking. For example, if you play a musical instrument well, you don't pay attention to each of the individual movements your hands make to produce each sound; instead, the individual movements are controlled in an automatic, intuitive manner by the Intuitive Behavior Control System.

The free-flowing nature of the dancer's movements suggest that her behavior is under the control of her *intuitive behavior control system,* which enables people to engage in behavior without paying attention to each step they are taking.

Mayank Mudnaney / EyeEm / Getty Images

4. **Discrepancy Detection System.** Finally, the fourth PSI system is a Discrepancy Detection System. This is the mental system that recognizes when something is going wrong—or, to phrase it more precisely, this is the mental system that is sensitive to differences between sensory experiences and prior expectations or goals. Sticking with our music example,

suppose you are playing a song and expect to hear yourself play a C major chord but, instead, hear yourself playing a C minor chord. Your Discrepancy Detection System will be aware of this difference between sensory input (the sound of C minor) and prior expectations (C major) and will produce a signal that something has gone wrong. Such signals can quickly change your state of mind. If you are playing in front of a crowd, the wrong-chord detection can shift you from a state of pleasant concentration on the music to an unpleasant, anxious thought about yourself and how the crowd is reacting to you.

Emotion and the Four Personality Systems

PSI theory takes an additional step that was not taken by Rogers. It identifies ways in which emotional states influence the ways in which people think about themselves (Kuhl & Joole, 2004). A core insight of PSI theory is that *changes in* emotions—specifically, increases or decreases in positive and negative emotions—activate the personality systems. These relations between emotions and personality systems are shown in Figure 6.2.

A key relation between emotion and personality systems is the one shown in the upper-right portion of the figure. According to PSI theory, decreases in negative emotion tend to activate the holistic thinking-and-feeling system. Reductions in negative emotion are a signal indicating the one is in a safe situation, and this safety signal allows a person to rely on the intuitive thinking-and-feeling system that is the integrated self (Kuhl & Koole, 2004). By contrast, *decreases* in positive emotion—or the sort one would experience in our musical example above, in which you hit a wrong note—signal that one's goals are not being met. This signal, in turn, causes people to engage in analytic thinking to figure out what is going wrong.

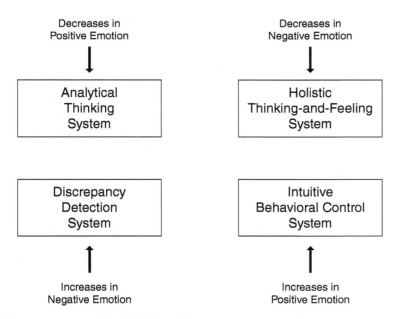

FIGURE 6.2 Four psychological systems identified by Personality Systems Interaction Theory and the ways in which changes in emotional states influence the activation of those systems. (This figure is not a complete presentation of all aspects of PSI theory; instead, it represents the theory's treatment of the regulation of behavior by cognitive systems that interact with emotional states. The terminology employed here simplifies some terminology employed originally. See Kuhl and Koole (2004), from which this figure is adapted).

Regarding the other two personality systems, increases in negative emotion are signals that there is a threat in the environment. These signals increase activity in the discrepancy detection system; the negative emotions cause this system to be "on the lookout for" problems that need to be detected and fixed. Finally, increases in positive emotion are associated with greater activation of the intuitive behavioral control system. Positive emotion states enable people to engage in creative, intuition-based actions.

Illustrative Research

Substantial lines of research support the theoretical claims of Personality Systems Interaction Theory. We will illustrate the approach by describing one example study, which explores the relation between emotion and intuitive, holistic styles of thinking.

To test the PSI prediction that decreases in negative emotion enables people to think holistically, Baumann and Kuhl (2002) asked participants to perform a "word triple" task. In this task, participated are presented with sets of three words. In some of the sets, the words are related to one another in ways that are hard to figure out; for example, you can see that the words "salt," "deep," and "foam" are related to one another only if you recognize that they are all linked to the word "sea". Identifying these relations requires holistic thinking; one has to consider the overall pattern that can be found in a whole set of information. The dependent measure in this study was participants' ability to solve word triple by providing a fourth word that was related to the other three ("sea" in the example above).

You might expect that word triples are entirely a cognitive task, that is, one whose success rests exclusively on the ability to think quickly. But PSI theory predicts that emotional states would influence task performance. People who are experiencing negative emotions that they are unable to control should perform less well on the task (see the upper right portion of Figure 6.2). To test this prediction, Baumann and Kuhl measured two qualities among their research participants: (1) the degree to which they currently were experiencing negative emotions (e.g., sadness, guilt) and (2) their tendency to stay in negative mood states rather than being able to get out of them (e.g., some people say that they "feel paralyzed" when things go wrong for them, whereas others say that bad news does not bother them for long).

The results of the study were just as predicted by PSI theory. Emotional states predicted the ability to think holistically. Specifically, the *lowest* level of performance on the word triple task was displayed by people who reported high levels of negative emotion that they could not control. The *highest* level of performance was achieved by people who said they were in a bad mood, but who also said that they *could* control their negative emotions. Reduced negative emotions enhance holistic thinking—a result with direct implications for Rogers's theory of personality, as we now discuss.

Implications for Rogers's Self Theory of Personality

PSI theory has two major implications for Rogers's theory of personality. The first concerns the concept of an integrated, whole self.

Scientific Basis for the Holistic, Integrated Self

As we noted, Rogers's was not able to identify the cognitive, emotional, and brain systems that enabled people to achieve a coherent sense of self. He proposed that the self exists, but did not provide a firm scientific basis for this proposal. This caused some psychologists, back in Rogers's day, to conclude that his theory was too speculative—in other words, that is was not sufficiently grounded in scientific evidence.

But today, PSI theory shows that the concept of an integrated self does, in fact, have a firm scientific basis (Kuhl et al., 2015). This is the major implication of the PSI analysis for Rogers's theory. The analysis of parallel process in human cognition, which is highlighted by PSI theory, supports Carl Rogers's central insight that the self is a coherent, integrated, holistic psychological system.

Demystifying Processes of Change in Client-Centered Therapy

A second implication concerns the process of therapy. As explained earlier in the chapter, Rogers felt that the central ingredient of his Client-Centered Theory was interpersonal. Rogers provided a warm, supportive interpersonal relationship in which clients experienced unconditional positive regard. This, in turn, changed the way clients thought about themselves, with the change being in the direction of positive personal growth.

The success of Rogerian therapy demonstrates the applied value of Rogers's approach. Yet, the psychological processes through which this change occurs remain, in Rogers's theory, a bit of a mystery. As you probably could detect in our coverage of "Presence" earlier in this chapter, even Rogers himself seemed a bit mystified that his therapeutic presence alone was sufficient to change clients' self and well-being. "Presence" is a compelling term to describe the therapeutic encounter. But it does not explain why the therapy works.

PSI theory demystifies the process of client-centered change in the following way. Clients entering therapy generally are experiencing distressed, negative emotions; these distressing emotions are, of course, a main reason why people seek therapy. An encounter with a supportive therapist is like to reduce these negative emotional states. In contrast to the stressful encounters that may make up the rest of the client's day, the therapeutic encounter is warm, positive, and uplifting. This positive interpersonal experience naturally would lower the client's level of negative emotions. Critically, this psychological process—a decrease in negative emotional states—is *exactly* the one that enhances holistic thinking according to PSI theory (see Figure 6.2) and research (Baumann & Kuhl, 2002). PSI theory thus suggests that the influence of Rogerian therapy on clients' thoughts and feelings is a special case of a more general psychological process. Whether a reduction in negative emotions occurs in everyday life, in a psychology experiment, or in client-centered therapy, lower levels of negative emotion enhance the holistic thinking-and-feeling system.

In sum, the implications of PSI theory for Rogers's theory of personality are quite positive. Some of Rogers's proposals about personality lacked firm scientific support when he stated them, but are more firmly supported today due to the advances provided by Kuhl's Personality Systems Interaction theory.

Critical Evaluation

We conclude our coverage of Rogers's theory by evaluating it critically. We do so in the same manner as we evaluated the psychodynamic approach, namely, by assessing its success in achieving five goals enumerated at the outset of our text, in Chapter 1. We then summarize the theory's major contributions.

Scientific Observation: The Database

The first goal is to build a personality theory on a database of solid scientific observations. In many respects the scientific observations on which Rogers based his theory are quite admirable. Far more than Freud, Rogers was sensitive to the fact that scientific observations must be objective. One must ensure that any personal biases are eliminated from the process of data collection. Rogers and his colleagues took a number of steps to achieve this objectivity. They used objective personality assessment techniques such as the Q-sort. They employed experimental methods to evaluate whether client-centered therapy is effective. Even when working with traditional clinical interview data, Rogers took a major step forward that was never taken by Freud. Rogers allowed (with his clients' permission) transcripts and recordings of his therapy sessions to be made public. Outside observers thus could verify Rogers's clinical reports.

Other features of Rogers's scientific observations seem limited in light of contemporary science. One limitation involves the type of personality assessment method he used. Rogers relied exclusively on measures that are explicit, that is, measures in which clients and research participants make statements about their personality that are formed through conscious self-reflection and are stated publicly. The limitation is that people may not be able—or willing—to put some aspects of their personality into words. There may exist personality qualities that people cannot articulate explicitly. Recognizing this, many contemporary researchers employ implicit measures of self-concept. Rather than relying on people's explicit, conscious self-reports, research employs subtle, indirect measures, such as indices of the speed with which people respond to certain words or ideas that are related to the self-concept (Asendorpf, Banse, & Mücke, 2002; Greenwald et al., 2002). These implicit measures often are correlated only modestly with explicit measures of self-concept. This, in turn, suggests that people possess implicit beliefs about the self that are not revealed by the explicitly self-reported methods on which Rogers relied. The general point is that the phenomenological approach may exclude from investigation critical psychological processes that occur outside of conscious experience. Rogers, a self-critical thinker, was aware of this problem. His response was that the phenomenological approach is a valuable, necessary one for psychology, but perhaps not the only one of value (Rogers, 1964).

A second limitation of Rogers's database is its relative lack of cultural diversity. Rogers devoted surprisingly little attention to the possibility of cultural variation in the nature of self-concept. The contemporary research reviewed in our discussion of culture and self processes suggests that Rogers's theorizing may be compromised by this limitation in its database.

Theory: Systematic?

Much of Rogers's writing is impressionistic rather than systematic. In keeping with his approach to therapy, Rogers relates, in an open and genuine manner, his own experiences and feelings as a psychologist. The relative absence of strict logical structures contrasts starkly with the writing of most of the other theorists you will learn about in this book and raises the question of whether Rogers's theorizing was systematically enough.

This question is answered—in the affirmative—by Rogers's 1959 essay in which he presented his theoretical ideas in a formal manner. His exposition of interactions among alternative types of parent–child interactions, self-concept, and psychological distress versus well-being affirms that his impressionistic style was accompanied by extremely admirable clarity of thought.

The main limitation to Rogers's theorizing does not involve quality (e.g., whether it is systematic) but quantity. There is rather little of it. A biographer notes that Rogers was "reluctant to begin theorizing in the first place" and that even when he began his theoretical work he was "still reluctant to place too great an emphasis on his own formulation" (Kirschenbaum, 1979, p. 240). Even Rogers himself recognized the lack of development of his theoretical work. Reflecting back on the propositions of his own theory, Rogers (1959; 1977, p. 232) laments its "immaturity . . . only the most general description can be given of . . . functional relationships" that, ideally, would be specified with mathematical rigor. In sum, Rogers provided a theory that was systematic, yet less systematic than that of some other theorists discussed in this text, if only because he composed less formal theoretical work than did others.

Theory: Testable?

If one asks whether Rogers provided a theory that is testable through standard scientific methods, the answer depends on which elements of his theory one is talking about. In some aspects of his work, Rogers defined constructs with great clarity and provided suggestions for personality assessments that could be used to measure those constructs. Rogers's work on the actual and ideal self stands out in this regard. He formulated these theoretical ideas with clarity. He indicated that the Q-sort is a viable method for assessing aspects of self-concept. As a result, he provided an overall theoretical conception of self-concept that was testable. In addition, to this day his work on the necessary and sufficient conditions for therapeutic change stands out as among the very best of research on the process of psychotherapy.

Other aspects of Rogers's work are far less testable. Consider his belief that there is a universal motive toward self-actualization. How would one test this idea? As we noted in Chapter 5, Rogers's writing about self-actualization sometimes is more poetic than scientific; Rogers does not provide the sort of clear definition of the construct that could guide research. He himself also provided no objective assessment tool for measuring a person's degree or level of self-actualization. Rogers also provided few conceptual tools for comparing his belief in a single self-actualizing motive to potential alternative beliefs, such as that there are a number of fundamentally distinct motives that each play a role in self-actualization (e.g., a motive to understand oneself, a motive to understand the spiritual world, a motive to be compassionate toward others, etc.). It is hard to know what kind of evidence Rogers would have accepted as proof that there is not, in fact, a single overarching motive for self-actualization. This element of this theory, then, is not clearly testable.

Theory: Comprehensive?

When introducing personality theories in Chapter 1, we explained that one task for the theorist is to develop a framework that is comprehensive. In psychology, theories abound. But the field houses few theories with the intellectual breadth to qualify as a theory of the whole person, or a theory of personality.

The first theory you learned about, Freud's, was extraordinarily comprehensive. It is difficult to formulate questions about personality, personality development, and individual differences that are not addressed, either directly or indirectly, in Freud's framework. The same cannot be said of the theory of Rogers. Consider some of the following questions. How does our evolutionary background contribute to the explanation of personality structure and functioning? How do emotional states influence thinking processes? If people are so self-actualizing, why are sexual and aggressive impulses so central to human experience? How does our genetic endowment interact with social influences in the course of development? Now consider the question "What does Rogers say about these issues?" A limitation of Rogers's work is that he simply does not say much at all about these issues. In this regard, and others, his work is not comprehensive.

Rogers at a Glance					
Structure	Process	Growth and Development	Pathology	Change	Illustrative Case
Self; ideal self	Self-actualization; congruence of self and experience; incongruence and defensive distortion and denial	Congruence and self-actualization versus incongruence and defensiveness	Defensive maintenance of self; incongruence	Therapeutic atmosphere: congruence, unconditional positive regard, empathic understanding	Mrs. Oak

If one were to ask why Rogers's work is relatively lacking in comprehensiveness, one simple answer is that he devoted much of his energies to developing individual and group therapies rather than to establishing basic theory and research on personality. A further answer, though, is that in Rogers's efforts—and the highly related efforts of other phenomenological, humanistic, and hermeneutic thinkers—to treat people as social beings, he sometimes fails fully to treat people as biological beings. Sometimes we feel bad because of our views of ourselves. But sometimes we feel bad owing to biochemical factors that influence our mood. Sometimes we are anxious because events are incongruent with self-perceptions. But sometimes we are anxious because of the activation of basic biological mechanisms that have nothing to do with self-perception (see Chapter 9). Integrating the biological and the social aspects of human nature is difficult. Rogers's failure to tackle this task head on makes his work less comprehensive than some of the other personality theories we review in this text.

Applications

Rogers's contributions to applied psychology are profoundly important. At least three aspects of his client-centered therapy are of enduring significance to the field. Rogers underscored the importance of the interpersonal relationship between client and therapist, while also providing techniques for building that relationship. He helped to establish objective methods for determining whether a given therapeutic approach actually benefited clients. Finally, and perhaps most importantly, he treated his clients as persons, not as patients. Rather than treating people as patients who harbored mental illnesses that needed to be diagnosed, he empowered clients by treating them as people who were capable, through the power of the self-actualizing motive, of improving their own lives. Few other figures in modern psychology can claim as strong a set of contributions to the field. Rogers's ability to generate not only abstract theory but also useful applications is a great strength of his work.

Major Contributions and Summary

Carl Rogers's contributions to personality theory must be understood in historical context. Today, in early 21st-century psychology, discussion of the role of the self is commonplace. Almost all personality psychologists recognize that cognitive and affective processes involving the self are central to personality structure and functioning. This, however, was not the case in Rogers's day. When he began his work in the mid-20th century, neither of the guiding theoretical models in the field, psychoanalysis and behaviorism, attended carefully to the role of self processes. Rogers and his colleagues in the phenomenological and humanistic traditions contributed importantly to a historical redirection of attention to aspects of human psychology that had been neglected.

We conclude by summarizing the strengths and limitations of Rogers's contributions (Table 6.1). We encourage you, the reader, to weigh these strengths and limitations against those of other theories you learn about in this text. We end by applauding Rogers for something he did uniquely. More than any other personality theorist, Rogers attempted to be objective about what is otherwise left to the artist:

> *Truly, nothing in the world has occupied my thoughts as much as the Self, this riddle, that I live, that I am one and am separate and different from everybody else, that I am Siddhartha; and about nothing in the world do I know less than about myself, about Siddhartha.*

Source: Hesse (1951, p. 40).

Table 6.1   Summary of Strengths and Limitations of Rogers's Theory and Phenomenology

Strengths	Limitations
1. Focuses on important aspects of human existence that are neglected in many other theories, including self-concept and the human potential for personal growth.	1. Less comprehensive than some other theories, with little attention devoted to the biological bases of human nature.
2. Provides concrete therapeutic strategies that have proven useful in bringing about psychological change in therapy.	2. May exclude from research and clinical concern phenomena that lie outside of conscious experience.
3. Brings scientific objectivity and rigor to difficult-to-study processes involving both interpersonal relations and phenomena experience.	3. Devotes little attention to the possibility of cultural variation or situation-to-situation variation in psychological structures and processes involving the self, and thus provides few tools for explaining those variations that exist.

MAJOR CONCEPTS

Authenticity	Contingencies of self-worth	Human potential movement	Unconditional positive
Client-centered therapy	Empathic understanding	Self-determination theory	regard
Congruence	Existentialism	Self-experience discrepancy	

REVIEW

1. For Rogers, the neurotic person is one who is in a state of incongruence between self and experience. Experiences that are incongruent with the self-structure are subceived as threatening and may be either denied or distorted.

2. Research in the area of psychopathology has focused on the discrepancy between the self and ideal self, and the extent to which individuals disown or are vague about their feelings.

3. Rogers's focus was on the therapeutic process. The critical variable in therapy was seen as the therapeutic climate. Conditions of congruence (genuineness), unconditional positive regard, and empathic understanding were seen as essential to therapeutic change.

4. The case of Mrs. Oak, an early case published by Rogers, illustrates his publication of recorded therapy sessions for research purposes.

5. Rogers's views are part of the human potential movement, which emphasizes self-actualization and the fulfillment of each individual's potential. Abraham H. Maslow and existentialists like Viktor Frankl are also representatives of this movement.

6. Contemporary work on existentialist concerns, including feelings of authenticity, internally motivated goals, and cultural variations in the perceptions of self, extend Rogers's theorizing while also raising some questions about the universality of some psychological motives posited by Rogers.

7 Trait Theories of Personality: Allport, Eysenck, and Cattell

Chapter Focus

Chris has just graduated from college and started a job in a new city. He feels lonely and wants to meet some new people. After some hesitation, he decides to place a personals ad. He stares at his blank computer screen—what should he write? What kinds of personality characteristics would you choose to describe yourself? He chooses "Unconventional, sensitive, fun-loving, happy, humorous, kind, slender graduate, 22, seeks similar qualities in sane soulmate." Somebody who can be described this way may indeed be a desirable date!

The personality characteristics that Chris has described are what are known as personality *traits*. Personality traits are psychological characteristics that are stable over time and across situations; it's a good bet that somebody who is sensitive and kind today will also be sensitive and kind a month from now. This chapter is about traits, defined as broad dispositions to behave in particular ways.

Specifically, in this chapter, you will learn about three personality trait theories and their associated research programs. Two of these theories—those of Hans Eysenck and of Raymond Cattell—attempt to identify the basic *dimensions* of personality traits, that is, basic characteristics that everyone shares to a greater or lesser degree. The two associated research programs rely on a particular statistical procedure, *factor analysis*; this statistical procedure is used to identify the most basic individual differences in personality traits.

Historically, the trait approach has been popular in American and British psychology and, in the field's recent era, in personality psychology in Europe as well. Part of this popularity reflects the methodological sophistication of factor-analytic research methods and the relatively consistent research results that they yield. Part of this popularity is also rooted in the commonsense nature of trait theory; the scientific theories of personality traits have an intuitive appeal because their basic units of analysis—personality traits—are similar to simple nonscientific, "folk" understandings of personality.

Questions to be Addressed in this Chapter

1. What are the main ways in which individuals differ from one another in their feelings, thoughts, and behavior? How many different traits are needed to adequately describe these personality differences?

2. Does every person have a unique set of personality traits, or is it possible to identify a set of traits that is universal and that can serve as a taxonomy of individual differences?

3. If individuals can be described in terms of their characteristic traits, how are we to explain variability in behavior across time and situations?

We now introduce a third main perspective on personality, that of the trait theories. The trait theories differ strikingly from the Freudian and Rogerian perspectives you learned about in previous chapters. As you will see, the differences involve not only the substantive claims of the theories but also the scientific database on which the theories rest.

Trait theorists emphasize that a central feature of the sciences is measurement. In the history of the physical sciences, scientific advances often could occur only after the development of tools for measuring physical phenomena precisely. If Galileo and Newton had not had relatively precise measures of time, mass, and other physical properties, they could not have verified that the motion of physical objects was lawful. If contemporary physicists did not have precise instruments for detecting the presence of subatomic particles, their science would be relatively speculative. Scientific progress often rests on precise measurement.

Contrast this emphasis with the approach of Freud and Rogers. Freud's work was virtually devoid of objective scientific measurement. He inferred the presence of mental structures of varying strength while providing no tools for measuring them. Freud relied merely on case study reports, which are more interpretative and thus more subjective than traditional scientific measurement. Rogers was more attentive to measurement principles. Yet, some of his central theoretical constructs (e.g., the self-actualization motive) were not accompanied by measurement principles. (Rogers never provided a measure of individual differences, or intraindividual variations, in self-actualizing tendencies.) Surveying this scene, the trait theorists asked, Could these prior thinkers be said to have made truly scientific progress? Their answer: no. The work of "Jung and Freud . . . amounted scientifically almost to a disaster" concluded the trait theorist Raymond Cattell (1965, pp. 16–17). Trait theorists called for a new approach to the study of personality, one whose measures of psychological attributes were as objective and reliable as those found in the physical sciences. This chapter and the next review the progress they made.

A View of the Trait Theorists

In our previous chapters, we introduced theoretical perspectives by reviewing the life of the primary theorist (Freud in Chapter 3 and Rogers in Chapter 5). Our approach to the trait theories is different. The difference reflects the nature of the theories and theorists. There simply is no single individual—no one dominant figure, no prime mover—in the trait theories of personality, in the way that there was in the psychodynamic and phenomenological traditions. In the 20th century, the foundations for trait psychology were laid by three investigators whose work is of particular significance: Gordon Allport, Raymond Cattell, and Hans Eysenck. Their contributions are reviewed in the present chapter. In the contemporary 21st-century field, much investigation centers around a theoretical perspective that endeavors to capitalize on the best aspects of the contributions of Allport, Cattell, and Eysenck. This approach, the five-factor model of personality, is reviewed in Chapter 8. Rather than providing biographical information for all these individuals right now, we include such information when introducing their respective contributions in the following sections.

Although the various trait theorists have made distinct contributions, their work features many common themes. There is a coherent "trait perspective" on personality. As you'll now see, it is a perspective that will seem immediately familiar. The trait theorist's main scientific constructs are quite similar to the words and ideas you use to discuss people in your everyday life.

Trait Theory's View of the Person

People love to talk about personality. We can spend hours discussing people's characteristics: Our boss is grumpy; our roommate, sloppy; our professor, quick witted. (Well, we hope your professor is quick witted rather than sloppy and grumpy.) We even discuss the loyalty of our dog and the laziness of our cat. When talking about people, we commonly use personality **trait** terms—words that describe people's typical styles of experience and action. Apparently, people think that traits are central to personality. Likewise, personality researchers associated with the trait approach consider traits to be the major units of personality. Obviously, there is more to personality than traits, but traits have loomed large throughout the history of personality psychology.

The Trait Concept

What, then, is a trait? Personality traits refer to consistent patterns in the way individuals behave, feel, and think. If we describe an individual with the trait term *kind*, we mean that this individual tends to act kindly over time (weeks, months, maybe years) and across situations (with friends, family, strangers, etc.). In addition, if we use the word *kind*, we usually mean that the person is at least as kind as the average person. If one believed that the person was less kind than average, he or she would not be described as "kind."

Trait terms, then, have two connotations: consistency and distinctiveness. By consistency, we mean that the trait describes a regularity in the person's behavior. The person seems predisposed to act in the way described by the trait term; indeed, traits often are referred to as "dispositions" or "dispositional constructs" (e.g., McCrae & Costa, 1999, 2008) to capture the idea that the person appears predisposed to act in a certain way. The idea of disposition highlights an important fact about trait terms as used by trait theorists of personality. If a trait theorist uses a trait term—for example, *sociable*—to describe someone, she does not mean that the person *always* will act sociably, across all settings of life. As the Dutch trait psychologist De Raad (2005) has emphasized, trait terms implicitly refer to behaviors in a type of social context. The trait theorist would expect the sociable person to be consistently sociable across settings that involve other people and in which sociable behavior is allowed by prevailing social norms. There is no expectation that the person would be sociable toward inanimate objects or act sociably when instructed by an authority figure to act otherwise.

By the other connotation, distinctiveness, we mean simply that the trait theorist is concerned primarily with psychological characteristics in which people differ—features that therefore make one person distinct compared to others. Trait theorists of personality are interested in traits for which there are significant differences among people.

The decision to build a personality theory on trait constructs implies a certain view of the person. It implies that there is substantial consistency to individuals' lives. Contemporary social life presents many changes: People change schools and jobs, meet new friends, marry, unmarry, remarry, and move to different communities if not different countries. At any one point in time, life may present multiple roles: student, employee, son or daughter, parent, community member. The trait theorist's fundamental message is that, despite all these variations, there is a consistent personality "in there." People possess psychological qualities that endure, almost regardless of time and place.

Trait Theory's View of the Science of Personality

The discussion that opened this chapter is revealing of the view of personality science implicit in most trait approaches. As you learned, a paramount interest of trait theorists is measurement. The ability to measure psychological traits reliably and validly is the utterly critical first step in building a science of personality in the trait-theoretical view.

This viewpoint displays a kind of conservatism that is valuable in the sciences. Both Freud and Rogers allowed themselves to create theories that went far beyond their available data; there were no direct, or indirect, measures of the strength of libidinal drives, of self-actualization motives, and so forth. Trait theorists of the mid-20th century rejected this sort of theorizing as too speculative. They felt that scientific measurement should constrain, and determine, theorizing. One should posit a personality structure if, and only if, the statistical analysis of carefully constructed measures suggests the existence of that structure.

Chris Ryan / Getty Images

Trait theories of personality are built on careful measurement. Researchers develop standardized personality tests and administer them to large numbers of individuals under identical testing conditions.

Scientific Functions Served by Trait Constructs

A main question to ask about the trait theory's view of science is, "Why posit trait constructs?" In other words, "What is it that trait constructs *do* in a science of personality?" Trait theorists use trait constructs to serve at least two, and sometimes three, scientific functions: description, prediction, and explanation.

Description

All personality trait theorists use trait constructs descriptively. Traits summarize a person's typical behavior and thus describe what a person typically is like. Since description is a critical first step in any scientific endeavor, trait theories could be seen as providing basic descriptive facts that need to be explained by any theory of personality.

Most trait theorists do not seek just to describe individual people, one at a time; rather, they try to establish an overall descriptive scheme within which any and all persons can be described. They try, in other words, to establish a personality *taxonomy*. In any science, a taxonomy is a scientist's way of classifying the things being studied. Since trait constructs refer to consistent styles of experience and behavior, a trait taxonomy is a way of classifying people according to their characteristic, average types of experience, and action.

Prediction

One question for a trait theorist is whether these classifications, within a taxonomy of personality traits, are of practical value. What can one do with knowledge of people's personality trait scores?

Throughout the history of the trait theories, a primary answer to this question has been as follows: You can predict things. People with different levels of a given personality trait may differ predictably in their everyday behavior. For example, if one knows college students' self-ratings on traits such as extraversion and conscientiousness, one can predict aspects of their personal environments, such as the decorations in, and degree of neatness of, their personal office spaces and dorm rooms (Gosling, Ko, Mannarelli, & Morris, 2002). Often, one can make predictions that have important practical value. Suppose you are running a business and want to hire employees who will be reliable, honest workers. You are faced with a job of prediction: How can you predict which applicants will be good employees? One way of making this prediction is by giving people tests that measure their characteristic personality traits; trait psychologists have been deeply involved in the practical task of predicting on-the-job performance (Roberts & Hogan, 2001). More controversially, in a recent US election, measures of personality traits obtained through social media sources were used to predict citizens' voting and responses to campaign materials, in support of the campaign of Donald J. Trump (Gonzales, 2017).

Explanation

In addition to description and prediction, a third scientific task is explanation. If personality psychology aspires to be a science, then it must tackle the most important challenge for a scientific theory, namely, explanation. Note that prediction and explanation are very different things (Toulmin, 1961). For example, in ancient times, Babylonians could describe and predict astronomical events such as lunar eclipses, but they appeared to have no scientific understanding whatsoever of why these events occurred as they did. In an opposite case, Darwin explained how organisms evolved through natural selection, but he did not literally predict the past evolutionary events (Toulmin, 1961).

Some trait theorists suggest that trait constructs can be used to explain a person's behavior. One might say that a student shows up on time for class and takes good lecture notes *because* the person is high on the trait of conscientiousness. However, not all trait psychologists use trait terms to accomplish this third scientific function: explanation. Some confine themselves to description and prediction. They view a trait taxonomy as being akin to a map. A map of the continents and oceans on Earth does not explain why the continents and oceans have their particular location; for that explanation, one needs additional scientific work (e.g., a theory of plate tectonics). Yet, the map is still a crucial step in scientific progress.

As you will see in this chapter and again in Chapter 9, some psychologists try to move from description to explanation by identifying biological factors underlying a given trait. People who obtain high versus low scores on a personality trait test might differ systematically in a neural or biochemical system, which could be interpreted as the causal basis of the trait and trait-related behavior. This possibility, which many trait theorists pursue, raises another aspect of trait theory's view of the person. It is strongly biological. Most trait theorists believe that inherited biological factors are a primary determinant of individual differences in traits. We discuss this possibility, and the related scientific evidence, both in the present chapter and in Chapter 9.

In sum, trait theorists differ in their claims about the explanatory status of trait constructs. This raises an important point for you to keep in mind. There is no one trait theory. The trait theories are a family of interrelated, but not identical, perspectives. In the next section, we review features that most, if not all, trait theories share.

Trait Theories of Personality: Basic Perspectives Shared by Trait Theorists

A set of shared assumptions jointly define the trait approach. The most basic assumption is that people possess broad predispositions, called traits, to respond in particular ways. In other words, it is assumed that personality can be characterized in terms of an individual's consistent likelihood of behaving, feeling, or thinking in a particular way (e.g., the likelihood of acting in an outgoing and friendly manner, or of feeling nervous and worried, or of being reliable and conscientious). People who have a strong tendency to behave in these ways are described as being high on these traits, whereas people with a lesser tendency to behave in these ways are described as low on the traits. The person who frequently is outgoing would be called high on extraversion, whereas the unreliable, forgetful individual might be low on conscientiousness. All trait theorists agree that these generalized tendencies to act in one versus another manner are the fundamental building blocks of personality.

A related assumption is that there is a direct correspondence between the person's performance of trait-related actions and his or her possession of the corresponding trait. People who act (or report that they act) in a more extraverted or conscientious manner than others are thought, by the trait theorist, to possess more of (to be higher on) the corresponding traits of extraversion and conscientiousness. This point may seem so obvious that it isn't even worth stating. You may be thinking, "Of course people who display more of the trait-related behavior have more of the trait." But note how this thinking contrasts with an earlier theory we covered, namely, psychoanalysis. To the psychoanalyst, someone who reports being more "calm and at ease" than other people may not, in reality, possess more of the psychological characteristic of calmness. Instead, such persons may be so anxious that they are repressing their anxieties and merely saying that they are calm. Psychoanalysis, as well as other personality theories we will cover later in this text, recognizes that there may be highly indirect relations between overt behavior and underlying personality characteristics. In contrast, the research procedures of trait theory assume that overt behavior and underlying traits are linked in a more direct, one-to-one manner. If someone reports a low amount of trait-related behavior on a test of personality traits, then he or she is said to possess low amounts of the given trait.

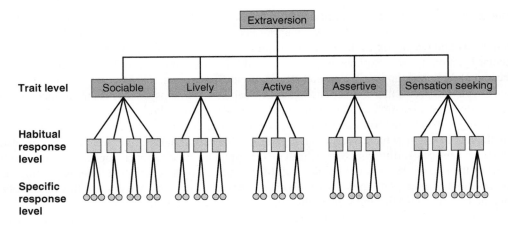

FIGURE 7.1 Diagrammatic representation of hierarchical organization of personality: extraversion–introversion (E). (Note: extraversion is one end of the E-I dimension. The other end, I, is not represented here.)
Adapted from Eysenck (1970, 1990).

Another shared assumption is that human behavior and personality can be organized into a hierarchy. A famous hierarchical analysis was provided by Eysenck (Figure 7.1), whose contributions are reviewed in more detail elsewhere in this chapter. Eysenck suggested that, at its simplest level, behavior can be considered in terms of specific responses. However, some of these responses are linked together and form more general habits. Groups of habits that tend to occur together form traits. For example, people who prefer meeting people to reading also generally enjoy themselves at a lively party; this bit of information suggests that these two habits can be grouped together under the trait of sociability. Finally, at the highest level of organization, various traits may be linked together to form what Eysenck called secondary, higher-order factors or superfactors (which also are traits, but at the highest, most abstract level of generalization). In sum, trait theories suggest that people display broad predispositions to respond in certain ways, that these dispositions are organized in a hierarchical manner, and that the trait concept can be a foundation for a scientific theory of personality.

The Trait Theory of Gordon W. Allport (1897–1967)

A figure of great historical importance to the development of trait theory, and personality psychology in general, was the Harvard University psychologist Gordon W. Allport. History remembers Allport as much for the issues he raised and the principles he emphasized than for a particular theory he created. Throughout his long and influential career, Allport highlighted the healthy and organized aspects of human behavior. This emphasis contrasted with other views of the time that emphasized the animalistic, neurotic, tension-reducing, and mechanistic aspects of behavior. Allport criticized psychoanalysis in this regard; he was particularly fond of telling the following story. While traveling through Europe at age 22, Allport decided it would be interesting to visit Freud. When he entered Freud's office, he was met with expectant silence as Freud waited to learn of Allport's mission. Finding himself unprepared for silence, Allport decided to start an informal conversation with the description of a four-year-old boy with a dirt phobia, whom he had met on the train. After he completed his description of the boy

Bettmann/Getty Images

Gordon W. Allport.

and his compulsive mother, Freud asked, "And was that little boy you?" Allport describes his response as follows:

> *Flabbergasted and feeling a bit guilty, I contrived to change the subject. While Freud's misunder-standing of my motivation was amusing, it also started a deep train of thought. I realized that he was accustomed to neurotic defenses and that my manifest motivation (a sort of rude curiosity and youth-ful ambition) escaped him. For therapeutic progress, he would have to cut through my defenses, but it so happened that therapeutic progress was not here an issue. This experience taught me that depth psychology, for all its merits, may plunge too deep and that psychologists would do well to give full recognition to manifest motives before probing the unconscious.*

Source: Allport (1967, p. 8).

A particularly amusing aspect of this episode is that Allport personally was very meticu-lous, punctual, neat, and orderly—possessing many of the characteristics Freud associated with the compulsive personality. Freud's question may not have been as far off as Allport suggested!

Allport's first publication, written with his older brother Floyd, centered on traits as an impor-tant aspect of personality theory (Allport & Allport, 1921). Allport believed that traits are the basic units of personality. According to him, traits actually exist and are based in the nervous system. They represent generalized personality dispositions that account for regularities in the functioning of a person across situations and over time. Traits can be defined by three proper-ties—frequency, intensity, and range of situations. For example, a very submissive person would frequently be very submissive over a wide range of situations.

Traits: Personality Structure in Allport's Theory

In a now classic analysis of personality descriptors, Allport and Odbert (1936) differentiated per-sonality traits from other units of analysis in personality research. They defined traits as "gener-alized and personalized determining tendencies—consistent and stable modes of an individual's adjustment to his environment" (1936, p. 26). Traits are different from psychological states or behavioral activities that are temporary and induced by external circumstances. Chaplin, John, and Goldberg (1988) replicated Allport and Odbert's classifications of personality descriptors into three categories: traits, states, and activities. For example, whereas a person may well be gentle throughout his or her lifetime, an infatuation (an internal state) typically does not last and even the most enjoyable carousing (activity) must come to an end.

Having distinguished traits from states and activities, the next question is whether there might exist different kinds of traits. Allport addressed this question by distinguishing among cardinal traits, central traits, and secondary dispositions. A **cardinal trait** expresses a disposition that is so pervasive and outstanding in a person's life that virtually every act is traceable to its influence. For example, we speak of the Machiavellian person, named after Niccolò Machiavelli's portrayal of the successful Renaissance ruler; of the sadistic person, named after the Marquis de Sade; and of the authoritarian personality who sees virtually everything in black-and-white, stereotyped ways. Generally, people have few, if any, such cardinal traits. **Central traits** (e.g., honesty, kindness, assertiveness) express dispositions that cover a more limited range of situations than is true for cardinal traits. **Secondary dispositions** are traits that are the least conspicuous, generalized, and consistent. In other words, people possess traits with varying degrees of significance and generality.

Allport did not claim that a trait is expressed in all situations, regardless of a situation's characteristics. He recognized that "traits are often aroused in one situation and not in another" (Allport, 1937, p. 331). For example, even the most aggressive people can be expected to modify their behavior if the situation calls for nonaggressive behavior, and even the most introverted person may behave in an extraverted fashion in certain situations. A trait expresses what a person generally does over many situations, not what will be done in any one situation. According to Allport, both trait and situation concepts are necessary to understand behavior. The trait concept is necessary to explain the consistency of behavior, whereas recognizing the importance of the situation is necessary to explain the variability of behavior.

Functional Autonomy

Allport analyzed not only stable traits but also motivational processes. He emphasized the **functional autonomy** of human motives. This means that although the motives of an adult may have their roots in the tension-reducing motives of the child, as Freud suggested, the adult grows out of the early motives. In adult life, motives become independent of, or autonomous from, earlier tension-reducing drives. What originally began as an effort to reduce hunger or anxiety can become a source of pleasure and motivation in its own right. What began as an activity designed to earn a living can become pleasurable and an end in itself. Although hard work and the pursuit of excellence can be motivated originally by a desire for approval from parents and other adults, they can become valued ends in themselves—pursued independently of whether they are emphasized by others. Thus, "what was once extrinsic and instrumental becomes intrinsic and impelling. The activity once served a drive or some simple need; it now serves itself or, in a larger sense, serves the self-image (self-ideal) of the person. Childhood is no longer in the saddle; maturity is" (Allport, 1961, p. 229). This of course sets Allport's work apart from Freud's, since Freud explained adult behaviors in terms of early childhood drives whose basic motivational force endured throughout adulthood.

Idiographic Research

A final distinguishing feature of Allport's contributions is his emphasis on the uniqueness of the individual. Unlike the other trait theorists we will discuss, Allport primarily endorsed an idiographic approach to research. An idiographic strategy, as we explained in Chapter 2, focuses on the potentially unique individual. In-depth studies of individual persons are viewed as a path for learning about people generally. This approach contrasts with that of other trait theorists, who generally adopt nomothetic procedures in which large numbers of individuals are described in terms of a common, universal set of personality traits.

One illustration of Allport's idiographic procedures was analysis of his use of materials unique to the individual case. For example, Allport published 172 letters from a particular woman. The letters were the basis of a clinical characterization of her personality, as well as for quantitative analysis. This sort of idiographic research highlights the pattern and organization of multiple traits *within* a person rather than a person's standing, relative to others, on isolated trait variables.

Comment on Allport

In personality psychology, Allport generally is revered. A biography (Nicholson, 2002) highlights his contributions not only to trait psychology but also to personality psychology's emergence as a unique scientific discipline. Nonetheless, Allport's empirical contributions were limited. He clarified the trait concept but did little research to establish its utility. He believed that many traits were hereditary but conducted no research on their genetic basis. He documented that people display distinctive patterns of trait-related behavior and that traits interact with situational influences, but provided no detailed processing that could explain these observations (Zuroff, 1986).

Furthermore, Allport's idiographic emphasis partly backfired. Some felt it was antiscientific, thinking that the study of individual idiosyncrasies conflicted with science's search for general laws. In retrospect, this was a poor reading of Allport's idiographic efforts. To build an adequate science of human beings, it may be necessary to study individual persons in detail. Idiographic strategies may advance, rather than impair, a general understanding of persons. Allport, like Freud, recognized that detailed case studies may yield insight into general principles that are found across individual cases. Scientists in other human sciences recognize this in a similar fashion; for example, a famed anthropologist who studies, in detail, the meaning systems of particular cultures concludes that, as a general principle of scientific understanding, "the road to the general, to the revelatory simplicities of science, lies through a concern with the particular, the circumstantial, the concrete" (Geertz, 1973, p. 53).

This idiographic approach, however, is *not* the one pursued by most trait theorists other than Allport. Subsequent trait theorists put little stock in idiographic studies. Instead, contrary to Allport's suggestions, they studied populations of individuals and tried to identify the most important individual differences in the population at large.

Before presenting these theories, we will explain (1) the primary scientific problem faced by the trait theorists discussed in the remainder of this chapter, as well as Chapter 8 and (2) the statistical tool they used to solve it, namely, the statistical technique of factor analysis. We then turn to the trait theories of Raymond B. Cattell and Hans J. Eysenck.

Identifying Primary Trait Dimensions: Factor Analysis

With the exception of Allport, trait psychologists generally have tried to identify a universal set of traits, that is, a set of traits that everyone possesses to a greater or lesser degree. Physically, everyone is more or less tall, heavy or thin, young or old, and so forth; height, weight, and age are universal dimensions that can be used to describe any and all persons. Psychologically, might there be a set of universal trait dimensions that can be used to describe the personality characteristics of any and all persons? If so, how can we identify those traits? Identifying a set of basic, universal traits is a scientific challenge that is fundamental to the history of trait theories of personality.

This challenge is made difficult by the fact that there seem to be so many traits. Some people are absentminded. Some people are agreeable. Some are aggressive. Some altruistic. Some antagonistic. Some argumentative. There are so many traits—and we're still in the A's! How can one possibly identify a simple yet comprehensive set of basic traits?

The key insight required to solve this problem is noticing that some traits go together, that is, that they tend to co-occur. When talking about physical characteristics, no one is bewildered by the large number of physical features: long left arms, long right arms, long left legs, long right legs, long fingers, and so on. We recognize that these qualities co-occur and summarize their co-occurrence with a simple dimension: height (or size). Height, then, is a more basic physical trait than "length of left leg"; the lengths of individual body parts are just manifestations of the person's overall height.

Psychological traits also co-occur. Consider our list of traits two paragraphs back. More often than not, if one finds someone who is extremely argumentative and extremely aggressive, it is unlikely that he or she will be extremely altruistic and extremely agreeable. Intuition tells us that certain traits co-occur, which suggests that some traits may be manifestations of other more basic traits. The question, then, is, How can one identify the basic traits? Clearly, one can't just rely on intuition. What is needed is a precise tool for identifying a basic structure of personality traits.

The tool that trait theorists have relied on is a statistical technique. The technique is called **factor analysis**. Factor analysis is a statistical tool for summarizing the ways in which a large number of variables go together, or co-occur. As you learned in Chapter 2, a correlation is a number that summarizes the degree to which *two* variables go together. If there were only two variables in which trait theorists were interested, then the technique of correlation would be sufficient for their purposes. However, the trait theorist is interested in a *lot* of variables. There seem to be hundreds of possible traits to measure. Once one measures them, there are hundreds and hundreds of correlations between one variable and another. Factor analysis is a statistical method for identifying patterns in this mass of correlations. Ideally, a factor analysis (i.e., a particular application of the general technique of factor analysis) will identify a small number of factors that summarize the intercorrelations among the large number of variables.

In a typical factor-analytic study, a large number of test items are administered to many subjects. Inevitably, some of these items are positively correlated with one another. People who answer a question (e.g., "Do you often go to loud and noisy parties?") in one way answer other questions (e.g., "Do you enjoy spending time with large groups of people?") in a similar manner. Some items are negatively correlated (e.g., responses to "Do you prefer to stay home at night rather than going out?" might be negatively correlated with answers to the two previous questions in this paragraph). In principle, large clusters of items might be correlated in this manner. These clusters might reflect the influence of an underlying factor, that is, something that is responsible for the correlations among the items (in the way that height is responsible for the correlations among long leg, long arm, and so on, in our previous example). Factor analysis identifies these patterns, or clusters, or correlations. The technique of factor analysis, then, simplifies the information contained in a large table of correlations by identifying a small set of factors, where each factor represents one cluster of correlations.

The factors technically are merely mathematical. Factor analysis is a technique of mathematical statistics, not psychology. However, using their knowledge of personality, psychologists generally attach psychological labels to the factors. The labels are meant to identify the primary psychological content in the test items that correlate with one another. In our example (the one with noisy parties, large groups of people, etc.), factor analysis would identify a mathematical factor that represents the correlations among the items, and the psychologist would give that factor a name such as "sociability."

Factor analysis is of the greatest importance to trait theories. It is the tool they use to identify the structures of personality. To most trait theorists, the factors that are identified in factor-analytic studies are the structures of personality. If a factor analysis identifies six mathematical factors that summarize correlations among personality test items, then the trait psychologist will usually refer to the resulting six-dimensional mathematical structure as the "structure of personality."

The use of factor analysis to identify personality structures has some significant advantages as compared to the procedures used by previous theorists. Previously (e.g., in the work of Freud, Jung, or Rogers), theorists relied heavily on their intuition. They observed clinical cases and intuited that certain personality structures were responsible for their clients' behavior. But human intuition can be faulty (Nisbett & Ross, 1980). Rather than relying on intuition to identify personality structures, the trait theorist relies on an objective statistical procedure: factor analysis.

Note that the statistical procedure identifies patterns of covariation in test responses. It does not answer the question of why the responses covary. It is the researcher, using his or her knowledge of psychology and relying on his or her theoretical beliefs, who infers the existence of some common entity (the factor) and interprets it. Different psychologists may make different interpretations. For example, in the contemporary field, some researchers conclude that the core of extraversion is reward sensitivity, that is, that extraverts are highly motivated to attain positive, goal-related rewards (Lucas, Diener, Grob, Suh, & Shao, 2000). Others, using similar correlational and factor-analytic methods, disagree, concluding instead that the core of extraversion is social attention; extraverts appear to enjoy being the object of attention (Ashton, Lee, & Paunonen, 2002).

Also, the exact nature of, and number of, factors one obtains hinges partly on subjective decisions about how exactly to conduct the analysis. Factor analysis is a complex set of techniques, not a simple arithmetic algorithm, and the researcher must choose exactly how to proceed. This is why, as you will now see, different investigators who each rely on factor-analytic methods end up with somewhat different factors, and different numbers of factors, in their theories of personality.

The Factor-Analytic Trait Theory of Raymond B. Cattell (1905–1998)

Raymond B. Cattell was born in 1905 in Devonshire, England. He obtained a B.Sc. degree in chemistry from the University of London in 1924. Cattell then turned to psychology, obtaining a Ph.D. degree at the same university in 1929. Cattell did personality research and acquired clinical experience in Britain, then moved to the United States in 1937. He spent much of his career as professor and director of the Laboratory of Personality Assessment at the University of Illinois. During his professional career, he was enormously prolific, publishing more than 200 articles and 15 books. Cattell stands as one of the most influential psychological scientists of the 20th century (Haggbloom et al., 2002).

Early in his career, Cattell gained knowledge of the newly developed (in his time) technique of factor analysis. He quickly exploited its potential. Specifically, with his background in chemistry Cattell recognized the importance to scientific advance of having a taxonomy of "basic elements," such as the periodic table of elements that is foundational to work in the physical sciences. Cattell judged that factor analysis could yield a set of basic psychological elements that would be foundational to personality psychology.

Surface and Source Traits: Personality Structure in Cattell's Theory

Cattell provided two conceptual distinctions that are both valuable for distinguishing among the multiplicity of personality traits. One distinction differentiates **surface traits** from **source traits**. Surface and source traits represent different levels of analysis; in this regard, Cattell relied on the idea that there are hierarchical relations among trait concepts. Surface traits represent behavioral tendencies that are literally superficial: They exist "on the surface" and can be observed. By examining patterns of intercorrelations among a large number of personality trait terms, Cattell was able to identify roughly 40 groups of trait terms that were highly intercorrelated. Each grouping, to Cattell, represented a surface trait.

The psychologist, of course, does not want merely to describe behavior "on the surface." The psychologist wants to identify psychological structures that underlie observable behavior tendencies. To this end, Cattell sought to identify source traits, that is, internal psychological structures that were the source, or underlying cause, of observed intercorrelations among surface traits.

Raymond B. Cattell.

To understand this co-occurrence of traits, Cattell relied on the technique of factor analysis. He developed systematic measures of each of the surface traits, administered these measures of surface traits to large numbers of people, and used factor analysis to identify patterns in the intercorrelations among the surface traits. The factors (i.e., the mathematical dimensions identified via factor analysis) that summarized the correlations among surface traits are, in Cattell's system, the source traits. These source traits that are revealed through factor analysis are the core personality structures in Cattell's theory of personality.

And what exactly are these source traits? Cattell identified 16 source traits. He grouped the 16 source traits into three categories: ability traits, temperament traits, and dynamic traits. **Ability traits** refer to skills and abilities that allow the individual to function effectively. Intelligence is an example of an ability trait. **Temperament traits** involve the emotional life and the stylistic quality of behavior. The tendency to work quickly versus slowly, to be calm versus emotional, or to act impulsively or only after deliberation are all qualities of temperament. Finally, **dynamic traits** concern the striving, motivational life of the individual. Individuals who are more or less motivated differ in dynamic traits. **Ability, temperament,** and **dynamic traits** are seen as capturing the major stable elements of personality.

Sources of Evidence: L-Data, Q-Data, and OT-Data

How did Cattell identify these traits? What exactly was his scientific database? A great virtue of Cattell's work is that there was no *one* database. Cattell relied on three different types—or three different sources—of data about personality. His distinctions among three different types of data are enduringly valuable to personality science.

Cattell's distinctions, presented here, should seem familiar; they are a basis of the LOTS classification of data sources we presented in Chapter 2. Cattell distinguished among

(1) life record data (**L-data**), (2) self-report questionnaire data (**Q-data**), and (3) objective-test data (**OT-data**).

The first, L-data, relates to behavior in actual, everyday situations such as school performance or interactions with peers. These may be actual counts of behaviors or ratings made on the basis of such observations. The second, Q-data, involves self-report data or responses to questionnaires, such as the Eysenck personality inventory discussed later in this chapter. The third, OT-data, involves behavioral miniature situations in which the subject is unaware of the relationship between the response and the personality characteristic being measured. Cattell himself developed a large number of these mini-situations; for example, a tendency to be assertive could be expressed in behaviors such as long exploratory distance on a finger maze test, fast tempo in arm–shoulder movement, and fast speed of letter comparisons. Ideally, the same factors or traits should be obtained from the three kinds of data.

Originally, Cattell began with the factor analyses of L-data and found 15 factors that appeared to account for most of an individual's personality. He then set out to determine whether comparable factors could be found in Q-data. Thousands of questionnaire items were written and administered to large numbers of people. Factor analyses were run to see which items went together. The main result of this research is a questionnaire known as the Sixteen Personality Factor (16 P.F.) Questionnaire. Initially, Cattell made up neologisms, such as "surgency," to name his personality trait factors, hoping to avoid misinterpretations of them. Nonetheless, the terms given in Table 7.1 roughly capture the meanings of these trait factors. As can be seen, they cover a wide variety of aspects of personality, particularly in terms of temperament (e.g., emotionality) and attitudes (e.g., conservative). In general, the factors found with Q-data appeared to be similar to those found with L-data, but some were unique to each kind of data. Illustrative L-data ratings and Q-data items for one trait are presented in Figure 7.1.

Cattell was committed to the use of questionnaires, in particular, those derived from a factor-analytic perspective, such as the 16 P.F. Questionnaire. At the same time, he expressed concern about the problems of motivated distortion and self-deception in relation to questionnaire

Table 7.1 **Cattell's 16 Personality Factors Derived from Questionnaire Data**

Reserved	Outgoing
Less intelligent	More intelligent
Stable, ego strength	Emotionality/neuroticism
Humble	Assertive
Sober	Happy-go-lucky
Expedient	Conscientious
Shy	Venturesome
Tough minded	Tender minded
Trusting	Suspicious
Practical	Imaginative
Forthright	Shrewd
Placid	Apprehensive
Conservative	Experimenting
Group dependent	Self-sufficient
Undisciplined	Controlled
Relaxed	Tense

responses. He also felt that the questionnaire is of particularly questionable utility with mental patients. Because of problems with L-data and Q-data, and because the original research strategy itself called for investigations with OT-data, Cattell's later efforts were concerned more with personality structure as derived from OT-data. It is the source traits as expressed in objective tests that are the "real coin" for personality research.

The results from L-data and Q-data research were important in guiding the development of miniature test situations; that is, the purpose was to develop objective tests that would measure the source traits already discovered. Thus, more than 500 tests were constructed to cover the hypothesized personality dimensions. These tests were administered to large groups of subjects, and repeated factoring of data from different research situations eventually led to the designation of 21 OT-data source traits.

As mentioned, the source traits or factors found in L-data and Q-data could, for the most part, be matched to one another. How, then, do the OT-data factors match those derived from L-data and Q-data? Despite the years of research effort, the results were disappointing: Although some relations were found across all three data sources, no direct one-to-one mapping of factors was possible.

In summary, we have described four steps in Cattell's research. (1) He set out to define the structure of personality in three areas of observation, called L-data, Q-data, and OT-data. (2) He started his research with L-data and through the factor analysis of ratings came up with 15 source traits. (3) Based on research findings, he developed the 16 P.F. Questionnaire, which contains 12 traits that match traits found in the L-data research and four traits that appear to be unique to questionnaire methods. (4) Using these results to guide his research in the development of objective tests, Cattell found 21 source traits in OT-data that appear to have a complex and low-level relation to the traits found in the other data.

The source traits found in the three types of observations do not complete Cattell's formulation of the structure of personality. However, the traits presented in this section do describe the general nature of the structure of personality as formulated by Cattell. In other words, here we have the foundation for psychology's table of the elements—its classification scheme. But what is the evidence for the existence of these traits? Cattell (1979) cited the following: (1) the results of factor analyses of different kinds of data, (2) similar results across cultures, (3) similar results across age groups, (4) utility in the prediction of behavior in the natural environment, and (5) evidence of significant genetic contributions to many traits.

Stability and Variability in Behavior

Cattell did not view persons as static entities who behaved the same way in all situations. Social action depends not only on traits but other factors as well. Cattell highlighted two other determinants: states and roles. **State** refers to emotion and mood at a particular, delimited point in time. One's psychological state is partly determined by one's immediate situation. Illustrative states are anxiety, depression, fatigue, arousal, and curiosity. To Cattell, the exact description of an individual at a given moment requires measurement of both traits and states: "Every practicing psychologist—indeed every intelligent observer of human nature and human history—realizes that the state of a person at a given moment determines his or her behavior as much as do his or her traits" (1979, p. 169).

Regarding the concept of **role**, Cattell noted that certain behaviors are more closely linked to social roles one must play than to personality traits one possesses. Social roles, not personality traits, explain why people shout at football games and not in churches (Cattell, 1979). Two people may act differently toward one another in different settings in which they play different roles. For example, a teacher may respond differently to a child's behavior in the classroom than when outside the classroom and no longer in the role of teacher.

In sum, although Cattell believed that traits foster stability in behavior across situations, he also recognized that a person's mood (state) and style of self-presentation in a given situation (role) contribute to behavior: "How vigorously Smith attacks his meal depends not only on how hungry he happens to be but also on his temperament and whether he is having dinner with his employer or is eating alone at home" (Nesselroade & Delhees, 1966, p. 583).

Comment on Cattell

One cannot help but be impressed with the scope of Cattell's efforts. His theorizing addressed all major aspects of personality theory, and his systematic research efforts laid a foundation for generations of trait-based researchers. One observer concluded that "Cattell's theory turns out to be a much more impressive achievement than has been generally recognized. . . . Cattell's original blueprint for personality study has resulted in an extraordinarily rich theoretical structure" (Wiggins, 1984, pp. 177, 190). His primary personality assessment device, the 16 P.F. Questionnaire, continues to be used widely in applied settings that require the assessment of individual differences.

Despite this, if Cattell were here today, he would be disappointed with the relative lack of impact his work exerts in contemporary personality science. This lack of impact may result, in part, from issues that are practical as much as they are scientific. Cattell provided a theoretical system with a lot of personality factors: 16. In practice, it is difficult for the basic or the applied psychologist to keep in mind this large number of factors when assessing the personality of individuals. Cattell would argue that this range of factors is necessary. Yet, in comparison to other theories, the approach is not parsimonious. As you will see in the remainder of this chapter and the next, other theorists tried to establish a simpler structure of personality traits.

Deeper problems may lie behind this practical concern. Cattell was fundamentally interested in the problem of measurement. In most respects, that is a very good thing; inadequate measurement impairs a scientific program. However, in Cattell's work, the measurement process was not used solely for the purpose of measurement. It was used for a second purpose: theorizing. In other words, the basic structure of Cattell's theory (the number of, and content of, the source traits) was determined entirely by the results of the measurement process (factor analyses of measures of the surface traits). Basing theory on measurement is a risky strategy. The risk is that there may exist important qualities that one *should* be studying in a comprehensive theory but that are not detected by one's measurement system. If this happens, the theory lacks coverage of the important topic. As one example, consider the fact that most people have a "life story" (McAdams, 2006). If you ask someone to tell you about themselves, they are likely to provide a narrative or autobiographical story about themselves. It is not at all clear that the numerical measurement of the sort employed by Cattell can capture the content of such stories. If, in a literature class, you are asked to analyze the meaning of a story, we would *not* suggest that you do so by employing the statistical technique of factor analysis! To the extent that individuals possess psychological attributes, such as a life story, that are not reducible to a set of numbers, these attributes are overlooked by Cattell's measurement system and, thus, his theory. If Carl Rogers were here today, he surely would think that this was an enormous limitation for a personality theory.

The Three-factor Theory of Hans J. Eysenck (1916–1997)

In our concluding comments on Cattell, we noted that his 16-factor theory had a practical drawback: It is cumbersome in practical applications to track such a large number of factors: 16. There may be a parallel scientific drawback. Sixteen factors may be too many on sheer scientific grounds. It might be that, hidden behind the 16 factors, there is a simpler and even more basic structure of personality traits. If one could identify this simpler trait structure, it might serve as the basis of a scientific model that is parsimonious and also of applications that are simple and practical. This possibility was pursued with unique creativity and energy by one of the giants of 20th-century psychology, Hans Eysenck.

Hans J. Eysenck was born in Germany in 1916 and later fled to England to escape Nazi persecution. Like Cattell, his work was influenced by advances in statistical techniques, especially factor analysis. He also was influenced intellectually by the work of European psychologists who studied personality types (especially Jung and Kretschmer), by research on the heredity of psychological characteristics, and by the experimental work on classical conditioning conducted by the Russian physiologist Pavlov (see Chapter 10).

Eysenck led a life characterized by enormous energy and productivity. His work included a broad sampling of both normal and pathological populations. He was an exceptionally prolific writer. In the scientific literature, he is one of the most influential and cited research psychologists of the 20th century (Haggbloom et al., 2002). In the 1980s, he founded and edited the journal *Personality and Individual Differences*, an international journal devoted primarily to research on personality traits, temperament, and the biological foundations of personality—all issues Eysenck cared about deeply. Eysenck died in 1997, after seeing through the republication of three of his early books and shortly after finishing his last book, *Intelligence: A New Look* (Eysenck, 1998).

Eysenck's role in the field was both constructive and critical. In addition to constructing a trait theory, he criticized other theories that he found flawed, particularly psychoanalysis. Eysenck, like Cattell, believed that the psychoanalysts' failure to provide precise, reliable measures of their psychological constructs was a serious shortcoming. In constructing a trait theory, Eysenck sought to avoid this problem through the use of reliable measures of individual differences. He felt that such measures also were necessary to identify the presumed biological foundations of each trait.

Hans J. Eysenck.

Stringer / Getty Images

Eysenck's emphasis on biological foundations of personality traits is particularly noteworthy. He recognized that, without understanding the biology of traits, trait explanations could be circular—explanations that go around in a conceptual circle, with a trait concept being used to explain the very behavior that served as the basis for inferring the existence of the trait in the first place. For example, think of a friend of yours who frequently talks in a friendly and outgoing manner to other people. How would you describe her behavior? You might say that she is "sociable." Now, consider another question: How would you *explain* her behavior? You might say that she is acting sociable because she has the trait of sociability. But if you said this, you wouldn't be providing a very good explanation; indeed, your explanation would violate basic principles of scientific explanation. The problem is that the only reason you know that your friend has the trait of sociability is because you saw her act in a sociable manner. Your explanation thus goes around in logical circles: It uses a word (*sociable*) to describe a pattern of behavior and then uses that same word to explain the existence of the pattern of behavior that was described. Eysenck recognized that trait theory can break out of such conceptual circles by going beyond the mere use of words and identifying biological systems that correspond to trait. We consider his degree of success in identifying such systems in the following pages.

"Superfactors": Personality Structure in Eysenck's Theory

To construct a personality theory, Eysenck conducted factor analyses of participants' responses, as did Cattell. But Eysenck also took another step, specifically a secondary application of the factor-analytic method. He conducted secondary factor analyses. A secondary factor analysis is a statistical analysis of an initial set of factors that are correlated with one another. In other words, when analyzing a broad spectrum of personality traits, an initial factor analysis might indicate the existence of a moderately large number of factors. In Cattell's case, in analyses of self-report data, this number was 16. However, these factors are not statistically independent. When one obtains this number of factors, different factors are commonly correlated; people who obtain low (high) scores on one factor tend to obtain low (high) scores on another. (A glance back at Table 7.1 would suggest, on intuitive grounds, that this is true for some of Cattell's factors, such as "reserved" and "shy.") Since the factors are correlated, and factor analysis is a tool for identifying patterns in a set of correlations, the intercorrelations among the factors could be factor analyzed. This is what is called a secondary factor analysis.

This, then, is what Eysenck did. He used secondary factor analysis to identify a simple set of factors that were independent, that is, not correlated with each other. These secondary factors of course also are traits: They are consistent styles of emotion or behavior that distinguish people from one another, and the superfactors are continuous dimensions, with a high and a low end and with most people falling in the middle. But they are factor-analytic trait dimensions at the highest level of a hierarchy of traits, and thus Eysenck called them **superfactors** ("super" in the sense of "high").

Eysenck at first identified two such superfactors, which he labeled (1) **introversion–extraversion** and (2) **neuroticism** (alternatively called emotional stability versus instability). The superordinate concept of extraversion organizes lower-level traits such as sociability, activity, liveliness, and excitability. Neuroticism organizes traits such as anxious, depressed, shy, and moody.

An interesting feature of Eysenck's system is that it captures individual differences identified in ancient times. The Greek physicians Hippocrates (around 400 B.C.) and Galen (around 200 A.D.) proposed the existence of four basic personality types: melancholic, phlegmatic, choleric, and sanguine. These four basic personality types could be represented by where the person falls on the introversion (I), extraversion (E), and stable-unstable (N) dimensions. For example, the melancholic person would be a combination of moody, anxious, quiet, and unsociable traits, while the sanguine person would be a combination of sociable, outgoing, carefree, and easygoing traits. Ancient Greek theorizing about the causes of personality types have since been repudiated. However, as Eysenck recognized, ancient scholars did validly identify important variations among people. People whom the Greeks saw as being of a particular personality type actually had a high amount of associated personality traits. The fact that these variations in personality were evident in both the ancient world and contemporary society suggests that they might be fundamental features of human nature, with a biological basis that transcends time and place.

Eysenck's initial work, then, identified two dimensions of normal variation in personality, that is, variations readily apparent in the personality qualities of people we know in our everyday life. We all recognize that our friends and family vary in the degree to which they are calm versus anxious, shy versus sociable, and Eysenck's model organizes these intuitions scientifically. After establishing these two dimensions, however, Eysenck added a third dimension. It organizes personality traits that, in the extreme, we might label as "abnormal": aggressiveness, a lack of empathy, interpersonal coldness, antisocial behavioral tendencies. This superfactor is called **psychoticism**. These resulting three factors—psychoticism, extraversion, and neuroticism—comprise Eysenck's complete model of personality structure. The factors are so well known in personality psychology that they commonly are referenced merely by their first letters: P, E, and N.

Measuring the Factors

With this model in hand, one then needs an assessment device to measure individual differences in P, E, and N. Eysenck provided this device, too. He developed questionnaire measures (e.g., the Eysenck Personality Questionnaire) that contained simple self-report items designed to tap each of the factors (Figure 7.2). The typical extravert will answer "yes" to questions such as these: Do other people think of you as very lively? Would you be unhappy if you could not see lots of people most of the time? Do you often long for excitement? The typical introvert will answer "yes" to questions such as these: Generally, do you prefer reading to meeting people? Are you mostly quiet when you are with people? Do you stop and think things over before doing anything? Note that Eysenck also included "lie scale" items to detect individuals who are faking responses in order to look good (Figure 7.2).

An important feature of Eysenck's work is that, like Cattell, he developed objective measures of traits, that is, measures that did not rely on subjective ratings in questionnaires. One such test, designed to differentiate extraverts from introverts, is Eysenck's "lemon drop test." A standard

		Yes	No
1.	Do you usually take the initiative in making new friends?	_____	_____
2.	Do ideas run through your head so that you cannot sleep?	_____	_____
3.	Are you inclined to keep in the background on social occasions?	_____	_____
4.	Do you sometimes laugh at a dirty joke?	_____	_____
5.	Are you inclined to be moody?	_____	_____
6.	Do you very much like good food?	_____	_____
7.	When you get annoyed, do you need someone friendly to talk about it?	_____	_____
8.	As a child did you always do as you were told immediately and without grumbling?	_____	_____
9.	Do you usually keeps "yourself to yourself" except with every close friends?	_____	_____
10.	Do you often make up your mind too late?	_____	_____

Note: The above items would be scored in the following way: *Extraversion:* 1 Yes, 3 No, 6 Yes, 9 No; *Neuroticism:* 2 Yes, 5 Yes, 7 Yes, 10 Yes; *Lie Scale:* 4 No, 8 Yes.

FIGURE 7.2 Illustrative items for extraversion, neuroticism, and lie scale from the Maudsley Personality Inventory and Eysenck Personality Inventory.

amount of lemon juice is placed on the subject's tongue. Introverts and extraverts (as identified by questionnaires) differ in the amount of saliva produced when this is done.

Why might this be (we hope you are asking yourself)? The idea is that there may be a biological basis to the individual differences.

Biological Bases of Personality Traits

Eysenck provided specific scientific models of the biological bases of individual differences. Note that, if you are Eysenck, you do need models (plural), not just one model. The traits (P, E, and N) are statistically independent. One therefore needs a separate biological model for each of the three traits. The trait for which Eysenck's theorizing about underlying biology has proven most successful is extraversion.

Personality and the Brain
Extraversion and Neuroticism

More than a half century ago, Hans Eysenck predicted that people with different scores on extraversion (E) and neuroticism (N) questionnaires would differ neurally. He anticipated, specifically, that they would differ in brain response when presented with emotionally arousing stimuli. With all the time that's elapsed, you might guess that this prediction would have been tested extensively, with the relevant brain systems being well understood. But guess again. Here in the contemporary era, authors (Kehoe, Toomey, Balsters, & Bokde, in press) still can state that "the relationship between extraversion and the neural substrates of emotional arousal processing are unknown" (ms, p. 2) and that, until recently, Eysenckian predictions about neuroticism and the brain "have never been investigated using functional magnetic resonance imaging (fMRI)" (ms, p. 1), the contemporary neuroscientist's favored tool.

This state of affairs is beginning to change. Kehoe et al. (in press) used fMRI to explore brain activity in a group of 23 women who differed in extraversion and neuroticism. After completing an Eysenck questionnaire that yielded E and N scores, the women participated in a laboratory experiment in which they viewed a series of photos showing faces that depicted varying emotional content. By analyzing brain scans taken while the photographs were viewed, the researchers could determine whether E and N were linked to brain activity, as Eysenck predicted.

So how did Eysenck's theory fare? Let's look at the two traits one at a time. Eysenck predicted that higher levels of extraversion would be associated with lower levels of cortical arousal—that is, arousal in the cortex of the brain—when people encounter environmental stimuli. This prediction was only partly supported by the fMRI evidence (Kehoe et al., in press). When the researchers examined arousal in the cerebellum (a brain region that influences motor movement but also is involved in emotional response), extraverts displayed lower levels of arousal, in accord with the Eysenckian prediction. But when they examined a different brain region, the insula (which contributes to the subjective conscious experience of emotion), extraverts displayed higher levels of brain arousal, contradicting Eysenck's theory.

fMRI evidence was more consistent with Eysenck's theory about the other trait, neuroticism. When emotionally arousing stimuli were presented, people higher in neuroticism displayed higher levels of brain activity in a region in the front of the brain, the prefrontal cortex (Kehoe et al., in press). This is not the exact region of the brain that Eysenck had linked to N; he anticipated that neuroticism would be associated with variations in lower-level regions of the brain, in the limbic system. Nonetheless, since the prefrontal cortex and limbic system are highly interconnected, the results are consistent with Eysenck's general expectations that the brains of people high in neuroticism would respond more strongly.

These findings represent a start in using fMRI to understand E and N. One would hope to see them replicated with larger and more diverse samples of participants and with a wider array of experimental stimuli. When it comes to the neural bases of extraversion and neuroticism, there's still a lot to learn.

Eysenck suggested that individual variations in introversion–extraversion reflect individual differences in the neurophysiological functioning of the brain's cortex. The idea is that introverts are more arousable; they experience more cortical arousal from events in the world. As a result, highly intense social stimuli (e.g., a loud party) make them *over*aroused—an aversive state that they avoid. The social behavior of introverts, then, is more inhibited because of the relatively greater arousal they experience. Conversely, extraverts experience less cortical arousal than introverts from a given stimulus and therefore seek out more intense social experiences. Research that directly measures the brain activity of introverts and extraverts provides some support for Eysenck's theorizing (Geen, 1997; also see *Personality and the Brain* feature, this chapter, and Chapter 9). Eysenck himself generated much relevant evidence on the biology of this dimension, including evidence that introverts are more influenced by punishments in learning, whereas extraverts are more influenced by rewards.

Since the trait has a biological basis, individual differences in introversion–extraversion should be at least partly hereditary. (Note that the biological basis does not imply that a trait would be entirely hereditary, since one's experiences during child development influence one's biological makeup.) Studies of identical and fraternal twins commonly suggest that heredity does, in fact, play a major part in accounting for differences between individuals in E scores (Krueger & Johnson, 2008; Loehlin, 1992; Plomin & Caspi, 1999). The following are other facts consistent with Eysenck's biological theorizing: the fact that the dimension of introversion–extraversion is found cross-culturally, that individual differences are stable over time, and that various indices of biological functioning (e.g., brain activity, heart rate, hormone level, sweat gland activity) correlate with E scores (Eysenck, 1990).

Regarding neuroticism, Eysenck hypothesized that the key neural systems are (a) the limbic system, a lower-level brain region involved in emotional arousal and (b) the autonomic nervous system, the part of the nervous system that influences bodily arousal (e.g., heart rate, sweat gland activity) and that, in turn, is regulated by the limbic system. In particular, Eysenck predicted that, among individuals high on neuroticism, the autonomic nervous system would respond particularly quickly to stress and would be slow to decrease its activity once danger disappears. The neurotic person thus seems "jumpy" and "stressed out." Unfortunately for Eysenckian theory, research has not consistently supported this physiological theory of neuroticism, as Eysenck himself fully recognized (Eysenck, 1990). Recent work using brain imaging methods unavailable to Eysenck, however, has been more promising (see this chapter's *Personality and the Brain* feature).

Less is known about the biological basis for the psychoticism (P) dimension. However, here a genetic association is suggested, in particular an association linked with maleness; aggressiveness, a component of (P), is higher in men and may be affected by levels of testosterone (Eysenck, 1990). A more recent suggestion involved a neurotransmitter in the brain, namely, dopamine. Research suggests that people with higher levels of psychoticism have higher levels of dopamine-based neural activity (Colzato, Slagter, van den Wildenberg, & Hommel, 2009). This result is intriguing in that dopamine also has been linked to the severe mental disorder schizophrenia.

Extraversion and Social Behavior

Do people who differ in extraversion–introversion scores also differ in their everyday social behavior? A mountain of evidence speaks to this question; extraversion is probably the most extensively studied of all traits, in part because relevant behaviors are relatively easy to observe (Gosling, John, Craik, & Robins, 1998). A review of the dimension presents an impressive array of findings (Watson & Clark, 1997). For example, introverts are more sensitive to pain than extraverts; they become fatigued more easily than extraverts; excitement interferes with their performance, whereas it enhances performance for extraverts; and they tend to be more careful but slower than extraverts. The following additional differences have been found:

1. Introverts do better in school than extraverts, particularly in more advanced subjects. Also, students withdrawing from college for academic reasons tend to be extraverts, whereas those who withdraw for psychiatric reasons tend to be introverts.

2. Extraverts prefer vocations involving interactions with other people, whereas introverts tend to prefer more solitary vocations. Extraverts seek diversion from job routine, whereas introverts have less need for novelty.

3. Extraverts enjoy explicit sexual and aggressive humor, whereas introverts prefer more intellectual forms of humor such as puns and subtle jokes.

4. Extraverts are more active sexually, in terms of frequency and different partners, than introverts.

5. Extraverts are more suggestible than introverts.

This last finding is illustrated in a study of a hyperventilating epidemic in England (Moss & McEvedy, 1966). An initial report by some girls of fainting and dizziness was followed by an outbreak of similar complaints, with 85 girls needing to be taken to the hospital by ambulance—"they were going down like ninepins." A comparison of the girls who were affected with those who were not, demonstrated that, as expected, the affected girls were higher in both neuroticism and extraversion. In other words, those individuals whose personalities were most predisposed to suggestion proved most susceptible to influence by suggestions of a real epidemic.

Finally, the results of an investigation of study habits among introverts and extraverts may be of particular interest to college students. The research examined whether such personality differences are associated with differing preferences for where to study and how to study, as would be predicted by Eysenck's theory. In accord with Eysenck's theory of individual differences, the

Sam Edwards / Getty Images

Where do you like to study? If you are an extravert, you probably prefer studying with a group of friends in a coffee shop to working by yourself in a quiet library.

following was found: (1) Extraverts more often chose to study in library locations that provided external stimulation than did introverts, (2) extraverts took more study breaks than did introverts, and (3) extraverts reported a preference for a higher level of noise and for more socializing opportunities while studying than did introverts (Campbell & Hawley, 1982). Extraverts and introverts differ in their physiological responses to the same noise level (introverts show a greater level of response), and each functions best at his or her preferred noise level (Geen, 1984). An important implication of such research is that different environmental designs for libraries and residence units might best fit the needs of introverts and extraverts.

Psychopathology and Behavior Change

Eysenck also developed a theory of abnormal psychology and behavior change. A core idea Eysenck espoused is that the type of symptoms or psychological difficulties a person experiences relate to basic personality traits and the nervous system functioning associated with the traits. A person develops neurotic symptoms because of the joint action of a biological system and environmental experiences that contribute to the learning of strong emotional reactions to fear-producing stimuli. Consistent with this suggestion of Eysenck's, the vast majority of neurotic patients tend to have high neuroticism and low extraversion scores (Eysenck, 1982, p. 25). In contrast, criminals and antisocial persons tend to have high neuroticism, high extraversion, and high psychoticism scores. Such individuals show weak learning of societal norms.

Despite the genetic component of personality traits and disorders, Eysenck was optimistic about treatment: "The fact that genetic factors play a large part in the initiation and maintenance of neurotic disorders and also of criminal activities is very unwelcome to many people who believe that such a state of affairs must lead to therapeutic nihilism. If heredity is so important, they say, then clearly behavior modification of any kind must be impossible. This is a completely erroneous interpretation of the facts. What is genetically determined are predispositions for a person to act and behave in a certain manner, when put in certain situations" (Eysenck, 1982, p. 29). It is possible for a person to avoid certain potentially traumatic situations, to unlearn fear responses, to learn appropriate social conduct, and thus to achieve a personality style that varies from his or her original predispositions. Eysenck thus was a major proponent of behavior therapy,

CURRENT QUESTIONS

Is it Better to be an Introvert or an Extravert?

Is it better to have the traits of being sociable, lively, active, and assertive or those of being shy, quiet, reserved, and passive? Most people would rate the former traits, those associated with extraversion, as more desirable than the latter traits, those associated with introversion. And, more objectively, extraversion is associated with leadership and business success. In fact, some go so far as to say that the most important aspect of personality is where we fall on the introversion–extraversion dimension, with introversion considered a second-class personality trait, "somewhere between a disappointment and a pathology" (Cain, 2012).

A recent book, however, questions this view and suggests that there is an introversion ideal as there is an extraversion

ideal. In the book *Quiet*, Cain (2012) suggests that there are advantages and disadvantages to each, and that many successful business leaders are introverts. Indeed, introverts tend to be more sensitive, empathic, creative, and persistent than extraverts, all many would consider to be desirable personality characteristics. In addition, there are cultural differences in what is valued—in Asia, for example, the introvert is not looked down upon but is respected and admired.

Ideally, it might be best to be flexible, able to be quiet and reserved or lively and assertive, depending on the situation. Would such flexibility and adaptiveness, however, create problems about the foundation of the introversion–extraversion dimension?

which is the systematic application of principles of learning and behavior change to therapy (see Chapter 10).

Evaluation of Eysenckian Theory

In many ways, Eysenck's contributions to personality science are exemplary. He upheld the highest standards of science while theorizing in a creative manner. He brought diverse forms of evidence to bear on questions of individual differences. His prolific writings delivered his messages about personality not only to fellow scientists but also to a wider intellectual public. If personality psychology had experienced ten Eysencks instead of one, it would today be a much stronger field.

Historically, Eysenck was always prepared to swim against the tide. "I have usually been against the establishment and in favor of the rebels (Eysenck, 1982, p. 298). Of course, this is Eysenck's view of himself. Many contemporary scholars would contend that the Eysenckian strategy of describing individual persons in terms of scores on a small number of universal personality dimensions is itself an establishment procedure against which the humanist might rebel.

Yet, one might ask why Eysenck has not been even more influential (see Loehlin, 1982). Some answers involve the social world of scientific activity. Eysenck's decision to found a new journal (see above) may partly have backfired. When a scientist starts a scientific journal, devotees of the scientist's position read it carefully, but others may not. Publications thus become isolated from the field's mainstream. Other answers involve scientific substance. As you will see in the next chapter of this book, some psychologists have judged that more than two personality factors are required to describe individual differences, and others have claimed that even Eysenck's basic two factors must be modified to align with knowledge of brain systems (Gray, 1990).

A recent review by Matthews (2016) argues strongly that, despite the historical significance of Eysenck's efforts, it is time for personality trait psychologists to abandon his framework. Mathews grounds his argument in a number of critiques of Eysenckian theory; they include the following:

1. **Measures did not align with theory.**   Eysenck's theory concerned neural factors such as levels of cortical arousal. But his major measurement efforts centered on the development of self-report questionnaires. Self-reports are not a good way of measuring brain activity. People cannot directly introspect about the working of their brain, and any behavioral tendencies on which they report may reflect an interaction of biological factors and sociocultural experiences, rather than being a direct indicator of activity in the brain.

2. **Eysenckian theory underestimated the complexity of the brain.**   Contemporary brain science reveals that higher-level cortical systems and lower-level perceptual and emotional systems are highly interconnected, and thus interacting, systems. Eysenck's focus on cortical arousal thus presented too simple a model of the brain and personality.

3. **Cognitive factors affect performance.**   When explaining behavior, Eysenckian theory focused on levels of arousal of a small set of brain systems that are possessed by humans and a wide variety of other mammalian species. Even if we were to presume that this arousal is correct, it is plainly inadequate for explaining individual differences among humans. People think. As Mathews emphasizes, humans are "differentiated from other animals by the use of linguistic representations that support schemas for future events and forward planning" (2016, p. 63).

Matthews central argument is that personality traits partly reflect individual's beliefs about themselves and the social world. This insight, which is foundational to Personal Construct Theory (Chapter 11) and Social Cognitive Theory (Chapters 12 and 13), "is alien to the Eysenckian perspective" (Matthews, 2016, p. 63).

MAJOR CONCEPTS

Ability, temperament, and
   dynamic traits
Cardinal trait
Central traits
Extraversion

Factor analysis
Functional autonomy
Introversion
L-data
Neuroticism

OT-data
Psychoticism
Q-data
Role
Secondary dispositions

Source traits
State
Superfactors
Surface traits
Trait

REVIEW

1. The trait concept represents people's broad dispositions to display a certain type of behavior or to have certain types of emotional experiences. Allport, one of the first trait theorists, differentiated among cardinal traits, central traits, and specific dispositions. He also suggested that some traits could only be identified through idiographic research strategies, that is, research strategies that are sensitive to potentially idiosyncratic qualities of particular individuals.

2. Many trait theorists use the statistical technique of factor analysis to develop a classification of traits. Through this technique, a group of items or responses (factors) are formed, the items in one group (factor) being closely related to one another and distinct from those in another group (factor).

3. Cattell distinguished among ability, temperament, and dynamic traits, as well as between surface and source traits.

4. According to Eysenck, the basic dimensions of personality are introversion–extraversion, neuroticism, and psychoticism. Questionnaires have been developed to assess people along these trait dimensions. Research has focused particularly on the introversion–extraversion trait dimension, where differences in activity level and activity preferences have been found. Eysenck suggests that individual differences in traits have a biological and genetic (inherited) basis.

Trait Theory: The Five-Factor Model and Contemporary Developments

8

Chapter Focus

People differ. You don't need to take a personality psychology course to know that. But *how* do they differ? On the first page of Chapter 1, you saw some of the ways that students like yourself describe the differences among individuals. Some people are abrasive. Others justice-oriented. Some shy-but-then-open-up. Others sweet-but-only-toward friends. There are "perfectionists." "Cynics." "Jackasses." Is the set of individual differences unending and unordered and the words for describing them a disjointed babble? Or might there be something systematic amidst the apparent chaos—and, if so, how could one find out?

Suppose that we proceed as follows. We ask a thousand people to write personality descriptions of a thousand others. Then we collect together all the trait-descriptive adjectives used in these descriptions. The result would be a list of personality descriptors that is not biased by any theoretical preconceptions. Certainly, with a thousand words, there would be considerable redundancy (e.g., *perfect* and *flawless* mean pretty much the same thing), permitting us to reduce the size of the list. If we then factor-analyze personality ratings on these traits, we should end up with the major dimensions of personality trait descriptions. The result may be a compromise that does not please everybody, but at least it is arrived at through a fair set of procedures, and its practicality and usefulness will determine whether it is generally accepted in the field.

This chapter first focuses on a finding that emerges when people engage in just this procedure; they obtain a set of five personality traits. After telling you how psychologists found the five, we will consider a range of follow-up questions about the traits: Do they predict behavior? Do they change over time? Are they found across cultures? And what are they, exactly?

Questions to be Addressed in this Chapter

1. How many and which trait dimensions are necessary for a basic description of personality?

2. What are the implications of individual differences in traits for career choice, physical health, and psychological well-being?

3. How stable are personality trait scores over time?

4. Is the nature of individual differences in personality consistent or variable across cultures?

5. What contemporary developments have advanced the traditional trait theories?

On Taxonomies of Personality

Any field of study may benefit from a taxonomy, that is, a system for classifying the field's objects of study. Is it a plant or an animal? An organic or inorganic compound? A planned or a free market economy? An impressionist or an expressionist painting?

Personality psychology is no exception. An agreed-upon taxonomy of personality traits would be a boon. With a simple taxonomic structure of personality in hand, researchers anywhere in the world could focus on a small set of personality trait categories rather than sifting through thousands of potential variables whenever they wanted to run a study.

So, does the field have one of these in hand: a consensually accepted, universally applicable, taxonomic structure of personality traits? It depends who you ask:

> *A strong consensus today suggests that. . .five factor-analytically-derived categories. . .do a reasonably good job of summarizing and organizing the universe of trait descriptors.*
>
> McAdams and Pals, p. 2006, p. 208

> *Although the Five Factor Model of personality continues to find cross-cultural support, new research suggests that the model may be difficult to replicate in less educated or preliterate groups. . .two or three broad dimensions may replicate better across cultures.*
>
> Church, 2016, p. 22

What do we mean by personality structure and how many structures are there?...We would say there is no single personality structure...Structural variation across individuals can reveal how individuals construe situations. Structural variation across cultures can reveal differences in culturally shared interpretations of situations and others' behavior.

Baumert et al. (2018, in press, p. 54)

The first author team says "yes." They claim that a taxonomy with five personality traits is consensually accepted. The second author tells us "no"—or, more specifically, he indicates that even if there is a consensus, it might be misplaced. When researchers represent the diversity of human experience in their data sets, the number of universal trait dimensions drops in half. Authors of the third quote go further. They do not even expect that any single universal structure of personality exists. Individuals and cultures may be too diverse, complex, and idiosyncratic for that. (It is noteworthy that the authors of the third quote were a team of 19 internationally renowned personality scientists.)

How, then, shall we proceed? This chapter begins by summarizing a taxonomy of personality traits that has been known to the field for more than a half-century and that came to great prominence in the latter decades of the 20th century: the five-factor or **Big Five** model. As you will see, substantial bodies of evidence indicate that individual differences can be usefully organized in terms of five broad, bipolar trait dimensions (John, Naumann, & Soto, 2008; McCrae & Costa, 2008). We will discuss where the model came from, how the five traits are measured, and how trait scores change or remain stable over time. We then will consider a deeply significant conceptual question: What *are* these traits – psychological structures that compose the core of human nature or merely efficient, handy descriptions of some ways in which people differ from one another? The chapter then (a) reviews research indicating that six, rather than five, dimensions are needed to describe significant differences among individuals; (b) presents a contemporary development in personality theory, *Reinforcement Sensitivity Theory*, that challenges aspects of the five-factor model; and (c) addresses the question of whether people's behavior is consistent across situations – a question crucial to trait theories since, as you saw in Chapter 7, accounting for consistency in behavior was an original *raison d'être* of the trait approach.

The five-factor model is *a factor-analytic* trait approach, just like the theories of Eysenck and Cattell. (Chapter 7; its views of the person and of personality science thus are the same as those presented at the beginning of Chapter 7.) So what's new about **five-factor theory**? In one word: evidence. A huge body of research evidence indicates that five factors—more than Eysenck's three, less than Cattell's sixteen—are necessary and reasonably sufficient for a taxonomy of individual differences. In this chapter, we review this evidence.

The Five-Factor Model of Personality: Research Evidence

The idea that five personality factors are the foundation of individual differences in personality rests on factor analysis—the same research tools that provided the basis for the theories of Cattell and Eysenck (Chapter 7). Specifically, the Big Five model receives strong support from two types of data: (1) factor analysis of trait terms in the natural language and (2) statistical analyses of relations among the resulting Big Five factors and other personality trait questionnaires and ratings. Once the Big Five factors were established in the analysis of natural language and questionnaires, psychologists could use the model to address questions of growth and development in personality. We consider these topics, as well as applications of the Big Five model, in the pages ahead.

Analysis of Trait Terms in Natural Language and in Questionnaires

As you have learned from previous chapters, psychologists build personality theories on different types of variables—different units of analysis (Chapter 1). Most scientific theories, including most theories of personality, describe their main variables using a specialized scientific language; terms such as *superego, collective unconscious, actualization motive,* and so forth are introduced to describe a feature of human psychology. The five-factor model is not like this. Instead of creating a scientific language, five-factor theorists put faith in the natural language, that is, the regular, everyday language people use to describe personality. Specifically, they place their faith in one aspect of the natural language: individual words (primarily adjectives) that describe persons.

The basic research procedure is to have individuals rate themselves or others on a wide variety of traits carefully sampled from the dictionary. The ratings are then factor-analyzed (see Chapter 7 for a discussion of factor analysis) to see which traits go together. The questions to be answered are these: (1) How many different factors are needed to understand the patterns of correlation in the data? and (2) What specifically are the factors?

Early work by Norman (1963), who drew upon research by Allport, Cattell, and others, indicated that five factors are necessary. Similar five-factor solutions were found repeatedly in studies that included a wide range of data sources, samples, and assessment instruments (John, 1990). All five factors were shown to possess considerable reliability and validity and to remain relatively stable throughout adulthood (McCrae & Costa, 2008, 2013). In 1981, Lewis Goldberg reviewed the existing research and, impressed with the consistency of its results, suggested that "any model for structuring individual differences will have to encompass at some level something like these 'Big Five' dimensions" (p. 159). "Big" was meant to refer to the finding that each factor subsumes a large number of more specific traits; the factors are almost as broad and abstract in the personality hierarchy as Eysenck's superfactors.

And what, exactly, are these factors? The terms Neuroticism (N), Extraversion (E), Openness (O), Agreeableness (A), and Conscientiousness (C) (Table 8.1) are used most commonly to label them. (They are made more memorable by the fact that their first letters spell the word **OCEAN**; John, 1990.) The meaning of the factors can best be seen by examining trait adjectives that describe individuals who score high and low on each (see Table 8.1). Neuroticism contrasts

Table 8.1 Illustrative Traits Associated With High and Low Scores on the Big Five Dimensions

High Score Traits	Low Score Traits
NEUROTICISM (N) Worrying, nervous, emotional, insecure, tense	Calm, relaxed, unemotional, secure, self-satisfied
EXTRAVERSION (E) Sociable, active, talkative, person-oriented, optimistic, fun-loving, affectionate	Reserved, aloof, task-oriented, retiring, quiet, timid
OPENNESS (O) Curious, broad interests, creative, original, imaginative, untraditional	Conventional, unimaginative, narrow interests, unartistic, unanalytical
AGREEABLENESS (A) Kind, cooperative, good-natured, trusting, helpful	Cynical, rude, suspicious, uncooperative, vengeful, ruthless, irritable, manipulative
CONSCIENTIOUSNESS (C) Organized, reliable, hard-working, self-disciplined, punctual, scrupulous, neat, ambitious, persevering	Aimless, unreliable, lazy, careless, lax, negligent, hedonistic

(Big 5 Traits)

dd

emotional stability with a broad range of negative feelings, including anxiety, sadness, irritability, and nervous tension. Openness to experience describes the breadth, depth, and complexity of an individual's mental and experiential life. Extraversion and Agreeableness both summarize traits that are interpersonal; that is, they capture what people do with each other and to each other. Finally, Conscientiousness primarily describes task- and goal-directed behavior and socially required impulse control.

Personality and the Brain
The Big Five

Personality psychologists first found the Big Five personality trait dimensions when analyzing questionnaire responses. Can they also find them when analyzing the brain?

Relating brain regions to Big Five scores is difficult. There are so many neural subsystems and so many interconnections among them in the brain that it's hard to know where to look. A theoretical analysis of psychological processes that are central to each Big Five dimension can be a helpful guide, as shown by recent theory and research by DeYoung and colleagues.

These investigators (DeYoung et al., 2010) obtained Big Five scores for a set of 116 adult research participants. They then obtained whole-brain images for each participant (using magnetic resonance imaging, MRI) and, using the images, looked for variations in brain volume that might be linked to variations in Big Five scores. The reasoning behind this approach is that greater volume in a specific brain region may indicate a greater psychological capacity to perform activities for which that region is needed. They found that:

— people with higher levels of extraversion had larger brain volume in a region of the frontal cortex that contributes to the processing of information about environmental rewards. This supports the idea that the pursuit of rewarding experiences is a core feature of extraversion.

— higher Neuroticism scores were correlated with great volume in brain regions known to be associated with the processing of environmental threats.

— Agreeableness scores correlated with brain volume in regions of the brain that contribute to people's ability to understand others' mental states—a

distinct psychological ability that has been linked to specific brain regions.

— Conscientiousness correlated with volume in a region of the frontal cortex known to be active when people plan events and follow rules.

— openness to experience was not significantly related to any of the examined brain regions.

So is it safe to conclude that these researchers have identified the neural origins of the Big Five traits? As the researchers themselves are aware, the answer is no. The findings are merely a first step in a newly emerging field, and they must be interpreted with caution, for at least three reasons: (1) In addition to results that were consistent with the researchers' theoretical conceptions, the study yielded a number of null results (where personality traits scores did not correlate with brain volume as expected) and unexpected results (where personality traits scores did correlate with brain volumes, but in areas of the brain that were unexpected). (2) Cause–effect relationships were impossible to determine. It may be that inherited differences in brain volume caused people to display a given personality disposition. Conversely, it may be that personality dispositions caused people to have different brain volumes. People who repeatedly engage in a behavior experience increases in brain volume in regions of the brain that are used to perform that behavior (Draganski et al., 2004). (3) The brain's various regions are enormously interconnected. During any complex task, a network of multiple interconnected regions becomes active (Bullmore & Sporns, 2009). Inevitably, then, focusing on volume in one region of the brain may yield an incomplete portrait of the complex brain networks that contribute to the multifaceted personality tendencies described by the Big Five personality traits.

The Fundamental Lexical Hypothesis

traits are not consistent across all languages [handwritten note in margin]

The Big Five were designed to capture those personality traits that people consider most important to personality. Goldberg has spelled out the rationale for this approach in terms of the **fundamental lexical** (language) **hypothesis**: "the most important individual differences in human transactions will come to be encoded as single terms in some or all of the world's languages" (Goldberg, 1990, p. 1216). The hypothesis, then, is that over time humans have found some individual differences particularly important in their interactions and have developed terms for easy reference to them. These trait terms communicate information about individual differences that are important to our own well-being or that of our group or clan. Thus, they are socially useful because they serve the purpose of prediction and control: They help us predict what others will do and thus control our life outcomes (Chaplin et al., 1988). They help answer questions about how an individual is likely to behave across a wide range of relevant situations.

The emphasis on universal terms for describing important individual differences ties trait theory to an evolutionary model: "The existence of cultural universals would be consistent with an evolutionary perspective. If the tasks most central to human survival are universal, then the most important individual differences, and the terms people use to label these individual differences, should be universal as well" (John, Naumann, & Soto, 2008, p. 121). On the other hand, culturally specific dimensions would suggest individual differences that are uniquely important to that culture. Presumably both could, perhaps should, exist, giving expression to what is basic to human nature and what is culturally distinct.

There are some counterexamples to the lexical hypothesis. For example, some writers note that individuals differ in the degree to which they need variety in their lives, or the degree to which they can tolerate ambiguity when making decisions; contrary to the lexical hypothesis, there is no single term in the English language that corresponds to these qualities (McCrae & Costa, 1997). Nonetheless, the lexical hypothesis has been an important stimulant to research and continues to guide much thinking in the field.

CURRENT QUESTIONS

Emotions and Traits: Other Animals?

Darwin's *The Origin of Species* suggested a continuity between humans and other species. In his book *The Expression of the Emotions in Man and Animals,* he suggested a continuity of expressions of emotions in animals and people—that is, that many of the same basic emotions and accompanying facial expressions exist in both. There is evidence of a similarity of expression of what are called basic emotions (e.g., anger, sadness, fear, joy) in nonhuman primates and humans, in infants as well as adults, and across cultures (Ekman, 1993, 1998). Evolutionary psychologists suggest that a continuity in traits exists between humans and other species; this view is bolstered by the fact that humans and the great apes share over 98% of the same genes. Is there evidence of such a continuity of traits?

Gosling and John (1998, 1999) set out to consider the question of whether there are dimensions of personality common to a wide range of species, raising the question: "What are the major dimensions of animal personality?" In a review of the literature of descriptions of 12 species, ranging from octopuses, guppies, and rats to gorillas and chimpanzees, they found evidence that three of the human five-factor dimensions showed generality across species—E, N, and A: "The evidence indicates that chimpanzees, various other primates, dogs, cats, donkeys, and pigs, even guppies and octopuses all show individual differences that can be organized along dimensions akin to E, N, and (with the exception of guppies and octopuses) A" (1999, p. 70). However, a separate C factor was found only in chimps (King & Figueredo, 1997), our closest relatives. This may be because traits related to C, such as following rules and norms, thinking before acting, and cognitively controlling impulses may be a relatively recent evolutionary development.

Are such similarities anthropomorphic projections on the part of humans, or are they actual attributes of the animals?

In a study of trait ratings of humans, dogs, and cats, Gosling and John again found evidence of three of the Big Five in dogs and cats as well as humans—E, N, and A, but no separate C factor. In a further study, they generated a list of "personality descriptors" of dogs, based on attributes human subjects most frequently used to describe dogs (e.g., affectionate, cuddly, energetic, happy, intelligent, nervous, lazy, loyal). One group of subjects then rated a human they knew on the "dog personality inventory," and another group of subjects rated a dog they knew on the same list of descriptors. Would the same factors emerge from the two groups of ratings, suggesting similar dimensions of personality for humans and dogs? Using the dog personality inventory for humans, they again found evidence of the Big Five: N, E, O, A, C. When the same rating items were applied to dogs,

three factors similar to E, N, and A again emerged, with no separate C factor.

Overall, studies on animal personality suggested the following conclusions: (1) Animal personality can be assessed reliably. (2) The structure of personality traits in humans resembles that of chimps. (3) Nonprimate mammals such as dogs and cats seem to have a less differentiated personality structure, with three dimensions showing considerable, though not perfect, generality across many species. (4) Personality descriptions of other species are not mere anthropomorphic projections; that is, such descriptions are not "all in the mind" of the human but instead reflect actual characteristics of the animal being rated.

Source: Ekman (1998), Gosling & John (1998, 1999), and Weinstein, Capitanio, & Gosling (2008).

The Big Five in Personality Questionnaires

A variety of questionnaires have been developed to measure the Big Five. These include very short tests where subjects rate themselves on traits such as those presented in Table 8.1 (Rammstedt & John, 2007) to more extensive personality questionnaires. A particularly well-developed questionnaire is the NEO-Personality Inventory Revised (**NEO-PI-R**).

The NEO-PI-R and Its Hierarchical Structure: Facets

Costa and McCrae (1985, 1989, 1992; McCrae & Costa, 2010) have developed a questionnaire, the NEO-PI-R, to measure the Big Five personality factors. Originally they had focused only on the three factors of Neuroticism, Extraversion, and Openness (thus the title NEO-Personality Inventory). Subsequently, they added the factors of Agreeableness and Conscientiousness to conform to the five-factor model. In addition to measuring the five factors, they differentiated each factor into six narrower **facets**; facets are more specific components that make up each of the broad Big Five factors. The six facets defining each Big Five factor are listed in Table 8.2.

When the NEO-PI-R is administered in research and clinical contexts, subjects indicate for each item the extent to which they agree or disagree, using a five-point rating scale. The resulting scales all have good reliability and show validity across different data sources, such as ratings by peers or spouses. McCrae and Costa (2003, 2010) argue strongly for the use of structured

Table 8.2 Each Big Five Factor Consists of Six Facets

Extraversion	Gregariousness; Activity Level; Assertiveness; Excitement Seeking; Positive Emotions; Warmth
Agreeableness	Straightforwardness; Trust; Altruism; Modesty; Tendermindedness; Compliance
Conscientiousness	Self-discipline; Dutifulness; Competence; Order; Deliberation; Achievement striving
Neuroticism	Anxiety; Self-consciousness; Depression; Vulnerability; Impulsiveness; Angry hostility
Openness to new experience	Fantasy; Aesthetics; Feelings; Ideas; Actions Values

questionnaires to assess personality and are critical of projective tests and clinical interviews, which they consider unsystematic and prone to biases. Evidence shows that their NEO-PI-R scales also agree well with other Big Five instruments, such as Goldberg's (1992) adjective inventories (Benet-Martinez & John, 1998; John & Srivastava, 1999). Nonetheless, it is important to point out that there are also some differences in which facets are emphasized on each instrument. For example, Costa and McCrae place the warmth facet on Extraversion, whereas other Big Five researchers find that warmth is more closely related to Agreeableness (John & Srivastava, 1999). Particular disagreement is found in the conceptualization of the fifth factor, Openness. Goldberg emphasizes intellectual and creative cognition, calling the factor Intellect or Imagination; McCrae (1996) criticizes this view as too narrow a definition of the Openness factor (see Table 8.2). Thus, there are still some inconsistencies among the various researchers that need to be worked out.

Integration of Eysenck's and Cattell's Factors within the Big Five

Assuming that the NEO-PI-R is an adequate measure of the five-factor model of personality, one can ask a question that harkens back to our previous chapter: Can the personality factors of Cattell and Eysenck be understood within the five-factor system? Much evidence suggests that the answer is yes. Scores on the NEO-PI-R correlate as predicted with scores on other personality questionnaires, including Eysenck's inventories and Cattell's 16 personality factors (Costa & McCrae, 1992, 1994).

These correlations are important theoretically. They allow one to integrate the older factor-analytic models with the Big Five and thus with each other. In particular, Eysenck's superfactors of Extraversion and Neuroticism are found to be virtually identical to the same-named dimensions in the Big Five, and Eysenck's Psychoticism superfactor corresponds to a combination of low Agreeableness and low Conscientiousness (Clark & Watson, 1999; Costa & McCrae, 1995; Goldberg & Rosolack, 1994). Cattell's 16 personality factors (Table 7.2) also map onto the broader Big Five dimensions (McCrae & Costa, 2003). For example, his scales Outgoing, Assertive, and Venturesome link with NEO-PI-R Extraversion. Based on findings of this sort, proponents of the Big Five model suggest that it provides a comprehensive framework within which Eysenckian and Cattellian constructs can be integrated.

Moreover, the NEO-PI-R questionnaire relates meaningfully to other forms of measurement (e.g., Q-sort ratings) and to questionnaires derived from other theoretical orientations. Individual differences identified in Murray's motivational model of personality can be understood within the Big Five system of traits, which is important because it suggests a link between traits and motives (Pervin, 1999). Individual differences identified in biological research on temperament (see Chapter 9) can be described within the Big Five system (De Fruyt, Wiele, & van Heeringen, 2000), which suggests that the factors might be reducible to underlying biological systems (see this chapter's *Personality and the Brain* feature).

Self-Ratings and Observer Ratings

Another important strength of the NEO-PI-R is that forms are available for both self-report and ratings by others. In several studies, subjects' self-ratings have been compared with ratings by their peers and spouses. McCrae and Costa (1990) report substantial agreement of self-ratings with ratings by peers and with ratings by spouses on all five factors. Agreement between self and spouse is greater than that between self and peer, perhaps because spouses generally know each other better than do friends or because spouses talk a lot about each others' personalities (see Kenny, 1994).

Three major findings have emerged from research using both self-report measures (S-data, as you learned in Chapter 2) and observer-report data (O-data) of the Big Five factors.

1. As noted above, the same five factors are found in both self-reports and observer ratings (McCrae & Costa, 2013).

2. Observers agree reasonably well with each other about the standing of individuals on each Big Five dimension. If you think you are conscientious, introverted, and neurotic, your friends probably think so, too (Connelly & Ones, 2010; McCrae & Costa, 1987).

3. O-data sometimes is a better predictor of performance than S-data. A meta-analysis (i.e., a statistical analysis of large numbers of prior studies) of the relationship between personality test scores and indices of the quality of job performance reveals that observer ratings of personality predict performance above and beyond the predictions that can be made by self-ratings of personality (Oh, Wang, & Mount, 2011).

How might observer ratings and self-ratings on the Big Five traits differ? Evidence suggests that differences are observed when ratings are made with respect to traits that are not highly visible. For example, Neuroticism (which involves inner feelings of anxiety that are not observable by others) may be more accurately measured by S-data than O-data (Vazire, 2010). Furthermore, people's desire to see themselves in a positive light may cause self-ratings to be more positive than other-ratings. A multinational data set shows that, although S-data and O-data often do correspond closely, people generally see themselves as higher in Neuroticism and lower in Conscientiousness than others believe them to be (Allik et al., 2010).

Growth and Development

Do people's scores on big five measures change systematically as they age? Or are levels of these personality traits stable throughout adulthood? Much research has explored age differences in personality traits across adulthood.

Age Differences Throughout Adulthood

The most direct way to answer questions about personality throughout adulthood is to study people over long periods of time and to administer the same personality trait measures at the different time periods. Research employing this strategy yields consistent findings. There is much stability (Caspi & Roberts, 1999; McCrae & Costa, 2008; Roberts & Del Vecchio, 2000). Even over long periods of time, the correlations between measures from one time to another remain significant (Fraley & Roberts, 2005). This does not mean that there are no significant changes whatsoever in personality for people in general. And it does not mean that individual people (who might differ from a group average) do not change. However, it does mean that personality trait psychologists can be confident in concluding that the personality trait variables of their theories are capturing personal qualities that are substantially stable, over substantial periods of time, for substantial numbers of people.

Despite this stability, it is also the case that change is found: "The 30-year-old extravert is still likely to be an extravert at age 70, though not quite as active or keen on excitement" (McCrae & Costa, 2008, p. 167). Older adults score significantly lower in Neuroticism, Extraversion, and Openness, and higher in Agreeableness and Conscientiousness than adolescents and young adults. On average, teenagers seem to be beset by more anxieties and concerns with acceptance and self-esteem (higher N), to spend more time on the phone and in social activities with their friends (higher E), are more open to all kinds of experience and experimentation (higher O), but also are more critical and demanding of specific others and society in general (lower A) and less conscientious and responsible than others (parents, teachers, police) expect them to be (lower C).

Not surprisingly, we speak of "angry young men," not of "angry middle-aged men" or "angry grandfathers." The teenage years and early 20s are the times of greatest discontent, turbulence, and revolt.

Age trends such as these are found to be relatively consistent across cultures (McCrae & Costa, 2013). Beyond this, raters across cultures tend to share similar beliefs about different age groups (Chan et al., 2012). This supports the view that age differences reflect intrinsic maturation, just like other biologically based systems.

At the same time, it should be noted that other researchers provide evidence that suggests somewhat greater degrees of change and a bigger role for social factors. Ravenna Helson and colleagues (e.g., Helson & Kwan, 2000; Helson, Kwan, John, & Jones, 2002) have studied a group of women residing in northern California over a particularly long period of time. The women were first studied around 1960, when they were seniors in college. Subsequent measures were taken as late as 40 years later, when the women were 61 years old. Clear evidence of *changes* in personality across adulthood was found. For example, women changed in self-reports of norm orientation (the degree to which one controls emotional impulses in accord with social norms, a quality that correlated with Big Five Agreeableness and Conscientiousness; Helson & Kwan, 2000). On most norm-orientation measures, women's scores consistently increased with increasing age. Conversely, on measures of social vitality (a measure that correlates with extraversion), consistent changes were found in the opposite direction; women scored lower in social vitality with increasing age. A particularly interesting aspect of this study is evidence that changes in women's personality were related to a sociocultural factor, namely, the women's movement, which began to usher in new ideas about gender and women's place in society during the 1960s and 1970s. Findings suggest that "women for whom the [women's] movement was important increased on Self-acceptance, Dominance, and Empathy scales, that is, they became more 'empowered,' more confident, assertive, and involved in the affective understanding of others" (Helson & Kwan, 2000, p. 96). A recent review (Helson et al., 2002) indicates that such changes are found consistently across different studies and in samples of research participants.

Further evidence of changes in personality trait scores during adulthood comes from work by Srivastava, John, Gosling, and Potter (2003). These researchers conducted an Internet survey in which a large sample of adults of varying ages from the United States and Canada completed a five-factor inventory. The analysis of survey responses revealed significant age-linked changes in most of the Big Five traits for both men and women. For example, self-ratings on the factor of Agreeableness increased significantly for both men and women between the ages of 31 and 50; as the authors note, these are years during which many adults are raising children and these nurturing experiences may alter agreeableness tendencies. The authors emphasize that these results "contradict the five-factor theory's brand of biologism" (Srivastava et al., 2003, p. 1051). In other words, they contradict the notion that personality trait levels are entirely inherited and are unaffected by social experience. Even though trait theories of personality devote less attention to social influences than do most of the other theoretical frameworks in the field, trait research increasingly provides evidence that personality develops across the course of life as a result of individuals' interactions with the social environment.

In sum, there is evidence of consistent age trends across cultures but the nature of the interplay between biological and cultural factors remains to be determined.

Stability And Change In Personality

What, then, can be said about how stable individuals are in regard to their basic tendencies during the life course? Is the rank ordering of individuals on the Big Five stable throughout life even if average levels change somewhat? We will have more to say about this issue in the

Findings suggest that social movements for women's rights and empowerment can affect personality qualities such as self-acceptance and dominance.

next chapter, but here we may note that differing points of view exist. For example, one view suggests that personality development is largely biologically determined and continuous, that "the child is father of the man" (Caspi, 2000, p. 158). Similarly, McCrae and Costa suggest that the evidence of traits having a large inherited component and the lack of evidence of a clear environmental impact suggest a biological basis for traits: "How was it possible that years of experience, marriage, divorce, career changes, chronic and acute illnesses, wars and depressions, and countless hours of television viewing could have so little impact on personality traits?" (2008, p. 169).

Another view is that although there is evidence of trait consistency across the life course, it is not so high as to warrant the conclusion that change does not occur (Roberts & Del Vecchio, 2000). And a third view is that although general trait structure and levels remain fairly stable, there is evidence of change in individual trait levels (Asendorpf & van Aken, 1999). Of particular note here is evidence that parenting practices can impact personality development and that work experiences can impact personality development during young adulthood (Roberts, 1997; Suomi, 1999).

At this point in time the data would appear to suggest the following: (1) Personality is more stable over short periods of time than over long periods of time. (2) Personality is more stable in adulthood than in childhood. (3) Although there is evidence of general trait stability, there are individual differences in stability during development. (4) Despite evidence of general trait stability, the limits of environmental influence on change, during childhood and adulthood, remain to be determined. (5) Some of the reasons for stability are genetic, and some are environmental in terms of environments that confirm already existing personality traits. In addition, some of the reasons for change are changes in life circumstances and active efforts toward change as in psychotherapy.

Applications of the Big Five Model

One of the great strengths of the Big Five model is that it provides psychologists with a comprehensive, widely accepted tool that can be used to solve applied problems. Employers, educators, clinical psychologists, and many others require a reliable means of assessing stable individual differences. Big Five assessments are one such means and thus have been applied widely, as we now review.

A possibility of interest to students of vocational (career) behavior is that variations in personality traits may predict the kinds of careers people choose and how they function in these occupations (De Fruyt & Salgado, 2003; Hogan & Ones, 1997; Roberts & Hogan, 2001). According to the five-factor model, individuals high in Extraversion should prefer and excel in social and enterprising occupations, relative to low-E individuals. People high on Openness to Experience should prefer and excel in artistic and investigative occupations (e.g., journalist, freelance writer) that require curiosity, creativity, and independent thinking—central features of high Openness. Indeed, much research does suggest that the five-factor model is useful in predicting job performance (Hogan & Ones, 1997). A review of a large number of existing studies indicated that Conscientiousness is related in a particularly consistent manner to performance across a variety of different types of jobs and a variety of different measures of job performance (Barrick & Mount, 1991). Nonetheless, some writers caution that personality characteristics beyond those in the Big Five model are important to predictions of workplace performance (Hough & Oswald, 2000; Matthews, 1997), and others find surprisingly weak results and caution that different measures of the same Big Five personality trait may fail to correspond with one another (Anderson & Ones, 2003, p. S62).

One area of application is that of *subjective well-being,* or the extent to which people think and feel that their life is going well. In general, there is an association between high scores on subjective well-being and the traits of high positive emotion and low negative emotion (Lucas & Diener,

Imperia Staffieri / Getty Images

Deciding whether to go in? According to Reinforcement Sensitivity Theory, you will be more likely to decide "yes" if you have a highly sensitive Behavior Approach System, a biological system that responds to pleasurable, desired stimuli.

2008). Although these associations tend to be stable and predictive over time, it does not mean that change in life satisfaction and subjective well-being is not possible. Change in personality as well as change in life circumstances can make a difference.

Another area of application is that of health. A long-term study indicates that more conscientious persons may live longer (Friedman et al., 1995a, 1995b). A large sample of children was followed for 70 years by several generations of researchers who kept track of which participants died and the causes of death. Adults who were conscientious as children (according to parent and teacher ratings at age 11) lived significantly longer and were about 30% less likely to die in any given year. Why do conscientious individuals live longer? That is, what are the causal mechanisms that lead to these differences in longevity? First, the researchers ruled out the possibility that environmental variables, such as parental divorce, explain the conscientiousness effects. Second, throughout their lives, conscientious individuals were less likely to die from violent deaths, whereas less conscientious individuals took risks that led to accidents and fights. Third, conscientious people were less likely to smoke and drink heavily. The researchers suggest that conscientiousness is likely to influence a whole pattern of health-relevant behaviors. Thus, in addition to less likelihood of smoking and drinking heavily, they were more likely to do the following: engage in regular exercise, eat a balanced diet, have regular physicals and observe medication regimens, and avoid environmental toxins (Friedman & Kern, 2014).

Hampson and colleagues (Hampson & Friedman, 2008) have recently presented related findings. Many of the studies establishing these linkages are longitudinal, suggesting that the effects of personality on health often are cumulative. Children who differ in Big Five traits in childhood, as rated by teachers, are found to differ in self-reports of health-related behaviors when they are studied 40 years later. Traits are linked to health partly through their relation to daily activities and habits. For example, children rated as more extraverted are, in later years, more likely to engage in physical activities and also more likely to smoke; adult health status predicts physical activity (positively) and smoking (negatively) (Hampson, Goldberg, Vogt, & Dubanoski, 2007).

Five-factor theorists also believe that their model of personality traits can inform clinical diagnosis and treatment. They see many kinds of abnormal behavior as exaggerated versions of normal personality traits (Costa & Widiger, 2001; Widiger & Costa, 2013; Widiger & Smith, 2008). In other words, many forms of psychopathology are seen as falling on a continuum with normal personality rather than as representing a distinct departure from the normal. For example, the compulsive personality might be seen as someone extremely high on both Conscientiousness and Neuroticism, and the antisocial personality as someone extremely low on both Agreeableness and Conscientiousness. Thus, it may be the pattern of scores on the five factors that are most important. This suggests that the five-factor framework would prove valuable not only as a taxonomy of individual differences in everyday personality functioning but also as a tool for clinical diagnosis.

There also has been interest in using the Big Five model in choosing and planning psychological treatments (Harkness & Lilienfeld, 1997). With an understanding of the individual's personality, the therapist may be in a better position to anticipate problems and plan the course of treatment. Another potentially important contribution may be the guidance that can be given in selecting the optimal form of therapy (Widiger & Smith, 2008). The principle here is that just as individuals with different personalities function better or worse in different vocations, so too they may profit more or less from different forms of psychological treatment. For example, individuals high in Openness may profit more from therapies that encourage exploration and fantasy than would individuals low on this factor. The latter may prefer and profit better from more directive forms of treatment, including the use of medication. One clinician writing about this notes that he has often heard a patient low on Openness say something like "Some people need to lie on a couch and talk about their mother. My 'therapy' is working out at the gym" (Miller, 1991, p. 426). In contrast, the person high on Openness may prefer the exploration of dreams found in psychoanalysis or the emphasis on self-actualization found in the humanistic-existential approach.

In summary, the five-factor model has proven to have numerous valuable applications across diverse areas of psychology. Its greatest strengths have been in those settings in which investigators wish to predict individual differences in psychological and social outcomes. In these domains, numerous positive findings attest to the worth of the model. In other domains, the model is more limited. For example, it offers little unique insight into the causal dynamics underlying psychopathology, and thus to the clinician it is more a way of merely describing disorders than explaining them. More generally, unlike the other theories covered in this book, the five-factor model has not generated unique therapeutic methods for helping people to change psychological qualities that are maladaptive for them.

Five-Factor Theory

Let's now return to a question introduced in our opening Chapter Focus: The big five trait variables—"What are they, exactly?" Phrased more formally, this is a question about the conceptual status of the trait constructs.

The terms—or "constructs"—that people use to describe one another come in more than one variety. Some are merely descriptions; they are "labels" that describe a person's qualities, actions, experiences, or life circumstances. For example, suppose you say that someone is "attractive." That is a descriptive label. The term does not refer to a specific biological system; the person does not "have an attractive" somewhere on their body. It merely describes, in a summary form, appealing characteristics that might involve physique, facial features, a cute smile, good hair, and so forth. Other terms, by comparison, refer to real things: structures or systems that exist in the world. If you say that the attractive person has "low blood pressure," that term refers to a real thing: blood that is under a low amount of pressure. If you start poking around in the person's body, you will find blood that is under low pressure, but you will not find "an attractive."

What about trait concepts such as the Big Five? Are they merely labels that describe psychological characteristics? Or might they also correspond to real psychological entities that individuals possess and that causally explain an individual's behavior? Many trait psychologists view the Big Five factors merely as descriptive. They view the constructs as a descriptive taxonomy of individual differences. However, McCrae and Costa (1999, 2008, 2013) offer a bolder theoretical view. They call their ideas five-factor theory. Five-factor theory claims that the five primary traits are more than mere descriptions of ways that people differ. The traits are treated as things that really exist; each is seen as a psychological structure that each and every person has in varying amounts (in the way that everyone has, for example, a certain degree of height in varying amounts) (McCrae, Gaines, & Wellington, 2013). The traits are said to causally influence each individual's psychological development. Phrased more technically, in a five-factor theory, the idea is that the five factors are basic dispositional tendencies that are possessed universally, that is, by all individuals.

McCrae and Costa (2013) propose that the factors have a biological basis. Behavioral differences linked to the Big Five are said to be determined by genetic influences on neural structures, brain chemistry, and so on. Multiple genes are assumed to contribute to each trait so that there is no 1:1 relationship between a single gene and a single trait. In proposing this model, McCrae and Costa felt that the biological basis of the factors was so strong that the basic five dispositional tendencies are not influenced directly by the environment; their contention was that "Personality traits, like temperaments, are endogenous dispositions that follow intrinsic paths of development essentially independent of environmental influences" (McCrae et al., 2000, p. 173). This position speaks to a classic issue in psychology: nature versus nurture. McCrae and Costa's theory is perhaps the strongest "nature" position possible—that is, the strongest possible claim that inherited biology (nature) determines personality and that social experience (nurture) has little effect. Culture is viewed as influencing the form of trait expression but not the basic structure of traits themselves; that is, in terms of basic structure there is cultural invariance (McCrae & Costa, 2013). The claim that external influences have no influence on an individual's personality traits is a relatively unique claim of five-factor theory.

The second unique feature of the theory is the one we discussed above, namely, the claim that the traits are not merely descriptions of individual differences (akin to *attractiveness* in the earlier example) but also causal structure. Five-factor theory views traits as causal factors that influence the life course of each and every individual. The five traits are said to be the "universal raw material of personality" (McCrae & Costa, 1996, p. 66). In five-factor theory, then, a trait construct such as Agreeableness serves two functions. It not only is (1) a "dimension of individual differences that applies to populations rather than people" but also is (2) "the underlying causal basis [of] consistent patterns of thoughts, feelings" where this causal analysis "applies directly to people" (McCrae & Costa, 2003).

What is one to think of five-factor theory? The model clearly has exceptional integrative potential. If it were correct, it would connect a biological view of traits and environmental influences to observable personality variables that are of such great concern to the other theoretical orientations represented in this book. Yet the model leaves open as many questions as it answers. Three issues seem particularly problematic for five-factor theory. Since they are of broad, general importance to personality theory, we will consider them in some detail.

The first problem is how to link personality structures to other personality processes. Trait theory has little to say about these processes; in McCrae and Costa's view, these are details to be filled in by other theoretical approaches to personality. This unquestionably is a significant theoretical limitation. A particular limitation is not merely that these dynamic processes are not filled in yet but that it is not at all clear how, even in principle, they could be filled in. In general, personality theorists connect structures to processes by specifying the psychological mechanisms that make up the personality structure, and then they explain how those mechanisms guide dynamic personality processing. For example, psychoanalysts posit that the basic mechanisms of the id involve unconscious, biologically based drives, and then they explain how these unconscious forces influence observable behavior. But in five-factor theory, the biological and psychological mechanisms associated with the trait structures are unspecified. The traits are thought of merely as tendencies. Since the causal mechanisms associated with the traits are unknown, it is difficult even to begin building a model that links them to dynamic processes.

The other two problems concern the two unique features of five-factor theory noted earlier. One is the idea that traits are not affected by social factors. The problem is that research findings contradict this theoretical idea. For example, some data suggest that personality trait scores have changed across historical periods. Twenge (2002) reasoned that cultural changes across periods of the 20th century might have caused changes in personality. Consider changes in the United States in the middle versus latter decades of the century. Compared to the 1950s, in the 1990s people experienced a culture with higher divorce rates, higher crime rates, smaller family size, and less contact with one's extended family (due to greater job and educational mobility of the population). These sociocultural changes, Twenge finds, were associated with higher levels of anxiety; anxiety increased significantly from the 1950s through 1990s (Twenge, 2002). A second compelling source of evidence is change in personality traits as a result of clinical interventions. An extensive meta-analysis by Roberts and colleagues indicates that therapeutic interventions substantially changes personality traits including neuroticism and extraversion (Roberts et al., 2017). When viewed from the perspective of theories of personality other than trait theory, this result is not surprising. Yet is does plainly contradict the five-factor theory view that external influences will have no effect on personality traits.

The third concern regarding five-factor theory is conceptually subtle, yet deeply important. Five-factor theory claims that all individuals possess the five factors. The claim, in other words, is that all individuals possess psychological structures corresponding to each of the factors, with individuals varying in their level on each trait. To five-factor theorists, the factors are analogous to bodily organs, which might vary in size from one person to another. The problem is that this theoretical claim does not follow, in any direct or logically necessary way, from the available research evidence. The evidence that supports the five-factor model involves statistical analyses of populations of persons. When one examines populations, one finds that the five factors do a good job of summarizing individual differences in the population at large. But this finding does not demonstrate that each and every individual in the population possesses each of the five factors. Questions about populations and about individual persons involve different levels of analysis. A statement that may be true about a population of persons but may not necessarily be true of any individual persons.

The question, then, is whether the factors identified when studying populations enable one to make any claims about psychological structures possessed by individual persons. Recently, Borsboom, Mellenbergh, and van Heerden (2003) have taken up this question in detail. These writers emphasize that analyses of populations and of individuals are entirely different things. The only way to claim validly that the five factors explain the personality functioning of individuals would be to conduct factor analyses of individuals one at a time and to find that, for each individual person, the five-factor model is recovered. As they write, "if one wants to know what happens in a person, one must study that person. This requires representing individual processes where they belong, namely, at the level of the individual one cannot expect between-subjects analyses to miraculously yield information at this level" (Borsboom et al., 2003, p. 216).

At present, relatively few researchers have even tried to find the five-factor structure at the level of the individual. Data that do exist suggest that the behavioral tendencies of individuals commonly differ from the tendencies described by the five-factor model (Borkenau & Ostendorf, 1998). This is why a variety of other personality theories exist despite the fact that the Big Five are so successful at describing individual differences. To most other personality theorists, the five factors do not solve the problem taken up by Freud, by Rogers, and by the theorists discussed in subsequent chapters of this book: identifying personality structures *in the head of the individual* that explain his or her typical experiences and action.

Maybe We Missed One? The Six-Factor Model

From the 1980s through the early years of the current century, the Big Five model was a consensus position among trait psychologists. The factors appear to be not only necessary, but reasonably sufficient to describe average differences among persons. Then something happened. Multiple data sets, compiled by an international team of researchers working with participants from a variety of nations, suggested that trait psychologists had "missed one." There appeared to be a sixth factor that was overlooked in prior analyses.

To get an intuitive sense of this factor, consider two hypothetical cases: (1) a smart, outgoing, hardworking, interpersonally agreeable, and socially skilled chief executive of a corporation; (2) a smart, outgoing, hardworking, interpersonally agreeable, and socially skilled chief executive of a corporation who engages in unfair business practices and lies about his company's finances. Clearly the people differ. But the differences seem not to be captured by the five-factor model. Both individuals may be similar in O, C, E, A, and N, but they differ in something else: honesty, or honesty/humility (Ashton et al., 2004, p. 363).

The question is whether this basic intuition—that people who are similar on Big Five traits might differ systematically on a sixth trait, the dimension of honesty/humility—holds up not only at an intuitive level but also scientifically. If one analyzes self-ratings made using personality trait adjectives, and if one is careful to include in the pool of personality adjectives a wide range of attributes (so that no important global traits will be missed), does one actually find this sixth factor? Based on findings across seven different languages, the answer is yes (Ashton et al., 2004). In addition to the original five factors (some of which change subtly in their meaning when the sixth factor is identified), there is indeed a sixth factor of honesty-humility. Individual differences in the tendency to be truthful and sincere, as opposed to cunning and disloyal, are a reliable sixth factor.

The six-factor model (i.e., the five-factor model plus this additional factor of honesty) is a new development in trait psychology. It has not yet been incorporated fully into either basic theory or applied research. Thus, as we now turn to applications, we will return to the basic five-factor model. However, as you read the material ahead, you should recognize that individual differences in honesty and humility, versus dishonesty and/or egotism, may be underrepresented in the five-dimensional model that has been so popular among trait psychologists. Furthermore, additional factors may be underrepresented. In a very recent study, De Raad (2006) noted that almost all research on the Big Five model has studied adjectives but that the study of nouns and verbs might convey additional information about people. Factor analyses of a database, including all three classes of words, revealed *eight* factors, including factors (such as competence) not identified clearly in the Big Five or Big Six models (De Raad, 2006).

Cross-cultural Research: Are the Big Five Dimensions Universal?

If there are universal questions concerning individual differences and human interaction, then one might expect the same basic trait dimensions to appear in many different languages; in other words, one might expect the Big Five factor structure to be universal. Fortunately, thanks to the efforts of international researchers conducting multinational studies, many research results begin to answer the question, Are the Big Five dimensions universal?

Before considering these research results, we will consider the research methods. When asking whether the Big Five is found universally, across languages and cultures, methodological issues can make a big difference. One issue involves translation. Many researchers study the universality of personality traits by translating a personality questionnaire written in one language (e.g., English) into others (German, Japanese, etc.). Such translations can be tricky. Languages may lack one-to-one translations, and even words that translate the same (e.g., English *aggressive* and the German word meaning aggressive) do not necessarily mean the same thing (the German word for aggressive means hostile rather than forceful–assertive). Thus, a word such as *outgoing* (an extraversion trait) mistranslated from Japanese into English as *affectionate* (an agreeableness trait) might lead researchers to question whether they have found the same factor in the two languages.

To illustrate such problems, Hofstede and colleagues (1997) identified 126 words that they could translate fairly directly across previous lexical studies in English, Dutch, and German and used them to compare the meanings of the factors in the three languages. Their findings showed considerable congruence across these three related languages, with one important exception: the Openness factor. The German and English were very similar, but the Dutch factor not only included the expected traits related to intellect and imagination (e.g., inventive, original, imaginative) but also emphasized traits related to unconventionality and rebelliousness. A similar variant of Openness was found in Italian and Hungarian trait studies (Caprara & Perugini, 1994).

Many reviews of the literature have suggested that factors similar to the Big Five are found in most languages (Benet-Martinez & Oishi, 2008; John, Naumann, & Soto, 2008; McCrae & Costa, 2013). In promoting their five-factor theory, McCrae and Costa (2013) have taken a very strong position, suggesting that the Big Five personality structure is a human universal. The evidence for their conclusion involves translations of their Big Five instrument (the NEO-PI-R, to be considered shortly) into many languages. When researchers work with such translations, the same five factors result with great regularity.

But you should note the potential limitation here. It is possible that the process of translating English-language questionnaires into another language forces the issue. The translation process may inadvertently impose certain psychological factors onto respondents in another culture, a culture where the factor may not arise spontaneously. For example, it might be that people in a given culture give relatively little thought to individual differences in Openness unless a psychologist asks them to think about this feature of personality.

This consideration highlights the importance of an alternative research strategy. Rather than imposing an English-language scale onto members of a different language group, one could study each language group's indigenous personality terms, that is, personality descriptors taken from the native language being studied. When this happens, findings become more complex (Saucier & Goldberg, 1996). Results often differ depending on whether the trait terms are imposed on members of a culture as opposed to being drawn from the language of that culture itself. As an example, consider research conducted by Di Blas and Forzi (1999), who explored the structure of personality terms in Italian.

Where's their neuroticism? When researchers have looked for the Big Five model in Italian, they have found three factors—extraversion, agreeableness, and conscientiousness—rather than the English-language five (Di Blas & Forzi, 1999). Such findings question the view that the Big Five is a universally applicable taxonomy of individual differences.

They did not do this by translating a scale from English into Italian; instead, they selected items directly from the indigenous language. They then asked people to rate themselves on these terms and used factor analysis to see if the Big Five structure, common in English, would replicate in Italian. It didn't; that is, not all five factors replicated consistently. Instead, Di Blas and Forzi (1999, p. 476) "found consistently that a three-factor solution was more stable across participants and observers"; Extraversion, Agreeableness, and Conscientiousness, which generally are more replicable than the other two components of the Big Five model (Saucier, 1997), were the factors found consistently in Italian. The traditional trait factor of Neuroticism was not found in the Italian language (Di Blas & Forzi, 1999), a null result similar to that of other investigators (Caprara & Perugini, 1994). The authors suggest that cultural variations in the perceptions of negative emotions in different interpersonal settings may explain the difference between Italian and English-language results (Di Blas & Forzi, 1999). Subsequently, De Raad and Peabody (2005) examined trait terms across 11 languages and concluded that "the Big Three—Extraversion, Agreeableness, and Conscientiousness—are cross lingually recurrent," whereas "the full Big Five Model is questionable" (De Raad & Peabody, 2005, p. 464).

The existence of variations from one country and language to another leads some to suggest that personality factors may exist that are unique to particular cultures. A potential example is a "Chinese tradition" factor (Cheung et al., 1996), which seems to capture values and attitudes considered important in traditional Chinese society. Such culture-specific factors are certainly possible, though further confirmation and replication are needed before we accept these factors as empirical fact. For example, it is possible that such factors do not reflect personality traits proper but other individual differences, such as attitudes and beliefs (e.g., conservative versus liberal).

In more recent years, psychologists increasingly have conducted research with populations of individuals who are outside of the North American, European, and East Asian societies in which a disproportionate percentage of psychological research is conducted. Their research results have sometimes presented stark challenges to the view that the language of personality, and the nature of individual differences, is universal. Findings, in other words, have revealed substantial cultural variations in personality structure. Consider three examples:

- One research team studied conceptions of personality among more than 1,000 people representing each of 11 different language and ethnic groups in South Africa (Valchev et al., 2012). Participants described the personal qualities of themselves and each of nine other individuals with whom they were acquainted. Rather than finding a single, universal language of personality description, the researchers identified differences among the groups. Black South Africans were relatively more likely to use social-relational personality descriptions, that is, terms referring to qualities that promote social harmony and good personal relationships. White South Africans more frequently employed concepts that either (a) referred to personal growth (e.g., terms referencing conscientiousness and achievement) or that were (b) abstract, that is, that referred to personal qualities (e.g., honest, loyal) without referencing concrete circumstances in which these qualities come into play. The findings raise the possibility that the trait perspective in general has underestimated the ways in which the natural language of personality description involves—at least for some cultural or ethnic groups—a language of concrete situated actions rather than abstract trait terms.

- Another research team determined whether the Big Five model could be found among the Tsiname, a population in Bolivia whose lifestyle is that of forager-farmers (Gurven, von Rueden, Massenkoff, Kaplan, & Vie, 2013). Members of the Tsiname culture are familiar with the contemporary industrialized world, but live in village communities that are isolated from it. What was the structure of individual differences in personality in this group? The researchers identified a "Tsiname Big Two" (Gurven et al., 2013, p. 365): two personality dimensions that did not correspond to any of the industrialized-world Big Five traits. The researchers judged that the Tsiname personality trait dimensions reflected patterns of social life specific to that culture; the dimensions corresponded to success in separate domestic (family) and public domains of cultural life.

- Finally, Singh, Misra, and De Raad (2013) studied personality trait structure among more than 500 Hindi-speaking citizens of India. India in some ways in similar to nations in the West; it is home to a democratic government and a market-based economy. One might therefore expect that most of the Big Five traits would replicate in Hindi. But instead, *none* of them replicated; "no apparent consistent relations with any of the Big Five. . .were observed" (Singh et al., p. 617). Individual differences instead aligned with the *triguna*, three personal qualities that have long been recognized in Hindu philosophy but that do not correspond directly to Western personality traits. For example, one of the Indian dimensions combined the qualities of restlessness, arrogance, prudishness, and disorganization—a combination clearly not found in any one Big Five trait.

De Raad and Mlačić (2017) have summarized cross-cultural studies of personality trait structure. They conclude that "when focusing on replicability of psycholexically based factors across most languages or cultures around the world, the Big Five *tends to lose* in competition with structures that have just two or three factors" (p. 209, emphasis added). Such findings have two implications. First, they plainly cast doubt on the claim that the five-factor structure of personality traits is universal. Second, if it is not universal, this fact opens the door to consideration of alternative models of personality traits that are not based on the study of language or the traditional Big Five dimensions. We consider one such alternative now.

Contemporary Developments in Trait Theory: Reinforcement Sensitivity Theory (RST)

The history of trait theory is long. As you saw in Chapter 7, the contributions of Eysenck and Cattell date back to the middle of the 20th century. The five-factor model is newer; yet, its outlines were evident by 1961 (Tupes & Christal, 1961). Are these relatively ancient foundations sturdy enough to support personality theorizing two decades into the 21st century?

Many contemporary commentators think not (e.g., Boag, 2011; Lamiell, 2013; Nilsson, 2014; Uher, 2013). Writers adopting a variety of theoretical perspectives (e.g., social-cognitive theorists; see Chapters 12 and 13) have identified limitations in the classic trait approach. One set of limitations is noted, and directly addressed, by a contemporary development in trait theory known as Reinforcement Sensitivity Theory (RST; Gray, 1991; Pickering & Corr, 2008). Let's first consider the limitations that RST highlights, and then outline the advance it provides.

Limitations of Classic Trait Theories

A limitation of classic trait theories (e.g., that of Eysenck or the five-factor theory of McCrae and Costa) becomes evident if you consider the relation between two things: (A) the goal of a personality theory and (B) the distinctive strategy of the classic trait approach.

Personality Theory and the Classic Trait Strategy

A major goal for all personality theories, as we said in Chapter 1, is to provide scientific explanation. If a person displays a distinctive style of emotion and behavior, a personality theory should be able to explain it.

A psychological explanation of a person's behavior must, at minimum, accomplish two goals. One must identify psychological systems (and, potentially, their biological bases) that (1) are actually possessed by the given individual and (2) have causal force, in other words, that contribute to the individual's personality style. Lots of everyday, non-scientific "explanations" do not meet these two criteria. If somebody says that you are emotional and intuitive because you are a Scorpio, "Scorpio" does not refer to anything that you possess and therefore not to anything that could have caused your behavior.

Now consider trait theory's distinctive strategy. As you have learned, to identify personality structure trait theorists rely on factor analysis. A typical research procedure is to ask a large number of people to complete personality questionnaires and to factor analyze their responses. The resulting statistical factors summarize the main ways that people differ from one another.

The Conceptual Status of Statistical Factors and "Top-Down" Explanation   Do these meet the goals of personality theory? In other words, are they qualities that (1) people actually possesses and that (2) causally influence their behavior?

Many classic trait theories say yes. Eysenck treated two factors, extraversion and neuroticism, as psychological structures that explain an individual's behavior, and searched for neural or biochemical factors that correspond to the factors (Chapter 7). Some current-day investigators similarly search for brain structures that correspond to Big Five factors (DeYoung et al., 2010). The assumption behind this search is that people with similar scores on a trait variable will be similar in terms of their underlying neurobiology.

This approach to identifying personality structures has been labeled a "top-down" strategy (Cervone, 1999). "Top-down" describes an approach in which one tries to identify a small set of "high-level" personality variables. Once they are identified, the high-level variables are said to explain a variety of lower-level tendencies and behaviors. Back in Chapter 7, Figure 7.1 visually displayed the top-down nature of Eysenck's theory. Two high-level variables, extraversion and neuroticism, were said to explain lower level tendencies and actions.

Five-factor theory is similarly top-down. Five individual-difference factors—the "Big Five"—are claimed to be personality structures that are possessed by individual persons and causally influence their development, experiences, and actions (McCrae & Costa, 1996).

The Risk of the Top-Down Approach

Top-down strategies are not without risk. A big risk is that the high-level individual-difference variables will not correspond in any consistent manner to psychological structures that individuals actually possess. This somewhat abstract point can be illustrated concretely with an example from outside of personality, per se.

Suppose that, in a large population, you measured each of a variety personal accomplishments that individuals have achieved. The accomplishments could be in various life domains: academics, finance, athletics, success in maintaining long-lasting friendships, or success in developing a talent or hobby. Inevitably, some people will have more achievements than others. Achievements in different domains may be positively correlated, if only because people who experience impoverished environments may have lower academic, professional, and social opportunities than others. Factor analysis thus might yield a "successfulness" factor.

Now ask yourself this: Does "successfulness" *explain* people's achievements? Obviously not. "Successfulness" summarizes what people have done, but plainly does not explain it.

Or ask yourself this: Is successfulness a structure inside of each individual, such that people with similar successfulness scores are necessarily similar psychologically or biologically? Again, obviously not. People with similar scores—a successful musician, a successful chemical engineer, and a successful professional wrestler—could have little in common. There is, in other words, no "one-to-one mapping" of successfulness scores to underlying psychology or biology.

The RST Alternative Strategy: Bottom-Up Trait Theory

The pioneers of Reinforcement Sensitivity Theory are keenly aware of these problems in the classic top-down trait approach. Their solution? Move in the opposite direction: bottom-up. Consider how they contrast their strategy with trait theories of the past.

As RST theorists explain, "Hans Eysenck adopted a. . .'top-down' method. His search for causal systems was determined by the structure of statistically derived personality factors/dimensions" (Pickering & Corr, 2008, all quotes p. 240). In other words, the statistics (the factor analysis) came first, and the hunt for underlying biological mechanisms came second. "By contrast," RST adopts a "bottom-up general approach." The RST strategy is to "first identify the fundamental properties of brain-behavioural systems" and "then relate variations in these systems to known measures of personality."

RST-inspired theorists similarly are critical of the five-factor model. The big five "describes between-person differences in personality but cannot explain how an individual's emotions and behaviors might vary across situations and over time" (Collins, Jackson, Walker, O'Connor, & Gardiner, 2016, p. 92). Just as "successfulness" does not explain why a person has (e.g.) a high income or a lot of good friends, five-factor "agreeableness" does not explain why a person displays cordial, affable behavior.

Let's now consider the RST strategy for identifying psychological systems that really exist, in the psychology and neurobiology of individual persons.

Reinforcement Sensitivity Theory

The specific goal of Reinforcement Sensitivity Theory (RST) is to identify neural subsystems in the brain that correspond to universal types of motivation and emotion. This goal was first pursued in the 20th century by the founder of RST, the eminent British scientist Jeffrey A. Gray (e.g., Gray, 1991).

Neural Subsystems

A neural subsystem, according to Gray, is not a single group of cells in one specific brain region. Instead, a neural subsystem is an interconnected collection of mechanisms that may be located in different parts of the brain, yet that work together to carry out a particular function. Gray (1991) gives the example of the visual system. It contains a lot of different parts, running from the eye through the middle of the brain and back to the visual cortex. Yet, it plainly is a singular, unified system, in that it carries out a single function, namely, vision. The visual system thus is a neural subsystem. RST tries to identify subsystems that carry out specific psychological functions, but ones related to emotion and motivation.

This effort is relevant to personality psychology for the following reason. If you can identify neural subsystems, you are in a good position to explain a question of major interest: individual differences. Just as individual differences in the visual system explain individual differences in sight (e.g., sharpness of eyesight or color vision ability), individual differences in other brain systems may explain person-to-person variations in emotion and motivation.

Three RST Systems

The scientific challenge is to identify these biological systems and their psychological implications. This originally was done by Gray through a review of research on brain systems and behavior in laboratory animals (e.g., rats). The reasoning behind such research is that significant aspects of brain functioning are preserved (i.e., are essentially the same) across mammalian species. Research on biological systems in animals thus provides insight into systems also possessed by humans (Gray, 1991).

A theoretical system presented by Gray and NcNaughton (2000) and later summarized and advanced by others (e.g., Pickering & Corr, 2008; Gray himself died in 2004) identified three

[Handwritten margin notes:] interconnected collection of mechanisms that may be located in different parts of the brain, but work together to carry out functions

identifying neural subsystems; explain individual differences biological systems of personality. As you read about these three systems, note how they differ from the variables of the Big Five model. The RST systems are not "global" traits; that is, they do not correspond to styles of behavior that are evident across any of a wide variety of life domains (or "globally"). Instead, RST systems respond to particular types of environmental stimuli. Just as, for example, your digestive or auditory systems respond to particular classes of stimuli (food, sound), each RST system responds to specific types of environmental events. Each system thus is relevant to a particular "domains" of life that features one versus another type of stimuli (Collins et al., 2016); for example, activities in which you are (a) doing something fun and enjoyable, rather than (b) trying to avoid something (or someone) who is stressful and threatening would be seen as different domains that activate different RST systems.

The three systems of RST are as follows:

1. **Behavioral Approach System (BAS).** The Behavioral Approach System is a biological system that responds to pleasurable, desired stimuli. These stimuli generally are called "appetitive," a term which indicates that they fulfill bodily needs. The BAS responds to appetitive stimuli that immediately fulfill those needs, as well as to other stimuli that are associated to them through classical conditioning. For example, if you are hungry, you BAS would become active if you smelled or saw some food. It also would become active if, when hungry and driving down a highway, you were to see a sign that said "EAT" in big letters, indicating that a restaurant was just ahead—the letters "EAT" having been associated with food through prior classical conditioning. The BAS produces the tendency to move toward—or "approach"—these pleasurable, rewarding stimuli. It also produces emotional experiences including "anticipatory pleasure," which is the positive feeling one has when looking forward to an upcoming positivity activity (e.g., the feeling you have when seeing the EAT sign).

[handwritten margin note: positive stimuli w/ a positive response]

The Big Five personality trait of conscientiousness predicts job performance. When searching for good workers, this result has practical benefits. But when building a personality theory, the implications are less clear. Instead of reflecting the influence of a broad personality trait, conscientiousness, the result could be due to one small component of the trait measure that overlaps with job outcomes (Mõttus, 2016). For example, one popular five-factor inventory asks people if they are "efficient" and "effective" workers who "do jobs carefully" (Costa & McCrae, 1992).

response due to fear [handwritten annotation]

• **Fight-Flight-Freeze System (FFFS).**   The Fight-Flight-Freeze System responds to aversive stimuli, that is, stimuli that are potentially harmful to an organism. As its name suggest, the system generates three types of responses depending on the details of the threat facing the organism: (i) confronting the threat (fighting), (ii) escaping from the threat (fleeing), or (iii) becoming completely immobility (freezing). The last of the three responses is unusual among people, but is seen in small animals; for example, if a squirrel notices you walking past, it may freeze in place rather than trying to run away. The emotion generated by activation of the FFFS is fear; organisms, including people, react fearfully when confronted with dangers to which the FFFS responds.

3. **Behavioral Inhibition System (BIS).**   The Behavioral Inhibition System resolves goal conflicts (Pickering & Corr, 2008). What is meant by "goal conflict" can be shown with a simple example. Imagine the experience of an animal foraging for food in the wild. Its Behavioral Approach System is active as it encounters rewarding food sources; yet, its Fight–Flight–Freeze System also is active if it is aware of the possibility of predators in the area. The two goals—getting food and avoiding becoming food—conflict; a bold search for food increases the chance of encountering a predator, whereas hiding in place to avoid predators eliminates the chance of finding food. The BIS responds to these conflicts. It does so by generating anxiety and "defensive approach" (Pickering & Corr, 2008, p. 245). The animal will still pursue rewards, but will do so hesitantly, with heightened sensitivity to environmental threats.

defensive response; combination of other two [handwritten annotation]

And what are the implications of these systems for the study of individual differences? Individual differences in the functioning of each system create individual differences in emotion and behavior (Pickering & Corr, 2008). Specifically,

• People with a particularly active BAS would be expected to be more impulsive than others.

• People with highly sensitive and active FFFS's would be prone to fear-related clinical disorders such as phobias.

• People with BIS are more active than others would be prone to experiencing anxiety (Pickering & Corr, 2008).

Even though the three neurobiological systems were first identified in laboratory research with animals, they may explain individual differences in the social behavior and emotions of people.

Implications for Classic Trait Theory

When contrasting RST with classic trait theory, three points stand out.

Identifiable RST Biological Mechanisms

One point is that the exact biological underpinnings of the RST systems are reasonably well understood. This is *not* something one can say about the Big Five variables. This understanding comes from research not only in personality science but also in psychological science and neuroscience more generally.

Consider, for example, the conflict resolution functions of the BIS. The question of how mental resources are allocated when people have conflicting goals has long been studied in cognitive science. A well-known task for studying these conflicts is the Stroop task, in which one sees a color name (e.g., BLUE) printed in ink of a different color (e.g., green) and has to name the ink color. The tendency to read "BLUE" conflicts with the need to provide the correct response, "green". This and other such conflict tasks are found to activate a particular region of the brain known as the Anterior Cingulate Cortex (ACC; Botvinick, Braver, Barch, Carter, & Cohen, 2001).

Thus, the ACC is a neural system that may carry out the psychological functions of the BIS (Collins et al., 2016).

There is No One-to-One Mapping of Big Five Variables to Underlying Biology

The second implication of RST is the one suggested by our "Successfulness" example above. As we said, there may be no one-to-one mapping of successfulness scores to underlying psychology or biology. A high school counselor, pop singer, and auto mechanic may be equally "successful," yet have little in common psychologically or biologically.

The implication of RST is that, similarly, there is no one-to-one mapping of Big Five variables to underlying psychology and biology. As Gray (1991) has long explained, the emotions of fear and anxiety illustrate the point. RST explains that fear and anxiety have different biological underpinning; fear results from FFFS activation whereas anxiety results from BIS activation. A theory of personality thus should identify different psychological structures that are associated, respectively, with anxiety and with fear. But consider the five-factor variable of neuroticism. It *combines* anxiety and fear together in one variable; questions about (a) apprehensive anxiety and (b) fear are both found in five-factor measures of neuroticism (Costa & McCrae, 1992). Furthermore, impulsiveness—which RST researchers explain is a product of a *third* neurobiological system, the BAS—also is a facet of five-factor neuroticism.

The RST conclusion is that neuroticism, and the other Big Five variables, do not "carve nature at its joints." There really are distinct biological systems of personality, according to RST. But they simply don't correspond to the variables of five-factor theory.

RST Makes Trait Theory "Interactionist"

A third implication of RST concerns "person–situation" interaction. The term person–situation interaction refers simultaneously to two facts; the first concerns psychology systems and the second involves observable behavior: (1) Any given personality structure may be activated in one situation but not another; psychological structures and situations thus interact. (2) People's behavior varies from one situation to another; almost everyone is outgoing in some setting but shy in others, conscientious about some things and not others. At the level of observable behavior, there are person-by-situation interactions.

An example illustrates both points. A college student might possess a long-standing belief that he or she is not good at math. This belief is not always active within the mind; instead, specific situations—for example, discussion of course planning with a college advisor—may activate the belief. The psychological structure, the belief that one is not good at math, this is activated in one setting but not another. At the level of observable behavior, one may see corresponding person–situation interactions; the student might be filled with self-confidence in discussions of life at school—unless those discussion turn to the question of math courses.

Trait theorists of course are aware of these interactions. The problem is that classic trait theory does little to explain them. Consider five-factor theory. The factors refer to average levels of behavior. They therefore do not speak to the question of when, and why, a person's behavior varies from one situation to another.

RST, by comparison, *does* speak to person–situation interactions, in two ways. One is that the theory specifies ways in which three RST systems are activated by environmental cues. The three RST systems are not global traits that pertain to any and all situations. Instead, situations that include cues involving reward, threat, and a need to resolve goal conflicts activate the BAS, FFFS, and BIS, respectively.

Work by Collins et al. (2016) identifies a second psychological process through which RST becomes a person–situation interaction theory: attention. Successful behavior requires the control of attention (also see MacKoon, Wallace, & Newman, 2004). If you sit down to study for an exam, but your attention shifts to social media, your good intentions may be doomed. People's ability to control the focus of their attention varies from one situation to another. When you are relaxed and alert early in the day, you can focus. When tired later in the day, attention wanders. If you are feeling anxious, your attention may become "locked in" to the source of your anxiety, causing you to *fail* to pay attention to opportunities that might reduce your anxiety. By combining (a) a situation-based analysis of attention with (b) the situation-linked processes of RST, one obtains a personality trait theory that advances far beyond classic theories of global traits (Collins et al., 2016).

Is RST a comprehensive theory of personality? It is hard to answer "yes." Although we humans may share BAS's, BIS's, and FFFS's with our furry friends in the animal kingdom, people plainly have a lot of other brain matter than gives us utterly distinct mental capacities—the ones highlight in personality theories discussed elsewhere in this book. Both RST and classic trait theories devote little attention, for example, to cognitive processes and social skills that are central to individual's life success (Matthews, 2017). Nevertheless, RST does represent a significant advance toward a biologically grounded theory of psychological mechanisms of personality.

The Case of Jim—Factor-Analytic Trait-Based Assessment

Let us now return to the case of Jim and consider how his personality is depicted by personality trait questionnaires. We begin with Cattell's 16 P.F. The following brief description of Jim's personality was written by a psychologist who assessed the results of Jim's 16 P.F. but was unaware of any of the other data on him.

> *Jim presents himself as a very bright and outgoing young man, although he is insecure, easily upset, and somewhat dependent. Less assertive, conscientious, and venturesome than he may initially appear, Jim is confused and conflicted about who he is and where he is going, tends toward introspection, and is quite anxious. His profile suggests that he may experience periodic mood swings and may also have a history of psychosomatic complaints. Since the 16 P.F. has been administered to college students throughout the country, we can also compare Jim with the average college student. Compared to other students, Jim is more outgoing, intelligent, and affected by feelings—easily upset, hypersensitive, and often depressed and anxious.*

The trait-based assessment classified Jim as extremely high on anxiety. This may relate to his dissatisfaction with his ability to meet the demands of life and to achieve what he desires. The high level of anxiety also suggests the possibility of physical disturbances and bodily symptoms. Also, Jim scored high on what Cattell called tender-minded emotionality. This suggests that rather than being enterprising and decisive, Jim is troubled by emotionality and often becomes discouraged and frustrated. Although sensitive to the subtleties of life, this sensitivity sometimes leads to preoccupation and to too much thought before he takes action. On other traits, Jim's scores were nearer to the average rather than being extremely high or low.

The 16 P.F. revealed two features of Jim's personality with particular clarity. The first is the frequency of his mood swings. In reading the results of the 16 P.F., Jim stated that he has frequent and extreme mood swings, ranging from extreme happiness to extreme depression. During the latter periods, he tends to take his feelings out on others and becomes hostile to them in a sarcastic, "biting," or "cutting" way. Second, Jim expressed many psychosomatic complaints. Jim has had considerable difficulty with an ulcer and frequently had to drink milk for the condition, as was recommended at that time. Notice that although this is a serious condition that gives him considerable trouble, Jim did not mention it at all in his autobiography.

Despite its informativeness, one is left wondering whether 16 dimensions are adequate for the description of personality. The clinician also wonders whether a score in the middle of the scale means that the trait is not important for understanding Jim or simply that he is not extreme on that characteristic; the latter appeared to be the case. Yet, when one writes up a personality description based on the results of the 16 P.F., the major emphasis tends to fall on scales with extreme scores.

Perhaps most serious, however, is that the results of the 16 P.F. are descriptive but not interpretive or dynamic. The test yields only a pattern of scores—not a whole individual. Although the Cattelian theory takes into consideration the dynamic interplay among motives, the results of the 16 P.F. appear to be unrelated to this portion of the theory. Jim is described as being anxious and frustrated, but anxious about what and frustrated for what reason? Why is Jim outgoing and shy? Why does he find it so hard to be decisive and enterprising? The results of the 16 P.F. tell us nothing about the nature of Jim's conflicts and how he tries to handle them. Note that the same problem would have arisen if Jim had been assessed in terms of five-factor scores; one still would have obtained a collection of test scores but little understanding of how and why one score might relate to another.

Personality Stability: Jim 5 and 20 Years Later

The material on Jim presented so far was written at approximately the time of his graduation from college. Since then, much time has elapsed, and Jim agreed to be reassessed. Five years after graduation, he was contacted and asked (1) to indicate whether there had been significant life experiences for him since graduation and, if so, how they affected him and (2) to describe his personality and any ways it had changed since graduation. He responded:

> After leaving college, I entered business school. I only got into one graduate school in psychology; it was not particularly prestigious, whereas I got into a number of excellent business schools, and so on that basis I chose to go to business school. I did not really enjoy business school, though it was not terribly noxious either, but it was clear to me that my interest really was in the field of psychology, so I applied to a couple of schools during the academic year but did not get in. I had a job in a New York import-export firm over the summer and disliked it intensely enough to once more write to graduate schools over the summer. I was accepted at two, and then went into a very difficult decision-making process. My parents explicitly wanted me to return to business school, but I eventually decided to try graduate school in psychology. My ability to make that decision in the face of parental opposition was very significant for me; it asserted my strength and independence as nothing else in my life ever had. Going through graduate school in the Midwest in clinical psychology was extremely significant for me. I have a keen professional identification as a clinician that is quite central to my self-concept. I have a system of thinking that is well-grounded and very central to the way I deal with my environment. I am entirely pleased with the decision I made, even though I still toy with the idea of returning to business school. Even if I do it, it would be to attain an adjunct degree; it would not change the fact that my primary identification is with psychology. I also fell in love during my first year in graduate school, for the first and only time in my life. The relationship did not work out, which was devastating to me, and I've not gotten completely over it yet. Despite the pain, however, it was a life-infusing experience.
>
> Last year I lived in a communal setting, and it was a watershed experience for me. We worked a lot on ourselves and each other during the year, in our formal once-a-week groups and informally at any time, and it was a frequently painful, frequently joyful, and always a growth-producing experience. Toward the end of last year, I began a relationship that has now become primary for me. I am living with a woman, Kathy, who is in a master's program in social work. She has been married twice. It is a sober relationship with problems involved; basically, there are some things about her

that I am not comfortable with. I do not feel "in love" at this point, but there are a great many things about her that I like and appreciate, and so I am remaining in the relationship to see what develops and how I feel about continuing to be with her. I have no plans to get married, nor much immediate interest in doing so. The relationship does not have the passionate feeling that my other significant relationship had, and I am presently trying to work through how much of my feeling at that time was idealization and how much real, and whether my more sober feelings for Kathy indicate that she's not the right woman for me or whether I need to come to grips with the fact that no woman is going to be "perfect" for me. In any event, my relationship with Kathy also feels like a wonderful growth-producing experience and is the most significant life experience I am currently involved in. I do not think I've changed in very basic ways since leaving college. As a result of going into psychology, I think of myself as somewhat more self-aware these days, which I think is helpful. As I remember your interpretation of the tests I took back then, you saw me as primarily depressive. At this point, however, I think of myself as being primarily obsessive. I think I am prone to depression but on balance see myself as happier these days—less frequently depressed. I see my obsessiveness as a deeply ingrained characterological pattern and have been thinking for some time now about going into analysis to work on it (among other things, of course). . ..I see myself as more similar to, than different from, the way I was five years ago. I think of myself as a witty, aware, interesting and fun-loving person. I continue to be quite moody, so sometimes none of these characteristics is in evidence at all. My sexual relationship with my girlfriend has put to rest my concern about my sexual adequacy (especially about premature ejaculation). I still see myself as having an "authority" issue (i.e., being quite sensitive and vulnerable to the way in which those who have authority over me treat me). I am extremely compulsive, I very efficiently get done what needs to be done, and I experience considerable anxiety when I am not on top of things.

By the time he reached his 40s, Jim was practicing as a consulting psychologist in a medium-size city on the West Coast. The most important subsequent events for him were marriage, the birth of a child, and the stabilization of a professional identity. He describes his wife as calm and peaceful, with a good sense of perspective on life. He feels that he has changed in a way that makes a lasting relationship possible: "I have a greater capacity for acceptance of the other and a clearer sense of boundaries between me and others—she is she and I am I. And she accepts me, foibles and all."

Jim feels that he has made progress in what he calls "getting out of myself" but feels that his narcissism remains an important issue: "I'm selectively perfectionistic with myself, unforgiving of myself. If I lose money I punish myself. As a teenager I lost twenty dollars and went without lunches all summer long. I didn't need the money. My family has plenty of it. But what I did was unforgivable. Is it perfectionistic or compulsive? I push myself all the time. I must read the newspaper thoroughly seven days a week. I feel imprisoned by it a lot of the time. Can I give up these rituals and self-indulgences with the birth of a child? I must."

Self-Ratings and Ratings by Wife on the NEO-PI

The NEO-PI was not available at the time of the original testing but was administered, via both self-ratings and ratings of Jim by his wife, at later time periods. In terms of self-ratings, the most distinctive feature of Jim's personality is his very low standing on Agreeableness. The test classified him as antagonistic and tending to be brusque or even rude with others. Two other significant features of Jim's responses were his very high ratings on Extraversion and Neuroticism. On specific subscale scores, the test indicated that he sees himself as forceful and dominant and prefers to be a group leader rather than a follower. In terms of Neuroticism, Jim's score is characteristic of individuals prone to have a high level of negative emotion and frequent episodes of psychological distress.

On the two remaining factors, Jim scored high on Conscientiousness and average on Openness. Additional personality correlates suggested in the report were that he likely uses ineffective coping responses in dealing with the stresses of everyday life and that he is overly sensitive to signs of physical problems and illnesses.

How similar a picture of Jim is given by his wife? On three of the five factors there is very close agreement. Both Jim and his wife saw him as very high on Extraversion, average on Openness, and very low on Agreeableness. There was a small difference in relation to Conscientiousness, with Jim rating himself slightly higher than his wife rated him. The big difference in ratings occurred in relation to Neuroticism, where Jim rated himself as very high and his wife rated him as low. Jim saw himself as much more anxious, hostile, and depressed than his wife rated him to be. In addition, whereas his responses suggest a person with ineffective devices for coping with stress and oversensitivity to physical problems, his wife's ratings portray an individual with effective coping devices and a tendency to discount physical and medical complaints.

How are we to evaluate such a level of agreement? In some ways, this is like asking whether a glass is half filled or half empty. The high level of agreement on some traits suggests that the self-ratings were basically accurate. Where there was disagreement, it is hard to know if Jim's wife was actually more accurate or if Jim successfully hides some aspects of his personality—even from his spouse. His Rorschach report from about 20 years earlier suggested that Jim hides some negative emotions behind a façade of poise. Is his wife's more positive view of Jim a result of his being excessively self-critical or a result of his hiding from her his more negative emotions?

The Person-Situation Controversy

When we began our coverage of the trait approach in Chapter 7, we explained that traits refer to "consistency. . .regularity in the person's behavior." At the time we skipped over a question: How much consistency is there? Consider your own experiences. Are you consistently extraverted? Or conscientious? Or agreeable? Or are you sometimes extraverted and, at other times, shy and inhibited? Conscientious in some respects but in others unreliable? Agreeable with some people some of the time but sometimes in a disagreeable mood?

Since the 1960s, various writers have questioned whether there is enough consistency in social behavior even to support the idea of trait concepts as a centerpiece of personality theory. The most influential of these writers was Walter Mischel, whose book *Personality and Assessment* (1968) profoundly affected the field. Mischel's review of research evidence led him to conclude that people's behavior often varies or is inconsistent from one situation to another. This inconsistency, he reasoned, reflects a basic human capability: the capability to discriminate between different situations and to vary one's actions in accord with the different opportunities, constraints, rules, and norms present in different circumstances. Mischel was not alone in his criticism; others similarly have noted the importance of situational factors in personality functioning and have explained that situational influences may contribute to the relative weakness of global personality traits in predicting behavior (e.g., Bandura, 1999; Pervin, 1994). In the 1970s and early 1980s, debate over these questions—what came to be known as the **person–situation controversy**—dominated much of the professional field.

In considering whether people are consistent in their personality traits, one must distinguish two aspects of such consistency: longitudinal stability and cross-situational consistency. Longitudinal stability asks whether people high on a trait at one point in time are also high on that trait at another point in time. Cross-situational consistency asks whether people high on that trait in some situations are also high on that trait in other situations. Trait theorists suggest that both are true, that is, that people are stable over time and across situations in their trait personality characteristics. The degree of cross-situational stability is what critics of trait theory question.

As we have seen, generally there is evidence of longitudinal stability of trait scores, although there exist individual differences in the degree of such stability. However, the issue of cross-situational consistency is perhaps more complex than that of longitudinal stability. One must consider a range of issues before one can make any sense of empirical results. One issue is how to decide that a person has acted, across situations, in a manner that we should call "consistent" or "inconsistent." It would not make sense for a person to behave the same way in all situations, nor would trait theorists expect this to happen. One would hardly expect evidence of aggressiveness in a religious ceremony or of agreeableness in a football game. The trait position that needs to be evaluated empirically is whether there is consistency across a range of situations where different behaviors are considered expressive of the same trait.

Concerning the issue of range of situations, trait psychologists suggest that it is an error to measure behavior in one situation as evidence of a person's standing on a trait. A single situation may not be relevant to the trait in question, and it is possible for an error in measurement to be made. On the other hand, sampling over a wide range of situations ensures that relevant and reliable measures will be obtained (Epstein, 1983). One reason trait psychologists like to use questionnaires is that they provide for the assessment of behavior in a wide range of situations that might be impossible to measure by other means.

So what happens if one takes these considerations into account and actually measures the consistency of trait-related behavior? One answer to this question comes from a study of the consistency of behaviors related to conscientiousness among college students, conducted by Mischel and Peake (1983). These investigators solved the problem of determining what counts as conscientiousness by asking students to nominate behaviors that represent the trait in a college environment (e.g., taking clear class notes). They solved the problem of error of measurement by measuring behaviors on multiple occasions and aggregating the measures together. Their results yielded impressive evidence of longitudinal stability of trait-related behaviors; people who were relatively high on conscientiousness at one point during the semester continued to act conscientiously later in the semester. However, levels of cross-situational consistency were relatively low. It was commonly the case that students were conscientious in some settings (e.g., they took good lecture notes) but not conscientious in other settings (e.g., their dorm room was a mess). It is important to note that levels of cross-situational consistency were not zero; people did display some consistency in their trait-related behaviors. Furthermore, levels of cross-situational consistency are higher if one focuses on a subset of the conscientious behaviors, specifically those within the same kinds of settings (e.g., school, home, or work) (Jackson & Paunonen, 1985). Nonetheless, Mischel and Peake (1983) emphasize that a basic fact of social life is that people may vary their behavior from one situation to another. In so doing, they commonly may display behaviors that are inconsistent with respect to a broad personality trait. This result was consistent with findings from much earlier in the field's history; a classic study by Hartshorne and May (1928) similarly indicated that levels of longitudinal stability could be quite high, whereas the cross-situational consistency of behaviors related to a broad trait might be low.

Note that trait questionnaires ask about general tendencies to display a given personality trait; they do not ask about how variable the behavior is. Even if we assume that people differ in their average display of trait-related behavior—and they clearly do, as findings reviewed previously indicate—it still might be that there is enormous variability *around* the average. An exciting recent advance in personality psychology is that researchers have developed methods for describing these variations around the average. In so doing, they have significantly expanded the field's understanding of personality and social behavior (e.g., Moskowitz & Herschberger, 2002; Moskowitz & Zuroff, 2005).

One important line of research is that of Fleeson (2001; Fleeson & Leicht, 2006). He asks research participants to record their current thoughts and feelings a few times a day, over a number of days. These ratings generally are done using Palm Pilots, that is, hand-held computers.

Rather than asking people merely to report their typical, overall level of a trait, Fleeson asks them to report on the degree to which they have exhibited a given type of trait-related behavior *during the past hour.* For example, a traditional extraversion item asks people whether they are talkative in general (e.g., "Are you a talkative person?"). Instead of this, Fleeson asks, "During the previous hour, how well does 'talkative' describe you?" (Fleeson, 2001). By asking this question repeatedly, over a series of days, one obtains a large amount of information per person. With this information, one can determine not only average levels of behavior but also the degree to which people's behavior varies around the average.

So how much variability in trait-related behavior is there? A lot! The results (see Figure 8.3) indicate that people show levels of variability that are "close to the maximum extreme possible" (Fleeson, 2001, p. 1016). Participants rated their behavior on a 7-point scale, with the values 1 and 7 being the low and high ends of the rating scale. As you can see from Figure 8.1, on the Big Five traits of Extraversion ("Extra" in the figure), Conscientiousness ("Cons"), and Openness/Intellect ("Intellect"), the distribution of people's personality characteristics ranged all the way from the low to the high end of the scale. In other words, "the average individual routinely and regularly manifests all levels of" these traits and also "most levels of Agreeableness and Emotional Stability" (Fleeson, 2001, p. 1016). People do differ in their average level of behavior. But that's only a part of the story. As they adapt to the diverse challenges and opportunities of daily life, people vary their behavior substantially, and these variations simply are not described, or explained, by trait constructs.

So where does this leave us in terms of the person–situation controversy? Can a conclusion based on the evidence be reached at this time? People are prepared to answer trait questionnaires, but they also report that their behavior varies from context to context. Do they know something personality psychologists have yet to conclude? A fair judgment at this time suggests that there is evidence of trait consistency, but this appears to be more within domains of situations (e.g.,

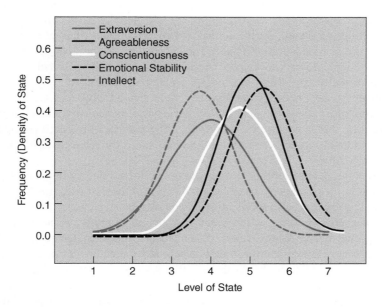

FIGURE 8.1 Graph displays the average individual's distributions of psychological states that generally are construed as manifestations of each of the Big Five traits. The graph indicates that there is substantial within-person variability in trait-related behavior; that is, the average individual shows both high and low levels of the trait.

home, school, work, friends, recreation) than across domains of situations. Since people tend to be observed over a limited range of situations, there may appear to be greater consistency than actually exists. Beyond this, the conclusions vary with the psychologist's point of view (Funder, 2008). There is evidence both for cross-situational consistency and for cross-situational variability, just as the nonprofessional suggests. To a certain extent people are the same regardless of context, and to a certain extent they also are different depending on the context. Trait theorists are impressed with the former and use such evidence to support their position, whereas situationist theorists are impressed with the latter and use such evidence to support their position. In Chapters 12 and 13 we will have the opportunity to consider theories that focus on the ways in which individuals perceive and adapt to different situations.

Critical Evaluation

We once again will evaluate a theoretical perspective by considering how well it achieves the five goals for a theory of personality that were reviewed back in Chapter 1. The evaluation of trait theory on these five criteria is a little more difficult than was the evaluation of psychodynamic and phenomenological theories (Chapters 4 and 6). This is because there is no one, single-trait theory. Critical evaluations might vary depending on whether one is considering the trait theory of Allport, or Eysenck, or Cattell, or the lexical Big Five model, or the five-factor theory of McCrae and Costa. In our evaluations, we will try to focus on main themes that are evident across the work of these different trait theorists.

Scientific Observation: The Database

The first of these five criteria, as you will recall, is whether a theory is based on a sound body of careful scientific observations. On this point, the trait theories excel. Thanks in particular to the pioneering efforts of Cattell, the theoretical edifice of trait theory has, almost from its outset, been built on a strong foundation of objective scientific data. Rather than relying on subjective interpretations of clinical interviews, trait theorists have employed statistical analyses of objectively scored personality tests. This objectivity is a major advantage.

The trait theorists' data not only are objective; they also are diverse. Large numbers of persons—of different ages, ethnicities, and sociocultural backgrounds—have taken part in the multinational enterprise that is personality trait testing. The number of research publications on the Big Five and trait theory more generally increased dramatically between 1990 and 2008 (John, Naumann, & Soto, 2008).

A third advantage of the trait-theory database is that it includes more than self-reports. It is true that self-report measures have been central to the trait theorists' efforts. Yet, many investigators have recognized that self-reports must be complemented by other forms of data: reports by observers, measures of objective life events, physiological indices of neural or biochemical systems that underlie a given trait (Chapter 9). In many respects, then, the quality of the scientific database of trait theory is far superior to that of psychodynamic or phenomenological theories. The one significant limitation to the database is that it so rarely employs the in-depth methods used by clinical theorists such as Rogers and Freud. In trait-theoretic assessments, one learns about a few general qualities of persons—their overall trait levels—but not about the inner psychological dynamics of the individual. This limitation has led one commentator to conclude that a trait analysis, by itself, yields "a psychology of the stranger" (McAdams, 1994, p. 145), that is, a superficial analysis that is similar to the information one might know about a stranger one only meets casually, rather than the deeper information that can be yielded by a detailed case study.

Stated differently, one might say that the Big Five are not adequate to capture the uniqueness of the individual (Grice, Jackson, & McDaniel, 2006).

Theory: Systematic?

Are the different elements of trait theory tied together systematically? Does the trait theorist provide a coherent, integrated account of personality structure, processes, and development?

For some theorists, the answer is yes. By analyzing not only traits but also states, roles, and motivational processes, Cattell did provide a statement about personality that was highly systematic. But Cattell's analyses of motivational processes had very little influence. By relating traits to biological mechanisms, Eysenck did provide a way of relating structures (enduring traits) to processes (of the nervous system). But except for work on the neurophysiology of extraversion, Eysenck's efforts to relate traits to biology were not entirely successful.

When one turns to more contemporary trait theories, one finds less in the way of systematic theory. As we noted earlier in this chapter, McCrae and Costa themselves readily admit that their five-factor theory does not actually specify the dynamic processes through which traits influence experience and behavior. Clearly, any theory that fails to specify these processes is one that fails to provide an integrated account of personality structures on the one hand and personality dynamics on the other. If you are "grading" the personality theories, contemporary trait theory receives a relatively low grade on the task of providing a systematic account of diverse aspects of personality.

Theory: Testable?

Trait theories deserve much higher marks on another task: developing a theory that is testable via objective evidence. Numerous aspects of trait theory can be tested objectively. Big Five theorists clearly make the prediction that factor analyses will yield five major dimensions of personality. Any other result—a six-factor solution, a three-factor solution, and so forth—clearly is a counterexample to the theoretical predictions. The fact that there can, in principle, be such clear-cut counterexamples means that trait theories have stated their ideas with admirable clarity.

Trait theorists make numerous other predictions that are open to unambiguous empirical tests. For example, they expect that individual differences on self-report personality traits will predict behavior, that genetically identical individuals will score similarly on such tests, and that trait scores will be relatively stable over time. In each case, the trait theorist could, in principle, be proven wrong. Their ideas are open to objective empirical testing.

Theory: Comprehensive?

In some respects, the trait theories are remarkably comprehensive. Trait theorists have been keenly aware that efforts to develop a taxonomy of personality traits would be of little value if important personality traits were left out of the taxonomy. They have tried to ensure, then, that all significant individual differences are incorporated into their factor-analytic studies of personality structure. They have gone to great efforts to ensure this, with lexical researchers combing the dictionary for all possible words that could be used to describe persons. In this way, their efforts are comprehensive.

Yet in other ways their efforts are lacking in comprehensiveness. This is evident if one thinks back to topics discussed in earlier chapters: the interplay of conscious and unconscious processes, the role of sexuality in personality development, the significance of dreams, the interpersonal relationship between a therapist and his or her client, the role of parents in fostering a sense of self-worth in children. What did trait theory say about these topics? Virtually nothing. These and many other topics of interest to other personality psychologists simply were not addressed by the primary trait theorists. Trait theorists have concentrated almost all their energies into identifying a comprehensive taxonomy of personality traits and determining whether individual differences in traits predict individual differences in social behaviors. These are important tasks. But there are many other tasks that also are important to a comprehensive analysis of personality.

Trait Approaches at a Glance

Structure	Process	Growth and Development
Traits	Neural and biochemical processes associated with traits	Genetic influences are primary determinant of trait levels

Trait theories lack comprehensiveness in two major ways. One is the relative absence of analyses of personality processes (Mischel & Shoda, 2008). The theories tell us far more about the stable "building blocks" of personality—personality trait structures—than about dynamic personality processes. The other is a relative lack of attention to the individual (Barenbaum & Winter, 2008). Except for Allport, trait theorists primarily focused on individual differences in the population rather than on the inner mental life of the individual person. This is a significant limitation.

By analogy, suppose that one knew nothing about the workings of the human body, wanted to create a science of human biology, and began one's efforts with an individual-differences strategy: factor-analyzing questionnaire reports of physical characteristics and tendencies among a large population of persons. In principle, one might identify factors such as attractiveness (a dimension of unattractive vs. attractive), athleticism (unathletic vs. athletic people), and healthiness (chronically sickly vs. healthy persons). Such factors clearly would provide valid descriptions of individual differences; some people really are more attractive, athletic, and healthy than others. But for a science of biology one also would want to identify factors such as "circulatory system" and "nervous system." The individual-differences strategy may fail to identify these biological systems; since everyone possesses them, there may be no significant individual differences that would produce a statistical factor.

The general point is that one cannot confidently assume that the traits identified in factor analyses of individual differences are qualities that exist in the psyche of each and every individual. Big Five researchers recognize this; Saucier, Hampson, and Goldberg (2000, p. 28) write: "Clearly, the study of different lexicons [of personality description] can lead to a useful and highly generalizable classification system for personality traits, but this classification system should not be reified into an explanatory one. A model of descriptions does not provide a model of causes, and the study of personality lexicons should not be equated with a study of personality." Some suggest that the Big Five was never intended as a comprehensive personality theory, while others, such as McCrae and Costa, appear to be much more committed to the five-factor theory as such a theory.

Applications

It is easy to describe how trait theory has been applied but trickier to evaluate the worth of these applications. This is because any such evaluations hinge on subjective judgments about the applied products that a personality theory should provide.

What trait theories do provide are tools for prediction. Trait theorists have identified a consensually accepted set of traits and have developed reliable scales for measuring them. In so doing, they have provided a simple and valuable technology for predicting individual differences in a wide variety of psychological outcomes (Barenbaum & Winter, 2008; John, Naumann, & Soto, 2008; McCrae & Costa, 2008). The widespread use of these measures attests to their applied utility. Educational psychologists, clinical psychologists, industrial/organizational psychologists, and many other applied investigators have long employed measures of individual differences in global personality traits. If the provision of tools for the prediction of individual differences is the main applied product one wants from a personality theory, then trait theory applications can be judged a success.

Pathology	Change	Illustrative Case
Extreme levels of traits (e.g., Neuroticism) predispose toward pathology	(No formal model)	Jim

However, other personality theorists want more. They want a theory of personality to be clinically useful, and they find trait theory lacking in this regard (Westen, Gabbard, & Ortigo, 2008). Every other personality theory discussed in this text provides not only a theory but also a therapy. Freud and Rogers—and, as you will see in subsequent chapters, behaviorists, personal construct theorists, and social-cognitive theorists—each provide novel therapy techniques that are based on their theories. These therapies are the main applications of the given theory. But there is no "trait theory therapy." Trait theory (with the exception of some efforts by Eysenck) is the one body of theorizing that has not generated therapies for bringing about psychological change.

The trait theorist may say that developing therapies simply is not what their work is about. Trait theories are theories of stable individual differences and the bases of those individual differences. They are not theories of psychological change. It thus may not be fair to evaluate trait theories negatively for their failure to produce novel forms of therapy.

Major Contributions and Summary

Psychologists working in the trait tradition rightly can claim to have made substantial gains (Table 8.3). This is most apparent by posing questions about personality that might be puzzling but that, thanks to the efforts of trait psychologists, have been answered convincingly: How many trait dimensions are needed to describe major individual differences in the population? Are people's standings in these dimensions consistent across time? Are there any relations between these individual differences and differences in social behavior? The answers "5 (or 6)," "yes," and "yes" can be provided with confidence, and enormous research backing, by the trait psychologist.

The ability to provide these answers is a major step forward. Outside of the halls of academia, people often desire a simple yet scientifically validated way of assessing individual differences in average psychological tendencies. There are so many potential individual differences that one might not even know how to get started on this task. But Cattell and Eysenck figured out a way to get started, and contemporary Big Five investigators provide a valuable and widely accepted solution to the problem.

Table 8.3   **Summary of Strengths and Limitations of Trait Theory**

1. Active research effort	1. The method: factor analysis
2. Interesting hypotheses	2. What does a trait include?
3. Potential ties to biology	3. What is left out or neglected?

Another major strength of the trait approach is its capacity to move from a psychological to a biological level of analysis. Work in genetics and neurophysiology has begun to identify biological foundations of individual differences, as we review in the chapter ahead. Although all personality psychologists recognize that persons are biological beings, the trait model particularly lends itself to the integration of biological findings into a comprehensive model of personality. We continue to consider this wedding of psychology to biology in the chapter ahead.

MAJOR CONCEPTS

Big Five	Five-factor theory	NEO-PI-R	Person–situation controversy
Facets	Fundamental lexical hypothesis	OCEAN	

REVIEW

1. In the later years of the 20th century, a consensus emerged among trait theorists around the Big Five, or five-factor (OCEAN), model of personality traits. Support for the model comes from the factor analysis of trait terms in language and the factor analysis of personality ratings and questionnaires.

2. The Big Five theorists' study of language rests on the fundamental lexical hypothesis, which is the hypothesis that the fundamental individual differences among people have been encoded into the natural language.

3. McCrae and Costa have proposed a theoretical model, the five-factor model, that emphasizes the biological basis of traits, which are construed in the model as basic tendencies. Substantial evidence of stability of overall trait structures and of individual differences in trait levels is consistent with this theoretical model. However, the model is questioned by evidence of change in personality trait levels and by uncertainty concerning the limits of environmental influence on personality development. In addition, there is evidence that at least one more trait factor is required to capture all major individual differences.

4. Research indicates that individual differences in five-factor scores significantly predict outcomes in domains of importance to applied psychologists, such as vocational guidance, personality diagnosis, work behavior, and psychological treatment. A limitation of the five-factor trait model as an applied tool, however, is that it offers no specific recommendations concerning the process of personality change.

5. Although there is evidence for longitudinal stability in personality traits, much research also suggests that people show significant variability in trait-related behavior when they encounter different social contexts. To some, this variability in trait-related behavior suggests that trait constructs are inadequate as a basis for personality theory. Yet others judge that the stability in behavior across time and place that does exist is sufficient to support the utility of trait theories (the person–situation controversy).

6. An overall evaluation of current trait theory suggests strengths in research, the formulation of interesting hypotheses, and the potential for ties to biology. At the same time, questions can be raised concerning the method of factor analysis and the neglect of such important areas of psychological functioning as the self and a theory of personality change.

❏ Big 5's conception on Mental Illness = traits can cause you to be predisposed to certain illnesses

Biological Foundations of Personality

9

Chapter Focus

Why are some people generally happy and others sad, some energetic and others lethargic, some impulsive and others cautious? Why do men's and women's behaviors differ; for example, why are women more likely to wear makeup and men more likely to pay for dinner on a first date? Why does everyone recognize that some acts (e.g., incest) are immoral or "taboo," even if they do not directly harm anyone? Do we learn these feelings and behaviors, or might they be part of our biological makeup?

Scholars have contemplated such questions for ages. In the 1880s, the British scientist Sir Francis Galton contrasted "nature" (heredity) with "nurture" (environment), setting the stage for decades of theory, research, and debate about their relative importance. In the recent era, scientific advances have brought many of the issues into sharper focus. This chapter presents some of those advances. We explore six topics: biologically based individual differences evident early in life, or *temperament*; the shaping of personality by processes from our ancestral past, or *evolution*; how personality is influenced by *genes*; the neuroscience of *mood and emotion*; environmental influences on biological structures, or *plasticity*; and the neural bases of cognitively "higher-level" functions, including those involving *self*.

Questions to be Addressed in this chapter

1. How, and why, do infants differ in temperament?

2. How can the study of human evolution inform our understanding of the personalities of contemporary humans?

3. What role do genes play in the formation of personality? How do they interact with the environment in the unfolding of personality?

4. What is the relation between brain processes and personality processes involving mood and self-concept?

Scientists sometimes learn from accidents. The story of an apple falling on Newton's head—even if it is apocryphal—wisely instructs us that an accident can inspire scientific insight.

Insight into the biological foundations of personality, the topic of this chapter, benefited greatly from an accident that took place in 1848. The accident was suffered by Phineas Gage, a railroad construction foreman who one day in 1848 had a "very bad day on the job": While executing a procedure to blast a path through hard rock—drill a hole in the ground, fill it with explosive powder, insert an iron rod, and light a fuse—Gage become distracted. The charge blew up in his face, and the explosion blew the iron rod up through his left cheek, the base of his skull, and the front of his brain. It destroyed a large section of Gage's frontal cortex before exiting the top of his head.

Gage was stunned but, miraculously, alive. He could walk and speak. Indeed, he could describe the accident in detail and communicate about it rationally. Yet, Gage had changed deeply. "Gage's disposition, his likes and dislikes, his dreams and aspirations are all to change. Gage's body may be alive and well, but there is a new spirit animating it. Gage was no longer Gage" (Damasio, 1994, p. 7). Previously serious, industrious, energetic, and responsible, Gage now was irresponsible, thoughtless of others, lacking in planfulness, and indifferent to the consequences of his actions.

Gage's story suggests that there are deep interconnections between brain functioning and personality functioning. If the explosion had blown a hole in his leg instead of his brain, it would have been a bad accident, but Gage would have been the same basic person as before. The simultaneity of Gage's (1) loss of frontal brain material and (2) change in personality qualities was—well, one might say it "was no accident".

Psychological science has systematically explored the body–personality connection suggested by Gage's accident. This chapter reviews some of their findings, and in doing so, it differs from

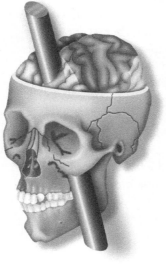

BSIP / UIG Via / Getty Images, Inc.

This illustration shows the location through which an iron rod blasted through the frontal cortex of Phineas Gage—who survived the accident but experienced a profound change in his personality.

our other chapters. Rather than focusing on a theory, the present chapter focuses on scientific *findings*. (The same is true for Chapter 14, which reviews findings on the relation between personality and social context.) They constitute a body of knowledge that must be taken into account by all personality theorists. Many of the findings relate strongly to the trait theories reviewed in Chapters 7 and 8. But others bear on distinct viewpoints, including a theoretical perspective called evolutionary psychology, which is reviewed later in this chapter.

Temperament

Right from the start, we differ. Children, even in infancy, vary in their styles of emotion and behavior. Since their experiences with the world are so limited, these variations cannot be the product of social experience; they must have biological roots. Temperament refers to biologically based individual differences in emotional and motivational tendencies that are evident early in life (Kagan, 1994; Rothbart, 2011). Early-life variations in the tendency to experience positive or negative moods, to become aroused in response to stimuli, or to calm oneself down after becoming upset are examples of temperament qualities.

[handwritten: deep interconnection between brain functioning and personality functioning]

Constitution and Temperament: Early Views

Scholars have long been interested in the possibility that psychological differences among people have a biological basis (reviewed in Kagan, 1994; Rothbart, 2011; Strelau, 1998). In ancient Greece, Hippocrates posited that variations in psychological characteristics reflect variations in bodily fluids (see Chapter 7, Figure 7.2). His view reflected the Greeks' beliefs about the universe. The Greeks thought nature was composed of four elements: air, earth, fire, and water. Hippocrates and other ancient scholars analyzed temperament through a similar fourfold scheme. The four elements of nature were said to be represented in the human body by four humors (blood, black bile, yellow bile, and phlegm), each corresponding to a temperament: sanguine, melancholic, choleric, and phlegmatic, respectively. Individual differences in temperament resulted from variations in the bodily humors. The Greeks, then, provided both taxonomy of temperament qualities and a biological theory of their cause.

This conception was remarkably long lasting. More than two millennia after Hippocrates, the great German philosopher Immanuel Kant distinguished four types of temperament and suggested that their basis was found in bodily fluids—a conception that was remarkably similar to that of the ancient Greeks. Needless to say, all contemporary psychological scientists reject the details of these bodily fluid theories.

Another view of historical note came from the 19th-century biologist Franz Joseph Gall. Gall founded the field of **phrenology,** which posited that specific areas of the brain are responsible for specific emotional and behavioral functions (Figure 9.1). Through postmortem inspections of brains, Gall attempted to relate differences in brain tissue to individuals' capacities, dispositions, and traits before death. Bumps on the head were examined, since they might be indicative of the development of underlying brain tissue. Phrenology gained great fame in the 19th century but subsequently was discredited. Contemporary research shows that the brain simply does not work in the way Gall assumed, with localized regions producing specific types of thought and behavior. Instead, most complex activities rest on the synchronized action of multiple, interconnected brain regions (Bressler, 2002; Edelman & Tononi, 2000; Sporns, 2011).

Efforts of more enduring value were seen in the mid-19th century. Three publications were critical: Charles Darwin's *The Origin of Species* (1859) and *The Expression of Emotions in Man and Animals* (1872) and Gregor Mendel's *Experiments on Plant Hybrids* (1865). Darwin's *Origin*, of course, was foundational to the contemporary science of biology. His *Expression of Emotions* documented numerous close relations between emotional expression in humans and emotional expression in other complex mammals; in doing so, it contributed indirectly to the study of temperament and also foreshadowed the development of contemporary evolutionary psychology (discussed later in this chapter). Mendel's work reported eight years of research on the breeding of pea plant characteristics and served as the foundation for modern genetics.

Two 20th-century investigators attempted to link temperament to an analysis of body types: the German psychiatrist Ernst Kretschmer (1925) and the American psychologist William Sheldon (1940, 1942). Their efforts were systematic, with careful measures of body type being related to indices of psychological qualities. Yet, in both cases, methodological problems limited the conclusions one can draw from their work; subsequent research indicates that the relationship between body type and personality are weak (Strelau, 1998).

Early 20th-century work of more lasting value was done by Pavlov. In addition to his research on how reflexes are changed by experience (see Chapter 10), Pavlov developed a theory of stable individual differences in nervous system functioning that highlighted the possibility of variations in nervous system "strength"—that is, in the degree to which normal nervous system functioning could be maintained in the face of high levels of stimuli or stress (Strelau, 1998).

Constitution and Temperament: Longitudinal Studies

The historical efforts to study temperament that we have just reviewed lacked an element that is crucial to contemporary research: *longitudinal* methods—that is, research methods in which a group of persons is studied repeatedly over an extended period of time. Longitudinal methods enable researchers to determine whether psychological qualities are evident early in life and are enduring, as one would expect if they are biologically based.

A pioneering longitudinal study, the New York Longitudinal Study (NYLS), was conducted by Alexander Thomas and Stella Chess (1977). They followed over 100 children from birth to adolescence, using parental reports of infants' reactions to a variety of situations to define variations in infant temperament. On the basis of ratings of infant characteristics such as activity level, general mood, attention span, and persistence, they defined three infant temperament types: easy babies who were playful and adaptable, difficult babies who were negative and unadaptable, and slow-to-warm-up babies who were low in reactivity and mild in their responses. This study and subsequent studies found a link between such early differences in temperament and later personality characteristics (Rothbart & Bates, 1998; Shiner, 1998). For example, difficult babies were found to have the greatest difficulty in later adjustment, whereas easy babies were found to have the least likelihood of later difficulties. In addition, Thomas and Chess suggested that the parental environment best suited for babies of one temperament type might not be best for those of a different temperament type. That is, there is a goodness of fit between infant temperament and parental environment.

Subsequently, Buss and Plomin (1975, 1984) used parental ratings of child behavior to identify dimensions of temperament that included *emotionality* (ease of arousal in upsetting situations; general distress), *activity* (tempo and vigor of motor movements; on the go all the time; fidgety), and *sociability* (responsiveness to other persons, makes friends easily versus shy). Individual differences in these temperament characteristics were found to be stable across time and substantially inherited, with identical twins being particularly similar on the temperament dimensions. Their strategy of relying on parental ratings is limited, for parents may be systematically biased when rating the personality of their own children; for example, they tend to overestimate the similarity of identical twins (Saudino, 1997). Nonetheless, Buss and Plomin's work was of enduring value. Many subsequent investigators adhered to their approach, searching for a small set of individual difference dimensions that characterize major variations in temperament characteristics in the population at large (Goldsmith & Campos, 1982; Gray, 1991; Strelau, 1998). These efforts partly informed the five-factor model of personality discussed earlier (Chapter 8).

These early longitudinal studies were limited, primarily because they did not identify the exact biological systems that underlie the observed temperament qualities. Doing so requires moving beyond parental self-report measures to direct measures of behavior and indices of biological response. Let's turn to such research now.

Biology, Temperament, and Personality Development: Contemporary Research

Inhibited and Uninhibited Children: Research of Kagan and Colleagues

Harvard psychologist Jerome Kagan has spearheaded a highly informative line of research on the biological bases of temperament (Kagan, 1994, 2003, 2011). A key to his research has been his use of direct, objective measures of behavior. Rather than merely asking parents to report about the characteristics of their children, Kagan observes the children directly, commonly in laboratory settings.

Based on these observations, Kagan noticed two clearly defined behavioral profiles in temperament: inhibited and uninhibited profiles. Relative to the uninhibited child, the inhibited child reacts to unfamiliar persons or events with restraint, avoidance, and distress, takes a longer time to relax in new situations, and has more unusual fears and phobias. Such a child behaves timidly and cautiously, the initial reaction to novelty being to become quiet, seek parental comfort, or run and hide. By contrast, the uninhibited child seems to enjoy these very same situations that seem so stressful to the inhibited child. Rather than being timid and fearful, the uninhibited child responds with spontaneity in novel situations, laughing and smiling easily.

Struck by such dramatic differences, Kagan set out to address the following questions: How early do such differences in temperament emerge? How stable are these differences in temperament over time? Can some biological bases for such differences in temperament be suggested? His central hypothesis was that infants inherit differences in biological functioning that lead them to be more or less reactive to novelty and that these inherited differences tend to be stable during development. According to the hypothesis, infants born highly reactive to novelty should become inhibited children, whereas those born with low reactivity should develop into uninhibited children.

To test this hypothesis, Kagan brought four-month-old infants into the laboratory and videotaped their behavior while they were exposed to familiar and novel stimuli (e.g., mother's face, voice of a strange female, colorful mobiles moving back and forth, a balloon popping). The videotapes then were scored on measures of reactivity such as arching of the back, vigorous flexing of limbs, and crying. About 20% of the infants were designated as high-reactive, characterized by arching of the back, intense crying, and unhappy facial expression in response to the novel stimuli. The behavioral profile suggested that they had been overaroused by the stimuli, particularly since the responses stopped when the stimuli were removed. In contrast, the low-reactive infants, about 40% of the group, appeared to be calm and laid-back in response to the novel stimuli. The remaining infants, about 40%, showed various mixtures of response.

To determine whether, as predicted, the high-reactive infants would become inhibited children and the low-reactive infants uninhibited children, Kagan again studied the children when they were 14 months old, 21 months old, and 4½ years old. Again, the children were brought to the laboratory and exposed to novel, unfamiliar situations (e.g., flashing lights, a toy clown striking a drum, a stranger in an unfamiliar costume, the noise of plastic balls rotating in a wheel at the first two ages, and meeting with an unfamiliar adult and unfamiliar children at the later age). In addition to behavioral observations, physiological measures such as heart rate and blood pressure in response to the unfamiliar situations were obtained. Again, findings revealed continuity in temperament. High-reactive infants showed greater fearful behavior, heart acceleration, and

Scary Claus, to some. Research on temperament explains why children differ greatly from one another in their reaction to unfamiliar people and situations.

increased blood pressure in response to the unfamiliar at 14 and 21 months and smiled and talked less than low-reactive children during social interactions at 4.5 years of age. Further testing at age 8 indicated continuing consistency, with a majority of the children assigned to each group at age 4 months retaining membership in that group. As you'll see later in the chapter, evidence of differences in biological functioning also was obtained.

Although there is consistency across time in temperament, there also is evidence of change (Fox et al., 2005). Many high-reactive infants did not become consistently fearful. Change in these children seemed particularly tied to having mothers who were not overly protective and placed reasonable demands on them (Kagan, Arcus, & Snidman, 1993). And some of the low-reactive infants lost their relaxed style. Despite an initial temperamental bias, environment played a role in the unfolding personality. "Any predisposition conferred by our genetic endowment is far from being a life sentence; there is no inevitable adult outcome of a particular infant temperament" (Kagan, 1999, p. 32). Yet, Kagan notes that not one of the high-reactive infants became a consistently uninhibited child, and it was rare for a low-reactive infant to become a consistently inhibited child. Thus, change was possible, but the temperamental bias did not vanish; it appeared to set constraints on the direction of development. As Kagan summarizes, "it is very difficult to change one's inherited predisposition completely" (1999, p. 41).

Another question is whether temperament qualities vary dimensionally (e.g., height) or categorically (e.g., eye color or biological sex). Woodward, Lenzenweger, Kagan, Snidman, and Arcus. (2000) employed statistical techniques that are designed to answer this question. These statistical methods are designed to identify categories or "classes" that may explain patterns of variation in data obtained from a large group of persons. To illustrate, suppose you did not know that some people are men and others are women. If you asked people a large number of questions about their personal habits, you might find out that there are distinct groups. A statistical analysis could indicate that some responses go together so strongly (e.g., people who say that they wear skirts also tend to say that they wear lipstick and own high-heel shoes) that they indicate a group of people that is a categorically distinct class (women). Woodward and colleagues (2000) found that the group of infants showing high reactivity (limb movements, crying) in response to novel situations is a distinct class. A distinct group of about 10% of a large population of children was found to be consistently more reactive than the population at large. This finding is important because it conflicts with the common assumption that individual differences in personality inevitably involve continuous dimensions.

Research also illuminates the brain regions that contribute to inhibited and uninhibited tendencies (Schmidt & Fox, 2002). More than one region appears to be involved, with behavioral tendencies reflecting interactions among the different neural systems. One important region is the amygdala, a region of the brain that, as we note below, is centrally involved in fear response. A second region is the frontal cortex, which is involved in regulating emotional response, in part by influencing the functioning of the amygdala. Interestingly, the functioning of these brain regions is not entirely determined by inherited factors; social experiences appear to modify brain functioning and thus influence children's emotional tendencies (Schmidt & Fox, 2002).

Neuroimaging methods provide particularly clear evidence of the role of the amygdala in inhibited versus uninhibited temperament (Schwartz, Wright, Shin, Kagan, & Rauch, 2003). Researchers studied a group of young adults who had been categorized as highly inhibited or uninhibited at age two. The adults participated in a laboratory study in which, while in an fMRI scanner, they viewed pictures of human faces of two sorts: (1) familiar faces (i.e., pictures of people that the participant had seen previously, in an earlier portion of the experiment) and (2) novel faces (faces that had not been seen previously). Brain imaging results supported the hypothesis that uninhibited versus inhibited persons differ in amygdala functioning. When they viewed the novel faces, adults who back when they were only two years old had been identified as inhibited children, showed higher levels of amygdala reactivity. Individual differences in a biological mechanism underlying inhibited behavior thus were stable across years of life.

More recent evidence suggests a molecular basis for fear—at least in animals, whose neural systems of fear may sufficiently resemble that of humans that results can be generalized. In this work (Shumyatsky et al., 2005), researchers identified a gene that contributes to levels of a protein, called stathmin, that influences the functioning of the amygdala. Mice with and without the stathmin gene differed in behavioral measures of fear, such as "freezing" in the presence of a potentially fear-provoking stimulus and exploring (or not) novel open spaces (Shumyatsky et al., 2005). A fascinating aspect of this work is that it was not only observational but truly experimental (see Chapter 2). The research included genetic "knockout" techniques in which genetic material is manipulated experimentally (Benson, 2004).

Interpreting Data on Biology and Personality

In summary, the evidence that genetically based biological processes contribute to individual differences in inhibition and fear in response to novelty is strong, as is the evidence that the amygdala is involved in fear responses. Nonetheless, it is important not to *over*interpret this evidence. Some interpretations that may at first appear appealing are overinterpretations, that is, conclusions that go beyond the actual data. Considering them is important to thinking critically about the biological foundations of personality.

One might conclude that the amygdala is a kind of fear-production machine: the necessary and sufficient cause of fear. This interpretation of the scientific evidence would be unwarranted for a number of reasons. First, the amygdala can be involved in many psychological functions *other than* fear responses; it is not specifically dedicated to the emotion of fear. Second, the amygdala is *the only* biological mechanism in fear responses. Some evidence suggests that it is not even necessary for the experience of emotions such as fear, even if it typically is involved in the fear response. Anderson and Phelps (2002) compared the daily emotional experiences of people with amygdala damage (lesions to and/or removal of portions of the amygdala, done surgically as a medical procedure to alleviate seizures these individuals had experienced) to people with normal, intact amygdalas. If the amygdala was necessary to the experience of emotions, these people's emotional life should have differed dramatically. But it turns out that they did not differ at all! People with amygdala damage experienced the same range of emotions as did biologically normal persons. The authors conclude that "the complexity and richness of human emotional life do not appear to be supported by the amygdala alone" (Anderson & Phelps, 2002, p. 717).

Furthermore, the amygdala may primarily be involved in the processing not of fear but of novelty. Kagan (2002) has reviewed evidence indicating that, in fact, "a state of surprise is a more reliable incentive for amygdalar activation than a state of fear" (p. 13).

Finally, the fact that inherited differences in a biological system, the amygdala, contribute to fearful behavior may prompt the interpretation that environmental experiences are unimportant and that a person's fearful tendencies cannot change. This conclusion, too, would be a mistake. Research (Fox et al., 2005) indicates that genetic factors interact with environmental ones in predicting behavioral inhibition in childhood. The environmental factor these researchers investigated was social support, specifically, the degree to which mothers provided nurturing, intimate social support when children were 4 years old. They also measured molecular genetic factors already known to be linked to inhibited behavioral tendencies. The genetic and environmental factors were used together to predict inhibited behavior with peers when children were 7 years of age. The main finding was that the link from genetics to behavior depended on the environmental factor, social support. Genetics were less strongly linked to behavior among children who received a high level of social support (Fox et al., 2005); high levels of social support, in other words, lessened the genetic differences that one would observe among children who experience less supportive environments.

In sum, "just because a person is born with a particular temperament . . . doesn't mean there is a simple set of instructions or blueprints. Nor . . . are [people] 'stuck' with their personalities from birth. On the contrary, one of the marvelous features of temperament is a built-in flexibility that allows us to adapt to life's hurdles and challenges. Everyone has the ability to grow and to change at every stage of life" (Hamer & Copeland, 1998, p. 7). It is always genes *and* environment rather than genes *versus* environment.

Evolution, Evolutionary Psychology, and Personality

When explaining the biological causes of a behavior, two types of causes can be cited; they often are labeled "proximate" and "ultimate" causes. **Proximate causes** refer to biological processes operating in the organism at the time the behavior is observed. Suppose that you take a break from reading this textbook to sit outside to get a tan. A proximate explanation of the tanning process would refer to the biological mechanisms in the skin that respond to sunlight, giving you a golden glow. (If, as a result of reading this example, you now are motivated to work on your tan, we note that you could always take your textbook out in the sun with you.) **Ultimate causes** ask a different question: Why is a given biological mechanism a part of the organism, and why does it respond to the environment in a given way? An ultimate-cause explanation of the tanning process would ask why it is that humans possess skin that tans in response to intense, prolonged sunlight.

Ever since Darwin, ultimate-cause explanations have invoked principles of natural selection. Scientists try to understand how and why a given biological mechanism evolved. These understandings are grounded in the basic principle that some biological features are better than others, at least for organisms living in a given environment. The organisms that possess those features are more likely to survive, to reproduce, and thus to be the ancestors of future generations. Organisms lacking the adaptive biological feature are less likely to pass on their genes to the next generation. Across a number of generations, the population as a whole is increasingly populated by beings who possess the adaptive biological mechanism. The biological mechanism, then,

Proximate = biological processes

Ultimate = why mechanisms respond to the environment

evolves. This historical view, grounded in Darwinian principles of evolution via natural selection, provides an "ultimate-cause" explanation.

In this section, we introduce you to ultimate-cause, evolutionary-based interpretations of personality functioning. We do so by reviewing developments in the field of evolutionary psychology (Buss, 2005, 2008, 2012) and their applications to questions of personality and individual differences. Subsequent sections of this chapter review proximate-cause explanations of personality functioning that involve the action of genes and neural systems.

Evolutionary Psychology

Many psychologists have tried to build such evolutionary explanations of psychological functioning. As a review by Linnda Caporael (2001) explains, these efforts have been of more than one type. Although all contemporary psychologists recognize the importance of analyzing evolutionary forces, their analyses differ. As a result, there exist "evolutionary psychologies" (Caporael, 2001)— that is, plural. The main points of difference involve the degree to which psychological tendency is seen as "hardwired" (i.e., as a biologically fixed, inevitable aspect of human nature) versus being a result of interactions between biology and culture. The latter perspective leaves open the possibility that different cultures will produce different psychological tendencies (Nisbett, 2003).

[handwritten margin note: Biology is fixed + unchanging]

In recent decades, writers who highlight the evolutionarily "hardwired" aspects of human nature (Buss, 2012; Buss & Hawley, 2011) have gained much prominence in personality psychology. Their work represents a startling challenge to many ways of thinking in the field. In this approach, contemporary human functioning is understood in relation to evolved solutions to adaptive problems faced by the species over millions of years. The idea is that basic psychological mechanisms are the result of evolution by selection; that is, they exist and have endured because they have been adaptive to survival and reproductive success. The fundamental components of human nature, then, can be understood in terms of **evolved psychological mechanisms** that have adaptive value in terms of survival and reproductive success. Such aspects of human nature, as our fundamental motives and emotions, can thereby be understood in terms of their adaptive value.

[handwritten margin note: Cause + effect = biology and experience]

Four points about evolution and the human mind are highlighted in this approach to evolutionary psychology (Pinker, 1997; Tooby & Cosmides, 1992). First, the features of mind that evolved are those that solve problems important to reproductive success. The critical feature in evolution is the passing on of genes. However, note that the reproduction-related problems do not merely involve acts of sexual reproduction. They include a wide range of problems relevant to the survival and reproduction of the organism. Consider the following simple example. Organisms need to see objects at a distance and to judge how near or far they are from objects. An organism that could not make these judgments commonly would be at a disadvantage (e.g., when hunting or trying to protect itself from a predator). To solve this problem, our nervous systems have evolved a solution: a pair of eyes that enables us to see in depth. The psychological capacity, depth perception, reflects a specific neural system that has evolved because of its usefulness in solving a recurrent problem faced throughout evolution. The intriguing feature of contemporary evolutionary psychology is that it extends this type of analysis to include patterns of social behavior that solve significant social problems faced across the eons of evolutionary history.

[handwritten margin note: - adaptivity]

A second point is that the evolved mental mechanisms are adaptive to the way of life of hundreds of centuries ago, when our ancestors were hunters and gatherers (Tooby & Cosmides, 1992). An implication is that we may have evolved psychological tendencies that no longer are good for us. For example, our taste preference for fat was "clearly adaptive in our evolutionary past because fat was a valuable source of calories but was very scarce. Now, however, with hamburger and pizza joints on every street corner, fat is no longer a scarce resource. Thus, our strong taste for fatty substances now causes us to over-consume fat. This leads to clogged arteries and heart attacks and hinders our survival" (D. M. Buss, 1999, p. 38).

[handwritten margin note: - needs are no longer a necessity]

Third, evolved psychological mechanisms are domain specific. According to evolutionary psychologists, we do not evolve a general tendency "to survive". Instead, the body and mind consist of evolved mechanisms that solve specific problems that occur in specific types of settings, or domains. Fundamental aspects of human nature, such as specific motives and emotions, apply to specific problems and contexts. For example, evolution does not give us a general tendency to be afraid, but instead selects for psychological mechanisms that cause us to fear specific stimuli that have been threats to humans across the course of evolution. Similarly, evolution gives us specific emotions, such as jealousy, because these emotional reactions have proven adaptive in solving specific problems of social living. These domain-specific motives and emotions have remained as part of our human nature because they facilitated survival and reproductive success given the problems to be faced in our ancestral environment. Note that this makes evolutionary psychology quite different than the trait approaches we discussed in the previous two chapters. In trait theory, a context-free variable such as "agreeableness" might be seen as responsible for actions such as being agreeable on a date and being agreeable toward a young niece or nephew. In evolutionary psychology, these acts would be seen as merely superficially similar. Even though they might both be described as "agreeable" behaviors, they would be caused by different psychological mechanisms, since, throughout the course of evolution, attracting opposite-sex mates and caring for children were distinctly different problems of social life.

The fourth point concerns the components and overall structure of the mind or its "architecture". One view of mental architecture is that the mind is like a computer with a central processing mechanism. All information—words, images, videos, games, regardless of their content—is processed by this one mechanism. Evolutionary psychologists reject this view of mental architecture. A core idea of evolutionary psychology is that the mind contains *multiple* information-processing devices, each of which processes information from one specific domain of life (Pinker, 1997). The concept of domain is critical. Different challenges that recurred throughout evolution—attracting mates, finding edible food, taking care of children, and so forth—each constitute a distinct problem domain. Some evolutionary psychologists suggest that we have evolved a distinct mental mechanism for solving problems in each domain. These mechanisms often are called mental "modules" (Fodor, 1983), a term implying that they are special-purpose mechanisms that carry out a domain-specific mental function.

What is important to recognize here, as with all human evolved psychological mechanisms, is that they are not rigid behaviors like instincts but rather provide for flexibility in meeting the demands of basic adaptive mechanisms.

Social Exchange and the Detection of Cheating

Which psychological mechanisms have evolved through selection, and which adaptive problems did they evolve to solve? Seminal work on this question was conducted by the evolutionary psychologist Leda Cosmides (1989). She explored a particular type of social setting and associated problem that, she reasoned, has been of significance throughout the course of evolution: "social exchange," that is, the exchange of goods and services. Throughout evolution, part of people's social interaction has involved the mutual exchange of beneficial goods. For example, a person may agree to help another with child-care tasks one day if that other person agrees to do the same on another day. People in a village that grows a large amount of a particular crop may agree to exchange some of their food with people from another village that produces a desired manufactured product. In any such exchange, it is important to avoid being cheated; the ability to detect cheating, in other words, has survival value. If you chronically fail to notice that a person needing change asked you for "two tens for a five" instead of "two fives for a ten," you lose resources that are required for social living, survival, and reproduction. Cosmides reasoned that cheating detection has been of such importance that a distinct mechanism for detecting cheating has evolved. She tested this idea in a clever manner that illustrates the overall approach of evolutionary psychologists to questions of mental architecture. Her work involved a particular type of logical reasoning task. In the task, people are asked to solve an "if then" problem—that is, to test a problem of logical relations in which one has to determine if a rule of the sort "if P then Q" is accurate.

As you might guess from this description, such abstract logical problems generally are difficult. People in psychology experiments commonly fail to solve them. However, Cosmides herself reasoned that people would be good at solving the problem if its content related to the detection of cheating. Although people might be poor at solving the problem "if P then Q?," they might be quite good at solving a problem such as "if person made a lot of money, did they pay taxes?" If the problem concerns potential cheating, then the particular subsystem of mind that processes information about social contracts and cheating should come into play, and people should be better at solving the problem. This is precisely what Cosmides (1989) found. Although a minority of people correctly solve abstract "P then Q" problems, a large majority correctly solve the same problem if the content of the problem involves the detection of cheating.

Evidence suggests that the ability to solve cheating problems is a human universal, precisely as evolutionary psychologists would expect. Both U.S. college students and nonliterate research participants in cultures isolated from the industrialized world solve such problems accurately (Sugiyama, Tooby, & Cosmides, 2002).

Other evidence has begun to identify brain regions that contribute to reasoning about social exchange. Researchers tested a neuropsychological patient who, in a bicycle accident, incurred a head injury that damaged portions of his brain's frontal cortex and amygdala. The patient performed normally (i.e., in a manner similar to persons without brain injury) on reasoning tasks *other than* social exchange but showed impaired performance when solving problems involving social contracts (Stone, Cosmides, Tooby, Kroll, & Knight, 2002).

Sex Differences: Evolutionary Origins?

Another domain to which evolutionary psychologists have turned their attention is sex differences. The evolutionary psychologist's reasoning is that, throughout evolution, male and female human beings have had different roles to play as a natural result of biological differences between the sexes. Differences, of course, are found in physical stature, as well as in child care (e.g., pregnancy, breast feeding). Since these differences have been consistent across the course of evolution, it is reasoned that the human mind has evolved sex-specific psychological tendencies. In other words, men and women, as a result of facing somewhat different problems across the course of evolution, are predicted to have somewhat different brains that predispose them to different patterns of thinking, feeling, and action.

Before considering this research, we note that drawing conclusions about psychological differences between men and women is a very tricky matter. Even if one finds such differences, it is hard to interpret them. True, men and women differ biologically. So one interpretation is that biology causes sex differences. But men and women also differ socially; specifically, they often develop within societies that do not treat men and women equally. Men commonly earn more money than women and hold more positions of power in society. It may be that, regardless of biological differences, any group within society that makes more money and holds more positions of power will differ, psychologically, from a group that earns less money and holds fewer positions of power. Sex differences, then, could be socially constructed, rather than being biologically caused. A core idea of evolutionary psychology, however, is that biology determines sex differences. Evolved psychological differences between men and women are seen as being responsible for the gender differences we observe in society. This notion has been advanced most vigorously by the evolutionary psychologist David Buss (1989, 1999). He has considered sex differences in two aspects of male–female relationships: mate preferences and causes of jealousy.

Male–Female Mate Preferences

Do you like men who are rich and professionally successful? Do you like women who appear youthful and have "curvey" hips? If so, evolutionary psychologists think they know why. According to evolutionary theory, as introduced by Darwin, selection pressures across the course of human evolution have produced sex differences in preferences for mates. The particular features of men that are attractive to women, and the features of women that are attractive to men, are thought to be a product of evolution.

Two ideas underlie the contemporary evolutionary psychologist's analysis of sex differences. One is something called **parental investment theory** (Trivers, 1972). The theory is an analysis of the different costs, or investments, that men versus women have made in parenting throughout the ages. The core idea is that biological differences between the sexes cause women to invest more in parenting. Women can pass their genes on to fewer offspring than men potentially can. This is because of both the limited time periods during which they are fertile and, relative to men, the more limited age range during which they can produce offspring. In other words, parental investment is greater for females because of the greater "replacement costs" for them. Also, women of course carry the biological burden of pregnancy, which lasts for nine months. Men not only do not have to bear the physical costs of pregnancy, but, unlike women, in principle they can be involved in multiple pregnancies at the same time. It follows that females will have stronger preferences about mating partners than will males and that males and females will have different criteria for the selection of mates (Trivers, 1972). Women need men to help with the burdens of pregnancy and child care and thus should seek men who have the potential for providing resources and protection. Men, in contrast, should be less interested in protection; instead, they are expected to focus on the reproductive potential of a partner (the person's youth and other biological markers of reproductive fitness). Although these preferences evolved ages ago, they still are present in the human mind. Thus, they should be evident in current social patterns. For example, since women are more interested than are men in a partner who can provide resources, the evolutionary psychologist would expect that, when on a dinner date, men would be more likely to pay for the dinner. Paying for dinner is viewed as an evolved strategy through which men display financial resources and thus add to their attractiveness to women.

In addition to parental investment theory, a second line of reasoning concerns parenthood. Since women carry their fertilized eggs, they can always be sure that they are the mothers of the offspring. On the other hand, males cannot be so sure that the offspring is their own and therefore must take steps to ensure that their investment is directed toward their own offspring and not those of another male (D. Buss, 1989, p. 3). Thus follows the suggestion that males have greater concerns about sexual rivals and place greater value on chastity in a potential mate than do females.

The following are some of the specific hypotheses that have been derived from parental investment and parenthood probability theories (Buss, 1989; Buss, Larsen, Westen, & Semmelroth, 1992):

1. A woman's "mate value" for a man should be determined by her reproductive capacity as suggested by youth and physical attractiveness. Chastity should also be valued in terms of increased probability of paternity.

2. A man's "mate value" for a woman should be determined less by reproductive value and more by evidence of the resources he can supply, as evidenced by characteristics such as earning capacity, ambition, and industriousness.

3. Males and females should differ in the events that activate jealousy, males being more jealous about sexual infidelity and the threat to paternal probability, and females more concerned about emotional attachments and the threat of loss of resources.

Buss (1989) obtained questionnaire responses from 37 samples, representing over 10,000 individuals, from 33 countries located on 6 continents and 5 islands. His samples reflected tremendous diversity in geographic locale, culture, ethnicity, and religion. What was found? First, in each of the 37 samples, males valued physical attractiveness and relative youth in potential mates more than did females, consistent with the hypothesis that males value mates with high reproductive capacity. The prediction that males would value chastity in potential mates more than would females was supported in 23 out of the 37 samples, providing moderate support for the hypothesis. Second, females were found to value the financial capacity of potential mates more than did males (36 of 37 samples) and valued the characteristics of ambition and industriousness in a potential mate to a greater extent than males (29 of 37 samples), consistent with the hypothesis that females value mates with high resource-providing capacity.

Causes of Jealousy

In subsequent research, three studies were conducted to test the hypothesis of sex differences in jealousy (D. M. Buss et al., 1992). In the first study, undergraduate students were asked whether they would experience greater distress in response to sexual infidelity or emotional infidelity. Whereas 60% of the male sample reported greater distress over a partner's sexual infidelity, 83% of the female sample reported greater distress over a partner's emotional attachment to a rival.

In the second study, physiological measures of distress were taken on undergraduates who imagined two scenarios, one in which their partner became sexually involved with someone else and one in which their partner became emotionally involved with someone else. Once more, males and females were found to have contrasting results, with males showing greater physiological distress in relation to imagery of their partner's sexual involvement and women showing greater physiological distress in relation to imagery of their partner's emotional involvement.

The third study explored the hypothesis that males and females who had experienced committed sexual relationships would show the same results as in the previous study but to a greater extent than would males and females who had not been involved in such a relationship. In other words, actual experience in a committed relationship was important in bringing out the differential effect. This was found to be the case for males for whom sexual jealousy was increasingly activated by experience with a committed sexual relationship. However, there was no significant difference in response to emotional infidelity between women who had and had not experienced a committed sexual relationship.

In sum, the authors interpreted the results as supporting the hypothesis of sex differences in activators of jealousy. Although alternative explanations for the results were recognized, the authors suggested that only the evolutionary psychological framework led to the specific predictions.

Evolutionary Origins of Sex Differences: How Strong Are the Data?

Based on our coverage so far, evolutionary psychology appears to provide a quite convincing explanation of sex differences. Indeed, many contemporary psychologists find the theory convincing in this regard. However, in recent years, new research findings have begun to raise questions about the validity of the theory as it applies to sex differences in social behavior. In evaluating evolutionary psychology, a major question is whether patterns of sex differences are found universally, that is, across all cultures of the world. Evolutionary psychology expects that sex differences will be universal. People share the same brain and physical anatomy. Humans share a common evolutionary past; throughout most of our species' evolutionary history, all humans lived in the same region of the world, Africa. If evolved psychological mechanisms are the cause of sex differences in social behavior, then those sex differences should be similar in all regions of the world and all human cultures.

A contrasting idea is that sex differences are a product of features of the society in which people live. In societies that treat men and women very differently, for example, in which there are particularly large differences in the work opportunities available to men versus women and in the income that they earn, sex difference may be larger than in societies in which men and women share more equally in the goods of society. Such a result would contradict the predictions of evolutionary psychology.

Eagly and Wood (1999) have provided evidence on this question. They reanalyzed data from a multinational study of men's and women's preferences in mates. The evolutionary psychology prediction is that the same pattern of sex differences would be found in all cultures, with women preferring men who have the capacity to earn money and men preferring young women with domestic skills. On the one hand, some of Eagly and Wood's findings were consistent with evolutionary psychology. For example, when looking for a mate, men did tend to value the quality of being a good cook to a greater degree than did women. However, other findings contradicted evolutionary psychology by demonstrating the existence of variations in the nature of sex differences. Specifically, sex differences were found to be smaller within societies in which men and women have more similar roles within the overall social structure. In societies in which there was greater gender equality, women were less concerned with men's earning capacity, men were less concerned with women's housekeeping skills, and sex differences on these measures were smaller (Eagly & Wood, 1999). A subsequent review of anthropological research on sex differences similarly was "not very supportive of evolutionary psychology" (Wood & Eagly, 2002, p. 718). Instead of pointing to universal patterns of sex differences that result from biology alone, the data were consistent with a biosocial view of sex differences. In a biosocial perspective, sex differences reflect interactions between biological qualities of men and women and social factors, particularly those involving economic conditions and the division of labor within society (Wood & Eagly, 2002).

Additional data question the original evolutionary psychology conclusions about sex differences. Miller, Putcha-Bhagavatula, and Pedersen (2002) noted that initial studies of sex differences in mate preferences by Buss and colleagues sometimes failed to compare men and women on all relevant psychological variables. When reanalyzing these mate-preference data, the Miller group (2002) found that "across the data, what men desired most in a mate women desired most in a mate. [There were] extraordinarily high correlations between men's and women's ratings for both short-term and long-term sexual partners" (p. 90).

The evolutionary psychologist's claim that men and women differ in the events that activate jealousy (Buss et al., 1992) is also contradicted by recent data (DeSteno, Bartlett, Braverman, & Salovey, 2002). These recent findings suggest that the original findings of evolutionary psychologists in this area may have resulted from a methodological artifact; an arbitrarily chosen feature of the research procedures may have artificially contributed to the results. Most of the evolutionary psychological original research on the topic involved a multiple-choice or "forced-choice" method. Participants in research are asked if they would be more distressed if they found that their romantic partner (a) had sexual relations with another person or (b) formed a close emotional bond with another person. Note, first, that this is an odd question, particularly from an evolutionary psychological perspective. Over the course of human evolution, it cannot possibly be the case that people frequently were faced with learning simultaneously about a partner's sexual and emotional relations and then having to decide which was worse. Recognizing the oddity of this forced-choice procedure, DeSteno and colleagues (2002) also asked participants to consider the sexual and emotional scenarios one at a time and to indicate how upset they would be by each one. With this change in procedure, the sex differences in jealousy predicted by evolutionary psychology were no longer found. Instead, men and women were highly similar. Both were more distressed by sexual infidelity than by news of a partner's emotionally close nonsexual relationship.

Related findings come from the analysis of men's and women's physiological responses to imagining sexual versus emotional infidelity (Harris, 2000). If men and women possess different evolved modules of the sort suggested by parental investment theory, then they should respond differently to these two scenarios: Men should react with stronger feelings of jealousy when imagining sexual infidelity, and women should react more when envisioning emotional infidelity. In Harris's careful research, women were not found to be more responsive to emotional (versus sexual) infidelity. Men did respond strongly to sexual infidelity, but, as Harris points out, that may not have resulted from the infidelity but merely from the idea that sex occurred; men simply may respond relatively strongly to any scenario involving sexual content. On her physiological measures, Harris (2000) indeed found that men responded strongly to imagined sexual encounters whether or not infidelity was involved. Subsequent work similarly failed to find the sex differences predicted by evolutionary psychology when research participants were asked to contemplate actual instances of infidelity they had experienced, rather than the hypothetical instances of infidelity that some previous researchers had studied (Harris, 2002). The overall findings, then, contradict the evolutionary psychological account of sex differences in jealousy—an account that, as Harris (2000) noted, had previously been seen as a "showcase example of evolutionary psychology" (p. 1082).

In summary, then, data do not provide consistent support for evolutionary psychological hypotheses about sex differences in mate attraction and jealousy. The exact nature of gender differences that might exist, and the roles of evolutionary hardwiring versus social structure in bringing them about, thus remain to be defined.

Genes and Personality

Whatever we inherit, we inherit it thanks to our genes. We possess 23 pairs of chromosomes, one of each pair from each of our biological parents. The chromosomes contain thousands of genes. Genes are made up of a molecule called DNA and direct the synthesis of protein molecules. Genes may be thought of as sources of information, directing the synthesis of protein molecules along particular lines. Information in the genes, then, directs the biological development of the organism.

In appreciating the relation of genes to behavior, it is important to understand that genes do not govern behavior directly. Thus, there is no "extraversion gene" or "introversion gene," and there is no "neuroticism gene." To the extent that genes influence the development of personality characteristics such as the Big Five, described in Chapter 8, they do so through the direction of the biological functioning of the body. In addition, a single gene does not determine a trait. Rather, a personality trait reflects the interaction of many genes with many environmental influences (Turkheimer, 2006).

Behavioral Genetics

The study of genetic contributions to behavior is called the field of **behavioral genetics**. Behavioral geneticists employ a variety of techniques to estimate the degree to which variation in psychological characteristics is due to genetic factors. As we shall see, the methods of behavioral genetics also can, and do, provide evidence of environmental effects on personality. Behavioral geneticists employ three primary research methods: selective breeding studies, twin studies, and adoption studies.

Selective Breeding Studies

In **selective breeding** studies, animals with a desired trait for study are selected and mated. This selection and reproduction process is used with successive generations of offspring to produce a strain of animals that is consistent within itself for the desired characteristic. Selective breeding is not only a research technique; it is used, for example, to breed race horses or breeds of dogs with desired characteristics.

Once one has created different strains of animals through selective breeding, one not only can study their typical behavioral tendencies. It also is possible to subject the different strains to different experimentally controlled developmental experiences. Researchers then can sort out the effects of genetic differences and environmental differences on the observed later behavior. For example, the roles of genetic and environmental factors in later barking behavior or fearfulness can be studied by subjecting genetically different breeds of dogs to different environmental rearing conditions (Scott & Fuller, 1965).

Selective breeding research has enhanced our understanding of how genes contribute to problems that often are blamed solely on the individual. Consider work on alcoholism (Ponomarev & Crabbe, 1999). The researchers bred various strains of mice that proved to exhibit qualitatively different responses to alcohol. This work illustrated that genes play a role in responsiveness to alcohol, addiction, and withdrawal. It contributed to a more complete understanding of the fact that genetic factors present some individuals with severe vulnerabilities to lifelong problems with alcohol (Hamer & Copeland, 1998).

Twin Studies

Even the most enthusiastic researcher realizes that selective breeding research cannot and should not be done with humans. Ethical factors force the researcher to consider alternatives. Fortunately for science, a ready alternative exists: human twins. Twins provide a naturally occurring experiment. What the scientist wants, ideally, is a circumstance in which there are known variations in degree of genetic similarity and/or environmental similarity. If two organisms are identical genetically, then any later observed differences can be attributed to differences in their environments. On the other hand, if two organisms are different genetically but experience the same environment, then any observed differences can be attributed to genetic factors. The existence of identical (monozygotic) twins and fraternal (dizygotic) twins offers a good approximation to this research ideal. Monozygotic (MZ) twins develop from the same fertilized egg and are genetically identical. Dizygotic (DZ) twins develop from two separately fertilized eggs and are as genetically similar as any pair of siblings, on the average sharing about 50% of their genes.

Researchers capitalize on these systematic differences between MZ and DZ twins by conducting **twin studies** to gauge the degree to which genetic factors explain person-to-person variations in psychological characteristics.

Two logical considerations underpin the twin method. The first is that, since MZ twins are genetically identical, any systematic difference between them must be due to environmental effects. Interestingly, then, the study of genetically identical persons is particularly valuable for revealing the effects of environmental experience. Second, it is the difference in similarity between MZ twin pairs and DZ twin pairs that is crucial to estimating the effects of genetics. Specifically, we know that MZ twins are more similar to one another genetically than DZ twins are similar to one another genetically. If genetics influence a given personality characteristic, then MZ twins, as a result of being more similar genetically, also should be more similar on the given personality characteristic than are DZ twins. If they are not, then there is no genetic effect. When studying both MZ and DZ twin pairs, then, the researcher can compare them (MZ similarity compared to DZ similarity on a trait of interest) to determine the magnitude of the influence of genetic factors. This genetic influence usually is expressed numerically in terms of a heritability coefficient (described below).

The twin strategy usually is conducted with twins who grow up in the same household. However, circumstances sometimes force parents to give up children for adoption early in life. As a result, MZ and DZ twins sometimes are reared apart. This creates a circumstance of remarkable interest to the psychological scientist and the public at large, namely, biologically identical people who are raised in different environments. What happens? Does biology win out, with genetically identical twins being psychologically identical despite their different experiences? Or do social experiences win out, with people differing substantially despite their identical genes?

Hero Images / Getty Images

A simple strategy for studying the influence of genetics on personality is to conduct research on twins. On each of a wide variety of psychological characteristics, identical twins are found to be more similar than fraternal twins. Such findings indicate that genetic factors contribute significantly to personality.

These questions can be answered thanks to an international data set that features large numbers of reared-apart twins who have completed various psychological measures (Bouchard, Lykken, McGue, Segal, & Tellegen, 1990). Results provide clear evidence that the effects of biology endure across different circumstances. On multiple personality trait measures, MZ twins raised apart were found to be similar to a significant degree; twin correlations indicating the degree of similarity between the twins were in the .45 to .50 range. Of particular interest is that MZ twins raised apart were about as similar to one another as were MZ twins raised together (Bouchard et al., 1990). Being raised in the same household did not make the twins more similar on broad personality trait measures. We return to this fascinating finding, and its interpretations and implications, after reviewing further research findings below.

Fascinating research by the psychologist Segal (2014) has compared identical and fraternal twins. The former, as aunts and uncles, are found to invest more in caring for the children of their twins than are the latter. They also mourn more for the loss of the twin sibling. Of particular interest is her research on what happens when identical and fraternal twins are reunited after being raised separately. She finds that reunited identical twins quickly establish much stronger bonds than do fraternal twins. She attributes these stronger bonds to their greater genetic similarity.

Adoption Studies

Studies of children who grow up with caregivers other than their biological parents are called **adoption studies**. (Adoption studies sometimes involve identical twins, as in the research reviewed in the paragraph immediately above, but commonly may involve nontwin siblings.) Adoption studies offer another method for studying genetic and environmental effects. When adequate records are kept, it is possible to consider the similarity of adopted children to their natural (biological) parents, who have not influenced them environmentally, and to compare this with the similarity to their adoptive parents, who share no genes in common with them. The extent of similarity to their biological parents is indicative of genetic factors, while the extent of similarity to their adoptive parents is indicative of environmental factors.

Finally, such comparisons can be extended to families that include both biological and adoptive children. Take, for example, a family of four children; two of the children are the biological offspring of the parents and two of the children have been adopted. The two biological offspring share a genetic similarity with one another and with the biological parents that is not true for the two adopted children. Assuming the two adopted children are unrelated, they share no genes in common but share a genetic similarity with their parents and any siblings who might exist in other environments. Thus, it is possible to compare different parent–offspring and biological sibling–adoptive sibling combinations in terms of similarity on personality characteristics. For example, one can ask whether the biological siblings are more similar to one another than are the adoptive siblings, whether they are more similar to the parents than the adoptive siblings, and whether the adoptive siblings are more similar to their biological parents than to their adoptive parents. A "yes" answer to such questions would be suggestive of the importance of genetic factors in the development of the particular personality characteristic.

It should now be clear that in twin and adoption studies, we have individuals of varying degrees of genetic similarity being exposed to varying degrees of environmental similarity. By measuring these individuals on the characteristics of interest, we can determine the extent to which their genetic similarity accounts for the similarity of scores on each characteristic. For example, we can compare the IQ scores of MZ and DZ twins reared together and apart, biological (nontwin) siblings reared together and apart, adoptive sibling and biological siblings with parents, and adoptive siblings with their biological and adoptive parents. Some representative correlations are presented in Table 9.1. The data clearly suggest a relationship between greater genetic similarity and greater IQ similarity.

Table 9.1   **Average Familial IQ Correlations**[®]

As genetic similarity increases, so does the magnitude of the correlations for IQ, suggesting a strong genetic contribution to intelligence.

Relationship	Average R	Number of Pairs
REARED-TOGETHER BIOLOGICAL RELATIVES		
MZ twins	0.86	4,672
DZ twins	0.60	5,533
Siblings	0.47	26,473
Parent offspring	0.42	8,433
Half-siblings	0.35	200
Cousins	0.15	1,176
REARED-APART BIOLOGICAL RELATIVES		
MZ twins	0.72	65
Siblings	0.24	203
Parent offspring	0.24	720
REARED-TOGETHER NONBIOLOGICAL RELATIVES		
Siblings	0.32	714
Parent offspring	0.24	720

Note: MZ, monozygotic; DZ, dizygotic.
Source: Adapted from "Familial Studies of Intelligence: A Review," by T. J. Bouchard and M. Mcgue, 1981, *Science*, 250, p. 1056. Reprinted from McGue et al., 1993, p. 60.

Heritability Coefficient

How, exactly, does the behavioral geneticist determine the degree to which genetic variations determine variations among people in a personality characteristic? This usually is done by computing what is called a **heritability coefficient**, or h^2 (it is h "squared" because numbers are squared when computing variations around an average score). The heritability coefficient represents the proportion of observed variance in scores that can be attributed to genetic factors. In a study involving both MZ and DZ twins, h^2 is based on the difference between the MZ and DZ correlations. If MZ twins (who share all their genes) are no more similar to one another than are DZ twins (who share half their genes), then there is no genetic effect: h^2 is zero. If MZ twins differ greatly from DZ twins, h^2 is large; its upper limit is 1.0, or 100% of the total variance. To the extent that h^2 is less than 1.0, there exists variance that is not accounted for by genetic factors; this remaining variance is explained by environmental variation.

Note that the heritability coefficient refers to variation in the population examined in a given study. This point has two implications. First, different heritability coefficients, for the same psychological trait, may be observed in different populations; for example, if one is studying a population in which many people have been subjected to environmental effects that exert a particular large influence on them (e.g., stress from disease or war), then the environmental effects in this group will be relatively large and h^2 will be relatively small (Grigorenko, 2002). Second, the heritability coefficient does not indicate the degree to which genetics accounts for the fact that a particular individual has a particular characteristic. It is a measure of variation in the population. For some attributes (e.g., a biological feature or psychological capacity possessed by all humans), there may be no person-to-person variation. The h^2 would be zero even if genetics explains why all people have the attribute. For other attributes (e.g., your ability to read), the attribute may be explained by an interaction of genetic and social factors, and it may make little sense to say that genetics versus the environment each accounted for X percent of the attribute. The h^2 is an estimate associated with a population and not a definitive measure of the action of genes.

Heritability of Personality: Findings

We now consider additional behavioral genetic findings and the conclusions about personality to which they lead. An interesting feature of this work is the consistency of findings across studies and across personality traits. As key investigators write, "It is difficult to find psychological traits that reliably show no genetic influence" (Plomin & Neiderhiser, 1992). "For almost every behavioral trait so far investigated, from reaction time to religiosity, an important fraction of the variation among people turns out to be associated with genetic variation. This fact need no longer be subject to debate" (Bouchard et al., 1990). These quotes reflect findings from numerous twin and adoption studies. These studies have been conducted on a wide variety of personality variables, often with large samples of research participants and with the work extending over significant periods of time. The evidence of genetic influence is sometimes startling, as when identical twins reared apart and brought together as adults are found not only to look and sound alike but to have the same attitudes and share the same hobbies and preferences for pets (Lykken, Bouchard, McGue, & Tellegen, 1993). But beyond such almost eerie observations is a pattern of results strongly suggesting an important role for heredity in almost all aspects of personality functioning (Plomin & Caspi, 1999). Recent estimates of the overall heritability of personality traits converge on roughly 40%. Table 9.2 presents heritability estimates for a wide variety of characteristics. For comparative purposes, heritability estimates for height and weight are included, as well as a few other characteristics that may be of interest.

Table 9.2 **Heritability Estimates**

The data indicate a strong genetic contribution to personality (overall estimate of 40% of the variance), a contribution not as large as that for height, weight, or IQ but larger than that for attitudes and behaviors such as TV viewing.

Trait	h² estimate
Weight	0.60
IQ	0.50
Specific cognitive ability	0.40
School achievement	0.40
BIG FIVE	
Extraversion	0.36
Neuroticism	0.31
Conscientiousness	0.28
Agreeableness	0.28
Openness to experience	0.46
EASI TEMPERAMENT	
Emotionality	0.40
Activity	0.25
Sociability	0.25
Impulsivity	0.45
ATTITUDES	
Conservatism	0.30
Religiosity	0.16
Racial integration	0.00
TV viewing	0.20

Note: EASI = Four dimensions of temperament identified by Buss and Plomin (1984).
E, Emotionality; A, Activity; S, Sociability; I, Impulsivity.
Sources: Bouchard et al., 1990; Dunn & Plomin, 1990; Loehlin, 1992; McGue et al., 1993; Pedersen et al., 1998; Pedersen et al., 1992; Plomin, 1990; Plomin et al., 1990; Plomin & Rende, 1991; Tellegen et al., 1998; Tesser, 1993; Zuckerman, 1991.

A criticism made of behavior-genetic research on personality is that most studies are based on self-report questionnaire methods. A recent study is important in this regard in that two independent peer reports as well as self-reports on the NEO Five-Factor Inventory were collected on a sample of 660 MZ twins and 304 DZ twins (200 same sex and 104 opposite sex). The investigators found good evidence of reliability of ratings in terms of peer–peer rating agreement, good evidence of the accuracy of self-report in terms of self-peer rating agreement, and general support for earlier findings concerning genetic influence on all of the Big Five personality factors (Table 9.3) (Riemann, Angleitner, & Strelau, 1997).

Some Caveats

Before concluding this section, we warn against two inappropriate conclusions that might otherwise be drawn from the behavioral genetic data. One is that heritability coefficients indicate the extent to which a characteristic is determined by heredity for a given individual. A heritability estimate of, for example, 40% for a personality trait does not mean that 40% of your own, individual personality trait is inherited. The heritability estimate is a population statistic; it describes variation *between* people in the overall population. At the level of the individual person,

Table 9.3 Peer–Peer, Self–Peer, MZ and DZ (Self-Report), and MZ and DZ (Average Peer Report) Correlations on the NEO Five-Factor Inventory

	Peer–Peer	Self–Peer	Self-Report		Averaged Peer Report	
			MZ	DZ	MZ	DZ
N	0.63	0.55	0.53	0.13	0.40	0.01
E	0.65	0.60	0.56	0.28	0.38	0.22
O	0.59	0.57	0.54	0.34	0.49	0.30
A	0.59	0.49	0.42	0.19	0.32	0.21
C	0.61	0.54	0.54	0.18	0.41	0.17
Mean	0.61	0.55	0.52	0.23	0.40	0.18

Note: MZ, monozygotic; DZ, dizygotic.
Sources: Adapted from Riemann, Angleitner, & Strelau, 1997, pp. 460, 461, 462.

psychological traits commonly involve such an interplay of biology and experience that it is not meaningful to say that "X%" of an individual's trait is due to one factor or another. (See discussions of gene–environment interaction and biological plasticity below.)

A second inappropriate conclusion would be that, because a characteristic has an inherited component, it cannot change. In reality, environmental experiences can alter even highly heritable qualities. Height is significantly determined by genes but can be influenced by environmental nutrition in childhood. Individual differences in weight are influenced by genes, yet your weight can vary greatly depending on your diet.

Molecular Genetic Paradigms

Researchers have moved beyond the traditional behavior-genetic paradigm. Instead of merely comparing different types of twins, they have turned to a direct examination of the underlying biology. This work employs molecular genetic techniques in an effort to identify specific genes that are linked with personality traits (Canli, 2008; Plomin & Caspi, 1999). By examining the genetic material of different individuals, researchers hope to show how genetic variations, or alleles, relate to individual differences in personality functioning. Ideally, one might be able to show how a genetic variation codes for alternative forms of a biological substance or system that, in turn, has psychological effects.

Initial research reported the discovery of a gene linked to the trait of novelty seeking, similar to Eysenck's P factor, and to low C on the Big Five (Benjamin et al., 1996; Ebstein et al., 1996). However, this finding has not been replicated uniformly in follow-up studies (Grigorenko, 2002). Perhaps more promising, researchers recently have identified an interaction between a specific genetic mechanism and the social environment. This research studied the effects of maltreatment in childhood on the development of antisocial behavior later in life (Caspi et al., 2003). Despite such unfortunate maltreatment, some children have good developmental outcomes; they seem to be resilient in the face of early life stress. The question, then, was whether there might be a genetic basis to this resilience.

To answer this question, the researchers identified a subset of the study's population of participants who possessed a gene that has an important property: It codes for an enzyme that lowers the activity of certain neurotransmitters in the brain that are linked to aggressive behavior. Among those who had experienced maltreatment in childhood, people with this genetic variation were found to differ from others. Specifically, people who experienced severe maltreatment but who had the gene that produced high levels of the enzyme were less likely to display antisocial behavior in adulthood. The genetic variation, in other words, seemed to lower the negative impact of maltreatment. This exciting finding requires replication. However, it suggests a promising feature for molecular genetic research on personality.

Subsequent work by this same research team has discovered molecular genetic factors that make individuals more or less vulnerable to becoming depressed (Caspi et al., 2003). The genetic factor that was studied is one that influences levels of serotonin in the brain. Specifically, the researchers studied a naturally occurring genetic variation that involves two different versions of a gene that affects serotonergic activity. The researchers' expectation was not that possessing a particular genetic background would lead inevitably to the experience of depression. Instead, they again expected an interaction: Genes should predict the onset of depression only in people who have certain types of environmental experiences. The environmental experiences they investigated were those that involve high levels of stress. Adults were surveyed to determine the degree to which they recently had experienced stressful life events involving factors such as finances, health, employment, and interpersonal relationships. The expectation of a gene X–environment interaction was confirmed. Individuals who were genetically predisposed to have lower levels of serotonergic activity and who experienced numerous stressful life events were much more likely to become depressed than were other individuals (Caspi et al., 2003). Again, then, molecular genetic research indicates that genes affect psychological outcomes in interaction with environmental experiences.

Environments and Gene–Environment Interactions

Genetic researchers realized early on that genetic and environmental influences are inextricably linked and interact in their influence on personality and behavior in adulthood. A classic study by Cooper and Zubek (1958) nicely illustrates such gene–environment interactions using the selective breeding research. In previous research, strains of maze-bright and maze-dull rats had been bred so that the strain of "bright" ones were much more likely to learn how to navigate a maze than were the "dull" ones. The researchers wanted to study how early environment experiences would influence the adult problem-solving capacity of these genetically different rats. Thus, they raised one group of each strain in an enriched, stimulating environment and another group of each strain in an impoverished environment. What happened? Compared to the normal lab environment, the enriched environment improved later learning ability in the dull rats but did not help the bright ones. Conversely, the impoverished environment markedly handicapped the bright rats but did not impair the dull group. Thus, even though these rats were not "prisoners" of their genetic predispositions, the environment interacted with their genes in a crucial way, modifying the way these predispositions were expressed.

For human personality, if the behavioral genetic data indicate that roughly 40 to 50% of the variance for single personality characteristics and personality overall are determined by genetic factors, then the rest of the population variance is made up of some combination of environmental effects and measurement error. Indeed, one interesting aspect of recent developments in behavioral genetics has been the effort to use twin and adoption data to determine environmental effects on personality variables. Thus, although Plomin (1990) suggests that "genetic influence is so ubiquitous and pervasive in behavior that a shift in emphasis is warranted: ask not what is heritable; ask instead what is not heritable" (p. 112), at the same time, he suggests that the "other message is that the same behavioral genetic data yield the strongest available evidence for the importance of environmental influence" (p. 115).

Shared and Nonshared Environment

Behavioral genetics has two messages: nature and nurture (Plomin, 1990). Research findings provide evidence of both genetic and environmental influence on personality. Behavioral geneticists estimate not only the proportion of variability in a characteristic that is due to heredity but also the proportion due to the environments.

Behavioral genetic research identifies environmental influences of two types: *shared* and *non-shared*. **Shared environments** are environmental <u>influences that make siblings more alike</u> (e.g., experiencing similar events while growing up in the same family). **Nonshared environments** are ones that <u>create differences among siblings</u> who grow up in the same family (e.g., siblings may be treated differently by parents or may develop different friendship patterns that affect their social development).

Behavioral geneticists compute numerical estimates of genetic, shared environmental, and nonshared environmental influences on individual differences. They most commonly do so by studying the similarity of identical and fraternal twins. Their studies yield a surprising finding about environments. Shared environmental effects on personality are negligible; nonshared effects are large. Put differently, the unique experiences siblings have inside and outside the family appear to be far more important for personality development than the shared experiences resulting from being in the same family. Literature reviews indicate that roughly 40% of the variability in personality trait is due to environmental factors that cause people—even people who grow up in the same household—to differ (Dunn & Plomin, 1990; Plomin & Daniels, 1987).

Loehlin, McCrae, Costa, and John (1998) examined genetic and environmental effects in three different measures of the Big Five, with results generally consistent with the above conclusions. Three findings stood out. First, all five of the Big Five dimensions showed substantial genetic influences of the same magnitude; that is, individual differences in A, C, and O were just as heritable as individual differences in E and N, which had been studied extensively in the context of Eysenck's model of these two superfactors (see Chapter 7). Second, these findings were independent of the effects of intellectual ability, which had also been measured and were controlled in the behavior-genetic analyses; that is, openness was found to be a personality dimension independent of intelligence, with its own genetic basis. Third, from a methodological perspective, having available three measures for each Big Five factor made it possible to test generalizability across instruments and to estimate error separately, rather than including it with the estimate of nonshared environment as in some previous research.

Nancy Ney / Getty Images

Same family, different experiences. Research on genetic and environmental influences on personality shows that siblings who grow up together in the same family often differ from one another psychologically. One possible reason is "nonshared" environmental effects. Despite being in the same household, siblings may have different day-to-day experiences that contribute to differences in personality.

In an analysis of the data from the self-peer ratings of MZ and DZ twins on the NEO scale (Riemann, Angleitner, & Strelau, 1997), Plomin calculated the percentage of the variance due to genetic factors, shared environments, and nonshared environments (including measurement error) for both self and peer ratings on the Big Five. The resulting percentages closely approximate those reported earlier, although the percentages for genetic factors tend to be lower for peer ratings than for self-ratings (Plomin & Caspi, 1999, p. 253).

Understanding Nonshared Environment Effects

These findings suggest that differences among families seem to matter less for the development of children than do differences within families. Recent research (Reiss, 1997; Reiss, Neiderhiser, Hetherington, & Plomin, 1999) has begun to focus on the particular processes linking genetic, family, and social influences on personality development during the important years of adolescence. This work focuses on the unique relationship between the parent and each adolescent sibling in terms of conflict and negativity, warmth and support, and so forth. In other words, the research seeks to separate out the effects of parenting common to siblings in a family from the effects of parenting unique to each sibling. The evidence to date shows substantial differences in the way siblings are treated by their parents. What is striking, however, is that much of the parenting unique to each child seems to be due to the genetic characteristics of that child. That is, differences in the way parents treat each child seem to be due to different behaviors evoked in the parent by that child, in line with earlier suggestions that children from the same family grow up to be different in part because of genetic differences that lead them to be treated differently by the parents. Most students with siblings can readily testify to such differences in parental treatment!

Does the finding that children from the same family differ due to nonshared environments mean that family experiences are unimportant? Not necessarily. Family influences may be very important but may also be unique to each child rather than shared by children in the same family. Rather than the family unit being the sole focus of study, researchers must focus on the potentially unique experiences of each child in the family.

Three Kinds of Nature–Nurture Interactions

Until now, we have considered the effects of genes and environment on personality separately. However, nature and nurture always are interacting with one another: "The critical point to remember in all of this is that in the dance of life, genes and environment are absolutely inextricable partners" (Hyman, 1999, p. 27). Along with the continuous unfolding of the effects of genes and experience, three particular forms of gene–environment interactions have been distinguished (Plomin, 1990; Plomin & Neiderhiser, 1992). First, the same environmental experiences may have different effects on individuals with different genetic constitutions. For example, the same behavior on the part of an anxious parent may have different effects on an irritable, unresponsive child than on a calm, responsive child. Rather than a straightforward effect of parental anxiety that is the same for both kinds of children, there is an interaction between parental behavior and child characteristic. In this case, the individual is a passive recipient of environmental events. Genetic factors are interacting with environmental factors but only in a passive, reactive sense.

In a second kind of nature–nurture interaction, individuals with different genetic constitutions may evoke different responses from the environment. For example, the irritable, withdrawn child may evoke a different response from the parent than will a calm, responsive child. Within the same family, siblings can evoke different parental behaviors that then set in motion two completely different patterns of parent–child interaction. Such differences were indicated in the research considered earlier on differential parental treatment of siblings associated with genetic differences in the children. Beyond this, differences in inherited characteristics lead to different responses from peers and others in the environment outside the family. Attractive children call forth different peer responses than do less attractive children. Athletic children call forth different responses than do unathletic children. In each case, a genetically determined characteristic evokes a differential response from the environment.

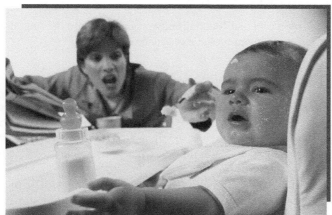

Genes and Environments Interact. A child's inherited tendency to be irritable will create stress in parents. As a result, the child will experience a different environment - one featuring higher levels of parental stress – than a child who inherits a lesser tendency to be irritable.

In the third form of gene–environment interaction, individuals with different constitutions select and create different environments. Once the individual is able to take an active form of interaction with the environment, which occurs at a fairly early age, genetic factors influence the selection and creation of environments. The extravert seeks out different environments than does the introvert, the athletic individual different environments than the unathletic individual, and the musically gifted individual different environments than the individual gifted in visual imagery. These effects increase over the course of time as individuals become increasingly able to select their own environments. By a certain point in time, it is impossible to determine the extent to which the individual has been the "recipient" as opposed to the "creator" of the environmental effect.

In sum, individuals can be relatively passive recipients of environments, they can play a role in environmental events through the responses they evoke, and they can play an active role in selecting and creating environments. In each case, there is a nature–nurture, gene–environment interaction. In considering the nature and nurture of personality, we must keep in mind that the development of personality is always a function of the interaction of genes with environments, that there is no nature without nurture and no nurture without nature (Manuck & McCasffrey 2014). We can separate the two for purposes of discussion and analysis, but the two never operate independently of one another. Indeed, genetic factors and environmental experiences are so intertwined that the usual formulation "nature versus nurture" may not even make sense any more. Instead, it may be better to think of "via nurture" (Ridley, 2003). The basic nature of genetic material, in other words, is that it "creates now possibilities for the organism" (Ridley, 2003, p. 250) that are realized only if the organism encounters particular environments—that is, only if it is nurtured in a particular way. Instead of asking how heritable a trait is, we might better ask about the circumstances under which the genetic contributions to the trait are enhanced or suppressed (Krueger & Johnson, 2008).

Mood, Emotion, and the Brain

All personality theorists are interested in mood and emotion. Freudians view emotional life as an expression of basic bodily instincts. Trait theorists see individual differences in mood as being at the heart of many personality traits. In the chapters ahead, you will see that behaviorists alter emotional responses through learning experiences and that cognitive and social-cognitive theorists, like humanistic theorists, posit that people's beliefs about themselves and the world shape their emotional life.

Here, in our chapter on biological foundation, we ask: What are the neural and biochemical bases of individual differences in emotional experience?

Left and Right Hemispheric Dominance

If you look at a brain, its most obvious anatomical feature is that it is comprised of two halves, or hemispheres. Research pioneered by the psychologist Richard Davidson (1994, 1995, 1998) reveals *hemispheric dominance* in emotion. The left and right hemispheres are active to different degrees in different emotional states, with the left (right) hemisphere dominating in activation during positive (negative) emotional states.

Evidence of this finding comes from EEG methods (see Chapter 2). In one study, EEG recordings of hemispheric activity were taken before and during the showing of film clips designed to elicit positive or negative emotion. Participants also rated their moods during the films. EEG measures of hemispheric dominance related closely to the psychological experience of mood. "Those individuals with more left-sided prefrontal activation at baseline reported more positive affect to the positive film clips and those with more right-sided prefrontal activation reported more negative affect to the negative film clips. These findings support the idea that individual differences in electrophysiological measures of prefrontal activation asymmetry mark some aspect of vulnerability to positive and negative emotion elicitors" (Davidson, 1998, p. 316).

What about stable individual differences in the experience of positive and negative mood? Currently depressed and previously depressed individuals are found to have decreased left anterior cortical activity relative to nondepressed individuals (Allen, Iacono, Depue, & Arbisi, 1993). Individuals with damage to the left anterior brain region are likely to become depressed, whereas those with damage to the right anterior brain region are likely to become manic (Robinson & Downhill, 1995). Research on infants suggests a relation between individual differences in measures of prefrontal activation and affective reactivity, with infants experiencing greater distress upon separation from their mothers showing greater right-sided prefrontal activation and less left-sided prefrontal activation than infants who showed little distress in this situation (Davidson & Fox, 1989).

Finally, research by Sharot (2011) and her colleagues suggests that desirable and undesirable information are encoded in different parts of the brain and that extreme optimists differ from pessimists in that their brains process undesirable information to a lesser extent.

EEG measures can differentiate between two different aspects of emotional experience that are both negative: anxious arousal during a task and worrying prior to a task (Heller, Schmidtke, Nitschke, Koven, & Miller, 2002). Worrying is associated with stronger left frontal brain activation than is anxious arousal (Hofmann et al., 2005). Worrying, then, is "a unique emotional state" (Hofmann et al., 2005, p. 472) and not just a variation on the state of anxious arousal during a task. This finding from neuroscience has interesting implications for the personality trait theories. The five-factor trait of neuroticism combines different aspects of anxiety into one factor, whereas this neuroscientific evidence indicates the existence of different types of negative emotion that truly are distinct.

CURRENT APPLICATIONS

Causes of Individual Differences: Genes, Social Experience—or Something Else?

Psychology's most famous question—"Nature or nurture?"—suggests that there are two causes of behavior: (1) information encoded into the genes from the moment of conception and (2) information acquired via social experience after one is born. Much of psychology's inquiry into the determinants of individual differences rests on this dichotomy between biological/genetic/nature factors and social/learned/nurture factors.

However, there is something else to consider: the prenatal environment, that is, the environment experienced after conception but before birth. Startling findings document a role for prenatal factors in determining a psychological quality of great interest, namely, sexual orientation.

One correlate of sexual orientation among males is the number of older brothers one has. People who have more older brothers are, on average, somewhat more likely to have a homosexual rather than a heterosexual orientation. (Note that this statement only holds on average; that is, it is a probabilistic statement that describes a pattern of results found only when one studies large numbers of people.) A question, then, is why this might be the case. What might link sexual orientation to the number of older brothers one has? One possibility is social experience. Maybe social interactions with large numbers of older males somehow influences sexual orientation. This, however, is *not* what recent findings suggest.

In a critical piece of research, the sexual orientation of males who were raised with varying numbers of older brothers living in their home was compared to the sexual orientation of a key comparison group: males who had the same number of older brothers, but whose brothers did *not* live in their household (e.g., people who were adopted or some of whose siblings were adopted). The findings revealed that sexual orientation was predicted by the number of older siblings one has *whether or not* those siblings grew up in one's own household! People with more older brothers were, probabilistically, more likely to have a homosexual orientation even in cases in which they were not raised with those older brothers.

How can this be? The investigator suggests that the key influence is in the prenatal environment. As women have more male children, they may develop an immune system response to male fetuses. This immune reaction could affect the biochemical environment of the subsequent male fetus, specifically influencing its brain development in such a way that the later child is less likely to develop a heterosexual orientation. Although these details are somewhat speculative and require further research, the existing findings do indicate a significant influence of prenatal factors on sexual orientation. In so doing, they expand the scope of factors that must be considered in analyses of personality development.

Source: Bogaert (2006).

Research on the emotion of anger has caused psychologists to modify the original idea that left/right hemispheric dominance is associated with variations in the valence of mood, that is, its positivity/negativity. Anger is a negative emotion. It arises in response to negative events, and people feel that it is an aversive state (compared to, e.g., calmness or happiness). But higher levels of anger are associated with *left* hemisphere activation (Harmon-Jones, 2003), the hemisphere previously associated with positive moods. This finding suggests that hemispheric dominance relates most closely to approach and avoidance motivation, that is, the motivation to move toward (approach) or away from (avoid) a stimulus. Both positive states such as happiness and the negative state of anger entail a behavioral approach: When happy, you approach an object to enjoy an interaction with it; when angry, you approach it to confront it.

Neurotransmitters and Temperament: Dopamine and Serotonin

The brain's neurons communicate using **neurotransmitters**, chemical substances that transmit information from one neuron to another. Much research links variations in neurotransmitter activity to individual differences in mood. Of the brain's various neurotransmitters, the two that have received most attention in the study of mood and personality are dopamine and serotonin.

An excess in the neurotransmitter dopamine is implicated in schizophrenia, while an underproduction of dopamine is implicated in Parkinson's disease. Dopamine also is associated with pleasure, being described as a "feel good" chemical (Hamer, 1997). Animals will perform responses that lead to administration of dopamine (Wise, 1996). Thus, dopamine appears to be central to the functioning of the reward system: "One way of characterizing the job of this dopamine circuit is that it's a reward system. It says, in effect, "That was good, let's do it again, and let's remember exactly how we did it" (Hyman, 1999, p. 25). Addictive drugs such as cocaine are viewed as "masquerading" as the neurotransmitter dopamine, leading to the experience of pleasure upon taking the drug but also to the experience of a low as the cocaine stops coming and the dopamine level drops.

The neurotransmitter serotonin also is involved in regulation of mood. Modern drugs, known as SSRIs (selective serotonin reuptake inhibitors), are thought to alleviate depression by prolonging the action of serotonin at the synapses of neurons. SSRIs administered to normal individuals have been found both to reduce negative affective experience and to increase social, affiliative behavior (Knutson et al., 1998). Finally, we know that the hormone cortisol is associated with the stress response. Again, returning to Kagan's (1994) research, inhibited children at the age of five were found to be high in reactivity to threat, as measured by cortisol response, although this was not as true at age seven.

The fact that neurotransmitters contribute to mood suggests that an analysis of brain chemistry can illuminate the topic with which we began this chapter: individual differences in temperament. Numerous investigators have explored the potential biochemical bases of temperament (Cloninger Svrakic, & Przybeck, 1993; Depue, 1995, 1996; Depue & Collins, 1999; Eysenck, 1990; Gray, 1987; Pickering & Gray, 1999; Tellegen, 1985; Zuckerman, 1991, 1996). Although similarities appear among almost all of these models, and many are similar to the five-factor model described in Chapter 8, they do not always overlap in clear ways with one another. Thus, rather than exploring a number of such models, we will follow the lead of Lee Anna Clark and David Watson (2008; Watson, 2000) in their analysis of personality temperament.

Three Dimensions of Temperament: PE, NE, and DvC

According to Clark and Watson's (2008) model, individual differences in temperament can be summarized in terms of three big superfactors similar to those suggested by Eysenck and also corresponding, roughly, to three of the Big Five dimensions: NE (Negative Emotionality), PE (Positive Emotionality), and DvC (disinhibition versus constraint). Individuals high on the NE factor experience elevated levels of negative emotions and see the world as threatening, problematic, and distressing, whereas those low on the trait are calm, emotionally stable, and self-satisfied. The PE factor relates to the individual's willingness to engage the environment, with high scorers (like extraverts) enjoying the company of others and approaching life actively, with energy, cheerfulness, and enthusiasm, whereas low scorers (like introverts) are reserved, socially aloof, and low in energy and confidence. It is important to note that although NE and PE have opposite-sounding qualities, they are independent of one another; that is, an individual can be high or low on each (Watson & Tellegen, 1999; Watson, Wiese, Vaidya, & Tellegen, 1999). This is because they are under the control of different internal biological systems. The third factor, DvC, does not involve affective tone, as was true for the first two factors, but rather relates to style of affective regulation, with high DvC scorers being impulsive, reckless, and oriented toward feelings and sensations of the moment, whereas low scorers are careful, controlled by long-term implications of their behavior, and avoiding risk or danger.

The question, then, is whether one can identify biological correlates of the three factors. Building on work by Depue (1996; Depue & Collins, 1999), Clark and Watson suggest that PE is associated with the action of dopamine, the "feel good" chemical. In animal research, high dopamine levels are associated with approach behaviors, whereas deficits in this neurotransmitter are associated with deficits in incentive motivation. In all, Clark and Watson suggest that "individual differences in the sensitivity of this biological system to the signals of reward that activate incentive motivation and positive affect, and supportive cognitive processes, form the basis of the PE dimension of tempera-ment" (1999, p. 414). Differences in hemispheric lateralization, with high PE scores being associ-ated with left hemispheric dominance, may also be involved (Davidson, 1994, 1998).

Turning to DvC, Clark and Watson suggest that the biological basis of this factor is serotonin. According to them, humans low in this neurotransmitter tend to be aggressive and to show increased use of dopamine-activating drugs such as alcohol. Alcoholism also is associated with reduced sero-tonin functioning. Hamer (1997) also associates the neurotransmitter dopamine with thrill seeking, impulsivity, and disinhibition. There also is evidence that high levels of the hormone testosterone are associated with competitiveness and aggressiveness, both linked with high scores on DvC.

Clark and Watson suggest that less is known about the neurobiology underlying NE. However, there is a relation between low serotonin levels at the neuron synapses and depression, anxiety, and obsessive–compulsive symptoms. Hamer and Copeland (1998) relate low serotonin levels to a dark view of the world, analogous to Galen's melancholic temperament. Depue (1995) reports that animals low in serotonin are excessively irritable, and Hamer (1997) describes serotonin as the "feel bad" chemical. In addition, there is the evidence noted of a relation between right hemi-spheric lateralization and the tendency to experience negative emotions. Finally, there is evidence that excessive sensitivity of the amygdala likely plays a role in the tendency to experience high levels of anxiety and distress (LeDoux, 1995, 1999).

In assessing this work, one must recall that there is no one-to-one correspondence between biological processes and personality traits. Rather, each biological component appears to be asso-ciated with the expression of more than one trait, and the expression of each trait is influenced by more than one biological factor: "Models of personality based on only one neurotransmitter are clearly too simplistic and will require the addition of other modifying factors" (Depue & Collins, 1999, p. 513). Thus, it is difficult to integrate all these neurobiological findings into the **three-dimensional temperament model** because we risk oversimplifying the neurobiology we know so far. The links between biology and temperament suggested in Table 9.4 are best described as initial hypotheses, as our best guesses of how things might hang together, to be tested further and revised as more data become available.

[handwritten margin notes: System of Brain Function = personality traits are linked with the functioning of patterning of elements in the biological system rather than by single elements]

Table 9.4   Suggested Links Between Biology and Personality

Amygdala Part of the primitive limbic system, the brain's emotional response center. Particularly important for aversive emotional learning.

Hemispheric Lateralization Dominance of the right frontal hemisphere associated with activation of negative emotions and personality traits of shyness and inhibition; dominance of the left frontal hemisphere associated with activation of positive emotions and personality traits of boldness and disinhibition.

Dopamine A neurotransmitter associated with reward, reinforcement, and pleasure. High dopamine levels are associated with positive emotions, high energy, disinhibition, and impulsivity. Low dopamine levels are associated with lethargy, anxiety, and constriction. Animals and people will self-administer drugs that trigger the release of dopamine.

Serotonin A neurotransmitter involved in mood, irritability, and impulsivity. Low serotonin levels are associated with depression but also with violence and impulsivity. Drugs known as SSRIs (selective serotonin reuptake inhibitors) (e.g., Prozac, Zoloft, Paxil) are used to treat depression as well as phobias and obsessive–compulsive disorders. Exactly how they operate is not totally clear.

Cortisol A stress-related hormone secreted by the adrenal cortex that facilitates reactions to threat. Although adaptive in relation to short-term stress, responses to long-term, chronic stress can be associated with depression and memory loss.

Testosterone A hormone important in the development of secondary sex characteristics and also associated with dominance, competitiveness, and aggression.

Sources: Hamer & Copeland, 1998; Sapolsky, 1994; Zuckerman, 1995.

In addition, although brain localization of functions has advanced significantly, it is important to consider the brain as a total system. According to Damasio (1994), Gall was correct in suggesting that the brain consists of subsystem parts that are specialized in the functions they serve, as opposed to being one large, undifferentiated mass. However, not only was Gall not able to identify correctly the parts and functions, he was unaware of how the brain functions as a system. As Damasio puts it: "I am not falling into the phrenological trap. To put it simply: The mind results from the operation of each of the separate components, and from the concerted operation of the multiple systems constituted by those separate systems" (1994, p. 15). There is both differentiation–localization and organization–system. In sum, personality traits are linked with the functioning of the patterning of elements in the biological system rather than by single elements: "Psychobiology is not for seekers of simplicity" (Zuckerman, 1996, p. 128).

Capacity of biological systems to change as a result of experience

Plasticity: Biology as Both Cause and Effect

When thinking about biology and personality, two thoughts are common: (1) biology is fixed, determined by genes and unchanging over time, and (2) in cause–effect relationships involving biology and experience, biology is a cause and psychological experience is its effect.

These two thoughts are only partly correct. Biology can change, and it changes, in part, as a result of behavioral experience. The capacity of biological systems to change as a result of experience is called plasticity. Like plastic, biology can be shaped and molded.

From Experience to Biology

Both neural systems and neurotransmitter systems display **plasticity** (Gould, Reeves, Graziano, & Gross, 1999; Raleigh & McGuire, 1991). For example, although leadership in a monkey hierarchy is associated with high levels of serotonin, if the troop is reorganized so that leadership ranks are reversed, the new leaders develop higher levels of serotonin than when they were on the bottom (Raleigh & McGuire, 1991). Similarly, the relation between testosterone and aggression or competitiveness is bidirectional, with high testosterone facilitating greater aggression and competitiveness but competition and aggression also increasing testosterone levels (Dabbs, 2000). Not only does losing a competitive sports event lower testosterone levels, but rooting for a loser does too (McCaul, Gladue, & Joppe, 1992). Merely winning in a coin toss can increase testosterone levels (Gladue, Boechler, & McCaul, 1989). Hamer and Copeland (1998) are led to conclude that "from song birds to squirrels, and mice to monkeys . . . winners get a blast of testosterone; losers get a drain. Humans are the same" (p. 112).

Experimental evidence showing the influence of experience on the brain comes from research employing a simple task: juggling (Draganski et al., 2004). After obtaining anatomical depictions of the brains of a group of research participants, Draganski and colleagues asked half, selected randomly, to learn how to juggle. These participants learned a simple three-ball juggling routine over a period of 3 months. At the end of this time period, both groups, jugglers and nonjugglers, returned to the lab for a second brain scan. Brain imaging revealed that the experience of juggling changed the anatomy of the brain. Jugglers experienced a significant expansion of gray matter in the brain, in particular in a brain region involved in the perception of motion. The results, the authors note, "contradict the traditionally held view that the anatomical structure of the adult human brain does not alter, except for changes in morphology caused by ageing or pathological conditions" (Draganski et al., 2004, p. 311).

In sum, advances in neuroscience are providing exciting evidence of the two-way street that runs between biology and experience. Future years surely will expand our understanding of the biological bases of personality functioning and of social and experiential contributions to the biology of the individual.

Neuroscientific Investigations of "Higher-Level" Psychological Functions

Much of the work we have just reviewed primarily addressed emotional and motivational processes. Investigators have related biological systems to psychological phenomena involving moods, basic impulses, and emotions such as fear. But what about the rest of personality functioning, including "higher-level" psychological functions (e.g., self-concept)? Those psychological functions also require a biological brain. In principle, then, neuroscience can shed light on these complex psychological functions. We now turn to some recent research that attempts to do just that.

Brain and Self

A uniquely human capacity is the ability to reflect on the self: one's features, potentials, appearance to others, and so forth. A question of basic research interest concerns the nature of this capacity. Does it reflect people's overall cognitive capabilities; in other words, is the self just "one of those things we happen to think about?" Or is it unique? Might there be functionally distinct systems in the brain that come into play when we are thinking about ourselves as opposed to thinking about other people or things?

Recent work (Kelley et al., 2002) has investigated this question by using a brain imaging technique, fMRI. An **fMRI** (or functional magnetic resonance imaging) enables researchers to identify specific regions of the brain that are active when people perform a given task. This technique involves analyzing changes in blood flow during task performance. If there is a particularly large change in blood flow in a given brain region during task performance, this provides evidence that the brain region is somehow involved in the performance of that task.

The task that participants performed in the Kelley et al. study (2002) involved the rating of trait adjectives (dependable, polite, etc.). Participants were asked to make three types of ratings about the words. They judged (1) whether the adjective (when presented to them) was in uppercase letters, (2) whether the adjective described George W. Bush, and (3) whether the adjective described themselves. The idea, then, is that some brain regions might be uniquely active when people think about themselves ("am I dependable?") as opposed to another person ("is Bush dependable?") or cues unrelated to a person ("is the word 'dependable' in uppercase type?"). An alternative possibility is that thinking about the self is no different than thinking about other people.

Kelley and colleagues (2002) found that, yes, there are regions of the brain that appear to be uniquely involved in judgments about the self. An area near the front of the brain, specifically the medial prefrontal cortex, or PFC was "selectively engaged during self-referential judgments" (p. 790). Compared to baseline recordings, fMRI recordings during task performance indicated that when participants were not performing the trait-rating task, the PFC was more involved in judgments about the self than about Bush or the typeface of the letters.

Such findings, of course, do not demonstrate that this particular region of the frontal cortex is the biological "home of the self". Judging oneself with respect to trait adjectives is only one aspect of self-concept, and multiple brain regions surely come into play when people engage in any complex mental activity involving self-reflection. Yet, the findings provide intriguing initial evidence that neuroscientific research can inform complex questions about personality functioning. Future years are sure to see growing interest, and scientific evidence, on the question of the neural foundations of self-concept (Churchland, 2002).

SUMMARY

In sum, in this chapter, we have reviewed an array of findings that are potentially "dizzying." They involve deep questions about personality and, simultaneously, complex techniques from the biological sciences. Yet, some simple themes emerge from this complexity. On the one hand, contemporary research in personality psychology has succeeded in identifying specific neural and biochemical systems that contribute to personality functioning and to significant differences among persons. On the other hand, research on biology and personality has, to a surprising degree, highlighted the influence of the environment. Identical twins are not identical in their personalities. Similar people who encounter different social settings and experiences differ biologically. In the broad context of the theories of personality, the research results we have reviewed do confirm the intuitions of trait theorists that biology is fundamental to personality and individual differences. Yet, they also support the intuitions of the theorists you will learn about in the chapters ahead, who commonly explore not only biology, but the environment, society, and culture, in their efforts to understand persons.

MAJOR CONCEPTS

adoption studies
behavioral genetics
Effortful control
fMRI (functional
    Magnetic Resonance
    Imaging).

evolved psychological mecha-
    nisms
heritability
inhibited-uninhibited tempera-
    ments
neurotransmitters

parental investment theory
phrenology
plasticity
proximate causes
selective breeding
Shared environments

temperament
three-dimensional tempera-
    ment model
twin studies
ultimate causes

REVIEW

1. Psychologists have long been interested in individual differences in temperament, relating such differences to constitutional factors. Advances in temperament research have come in the form of longitudinal studies and objective measures of behavior and constitutional-biological variables. Kagan's research on inhibited and uninhibited children is illustrative of such developments.

2. Evolutionary theory concerns ultimate causes of behavior—that is, why the behavior of interest evolved and the adaptive function it served. Work in the area of male–female mate preferences, emphasizing sex differences in parental investment and parenthood probability, and in male–female differences in causes of jealousy illustrate research associated with evolutionary interpretations of human behavioral characteristics.

3. Three methods used to establish genetic-behavior relationships are selective breeding, twin studies, and adoption studies. Twin and adoption studies lead to significant heritability estimates for intelligence and most personality characteristics. The overall heritability for personality has been estimated to be .4 to .5; that is, 40% to 50% of the variance in personality characteristics is due to genetic factors. However, there is evidence that heritability estimates are influenced by the population studied, personality characteristics studied, and measures used.

4. Associations between findings in neuroscience and personality have focused on the functioning of neurotransmitters such as dopamine and serotonin, on individual differences in hemispheric lateralization and emotional style, demonstrated in the work of Davidson, and on the functioning of parts of the brain such as the amygdala in relation to the processing of emotional stimuli and emotional memories. The three-dimensional temperament model proposed by Clark and Watson represents one attempt to systematize relations between the findings in neuroscience and personality. Many such links are suggested, although at this time a comprehensive model of biological processes and personality traits remains to be formulated.

5. In recent years, researchers in neuroscience have begun to identify specific brain regions that are involved in complex aspects of personality functioning, such as judgments about the self. This work generally relies on brain imaging techniques, particularly fMRI.

6. Although there is a tendency to think of biological processes as fixed, there is considerable evidence of plasticity or potential for change in neurobiological systems as a result of experience. Research on the biological foundations of personality, then, provides information not only about the role of genetics in personality but also about the role of the environment.

Behaviorism and The Learning Approaches To Personality

10

Questions to be Addressed in this Chapter

Behaviorism's View of the Person

Behaviorism's View of the Science of Personality

Watson, Pavlov, and Classical Conditioning

Skinner's Theory of Operant Conditioning

Critical Evaluation

Major Concepts

Review

Chapter Focus

Have you ever dated someone who did something that really annoyed you? A woman was particularly bothered by her boyfriend's constant moaning about how much schoolwork he had to do. She grew tired of constantly providing him with attention and sympathy—after all, she had just as much work! One day, she was struck with a new idea: What if she simply ignored her boyfriend every time he complained? It worked! When she stopped pampering him, his complaining gradually disappeared. In the language of behaviorism, her attention to his problems had been serving as a positive reinforcement that had taught him to complain in the first place.

Without realizing it, this woman was using some of the basic principles of learning theory to change her boyfriend's behavior. This chapter considers approaches to personality that are based on theories of learning and the overall approach to psychological science known as behaviorism. According to behaviorism, people gradually acquire their personality styles as a result of their experiences with the environment. Associated theories of learning specify the exact processes through which people are shaped by environmental experiences.

In this chapter, you will learn about theories that are of exceptional importance in the history of psychology: Pavlov's classical conditioning and Skinner's operant conditioning. These theories both share a commitment to the experimental testing of clearly defined hypotheses. Approaches to assessment and change are then considered, along with an overall critical evaluation of these approaches to personality.

Questions to be Addressed in this Chapter

1. Can principles of learning discovered in research on animals provide the basis for a theory of personality?

2. Is our behavior controlled by events (stimuli) in the environment?

3. If abnormal behavior is learned like all other behavior, can one base therapies on learning principles?

4. If our behavior is ultimately determined by the environment, as the behaviorists claim, do people have "free will"?

This chapter presents two theories of learning. They are not opposing views. Rather, they are complementary; they highlight different aspects of how people learn from environmental experiences. In combination, these two ideas—Pavlov's classical conditioning and Skinner's operant conditioning theories—provided the foundation for a view of psychology known as behaviorism.

During the middle of the 20th century, behaviorism was the predominant school of thought in scientific psychology. Later in the century, it experienced a precipitous decline in influence, although the study of operant and classical conditioning remains a part of the contemporary field (Domjan, 2005; Staddon & Cerutti, 2003). Why—you may already be asking—should I learn about a school of thought that already has declined in influence?

Three considerations motivate the study of behaviorism in contemporary personality theory and research. The first concerns the task of theory construction. Developing a comprehensive scientific theory of personality is no easy feat. It is instructive to see both the achievements and the limitations of past efforts. A second consideration involves applications. Despite whatever limits it may possess, behaviorism gave rise to therapeutic methods of unquestioned practical value, as you'll see in this chapter. Finally, behaviorism anticipated some of psychology's contemporary trends, with current researchers who may not label themselves "behaviorists" nonetheless exploring behavioristic themes. For example, social psychologists study how environmental stimuli control our actions (Bargh & Ferguson, 2000; Bargh & Gollwitzer, 1994) and how people's intuitions about the conscious self-control of behavior may be illusory (Wegner, 2003)—two main behavioristic themes. Writers also suggest that behavioristic theoretical writing (Skinner, 1948), despite being grounded in laboratory research with animals, anticipated psychology's 21st-century emphasis on the study of human virtues, potentials, and "positive" psychological characteristics (Adams, 2012).

Behaviorism's View of the Person

We begin by considering behaviorism's view of the person. (Views of the main theorists, especially B. F. Skinner, appear later in the chapter.) Its viewpoint on psychology is best understood by way of analogy. Consider how we think about people's anatomy and physiology. It is reasonable to conceive of the body as a kind of "machine". Like any complex machine, the body is a collection of mechanisms (heart, lungs, sweat glands, and so forth) that perform various functions (respiration, regulation of temperature, etc.). Now, return to our main topic: personality. Here, the idea of a machine seems odd. Bodies seem machinelike, but personalities do not. People are spontaneous and fun loving. They are conflicted and anxious, brave and imaginative. Machines are not spontaneous, fun loving, conflicted, anxious, brave, or imaginative. Intuitively, then, persons seem quite unlike machines.

Despite these intuitions, in the behaviorist view, persons are machinelike. To B. F. Skinner, behaviorism's greatest spokesperson and most influential theorist, the interesting thing about machines is that people have "created the machine in [their] *own image*" (Skinner, 1953, p. 46, emphasis added). With advances in science during the past two centuries, Skinner writes, "we have discovered more about how the living organism works and are better able to see its machine-like properties" (1953, p. 47). When seeking to build a science of persons, the behaviorist assumes that persons can be viewed as collections of machinelike mechanisms. The behaviorist explores how these mechanisms learn, that is, how they change in reaction to environmental input.

Viewing persons as machinelike has a major implication. This implication is a second important feature of behaviorism's view of the person. The implication is a philosophical position known as **determinism.** Determinism is the belief that an event is caused by, or determined by, some prior event, with the cause being something that can be understood according to basic laws of science. When applied to questions of human behavior, determinism is the belief that people's behavior is caused in a lawful scientific manner. Determinism stands in opposition to a different belief, namely, the belief in "free will". As we will explain in more detail, behaviorists do not believe that people have free will; that is, they do not think it is correct to say that a person freely chose to act in one way or another. Instead, they believe that people are part of a natural world and that in the natural world events—including the behavior of persons—are causally determined.

Behaviorism's View of the Science of Personality

As an approach to the science of personality, behaviorism differs enormously from the theories we discuss elsewhere in this book. The differences are revealed in the basic assumptions of the behavioral approach. There are two. The first is that behavior must be explained in terms of the causal influence of the environment on the person. Compare this to other theories. The other theories in this book primarily are theories about what's "in the head of" the person (psychodynamic structures, traits, etc.). They ask about how internal personality factors influence people's experiences and actions. Behaviorism, in contrast, is about what's in the environment. Behaviorists ask about how environmental factors causally determine people's behavior.

Behavior can be influenced by the environment

The second assumption is that an understanding of people should be built entirely on controlled laboratory research, where that research could involve either people or animals. Again, compare this to the other theories. One thing shared by the other personality theorists is that, in building theories of personality, the beings that were studied were persons. Behaviorists, in contrast, build a theory of persons in large part on a database involving animals. This may strike you as odd. Yet, as we will review, it exemplifies a strategy common in the sciences, a strategy of studying "simple systems".

personality is formed by experiences and environments.

Environmental Determinism and its Implications for the Concept of Personality

a conditioned response must be accompanied by a reinforcer

The most basic feature of behaviorism's view of the science of personality is that this science must study how environmental factors determine human behavior. They reason as follows. We human beings are physical objects in a physical universe. As such, we are subject to physical laws that can be understood through scientific analysis. Ever since the beginnings of modern physics hundreds of years ago, the behaviorists reason, scientists have recognized that the way to explain the behavior of any physical object is to identify the forces in the environment that act upon it, causing its behavior. Suppose we throw a rock into the air and observe its behavior: It travels in a curving, parabolic path back to the ground. How do we explain this? We don't say that the rock "enjoys traveling in parabolic paths" or that it has "the trait of fallingness". Instead, we recognize that the behavior of a rock is fully determined by lawful environmental forces (the force and direction of our throw, plus gravity and perhaps air pressure). To the behaviorist, the behavior of people should be explained in exactly this same way. Just as environmental forces determine the trajectory of the rock, environmental forces determine the trajectories of our lives as we come into contact with, and are influenced by, one environmental factor after another. To the behaviorist, then, there is no more need to explain a person's behavior in terms of his or her attitudes, feelings, or personality traits than there is to explain the rock's behavior in terms of its attitudes, feelings, or rock traits. The rock doesn't fall because it decided to fall but because gravity caused it to fall. Similarly, people do not act as they do because they decided to act that way but because environmental forces cause them to do so.

Behaviorists recognize that people have thoughts and feelings. But they view thoughts and feelings as behaviors that also are caused by the environment. If you say, "I took this personality psychology class because I thought it would be interesting" or "I broke up with my boyfriend because I felt our relationship wouldn't work out," a behaviorist would say that you were wrong. You didn't identify the right factor in your "because". To the behaviorist, the environment caused your behavior of taking the class. Furthermore, the environment caused your behavior of saying that you thought the class would be interesting! Similarly, features of the environment caused your feelings in the relationship and caused your decision to end it.

The most radical feature of the behaviorist worldview, then, is that it does not explain a person's actions in terms of thoughts and feelings. Instead, it explains people's actions, thoughts, and feelings in terms of environmental forces that shape the individual. This, to the behaviorist, is the only way to build a scientifically credible study of behavior. Suppose, by analogy, that we were studying evolution and wanted to explain why primates who once walked on four legs later evolved into upright primates who walked on two legs. We would never explain this by saying that the four-legged walkers "got tired of walking on all fours" or "decided to stand straight up". Such explanations would be absurd. They would have no scientific utility. The evolutionary change from four- to two-legged walking was, we recognize, caused entirely by adaptive pressures in the evolutionary environment. To the behaviorist, saying that people act a certain way "because they decided to" has no more scientific value than saying that the primates evolved because they decided to do so. Instead of such nonscientific explanations, behaviorists urge us to identify the environmental factors that are the true cause of people's feelings, thoughts, and actions. The behaviorist B. F. Skinner states this thesis with the greatest clarity:

> We can follow the path taken by physics and biology by turning directly to the relation between behavior and the environment and neglecting supposed mediating states of mind. Physics did not advance by looking more closely at the jubilance of a falling body, or biology by looking at the nature of vital spirits, and we do not need to try to discover what personalities, states of mind, feelings, traits of character, plans, purposes, [or] intentions really are in order to get on with a scientific analysis of behavior.
>
> Source: (Skinner, 1971), Beyond Freedom and Dignity, p. 15.

What does all this have to do with the study of personality? Suppose, hypothetically, that the behaviorist could in fact explain all behavior in terms of general laws of learning. This, the behaviorist would claim, would completely *eliminate the need* for a distinct field of study called "personality theory" or "personality psychology". The variables in all the other theories of personality—psychoanalytic conflicts, personality traits, and so forth—would not, according to the behaviorist, be referring to real psychological entities in persons' heads. Instead, the variables of other theories would be seen merely as descriptive labels—descriptions of patterns of psychological experience that are, in reality, caused by the environment. If the environment causes a person to feel hostility toward a same-sex parent and attraction toward an opposite-sex parent, the psychoanalyst labels this an "Oedipal complex". If the environment causes a person to engage in energetic, outgoing, sociable behaviors, the trait theorist labels the person an "extravert." In these and infinite other cases, the personality term does not identify the cause of the person's behavior. The behaviorist views the term as merely a label for a pattern of action that is caused by the environment.

To the behaviorists, then, an understanding of the laws of learning promises to replace any and all personality theories. If behavior can be explained by the laws of learning, and if "personality" is just a label that describes the type of behavior a person has learned to do, then there is no need for a scientific theory of personality that is distinct from learning theory. Behaviorists were quite explicit about this. They looked forward to a day when theories of personality would be "regarded as historical curiosities" (Farber, 1964, p. 37).

The belief in environmental determinism has additional implications. One is that it highlights the potential **situational specificity** of behavior. Since environmental factors are the causes of behavior, people's behavioral style is expected to vary significantly from one environment to another. Note how this expectation differs from the approach of the trait theories (Chapters 7 and 8). Trait variables corresponded to consistent styles of behavior; these variables were meant to explain why a person acts in a consistent manner across diverse situations. In contrast, behaviorists expect that there will be substantial variability in action as people adapt to situations that present different rewards and punishments for different types of behavior.

Another implication involves the causes and treatment of psychopathology. Psychopathology is not understood as an internal problem—an illness in the person's mind. Instead, the behaviorist assumes that maladaptive, "abnormal" behavior is caused by maladaptive environments to which the person has been exposed. The implication of this assumption is profound. It is that the task of therapy is not to analyze underlying conflicts or to reorganize the individual's personality. Instead, the goal is to provide a new environment, that is, new learning experiences for the client. The new environment should cause the client to learn new and more adaptive patterns of behavior, as we discuss later in this chapter.

Although rarely influential in its original form, learning approaches to personality are presented here because of their historical importance, because they set the stage for other developments, and because they present an interesting contrast to the cognitive approaches that follow in subsequent chapters.

Experimentation, Observable Variables, and Simple Systems

Another defining feature of the behavioral view of personality science is its research strategy. This strategy follows in a natural way from the belief in environmental determinism. If behavior is determined by the environment, then the way to do research is to manipulate environmental variables to learn how they influence behavior. Behaviorists base the study of human nature entirely on carefully controlled laboratory experiments of this sort.

In designing research, behaviorists emphasize that one must study things that are observable. The researcher must be able to see the environmental and behavioral variables, so he or she can measure them with accuracy and systematically relate them to one another. This point may seem obvious. Yet this feature—being able to observe the psychological variables about which one is theorizing—is *not* a part of the other theories we have discussed. One cannot directly observe the id, an Oedipal conflict, an extraverted tendency, a motive to self-actualize, and so forth. The behaviorist argues that these other theories are too speculative and thus not sufficiently scientific, because they contain variables that one cannot even observe. For this reason, behaviorists were harshly critical of virtually all other theories in psychology.

The attempt to study personality through experimental methods poses a severe challenge. It often may be impractical, as well as unethical, to manipulate environmental variables that may substantially affect people's everyday behaviors. Also, day-to-day human actions may be determined by such a large number of variables, and these variables may be so complexly related to one another that it is difficult to sort out the potentially lawful relations between any one environmental factor and behavior. These difficulties lead the behaviorist to adopt the following research strategy. Rather than researching complex social actions, the behaviorist commonly studies simple responses. And rather than study complex human beings, the behaviorist studies simpler organisms, such as rats and pigeons. The original body of data on which behavioral principles are based consists almost entirely of laboratory research on laboratory animals.

This research strategy may strike you as strange. "Why," you may be thinking, "would anyone think that they can learn about personality by studying animals?" This is a very good question. It

Table 10.1   Basic Points of Emphasis of Learning Approaches to Personality

1. Empirical research is the cornerstone of theory and practice
2. Personality theory and applied practice should be based on principles of learning
3. Behavior is responsive to reinforcement variables in the environment and is more situation specific than suggested by other personality theories (e.g., trait, psychoanalytic)
4. The medical symptom–disease view of psychopathology is rejected, and emphasis instead is placed on basic principles of learning and behavior change

is important, as one begins to learn about the behavioral approach, to recognize that the behaviorists' research strategy is not one that is unique to them. Instead, it is common in the sciences. It is the strategy of studying simple systems.

Suppose you were designing an airplane and were wondering if your craft would fly safely in windy weather. One strategy for answering this question would be to build an entire real plane, fill it with people, launch it into the sky, and see if it crashes when the wind kicks up. Of course, you would not do that. This strategy for learning about the flight characteristics of the plane is very costly and completely unethical. You would, instead, study something simpler than a real plane: perhaps a model plane in a wind tunnel or a computer simulation of an airline and wind flows. You would recognize that this simpler system is not the same thing as a real plane. Yet you would reason that it contains important features that are the same as the features of the system in which you are really interested, that is, the real plane. A similar strategy might be adopted by biologists seeking to understand the side effects of a new drug. Although the researchers are interested in the effects of the drug on people, they would first study its effects on laboratory animals, under the assumption that there is enough similarity in the makeup of animals and people that the animal study will, at the very least, provide some valuable information about the effects of the drug on people. Even if we do not think about it explicitly, we all recognize the value of studying simple systems.

This, then, is the simple system strategy. It is a research strategy in which, for both practical and ethical reasons, one conducts scientific studies on a system that is simpler than the one in which the researcher fundamentally is interested. This is the strategy adopted by the behaviorist.

Table 10.1 summarizes the basic points of emphasis in behaviorism that we have reviewed. With this background, we now begin our coverage of theories that were developed within this behavioral approach to psychological science. Specifically, we start where the approach itself began historically, with the ideas of John Watson and the associated research contributions of Ivan Pavlov.

Watson, Pavlov, and Classical Conditioning

Watson's Behaviorism

John B. Watson (1878–1958) was the founder of the approach to psychology known as **behaviorism.** He began his graduate study at the University of Chicago in philosophy and then switched to psychology. He took courses in neurology and physiology and began to do biological research with animals. During the year before he received his doctorate, Watson had an emotional breakdown and had sleepless nights for many weeks. He described this period as causing him to become interested in the work of Freud (Watson, 1936, p. 274). He eventually completed his dissertation, which caused him to develop a particular attitude regarding the use of human subjects:

> *At Chicago, I first began a tentative formulation of my later point of view. I never wanted to use human subjects. I hated to serve as a subject. I didn't like the stuffy, artificial instructions given to subjects. I always was uncomfortable and acted unnaturally. With animals I was at home. I felt that, in studying*

them, I was keeping close to biology with my feet on the ground. More and more the thought presented itself: Can't I find out by watching their behavior everything that the other students are finding by using O's (human subjects)?

Source: Watson, 1936, p. 276.

Watson left Chicago in 1908 to become a professor at Johns Hopkins University, where he served on the faculty until 1919. During his stay there, which was interrupted by a period of service during World War I, Watson developed his views on behaviorism as an approach to psychology. He first stated these views forcefully in a landmark paper published in psychology's leading journal, *Psychological Review*, in 1913. Public lectures and a book published in 1914 (*Watson's Behavior*) called further attention to a view of psychology that emphasized the study of observable behavior and rejected the use of introspection (observing one's own mental states) as a method of research. Watson's arguments were received enthusiastically by American psychologists. He was elected president of the American Psychological Association for 1915. He quickly expanded the theoretical base of his work by drawing on the findings of the Russian physiologist Pavlov (see below), incorporating them into his most significant book, *Psychology from the Standpoint of a Behaviorist* (1919). In 1920, he published a revolutionary study of the learning of emotional reactions with his student Rosalie Rayner (Watson & Rayner, 1920). At that time, he clearly was poised to be the dominant American psychologist of the 20th century.

This, however, is not how his career unfolded. In 1919, Watson divorced his wife and subsequently married his student Rayner. This scandalous turn of events forced his resignation from Johns Hopkins and caused him to entirely abandon his research career. Instead, he entered the business world, spending his years in advertising studying potential sales markets. Watson appeared to take this turn of events in good spirit, reporting "that it can be just as thrilling to watch the growth of a sales curve of a new product as to watch the learning curve of animals or men" (Watson, 1936, p. 280). After 1920, Watson did write some popular articles and a book, *Behaviorism* (1924). But his career as a theorist and experimenter had ended.

traveler1116 / Getty Images

Ivan Pavlov's work was of such significance that the government of the Society Union honored him with this stamp.

Theory of Classical Conditioning

Ivan Petrovich Pavlov (1849–1936) was a Russian physiologist who, in the course of his work on the digestive process, developed a procedure for studying behavior and a principle of learning that profoundly affected the field of psychology. Around the beginning of the 20th century, Pavlov was involved in the study of gastric secretions in dogs. As part of his research, he placed some food powder inside the mouth of a dog and measured the resulting amount of salivation. He noticed that after a number of such trials, the dog began to salivate, even before the food was put in its mouth, to certain stimuli: the sight of the food dish, the approach of the person who brought the food, and so forth. Stimuli that previously did not elicit salivation (called neutral stimuli) could now elicit the salivation response because of their association with the food powder that automatically caused the dog to salivate. To animal owners, this may not seem to be a startling observation. However, it led Pavlov to conduct significant research on the process known as classical conditioning.

Pavlov explored a broad range of scientific issues. In addition to his work on basic conditioning processes, he studied individual differences among his dogs, thereby stimulating a new field of temperament research (Strelau, 1997). He made important contributions to the understanding of abnormal behavior, using animal experiments to study disorganized behavior in dogs and human patients to study neuroses and psychoses, providing the foundation for forms of therapy based on principles of classical conditioning. In 1904, he was awarded the Nobel Prize for his work on digestive processes. His methods and concepts remain important today; they are among the most important in the history of psychology (Dewsbury, 1997).

Principles of Classical Conditioning

Classical conditioning is a process in which a stimulus that initially is neutral (i.e., that the organism initially does not respond to in any significant manner) eventually elicits a strong response. It elicits the response because the neutral stimulus becomes associated with some other stimulus that does produce a response. The process in which the organism learns to respond to the stimulus that originally was neutral is known as conditioning.

In the classic case studied in Pavlov's lab, a dog salivates the first time that food is presented. The response of salivation to food is *not* learned or conditioned; it is an automatic, built-in response of the organism. In the terminology of classical conditioning, food is an unconditioned stimulus (US), and the salivation in response to food is an unconditioned response (UR). "Unconditioned" here merely means that the connection between stimulus and response occurs without any learning or conditioning. Pavlov then introduces a new stimulus, such as the sound of a bell. Initially, this sound is neutral; it does not elicit any strong response on the part of the dog in Pavlov's lab. Then the critical step in research is taken. Over a series of trials, the bell is sounded just before the presentation of food. After these learning trials, the bell is sounded without any food being presented. What happens? The dog now salivates merely upon hearing the ring of the bell. Conditioning has occurred. The previously neutral stimulus now elicits a strong response. At this point, the bell is called a conditioned stimulus (CS), and the salivation in response to the bell is a conditioned response (CR).

The point of this work, of course, does not concern merely dogs, bells, and food. The point is general. In theory, any emotion could be associated with any stimulus. The emotional responses that dogs—and people!—experience to events in the world could be determined largely by classical conditioning.

Through classical conditioning, one also can learn to avoid a stimulus that initially is neutral. This is called conditioned withdrawal. In early research on conditioned withdrawal, a dog was strapped in a harness and electrodes were attached to its paw. The delivery of an electric shock (US) to the paw led to the withdrawal of the paw (UR), which was a reflex response on the part of the animal. If a bell was repeatedly presented just before the shock, eventually the bell alone (CS) was able to elicit the withdrawal response (CR).

The experimental arrangement designed by Pavlov to study classical conditioning allowed him to investigate a number of important phenomena. For example, would the conditioned response become associated with the specific neutral stimulus alone or would it become associated with other similar stimuli? Pavlov found that the response that had become conditioned to a previously neutral stimulus would also become associated with similar stimuli, a process called **generalization**. In other words, the salivation response to the bell would generalize to other sounds. Similarly, the withdrawal response to the bell would generalize to sounds similar to the bell.

What are the limits of such generalization? If repeated trials indicate that only some stimuli are followed by the unconditioned stimulus, the animal recognizes differences among stimuli, a process called **discrimination**. For example, if only certain sounds but not others are followed by shock and reflexive paw withdrawal, the dog will learn to discriminate among sounds. Thus, whereas the process of generalization leads to consistency of response across similar stimuli, the process of discrimination leads to increased specificity of response. Finally, if the originally neutral stimulus is presented repeatedly without being followed at least occasionally by the unconditioned stimulus, there is an undoing or progressive weakening of the conditioning or association, a process known as **extinction**. Whereas the association of the neutral stimulus with the unconditioned stimulus leads to the conditioned response, the repeated presentation of the conditioned stimulus without the unconditioned stimulus leads to extinction. For example, for the dog to continue to salivate to the bell, there must be at least occasional presentations of the food powder with the bell.

Although the illustrations used relate to animals, the principles can apply to humans as well. For example, consider a child who is bitten or merely treated roughly by a dog. The child's fear of this dog may now be extended to all dogs—the process of generalization. Suppose, however, by getting help, the child begins to discriminate among dogs of various kinds and begins to be afraid only of certain dogs. We can see here the process of discrimination. Over time, the child may have repeated positive experiences with all dogs, leading to the extinction of the fear response altogether. Thus, the classical conditioning model may be potentially very helpful in understanding the development, maintenance, and disappearance of many of our emotional reactions.

Psychopathology and Change

Pavlov extended his analysis of conditioning to the study of phenomena of clinical interest. He developed explanations for phenomena such as psychological conflict and the development of neuroses. A classic example explored what came to be known as experimental neuroses in animals. In this research, a dog was conditioned to salivate to the image of a circle. Differentiation between a circle and a similar figure, an ellipse, was then conditioned; this was done by not reinforcing the response to the ellipse, while response to the circle continued to be reinforced. Then, gradually, the ellipse was changed in shape. Its shape was made to be closer and closer to a circle. At first, the dog could still discriminate between the circle and the ellipse. But then, as the figures became extremely similar, it no longer could tell them apart. What happened to the dog? Its behavior became disorganized; as Pavlov himself described,

> After three weeks of work upon this discrimination not only did the discrimination fail to improve, but it became considerably worse, and finally disappeared altogether. The hitherto quiet dog began to squeal in its stand, kept wriggling about, tore off with its teeth the apparatus for mechanical stimulation of the skin, and bit through the tubes connecting the animal's room with the observer, a behavior which never happened before. On being taken into the experimental room the dog now barked violently, which was also contrary to its usual custom; in short, it presented all the symptoms of a condition of acute neurosis.

Source: Pavlov, 1927, p. 291.

Conditioned Emotional Reactions

Pavlov's work greatly influenced the thinking of John Watson. It inspired Watson to perform, with humans, the sort of conditioning research Pavlov had done with dogs. In 1920, Watson published one of the most famous, and infamous, studies in the history of psychology. It reported the conditioning of emotional reactions in an infant, an 11-month-old known as Little Albert.

In this research the experimenters, Watson and Rayner (1920), combined a stimulus that Little Albert was not afraid of—a small white laboratory rat—with an unconditioned stimulus that elicited fear—the noise produced by striking a hammer on a suspended steel bar. They then found that if the bar was struck immediately behind Albert's head just as he began to

John Watson and Rosalie Rayner conducting research on the classic conditioning of emotional reactions with the 11-month-old Little Albert.

reach for a rat, he began to develop fear of the rat. After a few experimental trials, the instant the rat alone (without the noise) was shown to Albert, he began to cry. He had developed what is called a **conditioned emotional reaction**. Furthermore, Albert's fear generalized, just as dogs' responses had generalized in Pavlov's lab. Albert began to fear not only white rats but also other white and furry objects—including, Watson and Rayner report, the white beard of a Santa Claus mask! Despite some evidence that Albert's emotional reaction was not as strong or as general as expected (Harris, 1979), Watson and Rayner concluded that many fears are conditioned emotional reactions. On this basis, they criticized the more complex psychoanalytic interpretations:

> *The Freudians twenty years from now, unless their hypotheses change, when they come to analyze Albert's fear of a seal skin coat will probably tease from him the recital of a dream upon which their analysis will show that Albert at three years of age attempted to play with the pubic hair of the mother and was scolded violently for it. If the analyst has sufficiently prepared Albert to accept such a dream when found as an explanation of his avoiding tendencies, and if the analyst has the authority and personality to put it over, Albert may be fully convinced that the dream was a true revealer of the factors which brought about the fear.*

> *Source*: Watson and Rayner, 1920, p. 14.

The "Unconditioning" of Fear of a Rabbit

For many psychologists, the classical conditioning of emotional reactions plays a critical role in the development of psychopathology and a potentially important role in behavioral change. Behavior therapy based on the classical conditioning model emphasizes the extinction of problematic responses, such as conditioned fears, or the conditioning of new responses to stimuli that elicit such undesired responses as anxiety.

An early utilization of this approach, one that followed Watson and Rayner's study of the conditioning of the fear emotional response in Albert, was the effort of Jones (1924) to remove a fear under laboratory conditions. In this study, described as one of the earliest, if not the first, systematic utilization of behavior therapy, Jones attempted to treat the exaggerated fear reaction in a boy, Peter, who then was two years and ten months old. Peter was described as a generally healthy, well-adjusted child with a fear of a white rat that also extended to a rabbit, fur coat, feather, and cotton wool. Jones carefully documented the nature of the child's fear response and the conditions that elicited the greatest fear. She then set out to determine whether she could "uncondition" the fear response to one stimulus and whether such unconditioning would then generalize to other stimuli. Jones chose to focus on Peter's fear of the rabbit since this seemed even greater than his fear of the rat. She proceeded by bringing Peter to play at a time when the rabbit was present, as well as the other children who were selected because they had no fear of the rabbit. Gradually Peter moved from almost complete terror at the sight of the rabbit to a completely positive response.

Peter was progressing well in his unconditioning until, unfortunately, he had to be taken to the hospital with scarlet fever. When he returned to the laboratory, his fear had returned to its original level, a not unusual occurrence in conditioning procedures. At this point, Jones began anew with another method of treatment, "direct conditioning." Here, Peter was seated in a chair and given food he liked as the experimenter gradually brought the rabbit in a wire cage closer to him: "Through the presence of a pleasant stimulus (food) whenever the rabbit was shown, the fear was eliminated gradually in favor of a positive response." In other words, the positive feelings associated with food were counterconditioned to the previously feared rabbit. However, even in the later sessions the influence of other children who were not afraid of the rabbit seemed to be significant.

And what of the other fears? Jones noted that after the unconditioning of Peter's fear of the rabbit, he completely lost his fear of the fur coat, feathers, and cotton wool as well. Despite the lack of any knowledge concerning the origins of Peter's fears, the unconditioning procedure was found to work successfully and to generalize to other stimuli as well.

Systematic Desensitization

A major advance in the application of classical conditioning principles to questions of psychopathology was the development of a therapeutic technique known as systematic desensitization. The technique was developed by Joseph Wolpe, a psychiatrist from South Africa, who became familiar with the writings of Pavlov.

Wolpe viewed persistent reactions of anxiety as a learned response that could be un-learned. He developed a therapy that was designed to provide this "unlearning." Phrased more technically, his therapy technique of **systematic desensitization** was designed to inhibit anxiety through **counterconditioning**. In counterconditioning, a person learns a new response that is physiologically incompatible with an existing response. If the existing response to a stimulus is fear or anxiety, then the goal might be to have the person learn a new response such as relaxation. Once the person learns, through new classical conditioning experiences, to experience relaxation in response to the previously feared stimulus, his or her fear should be eliminated.

In practice, systematic desensitization involves a number of phases (Wolpe, 1961). After determining whether the patient has a problem that can be treated by systematic desensitization, the therapist trains the patient to relax. This generally is done through deep muscle relaxation; the patient relaxes one part of the body after another. The next phase of treatment involves the construction of an anxiety hierarchy. In this procedure, the therapist tries to obtain from the patient a list of stimuli that arouse anxiety. These anxiety–arousing stimuli are grouped into themes such as fear of heights or fear of rejection. Within each group or theme, the anxiety–arousing stimuli are then arranged in order from most disturbing to least disturbing. For example, a theme of

Phobias such as spider phobia can be reduced through systematic desensitization, which is an application of basic principles of Pavlovian classical conditioning.

claustrophobia (fear of closed spaces) might involve placing the fear of being stuck in an elevator at the top of the list, an anxiety about being on a train in the middle of the list, and anxiety in response to reading of miners trapped underground at the bottom of the list. A theme of death might involve being at a burial as the most anxiety–arousing stimulus, the word "death" as somewhat anxiety–arousing, and driving past a cemetery as only slightly anxiety–arousing. Patients can have many or few themes and many or few items within each anxiety hierarchy.

With the construction of the anxiety hierarchies completed, the patient is ready for the desensitization procedure itself. The patient has learned to calm the self by relaxation, and the therapist has established the anxiety hierarchies. Now, the therapist encourages the patient to achieve a deep state of relaxation and then to imagine the least anxiety–arousing stimulus in the anxiety hierarchy. If the patient can imagine the stimulus without anxiety, then he or she is encouraged to imagine the next stimulus in the hierarchy while remaining relaxed. Periods of pure relaxation are interspersed with periods of relaxation and imagination of anxiety–arousing stimuli. If the patient feels anxious while imagining a stimulus, he or she is encouraged to relax and return to imagining a less anxiety–arousing stimulus. Ultimately, the patient is able to relax while imagining all stimuli in the anxiety hierarchies. Relaxation in relation to the imagined stimuli generalizes to relaxation in relation to these stimuli in everyday life. "It has consistently been found that at every stage a stimulus that evokes no anxiety when imagined in a state of relaxation will also evoke no anxiety when encountered in reality" (Wolpe, 1961, p. 191).

A number of clinical and laboratory studies have indicated that systematic desensitization is, in fact, an effective treatment procedure. These successful results led Wolpe and others to question the psychoanalytic view that, as long as the underlying conflicts remain untouched, the patient is prone to develop a new symptom in place of the one removed (symptom substitution) (Lazarus, 1965). According to the behavior therapy point of view, no symptom is caused by unconscious conflicts. There is only a maladaptive learned response, and once this response has been eliminated, there is no reason to believe that another maladaptive response will be substituted for it.

CURRENT APPLICATIONS

What Makes Some Foods a Treat and Others Disgusting?

Most people love some odors and food tastes and are disgusted by others. Often, these responses date back to childhood and seem nearly impossible to change. Can classical conditioning help us to understand them and their power?

Consider some research on food tastes. What makes some foods so unpleasant—even disgusting—that we have emotional reactions to just the thought of them? Eating worms or drinking milk that has a dead fly or dead cockroach in it are examples. The interesting thing about some of these reactions is that a food that evokes disgust in one culture can be considered a delicacy in another, and disgust might be evoked by a dead fly or cockroach in the milk even if one is told that the insect was sterilized before it was put in the milk. Having seen the dead insect in the milk, one might not even be prepared to drink a different glass of milk, the disgust reaction now having generalized to the milk itself.

According to the researchers of such reactions, a possible explanation lies in the strong emotional reaction that becomes associated with a previously neutral object. In classical conditioning terms, the disgust response becomes associated with, or conditioned to, a previously neutral object such as milk or another food: "We believe that Pavlovian conditioning is alive and well, in the flavor associations of billions of meals eaten each day, in the expression of affects of billions of eaters as they eat away, in the association of foods and offensive objects, and in the association of foods with some of their consequences."

If this is the case, then it suggests that many things that we like, perhaps even feel addicted to, are the result of classical conditioning. This being the case, it may be possible to change our emotional reactions to certain objects through the process of classical conditioning.

Source: Psychology Today, July 1985; Rozin & Zellner, 1985. Copyright © 1985 American Psychological Association. Reprinted by permission from Psychology Today.

Want some fried scorpion on a stick? They might not look too tasty to you. But if you had a different history of classical conditioning experiences, as a result of growing up in a different culture, you might be digging in.

Paul Biris / Getty Images

A Reinterpretation of the Case of Little Hans

In this section, the application of the learning theory approach will be observed in a case presented by Wolpe and Rachman (1960) that gives us an excellent opportunity to compare the behavioral approach with that of psychoanalysis. In fact, it is not a case in the same sense as other cases that have been presented. Rather, it is a critique and reformulation of Freud's case of Little Hans.

As we learned in Chapter 4, the case of Little Hans is a classic in psychoanalysis. In this case, Freud emphasized the importance of infantile sexuality and Oedipal conflicts in the development of a horse phobia, or fear. Wolpe and Rachman are extremely critical of Freud's approach to obtaining data and of his conclusions. They make the following points: (1) Nowhere is there evidence of Hans's wish to make love to his mother. (2) Hans never expressed fear or hatred of his father. (3) Hans consistently denied any relationship between the horse and his father. (4) Phobias can be induced in children by a simple conditioning process and need not be related to a theory of conflicts or anxiety and defense. The view that neuroses have a purpose is highly questionable. (5) There is no evidence that the phobia disappeared as a result of Hans's resolution of his Oedipal conflicts. Similarly, there is no evidence that insight occurred or that information was of therapeutic value.

Wolpe and Rachman feel handicapped in their own interpretation of the phobia because the data were gathered within a psychoanalytic framework. They do, however, attempt an explanation. A phobia is regarded as a conditioned anxiety reaction. As a child, Hans heard and saw a playmate being warned by her father that she should avoid a white horse lest it bite her: "Don't put your finger to the white horse." This incident sensitized Hans to a fear of horses. Also, there was the time when one of Hans's friends injured himself and bled while playing with horses. Finally, Hans was a sensitive child who felt uneasy about seeing merry-go-round horses being playfully beaten. These factors set the condition for the later development of the phobia. The phobia itself occurred as a consequence of the fright Hans experienced while watching a horse fall down. Whereas Freud suggested that this incident was an exciting cause that allowed the underlying conflicts to be expressed in terms of a phobia, Wolpe and Rachman suggest that this incident was *the* cause.

Wolpe and Rachman see a similarity here to Watson's conditioning of fear in Little Albert. Hans was frightened by the event with a horse and then generalized his fear to all things that were similar to or related to horses. The recovery from the phobia did not occur through the process of insight but probably through a process of either extinction or counterconditioning. As Hans developed, he experienced other emotional responses that inhibited the fear response. Alternatively, it is suggested that perhaps the father's constant reference to the horse in a nonthreatening context helped to extinguish the fear response. Whatever the details, it appears that the phobia disappeared gradually, as would be expected by this kind of learning interpretation, instead of dramatically, as might be suggested by a psychoanalytic, insight interpretation. The evidence in support of Freud is not clear, and the data, as opposed to the interpretations, can be accounted for in a more straightforward way through use of a learning theory interpretation.

Recent Developments

For some time, interest in classical conditioning declined among personality psychologists. However, more recently, there has been increased recognition of the potential contributions of concepts and procedures associated with classical conditioning theory. One illustrative area of research is the use of classical conditioning procedures to demonstrate that people can unconsciously develop fears and attitudes toward others (Krosnick, Betz, Jussim, Lynn, & Kirschenbaum, 1992; Ohman & Soares, 1993). For example, a stimulus, such as a picture with positive or negative affective value, can be presented subliminally (i.e., below the threshold of awareness) in association with another stimulus, such as another photo. Thus, a person will come to dislike a photo unconsciously associated with negative emotion and come to like a photo unconsciously associated with positive emotion. One can speculate in this regard how many of our attitudes and preferences are classically conditioned on a subliminal or unconscious basis. Consider, for example, the following conclusion of a leading social psychologist: "The aversive prejudice, once created, may be difficult to consciously eliminate." People can have egalitarian beliefs and still act prejudicial in certain situations—their impulsive, automatic reaction when faced with a member of that minority group may be negative. This doesn't mean that people are lying about nonprejudicial attitudes. It's that these attitudes reside coincidentally with a conditioned aversive reaction learned early in childhood (Cacioppo, 1999, p. 10).

In a surprising turn of events, researchers recently have related classical conditioning principles to a topic that we previously associated with the phenomenological theory of Carl Rogers, namely, self-esteem. Baccus, Baldwin, and Packer (2004) reasoned that expressions of high self-esteem are responses that could be altered through classical conditioning. Participants in their research took part in a conditioning task in which both words and pictures appeared on a computer screen. In an experimental condition, words that were self-relevant (i.e., words that the given participant said described himself or herself) appeared in combination with pictures of people who were smiling. This experimental condition was designed as a classical conditioning process in which positive emotions would be paired with the self. In another condition—a control condition—such words were paired with a mixture of pictures: some smiling, some frowning, some looking neutral. Afterward, participants completed self-esteem measures. The researchers compared the effects of the experimental condition (i.e., the condition with the faces that were consistently smiling) to the control condition for the group of participants overall and for subgroups of participants who, based on preexperimental measures, had low versus high self-esteem in general. The results demonstrated that classical conditioning increased feelings of self-esteem. People who saw smiling faces paired with words that are defining of them displayed higher levels of self-esteem than control group subjects.

Personality and the Brain
Classical Conditioning

Pavlov was a biologist. Yet, he was unable to study the biology of classical conditioning, that is, the nervous system mechanisms through which conditioning experiences alter an organism's responses. In Pavlov's time, the nervous system was not understood well enough, and technologies that might yield such an understanding were unavailable.

Times have changed. Today, the basic neural and biochemical processes that allow for classical conditioning in simple organisms is understood thoroughly. Significant advances have been made by Eric Kandel of Columbia University in New York, who was awarded the Nobel Prize in medicine in 2000 for his research on the topic.

Kandel's research is a classic example of the simple systems strategy we overviewed previously. In order to understand what happens in the brain when an organism learns a new response, Kandel studied an organism much simpler than the one Pavlov studied (the dog): Aplysia, a type of sea slug. Aplysia have relatively few nerve cells. This makes it relatively easy to identify the cell-by-cell changes that occur as a result of conditioning experiences.

Aplysia exhibit a simple response that can be modified through classic conditioning: the gill-withdrawal reflex. They withdraw their gill (the organ they use for breathing) when stimulated in another area of their body. Kandel and colleagues modified the gill-withdrawal behavior through classical conditioning and then explored the biological basis of the behavioral change (Kandel, 2000). The unconditioned stimulus in their conditioning trials was an electric shock applied to the Aplysia's tail. They paired this UCS with stimulation to the area of the body that, when stimulated, causes gill withdrawal.

At a behavioral level, they obtained exactly the sort of conditioning result that Pavlov had obtained. After the conditioning trials, the Aplysia's behavior changed. They exhibited a much stronger reflexive reaction (withdrawal of the gill) after the electric-shock trials.

At a biological level of analysis, they obtained the sort of finding that Pavlov could only dream of. To understand it, you need to distinguish between two types of neurons: (1) motor neurons (which connect to the gill, causing it to move) and (2) interneurons (which receive inputs from the stimulated part of the body and then connect to the motor neurons). Kandel and colleagues found that, after classical conditioning, interneurons become responsive. Specifically, they release more neurotransmitters after the conditioning trials with the UCS (the electric shock). These neurotransmitters reach the motor neuron, which raises motor neuron activity and thus enhances the gill-withdrawal reflex (Kandel, 2000).

Skinner's Theory of Operant Conditioning

Although John Watson left the field of psychology, others picked up the banner of behaviorism during the middle of the 20th century. These included historically significant figures such as Clark Hull, who developed a highly systematic drive theory of learning, and John Dollard and Neal Miller, who attempted to show how Hull's theory could address phenomena involving drives and intrapsychic conflicts that were of interest to psychoanalysts. Even these important contributions, however, were eventually overshadowed by those of another researcher who became one of the most influential figures in all of 20th-century psychology.

The most influential behavioral researcher, theorist, and spokesperson was the Harvard psychologist B. F. Skinner (1904–1990). Indeed, Skinner is probably the most well-known American psychologist of the last century; a recent quantitative analysis of the impact of individual psychologists on the field as a whole ranked Skinner as the singularly most eminent psychologist of the 20th century (Haggbloom et al., 2002). Skinner's eminence reflects his exceptional skill at articulating the broad implications of behavioral principles. In Skinner's hands, behaviorism was not just an approach to the psychology of learning. It was an all-encompassing philosophy that promised a comprehensive account of human behavior, as well as technologies for improving the human experience.

A View of The Theorist

The scientist, like any organism, is the product of a unique history. The practices which he finds most appropriate will depend in part upon his history.

In this passage, Skinner takes the point of view that has been argued in each of the theory chapters in this book—that is, that psychologists' orientations and research strategies are, in part, consequences of their own life history and expressions of their own personalities.

Bettmann / Contributor/Getty Images

B. F. Skinner.

B. F. Skinner was born in Pennsylvania, the son of a lawyer who was described by his son as having been desperately hungry for praise and a mother who had rigid standards of right and wrong. Still, Skinner (1967) described his home during his early years as a warm and stable environment. He reported a love for school and showed an early interest in building things. This desire to build things is particularly interesting in relation to the behavioral emphasis on laboratory equipment in the experimental setting and because it contrasts with the absence of such an interest in the lives and research of the clinical personality theorists.

At about the time Skinner entered college, his younger brother died. Skinner commented that he was not much moved by his brother's death and that he probably felt guilty for not being moved. Skinner went to Hamilton College and majored in English literature. At that time, his goal was to become a writer, and at one point, he sent three short stories to Robert Frost, from whom he received an encouraging reply. After college, Skinner spent a year trying to write but concluded that at that point in his life he had nothing to say. He then spent six months living in Greenwich Village in New York City. During this time he read Pavlov's *Conditioned Reflexes* and came across a series of articles by Bertrand Russell on Watson's behaviorism. Russell thought that he had demolished Watson in these articles, but they aroused Skinner's interest in behaviorism.

Although Skinner had not taken any psychology courses in college, he had begun to develop an interest in the field and was accepted for graduate work in psychology at Harvard. He justified his change in goals as follows: "A writer might portray human behavior accurately, but he did not therefore understand it. I was to remain interested in human behavior, but the literary method had failed me; I would turn to the scientific" (Skinner, 1967, p. 395). Psychology appeared to be the relevant science. Besides, Skinner had long been interested in animal behavior (recalling his fascination with the complex behaviors of a troupe of performing pigeons). Furthermore, there would now be many opportunities to make use of his interest in building gadgets.

During his graduate school years at Harvard, Skinner developed his interest in animal behavior and in explaining this behavior without reference to the functioning of the nervous system. After reading Pavlov, he disagreed with Pavlov's contention that, in explaining behavior, one could go "from the salivary reflexes to the important business of the organism in everyday life." However, Skinner believed that Pavlov had given him the key to understanding behavior. "Control your conditions (the environment) and you shall see order!" During these and the following years, Skinner (1959) developed some of his principles of scientific methodology: (1) When you run into something interesting, drop everything else and study it. (2) Some ways of doing research are easier than others. A mechanical apparatus often makes doing research easier. (3) Some people are lucky. (4) A piece of apparatus breaks down. This presents problems, but it can also lead to (5) serendipity—the art of finding one thing while looking for something else.

After Harvard, Skinner moved first to Minnesota, then to Indiana, and returned to Harvard in 1948. During this time, he became, in a sense, a sophisticated animal trainer; he was able to make organisms engage in specific behaviors at specific times. He turned from work with rats to work with pigeons. Finding that the behavior of any single animal did not necessarily reflect the average picture of learning based on many animals, he became interested in the manipulation and control of individual animal behavior. Special theories of learning and circuitous explanations of behavior were not necessary if one could manipulate the environment so as to produce orderly change in the individual case. In the meantime, as Skinner notes, his own behavior was becoming controlled by the positive results being given to him by the animals "under his control."

The basis of Skinner's **operant conditioning** procedure is the control of behavior through manipulation of rewards and punishments in the environment, particularly the laboratory environment. However, his conviction concerning the importance of the laws of behavior and his interest in building things led Skinner to take his thinking and research far beyond the laboratory. He built a "baby box" to mechanize the care of a baby, teaching machines that used rewards in the teaching of school subjects, and a procedure whereby pigeons could be used militarily to land a missile on target. He wrote a novel, *Walden Two* (1948), in which he describes a utopia based on the control of human behavior through positive reinforcement (reward) rather than punishment. Skinner committed himself to the view that a science of human behavior and the technology to be derived from it must be developed in the service of humankind. In an interview published within his obituary notice in the

New York Times (August 20, 1990), Skinner related that "all humans are controlled"—that is, it is inevitable that people's behavior is ultimately under the control of whatever environments they experience—"but the idea of behaviorism is to eliminate coercion, to apply controls by changing the environment in such a way as to reinforce the kind of behavior that benefits everyone" (pp. A1, A12).

Skinner was considered by many to be the greatest contemporary American psychologist. He received many awards, including the American Psychological Association's award for Distinguished Scientific Contribution (1958) and the National Medal of Science (1968). In 1990, shortly before his death, he became the first recipient of the American Psychological Association's Citation for Outstanding Lifetime Contribution to Psychology.

Skinner's Theory of Personality

Let's begin our discussion of Skinner's theory of personality by contrasting its general qualities with those of the theories you already have learned about in the previous chapters. Each of the previous theories (and, to give you a preview, each of the ones discussed subsequently in this book) emphasizes structural concepts. Freud used structural concepts such as id, ego, and superego; Rogers used concepts such as self and ideal self; and Allport, Eysenck, and Cattell used the concept of traits. Each theorist, then, inferred the existence of a psychological structure in the mind of the individual that accounted for the person's consistent styles of emotion and behavior. In contrast, Skinner's behavioral approach greatly deemphasizes structure. This is for two reasons. First, behaviorists view behavior as an adaptation to situational forces. They thus expect situational specificity in behavior: If the situational forces change, so does the behavior. If behavior varies from one situation to another, then there is little need to propose structural concepts to explain the supposed consistency of personality. The second reason involves a general approach to constructing a theory. As we explained earlier, the behaviorists wanted to build a theory based on observable variables. They felt that only observable variables could be verified by basic research. Inferring the existence of invisible personality structures was seen by Skinner, then, as a way of thinking that was not properly scientific.

The fact that Skinner does not propose a series of personality structures makes his work entirely different from the other personality theories. In fact, Skinner rejected the view that his ideas constituted a personality theory. He saw himself as replacing the personality theories with a new way of thinking about behavior.

Structure

The key structural unit for the behavioral approach in general, and Skinner's approach in particular, is the response. A response may range from a simple reflex response (e.g., salivation to food, startle to a loud noise) to a complex piece of behavior (e.g., solution to a math problem, subtle forms of aggression). What is critical to the definition of a response is that it represents an external, observable piece of behavior that can be related to environmental events. The learning process essentially involves the association or connection of responses to events in the environment.

In his approach to learning, Skinner distinguishes between responses elicited by known stimuli, such as an eyeblink reflex to a puff of air, and responses that cannot be associated with any stimuli. These responses are emitted by the organism and are called **operants**. Skinner's view is that stimuli in the environment do not force the organism to behave or incite it to act. The initial cause of behavior is in the organism itself. "There is no environmental eliciting stimulus for operant behavior; it simply occurs. In the terminology of operant conditioning, operants are emitted by the organism. The dog walks, runs, and romps; the bird flies; the monkey swings from tree to tree; the human infant babbles vocally. In each case, the behavior occurs without any specific eliciting stimulus. It is in the biological nature of organisms to emit operant behavior" (Reynolds, 1968, p. 8).

Process: Operant Conditioning

The most important concept in the Skinnerian analysis of psychological processes is reinforcer. A **reinforcer** is something that follows a response and increases the probability of the response occurring again in the future.

Suppose a pigeon is pecking at a disk. If the pecking is followed by the provision of some food and the pigeon therefore pecks at the disk more frequently in the future, the food is a reinforcer. Suppose a baby in a crib is crying. If the crying draws the attention of adults who rush over to care for the infant and the infant therefore cries more frequently in the future, the attention from adults is reinforced. Learning by reinforcement is a process in which the probability of a given response is altered by the presentation of a reinforcer.

What counts as a reinforcer in any given situation, then, is defined according to the effects of the potential reinforcer on behavior. Often, it is difficult to know ahead of time what will serve as a reinforcer. This may vary from individual to individual. Finding a reinforcer may turn out to be a trial-and-error operation. Stimuli that originally do not serve as reinforcers may come to do so through their association with other reinforcers. Some green rectangular pieces of paper (i.e., money) become **generalized reinforcers** because they are associated with many other reinforcing stimuli.

Skinner developed a specialized piece of laboratory apparatus to study the effects of reinforcers on behavior. It has become known as the Skinner box. The exact details of a Skinner box vary a bit depending on the organism for which it is designed. A Skinner box designed for research with a rat would have a lever that the rat may press and some mechanism for delivering a reinforcer such as a food pellet. One would present the reinforcer and determine whether it influenced the frequency with which the rat engaged in the behavior of pressing the lever. Skinner saw this simple environment as the best setting to observe the elementary laws of behavior.

These laws are discovered by varying the nature of the reinforcements and observing the effects on the behavior of the organism in the Skinner box. The variations are done according to different **schedules of reinforcement**. The term *schedules of reinforcement* refers to the relation between behavior and when a reinforcement occurs. The general idea is that reinforcements need not occur after every response. They may be given only some of the time. Different schedules are different patterns of occurrence of the reinforcers. One distinction between schedules of reinforcement differentiates reinforcements that are based on the passage of time from those based on numbers of responses. In a time-based schedule, known as a time interval schedule, the reinforcement appears after a certain time period (e.g., one minute) regardless of the number of responses. In contrast, in a response-based interval, reinforcements appear only after a certain *number* of responses (e.g., presses of a bar, pecks of a key) have been made, no matter how long it takes for the responses to occur.

A second distinction differentiates reinforcement schedules that are **fixed** from those that are **variable**. In fixed schedules, the relation of behaviors to reinforcers remains constant; in variable schedules, this relation changes unpredictably. To illustrate: Imagine yourself standing in front of each of two machines. Both require you to put money in the machine and to press a button, whereupon you may get a reinforcement. If the machine is a soft-drink dispenser, the experience is routine and uninteresting. If no soft drink (the reinforcer) comes out the first time, you stop putting money into the machine. If the machine is a slot machine in a casino, the same event—putting money into a machine, pressing a button—is exciting! If no money (the reinforcer) comes out, you do not stop putting money in. Instead, many people put more and more money into the machine. The difference between the two settings is the different **schedule of reinforcement**. The slot machine features a random schedule, the soda machine a fixed schedule. In both the Skinner lab with rats and the casino with people, the variable schedule produces higher rates of response.

The behaviorists were remarkably successful in identifying systematic relations between the schedule of reinforcement for a given behavior and the frequency with which that behavior occurred. In research with animals in Skinner boxes, the results were so reliable that they could be replicated with virtually every individual animal put in the box (Ferster & Skinner, 1957). Response-based schedules repeatedly generated higher levels of response than interval schedules. The highest response rates occurred with response-based schedules that were variable (i.e., like a slot machine or other gambling device). These highly consistent operant conditioning results, combined with the equally consistent research results Pavlov and colleagues found when studying classical conditioning, gave behaviorists an exceptionally solid set of findings on which to build their theorizing. These solid research findings contributed enormously to the appeal of behaviorism in the mid-20th century.

Why do people gamble, even after losing large amounts of money? Behaviorists explain that the cause is the schedule of reinforcement. Gambling devices feature variable ratio schedules of reinforcement that create high, persistent levels of behavior.

How do animals learn to do anything more complex than pressing a lever? According to Skinner, complex behavior results from a process known as **shaping** or (equivalently) **successive approximations**. Through a gradual, step-by-step process, one reinforces increasingly complex behaviors that approximate, to a greater and greater degree, the final behavior that is desired. The behavior of the organism is "shaped" until it matches a desired response. For example, suppose you want a rat in a Skinner box to run around in circles. You can't just wait until it runs around in circles and then reinforce it because it might never spontaneously run around in circles. Instead, you first reinforce a simple response such as running (whether or not in circles). You would then wait until the animal started to run in a curved path and reinforce it only then. Once this happened, you should wait until it ran in at least a half circle and reinforce it then. Eventually, you can train the animal to run in circles. Much animal training (in circuses, zoos, and Florida tourist attractions) is done in this manner. Skinner recognized that complex human learning also may occur in a step-by-step process of successive approximations.

In addition to the use of pleasant events as reinforcers, Skinnerians note that the removal or avoidance of an *un*pleasant stimulus also can be reinforcing. For example, suppose you are feeling so anxious about going to a social event that you suddenly decide not to go and that once you make this decision your anxiety goes away. The lessening of anxiety may reinforce the behavior of saying, "I'm not going to social events." The reduction of the negative occurrence, the anxiety, is reinforcing.

Skinnerians also recognize that the presentation of aversive stimuli can influence behaviors. In the behavioral vocabulary, these stimuli are **punishments**. In punishment, an aversive stimulus follows a response, decreasing the probability of that response occurring again. Skinnerians generally are against the use of punishment, whose effects tend to be temporary and whose administration may lead people to rebel against their use. Throughout his career, Skinner emphasized the value of positive reinforcement in shaping behavior.

Growth and Development

Skinner did not posit any principles of development other than the operant conditioning principles reviewed above. To Skinner, as children develop, they learn more and more responses as a result of naturally occurring reinforcement experiences. The process is no different, in terms of general principles, than the case of a rat which learns more and more responses as a result of systematic shaping experiences in a Skinner box.

This mechanistic view of development does have practical implications that may be beneficial. It suggests that parents should attend carefully to exactly how and when they are reinforcing the child's behavior. If one wants the child to behave in a certain way, the most effective procedure, according to Skinner, is not to lecture the child about proper forms of behavior or to punish the child for things it does wrong. The most effective procedure, according to Skinner, is to reinforce good behavior immediately after it occurs.

In its treatment of development, then, behaviorism differs from the other theories in this book. To Skinner, development does not occur in any particular sequences of stages. There are no conflicts that everyone necessarily experiences. No new structures spring up in the mind at one versus another point in development. Instead, the set of behaviors that a person can perform simply increases gradually, as he or she experiences more reinforcements.

Psychopathology

The learning theory position on psychopathology may be stated as follows: The basic principles of learning provide a completely adequate interpretation of psychopathology. Explanations in terms of symptoms with underlying causes are not necessary. According to the behavioral point of view, behavioral pathology is not a disease. Instead, it is a response pattern learned according to the same principles of behavior as are all response patterns.

The Skinnerians argue against any concept of the unconscious or a "sick personality". Individuals are not sick; they merely do not respond appropriately to stimuli. Either they fail to learn a response or they learn a maladaptive response. In the former case, there is a behavioral deficit. For example, individuals who are socially inadequate may have had faulty reinforcement histories in which social skills were not developed. Having failed to be reinforced for social skills during socialization as children, as adults they have an inadequate response repertoire with which to respond to social situations.

Reinforcement is important not only for the learning of responses but also for the maintenance of behavior. Thus, one possible result of an absence of reinforcement in the environment is depression. According to this view, depression represents a lessening of behavior or a lowered response rate. The depressed person is not responsive because positive reinforcement has been withdrawn (Ferster, 1973).

When a person learns a **maladaptive response**, the problem is that a response has been learned that is not considered acceptable by society or by others in the person's environment. This may be because the response itself is considered unacceptable (e.g., hostile behavior) or because the response occurs under unacceptable circumstances (e.g., joking at a formal business meeting). Related to this situation is the development of superstitious behavior (Skinner, 1948). Superstitious behavior develops because of an accidental relationship between a response and reinforcement. Thus, Skinner found that if he gave pigeons small amounts of food at regular intervals regardless of what they were doing, many birds came to associate the response that was coincidentally rewarded with systematic reinforcement. For example, if a pigeon was coincidentally rewarded while walking around in a counterclockwise direction, this response might become conditioned even though it had no cause–effect relationship with the reinforcement. The continuous performance of the behavior would result in occasional, again coincidental, reinforcement. Thus, the behavior could be maintained over long periods of time.

In sum, people develop faulty behavior repertoires, what others call "sick" behavior or psychopathology, because of the following: They were not reinforced for adaptive behaviors, they were punished for behaviors that later would be considered adaptive, they were reinforced for maladaptive behaviors, or they were reinforced under inappropriate circumstances for what would otherwise be adaptive behavior. In all cases, there is an emphasis on observable responses and schedules of reinforcement rather than on concepts such as drive, conflict, unconscious motives, or self-esteem.

Behavioral Assessment

How does one assess personality in a behavioral approach? Since the theory states that one must understand the relation between behavior and the environment, one does not assess the person in isolation. One assesses the person's responses to different environments. The behavioral approach to assessment, then, emphasizes three things: (1) identification of specific behaviors, often called **target behaviors or target responses**; (2) identification of specific environmental factors that elicit, cue, or reinforce the target behaviors; and (3) identification of specific environmental factors that can be manipulated to alter the behavior. A behavioral assessment of a child's temper tantrums, for example, would include a clear, objective definition of temper tantrum behavior in the child, a complete description of the situation that sets off the tantrum behavior, a complete description of the reactions of parents and others that may be reinforcing the behavior, and an analysis of the potential for eliciting and reinforcing other nontantrum behaviors (Kanfer & Saslow, 1965; O'Leary, 1972). This **functional analysis** of behavior, involving the effort to identify the environmental conditions that control behavior, sees behavior as a function of specific events in the environment. The approach has also been called the **ABC assessment**: One assesses the antecedent conditions of the behavior, the behavior itself, and the consequences of the behavior.

Behavioral assessment generally is closely tied to treatment objectives. For example, consider the task of assisting a mother who came to a clinic because she felt helpless in dealing with her four-year-old son's temper tantrums and general disobedience (Hawkins, Peterson, Schweid, & Bijou, 1966). The psychologists involved in this case followed a fairly typical behavioral procedure for assessment and treatment. First, the mother and child were observed in the home to determine the nature of the undesirable behaviors, when they occurred, and which reinforcers seemed to maintain them. The following nine behaviors were determined to constitute the major portion of the boy's objectionable behavior: (1) biting his shirt or arm; (2) sticking out his tongue; (3) kicking or biting himself, others, or objects; (4) calling someone or something a derogatory name; (5) removing or threatening to remove his clothing; (6) saying "No!" loudly and vigorously; (7) threatening to damage objects or persons; (8) throwing objects; and (9) pushing his sister. Observation of the mother–child interaction suggested that the objectionable behavior was being maintained by attention from the mother. For example, often she tried to distract him by offering him toys or food.

The treatment program began with a behavioral analysis of how frequently the boy expressed one of the objectionable behaviors during one-hour sessions conducted in the home two to three times a week. Two psychologists acted as observers to ensure that there was high reliability or good agreement concerning recording of the objectionable behavior. This first phase, known as a baseline period, lasted for 16 sessions. During this time, mother and child interacted in their usual way. Following this careful assessment of the objectionable behavior during the baseline period, the psychologists initiated their intervention, or treatment program. Now, the mother was instructed to tell her son to stop or to put him in his room by himself without toys each time he emitted an objectionable behavior. In other words, there was a withdrawal of the positive reinforcer for objectionable behavior. At the same time, the mother was instructed to give her son attention and approval when he behaved in a desirable way. In other words, the positive reinforcers were made contingent on desirable behavior. During this time, known as the first experimental period, the frequency of objectionable behaviors was again counted. The result was a marked decline in the frequency of objectionable behavior. In the preexperimental baseline phase, dozens of objectionable behaviors commonly were observed during any given one-hour period. In contrast, during the first experimental period, only 1 to 8 such responses per session were observed.

Following the first experimental treatment period, the mother was instructed to return to her former behavior to determine whether it was the shift in her reinforcement behavior that was determining the change in her son's behavior. During this second baseline period, her son's objectionable behavior ranged between 2 and 24 per session. There was an increase in this behavior, though not a return to the former baseline level. However, the mother reported that she had trouble responding in her previous way because she now felt more "sure of herself." Thus, even during this period, she gave her son firmer commands, gave in less after denying a request, and showed more affection in response to positive behaviors in her son than was previously the case. Following this, there was a return to a full emphasis on the treatment program, resulting in a decline in objectionable behavior (second experimental period). The rate of objectionable behavior was found to remain low after a 24-day interval (follow-up period), and the mother reported a continuing positive change in the relationship.

The study we just reviewed illustrates an experimental method known as an **ABA research design** (Krasner, 1971). In this research design, one measures behavior at one point in time (the "A" time period), introduces a reinforcer and measures behavior again at a second point in time (the "B" period), and then one takes away the reinforcer to see if the behavior returns to its original level (one returns to the "A" state of affairs). Instead of assigning groups of people to different experimental conditions, then, the Skinnerian studies a given individual at multiple time points in the presence or absence of a given reinforcer. Skinner believed that this was a more powerful method of research than are the typical experimental strategies used in psychology.

One last important point about behavioral assessment is that it illustrates the distinction between a **sign** and a **sample approach** to assessment (Mischel, 1968, 1971). In a **sign approach**, a given test response is seen as an indicator of (i.e., a "sign" of) some inner characteristic possessed by the individual. For example, if the person says, "I like parties!" a trait theorist implicitly embracing a sign approach might say that the response indicates that the person has a particular inner characteristic, such as the trait of extraversion. In a sign approach, then, the question one asks is, "What inner characteristic is the response a sign of?" This is not the question behaviorists ask. Behaviorists adopt a sample approach. When assessing a person who emits a certain response (does something, says something, etc.), the behaviorists view the response merely as a sample of behavior, that is, as one example of the sort of behavior the person engages in when faced with a particular stimulus. If the person says, "I like parties!" then the behaviorist will merely conclude that saying "I like parties!" is a behavior that, in the past, has been reinforced for this individual. There will be no additional inferences about unseen psychological structures in the mind of the individual. This approach may seem superficial. Yet it has big advantages. It stops the psychologist from engaging in highly speculative inferences about a person's inner mental life—inferences that may be little more than guesses. It also helps to identify reinforcers in the environment that, in principle, could be changed in a manner that helps a given individual.

Behavior Change

Behaviorists developed an applied technique for using reinforcement principles in real-world settings. This technique is known as a **token economy** (Ayllon & Azrin, 1965). A behavioral technician rewards, with tokens, behaviors that are considered desirable. The tokens, in turn, can be exchanged by the patient for desirable products, such as candy and cigarettes. For example, hospitalized psychiatric patients may receive reinforcing tokens for activities such as serving meals or cleaning floors. In a tightly controlled environment, such as a state hospital for long-term psychiatric patients, it is feasible to make almost anything that a patient wants contingent on the desired behaviors.

Research evidence supports the effectiveness of token economies. They are effective in increasing behaviors such as social interaction, self-care, and job performance in severely disturbed patients and mentally retarded individuals. They also have been used to decrease aggressive behavior in children and to lessen marital discord (Kazdin, 1977).

Token economy programs represent a very straightforward application of operant conditioning principles to the problem of behavior change. Target behaviors are selected, and reinforcement is made contingent on performance of the desired responses. This is completely consistent with the behavioral emphasis on how the environment acts upon people, as opposed to how people act upon the environment. The behaviorist working on human behavior change is, in essence, a social engineer. The scientific technology developed in the behavioral laboratory is applied directly to real-world problems of behavior change. Watson suggested that through control of the environment, he could train an infant to become any type of specialist he might select. Skinnerian social engineers take this principle one step further. As seen in the development of token economies, as well as in the development of communes based on Skinnerian principles, there is an interest in the design of environments that will control broad aspects of human behavior.

Free Will?

Skinner's operant behaviorism seems to have uplifting implications. By studying the influence of the environment on behavior, behaviorism gives rise to a technology of behavior change that can be usefully applied to the solution of human problems.

Yet, Skinner's behaviorism also has an implication that is disturbing. It is one that Skinner was quite aware of and that he explained in detail in a book titled *Beyond Freedom and Dignity* (Skinner, 1971). The implication is that people do not have free will. If the environment is the cause of our action, then we ourselves cannot be the cause of our behavior. And if we ourselves are not the cause of our behavior, then we do not truly have freedom to act. We do not make free choices. We do not have free will.

Skinner was quite aware that people believe that they have free will. But he concluded that this belief is an illusion. To illustrate how this could be, consider the following circumstances. Suppose that you are speeding down a highway in your red sports car; when you see a police car ahead, you slow down to avoid a ticket. If a passenger asks you, "Why did you slow down?" you are not likely to say, "Because I have free will and decided to." Instead, you will recognize that the environment caused your behavior. The presence of the police officer was an environmental cause of your slowing down. Now, suppose a passenger asks, "Why did you buy a red sports car?" Here, you are not likely to cite environmental causes. Instead, you are likely to say, "Because I decided to" or "Because I like red sports cars." You feel you had free will regarding your car purchase. But here is where Skinner says you are wrong. In Skinner's behaviorism, your behavior of slowing down and your behavior of buying a red sports car are both caused by the environment. But in the former case, the environment is simple, immediate, and obvious. You cannot miss the fact that the police officer is the cause of your slowing down. In the latter case, the environmental causes are complex and extend over a long period of time. Dozens of previous experiences (previous reinforcements and punishments) might have contributed to your behavior of buying a red sports car. It is impossible for you to remember all of them and assess their effects on your decision. But that does not mean that they were not there. In these cases, in which the environmental causes of behavior are complex, people essentially lose track of the multifaceted environmental causes and erroneously conclude that their behavior was caused by a single factor: themselves. Skinner concluded that people live with an illusion of free will—a conclusion similar to that reached by some contemporary research psychologists (Wegner, 2003).

Skinner did not argue against the notion of free will merely to disturb people. Quite the opposite: He felt that the solution of personal and social problems required a systematic application of behavioristic technology. Furthermore, he felt that people would not accept this technology if they thought that it infringed on their free will. Skinner recognized that people do not like to think that their behavior is being controlled and therefore that they would argue against an application of behavioral technology. But Skinner turned this argument on its head by contending that behavior is always controlled by the environment. Recognizing this fact and rejecting traditional notions of free will would, Skinner argued, open the door to a humane application of behavioral technology.

Before leaving this topic, we caution that many scholars have rejected Skinner's arguments about free will. Phenomenological theorists felt that Skinner's view underestimated the human being's inherent capacities; indeed, Rogers (1956) debated Skinner on the topic. More recent personality theorists (see Chapters 12 and 13) similarly contend that Skinner underestimated people's capacity to exert free will by failing to consider people's ability to think in a creative manner about the environment they face and how that environment can be changed.

Critical Evaluation

The behavioral perspective we have just reviewed contrasts starkly with the personality theories in previous chapters. The contrast is seen most clearly by considering what the behaviorist would say about those theories. Psychoanalysis would be seen as utterly nonscientific because it speculates about unseen internal variables that cannot be observed and measured. Phenomenological theory would be seen as a soft-headed view that falls into the trap of viewing people as the causes of their own behavior, rather than recognizing that the true cause is the environment. Trait theory would be just as bad in the behaviorist's eyes; it would be seen as dealing merely with superficial descriptions of behavior rather than with their causes. If behaviorism had been fully successful, all these other theories would have been swept aside.

But it was not successful. The theories reviewed in the previous chapters remain intellectually viable today. They fuel much basic and applied activity in contemporary personality science. Behaviorism, in contrast, has far fewer adherents today than in decades past. This is true despite the solid scientific contributions of Pavlov, Skinner, and their followers and despite the successful applications to which this basic research gave rise. This overall state of affairs prompts one to evaluate the strengths and the limits of the behavioral approach.

Scientific Observation: The Database

The behaviorists' commitment to basing theory on systematic research is a major strength of their work. Their respect for scientific methodology was beneficial on both scientific and administrative grounds. Scientifically, it contributed to an approach to persons that avoided the overly speculative qualities that were evident in previous perspectives. Administratively, the solid scientific database that behaviorists established made psychology seem more credible in the eyes of other scientists and thus contributed to the growth of the field in universities in the 20th century.

Yet in other ways, the scientific observations that formed the basis of behaviorism are limited. The limitation is obvious: The original database consisted primarily of research with animals (dogs, rats, pigeons). We humans possess psychological abilities not shared by our furry friends: the ability to use language, the ability to reason about events of the past, the ability to contemplate alternative potential outcomes in the future. These capacities are not represented in a database consisting of research with animals and, as a result, are not well represented in the behaviorists' theorizing. This is a major cause of the downfall of behaviorism in the last third of the 20th century.

Behaviorism lost influence in psychology primarily because it overlooked phenomena that are fundamental to human life. Perhaps the main phenomenon is the one that was so central to the phenomenological approaches, meaning that is, the question of how people assign subjective meaning to environmental events. In their research, the behaviorists skipped this question. Rats and pigeons in Skinner boxes simply do not engage in processes of meaning construction. They don't ask themselves questions such as "Hey, why is the guy in the lab coat over there giving me all this food just for pressing a lever?" But people ask themselves such questions all the time. Behavioristic theory and research simply provided little insight into the psychological processes involved in the construction of subjective meaning. Beginning in the 1960s, however, experimental psychologists working *outside of* the framework of behaviorism began making progress in the study of memory, language, emotions, belief systems—topics that informed the study of internal cognitive processes involved in the construction of meaning. There soon arose what came to be known as the cognitive revolution, the impact of which will be seen in the next three chapters.

Theory: Systematic?

Whatever the limits of behaviorism, the behaviorists were very systematic theorists. Pavlov and Skinner constructed careful, logically coherent accounts of classical and operant conditioning. Different phenomena—the rate with which an organism performs a response in response to reinforcement, the initial learning of that response, the persistence of the response if reinforcement ceases—are all explained through a single, coherent conceptual system.

In some ways, obtaining a theory whose parts are related systematically was easier for the behaviorists. This is because they have less theory; that is, theirs is an approach in which there is less theorizing about inner mental structures and processes than one finds in other theoretical accounts. The behaviorist thus does not face the task of relating numerous theoretical constructs to one another.

Theory: Testable?

Did the behaviorists provide a theory that is testable? If one asks about the behavior of animals in laboratory settings, the answer is yes. One can directly test predictions about the influence of classical and operant conditioning experiences on the emotional and behavioral responses of the organism in controlled laboratory settings. Within these settings, the behaviorists' ideas are as testable as are ideas one might find in the biological or physical sciences.

But what if one leaves the lab and enters the complex world of everyday human life? Here, behavioristic analyses sometimes become ambiguous. Consider an example suggested by Chomsky (1959) in a deservedly famous critique of Skinner's behaviorism. Suppose you are in an art museum gazing at a complex artistic composition. Skinner would say that your reactions to the piece are determined by your past history of operant and classical conditioning when exposed to similar stimuli. If you say, "I like it," that is because, in the past, similar stimuli have been positively reinforcing; they have caused the feelings we call "liking" and reinforced the behavior of saying, "I like it". How would you test this idea? Testing it presents a huge problem because, in the practical case presented here, it is hard to know what "stimuli" the person was responding to when saying "I like it". The composition of the painting? Its color? The originality of the artist? The picture frame? In a Skinner box, one can be confident in knowing the stimuli that control behavior because there are so few stimuli. But in the everyday world, it commonly is impossible to know what people are responding to in the first place. One might be able to find this out by asking the person after the fact; after they act, you could ask them what they were responding to. But if one has to ask people, after the fact, then there is no way to predict their behavior. One can only tell an after-the-fact behavioristic story. And if one only is providing after-the-fact stories, then one's theory is not testable.

Theory: Comprehensive?

Thanks in large part to the brilliant creativity of Skinner's writing, behaviorism is highly comprehensive. In just one of his books (Skinner, 1953), Skinner manages to extend behavioral principles to an analysis not only of individual behavior but also of group behavior, the functioning of government, and the rule of law, religion, psychotherapy, economics, education, and culture. In another volume (Skinner, 1974), he analyzes perception, language, emotion and motivation, and self-concept. Skinner and other behaviorists consider the full range of psychological and social phenomena that are to be addressed in a personality theory. Whatever the shortcomings of behaviorism, it does consider an exceptionally wide range of individual and social phenomena.

Learning Approaches at a Glance					
Structure	**Process**	**Growth and Development**	**Pathology**	**Change**	**Illustrative Case**
Response	Classical conditioning; operant conditioning	Schedules of reinforcement and successive approximations	Maladaptive learned response patterns	Extinction, discrimination earning, counterconditioning, positive reinforcement, systematic desensitization, behavior modification	Reinterpretation of Little Hans

Applications

The behaviorists displayed a valuable pragmatic bent. They moved quickly from research in laboratories with animals to practical applications designed to help people. Maybe they moved too quickly; however, behaviorists were not as careful as they should have been to raise the question of how the psychology of people may differ from the psychology of animals in Skinner boxes and classical conditioning studies. Nonetheless, behaviorists succeeded in developing practical applications that remain of value to psychology today. Indeed, they developed more valuable applications than did most theorists whose work today is more influential in personality psychology. In particular, the growth of behavior therapy is an application of immense practical value.

Major Contributions and Summary

The contributions of behaviorism are enormous (Table 10.2). The behaviorists showed how a comprehensive psychology could be built on an objective database of highly replicable research. They developed numerous applications that continue to be of practical benefit. They also valuably drew psychologists' attention to the impact of situational factors on behavior. By studying patients in their offices or asking people to fill out questionnaires in laboratories, the theorists whose work we covered previously removed individuals from the normal, everyday environments of their daily lives. The behaviorists explained that, to understand people's behavior, one must understand the environmental factors that are the behavior's cause.

Table 10.2 Summary of Strengths and Limitations of Learning Approaches

Strengths	Limitations
1. Committed to systematic research and theory development	1. Oversimplifies personality and neglects important phenomena
2. Recognizes the role of situational and environmental variables in influencing behavior	2. Lacks a single, unified theory
3. Takes a pragmatic approach to treatment, which can lead to important new developments	3. Requires further evidence to support claims of treatment effectiveness

BEHAVIORISM AND THE LEARNING APPROACHES TO PERSONALITY

A final contribution of behaviorism is indirect. The behaviorists provided clear and forceful statements about human nature that other, subsequent theorists thought were deeply wrong. The behaviorists, then, stimulated the thinking of most of the theorists discussed in the remaining chapters of this book. Each of these theorists was intimately familiar with the behaviorists' claims and was skeptical about those claims. This skepticism motivated them to provide alternative approaches to the study of personality, as you will see in the chapters ahead.

MAJOR CONCEPTS

ABA research design	Determinism	Operant conditioning	Situational specificity
ABC assessment	Discrimination	Operants	Successive
Behavioral assessment	Extinction	Punishments	approximations
Behaviorism	Fixed	Reinforcer	Systematic desensitization
Classical conditioning	Functional analysis	Sample approach	Target behaviors or target
Conditioned emotional	Generalization	Schedule of reinforcement	responses
reaction	Generalized reinforcers	Shaping	Token economy
Counterconditioning	Maladaptive response	Sign approach	Variable

REVIEW

1. The school of thought known as behaviorism promoted a learning approach to personality. The learning approach suggests that the patterns of social behavior that we see as indications of an individual's personality are learned through environmental experience.

2. Pavlov's work on classical conditioning, combined with Watson's extension of this work to humans in the case of Little Albert, provided the first foundation for a behavioral approach to the study of persons.

3. B. F. Skinner provided a second foundation for behaviorism in his work on operant conditioning. Skinner and his colleagues developed a highly systematic database showing how reinforcements determine the behavior of animals in Skinner boxes.

4. Skinner explained how principles of learning were relevant to questions of profound importance, including the question of whether people have free will.

5. Behaviorists did not merely conduct laboratory research with animals. They developed many useful applications of the principles of learning. These include clinical applications in which the goal of the clinician is to provide new environmental experiences through which the client can learn new, more adaptive forms of behavior. Systematic desensitization and token economy programs are two examples of the application of behavioral principles.

6. Behaviorism dominated psychology in the mid-20th century, but then its influence waned. This largely is because behaviorism failed to provide convincing research-based explanations for uniquely human phenomena, such as people's inherent tendency to assign subjective meaning to events. The growth of cognitive psychology, a foundation for theories discussed later in this book, caused the downfall of behaviorism.

☐ Behaviorism's Account of Mental Illness = individuals do not respond to stimuli appropriately. They fail to learn a response or learn a maladaptive response. Therapy is not to analyze conflicts; Goal is to provide new learning experiences for the client.

A Cognitive Theory: George A. Kelly's Personal Construct Theory of Personality

11

Chapter Focus

You've just finished a novel that you thoroughly enjoyed. Excitedly, you call a friend to recommend the book, telling him about the exquisitely detailed descriptions of the characters and the settings. To your dismay, your friend informs you that he has already read the book—and hated it! "Thin plot, slow moving," he complains. How could this be? Your "environment" (the book) was the same, yet you had utterly different experiences. You had completely different thoughts about exactly the same environmental stimulus.

This is what George Kelly's personal construct theory is all about: how each individual uniquely perceives, interprets, and conceptualizes the world. Just as you and your friend differed in your reading of the book, people differ in the way they "read" the persons and events of social life. To Kelly, these differences are at the heart of personality functioning. Our thoughts, emotional reactions, moods, goals, behavioral tendencies—virtually everything of interest to the personality psychologist—are, to Kelly, a product of our interpretations of the world. Individual differences in emotion and action, then, derive from individual differences in these interpretations. These ideas were the foundation of a cognitive theory of personality, a method of personality assessment, and an approach to therapy that were developed by one of the most innovative and impactful figures in the history of personality psychology: George Kelly.

Questions to be Addressed in this Chapter

1. What is the goal of the personality scientist when he or she constructs a theory?

2. In what ways are your thoughts, in your daily life, similar to the mental activities of the psychological scientist? What did Kelly mean by suggesting that people are like scientists (his **"person-as-scientist"** metaphor)?

3. How can one learn about people's beliefs and individual differences in belief systems?

4. How can an analysis of personal constructs explain psychological distress and inform the practice of psychotherapy?

In earlier chapters, you learned about two theories of personality that originated in clinical work: Freud's psychoanalysis and Rogers's phenomenological theory. This chapter considers a third theory that developed primarily out of contact with clients in therapy. Work as a therapist naturally directs one's attention to the "whole person". In other words, rather than focusing on one psychological variable or another, the therapist must confront whole, complex, intact individuals who experience multiple goals and feelings that cohere in meaningful ways. Like the clinician/theorists Freud and Rogers, George Kelly aimed to understand the whole individual.

Although Kelly shared these characteristics with Freud and Rogers, Kelly's overall theory differs from theirs. Freud emphasized animalistic forces in the unconscious. Kelly highlights the uniquely human capacity to reflect on oneself, the world, and the future. With regard to Rogers, Kelly's and Rogers's contributions are similar in some respects (see Epting & Eliot, 2006); both of them were concerned with creating a theory of the whole, coherent person. But Kelly, in his personal construct theory of personality, explored in much greater detail the specific cognitive processes through which individuals categorize people and things and construct meaning out of the events of their day.

Why is Kelly's work called a "personal construct" theory? Kelly used the word *construct* to refer to ideas or categories that people use to interpret their world. Some of these categories are universal. For example, if you and a friend both stare out the window during a boring moment in your professor's lectures and spot a 20-foot-tall green and brown leafy object, you probably will both categorize it as "a tree". We all have in our mind the category "tree," and we all apply this category to 20-foot-tall green and brown leafy objects. But some categories vary from person to person. People differ in whether they possess the given category and in where they use it.

Suppose that your professor sees you and your friend staring out the window at the tree, stops the lecture, and asks you both to start paying attention to class. You may categorize the professor as an "attentive teacher," whereas your friend may see her as a "condescending intellectual". In the language of Kelly's personal construct theory, you two will have used different personal constructs ("attentive teacher," "condescending intellectual") to interpret your professor's behavior. The use of these constructs would have great implications for your subsequent thoughts and feelings. You may admire the professor for her attention, whereas your friend may feel insulted by her condescension. To Kelly, an individual's personality can be understood in terms of the collection of personal constructs or the personal construct system that he or she uses to interpret the world.

In this text, we label Kelly's work a *cognitive* theory, a term that derives from the Latin verb that means "to know" and that, in contemporary psychology, generally refers to thinking processes. A cognitive theory of personality, then, is a theory that places the analysis of human thinking processes at the center point of the analysis of personality and individual differences. Kelly himself did not use the term *cognitive* to describe his theory, thinking it was too restrictive and that it suggested an artificial division between cognition (thinking) and affect (feeling). However, "cognitive" remains the most popular classification of Kelly's theory, and for good reason (Neimeyer, 1992; Winter, 1992). The constructs that people possess comprise their knowledge of the world, and these constructs are used in the acquisition of new knowledge. People apply their constructs to the interpretation of daily events through mental procedures that generally are termed *cognitive processes*; these include categorizing people and things, attributing meaning to events, and predicting events.

Kelly's major work in personality theory was published in 1955. Its immediate impact was not that large, for a number of reasons. In 1955, Kelly's emphasis on complex human cognitive processes was ahead of its time. Behaviorism, which eschewed study of subjective mental events, dominated academic psychology. Contemporary cognitive psychology, which directly addressed human thinking, had not yet developed. Furthermore, Kelly may have "shot himself in the foot" when it came to the question of quick, widespread acceptance of his theory. He employed an entirely novel, complex scientific terminology when presenting his work. "By adopting unfamiliar terminology," a recent reviewer writes, "it seems, in hindsight, that Kelly further alienated his theory from mainstream psychology" (Butler, 2009, p. 3).

Kelly's work, then, anticipated subsequent developments in the field. Throughout the last quarter of the 20th century—that is, years after Kelly's death—psychologists increasingly interpreted human behavior in terms of cognitive processes through which people interpret and understand their world. Here in the second decade of the 21st century, the study of future oriented thinking—the central phenomenon highlighted by Kelly—is attracting substantial new attention in cognitive science (Michaelian, Klein, & Szpunar, 2016). A supporter of personal construct theory has noted that "Kelly's theory enjoys the irony of becoming increasingly contemporary with age" (Neimeyer, 1992, p. 995). A more recent review suggests that not only was Kelly ahead of his time but also that his theory has opened new areas of research in a way that he would have welcomed (Walker & Winter, 2007).

Kelly provided not only an academic theory but also an approach to life. He challenged people—both the people he saw in therapy and the people who were his contemporaries in psychology—to think in new terms, to view the world in new ways, to try on new constructs. He similarly would invite and challenge you, the student, to "try on" the novel ideas of personal construct theory.

George A. Kelly (1905–1966): A View of the Theorist

The nature of George Kelly, the person, comes through in his writing. He appears to have been the kind of person he encouraged others to be—an adventuresome soul who is unafraid to think unorthodox thoughts and who dares to explore the unknown.

Kelly's philosophical and theoretical positions stem, in part, from the diversity of his experience (Sechrest, 1963). Kelly grew up in Kansas and obtained his undergraduate education there at Friends University and at Park College in Missouri. He pursued graduate studies at the University of Kansas, the University of Minnesota, and the University of Edinburgh and received his Ph.D from the State University of Iowa in 1931. He developed a traveling clinic in Kansas, was

Science Source.

George A. Kelly.

an aviation psychologist during World War II, and was a professor of psychology at Ohio State University and Brandeis University.

Kelly's early clinical experience was in the public schools of Kansas. He found that when teachers referred pupils to his traveling psychological clinic, their complaints appeared to say something about not only the pupils but also the teachers themselves. Kelly tried to understand the teachers' reports as an expression of their construction or interpretation of events. For example, if a teacher complained that a student was lazy, Kelly did not look at the pupil to see if the teacher was correct in the diagnosis; rather, he tried to understand the behaviors of the child and the way the teacher perceived these behaviors, that is, the teacher's construction of them that led to the complaint of laziness.

This was a significant reformulation of the problem. In practical terms, it led to an analysis of the teachers as well as the pupils and to a wider range of solutions to the problems. Furthermore, it led Kelly to the view that there is no objective, absolute truth—phenomena are meaningful only in relation to the ways in which they are construed or interpreted by the individual.

Kelly gradually came to reject "black or white" solutions to complex psychological problems. He instead preferred a more subtle and complex approach. His goal was to test interpretations of events, to reconstrue or reinterpret phenomena, and thereby to challenge traditional concepts of objective reality. He felt free to play in the world of make-believe, encouraging people to imagine alternative realities. He challenged the theorizing of others yet viewed his own theory as only a tentative formulation that eventually would be replaced. Kelly accepted the frustration and challenge, the threat and joy, of exploring the unknown.

Like all persons, Kelly can be viewed as a product of his times and his culture. He lived in an early/mid-20th-century Midwestern America that valued practical solutions to practical problems more than it valued esoteric theorizing about abstract metaphysical concerns. This was an America whose intellectual life was shaped by pragmatism, a philosophical school teaching that ideas should be evaluated on practical grounds, by asking how embracing the ideas would affect individuals and society in the long run (Menand, 2002). Kelly viewed his own theory as a construction—a kind of tool that had value if it achieved a practical goal, namely, the goal of enabling people to improve their lives by thinking in new ways about their problems and themselves.

Kelly's View of the Science of Personality

In previous chapters, we introduced personality theories by reviewing, in order, the given theorist's (1) view of the person and (2) view of the science of personality. Here, when presenting the work of Kelly, we reverse that order. Why? To Kelly himself, questions about science come first. This is for two reasons: (1) To a greater extent than other theorists, Kelly based his theory of persons on an explicit view of science and the nature of scientific inquiry. (2) Unlike other theorists, he used the contemporary notion of scientific inquiry as a metaphor for understanding the psychological activities of the everyday person (as we review in the next section). To best understand Kelly's theory, then, it is best to learn about his view of science and then his view of persons.

In developing a view of science, the fundamental question Kelly raised is, "What are scientists doing when they are constructing theories?" One view is that the scientist is searching for truth. Maybe there is a "true" theory out there, and armed with the methods of the sciences, the diligent scientist can find it. This conception implies that all theories can be evaluated as being true or false. A different view, adopted by Kelly (and many contemporary scientists and philosophers of science, e.g., Proctor & Capaldi, 2001), is that "true versus false" is not the right question to ask about a scientific theory. The problem is that any complex and well-formulated theory is likely to seem true in some respects but not others. An alternative question to ask, then, is whether and how a theory is useful. Does the theory enable one to do some useful things that one could not do without the theory? This question does raise another one: How does one evaluate a theory's usefulness? Kelly reasoned that scientists often are interested in predicting events; they find it useful to be able to predict how events will turn out. This reasoning converts questions about utility into questions about prediction: What important events can one predict using a given theory?

The simple idea of evaluating a theory according to its usefulness for making predictions has a significant implication. Different theories may enable one to make different types of predictions. Thus, every different theory may be uniquely useful. This implies that one does not need to choose between theories, accepting one as right and seeing the others as wrong. Instead, it may be valuable to see the world through the lens of different theories, each of which may enable one to see something interesting. Kelly called this idea **constructive alternativism**: Alternative scientific constructs each may provide a useful view of the world. According to this position, scientific theorizing does not involve the pursuit of a singular theory that is objectively "correct". Instead, scientists attempt to *construe* events—to interpret phenomena in order to make sense of them. Rather than there being a single correct theory, there are always alternative scientific constructions available from which to choose, each of which may be valuable for some purposes. (Kelly's argument should remind you of the toolkit metaphor introduced in Chapter 1.)

In Kelly's view, then, the enterprise of personality science is not concerned with the discovery of truth or, as Freud might have suggested, the uncovering of things in the mind previously hidden. Rather, it is an effort to develop scientific construct systems that are useful in predicting events. Different personality theories each may make unique and valid predictions about persons.

Kelly developed these ideas in part because he was concerned about the tendency toward dogma in psychology. He thought psychologists believed that constructs of inner states and traits actually existed rather than understanding them as "things" in a theoretician's head. If someone is described as an introvert, we tend to check to see whether he is an introvert, rather than checking the person who is responsible for the statement. Kelly's position against "truth" and dogma is of considerable significance. It allows one to establish an "invitational mood" in which one is free to invite many alternative interpretations of phenomena and to entertain propositions that initially may seem absurd. The invitational mood is a necessary part of the exploration of the world, for the professional scientist as well as for the patient in therapy.

According to Kelly, it is this invitational mood that allows one the freedom to develop creative hypotheses. A hypothesis should not be asserted as a fact but, instead, should allow the scientist to pursue its implications as if it were true. Kelly viewed a theory as a tentative expression of what has been observed and of what is expected. A theory has a **range of convenience**, indicating the boundaries of phenomena the theory can cover, and a **focus of convenience**, indicating the points within the boundaries where the theory works best. Different theories have different ranges and different foci of convenience.

For Kelly, theories were modifiable and ultimately expendable. A theory is modified or discarded when it stops leading to new predictions or leads to incorrect predictions. Among scientists, as well as among people in general, how long one holds on to a theory in the face of contradictory information is partly a matter of taste and style.

Kelly's view of science is not unique, yet its clarity of expression and points of emphasis remain important. In addition to highlighting the utility of a theory (rather than its truth versus falsity), Kelly also questioned other traditional assumptions. These include psychologists' extreme emphasis on measurement. In Kelly's time and today as well, much work in personality psychology is devoted to the precise measure of individual differences in one versus another psychological construct. Kelly felt that this emphasis on measurement leads personality theorists erroneously to view theoretical concepts as if they are real things in people's heads. The psychologist inadvertently becomes a technician whose primary expertise is in statistics, rather than a scientist whose primary expertise is in the study of the human mind. A third feature of Kelly's view of science is that it leaves room for clinical as opposed to purely experimental methods. He considered the clinical method useful because it speaks the language of hypothesis, because it leads to the emergence of new variables, and because it focuses on important questions. Here, we have a fourth significant aspect of Kelly's view of science: It should focus on important issues. Kelly felt that psychologists often feared doing anything that might not be recognized as science. This fear caused them to avoid studying important aspects of human experience that are difficult to test scientifically. Kelly urged that psychologists stop trying to look scientific and get on with the job of understanding people. He believed that a good scientific theory should encourage the invention of new approaches to the solution of the problems of people and society.

Kelly's View of the Person

Kelly's view of science connects directly to his view of persons. Kelly felt that scientists and laypersons (i.e., nonscientists in their everyday life) are engaged in the same task. They both use constructs to predict events. The scientists' constructs surely may differ from those of the layperson; they may be stated in a more precise manner and (depending on the science) may involve mathematical concepts rather than words. Yet the scientists' and laypersons' tasks are fundamentally similar. Both try to develop ideas (i.e., constructs) that enable them to predict events. The personality scientist may have a formal theory that enables her to make some types of predictions (e.g., a trait theorist might be able to predict your scores on personality traits five years from now based on your scores today). But your wise grandmother may have an informal, nonscientific theory that enables her to make a different set of predictions (e.g., whether one versus another type of discussion will cheer you up if you're having a down day). In both cases, the person is using accumulated knowledge to make predictions.

This reasoning underlies a metaphor that is central to Kelly's view of persons. It is the **person-as-scientist** metaphor. To Kelly, the central features of everyday life involve our attempts to develop ideas that enable us to predict significant events in our daily life. We want to be able to predict whether we will, for example, pass an upcoming exam, succeed in getting a date, or get out of a state of depression. We also want to predict which types of experiences might help us to achieve these goals. In making these predictions, Kelly argues, we operate as scientists. Like scientists, we develop theories ("Maybe I'm the sort of person who needs to work with friends when studying for exams"), we test hypotheses ("This time I'll try a different strategy of asking for a date and see what happens"), and we weigh evidence ("Last time I tried to relieve my depression by eating a lot of desserts, but that didn't work").

The person-as-scientist view has two further consequences. First, it highlights the fact that people are essentially oriented toward the future. "It is the future which tantalizes man, not the past. Always he reaches out to the future through the window of the present" (Kelly, 1955, p. 49). Much of human thinking indeed is directed toward future events. Of the personality theories we have discussed so far, Kelly's is the one that most directly confronts this basic fact of mental life.

The second consequence is this: If scientists can usefully adopt different theories to make different types of predictions, then so can laypersons. Just as there can be constructive alternativism in the domain of scientific constructs discussed previously, there can be constructive alternativism in the domain of personal constructs. People have the capacity to think constructively about the environment—to rethink their usual ways of construing the world. The individual can develop alternative theoretical formulations, can try on different constructs, and in so doing can devise novel strategies for dealing with the challenges and conflicts of life.

This view of people's capacity to think constructively about the world yields a new understanding of an issue discussed in the previous chapter of this book, namely, free will and determinism. To behaviorists such as Skinner, people merely responded to the environment. They thus were controlled by environmental forces and lacked free will. To Kelly, however, people do not respond passively to the environment. They think actively about it. Furthermore, they think actively about their own thinking processes. People can decide that they have not thought properly about something and can think about it differently. These thinking capacities make human beings both free and determined. "This personal construct system provides him [humankind] with both freedom of decision and limitations of action—freedom, because it permits him to deal with the meaning of events rather than forces him to be helplessly pushed about by them, and limitation, because he can never make choices outside the world of alternatives he has erected for himself" (Kelly, 1955, p. 58). Having "enslaved" ourselves with these constructions, we are able to win freedom again and again by reconstruing the environment and life. Thus, we are not victims of past history or of present circumstances unless we choose to construe ourselves in that way.[1]

These points are the general principles upon which Kelly built a theory of personality structures and processes. We now turn to the details of that theory.

The Personality Theory of George A. Kelly

Structure

The key structural variable in Kelly's theory of personality is the personal construct. A **construct** is an element of knowledge. It is a concept used to interpret, or construe, the world. People use constructs to categorize events. This is not something you necessarily do consciously; people do not say to themselves, "Um, I think I will use a construct now." It is something that happens automatically. When experiencing events, you try to make sense of them, and to make sense of them, you have to use some element of knowledge that you already possess. In Kelly's language, you use a personal construct.

The core idea of Kelly's theory is that a person anticipates events by observing patterns and regularities. People notice that some events share characteristics that distinguish them from other events. Individuals distinguish similarities and contrasts. They observe that some people are tall and some are short, that some are men and some are women, that some things are hard and some are soft. It is this construing of a similarity and a contrast that leads to the formation of a construct. Without constructs, life would be chaotic; we wouldn't be able to organize our world, to describe and classify events, objects, and people.

---

[1] Kelly's references to "man the scientist" and "man the biological organism" may strike students as sexist. It should be remembered that Kelly was writing in the 1950s, prior to efforts to remove sexism from language.

According to Kelly, at least three elements are necessary to form a construct: Two of the elements must be perceived as similar to each other, and the third element must be perceived as different from these two. The way in which two elements are construed to be similar forms the **similarity pole** of the construct; the way in which they are contrasted with the third element forms the **contrast pole** of the construct. For example, observing two people helping someone and a third hurting someone could lead to the construct kind/cruel, with kind forming the similarity pole and cruel the contrast pole. Kelly stressed the importance of recognizing that a construct is composed of a similarity/contrast comparison. This suggests that we do not understand the nature of a construct when it uses only the similarity pole or the contrast pole. We do not know what the construct respect means to a person until we know what events the person includes under this construct and what events are viewed as being opposed to it.

A construct is not dimensional in the sense of having many points between the similarity and contrast poles. Subtleties or refinements in construction of events are made through the use of other constructs, such as constructs of quantity and quality. For example, the construct black/white in combination with a quantity construct leads to the four-scale value of black, slightly black, slightly white, and white (Sechrest, 1963).

As we already noted, Kelly recognizes that human thinking is future oriented; we spend much of our time thinking about, and planning for, future events. This thinking also involves the use of personality constructs. People use constructs, then, not only to interpret events that have occurred to them but also to plan for future occurrences. As we explain in our coverage of the process aspects of Kelly's theory (discussed subsequently), the idea that people use constructs to anticipate events is the fundamental postulate of Kelly's theory.

Image Source / Getty Images

"My idea is fun, yours is boring." "No, my idea is safe, yours is dangerous." Kelly's personal construct theory explains that differences—and sometimes arguments—between people result from the use of different constructs (e.g., boring–fun, dangerous–safe).

Constructs and Their Interpersonal Consequences

It is fascinating to observe the diversity of constructs that individuals use. If you watch television and turn on a program with religious content, a speaker may describe people as moral versus immoral. If you turn on a political program, a speaker may describe people as liberal versus conservative. On a sports program, commentators may say that a person is a "clutch" player versus someone who "chokes". These bipolar ideas (moral/immoral, liberal/conservative, clutch/chokes) are examples of what Kelly called personal constructs.

Who are we learning about when we hear someone use constructs of this sort? Are we learning merely about the persons being described? Or are we learning also about the speakers—the people providing the descriptions? Kelly contends that people reveal aspects of their own personality in the constructs they use to describe others: "One cannot call another person a bastard without making bastardy a dimension of his own life also" (Kelly, 1955, p. 133).

Differences in construct systems have important interpersonal consequences. They often contribute to failures in communications between groups. You may find yourself in conversation with someone who uses constructs that conflict with yours. A friend of one of the authors once said, "Isn't there a winner and a loser in every relationship?" Well, maybe not; the friend seemed unaware that "winner/loser" is only a possible, not a necessary, construct. Another person might have used the construct compromising/uncompromising person or the compassionate/uncompassionate person.

Difficulties in communication could also result when groups who see themselves as being in opposition to one another fail to recognize that they actually have many constructs in common. Becoming aware of the commonalities in construct systems could benefit communication. Simpson, Large, and O'Brien (2004) recently used ideas from Kelly's theory to show how communication between two such groups can be improved. They worked with two groups of professionals who, they report, often experience tensions and failures to communicate in a particular professional setting, namely, a hospital. The two groups were (1) clinical health professionals who were responsible for patient care and (2) hospital managers who were responsible for the hospital's business operations and whose background often was outside of health care. Within a workshop to improve communication between the groups, Simpson and colleagues asked the clinicians and managers to enumerate the characteristics that they say was ideal for a clinician and for a manager. The idea was to make explicit the personal constructs that people held regarding an ideal professional of both types (clinician and manager). The groups then observed each other's personal construct lists. "What was . . . surprising to them," Simpson et al. (2004, p. 55) report, "was the areas of commonality between the two groups". The previously opposed groups learned that they held many constructs in common. This facilitated subsequent discussions between them.

Types of Constructs and the Construct System

People often express their personal constructs in words. Kelly refers to constructs that can be expressed in words as "verbal" constructs. Not all constructs have this quality, however. Kelly distinguished between two different types of constructs: **verbal** and **preverbal**. A **verbal construct** can be expressed in words, whereas a **preverbal construct** is one that is used even though the person has no words to express it. A preverbal construct is learned before the person develops the use of language. Kelly suggested that the verbal/preverbal distinction captures some phenomena that Freudians would call conscious versus unconscious.

Sometimes, one end of a bipolar construct is not available for verbalization; it is characterized as being **submerged**. If a person insists that people do only good things, one assumes that the other end of the construct has been submerged since the person must have been aware of contrasting behaviors to have formed the "good" end of the construct. Thus, constructs may not be available for verbalization, and the individual may not be able to report all the elements that are in the construct. In spite of the recognized importance of preverbal and **submerged constructs**, ways of studying them have not been highly developed by personal construct psychologists.

In addition to distinguishing between types of constructs (verbal and preverbal), another important aspect of Kelly's theoretical system concerns people's overall collection of constructs. The constructs people use are believed to be organized as part of a system. In the personal construct system, constructs differ in terms of the circumstances to which they apply. Each construct within the system has a range of convenience and a focus of convenience. A construct's range of convenience comprises all those events for which the user would find application of the construct useful. A construct's focus of convenience comprises the particular events for which application of the construct would be maximally useful. For example, the construct caring/uncaring, which might apply to people in all situations where help is given (range of convenience), would be particularly applicable in situations where special sensitivity and effort are required (focus of convenience).

In addition, some constructs are more central to the person's construct system than are others. There are **core constructs** that are basic to a person's functioning and that can be changed only with great consequences for the rest of the construct system. In contrast, **peripheral constructs** are much less basic and can be altered without serious modification of the core structure. If you have strong beliefs about religion and weaker beliefs about art, your conception of "creative/uncreative" art may be a peripheral construct that easily can be changed, whereas your conception of "sinful/holy" acts may be a core personal construct that is virtually unchangeable.

A person's construct system is organized hierarchically. An example of a hierarchy in the animal kingdom is ANIMAL/dog/golden retriever. In a hierarchy, the broadest and most inclusive constructs are the **superordinate constructs** at the top of the hierarchy (e.g., ANIMAL). These superordinate constructs include more narrow and specific constructs, such as dog, cat, and giraffe in our example. In turn, each of these middle-level constructs includes a large number of even more narrow **subordinate constructs** (e.g., golden retriever, German shepherd, poodle, etc.). Constructs, then, differ in their breadth and inclusiveness.

It is important to recognize that the constructs within the person's construct system are interrelated. Behavior, then, expresses the construct system rather than a single construct. Change in one construct can trigger changes in other parts of the system. Although constructs generally are consistent with one another, some constructs conflict with others, which produces strain and difficulties for a person in making choices (Landfield, 1982).

To summarize, according to Kelly's theory of personal constructs, an individual's personality is made up of his or her construct system. A person uses constructs to interpret the world and to anticipate events. The constructs a person uses thus define his or her world. People naturally differ from one another in the constructs they use and in the organization among constructs in their overall system of knowledge. If you want to understand a person, you must know something about the constructs that person uses, the events subsumed under these constructs, the way in which these constructs tend to function, and the way in which they are organized in relation to one another to form a system (Adams-Webber, 1998).

Assessment: The Role Construct Repertory (Rep) Test

How does the psychologist learn about a person's construct system? How, in other words, does one go about the task of personality assessment in personal construct theory?

Kelly's first step in answering this question is to express faith in the wisdom of the person who is being assessed. "If you don't know what is going on in a person's mind, ask him; he may tell you" (1958, p. 330). Kelly placed great faith in people's ability to report on their own personality; in this way, he differed strikingly from Freud.

As part of his personal construct theory, Kelly developed his own assessment technique: the **Role Construct Repertory Test (Rep test).** Kelly's assessment procedure is very closely tied to his theory; the Rep test is perhaps the singularly best example of an assessment instrument that is directly related to the core elements of a given personality theory.

The Rep test consists of two steps: (1) the development of a list of persons about whom personality ratings will be made (the role title list) and (2) the elicitation of constructs; that is, the test taker is asked to engage in a task that will elicit his or her personal constructs. In the first step, people are asked to indicate the names of specific people who fill various roles in their life: mother, father, a teacher you liked, a neighbor you find hard to understand, and so forth. Generally, people fitting 20 to 30 roles are identified. Next comes the critical novel step in Kelly's testing procedure. The examiner picks three specific figures from the list and asks the test taker to indicate how two of these people are alike and are different from the third. For example, suppose that a test taker is given the names of persons identified in the roles of mother, father, and liked teacher. They might say that the father and the liked teacher are similar and are different from the mother. They might then say that father and liked teacher are similar in that they are "outgoing" and different from mother who is "shy". The point is *not* that one is learning about the mother, father, and teacher of the person taking the test! The point is that one is learning about *the person who is taking the test*; one learns that the person has, in his or her mind, the construct "shy/outgoing". With each presentation of a new triad, the test taker generates a construct. The construct given may be the same as a previous one or a new construct. Illustrative constructs given by one person are presented in Table 11.1.

Note how the structure of the Rep test follows directly from Kelly's theory. The theory says that constructs are used to evaluate how two entities are similar and different from others. The test directly taps this form of thinking. The theory says that people cannot be fit into any simple taxonomy of personality traits or types. The test is highly flexible; it allows people to express how they construe the world and makes no attempt to fit them into a preexisting taxonomy of personality types.

Unique Information Revealed by Personal Construct Testing

As you can tell from the preceding description, the Rep test is rather complicated. Administering and scoring the test is a more complex, time-consuming procedure than, for example, merely giving people a small set of standard personality trait tests and computing Big Five scores (see Chapter 8). Is the effort worth it? Does one actually learn unique information about the individual being tested by following the procedures suggested by Kelly? Or might it be possible to get the same information by using simpler procedures based on trait theory?

Table 11.1   Role Construct Repertory Test: Illustrative Constructs

Similar Figures	Similarity Construct	Dissimilar Figure	Contrasting Construct
Self, father	Emphasis on happiness	Mother	Emphasis on practicality
Teacher, happy person	Calm	Sister	Anxious
Male friend, female friend	Good listener	Past friend	Trouble expressing feelings
Disliked person, employer	Uses people for own ends	Liked person	Considerate of others
Father, successful person	Active in the community	Employer	Not active in the community
Disliked person, employer	Cuts others down	Sister	Respectful of others
Mother, male friend	Introvert	Past friend	Extravert
Self, teacher	Self-sufficient	Person helped	Dependent
Self, female friend	Artistic	Male friend	Uncreative
Employer, female friend	Sophisticated	Brother	Unsophisticated

This question has been examined systematically in research by Grice (2004). He administered two types of tests to a sample of research participants: (1) an idiographic grid procedure that was modeled closely after Kelly's Rep test for assessing personal constructs and (2) a nomothetic grid technique in which people made personality ratings using a fixed set of Big Five markers, rather than using the potentially unique personality descriptors that are revealed by Kelly's procedure. The question, then, is the degree to which the idiographic personal construct procedure reveals information that is unique—that is, information that is not revealed by the nomothetic Big Five procedure.

This question was addressed by statistical analyses of these two forms of personality assessment. The findings revealed that the procedures overlapped only partly. Specifically, about half of the variation in personality ratings made in personal construct testing was predictable from Big Five scores, whereas the other half was unique (Grice, 2004). Kelly's personal construct method would, then, appear to be well worth the effort. Half of the information that is learned about individuals through Kelly's test would be lost if one employed merely Big Five testing methods. As Grice (2004, p. 227) explains, "when left to their own devices" in Kelly's idiographic procedure, people commonly go "beyond personality traits (viz. the Big Five) to describe themselves and other people".

Cognitive Complexity/Simplicity

As noted, people may differ not only in the content of individual constructs they possess but also in the overall structure and organization of their construct systems. How, exactly, might people's construct systems differ? One difference involves the **cognitive complexity versus simplicity** of construct systems.

A cognitively complex construct system is one that contains many constructs that do not overlap. (If one of your constructs for thinking about people is "smart/dumb" and another is "intelligent/unintelligent," these two constructs would be said to overlap.) Greater cognitive complexity provides expertise. A person with a more complex construct system is able to identify distinctions among people and events that may be overlooked by someone with fewer constructs. If you've got a lot of constructs that pertain to symphonic music, you can distinguish among symphonies. If you don't, they all sound pretty much the same.

Research on cognitive complexity began soon after Kelly first proposed his personality theory. James Bieri (1955) hypothesized. "It appears that, unlike all previous editions, in this edition Wiley USA has suggested that we add the individual's first name; there is a "James" insertion. I would like to request that we *not* change the text, that is, that we not add the person's first name. Note: (a) We do not, in general, include people's first names unless the individual is a major theorist. Cf. top of this same page, reference to Grice. (b) Pedagogically, I'm trying to call student's attention to the ideas not the people, *except for* the special case in which the person is a major personality theorist (which is not the case for Bieri).

Bieri tested this prediction among a group of students in a college class. Students first described the personalities of others in the class via a Rep test in which they indicated a construct that made two classmates similar and different from a third. This Rep test procedure was conducted for each of a series of sets of three class members. Bieri analyzed each student's responses, gauging the complexity of the construct systems that the person displayed; someone who used a small set of constructs received a low cognitive complexity score, whereas someone who used numerous, nonoverlapping constructs received a high score. Then, separately, students completed a multiple-choice test in which they had to predict how other students in the class would behave in a variety of hypothetical social situations. (People also rated their own likely behavior in those situations, and these self-ratings were taken as the "correct" test responses.) As predicted, individual differences in cognitive complexity predicted individual differences in the accuracy of behavioral prediction: Cognitively complex students predicted others' behavior more accurately. A particular capacity display by cognitively complex students was the ability to recognize differences between themselves and others. They were less likely to mistakenly conclude that other people would respond to social situations in the same manner that they themselves would. Just

Personality and the Brain
Constructs and Expertise

Kelly's theory of personality addressed psychological questions, not biological ones. Kelly was interested in how people create meaning out of the events of their lives, and he was relatively uninterested in the biological matter that makes meaning construction possible. Nonetheless, one can derive two predictions about the brain from Kelly's work.

One prediction is simple: The brains of people with complex construct systems should differ from those with less complex systems. Since thinking relies on the brain, there must be some difference, somewhere in the brain, between people who display qualitatively different thinking abilities—cognitively complex thinking of the sort we associate with "experts" in a domain versus cognitively simple thinking displayed by "novices".

The other prediction is a little more complex. It concerns the question of how, exactly, the brains of experts and novices should differ. In Kelly's psychological theory, people are said to possess a singular construct system. When they acquire greater cognitive complexity, they do not develop a second construct system; instead, their one construct system becomes more complex. When formulating a biological prediction, then, one might expect that novice and expert thinkers would differ in the following way. They would use the same neural system—the same region of brain—to construe the world, since they both possess one construct system. But in the brains of cognitively complex experts, that region of brain (wherever it may be) would be more developed biologically; for example, it would have a greater density of brain cells.

This question can be addressed through brain-scanning methods. The general strategy is (1) to identify people who vary in cognitive complexity with regard to a topic; (2) to ask them to think about the topic, plus an unrelated topic that functions as an experimental control condition; and (3) to obtain and analyze brain images that are taken while the participants are thinking. In one study, the topic was hockey (Beilock, Lyons, Mattarella-Micke, Nusbaum, & Small, 2008). The participants included both collegiate hockey players and others who were unfamiliar with the sport. (It can be assumed that the expert hockey players had a more complex set of constructs regarding the sport of hockey than did other participants.) Researchers presented, to all participants, both hockey-related sentences (e.g., "The hockey player finished the shot") and nonhockey sentences (e.g., "The individual pushed the card"). Brain imaging revealed the regions of brain that were most active while participants thought about the sentences.

When thinking about the nonhockey sentences, all participants experienced activation in a region of the brain that is known to be active during the processing of words. And what about the hockey-related sentences? Based on Kelly's theory, you might expect that hockey players would have greater activation in this same brain region, which might be the neural basis of their construct system. But, instead, they displayed brain activation in a second, separate area of the brain: the premotor cortex (Beilock et al., 2008). Everyone uses the premotor cortex when planning and executing their own motor movements. It turns out that cognitively complex experts also use it when comprehending the motor movements of other people. This result was confirmed in a subsequent study (Lyons et al., 2010). It also is consistent with a large body of research on *embodied cognition* (Shapiro, 2011), where findings consistently show that people use multiple, distinct regions of the brain (e.g., the motor cortex, the visual cortex) when assigning meaning to events.

Does this result show that Kelly's theory was wrong? No; one can't say that, since Kelly's theory did not make any predictions whatsoever about the neural underpinnings of construct systems. Nonetheless, the finding does underscore a drawback of personal construct theory. It can be understood in the terms provided by Kelly himself. Kelly's theory did not anticipate the neuroscience result. There are no scientific constructs within personal construct theory that would enable one to predict that some people, but not others, would use their premotor cortex to construe events. The finding is outside of the *range of convenience* of Kelly's theory. With the rapid advance of research on personality and the brain, an ever-growing body of findings lies outside of Kelly's range of convenience. This, in the 21st century, may be personal construct theory's greatest limitation.

as Kelly's theory predicted, then, complex construct systems gave people the capacity to think flexibly, making them expert judges of others' behavior.

Subsequent work revealed more about cognitive complexity/simplicity. People high in complexity differ from those low in complexity in the way that they handle inconsistent information about a person. High-complex persons try to use the inconsistent information in forming an impression, whereas low-complex persons commonly form an impression that is consistent by rejecting all information inconsistent with that impression (Mayo & Crockett, 1964). More complex individuals are better able to understand and take on the role of others (Adams-Webber, 1979, 1982; Crockett, 1982). In terms of the Big Five dimensions described in Chapter 8, complexity is related most strongly to the fifth factor, openness to new experiences (Tetlock, Peterson, & Berry, 1993).

Contemporary researchers continue to study the complexity versus simplicity of cognitive construct systems. They are particularly interested in the complexity of beliefs about the self, or "self-complexity". Much of this interest was spurred by seminal research conducted by Linville (1985). Linville reasoned that people may differ significantly in their levels of self-complexity. Some people may possess a small number of central beliefs about the self that come into play repeatedly in one or two central circumstances in their lives. Other people may be involved in numerous life roles and may possess a rich array of different skills and personal tendencies, each of which comes into play in different settings. For example, you might have two friends, one of whom is a pre-med student who studies 60 hours a week and describes himself as being "smart" and "diligent" and the other is a student, parent, church volunteer, part-time employee, and weekend athlete who sees herself as having a distinct personal style in each of these different settings. The latter person would be seen as being higher in self-complexity.

Research by Linville (1985, 1987) indicated that higher levels of complexity serve as a buffer against stress. People with high self-complexity, in other words, seemed emotionally better off when things were particularly stressful in their lives. For example, if a student high in self-complexity were to fail a test, the existence of other life roles (parent, employee, etc.) seemed to serve as a useful cognitive distraction that helped avoid prolonged negative mood. A recent review indicates, however, that self-complexity is not consistently found to be a buffer against stress and suggests that improvements in the measurement of self-complexity are needed (Rafaeli-Mor & Steinberg, 2002).

Finally, another promising area of contemporary study is "social identity complexity" (Roccas & Brewer, 2002). Social identity complexity refers to the complexity of people's mental representations of the social groups to which they belong. People who live in a multicultural society may recognize complex interrelations among multiple group identities.

In sum, then, the study of cognitive complexity versus simplicity stands as the most highly investigated aspect of individual differences in personal construct systems.

Process

The process aspects of **Kelly's personal construct theory** radically departed from traditional theories of motivation available in his time. As already mentioned, the psychology of personal constructs does not interpret behavior in terms of motivation, drives, and needs. For personal construct theory, the term *motivation* is redundant. This term assumes that a person is inert and needs something to get started. If we assume, however, that people are basically active, the controversy as to what prods an inert organism into action becomes a dead issue. "Instead, the organism is delivered fresh into the psychological world alive and struggling" (Kelly, 1955, p. 37). Kelly contrasted his own position with other theories of motivation. He did so using a colorful pitchfork/carrot metaphor. Kelly suggested that some motivation theories are "pitchfork" theories which posit drives that push the organism forward, whereas others are "carrot" theories that highlight purposes and values that pull the organism ahead. Kelly said

CURRENT APPLICATIONS

A Rep Test for Children: How Do They Construe Personality?

What kinds of constructs do you use to differentiate among people you know? For example, how are your mother and father similar to each other but different from yourself? Has the way you construe the similarities and differences between your parents and yourself changed since you were a child? A study by Donahue (1994) suggests that your construct system has changed both in content and in form. Donahue used a simplified version of Kelly's Rep test to elicit the constructs 11-year-olds use to describe personality. The children nominated nine individuals: self, best friend, an opposite-sex peer "who sits near you at school," a disliked peer, mother (or mother figure), father (or father figure), a liked teacher, the ideal self, and a disliked adult. The individuals' names were written on cards and presented in sets of three. For example, to elicit the first construct, the children had to consider the self, the best friend, and the liked teacher. They then generated a word or phrase to describe how two of the individuals were alike and an opposite word to describe how the third person was different from the other two. In this way, each child generated nine constructs.

What kinds of constructs did the children use? In terms of content, Donahue categorized the constructs according to the Big Five dimensions of personality description—extraversion, agreeableness, conscientiousness, emotional stability, and openness to experience (see Chapter 8). Although the children used constructs from all Big Five domains, the vast majority of their constructs dealt with agreeableness (e.g., "is

nice" versus "gets into fights") and extraversion ("wants to be in charge" versus "likes to play quietly"). In contrast to the personality descriptions of adults, the children used the other three Big Five dimensions much less frequently. Thus, most of their constructs were interpersonal in nature—reflecting the importance of getting along with their peers, parents, and teachers.

In terms of form, Donahue coded six distinct ways of structuring or expressing personal constructs: facts ("from Oklahoma"), habits ("eats lots of sweets"), skills ("is the marble champion"), preferences ("likes comic books"), behavioral trends ("always in trouble with the teacher"), and traits ("shy"). As expected, the children used fewer trait descriptors and many more facts than adults. These findings suggest that children's construct systems are more concrete and become more abstract and psychological as they mature into adults.

These findings show that the Rep test allows us to see how personal construct systems are defined across ages in terms of both content and form. Of course, many other interesting comparisons are possible. For example, how do you think the construct systems of women and men differ? What about those of different ethnic groups or cultures? The Rep test allows us to explore both what is unique and what is shared in the way we construe the world around us.

Source: Donahue (1994).

---

his theory was neither of these. His, instead, was a "jackass" theory that took seriously the nature of the animal itself.

Anticipating Events

A basic task for scientific psychology is to explain why humans are active and why they direct their actions toward one goal versus another. In Kelly's time, the traditional way to explain such human capacities was in terms of motives. Different motives presumably powered different forms of behavior. Kelly, as we noted, rejected the concept of motive. How, then, did he explain the direction of activity?

Kelly addressed this issue in what he termed the **fundamental postulate of personal construct theory**. According to this postulate, people's psychological processes are channeled by the ways in which they anticipate events. Kelly felt that the entire range of psychological outcomes that are of interest to the personality psychologist are shaped by people's anticipations of the future. People use their personal construct system to anticipate what the future will bring. Thus, the fundamental postulate links the structure aspects of Kelly's theory (the personal construct system) to ongoing dynamic processes.

Unlike prior theories of personality, in Kelly's personal construct the central personality process is thinking about the future - or, in Kelly's language, people's "anticipation of events".

When experiencing events, people observe similarities and contrasts, thereby developing constructs. On the basis of these constructs, individuals, like true scientists, anticipate the future. As we see the same events repeated over and over, we modify our constructs so that they will lead to more accurate predictions. Constructs are tested in terms of their predictive efficiency. But what accounts for the direction of behavior? Again, like the scientist, people choose the course of behavior that they believe offers the greatest opportunity for anticipating future events. Scientists

CURRENT APPLICATIONS

Cognitive Complexity, Leadership, and International Crises

Studies in the field of political psychology have related cognitive complexity–simplicity (an aspect of personality important to personal construct theory) to the behavior of political and governmental leaders. Findings have fascinating implications for politics, leadership, and international relations.

For example, would one suspect that greater or lesser cognitive complexity would be advantageous for a revolutionary leader? A study of successful and unsuccessful leaders of four revolutions (American, Russian, Chinese, Cuban) found that low cognitive complexity was associated with success during the phase of revolutionary struggle but high complexity was associated with success in the post-struggle consolidation phase. A categorical, single-minded approach appears desirable at first, but a more complex, integrative style succeeds during the later phase. This may help to explain why revolutionary leaders sometimes fare poorly as leaders of postrevolutionary democratic governments.

Studies of international relations suggest that complexity of communications predicts the likelihood of war. War is less likely when diplomatic communications are of greater cognitive complexity. The complexity of Israeli and Arab speeches delivered to the United Nations General Assembly was significantly reduced prior to each of the four wars in the Middle East (1948, 1956, 1967, 1973). Communications between the United States and the Soviet Union were much less complex prior to the outbreak of the Korean War than prior to crises resolved without war, such as the Berlin blockade and the Cuban missile crisis. Indeed, if one examines transcripts (May & Zelikow, 1997) of communications among U.S. government officials during the Cuban missile crisis and between U.S. and Soviet leaders at the time, one finds that President Kennedy's success in averting nuclear holocaust rested on an exceptionally cognitively complex and subtle analysis of military and diplomatic maneuvers.

Source: Suedfeld & Tetlock (1991).

try to develop better theories, theories that lead to the efficient prediction of events, and individuals try to develop better construct systems. Thus, according to Kelly, a person chooses the alternative that promises the greatest further development of the construct system.

In essence, then, individuals make predictions and consider further changes in their construct systems on the basis of whether those changes have led to accurate predictions. Notice that individuals do not seek reinforcement or the avoidance of pain; instead, they seek validation and expansion of their construct systems. If a person expects something unpleasant and that event occurs, he or she experiences validation regardless of the fact that it was a negative, unpleasant event. Indeed, a painful event may even be preferred to a neutral or pleasant event if it confirms the predictive system (Pervin, 1964).

One should understand that Kelly is not suggesting that the individual seeks certainty, such as would be found in the repetitive ticking of a clock. The boredom people feel with repeated events and the fatalism that comes as a result of the inevitable are usually avoided wherever possible. Rather, individuals seek to anticipate events and to increase the range of convenience or boundaries of their construct systems. This point leads to a distinction between the views of Kelly and the views of Rogers. According to Kelly, individuals do not seek consistency for consistency's sake or even for self-consistency. Instead, individuals seek to anticipate events, and it is a consistent system that allows them to do this.

Anxiety, Fear, and Threat

Thus far, Kelly's system appears to be reasonably simple and straightforward. The process view becomes more complicated with the introduction of the concepts of anxiety, fear, and threat. Kelly defined anxiety in the following way: **Anxiety** is the recognition that the events with which one is confronted lie outside the range of convenience of one's construct system. One is anxious when one is without constructs, when one has "lost his structural grip on events," when one is "caught with his constructs down." People protect themselves from anxiety in various ways. Confronted by events they cannot construe—that is, that lie outside their range of convenience—individuals may broaden a construct and permit it to apply to a greater variety of events, or they may narrow their constructs and focus on minute details. For example, suppose that an individual who has the construct caring person/selfish person and considers herself a caring person finds herself acting in a selfish way. How can she construe herself and events? She can broaden the construct caring person to include selfish behavior or probably more easily in this case restrict the construct caring person to important people in her life, rather than people generally. In the latter case, the construct applies to a more limited set of people or events.

In contrast to anxiety, one experiences **fear** when a new construct appears to be about to enter the construct system. Of even greater significance is the experience of threat. **Threat** is defined as the awareness of imminent comprehensive change in one's core structure. A person feels threatened when a major shakeup in the construct system is about to occur. One feels threatened by death if it is perceived as imminent and if it involves a drastic change in one's core constructs. Death is not threatening when it does not seem imminent or when it is not construed as being fundamental to the meaning of one's life.

Threat, in particular, has a wide range of ramifications. Whenever people undertake some new activity, they expose themselves to confusion and threat. Individuals experience threat when they realize that their construct system is about to be drastically affected by what has been discovered. "This is the moment of threat. It is the threshold between confusion and certainty, between anxiety and boredom. It is precisely at this moment when we are most tempted to turn back" (Kelly, 1964, p. 141). The response to threat may be to give up the adventure to regress to old constructs to avoid panic. Threat occurs as we venture into human understanding and when we stand on the brink of a profound change in ourselves.

Response to
Threat
is to
avoid panic

Threat, the awareness of imminent comprehensive change in one's core structure, can be experienced in relation to many things. Consider, for example, the experience of music majors who are going to perform before a music jury that will determine whether they pass for the semester. To what extent can they be expected to experience threat associated with the possibility of failure? Why should some music majors experience more performance anxiety than others? Following Kelly, two psychologists tested the hypothesis that students would feel threatened by the possibility of failure by a music jury to the extent that such failure implied reorganization of the self-construal component of their construct system. To test this hypothesis, at the beginning of the semester, music majors were administered a threat index consisting of 40 core constructs (e.g., competent/incompetent, productive/unproductive, bad/good) in relation to which they first rated the self and then the self if performed poorly for the jury. The threat index score consisted of the number of core constructs on which the self and self if performed poorly were rated on opposite poles. Anxiety was measured through the use of a questionnaire at the beginning of the semester and three days before the onset of the music performance(s). Consistent with personal construct theory, those students who reported that failure would result in the most comprehensive change in self-construal were also those who reported the greatest increase in anxiety as the date of the jury approached (Tobacyk & Downs, 1986).

Unfortunately, the investigators in this study used the concept of anxiety in a way that was not necessarily consistent with Kelly's views. Even more significant, what was not studied in this case was the experiences of students anticipating the possibility of performing much better before the jury than would be expected on the basis of their self-construal; that is, would comprehensive change as a result of unexpected exceptional performance also be associated with threat? This is important since in Kelly's view it is the awareness of imminent comprehensive change in the construct system that is threatening, not failure per se.

Some personal construct psychologists have focused their research attention on attitudes toward death, both in terms of the ways in which death is construed and the amount of threat associated with death (Neimeyer, 1994). In terms of how death is construed, research suggests that people use constructs such as purposeful/purposeless, positive/negative, acceptance/rejection, anticipated/unanticipated, and final/afterlife. In terms of the amount of threat associated with death, research has involved measurement of the discrepancy between the ways in which individuals construe themselves and the ways in which they construe death. In other words, in personal construct theory terms, death threat is high when the person is unable to construe death as relevant to the self. As measured by the threat index, individuals rate themselves and their own death on constructs such as healthy/sick, strong/weak, predictable/random, and useful/useless. An individual's threat score represents the difference between the two sets of ratings. Presumably in the case of a large self/death discrepancy, interpretation of the death construct as relevant to the self would involve comprehensive change in one's construct system. Death threat, as defined in this way, has been found to be lower in hospice patients than general hospital patients, lower in individuals open to feelings as opposed to those who repress feelings, and lower in self-actualizing individuals as opposed to individuals less oriented toward growth and self-actualization.

What makes the concepts of anxiety, fear, and threat so significant is that they suggest a new dimension to Kelly's view of human functioning. The dynamics of functioning can now be seen to involve the interplay between the individual's wish to expand the construct system and the desire to avoid the threat of disruption of that system. Individuals always seek to maintain and enhance their predictive systems. However, in the face of anxiety and threat, individuals may rigidly adhere to a constricted system instead of venturing out into the risky realm of expansion of their construct systems.

To summarize the process aspects of personal construct theory, Kelly assumes an active organism, and he does not posit any motivational forces. For Kelly, people behave as scientists in construing events, in making predictions, and in seeking expansion of the construct system.

Encountering people from different cultures may expand one's construct system.

Sometimes, not unlike the scientist, we are made so anxious by the unknowns and so threatened by the unfamiliar that we seek to hold on to absolute truths and become dogmatic. On the other hand, when we are behaving as good scientists, we are able to adopt the invitational mood and to expose our construct systems to the diversity of events that make up life.

Growth and Development

No personality theory is completely comprehensive. All have areas in which they are less fully developed than would be ideal. An area in which personal construct theory is not fully developed is its treatment of growth and development.

Kelly was never explicit about the origins of construct systems. He stated that constructs are derived from observing repeated patterns of events. But he did little to elaborate on the kinds of events that lead to differences like the ones between simple and complex construct systems. Kelly's comments relating to growth and development thus are limited. He emphasizes the development of preverbal constructs in infancy and the interpretation of culture as involving a process of learned expectations. People belong to the same cultural group in that they share certain ways of construing events and have the same kinds of expectations regarding behavior.

Developmental research associated with personal construct theory generally has emphasized two kinds of change. First, there has been exploration of increases in complexity of the construct system associated with age (Crockett, 1982; Hayden, 1982; Loevinger, 1993). Second, there has been exploration of qualitative changes in the nature of the constructs formed and in the ability of children to be more empathic or aware of the construct systems of others (Adams-Webber, 1982; Donahue, 1994; Morrison & Cometa, 1982; Sigel, 1981). In terms of construct system complexity, there is evidence that as children develop they increase the number of constructs available to them, make finer differentiations, and show more hierarchical organization or integration. In terms of empathy, there is evidence that as children develop they become increasingly aware that many events are not related to the self and increasingly able to appreciate the constructs of others (Sigel, 1981).

Two studies have been reported that are relevant to the question of the determinants of complex cognitive structures. In one study, the subjects' level of cognitive complexity was found to be related to the variety of cultural backgrounds to which they had been exposed in childhood (Sechrest & Jackson, 1961). In another study, parents of cognitively complex children were found to be more likely to grant autonomy and less likely to be authoritarian than were the parents of children low in cognitive complexity (Cross, 1966). Presumably, the opportunity to examine many different events and to have many different experiences is conducive to the development of a complex structure. One would also expect to find that children who experience a long-standing and severe threat from authoritarian parents would develop constricted and inflexible construct systems.

The question of factors determining the content of constructs and the complexity of construct systems is of critical importance. In particular, it is relevant to the field of education, since a part of education appears to be the development of complex, flexible, and adaptive construct systems. Unfortunately, Kelly himself made few statements in this area. Kelly's theory simply did not treat questions of development as thoroughly as would have been ideal. Relatively little contemporary research on personality development is directly guided by the postulates of personal construct theory.

Clinical Applications

Psychopathology

Although Kelly's analysis of development may have been insufficiently developed, the same cannot be said for his treatment of psychopathology. Kelly devoted volume 2 of his monumental 1955 work to clinical applications of personal construct theory.

According to Kelly, psychopathology is a disordered response to anxiety. For Kelly, psychopathology is defined in terms of disordered functioning of a construct system. The person-as-scientist metaphor remains relevant here. Only a poor scientist retains a theory and makes the same predictions despite repeated research failures. Similarly, only a poorly functioning person retains his or her construct system, unchanged, if it repeatedly yields incorrect predictions.

At the root of such rigid adherence to a construct system are feelings of anxiety, fear, and threat. Kelly stated that one could construe human behavior as being directed away from ultimate anxiety. Psychological disorders are disorders involving anxiety and faulty efforts to reestablish the sense of being able to anticipate events:

> A "neurotic" person casts about frantically for new ways of construing the events of his world . . . A "psychotic" person appears to have found some temporary solution for his anxiety. But it is a precarious solution, at best, and must be sustained in the face of evidence which, for most of us, would be invalidating.
>
> Source: Kelly, 1955, pp. 895–896.

Fundamental to Kelly's view of psychopathology, then, are people's efforts to avoid anxiety (the experience that one's construct system is not applicable to events) and to avoid threat (the awareness of imminent comprehensive change in the construct system). To protect against anxiety and threat, an individual employs protective devices. This view resembles that of Freud. Indeed, Kelly suggested that in the face of anxiety, individuals may act in ways that will make their constructs unavailable for verbalization, that is, not consciously available. Thus, for example, in the face of anxiety, individuals may submerge one end of a construct or suspend elements that do not fit well into a construct. These are responses to anxiety that seem very similar to the concept of repression. In some cases, individuals make the same predictions regardless of changes in events, and in other cases, they try to force people to behave in ways that will conform to their construct system. In all cases, psychopathology involves the use of poor constructs or the use of a maladaptive construct system.

Change and Fixed-Role Therapy

In personal construct theory, the target of change is the client's personal construct system. Therapists try to foster the development of better construct systems. If the continued use of invalid constructs is pathological, then psychotherapy is the process of helping clients to improve their predictions by developing better constructs. One strives to make the client a better scientist. Psychotherapy is a process, then, of reconstructing the construct system. Some constructs are replaced, some new ones added, some connections are dropped, others are added. Whatever the details of the process, psychotherapy is the psychological reconstruction of life.

How does one do this? Kelly developed a specific technique called **fixed-role therapy**. The goal of fixed-role therapy is to enable clients to think about themselves in new ways. The therapist wants clients to behave in new ways, to construe themselves in new ways, and thereby to become new people. One technique for accomplishing this goal is the use of a personality sketch. In therapy, after establishing a basic understanding of the client, a psychologist or a team of psychologists writes a sketch of a new person, an alternative type of person that the client can "try out" as a way of expanding his or her construct system. After the personality sketch is drawn up, it is presented to the client. The client decides whether the sketch sounds like someone he would like to know and whether he would feel comfortable with such a person. This is done to ensure that the new personality will not be excessively threatening to the client.

In the next phase of fixed-role therapy, the therapist invites the client to act as if he were that person. For about 2 weeks, the client is asked to forget who he is and to be this other person. If the new person is called Tom Jones, then the client is told the following: "For 2 weeks, try to forget who you are or that you ever were. You are Tom Jones. You act like him. You think like him. You talk to your friends the way you think he would talk. You do the things you think he would do. You even have his interests, and you enjoy the things he would enjoy." The client may resist; he may feel that this is play-acting and that it is hypocritical, but he is encouraged, in an accepting manner, to try it and see how it works. The client is not told that this is what he should eventually be, but he is asked to assume the new personality. He is asked to give up being himself temporarily so that he can discover himself:

> The therapist must be prepared to act as if he or she (the client) were various persons and to accept the invitational mood. The therapist must at every moment "play in strong support of an actor the client who is continually fumbling his lines and contaminating his role."
>
> *Source:* Kelly (1955, p. 399).

Many characteristics in the sketch contrast sharply with the person's current functioning; Kelly suggested that it might be easier for people to play up what they believe to be the opposite of the way they generally behave than to behave just a little bit differently. Behaving in accord with the sketch is thought to set in motion processes that will have effects throughout the construct system. Fixed-role therapy, then, does not aim at the readjustment of minor parts of personality. Instead, it aims thoroughly to reconstruct a personality. It does so by offering a new role, a new personality that the client can try out in the safe setting of therapy.

Fixed-role therapy was not the only therapeutic technique discussed or used by Kelly (Bieri, 1986). However, it is the one that is particularly associated with personal construct theory, and it does exemplify some of the principles of the personal construct theory of change. The goal of therapeutic change is the individual's reconstruction of the self. The individual drops some constructs, creates new ones, does some tightening and loosening, and develops a construct system that leads to more accurate predictions. The therapist encourages the client to make believe, to experiment, to spell out alternatives, and to reconstrue the past in the light of new constructs. The process of therapy is complex. Different clients must be treated differently, and the resistance

Hill Street Studios / Getty Images

Fixed-Role Therapy. In Kelly's fixed-role therapy, clients are encouraged to try on new "roles" in their interactions with others. Kelly (1955) felt that the new role would be a "construct-shaking experience" (p. 412)—in other words, it would cause the client to think in new ways.

to change must be overcome. However, positive change is possible in a situation where a good director assists in the playing of the human drama or a good teacher assists in the development of a creative scientist. Evidence suggests that therapy conducted within the framework of personal construct theory is effective with a wide variety of psychological disorders (Winter & Viney, 2005).

The Case of Jim

Rep Test: Personal Construct Theory

Jim took the group form of Kelly's Rep test separately from the other tests (Figure 11.1). Here, we have a test that is structured in terms of the roles given to the subject and the task of formulating a similarity/contrast construct. However, the subject is given total freedom in the content of the construct formed. As noted previously in this chapter, the Rep test is derived logically from Kelly's theory of personal constructs. Two major themes appear in these constructs. The first theme is the quality of interpersonal relationships. Basically, this involves whether people are warm and giving or cold and narcissistic. This theme is expressed in constructs such as gives love/is self-oriented, sensitive/insensitive, and communicates with others as people/is uninterested in others. A second major theme concerns security and is expressed in constructs such as hung up/healthy, unsure/self-confident, and satisfied with life/unhappy. The frequency

CONSTRUCT	CONTRAST
Self-satisfied	Self-doubting
Uninterested in communicating with students as people	Interested in communicating with students as people
Nice	Obnoxious
Sensitive to cues from other people	Insensitive to cues
Outgoing–gregarious	Introverted–retiring
Introspective–hung up	Self-satisfied
Intellectually dynamic	Mundane and predictable
Outstanding, successful	Mediocre
Obnoxious	Very likable
Satisfied with life	Unhappy
Shy, unsure of self	Self-confident
Worldly, openminded	Parochial, closeminded
Open, simple to understand	Complex, hard to get to know
Capable of giving great love	Somewhat self-oriented
Self-sufficient	Needs other people
Concerned with others	Oblivious to all but his own interests
So hung up that psychological health is questionable	Basically healthy and stable
Willing to hurt people in order to be "objective"	Unwilling to hurt people if he can help it
Closeminded, conservative	Openminded, liberal
Lacking in self-confidence	Self-confident
Sensitive	Insensitive, self-centered
Lacking social poise	Secure and socially poised
Bright, articulate	Average intelligence

FIGURE 11.1 Rep test data—case of Jim.

with which constructs relevant to these two themes appear suggests that Jim has a relatively constricted view of the world—that is, much of Jim's understanding of events is in terms of the warm/cold and secure/insecure dimensions.

How do the constructs given relate to specific people? On the sorts that involved himself, Jim used constructs expressing insecurity. Thus, Jim views himself as being like his sister (so hung up that her psychological health is questionable), in contrast to his brother, who is basically healthy and stable. In two other sorts of constructs, he sees himself as lacking self-confidence and social poise. These ways of construing himself contrast with those involving his father. His father is construed as being introverted and retiring but also as self-sufficient, open-minded, outstanding, and successful.

The constructs used in relation to Jim's mother are interesting and again suggest conflict. On the one hand, his mother is construed to be outgoing, gregarious, and loving; on the other, she is construed to be mundane, predictable, closed-minded, and conservative. The closed-minded, conservative construct is particularly interesting since, in that sort, Jim's mother is paired with the person with whom he feels most uncomfortable. Thus, the mother and the person with whom he feels most uncomfortable are contrasted with his father, who is construed to be open-minded and liberal. The combination of sorts for all persons suggests that Jim's ideal person is someone who is warm, sensitive, secure, intelligent, open-minded, and successful. The women in his life—his mother, sister, girlfriend, and previous girlfriend—are construed as having some of these characteristics but also as missing others.

Comments on the Data

The Rep test gives us valuable data about how Jim construes his environment. Jim's world tends to be perceived in terms of two major constructs: warm interpersonal/cold interpersonal relationships and secure, confident/insecure, unhappy people. Through the Rep test, we gain an understanding of why Jim is so limited in his relationships to others and why he has so much difficulty in being creative. His restriction to only two constructs hardly leaves him free to relate to people as individuals and instead forces him to perceive people and problems in stereotyped or conventional ways. A world filled with so little perceived diversity can hardly be exciting, and the constant threat of insensitivity and rejection can be expected to fill Jim with a sense of gloom.

The data from the Rep test, like Kelly's theory, are tantalizing. What is there seems so clear and valuable, but one is left wondering about what is missing. There is a sense of the skeleton for the structure of personality, but one is left with only the bones. Jim's ways of construing himself and his environment are an important part of his personality. Assessing his constructs and his construct system helps us to understand how he interprets events and how he is led to predict the future. But where is the flesh on the bones—the sense of an individual who cannot be what he feels, the person struggling to be warm amid feelings of hostility and struggling to relate to women, although confused about his feelings toward them?

Related Points of View and Recent Developments

Psychology is different today than it was in Kelly's time. In his day, Kelly's emphasis on human cognitive processes was radical; today, such an emphasis is mainstream. It is in this sense that Kelly anticipated future developments in the field. As we will see in the next chapter, contemporary social–cognitive approaches to personality embrace many of the same assumptions about human nature that are found in personal construct theory.

Although Kelly's theory attracted considerable attention when it was presented in 1955, it differed so greatly from the field's traditions that it spawned little research in the following decade. It was only in later years that many leads suggested by personal construct theory were explored (Neimeyer & Neimeyer, 1992). A major focus has been the Rep test and the structure of construct systems. Studies of the reliability of the Rep test suggest that the responses of individuals to the role title list and constructs used are reasonably stable over time (Landfield, 1971). Beyond this, the Rep test has been used to study a variety of individuals with psychological problems, the construct systems of married couples, and people with varied interpersonal relationships (Duck, 1982). Modifications of the Rep test have been used to study the structural complexity of construct systems, the perception of situations, and, as noted, the use of nonverbal constructs. Almost every aspect of Kelly's theory has received at least some study (Mancuso & Adams-Webber, 1982). The organization of the construct system and changes in this organization associated with development are particularly noteworthy topics (Crockett, 1982). The developmental principles emphasized suggest many similarities in the developmental theories of Kelly and Piaget: (1) an emphasis on progression from a global, undifferentiated system to a differentiated, integrated one; (2) increasing use of abstract structures to handle more information more economically; (3) development in response to efforts to accommodate new elements in the cognitive system; and (4) development of the cognitive system as a system, as opposed to a simple addition of new parts or elements.

Other relevant research has roots in Kelly's personal construct theory, although it is conducted within the framework of more contemporary approaches to personality (Chapters 12 and 13). For example, the psychologist Tory Higgins (1999) has developed an approach to cognitive constructs and personality functioning that is highly compatible with Kelly's. In his research, Higgins (Higgins & Scholer, 2008) focuses on the importance of *chronically accessible constructs*, defined as constructs that are readily activated on the basis of little information. Such constructs, which may be conscious or unconscious, bias our perception and memory of events. Along similar lines, the social–cognitive theorist Walter Mischel, a former student of Kelly's, has directly extended Kelly's analysis of encoding constructs as a core feature of personality (Chapter 12). Other investigators have recently considered a question to which Kelly devoted relatively little attention, namely, the possibility of cultural differences in the constructs used and how constructs are formed (Chapter 14). These contemporary developments relate to personal construct theory but only in an indirect way.

The contemporary personality psychologist has, at his or her disposal, a battery of findings, theoretical concepts, and research methods in the study of human cognition that were unavailable to Kelly. Contemporary investigators commonly use these tools to analyze precisely the same phenomena that interested Kelly. Yet, they rarely do so by using the precise terms and theoretical formulations of personal construct theory. Even though Kelly remains an extraordinarily respected figure, today, the details of his theory often are viewed as expendable precisely as Kelly himself might have anticipated.

Critical Evaluation

Scientific Observation: The Database

How does Kelly's theory fare on the five criteria with which we have been evaluating the theories of personality? On criterion #1, scientific observations, Kelly fares well. As a clinician, his observations included detailed, in-depth analyses of the kind one associated with theorists such as Freud and Rogers. Yet, as a person who developed a testing instrument, the Rep test, he succeeded in providing a reliable, objective means of assessing the personality attributes of the individual. The Rep test is particularly noteworthy in that it fit his theory ideally. By the standards of mid-20th-century psychology, then, Kelly's database of scientific observations was quite admirable.

By contemporary standards, however, Kelly's database seems limited. His observations of personality did not thoroughly include cultural diversity; he did his work exclusively within a North American culture (the United States). He did not have at his disposal a diversity of methodological tools, such as the reaction-time techniques and priming techniques employed by social–cognitive psychologists who share Kelly's interest in construct systems and personality (Chapters 12 and 13). One can hardly blame Kelly for failing to invoke research procedures that developed only after his time. Nonetheless, by contemporary standards, Kelly's scientific database is lacking in diversity.

Theory: Systematic?

Personal construct theory is highly systematic. Kelly was a careful theorist, and he composed his theoretical writing in a logical, formal style. Personal construct theory features a well-specified series of theoretical postulates and associated corollaries. By constructing his theory in this formal style, Kelly was able coherently to relate each element of his theory to his overall conceptual framework.

Kelly did have one advantage over most other personality theorists. Notably, he presented his entire theory at one point in time, in one place: his 1955 volumes. It is easier to achieve systematic coherence in one's career contributions if all those contributions are made within one book rather than being expressed in a series of books and papers written over a long period of time, during which one's theoretical views may shift.

Theory: Testable?

Kelly took two key steps that make his theory testable. He defined the terms of personal construct theory quite precisely. Second, he developed an objective assessment procedure that perfectly matched the theory: the Rep test. By combining theoretical precision with objective measurement, one can derive and test numerous theory-based predictions: that variations in cognitive complexity will correlate with the accuracy of social predictions, that anxiety will result when events fall outside one's construct system, that fixed-role therapy will foster the development of new constructs in clients, and so forth.

Nonetheless, Kelly's work also contains central features that are not open to test. Imagine that you went up to Kelly and said that "I don't think people are like scientists" or "I don't believe that psychological processes are channeled by the way people anticipate events" or "I don't believe in constructive alternativism as a general principle of human psychology." It is hard to imagine that Kelly would think that these disagreements, which involve bedrock features of personal construct theory, could be resolved by empirical test. These challenges do not involve testable predictions but, instead, theoretical *assumptions*. Kelly makes certain assumptions about personality, states them as basic premises and postulates, and then builds his theory logically from those premises. This, of course, is true of all theorists. For example, for Freud, the idea that the mind is an energy system was an assumption, not a conclusion based on systematic data and not, in and of itself, a testable prediction. Kelly's theory, then, is not unique in resting on theoretical assumptions that are not open to direct test. However, in Kelly's case, the number and range of such assumptions seem particularly significant. One can imagine reformulating psychoanalytic theory while dropping the assumption that the mind is an energy system. But if one dropped the assumption that psychological processes are channeled by the way people anticipate events or the assumption that people can engage in constructive alternativism, one would no longer have anything that resembled personal construct theory. The untestable assumptions are particularly significant in Kelly's work. Another point to be made is that although construct systems have been widely studied, there is little evidence that measures of these systems are related to overt behavior. The theory would suggest that this is the case, but evidence is needed.

Theory: Comprehensive?

If one accepts the fundamental postulate of Kelly's theory—that all psychological processes are channeled by the ways in which people anticipate events—then Kelly's theory is seen as comprehensive. In principle, the theory applies to all circumstances in which people use their personal

Kelly at a Glance

	Structure	Process	Growth and Development	Pathology	Change
	Constructs	Processes channelized by anticipation of events	Increased complexity and definition to construct system	Disordered functioning of the construct system	Psychological reconstruction of life; fixed-role therapy

constructs to anticipate events—and this, to Kelly, is essentially all the circumstances of interest to the personality psychologist.

However, if one questions the fundamental postulate rather than merely accepting it on faith, then personality construct theory appears to lack comprehensiveness. It provides a wonderful portrait of those circumstances in which people act "like scientists." But what about other circumstances in which people act like members of a crazed mob, or like drunks, or like irrational love-struck Romeos and Juliets? An early reviewer of Kelly's work suggested that "I rather suspect that when some people get angry or inspired or in love, they couldn't care less about their [personal construct] systems as a whole! One gets the impression that the author is, in his personality theory, overreacting against a generation of irrationalism" (Bruner, 1956, p. 356).

There are additional ways in which Kelly's work is less comprehensive than some other theories presented in our text. The process aspects of the theory are not as well specified as would be ideal. For example, how does the individual know which construct will be the best predictor? How does one know which end of the construct (similarity or contrast) to use? There is less discussion of personality growth and development than would be optimal; in an ideal world, Kelly would have specified and tested ideas about how, through the course of child development, people acquire one versus another type of construct system. There is relatively little discussion of emotions by Kelly, though some subsequent personal construct theorists have addressed this shortcoming (McCoy, 1981). A particular limitation, with regard to emotions, is that Kelly primarily takes a unidirectional view of personal constructs and emotion; his theory explains how personal constructs influence emotional experience but says little about how emotions influence the personal constructs that come to mind for the individual at a given point in time. Contemporary research documents the importance of this "other direction," in which emotional states influence cognitive contents and processes (Forgas, 1995).

Finally, we saw a limitation in the work of Rogers, whose theoretical approach is similar to that of Kelly in significant ways. Like Rogers, Kelly tells us more about humans as cognitive and social beings than as biological beings. Questions of evolution, genetics, and inherited individual differences in temperament receive far less attention than is required for a truly comprehensive theory of persons. Contemporary developments in the study of biology and mind, for example, would force significant expansions of, and probably alterations in, personal construct theory. For example, one recent development is the study of "embodied" cognition (Lakoff & Johnson, 1999; Niedenthal, Barsa-lou, Winkielman, Krauth-Gruber, and Ric, 2005). The idea is that conceptual processes such as reasoning, categorization, and judgment (what Kelly called construing) are not carried out by one single cognitive system (what Kelly called the personal construct system). Instead, a number of distinct systems are involved.

Applications

Applications are a strong point for personal construct theory. Like Freud and Rogers, Kelly was a clinical psychologist. He based his theorizing on clinical experience and accompanied his theory of personality with detailed principles for conducting theory. He developed an objective personality assessment method that, in principle, can be used whenever the applied psychologist wishes to predict individual differences in some psychological outcome. (We say "in principle" only because Kelly's Rep test has been used in such applications much less frequently than have methods based on the trait theories of personality.)

The entire second volume of Kelly's (1955) main published work, *The Psychology of Personal Constructs*, is devoted to therapeutic applications of his theoretical system. Kelly, then, deserves high marks for translating theory to practice. Indeed, one's sense from reading Kelly's work is that his theoretical efforts were fundamentally motivated by, and thus in the service of, an applied goal: enabling people to improve their lives by reconstruing their circumstances.

Major Contributions and Summary

Kelly's structural model of personality made a significant contribution to personality theory. Soon after its publication, Bruner (1956) called personal construct theory the single greatest contribution of the decade between 1945 and 1955 to the theory of personality functioning. Kelly displayed exceptional imagination and boldness in forging a theory that was so *unlike* the behavioristic and psychodynamic perspectives that dominated psychology in his day. For this achievement, Kelly is to be applauded.

In the decades after Kelly presented the theory, however, his perspective did not develop and flourish as much as one might have expected. Some have suggested that progress was stymied by reverence for Kelly, insularity, and orthodoxy (Rosenberg, 1980; Schneider, 1982). As noted by one of Kelly's followers, without new ideas, no theory of personality can survive (Sechrest, 1977). By the late 1980s, a review concluded that, except among a group of enthusiasts, Kelly's ideas often were neglected (Jankowicz, 1987). This was less true in England, where Kelly's ideas are widely known and are still part of the training of most clinicians. However, in the United States, the high respect accorded to Kelly's ideas has not been matched by a high degree of overall attention and impact on the field (Winter, 1992). In the contemporary field, Kelly's biggest impact is indirect. His work significantly contributed to the thinking of social–cognitive theorists, whose contributions are discussed in the next two chapters.

In sum, personal construct theory has both strengths and limitations (Table 11.2). On the positive side, consider the following strengths: (1) The theory makes a significant contribution by bringing to the forefront of personality the importance of cognition and construct systems. (2) It is an approach to personality that attempts to capture both the uniqueness of the individual and the lawfulness of people generally. (3) It has developed a new, interesting, and theoretically relevant assessment technique, the Rep test. On the negative side, there are a number of limitations: (1) The theory shows relative neglect of certain important areas, especially development. (2) It has remained outside of mainstream research relating work in cognitive psychology to personality. Many of these approaches give lip service to Kelly's contributions but proceed along independent lines.

Table 11.2 **Summary of Strengths and Limitations of Personal Construct Theory**

Strengths	Limitations
1. Places emphasis on cognitive processes as a central aspect of personality	1. Has not led to research that *extends* the theory
2. Presents a model of personality that provides for both the lawfulness of general personality functioning and the uniqueness of individual construct systems	2. Leaves out or makes minimal contributions to our understanding of some significant aspects of personality (growth and development, emotions)
3. Includes a theory-related technique for personality assessment and research (Rep test)	3. Is not as yet connected with more general research and theory in cognitive psychology

MAJOR CONCEPTS

Anxiety	Core constructs	Peripheral constructs	Similarity pole
Cognitive complexity versus simplicity	Fear	Person-as-scientist	Submerged construct
Construct	Fixed-role therapy	Preverbal construct	Subordinate construct
Constructive alternativism	Focus of convenience	Range of convenience	Superordinate construct
Contrast pole	Fundamental postulate of personal construct theory	Role Construct Repertory Test (Rep test)	Threat
			Verbal construct

REVIEW

1. The personal construct theory of George Kelly emphasizes the way in which the person construes or interprets events. Kelly viewed the person as a scientist—an observer of events who formulates concepts or constructs to organize phenomena and uses these constructs to predict the future. People always are free to reconstrue events.

2. Kelly viewed personality in terms of the person's construct system—the types of constructs the person formed and how they were organized. Constructs are formed on the basis of observations of similarities among events. Core constructs are basic to the system, whereas peripheral constructs are less important. Superordinate constructs are higher in the hierarchy and include other constructs under them, whereas subordinate constructs are lower in the hierarchy.

3. Kelly developed the Role Construct Repertory Test (Rep test) to assess the content and structure of the person's construct system. The Rep test has been used to study the extent to which the person can be described as cognitively complex or simple, indicating the extent to which the person can view the world in differentiated terms.

4. According to Kelly, the person experiences anxiety when aware that events lie outside the construct system, experiences fear when a new construct is about to emerge, and experiences threat when there is the danger of comprehensive change in the construct system. Disordered responses to anxiety can be seen in the way constructs are applied to new events, in the way constructs are used to make predictions, and in the organization of the entire construct system. Psychotherapy is the process of reconstructing the construct system. In Kelly's fixed-role therapy, clients are encouraged to represent themselves in new ways, behave in new ways, and construe themselves in new ways.

5. Research on personal construct theory has focused mainly on the Rep test. Recent research has shown that Kelly's idiographic assessment procedures reveal much information about the individual that is not revealed by nomothetic tests based on trait theory. Other work has explored the complexity/simplicity of construct systems in a manner that is related to, yet not directly guided by, the postulates of personal construct theory.

12 Social-Cognitive Theory: Bandura and Mischel

Chapter Focus

Do you remember your first day of high school? Perhaps, you don't care to! What could be more unnerving than not knowing how to act, especially in an environment where "fitting in" is paramount? Although she was really anxious and unsure of what to expect, one young woman decided to approach the first day of high school as an opportunity to learn. Her plan was to model herself after the most successful seniors in the school. She paid close attention to what they talked about, what they wore, where they went, and when they went there. Soon, she was the coolest freshman in the class.

This young woman was very influenced by her new environment, but she was also an active agent in choosing how to respond to that influence. This idea, that behavior is the result of an interaction between the person and the environment, is a key concept in the social-cognitive theory of personality. This theory is distinctive in its emphasis on the social origins of behavior and the importance of cognition (thought processes) in human functioning. People are viewed as capable of actively directing their own lives and learning complex patterns of behavior in the absence of rewards. Social-cognitive theory has developed considerably during the past few decades and today is an important force in the science of personality.

Questions to be Addressed in this Chapter

1. What is the role of thinking, or "cognitive," processes in personality?

2. How do people learn complex social behaviors?

3. How can one scientifically analyze people's capacity for personal agency, that is, their ability to influence their actions and the course of their own development?

4. In what ways do variations—as opposed to consistencies—in a person's behavior reveal the nature of his or her personality?

Social-cognitive theory has roots in the behavioral/learning tradition (Chapter 10). Beginning in the 1950s, some theorists tried to shift learning theory's focus from animals in boxes to *social* learning: the acquisition of new patterns of behavior by humans acting in a social world. It is also rooted, in part, in the tradition pioneered by George Kelly: the study of *cognition*, including the cognitive structures that people use to interpret events. By synthesizing and advancing beyond these past traditions, theorists created a *social-cognitive* approach that has risen to prominence in contemporary personality science.

Relating Social-Cognitive Theory to the Previous Theories

In crafting their theory, social-cognitivists tried to overcome the limitations of prior theories of personality (the ones covered in our previous chapters). Their critiques of past theories constitute a good introduction to the social-cognitive approach (see Bandura, 1986, 1999, 2012; Mischel, 1999, 2001).

To the social-cognitivist, psychoanalysts *over*emphasize unconscious forces and the influence of early childhood experience. Social-cognitive theorists place greater emphasis on conscious self-reflection and argue that critical developmental processes occur not only in early childhood but also throughout the life course (Artistico et al., 2011).

Social-cognitive theorists question the core premise of trait theory: that personality can be understood in terms of overall, average tendencies (i.e., average trait levels). They believe that personality is revealed in both average levels of behavior and patterns of *variability* in action. Are you shy with some people but outgoing with others? Motivated on some tasks but lazy on others? Social-cognitive theory sees such variability as revealing of personality structure (Mischel & Shoda, 2008).

Social-cognitive theorists question the adequacy of evolutionary psychology. How, they ask, can an evolutionary perspective explain the vast changes in human social life observed from one historical period to another (Bandura, 2006; Bussey & Bandura, 1999)? A century ago, evolutionary psychologists might have explained why women are evolutionarily predisposed to stay at home rather than entering the workforce. Now that women have entered the workforce in massive numbers, such an explanation makes little sense.

Finally, social-cognitive theory rejects the behavioristic argument that environmental stimuli control behavior. People also have a capacity for self-control. Cognitive capabilities, they argue, enable people to shape the course of their own development (Bandura, 2006). These capabilities also allow people to learn new patterns of behavior by observation, or "modeling," even in the absence of reinforcement (Table 12.1).

Many contemporary personality psychologists have contributed to social-cognitive theory (Cervone & Shoda, 1999b). However, two of them have made extraordinarily seminal

Table 12.1   Distinguishing Features of Social-Cognitive Theory

1. Emphasis on people as active agents
2. Emphasis on social origins of behavior
3. Emphasis on cognitive (thought) processes
4. Emphasis on both average behavioral tendencies and variability in behavior
5. Emphasis on the learning of complex patterns of behavior in the absence of rewards

contributions that mark them as the primary social-cognitive personality theorists: Albert Bandura and Walter Mischel. Although they focus on somewhat different aspects of personality functioning, their contributions complement one another and contribute to a coherent body of social-cognitive theory and research.

A View of the Theorists

Albert Bandura (1925–)

Albert Bandura grew up in northern Alberta, Canada. After graduating from the University of British Columbia, he pursued graduate work in clinical psychology at the University of Iowa, known for its excellence in research on learning processes. In an interview, Bandura indicated that he "had a strong interest in conceptualizing clinical phenomena in ways that would make them amenable to experimental test, with the view that as practitioners we have a responsibility for assessing the efficacy of a procedure, so that people are not subjected to treatments before we know their effects" (quoted in Evans, 1976, p. 243).

After obtaining his Ph.D. at Iowa in 1952, Bandura joined the faculty at Stanford University, where he has spent his entire career. Work on social factors that contribute to children's development of aggressive behavior resulted in two books with Richard Walters, his first graduate student: *Adolescent Aggression* (Bandura & Walters, 1959) and *Social Learning and Personality Development* (Bandura & Walters, 1963). The latter volume, in particular, laid the foundations for the social-cognitive perspective Bandura developed throughout the latter third of the 20th century. In 1969, *Principles of Behavior Modification* (Bandura, 1969) reformulated the practice of behavior therapy by directing therapists' attention to the thinking processes of their clients, rather than to the environmental factors and conditioning processes emphasized by behaviorists (Chapter 10).

Since the 1970s, Bandura has focused on "self-processes," that is, thinking processes involving self-conceptions and personal goals (1977, 1997). He contends that self-processes give people the capacity for personal agency, that is, the capacity to affect their own behavior and experiences. Bandura's social-cognitive theory thus is an "agentic" conception of human nature (Bandura, 1999, 2001, 2012). Bandura examines how interpersonal, social, and socioeconomic conditions influence people's self-referent beliefs (Bandura, 2006).

Bandura's monumental *Social Foundations of Thought and Action* (Bandura, 1986) organized a vast body of knowledge about personality processes, structures, and development within a social-cognitive framework. It stands as the definitive statement of his theoretical position. He has remained active well past traditional "retirement age"; Bandura's most recent book, a comprehensive analysis of ways in which otherwise good people sometimes commit unethical and immoral acts, was published in 2015.

Bandura has received innumerable rewards and honors. They include the presidency of the American Psychological Association APA's Distinguished Scientific Contribution Award, the William James Award from the Association for Psychological Science (APS) for Outstanding

NurPhoto / Contributor / Getty Images

Albert Bandura, creator of Social Cognitive Theory, receiving the United States National Medal of Science from former U.S. President Barack Obama.

Lifetime Contribution to Psychology, and honorary degrees from universities throughout North America and Europe. In a fitting capstone to his career in 2016, Bandura became the first figure in the history of personality theory and research to receive the U.S. National Medal of Science.

Walter Mischel (1930–)

Walter Mischel was born in Vienna and lived his first nine years "in easy playing distance of Freud's house." He describes the possible influence of this period as follows:

> *When I began to read psychology Freud fascinated me most. As a student at City College (in New York, where my family settled after the Hitler-caused forced exodus from Europe in 1939), psychoanalysis seemed to provide a comprehensive view of man. But my excitement fizzled when I tried to apply ideas as a social worker with "juvenile delinquents" in New York's Lower East Side: somehow trying to give those youngsters "insight" didn't help either them or me. The concepts did not fit what I saw, and I went looking for more useful ones.*

> *Source:* Mischel, 1978, personal communication.

> *Characterizations of individuals on common trait dimensions (such as "Conscientiousness" or "Sociability") provided useful overall summaries of their average levels of behavior but missed, it*

seemed to me, the striking discriminativeness often visible within the same person if closely observed over time and across situations. Might the same person who is more caring, giving, and supportive than most people in relation to his family also be less caring and altruistic than most people in other contexts? Might these variations across situations be meaningful stable patterns that characterize the person enduringly rather than random fluctuations? If so, how could they be understood and what did they reflect? Might they be worth taking into account in personality assessment for the conceptualization of the stability and flexibility of human behavior and qualities? These questions began to gnaw at me and the effort to answer them became a fundamental goal for the rest of my life.

Source: Mischel, as quoted in Pervin, 1996, p. 76.

Courtesy Walter Mischel.

Walter Mischel.

In addition to critiquing previous approaches, in 1973, Mischel provided an alternative: a set of cognitive-social personal variables (Mischel, 1973; discussed below). They were designed to explain the discriminativeness of behavior, that is, how people distinguish between situations (even seemingly similar ones) and vary their actions adaptively from one situation to the next. "Might the same person who is more caring, giving, and supportive than most people in relation to his family also be less caring and altruistic than most people in other contexts?" Mischel asks. "Might these variations across situations be meaningful stable patterns that characterize the person enduringly?" (Mischel, in Pervin, 1996, p. 76). Such questions drove Mischel's work, including his development of a "systems" perspective in which personality is understood as a complex, interconnected system of cognitive and affective processes that are activated by features of social situations (Mischel & Shoda, 2008).

Mischel also has become extremely well known thanks to "the marshmallow test" (Mischel, 2014), a simple research paradigm (described below) that revealed highly consequential individual differences in people's ability to control their impulsive tendencies.

In terms of his view of human nature, Mischel suggests that while genes are important in shaping personality, there remains great potential for personality change: "I think, therefore I can change what I am" (2014, p. 278).

Mischel's numerous honors include APA's Award for Distinguished Scientific Contributions, APS's William James Award, the Ludwig Wittgenstein Prize from the Austrian Research Foundation, and election to the U.S. National Academy of Sciences. He also has served as Editor of *Psychological Review*, psychology's leading publication outlet for theoretical papers.

Bandura's and Mischel's scientific impact is particularly noteworthy. A quantitative review (Haggbloom et al., 2002) of the impact of 20th-century psychologists found that both Bandura and Mischel were among that century's top 25 most influential figures, with the work of only three psychologists—Skinner, Piaget, and Freud—having greater impact than Bandura's. A 2007 analysis of the most cited book authors in the humanities and social sciences found Bandura's work to be more frequently cited than that of any other psychologist.

Social-Cognitive Theory's View of the Person

The simplest way to understand the social-cognitive theory view of the person is to ask, "What is a person?" What makes some beings "persons" and others "not persons"? Three psychological qualities of persons are unique. People (1) reason about the world using language; (2) contemplate not only present circumstances but also past and hypothetical future events; and (3) reflect on themselves, thinking about themselves and their own thinking.

Curiously, many prior personality theories did not emphasize these uniquely human abilities. Psychoanalysts highlighted animalistic impulsive forces. Behaviorists treated people as machines and based theories on research with animals. Trait theorists report that the Big Five personality traits are found in animals, too (Gosling & John, 1999). Social-cognitive theory, by contrast, centers its attention on uniquely human cognitive capacities (Bandura, 1999). As Mischel puts it:

> The image is one of the human being as an active, aware problem-solver, capable of profiting from an enormous range of experiences and cognitive capacities, possessing great potential for good or ill, actively constructing his or her psychological world, and influencing the environment but also being influenced by it in lawful ways. . . . It is an image that has moved a long way from the instinctual drive-reduction models, the static global traits, and the automatic stimulus-response bonds of traditional personality theories.
>
> *Source:* Mischel, 1976, p. 253.

Social-Cognitive Theory's View of the Science of Personality

Many personality theorists have remained outside of the mainstream of psychological science. Freud, Rogers, and Kelly, for example, barely took notice of advances in the overall science of psychology. Social-cognitivists take a different approach. They try to capitalize on advances throughout psychology, as well as related sciences of human nature (Cervone & Mischel, 2002). They pursue an integrative task: to synthesize knowledge from diverse fields into a coherent portrait of human nature and the differences among persons.

A second feature of the social-cognitive view of personality science is its emphasis on the uniqueness of the individual. Social-cognitive theorists employ idiographic (see Chapter 7) methods to capture the idiosyncrasies of individuals (cf. Molenaar & Campbell, 2009).

Finally, Bandura and Mischel have pursued practical applications of their theoretical ideas. They stress that a bottom line for evaluating a theory is whether it yields practical tools that benefit human welfare.

Social-Cognitive Theory of Personality: Structure

The personality structures emphasized by social-cognitive theory mainly involve cognitive processes. Four structural concepts are particularly noteworthy: competencies and skills, expectancies and beliefs, behavioral standards, and personal goals.

Competencies and Skills

The first type of personality structure in social-cognitive theory is skills, or **competencies**. The core insight of the theory is that differences between people we observe may not be caused only by differences in emotions or motivational impulses, as other theories have emphasized. Instead, the differences may reflect variations in people's skill in executing different types of action. Some people may, for example, act in an introverted manner because they lack the social skills that are required to execute socially effective extraverted acts. Others may be conscientious because they have acquired a large degree of cognitive skills that enable them to adhere to social norms.

Of particular interest to social-cognitive theorists, then, are cognitive competencies and skills in solving problems and coping with the challenges of life (Cantor, 1990; Mischel & Shoda, 1999, 2008). Competencies involve both ways of thinking about life problems and behavioral skills in executing solutions to them. They involve two types of knowledge: procedural and declarative knowledge (Cantor & Kihlstrom, 1987). Declarative knowledge is knowledge that we can state in words. Procedural knowledge refers to cognitive and behavioral capacities that a person may have without being able to articulate the exact nature of those capacities; the person can execute the behavioral "procedure" without being able to say how he or she did it. For example, you may be good at cheering up a friend who is feeling depressed, yet you may not be able to say in words precisely what it is that you do that enables you to succeed at this task. Competencies, then, involve a combination of declarative and procedural knowledge.

A focus on competencies has two implications. The first involves **context specificity**. The term refers to the fact that psychological structures that are relevant to some social situations, or contexts, may be irrelevant to others. Context specificity is a natural feature of skills (Cantor & Kihlstrom, 1987). A person may have excellent study skills, but these are of little use when it comes to getting a date or resolving an argument. Different contexts present different challenges that require different competencies. A person who is competent in one context may not be competent in another. This emphasis on context specificity (also see Chapter 14) differentiates social-cognitive theory from trait approaches (Chapters 7 and 8), which feature context-free personality variables. Social-cognitive theory generally rejects context-free variables—particularly when discussing cognitive competencies. The last thing social-cognitivists would do is to assume that one person is "generally more competent" than another. Instead, they recognize that any person's competencies may vary considerably from one domain of life to another.

The second implication involves psychological change. Competencies are acquired through social interaction and observation of the social world (Bandura, 1986). People who lack skills in a particular area of life can change. They can engage in new interactions and new observations of the world and thereby acquire new competencies. The ideas of social-cognitive theory therefore can be applied directly to clinical applications that are designed to boost people's life skills (Chapter 13).

Beliefs and Expectancies

The other three social-cognitive structures can be understood by considering three different ways that people may think about the world (Cervone, 2004). One set of thoughts involves beliefs about what the world *actually is like* and what things probably will be like in the future. These thoughts are called beliefs and—when the beliefs are directed to the future—**expectancies**. A second class of thinking involves thoughts about what things *should* be like. These thoughts are **evaluative standards**, that is, mental criteria (or standards) for evaluating the goodness or worth of events. A third class of thinking involves thoughts about what one *wants to achieve in the future*. These thoughts are called personal **goals**. In addition to competencies, then, the other three main social-cognitive personality structures are beliefs and expectancies, evaluative standards, and goals.

First, we will consider beliefs and expectancies, which we will refer to simply as "expectancies" here because social-cognitive theory so strongly emphasizes the role people's beliefs about prospective future events have in personality functioning.

Social-cognitive theory contends that a primary determinant of our actions and emotions is our expectations about the future. People have expectancies concerning topics such as the likely behavior of other people, the rewards or punishments that may follow a certain type of behavior, or their own ability to handle the stress and challenges. It is this system of thoughts about the future that constitutes the person's expectancies.

As was the case with skills and competencies, a person's expectations may vary considerably from one situation to another. Everyone expects that the same action might elicit different reactions in different situations (e.g., loud, jovial behavior at a party versus a church). People naturally discriminate among situations, expecting different opportunities, rewards, and constraints in different settings. Although researchers sometimes do study generalized expectations, most social-cognitive investigators study expectancies in a domain-linked manner. In other words, they assess people's expectancies with regard to specific areas, or domains, of their life. Social-cognitive theorists recognize that the capacity to vary expectations and behavior from one situation to another is basic to survival. No animal could survive if it failed to make such discriminations. Because of their tremendous cognitive capacity, humans make an incredible variety of discriminations among situations.

A key point in the social-cognitive approach is that, when forming expectancies, people may group together situations in ways that are highly idiosyncratic. One person may group together situations involving school versus social life and, perhaps, have high expectations in one domain and low expectations in the other. Another person may think of situations in terms of relaxing circumstances versus circumstances that make him or her anxious—where both relaxing and anxiety-provoking circumstances could occur both at school and in social life. Yet another person may possess a cognitive category that involves "opportunities to get a date"—where those opportunities could be relaxing or anxiety provoking and could arise in social settings or at school. People naturally "slice up" the situations of their lives in different ways and, thus, may display idiosyncratic patterns of expectancies and social behavior. According to social-cognitive theorists, the essence of personality lies in these differing ways in which unique individuals perceive situations, develop expectations about future circumstances, and display distinct behavior patterns as a result of these differing perceptions and expectations.

This focus on expectancies differentiates social-cognitive theory from behaviorism. In behaviorism, behavior was understood as being caused by reinforcements and punishments in the environment. In contrast, in social-cognitive theory, behavior is explained in terms of people's *expectations about* rewards and punishments in the environment. This is an important difference. The shift to studying expectations, as opposed to merely environmental events, enables the social-cognitive theorist to explain why two different people may react differently to the same environment. The two people may experience similar environmental events, yet develop different expectations about what is likely to happen in the future.

The Self and Self-Efficacy Beliefs

Although some of our expectations concern other people, expectations of particular importance to personality functioning involve the self. Bandura (1997, 2001) has been at the forefront in emphasizing that people's expectations about their own capabilities for performance are the key ingredient in human achievement and well-being. He refers to these expectations as perceptions of self-efficacy. Perceived self-efficacy, then, refers to people's perceptions of their own capabilities for action in future situations.

Why are self-efficacy perceptions so important? It is because self-efficacy perceptions influence a number of different types of behavior that, in turn, are necessary for human achievement.

Consider some area of life in which you have achieved success. For example, if you are a reader of this textbook, you probably were quite successful in high school and thereby succeeded in gaining admission to college. What was required for this success? You had to (1) decide to commit yourself to college admission, (2) persist in study in order to learn material in high school and achieve high grades, and when taking important exams, you had to (3) remain calm, and (4) think in a highly analytical manner. It is precisely these four behavioral mechanisms that are influenced by self-efficacy perceptions (Bandura, 1997). People with a higher sense of self-efficacy are more likely to decide to attempt difficult tasks, to persist in their efforts, to be calm rather than anxious during task performance, and to organize their thoughts in an analytical manner. In contrast, people who question their own capabilities for performance may fail even to attempt valuable activities, may give up when the going gets rough, tend to become anxious during task performance, and often become rattled and fail to think and act in a calm, analytical manner (colloquially speaking, one might say that a person with a low sense of self-efficacy tends to choke on difficult activities).

It is important to recognize that Bandura conceptualizes perceived self-efficacy as different from self-esteem. Self-esteem refers to people's overall evaluation of their personal worth. Perceived self-efficacy, in contrast, refers to people's appraisals of what they are capable of accomplishing in a specific situation.

Sometimes people with high ability lack perceived self-efficacy. Adele is one of the most talented and successful musical artists of the 21st century. Yet, for a period of time after her Grammy Award winning Album, 21, she developed self-doubts: "I lost my confidence . . . for a while I was just a mum." Adele reported that she was 'frightened' by her album's success and, for a while "didn't believe in [herself]." http://www.dailymail.co.uk/tvshowbiz/article-3329116/Adele-reveals-struggled-believe-music-removing-spotlight-three-years-raise-son.html

A second distinction of importance concerns the difference between self-efficacy expectations and outcome expectations (Bandura, 1977). Outcome expectations are beliefs about rewards and punishments that will occur if one performs a given type of behavior. Self-efficacy expectations are beliefs about whether one can perform the behavior in the first place. Suppose that you are considering what major to choose in college. You might believe that there are high rewards (e.g., high financial income in the future) if you were to major in electrical engineering. You would, then, have high outcome expectations with respect to electrical engineering. But you might also think that you are not personally capable of executing the behaviors (e.g., passing all the math, physics, and engineering courses) required to major in electrical engineering. You would have low self-efficacy expectations with respect to electrical engineering. Social-cognitive theory contends that efficacy expectations generally are more important than are outcome expectations as a determinant of behavior. If people lack a sense of efficacy for accomplishing something, the rewards associated with accomplishing that goal are probably irrelevant to them. You are unlikely to select electrical engineering as your major, despite its financial attractions, if you have a low sense of self-efficacy for completing the required courses.

In terms of assessment, Bandura emphasizes what he calls a **microanalytic research** strategy. According to this strategy, detailed measures of perceived self-efficacy are taken before performance of behaviors in specific situations. Specifically, people are asked to indicate their degree of certainty in performing specific behaviors in designated contexts. A self-efficacy scale for athletic performance in, for example, the sport of basketball would *not* ask a vague question such as "Do you think you are a good basketball player?" (The question is vague because the word "good" is so ambiguous: Good compared to your teammates? Compared to an NBA player? Compared to your little brother?) Instead, test items describe specific actions and accomplishments and ask people to indicate their confidence in attaining them: For example, "How confident are you that you can make at least 75% of your free throws during a basketball game?" or "How confident are you that you can dribble upcourt with a basketball even if you are covered by a skilled defensive player?" This assessment strategy follows directly from the theoretical considerations above. In terms of theory, Bandura recognizes that self-efficacy perceptions may vary, for any individual, from one situation to another. In terms of assessment methods, then, situation-specific measures are employed in order to capture this variability. Such measures are much better for capturing the psychological characteristics of the individual. Global self-concept measures are criticized because they "[do] not do justice to the complexity of self-efficacy perceptions, which vary across different activities, different levels of the same activity, and different situational circumstances" (Bandura, 1986, p. 41).

Self-Efficacy and Performance

A basic claim of social-cognitive theory is that self-efficacy perceptions causally influence behavior. If you think critically about such claims, you may already have a counterargument: Maybe self-efficacy perceptions do not really play a causal role. Maybe some other factor is really the cause. Another possible factor is a person's actual level of skill. Skill levels might influence both self-efficacy perceptions and behavior and account for the relation between perceived self-efficacy and motivated action. For example, everyone has a high sense of self-efficacy for picking up a 5-pound weight (we're confident that we can do it) and a low sense of self-efficacy for picking up a 500-pound weight (we perceive ourselves as incapable of doing it). But there's no need to appeal to the notion of perceived self-efficacy to explain why we actually can lift the light weight and not the heavy one. Our behavior can be understood simply in terms of our inherent physical capacities. How, then, do we know that we ever need to appeal to the notion of perceived self-efficacy to explain behavior?

Social-cognitivists have addressed this question through experimental strategies. The idea is to experimentally manipulate perceived self-efficacy while holding other factors—such as people's actual skills—constant. Once self-efficacy perceptions are manipulated experimentally, one can see whether the variations in perceived self-efficacy causally influence behavior.

Of course, one needs a strategy for manipulating perceived self-efficacy. Ideally, the manipulation would be simple and subtle, to ensure that it influenced perceived self-efficacy but did not also influence people's actual skills on the task.

One research strategy has been to employ a technique known as "anchoring" manipulations. Anchoring refers to a thinking process that comes into play when people try to figure out the answer to a problem. What often happens is that the final answer that people reach is greatly influenced by whatever people happen to think of *first* when they try to solve the problem; their final answer is "anchored on" their initial guess. Surprisingly, this occurs even when the initial guess is determined by factors that are completely random and obviously irrelevant to the problem (Tversky & Kahneman, 1974). For example, imagine you are trying to guess a numerical quantity such as the population in millions of the nation of Russia. Suppose that just before you make your estimate, someone pulls a random number out of a hat, reads it aloud—"639"—and then asks, "Do you think there are more or less than 639 million people living in Russia?" You would know that 639 is way too high, and you would know that it also is irrelevant to the real answer because it was chosen randomly. Nonetheless, if you respond like most research participants in anchoring studies, when you then guessed the actual population, your guess would be much higher than if you never had been exposed to the random value. ("Hmm," you might think, "it can't be 639 million. Um . . . maybe it's 400 million.") Your final guess would be "anchored" in the direction of the large number. Conversely, if you first were exposed to a *low* anchor value (e.g., in our population example, the value 20 million), your final guess would probably end up lower. ("Hmm, 20 million, that can't be right. Maybe it's, um . . . 70 million.") The presentation of random anchor values, then, is a way of experimentally manipulating people's judgments.

Cervone and Peake (1986) applied anchoring techniques to the question of self-efficacy judgment and behavior. Prior to performing a task that had a series of items, participants were asked to judge whether they could solve "more or less than X" of the items. In high and low anchor conditions, the "X" was a number that corresponded to a high versus low level of performance. This number appeared to be random, literally drawn out of a hat. People then judged exactly how many items they could solve (their level of self-efficacy on the task). Findings indicated that the anchoring manipulation affected perceived self-efficacy; participants exposed to high and low random numbers had high and low self-efficacy perceptions (Figure 12.1, left panel). This circumstance, then, is exactly what one needs to test the claim that self-efficacy causally influences behavior; thanks to the anchoring manipulation, people *differ* in perceived self-efficacy while being the *same* on other factors, such as actual skills on the task. To provide this test, the experimenters asked people to work on the task and measured their behavioral persistence (i.e., how long they tried working on the problems before giving up). Variations in self-efficacy were

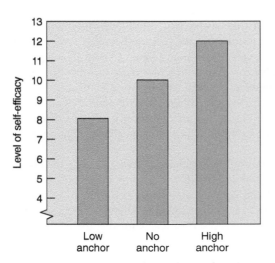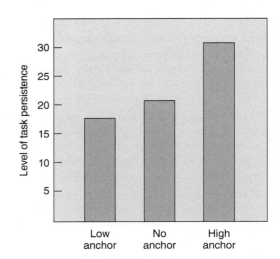

FIGURE 12.1 Mean levels of perceived self-efficacy and behavior as a function of exposure to apparently random high versus low anchor values.
Source: Cervone & Peake, 1986.

found to create corresponding variations in behavior (Figure 12.1, right panel). The groups that had high versus low self-efficacy perceptions differed in their subsequent behavior—even though the high versus low differences were created experimentally and merely by presenting random anchor values.

Such findings provide strong evidence for a central aspect of social-cognitive theory, namely, that people's subjective perceptions of themselves have a unique causal influence on their own behavior. Even when a seemingly irrelevant situational factor causes people to have relatively high or low judgments of self-efficacy, these judgments can affect subsequent decisions and actions.

Self-efficacy beliefs also influence how people cope with disappointments and stress in the pursuit of life goals. Research generally suggests that human functioning is facilitated by a personal sense of control (Schwarzer, 1992). Self-efficacy beliefs represent one aspect of such a sense of control. A study of women coping with abortion demonstrated the importance of self-efficacy beliefs in coping with stressful life events (Cozzarelli, 1993). In this research, women about to obtain an abortion completed questionnaire measures of personality variables such as self-esteem and optimism, as well as a self-efficacy scale measuring expectations concerning successful post abortion coping. For example, the scale included items asking about whether the women thought they would be able to spend time around children or babies comfortably and whether they would continue to have good sexual relations following abortion. Following abortion and then three weeks later, measures of mood and depression were obtained (e.g., the degree to which the women were feeling depressed, regretful, relieved, guilty, sad, good). The results clearly supported the hypothesis that self-efficacy was a key determinant of post abortion adjustment. The contribution of personality variables such as self-esteem and optimism was also related to post abortion adjustment. However, their effects appeared to occur through their contribution to feelings of self-efficacy.

In sum, perceptions of self-efficacy have been shown to have diverse effects on experience and action, in the following ways:

Selection: Self-efficacy beliefs influence the goals individuals select (e.g., individuals with high self-efficacy beliefs select more difficult, challenging goals than do those with low self-efficacy beliefs).

Effort, persistence, and performance: Individuals with high self-efficacy beliefs show greater effort and persistence and perform better relative to individuals with low self-efficacy beliefs (Stajkovic & Luthans, 1998).

Emotion: Individuals with high self-efficacy beliefs approach tasks with better moods (i.e., less anxiety and depression) than individuals with low self-efficacy beliefs.

Coping: Individuals with high self-efficacy beliefs are better able to cope with stress and disappointments than are individuals with low self-efficacy beliefs. Bandura summarizes the evidence concerning the effects of self-efficacy beliefs on motivation and performance as follows: "Human betterment has been advanced more by persisters than by pessimists. Self-belief does not necessarily ensure success, but self-disbelief assuredly spawns failure" (1997, p. 77).

Although self-efficacy beliefs are discussed here in the section on structure, one can correctly infer that they play an important role in the social-cognitive view of motivation.

Goals

The third type of personality structure in social-cognitive theory is goals. A goal is a mental representation of the aim of an action or course of actions. A basic tenet of social-cognitive theory is that people's ability to envision the future enables them to set specific goals for action and, thus, to motivate and direct their own behavior. Goals, then, contribute to the human capacity for self-control. Goals guide us in establishing priorities and in selecting among situations. They enable us to go beyond momentary influences and to organize our behavior over extended periods of time.

A person's goals are organized in a system. In a goal system, some goals are more central or important than others. Goal systems often are understood as having a hierarchical structure. Goals at a higher level in the hierarchy (e.g., get accepted into law school) organize lower-level goals (e.g., get good grades in college), which, in turn, organize lower-level aims (e.g., study for exams). Goal systems, however, are not rigid or fixed. People may select among goals, depending on what seems most important to them at the time, what the opportunities in the environment appear to be, and their judgments of self-efficacy for goal attainment.

People's goals on a task may differ in a variety of ways (Locke & Latham, 1990, 2002). One obvious variation is in the level of challenge, or difficulty, of goals. For example, in a college class, some people may have the goal merely of passing the course, whereas others may adopt the challenging goal of getting an A in the class. Another variation involves the nearness, or proximity, of goals. One person may set a proximal goal, that is, a goal that involves an aim that is coming up soon. Others may set distal goals, that is, goals that specify achievements that are far in the future. For example, if one's goal is to lose weight, a proximal goal might be losing 1 pound each week, whereas a distal goal would be losing 12 pounds in the next 3 months. Research findings indicate that proximal goals often have a bigger influence on one's current behavior than do distal goals (Bandura & Schunk, 1981; Stock & Cervone, 1990). In part, this is because distal goals allow one to "slack off" in the present. For example, the person who wants to lose 12 pounds in 3 months might convince herself that she can go off her diet 1 week and still meet the long-term aim.

In addition, goals may differ in a manner that involves the subjective meaning of an activity. On any challenging task, some people may have the goal of developing more knowledge and skills on the task; the meaning of the task is that it is an opportunity to learn. Others, in contrast, may be more concerned with goals such as not embarrassing themselves in front of others. These differences between "learning" and "performance" goals (Dweck & Leggett, 1988) are discussed in Chapter 13.

Goals are related to the previous social-cognitive personality construct: expectancies. Expectancies influence the process of goal setting. When selecting goals, people generally reflect on their expectations about their performance. People with higher perceptions of self-efficacy often set higher goals and remain more committed to them (Locke & Latham, 2002). Conversely, goals may influence expectancies and may interact systematically with expectancies as people work on tasks and receive feedback on their performance (Grant & Dweck, 1999). For example, suppose that you take an exam and learn that your score was identical to the average score in the class. If your goal was merely to learn something about the course material and to earn a passing grade, then you might be perfectly satisfied with your performance. However, if your goal was to perform exceptionally well in the course in order to impress your friends and your professor, then you might interpret the average grade very negatively and become discouraged, especially if your expectations are that you no longer can achieve your ultimate aims in the course.

Evaluative Standards

The fourth personality structure in social-cognitive theory is evaluative standards. A mental standard is a criterion for judging the goodness, or worth, of a person, thing, or event. The study of evaluative standards, then, addresses the ways in which people acquire criteria for evaluating events and how these evaluations influence their emotions and actions.

Of particular importance in social-cognitive theory are evaluative standards concerning one's self, or "personal standards". Personal standards are fundamental to human motivation and performance. Social-cognitive theory recognizes that people commonly evaluate their ongoing behavior in accordance with internalized personal standards. As an example, imagine that you are writing a term paper for a course. What are you thinking about? On the one hand, you have in mind the content of the material for the paper: the main facts you have to cover, the thesis you are trying to develop, and so forth. On the other hand, inevitably you will find yourself thinking of something else. You will be thinking about the quality of your own writing. You will evaluate whether the sentences you have written are good enough or have to be revised. In other words, you have in mind evaluative standards that you use to judge the goodness or worth of your own behavior. Much of the writing and revising process is one in which you try to alter your own behavior (i.e., your writing) to bring it in line with your own personal standards for writing.

Evaluative standards often trigger emotional reactions. We react with pride when we meet our standards for performance, and we are dissatisfied with ourselves when we fail to meet our own standards. Bandura refers to such emotions as **self-evaluative reactions**; we evaluate our own actions and then respond in an emotionally satisfied or dissatisfied way toward ourselves as a result of this self-evaluation (Bandura, 1986). These emotional reactions constitute self-reinforcements and are important in maintaining behavior over extended periods of time, particularly in the absence of external reinforcers. Thus, through such internal self-evaluative responses as praise and guilt, we are able to reward ourselves for meeting standards and to punish ourselves for violating them.

Social-cognitive theory thus emphasizes that evaluative standards are central to behavior that we call "moral" versus "immoral". Some of the evaluative standards that we learn involve ethical and moral principles concerning the treatment of other people. Although everyone in a given society may be familiar with such principles, sometimes people do not use them to regulate their own behavior. For example, everyone knows that it is wrong to steal things from a store or to include plagiarized material in a term paper, yet some people still do these things; they selectively "disengage" their moral standards when it is to their personal advantage to do so (Bandura, Barbaranelli, Caprara, & Pastorelli, 1996). People who disengage their moral standards say things to themselves that temporarily enable them to disregard their own standards for behavior. For example, a student who is tempted to cheat on a test might say something like "Everybody cheats on tests, so it must be ok." The disengagement of evaluative standards enables people to perform acts that they normally would not perform due to internalized moral sanctions.

A study by Osofsky, Bandura, and Zimbardo (2005) provides a striking example of this point. The evaluative standard of relevance to their study was the moral sanction against killing a fellow human being. Everyone possesses moral standards indicating that killing is wrong. Yet some people in U.S. society kill people as part of their profession; they are executioners who carry out death penalties. How do they do it? How can people who, in general, believe that killing is bad execute prisoners? To answer this question, Osofsky et al. studied personnel who work at maximum-security prisons. Prison personnel differed in the degree to which they were involved in the execution process. Some personnel were relatively uninvolved in executions (e.g., they counseled the prisoner's family members), whereas others were highly involved (e.g., they administered lethal injections). Osofsky et al. asked all participants to complete a scale measuring the tendency to disengage from moral standards involving executions. They found that the degree to which people displayed moral disengagement varied as a function of their level of involvement in executions. Prison personnel who were directly involved in executions displayed much higher levels of moral disengagement than did others; they were more likely to endorse statements such as "An execution is merciful compared to a murder" and "Nowadays the death penalty is done in ways that minimize the suffering of the person being executed"

(Osofsky et al., 2005). Such statements enable one temporarily to disregard, or "disengage," prohibitions against killing.

The study of evaluative standards is another point that differentiates social-cognitive theory from behaviorism. In a behavioristic experiment, the experimenter determines the evaluative standards. He or she decides that a given number of lever presses by a rat, for example, are enough presses to receive a reinforcement. Social-cognitive theorists note that such experiments fail to address a basic fact of human life. In the human case, evaluative standards are not always set by an outside agent. They are determined by the individual. People have their own personal standards for evaluating their own behavior. Ongoing behavior, then, is determined by this internal psychological system, not by forces in the environment, as the behaviorists had argued.

The Nature of Social-Cognitive Personality Structures

In social-cognitive theory, the four personality structures we have reviewed—beliefs and expectancies, goals, evaluative standards, and competencies and skills—are not treated as four independent "objects" in one's mind. Instead, these four personality structures should be understood as referring to distinct classes of thinking. Each of the four is a cognitive subsystem within the overall system of personality. The theoretical claim is that cognitions about what the world actually is like (beliefs), about one's aims for the future (goals), and about how things normatively should be (standards) play distinct roles in personality functioning and, thus, should be treated as distinct personality structures. Similarly, the declarative and procedural knowledge that gives people the capacity to act in an intelligent, skilled manner (competencies) is seen as being psychologically distinct from beliefs, goals, and evaluative standards and, thus, as constituting a distinct personality structure.

Given this view of cognition and personality, the social-cognitive theorist would never assign to a person a single score that is supposed to represent "how much" of each variable the person has. Social-cognitive theorists believe that personality is far too complex to be reduced to any simple set of scores. Instead, each of these four personality structures refers to a complex system of social cognition. People have a large number of goals, a wide spectrum of beliefs, an array of evaluative standards, and a diversity of skills. Different personality structures come into play in different social situations. By studying this complex system of social-cognitive structures, and its interaction with the social world, the social-cognitive theorist tries to grapple with the true complexity of the individual.

Social-Cognitive Theory of Personality: Process

Social-cognitive theory addresses the dynamics of personality processes in two different ways. The first involves general theoretical principles. Social-cognitive theorists have presented two theoretical principles that they think scientists should use when analyzing the dynamics of personality processes. One is an analysis of the causes of behavior, which is called reciprocal determinism. The other is a framework for thinking about internal personality processes, which is called a cognitive–affective processing system (CAPS) framework.

After we review these two ideas—reciprocal determinism and the CAPS model—we will consider the second way in which social-cognitive theory addresses personality processes. By way of preview, this second way is by analyzing psychological functions that are of particular importance in a scientific analysis of personality and individual differences. Three types of psychological functions have received particular attention: (1) observational learning (or learning through "modeling"), (2) motivation, and (3) self-control.

Reciprocal Determinism

Bandura (1986) has introduced a theoretical principle known as **reciprocal determinism**. This principle addresses the issue of cause and effect in the study of personality processes.

The problem Bandura is trying to solve is the following. When analyzing a person's behavior, one generally needs to consider three factors: the person, his or her behavior, and the environmental setting in which the person acts. In this three-part system, how are we to analyze causes and effects? What causes what? Should one say that the person, with his or her personality attributes, is the cause of behavior (as implied in some trait theories of personality)? Should one say that the environment is the real cause of behavior (as argued by the behaviorists)? Bandura thinks we should not say either of these things because both statements are too simplistic. Instead, he argues that causality is a "two-way street." Stated more formally, causality is reciprocal. The three factors under consideration—behavior, personality characteristics, and the environment— are each a cause of one another. The factors are reciprocal determinants. Bandura's principle of reciprocal determinism, then, contends that personality, behavior, and the environment must be understood as a system of forces that mutually influence one another across the course of time.

To understand this principle intuitively, imagine yourself in conversation with someone whom you find attractive. You might smile, look attentive, and try to alter the topics of conversation in a manner that makes a good impression on the other person. Now, from the perspective of a personality scientist, how are we to understand causality in this conversation? What causes what? On the one hand, one could say that the environment causes your behavior. The other person's physical and social attractiveness has caused you to act in a certain way. This is not incorrect; yet it is insufficient. The environment is something that you interpreted, and your particular interpretations are influenced by beliefs and feelings of yours—that is, your personality characteristics. Further, your ability to make a good impression depends on your social skills—another feature of your personality. In addition, your behavior alters the environment you experience. If you skillfully make a good impression, then the other person will be in a better mood, will like you more, will be smiling, will be attentive to you, and so on. In other words, through your own actions, you will have created a more positive social environment. Finally, if you are successful, your behavioral success may alter your mood and your sense of self; there will be an influence of your own behavior on your own personality. It is futile to isolate one factor as "the cause" and the

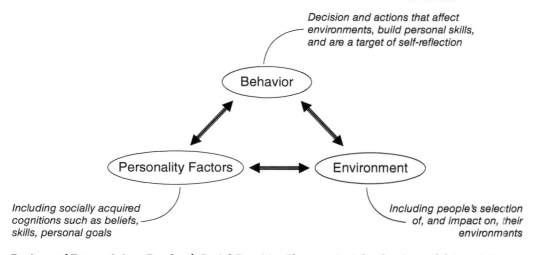

Reciprocal Determinism. Bandura's Social Cognitive Theory principle of reciprocal determinism contrasts with Behaviorism (Chapter 10), which attempted to explain behavior and experience solely in terms of environmental influences. Adapted from Bandura (1978).

other as "the effect" in such a system. Instead, personality, behavior, and the environment must be understood as factors that reciprocally determine one another.

The principle of reciprocal determinism constitutes a rejection of the views of other theories. Some theories explain behavior primarily in terms of inner forces: the inner conflicts of psychoanalysis, the motive for self-actualization of the phenomenological theories, the genetically determined dispositions of the trait theories, and the evolved psychological modules of evolutionary psychology. Others explain behavior in terms of external forces—behaviorism being the paradigm case. Bandura rejects this entire discourse about "inner versus outer" or "internal versus external" forces as woefully inadequate because it fails to recognize that the person's internal psychology and the social environment influence one another reciprocally. People are influenced by environmental forces, but they also choose how to behave. The person is both responsive to situations and actively constructs and influences situations. People select situations as well as are shaped by them; social-cognitive theorists regard the capacity to choose the type of situation that one will encounter as a critical element of people's capacity to be active agents influencing the course of their own development.

Personality as A Cognitive–Affective Processing System (CAPS)

In recent years, social-cognitive theorists increasingly have emphasized that personality should be understood as a system. The term *system* generally refers to something that has a large number of interacting parts. The behavior of the system reflects not only the isolated parts but also the ways in which the parts are interconnected. Systems with a very large number of highly integrated parts often exhibit highly complex and coherent forms of behavior, even if the parts are relatively simple. Dynamic interactions among the parts give rise to the system's complexity. An example of this is the brain. It performs remarkably complex actions despite the fact that its parts—neurons—are relatively simple. The complex interconnections among the parts give rise to the brain's complex capabilities (Damasio, 1994; Edelman & Tononi, 2000).

Social-cognitive theory views personality as a complex system. Social-cognitive variables do not operate in isolation from one another. Instead, the various cognitions and affects interact with one another in an organized fashion; as a result, there is an overall coherence to personality functioning (Cervone & Shoda, 1999b).

A systems view of structure has been articulated by Mischel and Shoda (2008). They present a **cognitive–affective processing system (CAPS)** model of personality. The CAPS model has three essential features. First, cognitive and emotional personality variables are seen as being complexly linked to one another. It is not merely the case that people have a goal (e.g., get more dates), a level of competency (e.g., low dating skills), a particular expectancy (e.g., low perceived self-efficacy for dating), and certain evaluative standards and self-evaluative reactions (e.g., feeling emotionally dissatisfied with oneself when it comes to dating). Instead, their personality system features these cognitions and affects *and* interrelations among them. Thoughts about one's goals may trigger thoughts about skills, which in turn trigger thoughts about self-efficacy, all of which may affect one's self-evaluations and emotions.

The second key feature of the CAPS model concerns the social environment. In this model, different aspects of social situations, or "situational features," activate subsets of the overall personality system. For example, a situation in which you are in a conversation with someone about a date they had last weekend may activate the system of goals and expectancies involving dates outlined in the preceding paragraph. In contrast, a conversation about politics, sports, or classes at school may activate an entirely different set of cognitions and affects.

The third feature follows naturally from the second one. If different situational features activate different parts of the overall personality system, then people's behavior should *vary* from one situation to another. Suppose, hypothetically, that an individual's personality system contains

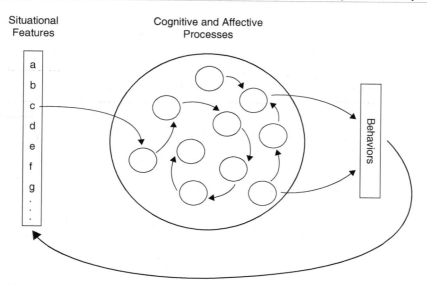

The CAPS model. In the CAPS model of Mischel and Shoda, personality consists of an interacting system of cognitive and affective processes. People's encoding of features of situations that they experience activates these processes which, in turn, generate behavior. As in Bandura's model of reciprocal determinism, behaviors, in turn, influence the environment. Adapted from Mischel and Shoda (1995).

negative thoughts and feelings about their dating skills but positive thoughts and feelings about their academic abilities. Situational features that activate one versus the other concern (dating versus academic performance) should produce, in the individual, entirely different patterns of emotion and action. Although the individual's personality system is stable, his or her experiences and action nonetheless should change from one situation to another as different subsets of the overall personality system become active. This is perhaps the most distinctive feature of the CAPS model. It contends that not only average levels of behavior but also *variations* in behavior are a defining aspect of personality.

Empirical research by Mischel and his associates illustrates the CAPS approach (Shoda, Mischel, & Wright, 1994). Children were observed in various settings—for example, woodworking, cabin meeting, classroom, mealtime, playground, watching TV—for six weeks during summer camp. Researchers coded the type of social interaction that occurred in each of the situations, for example, whether the given child was interacting with a peer or an adult counselor and whether the interaction was positive (e.g., child praised) or negative (e.g., child teased). The researchers also recorded the child's behavior in that situation, attending to behavior of different types: verbal aggression (e.g., provoking, threatening); physical aggression (hitting, pushing); whining or babyish behavior; complying or giving in; talking prosocially. These observations were hourly, five hours a day, six days a week, for 6 weeks—an average of 167 hours of observation per child. This yielded an extensive record of expressions of personality in social context.

When analyzing these data, the investigators plotted *if–then* profiles. In an *if–then* profile analysis, one plots an individual person's behavior in each of a variety of different situations. One then determines if the individual's behavior varies systematically from one situation to another. One might be able to determine that "if" the person encounters a particular type of situation, "then" that person tends to act in a certain manner. The "ifs" and "thens" may vary from one person to another. The profile analysis thus captures idiosyncratic tendencies exhibited by unique individuals.

What, then, were the findings? Of course, there was evidence of considerable differences in behaviors expressed in different situations. People do behave differently in different types of situations. In general, behavior is different on the playground than in the classroom, in a cabin meeting than in woodworking. And, of course, there were individual differences in average expressions of each of the five observed types of behavior. As trait theorists suggest, there are individual differences in average expressions of behavior across situations. However, the more critical question for social-cognitive theory is whether individuals can be described in terms of their distinctive patterns of situation–behavior relationships. In other words, do individuals differ in their patterns of behavior even if their overall levels are the same? Can two individuals express the same average level of aggressive behavior, be the same on a trait such as aggressiveness, but differ in the kinds of situations in which they express their aggressiveness? Mischel and his associates indeed found clear evidence that individuals have distinctive, stable profiles of expressing particular behaviors in specific groups of situations.

Consider, for example, the verbal aggression profiles of two individuals in relation to five types of psychological situations (Figure 12.2). Clearly, the two differ in their profiles of expressing verbal aggression across the various situations. Each behaves reasonably consistently within specific groups of situations but differently between groups of situations. Averaging behavior across situations would mask such distinctive patterns of situation–behavior relationships.

Interestingly, laypersons—that is, people who are not trained professionally in psychology—appear naturally to recognize the importance of *if . . .then . . .* variability in action. This was demonstrated in recent studies by Kammrath, Mendoza-Denton, and Mischel (2005). In one study, laypersons were asked how they expected people with different personality characteristics to behave in different situations. Results indicated that laypersons did not anticipate that people would act in a uniform, consistent manner in different contexts. Instead, they anticipated *if–then* variability; they expected that people's behavior would vary substantially from one situation to another. In a second study, participants were told about the actions of individuals whose behavior varied distinctively across different situations. Research participants were not befuddled by these violations of traitlike consistency in behavior. Instead, they inferred that people possessed motives that explained their patterns of variability in conduct (Kammrath et al., 2005).

What can be concluded from this program of research? Mischel and his associates suggest that individuals have distinctive profiles of situation–behavior relationships, which are called **behavioral signatures**. "It is this type of intra individual stability in the pattern and organization of behavior that seems especially central for a psychology of personality ultimately devoted to understanding and capturing the uniqueness of individual functioning" (Shoda, Mischel, &

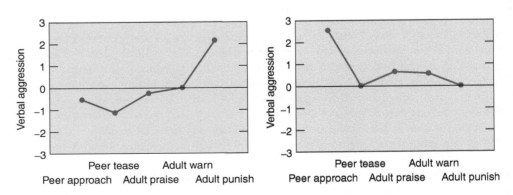

FIGURE 12.2 Illustrative intra individual profiles of verbal aggression for two individuals across five types of psychological situations.

Adapted from Shoda, Mischel, & Wright, 1994, p. 6.

Wright, 1994, p. 683). Mischel and colleagues emphasized that these unique patterns of behavior would be completely overlooked if one merely asked about people's overall, average behavioral tendencies. Two people who, for example, display the same average level of anxiety may be fundamentally different people. An *if–then* profile analysis might reveal that one person is anxious in achievement settings and the other is anxious when it comes to romantic relationships. The analysis would indicate that the different people have different personality dynamics—despite the fact that they might happen to get the same score on "global trait anxiety" if a researcher averages together their responses in the different situations of their lives. The basic message Mischel and colleagues send to other psychologists, then, is this: Don't average together the different situations of their lives! Instead, look closely at individuals and the distinctive patterns of variability in action that they display in different circumstances.

To summarize the social-cognitive view of motivation, a person develops goals or standards that serve as the basis for action. People consider alternative courses of action and make decisions on the basis of the anticipated outcomes (external and internal) and the perceived self-efficacy for performing the necessary behaviors. Once action has been taken, the outcome is assessed in terms of the external rewards from others and one's own internal self-evaluations. Successful performance may lead to enhanced self-efficacy and either a relaxation of effort or the setting of higher standards for further effort. Unsuccessful performance or failure may lead to giving up or continued striving, depending on the value of the outcome to an individual and to his or her sense of self-efficacy in relation to further effort.

Social-Cognitive Theory of Growth and Development

Observational Learning (Modeling)

So far, we have outlined four personality structures that are central to social-cognitive theory and have reviewed two theoretical principles that Bandura and Mischel use to understand the nature of personality and the causes of behavior. We now can see these theoretical ideas put into action. Social-cognitive theorists use these theoretical principles to understand two main psychological activities, or what we will call here two psychological functions: (1) acquiring new knowledge and skills, particularly through processes of observational learning and (2) exerting control over, or self-regulating, one's own actions and emotional experiences.

The first of these two psychological functions concerns the question of how people acquire knowledge and skills. How do we learn social skills? How do we acquire particular beliefs, goals, and standards for evaluating our behavior? Previous theories commonly have overlooked these questions. There is little explicit discussion of the acquisition of beliefs and social skills in most of the previous theories we have discussed. The theory that addressed the topic most explicitly was behaviorism. As you will recall, behaviorists claim that people learn things through a trial-and-error learning process called shaping, or successive approximation. Over a large series of learning trials, reinforcements gradually shape a complex pattern of behavior. Although there are lots of errors at first, through reinforcement processes, behavior gradually approximates a desired pattern.

In a profoundly important development for psychology, Albert Bandura succeeded in explaining the shortcomings of this behavioral theory and in providing psychology with an alternative theoretical explanation. In retrospect, the shortcomings of the behavioral approach seem obvious. Sometimes, learning simply cannot be through trial and error because the errors are too costly.

As an example, consider the first time you ever drove a car. According to the behaviorists, reinforcements and punishments would gradually shape your safe driving behavior. On Day 1 of driving, you might get into 9 or 10 traffic accidents, but due to reinforcement processes on Day 2, you might only have 5 or 6 accidents, and after a few more trials, the errors would disappear and the environment would have shaped safe driving behavior. Is this what actually happened? We sure hope not! In reality, the first time you sat behind the wheel—before you ever had been reinforced or punished for specific driving behaviors—you already were able to drive a car fairly adequately. What needs to be explained is the human capacity to learn such skills in the absence of prior rewards and punishments.

Social-cognitive theory explains that people can learn merely by observing the behaviors of others. The person being observed is called a model, and this **observational learning** process is also known as **modeling**. People's cognitive capacities enable them to learn complex forms of behavior merely by observing a model performing these behaviors. As Bandura (1986) has detailed, people can form an internal mental representation of the behavior they have observed and then can draw upon that mental representation at a later time. Learning by modeling is evident in innumerable domains of life. A child may learn language by observing parents and other people speaking. You may have learned some of the basic skills for driving (where to put your hands and feet, how to start the car, how to turn the wheel) merely by observing other drivers. People learn what types of behavior are acceptable and unacceptable in different social settings by observing the actions of others.

What's on? Bandura's research on observational learning drew attention to the possibility that children were learning negative patterns of behavior, such as aggression, merely by watching TV.

This modeling process can be much more complex than simple imitation or mimicry. The notion of "imitation" generally implies the exact replication of a narrow response pattern. In modeling, however, people may learn general rules of behavior by observing others. They then can use those rules to self-direct a variety of types of behavior in the future. Bandura's conceptualization of modeling also is narrower than the psychodynamic notion of identification. Identification implies an incorporation of broad patterns of behavior exhibited by a specific other individual. Modeling, in contrast, involves the acquisition of information through observation of others, without implying that the observer internalizes entire styles of action exhibited by the other individual. The individual who is observed in the process of observational learning (i.e., the model) need not be someone who is physically present. In contemporary society, much modeling occurs through the media. We may learn styles of thought and action from people whom we never meet but whom we merely observe on television or other media sources. A social concern is that television often models antisocial behavior such as aggression; research indicates that exposure to high levels of aggression in the media when one is a child can cause people to learn aggressive patterns of behavior that are evident later in life. Huesmann and colleagues (Huesmann, Moise-Titus, Podolski, & Eron, 2003) performed a long-term longitudinal study on the question of whether exposure to violence in the media during childhood leads to higher levels of aggression later in life. Among both men and women, people who witnessed high levels of violence when they were 6–10 years old turned out to be more aggressive in early adulthood. The link between media violence in childhood and aggression in adulthood held up even when the researchers statistically controlled for factors other than media exposure (e.g., socioeconomic status) that might possibly be correlated with levels of aggression. Bandura's research on modeling clearly has important social implications.

Acquisition versus Performance

An important part of the theory of modeling is the distinction between **acquisition** and **performance**. A new, complex pattern of behavior can be learned or acquired regardless of reinforcers, but whether or not the behavior is performed will depend on rewards and punishments. Consider, for example, the classic study by Bandura and his associates to illustrate this distinction (Bandura, Ross, & Ross, 1963). In this study, three groups of children observed a model expressing aggressive behavior toward a plastic Bobo doll. In the first group, the aggressive behavior by the model was not followed by any consequences (No Consequences); in the second group, the model's aggressive behavior was followed by rewards (Reward); and in the third group it was followed by punishment (Punishment). Following observation of the model's aggressive behavior, children from the three groups were presented with two conditions. In the first condition, the children were left alone in a room with many toys, including a Bobo doll. They were then observed through a one-way mirror to see if they would express the aggressive behaviors of the model (No Incentive condition). In the next condition, the children were given attractive incentives for reproducing the model's behavior (Positive Incentive condition).

Two relevant questions can be asked. First, did the children behave aggressively when they were given an incentive to do so as opposed to when they were not? Many more imitative aggressive behaviors were shown in the Incentive condition than in the No Incentive condition (Figure 12.3). In other words, the children had learned (acquired) many aggressive behaviors that were not performed under the No Incentive condition but were performed under the Incentive condition. This result demonstrated the use of the distinction between acquisition and performance. Second, did the consequences to the model affect the children's display of aggressive

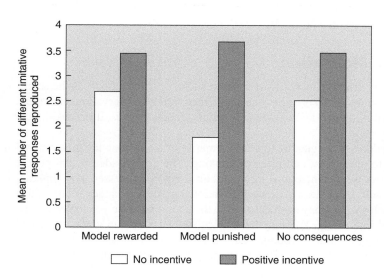

FIGURE 12.3 Mean number of different imitative responses reproduced by children as a function of response consequences to the model and positive incentives.

Bandura (1965). Copyright 1965 by the American Psychological Association. Reprinted by permission.

behavior? Observation of behavior in the No Incentive condition indicated clear differences; children who observed the model being punished performed far fewer imitative acts than did children in the model Rewarded and No Consequences groups (Figure 12.3). This difference, however, was wiped out by offering the children attractive incentives for reproducing the model's behavior (Positive Incentive). In sum, the consequences to the model had an effect on the children's performance of the aggressive acts but not on the learning of them.

Vicarious Conditioning

A number of other studies have since demonstrated that the observation of consequences to a model affects performance but not acquisition. The difference between acquisition and performance suggests, however, that in some way the children were being affected by what happened to the model; that is, either on a cognitive basis, on an emotional basis, or both, the children were responding to the consequences to the model. The suggestion here is that the children learned certain emotional responses by sympathizing with the model, that is, vicariously by observing the model. Not only can behavior be learned through observation, but emotional reactions such as fear and joy can also be conditioned on a vicarious basis: "It is not uncommon for individuals to develop strong emotional reactions toward places, persons, and things without having had any personal contact with them" (Bandura, 1986, p. 185).

emotions

The process of learning emotional reactions through observing others, known as **vicarious conditioning,** has been demonstrated in both humans and animals. Thus, human subjects who observed a model expressing a conditioned fear response were found to develop a vicariously conditioned emotional response to a previously neutral stimulus (Bandura & Rosenthal, 1966). Similarly, in an experiment with animals, it was found that an intense and persistent fear of snakes developed in younger monkeys who observed their parents behave fearfully in the presence of real or toy snakes. What was particularly striking about this research is that the period of observation of their parents' emotional reaction was sometimes very brief. Further, once the vicarious conditioning took place, the fear was found to be intense, long lasting, and present in situations different from those in which the emotional reaction was first observed (Mineka, Davidson, Cook, & Kleir, 1984).

Although observational learning can be a powerful process, one should not think that it is automatic or that one is bound to follow in the footsteps of others. Children, for example, have multiple models and can learn from parents, siblings, teachers, peers, and television. In addition, they learn from their own direct experience. Beyond this, as children get older, they may actively select which models they will observe and attempt to emulate.

Self-Regulation and Motivation

As we have just reviewed, one central personality process in social-cognitive theory is the acquisition of knowledge and skills, which is commonly accomplished through observational learning. A second process concerns putting that knowledge into action. In other words, it involves questions of human motivation.

Social-cognitive theory addresses human motivation primarily by examining the motivational impact of thoughts related to oneself, or self-referent thinking. The general idea is that people commonly guide and motivate their own actions through their thinking processes. Key thinking processes often involve the self. Consider your own motivational processes as they relate to this course in personality psychology. You may have enrolled in the course because you expected that you would find the material interesting. You may have calculated an expected grade you could earn in the course; in selecting this course, you may have avoided other course options in which you expected that you might earn a low grade. During the time you have been in the course, you

CURRENT APPLICATIONS

Don't Blame Me—It was that Video Game!

In November 2002, a teenager in the state of Wisconsin was arrested for auto theft. This was no minor case of theft: The teen was charged with stealing about a hundred vehicles! What could cause such behavior? Hostile impulses buried deep in the teen's unconscious? A lifelong trait of criminality?

As reported by the Associated Press, the teenager himself had a much simpler explanation: "He had been inspired by the video game "Grand Theft Auto". In the game, players control animated figures who violently battle law enforcement officials as they go on crime rampages, including the theft of autos. As the local police chief in Wisconsin reported, after playing this game for many hours, the teenager felt that stealing real cars would be "challenging and fun". In the language of social-cognitive theory, the game provided psychological models of illegal behavior, including the anticipated benefits (fun, challenge) of that behavior.

This, of course, is just a single, isolated case. It does not provide scientific evidence that playing video games actually contributed to this particular teenager's behavior. Nor does it answer the key question: In general, does playing a lot of violent video games cause a person to act more violently in the real world?

This question can be answered. It can be done by evaluating a large number of cases in which one can measure both game playing and real-world aggression. One then can determine the overall degree to which exposure to violent and criminal acts in video games is related to real-world aggressive behavior.

The psychologists Craig Anderson and Brad Bushman have provided an analysis of this sort. They analyzed the results obtained in 35 research reports examining the relation between violent video game playing and various measures of real-world aggression. Their sample included more than 4,000 participants who had taken part in both correlational studies (i.e., studies correlating game playing and aggression) and experimental studies (i.e., studies in which exposure to violence in video games was controlled experimentally).

As the authors summarize, the results of their analyses "clearly support the hypothesis that exposure to violent video games poses a public-health threat to children and youths, including college-age individuals" (Anderson & Bushman, 2001, p. 358). In both experimental and nonexperimental

PeopleImages / Getty Images, Inc.

studies, higher exposure to violence in video games was linked to higher levels of aggression, as well as to lower levels of prosocial behavior. The overall correlation between levels of violent game playing and levels of aggression was a little under .2. Although a correlation of this size means that there are many people who play violent video games and yet are not violent in other aspects of their life, it nonetheless is large enough to indicate that violent game playing can have a detrimental effect on large numbers of people.

Subsequent research by the authors indicates one way in which game playing has its effects (Bushman & Anderson, 2002). Playing violent games produces a "hostile expectation bias". In this experimental research, people played either a nonviolent or a violent video game. They subsequently were asked whether various interpersonal conflicts depicted in stories (that were not part of the game) involved feelings of aggression and hostility on the part of the story characters. People who had played the violent game subsequently were biased to think that the story characters were feeling and acting aggressively and were having aggressive thoughts. This result implies that people who play violent video games may, in their day-to-day life, more frequently think that other people around them are having hostile, aggressive thoughts. This, of course, could contribute to hostile feelings and actions on their part.

It appears, then, that "fun" and "challenge" are not the only feelings created by violent video games.

Sources: Anderson & Bushman, 2001; Associated Press, November 14, 2002. Bushman & Anderson, 2002.

may have set personal goals for performance in the class and may have guided your own studying by reminding yourself that "I've got to finish reading these chapters before the midterm exam!" It is these personal expectations, personal goals, and talking to oneself that social-cognitive theory sees as being at the heart of human motivation.

The general term for personality processes that involve the self-directed motivation of behavior is **self-regulation** (Gailliot Mead, & Baumeister, 2008). The term is meant to imply that people have the capacity to motivate themselves: to set personal goals, to plan strategies, and to evaluate and modify their ongoing behavior. Self-regulation involves not only getting started in goal attainment but also avoiding environmental distractions and emotional impulses that might interfere with one's progress.

The process of self-regulation inherently involves all of the social-cognitive personality structures that we have reviewed thus far. People regulate their behavior by setting personal goals and by evaluating their ongoing behavior according to evaluative standards for performance. Expectancies also are critical; in particular, high expectations of self-efficacy may be necessary if people are to persevere in their goals despite running into setbacks along the way.

In its study of self-regulation, social-cognitive theory emphasizes the human capacity for foresight—our ability to anticipate outcomes and make plans accordingly (Bandura, 1990). Thus, according to Bandura, "most human motivation is cognitively generated" (1992, p. 18). People vary in the standards they set for themselves. Some individuals set challenging goals, others easy goals; some individuals have very specific goals, others ambiguous goals; some emphasize short-term, proximal goals, while others emphasize long-range, distal goals (Cervone & Williams, 1992). In all cases, however, it is the anticipation of satisfaction with desired accomplishments and dissatisfaction with insufficient accomplishments that provides the incentives for our efforts. In this analysis, people are seen as proactive rather than as merely reactive. People set their own standards and goals, rather than merely responding to demands from the environment. Through the development of cognitive mechanisms such as expectancies, standards, and self-evaluation, we are able to establish goals for the future and gain control over our own destiny (Bandura, 1989a, 1989b, 1990). Thus, growth and development involve changes in cognitive mechanisms associated with self-regulation. With such development, there is increased potential for self-regulation.

Self-Efficacy, Goals, and Self-Evaluative Reactions

Research in social-cognitive theory has examined how these multiple personality processes—self-efficacy perceptions, goals, and self-evaluation of one's ongoing behavior—combine to contribute to self-regulation. Bandura and Cervone (1983) studied the effects of goals and performance feedback on motivation. The hypothesis tested was that performance motivation reflects both the presence of goals and the awareness of how one is doing relative to standards: "Simply adopting goals, whether easy or personally challenging ones, without knowing how one is doing seems to have no appreciable motivational effects" (p. 123). The assumption was that greater discrepancies between standards and performances would generally lead to greater self-dissatisfaction and efforts to improve performance. However, a critical ingredient of such efforts is self-efficacy judgments. Thus, the research tested the hypothesis that self-efficacy judgments, as well as self-evaluative judgments, mediate between goals and goal-directed effort.

In this research, subjects performed a strenuous activity under one of four conditions: goals with feedback on their performance, goals alone, feedback alone, and absence of goals and feedback. Following this activity, described as part of a project to plan and evaluate exercise programs for postcoronary rehabilitation, subjects rated how self-satisfied or self-dissatisfied they would be with the same level of performance in a following session. In addition, they recorded their perceived self-efficacy for various possible performance levels. Their effortful performance was then again measured. In accord with the hypothesis, the condition combining goals and performance

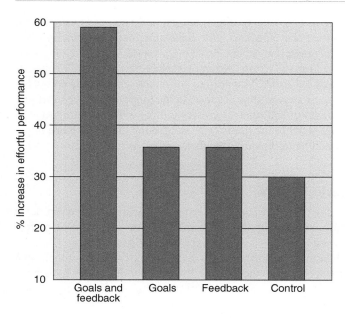

FIGURE 12.4 Mean percentage increase in effortful performance under conditions varying in goals and performance feedback.

Bandura and Cervone (1983). Copyright © 1983 by the American Psychological Association. Reprinted by permission.

feedback had a strong motivational impact, whereas neither goals alone nor feedback alone had comparable motivational significance (Figure 12.4). Also, subsequent effort was most intense when subjects were both dissatisfied with substandard performance and high on self-efficacy judgments for good attainment. Neither dissatisfaction alone nor positive self-efficacy judgments alone had a comparable effect. Often, effort was reduced where there were both low dissatisfaction with performance and low perceived self-efficacy. There was, then, clear evidence that goals have motivating power through self-evaluative and self-efficacy judgments.

Performance feedback and self-efficacy judgments also are important to the development of intrinsic interest. Psychologists have been able to enhance students' interest in learning and performance by helping them to break down tasks into subgoals, helping them to monitor their own performance, and providing them with feedback that increased their sense of self-efficacy (Bandura & Schunk, 1981; Schunk & Cox, 1986). Intrinsic interest thus develops when the person has challenging standards that provide for positive self-evaluation when met, as well as the sense of self-efficacy in the potential for meeting those standards. It is such intrinsic interest that facilitates effort over extended periods of time in the absence of external rewards. Conversely, it is difficult to sustain motivation where one feels that the external or internal self-evaluative rewards are insufficient or where one's sense of efficacy is so low that a positive outcome seems impossible. Self-perceived inefficacy can nullify the motivating potential of even the most desirable outcomes. For example, no matter how attractive it might seem to become a movie star, people will not be motivated in that direction unless they feel that they have the necessary skills. In the absence of such a sense of self-efficacy, becoming a movie star remains a fantasy rather than a goal that is pursued in action.

Self-Control and Delay of Gratification

Sometimes you need to *do* something, but you can't get yourself to do it. For example, you might need to start working on a term paper that is due at the end of the semester, but for some reason, you can't get yourself to start actually doing the writing. It is under these circumstances that clear goals and standards for performance and a strong sense of self-efficacy are beneficial.

Now, we turn to a different type of psychological problem. Sometimes, you need to *stop* doing something. There may be some behavior that you find quite enjoyable, but it is socially inappropriate and/or potentially harmful to yourself or others. Smoking, overeating, and driving your car down the highway at 100 miles per hour are obvious examples. Here, the psychological challenge is the opposite of the one we analyzed above. You need to curtail the intrinsically enjoyable behavior. You need to control your impulsive reactions because, in the long run, it is better if you do not give in to them. When these cases of self-control involve putting off something good in the present in order to attain something better in the future (e.g., not having that extra piece of pie now so that, in the future, one will be in better health), the phenomenon is referred to as "delay of gratification".

Learning Delay of Gratification Skills

Research in social-cognitive theory suggests that people's capacity to delay gratification has a social basis. Modeling and observational learning are important to the development of performance standards for success and reward that serve as a basis for delay of gratification. Children exposed to models who set high standards of performance for self-reward tend to limit their own self-rewards to exceptional performance to a greater degree than do children who have been exposed to models who set lower standards or to no models at all (Bandura & Kupers, 1964). Children will model standards even if they result in self-denial of available rewards (Bandura, Grusec, & Menlove, 1967) and will also impose learned standards on other children (Mischel & Liebert, 1966). Children can be made to tolerate greater delays in receiving gratification if they are exposed to models exhibiting such delay behavior.

The effects of a model on delay behavior in children are well illustrated in research by Bandura and Mischel (1965). Children found to be high and low in delay of gratification were exposed to models of the opposite behavior. In a live-model condition, each child individually observed a testing situation in which an adult model was asked to choose between an immediate reward and a more valued object at a later date. The high-delay children observed a model who selected the immediately available reward and commented on its benefits, whereas the low-delay children observed a model who selected the delayed reward and commented on the virtues of delay. In a symbolic-model condition, children read verbal accounts of these behaviors, the verbal account again being the opposite of the child's pattern of response. Finally, in a no-model condition, children were just apprised of the choices given the adults. Following exposure to one of these three procedures, the children were again given a choice between an immediate reward and a more valuable reward. The results were that the high-delay children in all three conditions significantly altered their delay of reward behavior in favor of immediate gratification. The live-model condition produced the greatest effect (Figure 12.5). The low-delay children exposed to a delay model significantly altered their behavior in terms of greater delay, but there was no significant difference between the effects of live and symbolic models. Finally, for both groups of children, the effects were found to be stable when the tests were readministered four to five weeks later.

As mentioned previously, the performance of observed behaviors clearly is influenced by the observed consequences to the model. For example, children who watch a film in which a child is not punished for playing with toys that were prohibited by the mother are more likely to play with prohibited toys than are children who see no film or see a film in which the child is punished (Walters & Parke, 1964). The old saying "Monkey see, monkey do" is not completely true. It would be more appropriate to say "Monkey sees reward or is not punished, monkey does." After all, the monkey is no fool.

Mischel's Delay of Gratification Paradigm

In addition to the issue of social influences such as modeling on delay of gratification, another question involves the exact cognitive processes that enable people to control their impulses. What can you do if you want to control your impulses? What mental strategies enable people to delay

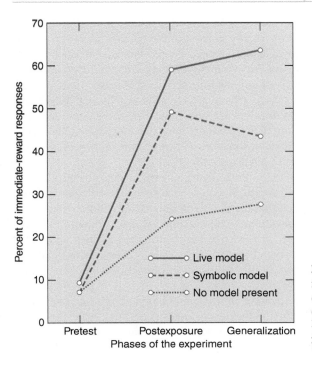

FIGURE 12.5 Mean percentage of immediate-reward responses by high-delay children on each of three test periods for each of three experimental conditions. Bandura & Mischel, 1965. Copyright © by the American Psychological Association. Reprinted by permission.

gratification? Much insight into this question comes from an exceptionally informative line of research pioneered by Mischel (1974) and Metcalfe & Mischel (1999).

In Mischel's **delay of gratification** paradigm, often described as "the marshmallow experiment," an adult who is interacting with a young child (usually one of preschool age) informs the child that she needs to leave the child alone for a few minutes. Before leaving, the adult teaches the child a game. The game involves two different rewards. If the child can wait patiently until the adult comes back, she gets a large reward (e.g., a few marshmallows). If the child simply cannot wait for the adult to return, the child can ring a bell and the adult will return immediately; however, if this happens, the child earns only a smaller reward (e.g., one marshmallow). The child, then, can earn the larger reward only by delaying gratification. The dependent measure is how long children are able to wait before ringing the bell.

A critical experimental manipulation in this setting is whether children can see the reward—or, phrased more technically, whether the rewards are available for attention. In one experimental condition, children could see the rewards. In another, the rewards were not available for attention; they simply were covered up. This simple experimental manipulation proved to have a huge effect on children's delay abilities. When the rewards were covered up, most children were able to wait a relatively long time. But when the children were looking at the rewards, they had an enormously hard time controlling their impulses. It appears that looking at rewards that one is not supposed to have primarily is a frustrating experience that children have a hard time handling (Mischel, 1974). Being unable to look at the rewards, then, makes the situation easier to handle.

Subsequent work showed that the key factor in delay of gratification is what is going on in children's minds as they try to wait for the large reward. Children do well at the task if they employ cognitive strategies that distract them from the attractive qualities of the rewards. If children are taught to think about how marshmallows resemble some nonfood object (e.g., clouds), or are asked to form mental images in which they think of the rewards as if they are merely photos rather than real things, or are taught to sing songs to themselves or play other mentally distracting games during the delay period, then they are able to delay gratification even if the rewards are in sight (Mischel & Baker, 1975; Mischel & Moore, 1973; Moore, Mischel, & Zeiss, 1976). "Thus, what is in the children's heads—not what is physically in front of them—crucially affects their ability to purposefully sustain delay in order to achieve their preferred but delayed goals. . . . If the children imagine the real objects as present they cannot wait long for them. In contrast, if they imagine pictures of the objects, they can wait for long time periods" (Mischel, 1990, p. 123). Imagining a mere picture of the object is a "cool" encoding (Metcalfe & Mischel, 1999), that is, a way of thinking about the stimulus that does not activate "hot," impulsive emotional systems. People seem more capable of controlling their emotional reactions, then, when they focus their attention on less emotional features of a given situation. The impact of "hot" versus "cool" encoding for interpersonal behavior is reviewed in Chapter 14.

Mischel's delay of gratification findings vividly illustrate the human capacity for self-control. It is instructive to contrast his social-cognitive approach with behaviorism. The behaviorist looking at Mischel's paradigm might have argued that the main determinant of children's behavior would be the reward contingencies. The problem with that argument is that children in the different experimental conditions all had *exactly the same* reward contingencies; they all got the same small and large rewards based on the same behavior. Mischel's research, then, illustrates the power of something that classic behaviorism never thought of, namely, *mental representations* of rewards.

Do individual differences in delay of gratification ability in childhood persist into later years of life? To find out, researchers studied children in the delay studies years later, when they were adolescents. They related delay of gratification scores in preschool to adolescent measures of cognitive and social competence (as rated by parents) and to the adolescents' verbal and quantitative SAT scores. Childhood delay of gratification ability predicted adolescent outcomes, with high-delay children becoming adolescents who were more able to control their emotions and who obtained higher SAT scores (Shoda, Mischel, & Peake, 1990).

CURRENT QUESTIONS

What Does the Marshmallow Test Measure and What are Its Social Policy Implications?

Mischel's marshmallow experiment has been described as "one of the most famous and delightful experiments in modern psychology" (Brooks, 2011; Mischel, 2014). The concept of delay of gratification and related concepts (e.g., self-regulation, willpower, ego strength, conscientiousness) are among the most widely studied in the social sciences (Duckworth, 2011). But questions have been raised about the concept, its measurement, and its social policy implications.

Does the marshmallow test measure the ability to delay gratification or might it measure something else, such as trust, the ability to think about and have confidence in the future, or perhaps even intelligence (Bourne, 2014; Konnikova, 2013)? Are all the seemingly related concepts really the same or are they different? Is it really self-control and do early measures of it really have predictive power? Recent research addressing these issues suggests the following conclusions: 1) The various self-control concepts and related measure are associated with one another but are not identical (Duckworth & Kern, 2011). 2) The concept of self-control is distinct from that of intelligence or socioeconomic status (Duckworth, 2011; Moffitt et al., 2011). 3) Measures of self-control, including the marshmallow task, have significant predictive power in terms of later functioning in areas such as school success, occupational success, physical and mental health, and lack of criminal convictions (Duckworth & Carlson, in press; Duckworth, Tsukayama, & Kirby, 2013; Moffitt et al., 2011).

But what of the social policy implications? Is self-control a fixed personality characteristic, either by genes or by the earliest years of the environment (or the interaction between the two), or can it be modified by early intervention programs, to the benefit of individuals and society? According to one recent review, there is evidence that school-based interventions, targeting both individual cognitive strategies and the school culture, provide proof that self-regulation can be cultivated (Duckworth & Carlson, in press).

Delay ability in childhood also predicts health-related outcomes. When researchers related delay ability at age 4 to body mass index measured at age 11, they found that children who were poor at delaying gratification were more likely to become overweight (Schlam et al., 2013; Seeyave et al., 2009). This result is consistent with research showing that the ability to control impulses and emotions is relatively stable across the life span and contributes to important life outcomes such as academic performance, alcohol and drug abuse, overeating, and monetary spending (Gailliot, Mead, & Baumeister, 2008).

Personality and the Brain
Delay of Gratification

As you've just seen, individual differences in the ability to delay gratification are detectable early in childhood and often persist into the later years of life. A challenge for research on personality and the brain is to identify the neural bases of these differences among individuals.

Note that we said neural "bases," plural. At a psychological level of analysis, there is not one, but two, components to delay of gratification: (1) the impulsive desire to attain a reward and (2) cognitive strategies that people use to avoid acting on that impulse. One should expect, then, that a biological analysis will identify at least two areas of the brain that might contribute to individual differences in delay ability: a brain system underlying impulsive reactions to rewards and another brain system that underlies the ability to devise cognitive strategies.

Researchers who have searched for these brain regions have done so in a study that was conducted with an interesting group of participants: adults who, when they were children, participated in Mischel's delay of gratification experiments (Casey et al., 2011). By studying this population, the researchers could relate childhood delay of gratification abilities to adulthood brain activity. They expected to find links from childhood to adulthood because self-control abilities are relatively consistent across the life course.

Two types of participants were identified: people who were either (1) consistently good or (2) consistently poor at delaying gratification in childhood. These people, as adults, were asked to attempt a task that required them to control their impulses. In the task, called a go/no-go task, the participants have to either press a button (go) or inhibit their tendency to press the button (no go) in response to different stimuli that are shown rapidly on a video screen. The ability to control the urge to press the button (when pressing it is inappropriate) taps some of the same mental control abilities that are needed to delay gratification in the original Mischel research paradigm. Participants performed the go/no-go task while in a brain scanner. The researchers thus could search for variations in the brain that corresponded to variations in delay of gratification ability.

As expected, they found such variations in not one but two regions of the brain:

- One region was in the frontal lobes. The brain's frontal lobes are a higher-level brain region critical to the human ability to make plans and to control the flow of one's own actions, especially when choosing between two courses of action. Delay ability was found to be positively related to activity within the frontal lobes. People who (as children) were better at self-control displayed (as adults) more activity in this brain region.

- The other was a brain structure known as the *striatum*, which is found in a lower region of the brain. The striatum is known to be involved in the processing of information about rewards. Delay ability related *negatively* to activation in this region. People who had *less* delay of gratification ability in childhood displayed *more* brain activation in this reward-processing area of the brain as adults. The researchers suggest that this high level of activation in the striatum may overwhelm the frontal lobes' ability to control behavior (Casey et al., 2011).

The research, then, provides insight into two neural bases of individual differences in the ability to delay gratification.

In addition, there is an action component to this research in terms of school-based intervention programs to improve self-control mechanisms in young children (Duckworth & Carlson, in press).

Summary of the Social-Cognitive View of Growth and Development

In addition to the importance of direct experience, social-cognitive theory emphasizes the importance of models and observational learning in personality development. Individuals acquire emotional responses and behaviors through observing the behaviors and emotional responses of models (i.e., the processes of observational learning and vicarious conditioning). Whether acquired behaviors are performed similarly depends on directly experienced consequences and the observed consequences to models. By experiencing direct external consequences, individuals learn to expect rewards and punishments for specific behaviors in specific contexts. Through vicarious experiencing of consequences to others, individuals acquire emotional reactions and learn expectancies without going through the often painful step of experiencing consequences directly. Thus, through direct experience and observation, through direct experiencing of rewards and punishments, and through vicarious conditioning, individuals acquire such important personality characteristics as competencies, expectancies, goals/standards, and self-efficacy beliefs. In addition, through such processes, individuals acquire self-regulatory capacities. Thus, through the development of cognitive competencies and standards, people are able to anticipate the future and reward or punish themselves for relative progress in meeting chosen goals. The latter self-produced consequences are of particular significance in maintaining behavior over extended periods of time in the absence of external reinforcers.

It is important to recognize that social-cognitive theory is opposed to views that emphasize fixed stages of development and broad personality types. According to Bandura and Mischel, people develop skills and competencies in particular areas. Rather than developing consciences or healthy egos, they develop competencies and motivational guides for action that are attuned to specific contexts. Such a view emphasizes the ability of people to discriminate among situations and to regulate behavior flexibly according to internal goals and the demands of the situation.

MAJOR CONCEPTS

A cognitive–affective processing system	Competencies	Goals	Reciprocal determinism
Acquisition	Context specificity	Microanalytic research	Self-evaluative reactions
Behavioral signatures	Delay of gratification	Observational learning	Self-regulation
Cognitive–affective processing system (CAPS)	Evaluative standards	Perceived self-efficacy	Vicarious conditioning
	Expectancies	Performance	

REVIEW

1. Social-cognitive theory centers its analyses of personality on uniquely human cognitive capacities. Thanks to their ability to think about themselves, their past, and their future, individuals are seen to have the capacity to influence their own experiences and development. Since these thinking processes develop through interaction with the social environment, they are called social-cognitive. Two theorists who have made primary contributions to the development of the social-cognitive approach are Albert Bandura and Walter Mischel.

2. The personality structures emphasized in social-cognitive theory are competencies and skills, expectancies and beliefs, behavioral standards, and personal goals. These four personality variables refer to four distinct classes of cognition; they thus

can be seen as distinct subsystems within the overall system of personality. Any given person may have different skills, beliefs, standards, and goals in different situations. Thus, behavior naturally varies across situations in a meaningful manner that reflects the individual's personality characteristics.

3. Social-cognitive theory addresses personality processes in two primary ways. First, the principle of reciprocal determinism captures the back-and-forth influences between personality and the environment. Second, personality is construed as **a cognitive–affective processing system**. Much research on personality processes from a social-cognitive perspective has explored the phenomena of observational learning, self-regulation, and self-control.

4. The social-cognitive theory analysis of observational learning emphasizes that people's knowledge and skills primarily are acquired by observing others. Observational learning processes include the learning of emotional reactions through observation of models or "vicarious conditioning". An important distinction is made between *acquiring* patterns of behavior in the absence of rewards and *performing* those behaviors.

5. The social-cognitive theory analysis of motivation emphasizes the role of people's thoughts about themselves. Self-efficacy judgments, or perceptions of one's capability to execute behaviors, are key to motivation; self-efficacy beliefs influence people's selection of goals, effort and persistence toward achieving the goal, emotions prior to and during task performance, and success in coping with stress and negative events. In addition, much work examines processes of goal setting and the role that people's evaluations of their own actions play in goal-directed motivation.

6. Research on the development of cognitive and behavioral competencies associated with delay in gratification illustrates the social-cognitive approach to questions of both self-control and personality development. Standards for self-control are learned through the observation of models and through reinforcement. The ability to delay gratification involves the development of cognitive competencies, especially involving the control of attention; people who distract themselves from frustrating situations are better able to control their negative emotions and impulses. Research also indicates that individual differences in the capacity to delay gratification are remarkably stable across the course of development.

Social-Cognitive = thinking processes developed through a social environment

13

Social-Cognitive Theory: Applications, Related Theoretical Conceptions, and Contemporary Developments

Chapter Focus

A college senior working on medical school applications was filled with anxiety. How could he cope with the possibility of not getting accepted anywhere? His family is counting on him to be a doctor. His friends would think he was a big braggart if he was rejected after years of boasting about his professional plans. These thoughts distracted him so much that his work progressed slowly, he submitted some applications late, and he thereby worsened his chances of admission.

The case is not uncommon. People's success in life depends, in part, on what they think about themselves. When facing a challenge, people often think about not only the task at hand ("what should I include in this application?") but also their hopes, fears, and obligations to others ("what if I don't get in?!"). Depending on how people think about themselves, their thoughts can distract them from the task at hand, create anxiety, and thus undermine performance.

Basic research in social-cognitive theory has tried to understand the impact of beliefs, goals, and standards on people's emotions and behavior, including negative emotions that undermine performance. In clinical applications, psychologists have aimed to alter self-defeating negative beliefs. These challenges are the focus of this chapter.

Questions to be Addressed in this Chapter

1. How do knowledge structures—especially cognitive "schemas"—contribute to personality functioning and help to explain individual differences?

2. How do personal goals and standards of self-evaluation differ from one person to another, and how do these differences relate to motivation and emotional life?

3. What is the role of self-efficacy beliefs and other self-referent thinking processes in psychological disorders and therapeutic change?

4. What are some scientific challenges that were not addressed in the original formulations of social-cognitive theory and how have they been addressed by contemporary developments in personality theory?

In Chapter 12, you learned that social-cognitive theory explains personality in terms of basic thinking—or cognitive—capacities. The main theorists, Albert Bandura and Walter Mischel, try to understand how people's cognitive capacities develop as people interact with the social world. As you will recall, three social-cognitive personality variables were as follows:

- People's *beliefs* about the self and the world

- Their personal aims or *goals*

- The *evaluative standards* that people use to judge the goodness or worth of their own actions and those of others

Social-cognitive theory advanced a straightforward idea: Beliefs, goals, and standards—as well as competencies for performing behaviors—are cognitive variables that help to explain the uniqueness and coherence of individuals' personalities. Consider an example close at hand. Why are you spending a lot of time these days reading textbooks, going to classes, and studying for exams, when you could just be hanging out with friends, listening to music, and snacking? It probably is because you (1) *believe* you need to study to excel at school and believe you have the ability to do so, (2) have the goal of doing well in courses and graduating, and (3) know you would *evaluate* yourself negatively (i.e., you'd feel bad about yourself) if you spent your whole day just hanging out, snacking; that behavior would fall below your standards for evaluating yourself. Although your personality style might be *described* by a personality trait term such as "conscientious" (Chapter 8), the *explanation* of your behavior can be found in social-cognitive variables: your (1) beliefs, (2) goals, and (3) standards for self-evaluations.

In this chapter, we review research programs on each of these three social-cognitive components of personality. Some of the research was spearheaded by Bandura or Mischel, the primary social-cognitive theorists you have learned about in Chapter 12, whereas others were initiated by other personality scientists; many psychologists contribute to the social-cognitive approach to personality. Finally, at the end of the chapter, we will review consider a contemporary development in personality theory that addresses some limitations in the original 20th-century formulation of social-cognitive theory.

Cognitive Components of Personality: Beliefs, Goals, and Evaluative Standards

Beliefs About The Self And Self-Schemas

As noted in our opening *Chapter Focus*, it is human nature to think about oneself. Your day may be filled with external challenges—at school, at work, or with family and friends. Yet you inevitably spend much time reflecting on your internal mental life: your feelings, your goals, and the personality characteristics you possess. People contemplate not only the challenges they face but also their own thoughts and feelings as they face those challenges. And you have been doing this for years.

Over the course of time, people's self-reflections usually coalesce into a stable self-concept: a set of beliefs about one's primary personal qualities and aspirations (Dweck, 2017; Harter, 2012). Once formed, this self-concept is influential. Beliefs about the self-affect emotions, motivation, and even the content of the ideas that "pop into mind" as we go about our day (Klinger, Marchetti, & Koster, in press).

Historically, psychology's attention to self-concept has been inconsistent. With some exceptions (see Chapter 5), psychologists devoted relatively little attention to self-concept during the first three-fourths of the 20th century. The intellectual scene shifted rapidly only after the century's three-quarter mark, with a turning point being the year 1977. It witnessed the publication of seminal papers in which self-concept figured prominently, including Bandura's (1977) initial statement of self-efficacy theory (see Chapter 12), research documenting that self-relevant information is more memorable than other types of information (Rogers, Kuiper, & Kirker, 1977), and novel analyses of "self-schemas," reviewed immediately below.

A Google Scholar search (conducted by your Author) indicates the magnitude of this shift in the field. In the two decades from 1980 to 2000, the number of published papers whose titles contained both the words "self" and "psychology" was 2270. In the two decades from 1930 to 1950, the number of such papers was only 28.

Schemas and Self-Schemas

The idea that the mind contains *schemas* has a long history. The 18th-century German philosopher Immanuel Kant recognized that people make sense out of new experiences by interpreting events in terms of preexisting ideas that he called schemas (Watson, 1963). Schemas are knowledge structures; specifically, they are highly developed, informationally elaborate structures of knowledge that people use to make sense out of what otherwise might be a confusing jumble of stimuli. Here is an example. Suppose you hear a new song on the radio. In terms of sheer physical stimuli reaching your ears, it might seem chaotic: There's some banging on a drum, some noises from a synthesizer, a few guitar chords, somebody singing something, somebody else singing something else—and all at the same time! Yet, of course, it isn't chaotic. To you, it is a structured, meaningful, memorable piece of music. It sounds this way because you have acquired mental schemas for song structures that guide your interpretation of the sounds. The role of schemas becomes clear if you hear music of a type that is unfamiliar to you (e.g., music from an unfamiliar culture or free jazz that abandons traditional rhythms and melodic structures). It might sound chaotic to you—even though it surely sounds structured and orderly to its composer. This is because you lack the musical schemas that are necessary to make sense of the sounds.

Schemas are not just lists of facts stored in memory but, instead, are organized networks of knowledge (Fiske & Taylor, 1991; Smith, 1998). These networks may be of such complexity that it is impossible to put all your knowledge into words. For example, you have a schema for music but if somebody asks even a simple question such as "What does a guitar sound like?," it's hard to say anything other than "um, like a guitar".

Hazel Markus (1977) recognized that many of our most important schemas concern ourselves. Self-schemas are highly developed, elaborate knowledge structures that contain knowledge of one's own personal qualities. Once formed, self-schemas affect our thinking; they draw attention to schema-relevant information and influence the way we interpret situations. Here is an example. Suppose you have a "shy around strangers" self-schema, that is, a schema that represents your belief that you are shy around people who have not previously met. The schema may (a) draw your attention to related information (e.g., if somebody invites you over for a party, you will notice if they mention a lot of other invitees who you do not know) and (b) shape your thinking during the event (once you get to the party, you might start worrying that you are acting too shy). Your personality dynamics—your thoughts and feelings—are influenced by your self-schema.

Different people—with their different interpersonal, social, and cultural life experiences—inevitably develop different self-schemas, that is, schemas with different content. For example, one person might have an independence/dependence self-schema; in other words, she might commonly think of herself as an independent person, might possess a lot of knowledge about this personality characteristic of hers, and might interpret situations according to their relevance to independence. Another person might possess a schema organized around the concept of guilt/innocence and might use this schema to interpret many situations, even though a guilt/innocence schema might not even be present in most other persons. Self-schemas, then, may account for the relatively unique ways in which idiosyncratic individuals think about the world around them.

Self-Schemas and Reaction-Time Methods

Importantly, Markus (1977) did not merely analyze self-schemas theoretically. She also employed a measurement tool for studying them in research: *reaction-time* measures. In reaction-time measures, researchers record not only the content of people's responses to questions but also how long they take to respond. Reaction times are relevant to self-schemas for the following reason. If self-schemas guide information processing, then people who possess a self-schema should think more quickly; self-schemas should *lower* reaction times. Specifically, they should lower reaction times in the domain of life in which people are "schematic" (i.e., possess a self-schema). Here's an example.

Suppose you meet two people. One does volunteer community service for hours every week. The other volunteers for something only once a year. If you ask both people, "are you helpful to others," they may both say yes. From these two responses – "yes" and "yes"—you could not tell one person from the other. But now imagine that you had *timed* their responses to your question. The person who volunteers only once a year may have paused for a moment, thought about their activities, and eventually concluded that "yes, I'm helpful." But the other person may have said "yes" immediately. Thanks to their frequent volunteer service, they have developed a self-schema for the characteristic "helpfulness". This knowledge structure is activated by the content of the question and triggers an immediate "yes" response. Reaction times thus reveal cognitive schemas.

This is exactly the sort of result found by Markus (1977). In one study, she identified three groups of people: individuals who said that (1) they are highly independent and independence is important to them; (2) they are highly *de*pendent on others and dependence is important to them; and (3) the personal qualities of independence and dependence are not important to them. Groups 1 and 2 were expected to possess a self-schema regarding (in)dependence. Participants then were asked to rate whether a series of adjectives that are semantically related to independence/dependence (e.g., individualistic, adventurous, dependable, conforming) were descriptive of themselves. As predicted, participants who possessed a schema made schema-consistent judgments more quickly.

People may develop self-schemas about any domain of life. You may be schematic, for example, about your intelligence, or sense of humor, or physical appearance. Some schemas are relatively idiosyncratic; in other words, people may have beliefs about themselves that are unique. Others are widely shared. For example, one research team studied the role of sexual self-schemas, in order to test the hypothesis that women with differing sexual self-schemas would process interpersonal information differently and behave differently in their sexual and romantic relationships (Andersen & Cyranowski, 1994). In this research, women were asked to rate themselves on a list of 50 adjectives, 26 of which were used to form a Sexual Self-Schema Scale (e.g., uninhibited, loving, romantic, passionate, direct). They also were asked to respond to measures that asked about sexual experiences and romantic involvement. Clear evidence was found that women with high scores on the Sexual Self-Schema Scale, particularly those with positive sexual self-schemas, were more sexually active, experienced greater sexual arousal and sexual pleasure, and were more able to be involved in romantic love relationships relative to women with low scores on the scale. "Co-schematics," that is, women who had both positive schemas organized around their ability to experience sexual passion and negative schemas involving sexual conservatism or embarrassment, were found to experience high levels of involvement with sexual partners, yet also to experience relatively high levels of sexual anxiety (Cyranowski & Andersen, 1998). These experiences, in turn, could further influence views about the self, creating a self-confirming bias in which schemas contribute to experiences that, in turn, confirm the original schemas.

Any given individual does *not* possess merely one self-schema. Instead, people tend to live complex lives in which they develop a number of different views of themselves. For example, it may not be the case that you are either a hard-working student, or a loyal friend, or a good dancer at parties, or an anxious test-taker. Instead, you well could be all four of these things; that is, you may possess self-schemas concerning all four of these aspects of self. The different self-schemas would tend to come to mind in different settings. Different situational cues may cause different self-schemas to enter working memory and, thus, to be part of the **working self-concept** (Markus & Wurf, 1987), that is, the subset of self-concept that is in working memory at any given time. Self-concept thus is dynamic; the information about the self that is in consciousness, and guides behavior, at any given time, changes dynamically as people interact with the ever-changing events of the social world (Figure 13.1).

Note an implication of this research on self-schemas: The self is not a single, unitary element of the mind. Instead, people commonly possess multiple self-schemas that are each an aspect of their self-concept. The different self-schemas may be related to one another; for example, a person who thinks they are "hard working," "anxiety prone," and "fun at parties" may understand that partying is a way of relieving anxiety experienced at work. People tend to possess a "family of selves" (Cantor & Kihlstrom, 1987)—that is, a collection of self-views that may be as diverse as are different members of the same family, yet that may share some family resemblances. According to this view, you are many things, in many places, with many people. Thus, you have many contextualized selves, each with a set of features. The features of these contextualized

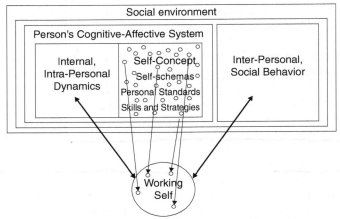

FIGURE 13.1 Markus and Wurf's (1987) model of the dynamic self-concept. In the model, people possess a large number of mental representations involving the self ("Self-Concept"). A subset of them is in working memory, and thus constitutes the "Working" self, at any given time.

selves, this family of selves, will overlap in some ways and be distinctive in others. Each of us, then, has a family of selves, the contents and organization of which are unique. Within this family of selves there may be a prototypic self, a self-concept in relation to which we say "This is what I am really like." And within this family of selves there may be fuzzy selves, or parts of us that we are not sure how they fit in relation to the other selves.

Self-Based Motives and Motivated Information Processing

Self-schemas do not merely provide information that is used in thinking, in the way that Wikipedia provides information used to answer a trivia question. Self-schemas also *motivate* information processing. The way you think—the information you seek out; the conclusions you draw—may reflect your views of yourself and your desire to maintain your self-image (Kwan, John, Kenny, Bond, & Robins, 2004; Leary, 2007). Researchers have identified two self-based motives that influence thinking: **self-enhancement** and **self-verification** (Swann, 2012; Swann & Bosson, 2008).

Self-enhancement is familiar to you intuitively. You know that if somebody gets a bad exam grade, they may conclude that the exam was unfair, and if they get a good grade that will discuss their inherent brilliance. Much research is consistent with such intuitions; people often are biased to maintain a positive view of themselves (Tesser, Pilkington, & McIntosh, 1989). These biases can be explained by positing a self-enhancement motive: a motive to maintain a positive self-image. This motive causes people to overestimate their positive attributes (Dunning, Heath, & Suls, 2004) and to enhance self-image by selectively comparing themselves to people who are faring less well (Wood, 1989).

The second motive is less intuitive, yet may be equally influential. People also may be motivated to experience themselves as consistent and predictable—as being basically the same person from one day to the next. The psychologist William Swann explains this by positing a self-verification motive (Swann, 2012; Swann & Bosson, 2008; Swann, Rentfrow, & Guinn, 2003), which is a motive to obtain information that confirms one's own self-concept. A self-identified introvert, for example, may start a discussion about how she stayed at home reading a book all weekend. The discussion is a social setting that verifies her sense of self.

As the example suggests, people will even seek to verify negative qualities. People who are depressed and have negative self-schemas may seek out self-verifying information. If they obtain it, the information not only maintains their negative self-image; it may also serve to maintain their depression (Giesler, Josephs, & Swann, 1996). More generally, people gravitate toward relationships with others who see them as they see themselves. People with positive (negative) self-concepts are more committed to spouses who think highly of them positively (negatively; De La Ronde & Swann, 1998; Swann, De La Ronde, & Hixon, 1994).

Learning Versus Performance Goals

Self-schemas, discussed above, concern people's beliefs: what they believe are their most significant personal qualities. Another element of personality important to social-cognitive approaches is people's goals (see Chapter 12). Goals, which are mental representations of the aim of an action or set of actions, are central to human motivation.

People's goal can differ in a variety of ways. One is the people may have differ goal *levels*; for example, a friend of yours might have the goal of earning a B in a psychology class whereas you might be aiming for an A (a higher level goal). In addition, there are different *types of* goals. Different people, in other words, may think differently about the aim, or purpose, or any given activity. Influential theory and research on social-cognitive processes and different types of goals comes from the psychologist Carol Dweck, who distinguished between "learning" and "performance" goals.

Bryan Hainer / Getty Images

Is all the world a stage? Research by Carol Dweck indicates that, rather than focusing exclusively on learning, some students become concerned that they are being observed and evaluated by others, and try to "put on a good performance."

In the theory of goals and motivation developed by Dweck and her colleagues (Dweck & Leggett, 1988; Grant & Dweck, 1999; Olson & Dweck, 2008), **learning goals** and **performance goals** are different ways of thinking about what you are trying to accomplish on an activity. The difference can be understood through a simple example. Suppose that you are working on a group project and are about to present your part of the project to others in the group who will discuss its strong and weak points. Right before the presentation, you might focus your attention on how their feedback will provide information that can help you to improve your work. If so, you have a *learning* goal: You are striving to learn from others, in order to increase your ability and achievement. Alternatively, you might focus on the personal impression you'll make on the other people; you might try to "look smart" and to avoid doing anything that will make you look stupid. If so, you would have a *performance* goal: the aim of "putting on a good performance" for others who will be evaluating your abilities.

People with learning versus performance goals experience activities differently, particularly if they are not confident in their abilities. In one study (Elliott & Dweck, 1988), students were given information designed to induce either learning goals (students were told that the task would sharpen their mental skills) or performance goals (students were told their performance would be evaluated by experts) on a problem-solving task. Students' beliefs in their ability on the task were also manipulated through provision of bogus feedback on a prior activity. The researchers measured task performance and also asked students to think out loud while they attempted the task; the think-aloud process provided a record of the thoughts running through their minds during task performance. The research yielded two key results:

—Students with performance goals and low beliefs in their ability performed poorly. The measure of task performance indicated that they were less likely than others to devise useful strategies for solving the task.

—Students with performance goals and low beliefs in their ability also become distracted from the task itself. The think-aloud measure indicated that, unlike students with learning goals, those with performance goals became tense, anxious, and worried about why they weren't doing better on the task. ("My stomach hurts" [Elliott & Dweck, 1988, p. 10], one of them said.)

The findings show that performance goals can create a pattern of thought and emotion that we commonly call "test anxiety". As you know, some people become highly anxious when taking a test and, as a result, perform more poorly than they would have if they had remained calm. Dweck's social-cognitive approach identifies a type of thinking that is an underlying cause of this anxiety.

Causes of Learning versus Performance Goals: Implicit Theories

Why do some people adopt learning goals on tasks, whereas others adopt performance goals? A primary factor is that different people hold different **implicit theories** about intelligence. Different implicit theories prompt people to adopt different types of goals (Dweck, 2012).

Implicit theories are ideas that guide our thinking, but that we may not usually state in words; we possess the ideas implicitly, even if we do not state them explicitly. Dweck and colleagues are particularly interested in one aspect of people's implicit theories about intelligence: whether intelligence is fixed or changeable (e.g., Dweck, 1991, 1999; Dweck, Chiu, & Hong, 1995). People who hold an *entity theory* of intelligence believe that intelligence levels are fixed. According to another set of beliefs, known as an *incremental theory*, intelligence is acquired gradually and naturally changes over time.

Differences in implicit theories have implications for the goals people set and their responses to failure (Dweck & Leggett, 1988). Children with an entity view of intelligence tend to set performance goals; if one thinks that intelligence is a fixed entity, then it is only natural to interpret activities as a test of one's intelligence—that is, as a "performance" in which one's intelligence is evaluated. Conversely, children with an incremental view of intelligence tend to set learning goals. If intelligence can be increased, then, it is natural to set the learning goal of acquiring experiences that increase one's intelligence. Thus, different implicit theories lead people to set different goals that, in turn, have different implications for emotion and motivation.

This theoretical analysis has practical implications. If one could change people's implicit theories—turning entity theorists into incremental theorists—one should be able to reduce their test anxiety and boost their performance. With this goal in mind, Blackwell, Trzesniewski, and Dweck (2007) enrolled 7th-graders in an educational intervention designed to induce an incremental theory of intelligence: Students learned that the human brain changes when people study, growing new connections among neurons that increase a person's mental abilities. A separate group of students did not receive this instruction. The academic performance of both groups was monitored during an academic year. By the end of the year, students who had been exposed to the intervention began to outperform the other students. The findings, then, suggest that an intervention can change this social-cognitive personality structure, implicit theories, and that the change can have beneficial effects.

Dweck's analysis of implicit theories applies to domains beyond theories of intelligence. People also differ in theories about emotions. Some believe emotions to be malleable and controllable ("Everyone can learn to control their emotions"), whereas other see emotions as fixed and uncontrollable ("No matter how hard they try, people can't really change the emotions that they have"). Research conducted with students making the transition from high school to college shows that people with these different theories have substantially different outcomes. Students with incremental (malleable) beliefs are better able to regulate their emotions and receive more social support from new friends they meet at college. By the end of the freshman year, those with incremental beliefs were found to have more positive moods and generally better levels of adjustment than those with entity beliefs (Tamir, John, Srivastava, & Gross, 2007).

In conclusion, it should be noted that Dweck (2008) sees these beliefs and implicit theories as central to personality functioning and as potential areas of therapeutic change.

Personality and the Brain

Goals

As you've seen, *goals* are distinct psychological variables in the social-cognitives approach to personality. Are they also distinct biologically? In other words, might there be unique activity in the brain when people think about goals and standards for evaluating performance? Recent advances in the study of personality and the brain indicate that the answer is yes.

Before turning to these advances, note that a key word in the paragraph above is "distinctive." There is no question that when people set goals and contemplate standards of evaluation, they do so using their brains. The question is whether these thoughts are underpinned by regions of the brain that differ from those that are active when people think about other types of cognitive content.

A research team in Europe has investigated neural systems that underlie people's ability to formulate personal goals (D'Argembeau et al., 2009). To determine whether goal-related thinking activates unique neural systems, the researchers asked participants to imagine future outcomes that either were or were not personal goals for them. (For example, if you had the goal of becoming a doctor and had no particular interest in ever going deep-sea fishing, those future outcomes respectively would, and would not, represent personal goals.) Participants were in a brain scanner while imagining these two types of outcomes.

The brain-imaging results revealed two brain regions that were more active when people thought about personal goals than about future activities that were not goals for them: the medial prefrontal cortex (MPFC) and the posterior cingulate cortex (PCC). These regions are significant for the following reasons.

—The MPFC is needed to determine the self-relevance of events. Many everyday occurrences (a passing car; a randomly overhead conversation) are irrelevant to your well-being, but some (a passing car containing a friend you were looking for; a conversation about someone you're hoping to get to know better) are highly relevant to you. The MPFC is active in detecting and processing information about the self-relevant events.

—The PCC has been shown to be active during autobiographical memory, that is, memory of events that one has experienced in the past. PCC activation during the personal goals task, then, suggests that activity in the brain relates here-and-now goals to memories of past events. (Using our example above, if you contemplated your goal of becoming a doctor, the goal-related thinking would, thanks to the PCC, activate autobiographical memories, such as discussions you've had with friends and family about becoming a physician.)

This brain research, then, has psychological implications. It reminds us that goals are psychologically rich mental contents that combine the detection of personally relevant occurrences in the environment with information stored in your "library" of autobiographical memories.

Standards of Evaluation

In Chapter 12, you learned that another personality variable important to social-cognitive theory is self-evaluative standards, which are criteria people use to evaluate the goodness or worth of themselves and their actions. Standards are related to, yet differ from, goals (Boldero & Francis, 2002; Cervone, 2004). Goals are aims one hopes to achieve in the future. Standards are criteria used to evaluate events in the present. For example, if you are watching an ice skating performance, you might evaluate the performance as good or bad according to standards you have used for judging the performance of skaters. You might have these standards whether or not you, personally, have the goal of being a figure skater. Goals and standards, then, are psychologically distinct mechanisms. Much work in personality psychology indicates that people regulate their behavior by evaluating whether their actions are consistent with internalized standards for performance (e.g., Baumeister & Vohs, 2004; Carver, Scheier, & Fulford, 2008; Cervone, Shadel, Smith, & Fiori, 2006).

Our review of Dweck's work, above, showed that it is valuable to distinguish among qualitatively different types of goals. Similarly, it is valuable to distinguish among qualitatively different types of evaluative standards (Dweck, Higgins, & Grant-Pillow, 2003). An exceptionally fruitful line of theory and research by the psychologist Tory Higgins (2006, 2012, 2014; Higgins & Scholer, 2008) has expanded the scope of social-cognitive analyses of personality by showing how different types of evaluative standards relate to different types of emotional experiences and motivation.

Self-Standards, Self-Discrepancies, Emotion, and Motivation

The psychological phenomenon of interest to Higgins can be illustrated with an example. Suppose two people are reading in a college library some night late in the semester, both are unhappy with how they have been doing in a course, and both are behind in course readings as the semester draws to a close. And imagine they take a break from their work to discuss how they're doing. "I'm really anxious about this class," one person says tensely. "I wanted an A, but I don't even think I can get a B." "I'm not anxious" says the other, dejectedly. "I'm really *depressed* about this class. I wanted an A, but I don't even think I can get a B."

What's going on here? How can one explain why the two people have different emotional reactions to the same event? Why is one vulnerable to becoming anxious, the other to becoming depressed? Higgins suggests it is because they are evaluating the event with different types of standards. Although they both "want" the same thing, an A, the subjective nature of that standard of performance differs from one person to the other. The critical distinction is the difference between standards that represent "ideals" versus "oughts". Some evaluative standards represent achievement that people *ideally would like* to reach. They represent types of behavior that one values positively. Higgins calls these ideal standards, or aspects of the "ideal self." (In this way, Higgins's analysis is similar to that of Rogers, Chapter 5.) Alternatively, some evaluative standards represent standards of achievement that people feel they *should* or *ought to* achieve. The standards represent duties or responsibilities. These are termed *ought* standards, or elements of the "ought self".

Higgins's analysis is important to the study of personality and individual differences because different individuals may evaluate the same type of behavior using different standards. Recent work demonstrates this point with a behavior of importance to health: smoking. People who are similar in that they all want to quit nonetheless differ in their evaluative standards regarding quitting. Some wish to quit primarily because they ideally would like to be healthier; smoking for them violates an ideal standard. Others primarily feel a sense of responsibility to others to quit smoking (e.g., to avoid bothering others with cigarette smoke); smoking for them violates an ought standard (Shadel & Cervone, 2006).

A key insight of Higgins's is that different types of standards, ought versus ideal, trigger different types of negative emotions (Higgins, 1987, 1996). There are two steps to Higgins's reasoning: (1) People experience negative emotions when they detect a discrepancy between how things really are going for them—or their "actual self"—and a personal standard. These self-discrepancies are cognitive mechanisms that contribute to emotional experience. (2) Discrepancies with *different* (ideal versus ought) standards trigger *different* emotions. Discrepancies between the actual and ideal self cause people to feel sad or dejected; failing to meet one's ideal standards is a loss of positive outcomes that brings on sadness. Discrepancies between the actual and ought self cause agitation and anxiety; the possibility of not achieving one's obligations is a potential negative outcome that is threatening.

To test these ideas, Higgins, Bond, Klein, and Strauman (1986) first assessed individual differences in self-discrepancies. They identified one group of people who predominantly have actual/ideal discrepancies and a second set who predominantly have actual/ought discrepancies. To do this, Higgins and colleagues employed a simple questionnaire in which people listed attributes they believed they (a) actually possessed, (b) ideally would like to possess, and (c) believed they should, or ought to, possess. In a subsequent experimental session, these people's emotional reactions were assessed as they envisioned themselves experiencing a negative life event. Although all participants envisioned the *same* event, they experienced *different* emotions. People whose self-descriptions featured many actual/ideal discrepancies tended to become sad but not anxious when thinking about the negative outcome. People whose self-described attributes featured mostly actual/ought discrepancies became anxious but not sad.

If you are thinking critically, you might complain that these findings are only correlational; different types of self-discrepancies are correlated with different emotional reactions. As we discussed in Chapter 2, experimental—rather than merely correlational—research would provide evidence that is more convincing. Recognizing this fact, Higgins and colleagues also studied self-discrepancies experimentally. They did so by manipulating self-discrepancies through cognitive priming. People who possessed both actual/ideal and actual/ought self-discrepancies were randomly assigned to conditions that primed either ideal standards or ought standards. In different experimental conditions, participants were asked to briefly discuss either their personal hopes (to prime the ideal self) or their duties and obligations (to prime the ought self). Priming alternative standards led to different emotional reactions. When ideal self-discrepancies were primed, participants felt dejected. When ought standards were primed, they felt agitated. Thus, an experimental manipulation of cognition led to changes in emotion.

Much subsequent research has yielded evidence consistent with Higgins's core idea that discrepancies with ideal versus ought standards lead to different emotional experiences. This includes clinical research with social phobics and clinically depressed patients, who exhibit predominantly actual/ought and actual/ideal discrepancies, respectively (Strauman, 1989). Higher levels of neuroticism and lower levels of subjective well-being are experienced by people whose self-descriptions indicate a discrepancy between how they really think they are and how they judge who they think they ought to be (Pavot, Fujita, & Diener, 1997). The existence of self-discrepancies has health implications, having been found to decrease the effectiveness of the functioning of our immunological system in fighting disease (Strauman, Lemieux, & Coe, 1993). Clinical researchers have begun to develop therapeutic techniques to reduce discrepancies between the actual and ideal self (Strauman et al., 2001).

Higgins (2006, 2014) emphasizes that evaluative standards have implications not only for emotional experience but also for motivation. People who evaluate their actions primarily through ideal standards tend to have a "promotion" approach to their activities. In other words, they are motivated toward promoting well-being, which they do by focusing on positive outcomes (either attaining positive outcomes or avoiding their loss once they have been attained). A pre-med student with a promotion focus might dwell on the benefits of a medical career or the importance of not lowering his or her high grade point average. In contrast, a focus on ought standards tends to make one prevention-focused, that is, focused on preventing the occurrence of (or gaining an absence of) negative outcomes. In our previous example, a prevention-focused pre-med student might focus on the possibility of not being admitted to med school and might view good class performance primarily as a way in which one avoids this negative outcome. Different motivational processes come into play when one is prevention versus promotion-focused (Shah & Higgins, 1997), and people's actions feel more natural to them when their activities fit their primary motivational orientation (Higgins, 2006).

A "General Principles" Approach to Personality

Higgins's analysis of cognition, emotion, and individual differences has a theoretical advantage that is a bit subtle, yet highly significant. It concerns the explanation of consistency and variability in behavior as people encounter diverse situations. As we have discussed previously (see especially Chap. 8), some personality psychologists embrace the following two-step logic: (1) consistencies in behavior reveals an individual's personality, whereas (2) variability in behavior reflect the power of social situations. In this approach, "personality variables" explain what people do on average and "situational factors" variability around the average. As Higgins (1999) recognizes, this thinking yields a very unsatisfying science of persons. It is unsatisfying because entirely different scientific principles—personal factors versus situational influences—are invoked to explain the same type of behavior, exhibited in different circumstances.

In contrast, Higgins (1999) provides a **general principles approach**. A common set of principles, involving personal knowledge and standards for performance, explains both consistency and variability in personality functioning. Personal knowledge is an enduring structure of mind that contributes to behavioral consistency. Different situations activate different aspects of knowledge which, in turn, fosters variability. In this approach, one of personality psychology's "classic" distinctions—(1) consistency and personality effects versus (2) variability and situation effects—becomes a relic (Cervone, Caldwell, & Orom, 2008). Instead of disconnected "person" and "situation" effects, one obtains an integrated account of personal and situational influences, and of the consistency and variability of behavior. Higgins' analysis is closely related to the contemporary development in social-cognitive theory to which we turn next.

Contemporary Developments in Personality Theory: The KAPA Model

You have just learned about advances in the study of social cognition and personality that were spearheaded by Hazel Markus, Carol Dweck, and Tory Higgins. Each focused primarily on one or two social-cognitive variables: self-schemas (Markus); goals and implicit beliefs (Dweck); and evaluative standards and emotion (Higgins). This type of focus is a primary way that science progresses; investigators analyze specific processes in detail. Yet a larger question remains: Have there been recent developments in the *overall* social-cognitive approach, that is, in efforts to comprehensively address the challenges of personality theory from a social-cognitive perspective?

This question raises another: Are any such developments needed? Did 20th-century social-cognitive theory possess limitations that would motivate a new development?

After outlining some limitations, we review one contemporary development: the **Knowledge-and-Appraisal Personality Architecture or KAPA** model (Cervone, 2004). A caution to the reader: The primary developer of the KAPA model (Cervone, 2004, 2005, 2007, in press) is your textbook author. The upcoming coverage thus may be biased; I might overemphasize the KAPA model's merits and "repress" its limitations. At this point in our journey through personality theory and research, you are in a good position to evaluate the KAPA model yourself.

Social-Cognitive Theory: Three Limitations of 20th-Century Theory and Research

In many respects, 20th-century social-cognitive theory was a success. Compelling research findings spurred a novel theoretical perspective that, in turn, yielded valuable applications. Yet one can identify limitations in three areas (1) personality theory, (2) personality assessment, and (3) identifying cross-situational consistency in personality.

Social-Cognitive Personality Structures and Processes

In Chapter 1, you learned that personality theories contain both "structure" and "process" components. Theorists generally are careful to differentiate structure variables from process variables. Freud, for example, distinguished psychoanalytic structures (the id, ego, and superego) from dynamic processes (flows of mental energy).

In social-cognitive theory, the structure/process distinction is less clear. A particular ambiguity is the following. In many cases, a variable (i.e., a theoretical construct in social-cognitive theory) is used in two different ways: Sometimes the variable refers to an enduring personality structure and other times it refers to a dynamic personality process. Consider the social-cognitive personality variable "goals". If someone, for years, someone has had the goal of becoming a professional soccer player, her "goal" is an enduring social-cognitive structure. If, while playing in a game, she rushes upfield with the goal of scoring but encounters a defender and changes her goal to that of passing to a teammate, but the pass goes awry and she adopts a new goal of defending, her "goals" are rapidly changing processes.

In informal discussions, this dual use of the word "goals" is fine. But in a formal scientific theory of personality, it can be confusing. (Imagine the confusion if Freud had sometimes used the term "superego" to refer to an enduring personality structure and other times to refer to rapidly changing psychological processes.) The general point is that when social-cognitive theorists proposed variables such as "goals" (or "expectancies" and "values," Mischel, 1973), they did not indicate whether a given variable was a personality processes or a personality structure (or both). They thus did not adequately address the process versus structure components of personality theory. This is one limitation of the 20th-century social-cognitive perspective.

Social-Cognitive Personality Assessment

A second limitation involves assessment. Recall that social-cognitive theory views personality as a "system": a set of interacting cognitive and affective processes (Bandura, 1999; Mischel & Shoda, 1995). This implies that, in assessment, one should assess a system of interacting social-cognitive variables. Since they are *social*-cognitive variables, one might also assess the situations that activate one versus another self-cognitive variable for any given person.

Unfortunately, in 20th-century social-cognitive theory, assessment methods did not keep up with theoretical developments. Social-cognitive theorists did not develop such assessments. They tended to assess one or two variables at a time (e.g., self-efficacy perceptions; self-control abilities). Tools to assess a more complex system of social-cognitive structures and processes were lacking. In retrospect, assessment methods did not keep pace with theoretical developments.

From Social-Cognitive Systems to Personality Consistency

The third limitation concerns a topic you read about back in Chapter 8: the cross-situational consistency of personality. Walter Mischel (1968) addressed this topic in the early days of social-cognitive theory. As he explained in a critique of the trait approach, although personality trait variables were designed to explain personality consistency (i.e., consistent styles of personality evident across different situations), they encounter two problems. First, people's trait-related behavior is often *in*consistent. A person might, for example, be highly conscientiousness in some situations and much less conscientious in others (Mischel & Peake, 1982). Second, even when behavior is consistent, trait variables cannot *explain* the consistency. To say that a person consistently behaved conscientiously "because of her conscientiousness" is to go around in conceptual circles.

In retrospect, after crafting this critique the social-cognitive theorists might have done something more: They might have shown how their approach can succeed where trait theory failed. In other words, they might have developed a social-cognitive explanation of where, and why, people display cross-situationally consistent personality styles. But this was not accomplished in the 20th-century social-cognitive approach.

Addressing the Limitations: The KAPA Model

The KAPA model (Cervone, 2004) was designed to address these three limitations. Let's first consider its approach to personality structures and processes.

Knowledge Structures and Appraisal Processes

The KAPA model's central claim is that there are two types of social-cognitive personality variables: knowledge and appraisals (Cervone, 2004; also see Lazarus, 1991). Knowledge is enduring; it is a social-cognitive structure. Appraisals shift rapidly over time; they are social-cognitive processes. We will illustrate the knowledge/appraisal distinction with an example.

Knowledg=structure
Appraisals = process

Consider two types of thoughts you may have about yourself:

A. You may believe you are an "intelligent person" who "has trouble dealing with stress." You may have thought about yourself this way for years. These two beliefs are unlikely to change any time soon; you will *not* wake up next week or next month thinking "I'm actually an unintelligent person who has no trouble at all dealing with stress."

B. When contemplating the end of your academic semester, you might think "I'll do great on my personality final exam!" But a moment later you might realize, "Oh no, with all my other exams, I might not have time to study—and I'll do badly." Yet another moment later, you might devise a strategy: "I'll spend less time on my boring Sociology class, freeing up time for Personality—and I will get an A!"

In the language of 20th-century social-cognitive theory, both sets of thoughts, A and B, are self-referent social cognitions: thoughts about oneself in interaction with the social world. Yet they plainly differ. The "A" cognitions are long-lasting, stable beliefs. The "B" cognitions are a rapidly changing flow of thought. In the KAPA model, the A's are knowledge structures and the B's are appraisal processes (Cervone, 2004; also see Lazarus, 1991; Smith & Lazarus, 1990).

Knowledge refers to enduring mental representations, that is, long-lasting concepts about oneself, other people, and the world at large. In the study of personality, a particularly important aspect of knowledge is *self*-knowledge: enduring mental representations of one's own personal qualities and aspirations. We already covered one type of self-knowledge structure earlier in this chapter, when discussing self-schemas.

Appraisals are ongoing evaluations of the relation between oneself and the surrounding (or upcoming) environment. The thoughts that run through your head whenever you encounter a challenge—"ugh, I'm not doing as well as I should," "can I do better?" "how—what should I do next?"—are appraisals. Much research establishes that people's appraisals influence their emotions and behavior (Moors, Ellsworth, Scherer, & Fridja, 2013). Many of the social-cognitive processes you read about in Chapter 12, such as the flow of thoughts (self-efficacy perceptions and self-evaluative reactions) that occur when people receive feedback on challenging tasks, are appraisals.

Knowledge and appraisal are systematically related. Knowledge structures influence appraisal processes (Higgins, 1996; Markus & Wurf, 1987). The way people think about an event (their appraisals) is affected by beliefs, plans, and memories they have stored in memory (knowledge). Knowledge influences appraisals particularly strongly when situations are ambiguous and you have to figure out what is going on. "Does that person like me, or not?," "Should I talk to them more to find out, or not?" When trying to figure out ambiguous circumstances, people draw on knowledge they have stored in memory.

Social-Cognitive Personality Assessment

The knowledge/appraisal distinction establishes a goal for personality assessment. In the KAPA model, the main assessment goal is to identify the knowledge structures that are most significant to an individual and the appraisals the person engages in when thinking about the challenges of his or her life. Two assessment principles guide this search (Cervone, Shadel, & Jencius, 2001).

1. *Assess Knowledge and Appraisal Contextually.*   People's thoughts often vary a lot from one situation to another. You may feel confident around your friends but not around strangers. You may know that you are a responsible, reliable parent—and a procrastinator when it comes to studying. KAPA model assessments thus are contextual. Rather than asking what people are like "in general," KAPA assessments try to identify people's primary thoughts as they encounter the varying contexts (e.g., with friends, with strangers, in the role of parenting, in the role of student) that make up their day.

2. *Be Sensitive to Idiosyncrasy.*   People's beliefs about themselves may vary idiosyncratically. A second principle of KAPA assessments is that one should be sensitive to this idiosyncrasy. Rather than administering brief personality questionnaires with a fixed sets of items, KAPA assessments allow people to describe themselves in their own words (this, too, is illustrated below). In its attention to the potentially unique content of people's belief systems, the KAPA approach is similar to the personal construct assessments pioneered by George Kelly (Chapter 11).

Cross-Situational Coherence in Self-Appraisals: Self-Schemas and Self-Efficacy Appraisals

The first two points—the knowledge/appraisal distinction and the KAPA model assessment strategy—lead naturally to the third. The KAPA model aims to understand how knowledge structures produce cross-situationally consistent patterns of personality functioning. It uses personality assessment strategies that can detect idiosyncratic patterns of personality consistency displayed by unique individuals.

The KAPA model's approach can be understood by contrasting it an alternative you saw in Chapter 8. That chapter discussed trait theory and the "person—situation controversy." The "controversy" concerned research findings: Psychologists drew different conclusions from research results. However, there was a common set of research *methods*. Almost all studies employed the strategy depicted in the left side of Figure 13.1. Researchers (a) selected a trait construct to study (e.g., conscientiousness); (b) identified a set of situations, and associated response, that were thought to be good measures of the trait (e.g., "if you have a tedious job to do, complete it conscientiously;" "if you have an early morning class, show up for every class meeting on time"); and (c) determine whether a group of people responds consistently across this fixed set of situations.

This strategy possesses the problems identified by Mischel (1968): (1) cross-situational consistency often is low and (2) even if it were high, the approach fails to identify psychological processes that might explain why people respond consistently. In addition, there is a third problem: (3) The research strategy is not sensitive to the idiosyncrasy. If a person displays a meaningful pattern of behavior that is consistent with their own personal qualities but inconsistent with the researcher's trait construct, the research strategy will overlook it.

For example, suppose you are in a study of "conscientiousness" that is conducted a week before final exams. If your goal is to excel on the exams, you might (a) spend a lot of time studying, (b) *not* spend time on distracting activities (e.g., paying bills, doing laundry, etc.), and also (c) try to hang out socially with some people in your classes who seem smart, so you can then be in a study group with them. Your behavior is consistent with your goal. But it is inconsistent with traditional personality traits. The "a" and "b" behaviors are inconsistently conscientious. The "c" behavior, hanging out with friends, would be overlooked in a study of conscientiousness because it is, in trait theory, an example of "extraversion." The trait strategy may make sense for people in general, but it overlooks the idiosyncrasies of your particular case.

The KAPA model suggests an alternative strategy for studying personality consistency. It is depicted in the right side of Figure 13.2. The KAPA strategy rests on two ideas:

— *Self-schemas can produce cross-situational consistency in personality.* A given self-schema might come to mind in any of a variety of situations. If, for example, someone possesses a self-schema about their being "shy," the self-schema might come to mind in settings involving social groups (e.g., meeting new people in one's neighborhood), work (e.g., a job interview), or relationships (e.g., "opening up" to a relationship partner about one's feelings). Since schematic knowledge structures influence appraisal processes, the self-schema should produce consistent styles of personality across these different settings.

— *Patterns of cross-situational consistency may vary idiosyncratically.* Any given person might have a unique set of beliefs about themselves. Furthermore, the situations that are important to an individual's day-to-day life, and in which those beliefs come into play, may vary idiosyncratically. This suggests that research should search for personality consistency in a manner that is sensitive to idiosyncrasy.

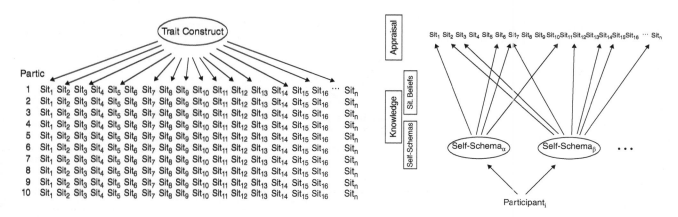

FIGURE 13.2 These figures contrast two strategies for studying personality consistency. In a trait approach (see Chapters 7-8), researchers determine the degree to which people are consistent with respect to a fixed personality trait (left side of figure). By contrast, in the social-cognitive KAPA model (right side of figure), researchers consider the possibility that an individual's personality consistency may be revealed in a unique set of situations that are particularly relevant to that person's self-schemas (i.e., central beliefs about the self). Adapted from Cervone (2004).

An example from KAPA model research (Cervone, 2004) will make these somewhat abstract theoretical points more concrete.

The individual shown in Figure 13.3 was participating in a study in which, in a first step of personality assessment, people first were asked to write a description of their personal strengths and weaknesses. Personal strengths and weaknesses that people identified as being particularly important to them are the "schematic" personality qualities in this study (cf. Markus, 1977). Two boxes near the bottom of the figure display this particular individual's two primary self-schemas. As you can see, thought her strongest personal quality is that she can "have a good time naturally." At the same time, she possessed a negative self-schema (her personal weakness) in which she thought of herself as being "crabby and bitchy."

It may immediately cross your mind that these self-descriptions are hard to reconcile with trait theories of personality. This person is, according to her own descriptions, *both high and low* on the personality trait of agreeableness. Yet her self-description is perfectly sensible; lots of people are relaxed and agreeable in some settings and unpleasantly disagreeable in others.

The rest of the figure, on the top, displays situations that this person thought were relevant to her two main personality qualities; these situations are identified through a task in which people are asked whether a given personality quality would influence a person's behavior in each of a large number of situations (Cervone, Shadel, & Jencius, 2001). As shown, she saw different personal qualities as being relevant to different situations. Her ability to "have a good time naturally" was, in her view, relevant to social settings that included a lot of strangers. Her crabby/bitchy qualities were relevant to circumstances involving work, driving, or her boyfriend. These are the sort of individualized social-cognitive "maps" that are central to KAPA model assessments.

KAPA model research not only produces individualized portraits like the one in Figure 13.2. It also yields a research finding in the study of personality consistency. People are found to display consistent self-efficacy appraisals across distinctive sets of situations—specifically, those situations in which their self-schemas come into play. When self-schemas are used to predict self-efficacy appraisals, people are found to have a much higher appraisals of self-efficacy in

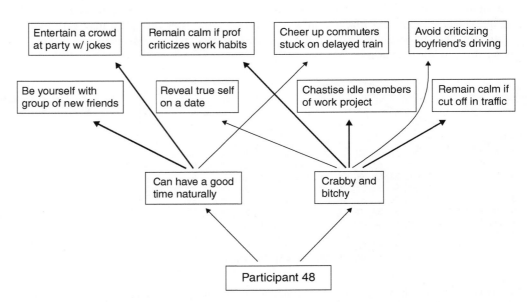

FIGURE 13.3 This figure depicts the self-knowledge and situational beliefs of a participant in a KAPA model study. Her self-knowledge included the beliefs that she is "crabby and bitchy" yet also "can have a good time naturally." The arrows pointing up from these two elements of self-knowledge display the situations that she saw as relevant to one versus the other personal quality. From Cervone (2004).

those situations in which their positive self-schemas (their "personal strengths") come to mind, as compared to situations in which their negative self-schemas come to mind (Cervone, 1997).

This result has been found in a wide variety of studies. Schematic knowledge structures have been found to predict cross-situational patterns of appraisal in studies of adults contemplating their self-efficacy for performing everyday behaviors (Cervone, 1997, 2004; Di Blas, 2017; Orom & Cervone, 2009); smokers contemplating situations in which they need to resist smoking urges (Cervone et al., 2007; 2008; Shadel, Cervone, Niaura, & Abrams, 2004); people seeking exercise who think about their ability to engage in different types of recreational activities (Wise, 2007, 2009); adults considering the use of a strategic interpersonal behavior, humor, in different situations (Caldwell, Cervone, & Rubin, 2008); and older adults reflecting on how their strengths and weaknesses might influence their ability to perform challenging everyday tasks (Artistico, et al., 2018). In all these studies, people have higher appraisals of self-efficacy in situations that are relevant to their positive self-schemas.

One last distinctive feature of the KAPA model is that is can be tested experimentally. Priming procedures (of the sort you saw in Higgins's research on self-discrepancies) enable researchers to activate one versus another aspect of self-knowledge. The KAPA model predicts that such priming manipulations should, in turn, influence people's appraisals of self-efficacy for handling everyday challenges. Priming has been accomplished by asking participants to perform a memory task that is seemingly unrelated to other aspects of the study. On different days, the task presented to participants includes words that are synonymous with either their schematic personal strength of their schematic personal weakness (Cervone et al., 2008). After the priming procedures, people are asked to consider some challenging tasks and appraise their self-efficacy for success on those tasks. Findings confirm the KAPA model prediction; the priming of positive self-schemas raises self-efficacy appraisals in situations relevant to the self-schema (see Figure 13.4).

In sum, the KAPA model extends the pioneering efforts of Bandura, Mischel, and other prior social-cognitive investigators. It does so by putting social-cognitive tools to work on classic problems in the psychology of personality. The result is a theory that combines the nomothetic with the idiographic (cf. Chapter 7). A set of general, nomothetic principles distinguishes personality structures and processes. Individualized, idiographic assessments shed light on personality psychology's fundamental target: the psychological dynamics of the individual.

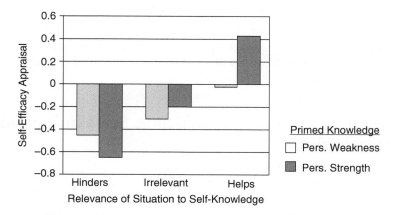

FIGURE 13.4 The KAPA model predicts that beliefs about oneself (self-knowledge) that are active in mind will influence appraisals of capabilities for performance, or self-efficacy appraisals. The graph displays results from a study in which this prediction was tested experimentally. Cognitive priming was used to bring beliefs about either personal strengths or personal weaknesses to mind. Priming personal strengths increased self-efficacy appraisals – but, as predicted, only in those specific situations in which participants believed that their personal strengths were relevant and helpful. From Cervone, Caldwell, Fiori, Orom, Shadel et al. (2004).

Clinical Applications

Thus far in discussing social-cognitive theory, we primarily have reviewed core theoretical principles and basic research findings. We now turn to a key arena in which this work is applied: the psychological clinic. Clinical applications of cognitive theory have been of enormous significance in the past quarter-century. Indeed, in many clinical settings and training programs, the cognitive approach has become the most predominant of all theoretical orientations.

There is no one theory or technique of cognitive therapy. Instead, there are different approaches, often tailored to specific problems, that share some common assumptions:

1. Cognitions (attributions, beliefs, expectancies, memories concerning the self and others) are viewed as critical in determining feelings and behaviors. Thus, there is an interest in what people think and say to themselves.

2. The cognitions of interest tend to be specific to situations or categories of situations, though the importance of some generalized expectancies and beliefs is recognized.

3. Psychopathology is viewed as arising from distorted, incorrect, maladaptive cognitions concerning the self, others, and events in the world. Different forms of pathology are viewed as resulting from different cognitions or ways of processing information.

4. Faulty, maladaptive cognitions lead to problematic feelings and behaviors, and these in turn lead to further problematic cognitions. Thus, a self-fulfilling cycle may set in whereby persons act so as to confirm and maintain their distorted beliefs.

5. Cognitive therapy involves a collaborative effort between therapist and patient to determine which distorted, maladaptive cognitions are creating the difficulty and then to replace them with other more realistic, adaptive cognitions. The therapeutic approach tends to be active, structured, and focused on the present.

6. In contrast with other approaches, cognitive approaches do not see the unconscious as important, except insofar as patients may not be aware of their routine, habitual ways of thinking about themselves and life. Further, there is an emphasis on changes in specific problematic cognitions rather than on global personality change.

In this section first we will consider the clinical applications that follow directly from social-cognitive theory, and then we will consider other clinical applications that, while they do not follow directly from the work of Bandura and Mischel, are part of the more general social-cognitive approach to pathology and change.

Psychopathology and Change: Modeling, Self-Conceptions, and Perceived Self-Efficacy

Why do people experience psychological distress and how can it be reduced? The theories of personality provide different answers to this question. Psychoanalysis tells us that psychological problems experienced in adulthood are symptoms of an underlying psychological pathology that originated in childhood. Humanistic theories claim that interpersonal relationships that are experienced throughout life affect self-concept and well-being. Trait theories highlight genetic factors that predispose some people to experience distressful emotions. Social-cognitive theory provides a different answer. It contains two key parts.

First, social-cognitive theory emphasizes the role of behavioral experience (Bandura, 1969). People may experience environments in which they learn behaviors that are maladaptive or fail to experience settings that teach skills that would help them to cope with life's challenges. A major task for the therapist therefore is to provide clients with new experiences that teach new, adaptive behaviors. Note how this approach differs from a "medical model" of psychological disorder. In a medical model, a therapist might primarily try to identify early-life experiences or predisposing biological factors that are an underlying cause of a client's symptoms. In the social-cognitive approach, the therapist instead directly confronts the challenge of modifying the problematic behavior that caused the client to seek professional help.

The second distinguishing feature is a focus on cognition, including **dysfunctional expectancies** and **dysfunctional self-evaluations**. If people erroneously expect that negative outcomes will occur to them, these expectations may create the outcomes they hope to avoid. For example, a person who expects that interpersonal closeness with a partner will inevitably bring pain may act in a hostile way toward the partner, thereby harming the relationship. **Dysfunctional self-evaluations** include perfectionistic standards for evaluating oneself. As Rogers also recognized in his analysis of the idea self, people who adopt overly-stringent standards of self-evaluation—who are happy only if they are the absolutely best player on their team or the best student in class—may doom themselves to repeated disappointed when their impossibly-high standards are not met.

Self-Efficacy, Anxiety, and Depression

The social-cognitive analysis of psychopathology is multifaceted; a variety of beliefs, actions, and skill deficits can foster psychological distress. Yet the theory does give a central role to perceived self-efficacy. Let us first consider the role of self-efficacy perceptions in anxiety.

According to social-cognitive theory, low self-efficacy for coping with threats directly causes high anxiety arousal. It is not the threatening event per se but the perceived inefficacy in coping with it that is fundamental to anxiety. Research indeed indicates that those who believe they cannot manage threatening events experience relatively greater distress. They also may focus attention on the expected disaster that lies ahead rather than on strategies to cope with a challenge, and may become concerned about their own tendency to panic—a fear-of-fear response that can lead to actual panic (Barlow, 1991).

Perceived inefficacy also plays a role in depression. A perceived inability to achieve desired outcome creates a sense of loss that is depressing. Furthermore, low self-efficacy beliefs may contribute to diminished performance, leading to further depression and self-blame (Kavanagh, 1992). Just such a relationship was found in a study of childhood depression. In this study, perceived social and academic inefficacy was found to contribute to depression directly as well as indirectly through problem behaviors that interfered with future social and academic success (Bandura, Pastorelli, Barbaranelli, & Caprara, 1999). Thus, a self-defeating cycle was established wherein low self-efficacy contributed to depression and problem behaviors, which in turn contributed to further perceived inefficacy and depression.

Bandura (1992) raises the interesting point that discrepancies between standards and performance can have varied effects ranging from greater effort to apathy to depression. What determines which effect will occur? According to Bandura, discrepancies between performance and standards lead to high motivation when people believe they have the efficacy to accomplish the goal. Beliefs that the goals are beyond one's capabilities because they are unrealistic will lead to abandoning the goal and perhaps to apathy but not to depression. For example, a person may say "This task is just too hard" and give up, perhaps becoming frustrated and angry but not depressed. Depression occurs when a person feels ineffective in relation to a goal but believes the goal to be reasonable; therefore that person feels he or she must continue to strive to meet the standard. Thus, the effects of a discrepancy between standards and performance on effort and mood depend on self-efficacy beliefs and on whether the standard is perceived to be reasonable, possible to achieve, and important.

The relations between (a) depressed mood and (b) discrepancies between standards and performance is bidirectional. Not only do cognitive discrepancies create depressed emotions; depressed emotions contribute to the existence of these discrepancies. Evidence comes from research that experimentally manipulates people's moods (Cervone, Kopp, Schaumann, & Scott, 1994; Scott & Cervone, 2002) as well as work that compares depressed and nondepressed persons (Tillema, Cervone, & Scott, 2001). The findings indicate that when people are feeling bad, they tend to adopt performance standards that are more perfectionistic. When in a bad mood, routine outcomes seem less satisfactory; as a result, people are satisfied only with superior attainments. These higher standards for performance commonly exceed the level of performance people think they actually can attain (Cervone et al., 1994).

Self-Efficacy and Health

One active area of social-cognitive research has related self-efficacy beliefs to health. The social-cognitive theory of health promotion and disease prevention focuses on four structures previously noted: *knowledge* of health risks and benefits of different health practices; *perceived self-efficacy* that one can control one's health habits; *outcome* expectancies about the expected costs and benefits of different health practices; and the *health goals* people set for themselves and strategies for realizing them (Bandura, 2004). Not surprisingly, self-efficacy beliefs are the focus of much health-related research. The results of this research can be easily summarized: Strong, positive self-efficacy beliefs are good for your health; conversely, weak and negative self-efficacy beliefs are bad for your health (Schwarzer, 1992). Self-efficacy beliefs affect health in two major ways: they affect health-related behaviors and they impact physiological functioning (Contrada, Leventhal, & O'Leary, 1990; Miller, Shoda, & Hurley, 1996). Self-efficacy beliefs affect both the likelihood of developing various illnesses and the process of recovery from illness (O'Leary, 1992).

Self-efficacy beliefs have been related to a variety of health-relevant behaviors (O'Leary, 1992). For example, in the study of safe sex practices, higher self-efficacy perceptions predict a higher likelihood of safe sexual behavior (Burns & Dillon, 2005). Among individuals recovering from a heart attack, self-efficacy perceptions that are optimistic, yet also appropriate to the patient's health status, promote healthier exercise patterns (Ewart, 1992).

Self-efficacy beliefs also have been related to specific physiological functions. Evidence indicates that high self-efficacy beliefs buffer the effects of stress and enhance the functioning of the body's immune (disease-fighting) system (O'Leary, 1990). In one experiment on perceived self and immune system functioning (Wiedenfeld et al., 1990), participants experiencing snake phobia were tested under three conditions: a baseline involving no exposure to a snake, a perceived self-efficacy acquisition phase during which they were assisted in gaining a sense of coping efficacy, and a maximal self-efficacy phase in which they had achieved a complete sense of coping efficacy. During these phases, a small amount of blood was drawn from the subjects and analyzed for the presence of cells known to help regulate the immune system, including helper T cells that play a role in destroying cancerous cells and viruses. Increases in self-efficacy beliefs were associated with increases in immune system functioning, including helper T cell levels.

Therapeutic Change: Modeling and Guided Mastery

Bringing about beneficial behavior change is a critical goal to Bandura and other social-cognitivists. Bandura embraces this goal while warning that it should be pursued cautiously; therapeutic procedures should be applied clinically only after the basic psychological mechanisms underlying change are understood.

To Bandura (1977), a central mechanism of change is cognitive: perceived self-efficacy. But the most powerful means of affecting this mechanism is behavioral: mastery experiences. If therapists can guide patients in the behavioral process of mastering challenges, changes in self-efficacy beliefs are likely to follow.

A primary therapy strategy for Bandura is modeling and **guided mastery**. In modeling, a client observes someone (e.g., the therapist) who displays a skill the client hopes to acquire. In guided mastery, the individual not only views a model performing beneficial behaviors, but clients also are assisted in performing the behaviors themselves. Much research indicates that guided mastery therapies are powerful and efficient (Bandura, 1997). Preliminary investigations documented their ability to reduce snake phobias, irrational fears of snakes that can interfere with daily life.

In this work, Bandura and colleagues evaluated the relation between self-efficacy perceptions and behavior change using a "microanalytic" research strategy. In this strategy, self-efficacy and behavior are related at the level of individual acts. The strategy was executed is an experiment in which chronic snake phobics were assigned to one of three conditions: participant modeling (the therapist models the threatening activities and subjects gradually perform the tasks, with therapist assistance, until they can be performed alone); modeling (subjects observe the therapist perform the tasks but do not engage in them); and a control condition (Bandura, Adams, & Beyer, 1977). Both before and after these conditions, the subjects were tested on a Behavioral Avoidance Test (BAT), which consisted of 29 performance tasks of increasing difficulty (the final task involved letting the snake crawl in one's lap). To test the role of perceived self-efficacy, the researchers conducted a highly detailed assessment in which they measured snake phobics' perceived self-efficacy for performing each of a the BAT behaviors, with the self-efficacy assessments being taken both before and after treatment.

The results indicated that, as expected, participant modeling produced the strongest changes in behavior. More important for the study of perceived self-efficacy, changes in self-efficacy perceptions and changes in behavior were extremely closely related. At the between-group level, the groups that achieved the greatest changes in self-efficacy perceptions also achieved the greatest changes in behavior. At the individual level, self-efficacy judgments were uniformly accurate predictors of performance. Indeed, self-efficacy/behavior relations were remarkably large; Bandura and colleagues (1977) report a correlation of .84 between level of self-efficacy and subsequent approach behavior. In sum, the data indicate not only that guided mastery is a powerful treatment, but that its power comes from its effects on self-efficacy perceptions (also see Bandura & Adams, 1977; Bandura, Adams, & Beyer, 1977; Bandura, Reese, & Adams, 1982; Williams, 1992).

This social-cognitive approach subsequently has been applied more widely. Studies have demonstrated the role of mastery experiences and self-efficacy perceptions in behavior change among students coping with test anxiety (Smith, 1989), combat veterans dealing with post-traumatic stress (Benight & Bandura, 2004), athletes concerned about prospective injuries (Chase, Magyar, & Drake, 2005), and women concerned about their vulnerability to assault (Ozer & Bandura, 1990; Weitlauf, Cervone, & Smith, 2001). In the latter application, women who participated in a modeling program in which they mastered the physical skills needed to defend themselves against unarmed sexual assailants gained increased freedom of action and decreased avoidant behavior. Fundamental to all of these studies is that the experience of mastery creates a therapeutically beneficial increase in perceived self-efficacy.

Stress-Vulnerability Signatures

The CAPS model of Mischel and Shoda also has been employed to benefit therapeutic change. In one study, Shoda and colleagues (2013) sought to identify the situations that a client experiences as highly stressful and the psychological reactions they trigger. To obtain a *stress vulnerability signature,* the client is asked to make a daily diary of ratings of stressful situations and the situational characteristics of them. Note the emphasis on situations that are specific to the individual client, in particular the psychological situation, a procedure that is termed the *Highly Repeated Within Person (HRWP)* approach. In keeping with the CAPS approach, rather than an emphasis on generally stressful situations or mean levels of stress for the individual, it is the situational variability within the individual that is of interest. Whereas one client may be vulnerable to feeling excluded, another may be vulnerable to feeling irritated, and a third to feeling he or she has let others down.

In addition to the mapping of the stress vulnerability signature, there is an assessment of maladaptive coping strategies. Illustrative of such strategies are blaming the self or others, avoidance, and wishful thinking. Again, these are assessed in terms of the individual client rather than some general emphasis on maladaptive strategies. Following assessment of situations and strategies, a stress management program is introduced, called the *cognitive-affective stress management training (C-ASMT)* program. This is a six-session intervention program that targets the maladaptive cognitions through procedures such as cognitive restructuring and relaxation. For example, the client may be instructed to consider statements to the self such as "What is the worst possible outcome? How likely is this?" and to apply relaxation procedures that have been taught in the sessions. In other words, the focus is on altering specific problematic cognitions and increasing specific coping skills.

The work we have just reviewed involves direct applications of social-cognitive personality theory to clinical change. These social-cognitive applications can be understood as part of a broad effort in psychology to identify cognitive processes that contribute to psychological distress and that can be modified to enhance well-being. We close this chapter by briefly overviewing these efforts.

Stress, Coping, and Cognitive Therapy

Ever feel stressed? You're not alone. A recent survey of thousands of college students asked about factors that negatively impacted their performance at school. Students mentioned a range of challenges: homesickness, roommates, computer games, and so forth. But the difficulty that was the singularly most cited was stress. Furthermore, the next two most-cited problems are ones that can be created by stress: feelings of anxiety and trouble getting a good night's sleep (American College Health Association, 2016).

The study of stress, and of strategies to cope with it, has received much attention from personality and clinical psychologists (e.g., Folkman & Moskowitz, 2004). One primary approach is that of cognitively-oriented researchers whose work complements social-cognitive personality theory. A major figure in this effort was the psychologist Richard Lazarus.

Lazarus explained that the experience of stress often results from the way in which individuals appraise the relation between themselves and the environment (Lazarus, 1990). Specifically, stress occurs when the person views circumstances as taxing or exceeding his or her resources and endangering well-being. Two stages of cognitive appraisal can be distinguished. In *primary* appraisal, the person evaluates whether there is anything at stake in the encounter, whether there is a threat or danger. For example, is there potential harm or benefit to self-esteem? Is one's personal health or that of a loved one at risk? In *secondary* appraisal, the person evaluates what, if anything, can be done to overcome harm, prevent harm, or improve the prospects for benefit. In other words, secondary appraisal involves an evaluation of the person's resources to cope with the potential harm or benefit evaluated in the stage of primary appraisal.

There are different ways of coping with any given situation. A key distinction is one that differentiates between **problem-focused coping**, which refers to attempts to cope by altering features of a stressful situation, and **emotion-focused coping**, which refers to coping in which an individual strives to improve his or her internal emotional state, for example, by emotional distancing or the seeking of social support. Research by Folkman, Lazarus, and colleagues has developed a questionnaire to assess coping, the Ways of Coping Scale, and has explored the health implications of different coping strategies.

This research suggests the following conclusions (Folkman, Lazarus, Gruen, & DeLongis, 1986; Lazarus, 1993):

1. There is evidence of both stability and variability in the methods individuals use to cope with stressful situations. Although the use of some coping methods appears to be influenced by personality factors, the use of many coping methods appears to be strongly influenced by the situational context.

2. In general, the greater the reported level of stress and efforts to cope, the poorer the physical health and the greater the likelihood of psychological symptoms. In contrast, the greater the sense of mastery, the better is the physical and psychological health.

3. Although the value of a particular form of coping depends on the context in which it is used, in general, planful problem solving ("I made a plan of action and followed it" or "Just concentrate on the next step") is a more adaptive form of coping than escape avoidance ("I hoped a miracle would happen" or "I tried to reduce tension by eating, drinking, or using drugs") or confrontative coping ("I let my feelings out somehow" or "I expressed anger to those who caused the problem").

In addition to this conceptual analysis of stress, one wants practical procedures to reduce it. One strategy is **stress inoculation training** (Meichenbaum, 1995). In stress inoculation training, therapists teach clients the cognitive nature of stress. Clients learn about stress-inducing thoughts that may pop into mind automatically (e.g., "It is such an effort to do anything") and are instructed in new stress-*reducing* ways of thinking. These new cognitive skills are designed to prepare people for—or "inoculate them against"—stressful events that will inevitably occur in the future. The training combines verbal and visual ways of thinking. In addition to learning coping statement such as "I can do it," "One step at time," and "Focus on the present; what is it I have to do?," clients engage in imagery in which they mentally simulate prospective future situations that present a high risk for experiencing stress.

The stress inoculation training procedure is active, focused, structured, and brief. It has been used with patients about to undergo surgery, women coping with pregnancy, athletes dealing with the stress of performance, rape victims dealing with the trauma of assault, and employees who need to work effectively in teams. Research findings document the effectiveness of this strategy for reducing stress (e.g., Khorsandi et al., 2015; Saunders, Driskell, Johnston, & Salas, 1996).

Ellis's Rational-Emotive Therapy

Albert Ellis was a former psychoanalyst who developed a therapeutic system of personality change known as rational emotive-therapy (RET) (Ellis, 1962, 1987; Ellis & Harper, 1975) or, equivalently, rational-emotion behavior theory (REBT; e.g., Ellis & Tafrate, 1997). There are two primary theses behind Ellis's work on psychological distress and its treatment.

The first thesis is that people do not respond emotionally to events in the world but to their *beliefs about* those events. Ellis conveys this idea simply, by suggesting an "ABC" of rational-emotive therapy (Ellis, 1997). An activating (A) event may lead to a consequence (C) such as an emotional reaction. A person unfamiliar with Ellis's analyses may think that the A caused the C, that is, that the activating event is the cause of the emotional consequence. But not so, according to Ellis. "We . . . create Beliefs (Bs) between A and C. Our Bs about A largely determine our response to it" (Ellis & Tafrate, 1997, p. 31). This first premise of rational-emotive therapy, then, is identical to the central premise of the social-cognitive approach to personality, namely, that people's enduring belief systems are immediate determinants of their experiences and actions.

Ellis's second thesis is more unique. It is his claim that the beliefs that cause psychological distress have a particular quality: They are *irrational;* that is, they are beliefs that no rational person would, upon reflection, wish to have because the beliefs are sure to bring about one's own psychological distress.

According to Ellis, then, the causes of psychological difficulties are irrational beliefs or irrational statements we make to ourselves: beliefs, for example, that we *must* do something, that we *have to* feel some way, that other people *always should* treat us in a certain manner. Suppose a person thinks "If good things happen, bad things must be on the way" or "If I express my needs, others will reject me." These thoughts are irrational in that persons who think these things are dooming themselves to psychological distress.

Cognitive therapists often distinguish among alternative types of thinking that are maladaptive. The distinctions among them are not terribly important; nonetheless, listing a few can give you an idea of the type of negative thinking that Ellis and similar therapists wish to change in therapy:

Faulty reasoning. "I failed on this effort, so I must be incompetent." "They didn't respond the way I wanted them to, so they must not think much of me."

Dysfunctional expectancies. "If something can go wrong for me, it will." "Catastrophe is just around the corner."

Negative self-views. "I always tend to feel that others are better than me." "Nothing I do ever turns out right."

Maladaptive attributions. "I'm a poor test-taker because I am a nervous person." "When I win, it's luck; when I lose, it's me."

Memory distortions. "Life is horrible now and always has been this way." "I've never succeeded in anything."

Maladaptive attention. "All I can think about is how horrible it will be if I fail." "It's better not to think about things; there's nothing you can do anyway."

Self-defeating strategies. "I'll put myself down before others do." "I'll reject others before they reject me and see if people still like me."

Ellis's therapy techniques are designed to force people to reflect on their own thinking. Rational-emotion therapists try to make people aware of the irrationality of their own thoughts, so that they can replace these thoughts with calm, rational thinking. Therapists use a variety of techniques—logic, argument, persuasion, ridicule, humor—in an effort to change the irrational beliefs that cause psychological distress.

Beck's Cognitive Therapy for Depression

Like Albert Ellis, Aaron Beck is a former psychoanalyst who became disenchanted with psychoanalytic techniques and gradually developed a cognitive approach to therapy. His therapy is best known for its relevance to the treatment of depression, but it has relevance to a wider variety of psychological disorders. According to Beck (1987), psychological difficulties are due to automatic thoughts, dysfunctional assumptions, and negative self-statements.

The Cognitive Triad of Depression

Beck's cognitive model of depression emphasizes that a depressed person systematically misevaluates ongoing and past experiences, leading to views of the self as a loser, the world as frustrating, and the future as bleak. These three negative views are known as the cognitive triad and include negative views of the self such as "I am inadequate, undesirable, worthless," negative views of the world such as "The world makes too many demands on me and life represents constant defeat," and negative views of the future such as "Life will always involve the suffering and deprivation it has for me now." In addition, a depressed person is prone to faulty information processing, such as in magnifying everyday difficulties into disasters and overgeneralizing from a single instance of rejection to the belief that "Nobody likes me." It is these thinking problems, these negative schemas and cognitive errors, that cause depression.

Research on Faulty Cognitions

Considerable research has examined whether faulty cognitions are related to symptoms of depression, as Beck's theory anticipates. Much research in the 1980s and 1990s provided evidence that was consistent with Beck's model (Segal & Dobson, 1992). Compared to nondepressed individuals, depressed persons appeared to focus more on themselves (Wood, Saltzberg, & Goldsamt, 1990), to have more accessible negative self-constructs (Bargh & Tota, 1988; Strauman, 1990), and to have a bias toward pessimism rather than optimism, particularly in relation to the self (Epstein, 1992; Taylor & Brown, 1988).

Much of the early research on cognition and depression employed "concurrent" research designs, that is, research plans in which cognitions and depressive symptoms are measured at the same time. Concurrent designs have a big drawback: It is hard to know if relations between cognition and depression reflect (1) the influence of cognition on depression (as Beck and other cognitive theorists predict), (2) the influence of depressed emotions on cognition, or (3) the influence of some third factor that affects both cognition and depression (e.g., negative life events that affect people's beliefs and emotional experiences). Cognitive theories can be evaluated more convincingly through the use of "prospective" research designs, that is, research in which cognitive factors are measured at one point in time and are used to predict the development of depressive symptoms at later times.

Fortunately, in recent years, investigators have turned to prospective research designs. For example, Hankin, Fraley, and Abela (2005) asked participants, at the outset of a study, to complete a questionnaire that measured their tendencies to engage in negative patterns of thinking that were thought to predispose persons to becoming depressed. They then asked these same research participants to complete a daily diary for a period of 35 days. Individual differences in the tendency to thinking negatively, as assessed at the outset of the study, predicted the subsequent occurrence of depressive symptoms; that is, the cognitive factor predicted depressive symptoms during the following 35 days during which people completed the diary (Hankin et al., 2005).

One of the puzzling questions for psychologists who emphasize the role of faulty cognitions in depression is the following: What happens to the faulty cognitions when the depression has lifted? This question is important because once a person has experienced a serious depression, the tendency for that person is to fall into a relapse or another depression. Why should this be the case if the faulty cognitions are gone? There is some evidence that the faulty cognitions that make the person vulnerable to depression are latent and become manifest only under conditions of stress (Alloy, Abramson, & Francis, 1999. For example, people vulnerable to depression may retain negative attitudes toward the self that only become manifest and operational when they experience blows to their self-esteem. The task of therapy, then, is to affect fundamental change in these cognitions as well as to make the person aware of the conditions under which they become operational.

Cognitive Therapy

Cognitive therapy of depression is designed to identify and correct distorted conceptualizations and dysfunctional beliefs (Beck, 1993; Brewin, 1996). Therapy generally consists of 15–25 sessions at weekly intervals. The approach is described as involving highly specific learning experiences designed to teach the patient to monitor negative, automatic thoughts, to recognize how these thoughts lead to problematic feelings and behaviors, to examine the evidence for and against these thoughts, and to substitute more reality-oriented interpretations for these biased cognitions. The therapist helps the patient to see that interpretations of events lead to depressed feelings. For example, the following exchange between therapist (T) and patient (P) might occur:

P: I get depressed when things go wrong. Like when I fail a test.
T: How can failing a test make you depressed?
P: Well, if I fail I'll never get into law school.
T: So failing the test means a lot to you. But if failing a test could drive people into clinical depression, wouldn't you expect everyone who failed the test to have a depression? Did everyone who failed get depressed enough to require treatment?
P: No, but it depends on how important the test was to the person.
T: Right, and who decides the importance?
p: I do.

Source: Beck, Rush, Shaw, & Emery, 1979, p. 146.

In addition to the examination of beliefs for their logic, validity, and adaptiveness, behavioral assignments are used to help the patient test certain maladaptive cognitions and assumptions. This may involve the assignment of activities designed to result in success and pleasure. In general, the therapy focuses on specific target cognitions that are seen as contributing to the depression. Beck contrasts cognitive therapy with traditional analytic therapy in terms of the therapist's being continuously active in structuring the therapy, in the focus on the here and now, and in the emphasis on conscious factors.

Beck's cognitive therapy has been expanded to include the treatment of other psychological difficulties, including anxiety, personality disorders, drug abuse, and marital difficulties (Beck, 1993). The idea is that each difficulty is associated with a distinctive pattern of beliefs. Whereas in depression the beliefs concern failure and self-worth, in anxiety, for example, they concern danger. There is evidence for the effectiveness of cognitive therapy (Antonuccio, Thomas, & Danton, 1997). Although the distinctive therapeutic features of cognitive therapy and whether changes in beliefs are the key therapeutic ingredients remain to be determined (Dobson & Shaw, 1995), evidence suggests that therapeutic change indeed follows cognitive change (Tang & De Rubeis, 1999a, 1999b).

The Case of Jim

Twenty years ago Jim was assessed from various theoretical points of view: psychoanalytic, phenomenological, personal construct, and trait. At the time, social-cognitive theory was just beginning to evolve, and thus he was not considered from this standpoint. Later, however, it was possible to gather at least some data from this theoretical standpoint as well. Although comparisons with earlier data may be problematic because of the time lapse, we can gain at least some insight into Jim's personality from this theoretical point of view. We do so by considering Jim's goals, reinforcers he experiences, and his self-efficacy beliefs.

Jim was asked about his goals for the immediate future and for the long-range future. He felt that his immediate and long-term goals were pretty much the same: (1) getting to know his son and being a good parent, (2) becoming more accepting and less critical of his wife and others, and (3) feeling good about his professional work as a consultant. Generally, he feels that there is a good chance of achieving these goals but is guarded in that estimate, with some uncertainty about just how much he will be able to "get out of myself" and thereby be more able to give to his wife and child.

Jim also was asked about positive and aversive reinforcers, things that were important to him that he found rewarding or unpleasant. Concerning positive reinforcers, Jim reported that money was "a biggie". In addition, he emphasized time with loved ones, the glamour of going to an opening night, and generally going to the theater or movies. He had a difficult time thinking of aversive reinforcers. He described writing as a struggle and then noted, "I'm having trouble with this."

Jim also discussed another social-cognitive variable: his competencies or skills (both intellectual and social). He reported that he considered himself to be very bright and functioning at a very high intellectual level. He felt that he writes well from the standpoint of a clear, organized presentation, but he had not written anything that is innovative or creative. Jim also felt that he was very skilled socially: "I do it naturally, easily, well. I can pull off anything and have a lot of confidence in myself socially. I am at ease with both men and women, in both professional and social contexts." The one social concern noted was his constant struggle with "how egocentric I should be, how personally to take things." He felt that sometimes he takes things too personally: "My security is based on how I'm doing with others. I put a lot of energy into friendships, and when I'm relating well I feel good."

In terms of self-efficacy beliefs, Jim had many positive views of himself. He believes that he does most things well; he is a good athlete, a competent consultant, bright, and socially skilled. Does he have areas of low self-efficacy? Jim mentioned three: that he does not genuinely accept his wife; a difficulty "getting out of myself so that I can be genuinely devoted to others"; and, third, creativity: "I know I'm not good at being creative, so I don't try it."

It also was informative to consider irrational beliefs, dysfunctional thoughts, and cognitive distortions. Jim described his tendency to overpersonalize: "This is a problem of mine. If someone doesn't call, I attribute it to a feeling state in relation to me. I can feel terribly injured at times." In his responses to the Automatic Thoughts Questionnaire (Hollon & Kendall, 1980) he reported having the following thoughts frequently: "I've let people down," "I wish I were a better person," "I'm disappointed in myself," and "I can't stand this." These frequent thoughts have to do with his not being as loving or generous as he would like, his being very demanding of himself professionally and in athletics, his obsession about things that might go wrong, and his intolerance of things not going his way. For example, he cannot stand to be in traffic and will say "I can't stand this. This is intolerable." Jim did not think much of Ellis's work, and an interview suggested that he didn't have many irrational beliefs, yet on a questionnaire he checked four out of nine items as frequent thoughts of his: "I must have love or approval," "When people act badly, I blame them," "I tend to view it as a catastrophe when I get seriously frustrated or feel rejected," and "I tend to get preoccupied with things that seem fearsome." He also described his tendency to catastrophize if he is going to be late for a movie: "It's a calamity if I'm going to be one minute late. It becomes a life and death emergency. I go through red lights, honk the horn, and pound on the wheel." This is in contrast to his own tendency to be at least a few minutes late for virtually all appointments, though rarely by more than a few minutes.

In some ways the social-cognitive data on Jim are more limited than those associated with the previous theories of personality. We learn about important aspects of Jim's life, but clearly there also are major gaps. There are two reasons for this. First, only a limited amount of time was available for assessment. Second, and perhaps more important, social-cognitive theorists have not developed comprehensive personality assessment tests; only recently have social-cognitive investigators turned their attention explicitly to questions of personality assessment (Cervone, Shadel, & Jencius, 2001). In part, the previous lack of attention reflected social-cognitive theory's conviction that systematic research and the testing of hypotheses, rather than the in-depth study of individuals, is critical to building a scientifically valid personality theory. It perhaps also reflected the social-cognitive criticism of traditional approaches to assessment that emphasize broad personality consistencies across many domains. In this regard, it is interesting that Jim had difficulty articulating differences in his functioning in various areas. In this sense, he functions much more like a traditional personality theorist than like a social-cognitive theorist, although with further questioning he probably would have been able to specify ways in which his goals, reinforcers, competencies, and self-efficacy beliefs varied from context to context.

From a social-cognitive perspective, what can be said about Jim as he approaches midlife? We see that in general Jim has a strong sense of self-efficacy in relation to intellectual and social skills, though he feels less efficacious in relation to creative thought and the ability to be loving, generous, and giving to people who are dear to him. He values money and financial success but has settled more on family intimacy and the quality of his work as a consultant as goals for the future. He has a strong sense of individual responsibility and belief in personal control over events. There is a streak of pessimism and depression to him. He is bothered by concerns about the approval of others, by his perfectionism and impatience, and by a tendency to worry about things. He tends to be self-controlled in coping with stress rather than avoiding problems or escaping from them. Generally he sees himself as a competent person and is guardedly optimistic about his chances of achieving his goals in the future.

Critical Evaluation

Scientific Observation: The Database

We turn now to a critical evaluation of this last of the personality theories we present, social-cognitive theory (Table 13.1). As in our prior evaluations, we first assess the quality of the scientific observations that furnish the database on which the theory rests.

On this criterion, social-cognitive theory excels. Bandura, Mischel, and colleagues have built their theory on a systematic accumulation of objective scientific evidence. A particularly outstanding feature of this database is its diversity. To test claims that social-cognitive processes causally influence personality functioning, social-cognitivists have run controlled laboratory experiments. To study the development of individual differences, they have run correlational studies and employed longitudinal methods. To study behavior change, they have conducted clinical outcome studies. The participants in their studies have been diverse: children, adolescents, and adults; people suffering from psychological distress; high-functioning members of the population at large. They have employed a variety of research methods: self-report questionnaires; parental and peer reports of personality; direct observations of behavior in natural settings; measures of cognitive processes in the laboratory.

Table 13.1   Summary of Strengths and Limitations of Social-Cognitive Theory

Strengths	Limitations
1. Has impressive research record	1. Is not a systematic, unified theory
2. Considers important phenomena	2. Contains potential problems associated with the use of verbal self-report
3. Shows consistent development	3. Requires more exploration and elaboration as a theory development in certain areas (e.g., motivation, affect, system properties of personality organization)
4. Focuses attention on important	4. Provides findings concerning therapy theoretical issues that are tentative rather than conclusive

Of all the approaches to personality, social-cognitive theory and the trait theories are built on the largest and most systematic sets of scientific evidence. This surely is why they long have been the two most influential frameworks in modern personality science (Cervone, 1991).

Theory: Systematic?

Social-cognitive theory has many strengths. But its ability to provide a theory that is systematic—that is, in which all theoretical elements are coherently interrelated—traditionally has not been one of them. For many years, social-cognitive theory did not provide an over-arching network of assumptions that coherently tied together all elements of the theoretical perspective. The approach sometimes functions more as a strategy or framework for studying personality than a fully specified theory. Investigators have been aware of this; for example, Shoda and Mischel (2006) have referred to their CAPS model as a "meta-theory": not a full-fledged theory of personality, but a conceptual framework within which further theorizing could develop.

This is the limitation that the KAPA model of personality architecture was designed to address. Two main steps taken by the KAPA model were to identify (a) principles with which one can distinguish between social-cognitive structure and process variables and (b) psychological dynamics through which structures and processes are related. These were designed as steps in the direction of a more systematic social-cognitive theory—one that provides theoretical tools that are sufficient to guide the practical task of personality assessment and the scientific challenge of identifying cross-situational consistency in experience and behavior.

Theory: Testable?

Social-cognitive theorists unquestionably have succeeded in providing a personality theory that is testable. This is evident if one reflects on the research studies we have reviewed in the past two chapters. They could have come out differently; the social-cognitive hypotheses could have been proven wrong. It is possible that participant modeling would not have been such a success, or that attentional factors would not have been so important to delay of gratification, or that self-efficacy beliefs would have been unrelated to behavior once one controlled for "third variables". In these and numerous other cases, social-cognitive theorists defined their constructs with clarity and provided measurement tools and experimental methods that enabled their ideas to be tested. On this criterion, social-cognitive theory gets high marks.

Theory: Comprehensive?

Social-cognitive theory is quite comprehensive. Theorists have addressed questions of motivation, development, self-concept, self-control, and behavioral change. The approach even addresses a topic that is skipped in most other personality theories: the learning of social skills and other behavioral competencies.

Yet there also are ways in which social-cognitive theory lacks comprehensiveness. Some aspects of the human experience simply have received little attention from social-cognitive theorists. For example, biological forces of maturation would appear important to people's experiences of the world; sexual feelings in adolescence or a desire for parenting in adulthood may reflect biological rather than social and cognitive features of personality. But these maturational factors receive relatively little formal attention in social-cognitive theory. Inherited temperament may interact with social experience in the development of social-cognitive systems, but these interactions have received less attention in research than they deserve. Other important types of experience—for example, mental conflict, feelings of alienation or anomie, existential concerns about death—similarly have not been systematically targeted in social-cognitive theorizing. Social-cognitive theory has expanded gradually over the years. Expansions that include topics such as those listed here are a challenge for future work.

Social-Cognitive Theory at a Glance		
Theorist or Theory	**Structure**	**Process**
Social-Cognitive Theory	Competencies, Beliefs, Goals, Evaluative Standards	Cognitive and affective processing system functions in reciprocal interaction with the social environment, especially in observational learning, self-regulated motivation, and self-control

Applications

Social-cognitive theorists have succeeded admirably in applying their theory to the solution of social problems and the alleviation of psychological distress. Indeed, no personality theory exceeds the social-cognitive theorists' level of success on this point. Both Bandura and Mischel were trained as clinicians, and this surely heightened their awareness of the need to apply basic theory to practical concerns.

Two features contribute greatly to social-cognitive theorists' success in relating theory to practice. One is that they did not artificially separate "basic" and "clinical" research. Instead, they pursued basic research questions in clinical contexts; for example, the first experimental tests of self-efficacy theory were done in a clinical setting (with snake phobics). The other is that the social-cognitive theorists wrote books that were central to the professional training of many other psychologists who, in turn, advanced psychological applications. Bandura's (1969) volume on behavior therapy was used as a textbook by many clinicians who advanced cognitive-behavioral therapy in the last third of the 20th century. Mischel's (1968) volume on personality assessment and prediction taught applied psychologists lessons about the limitations of behavioral predictions based on traditional psychodynamic or trait-theoretic assessments.

Growth and Development	**Pathology**	**Change**
Social learning through observation and direct experience; development of self-efficacy judgments and standards for self-regulation	Learned response patterns; excessive self-standards; problems in self-efficacy	Modeling; guided mastery; increased self-efficacy

Major Contributions and Summary

Social-cognitive theory is a current favorite among academic personality psychologists. Many clinicians also would label themselves social-cognitive psychologists. The two main social-cognitive theorists, Bandura and Mischel, are two of the most eminent figures to be found in any branch of the psychological sciences. Numerous factors have contributed to the success of the approach. Some were cited in this chapter: its large and systematic database, the testability of its formulations, the applicability of its theoretical principles. Yet one last meritorious feature should be noted. It is that social-cognitive theorists have been open to change. They have incorporated ongoing scientific advances into their theory, modifying features of the work as facts dictate. A comparison of *Social Learning and Personality Development* (1963) by Bandura and Walters with the latest formulations of social-cognitive theory (Bandura, 2006; Mischel & Shoda, 2008) testifies to the rapid evolution of the approach. The early work is described by the authors them-selves as a "socio-behavioristic approach" (Bandura & Walters, 1963, p. 1). Contemporary work is miles from behaviorism, with theorists now explicating the uniquely human cognitive capabilities that are the basis of human agency. We anticipate that social-cognitive theory will continue to evolve in the years ahead.

MAJOR CONCEPTS

Dysfunctional expectancies	Implicit theories	Problem-focused coping	Self-schemas
Dysfunctional self-evaluations	Knowledge-and-appraisal per-	Schemas	Stress inoculation training
Emotion-focused coping	sonality architecture or KAPA	Self-discrepancies	Working self-concept
General principles approach	Learning goals	Self-enhancement	
Guided mastery	Performance goals	Self-verification	

REVIEW

1. Much research in the social-cognitive tradition has explored three cognitive components of personality: beliefs, goals, and evaluative standards. The study of beliefs has included research on the role of cognitive generalizations about the self, or self-schemas. Research on goals has explored differences between types of goals, including learning versus performance goals. Work on evaluative standards has explored discrepancies between people's views of their actual self and standards representing ideals versus oughts, or obligations.

2. Research has established that people's thoughts about the causes of significant life events, or attributions about the events, significantly influence motivation and emotional reactions.

3. In clinical applications, social-cognitive theory rejects the medical symptom/disease model of psychopathology, emphasizing instead the dysfunctional learning of behaviors, expectancies, standards for self-reward, and, most significantly, self-efficacy beliefs. Dysfunctional learning can occur through the observation of models, in particular through vicarious conditioning, or through direct experience.

4. According to social-cognitive theory, there are two key points in bringing about psychological change in therapy. One is that low levels of perceived self-efficacy contribute to a wide variety of psychological dysfunctions, including anxiety and depression.

The other is that self-efficacy perceptions can be increased therapeutically, especially through modeling and guided mastery therapies. In modeling, models demonstrate the skills and sub-skills necessary in specific situations. In guided participation, the person is assisted in performing these modeled behaviors. Research supports the use of these procedures in raising the perception of self-efficacy.

5. In relation to the theories considered previously, social-cognitive theory emphasizes (a) conscious cognitive processes and experimental data as opposed to the psychoanalytic emphasis on unconscious processes and clinical data; (b) the role of social context and contextual variability in cognition and action, as opposed to the global self-conceptions emphasized by Rogers; and (c) personal capabilities for action, including people's potential to control and alter their own typical patterns of behavior, rather than the stable dispositional tendencies emphasized in the trait conceptions of personality.

6. Social-cognitive theory's strengths include its ability to bring systematic research to bear on important problems of personality functioning and social behavior. Its primary limit is that it is not yet a wholly unified, systematic theory. A primary challenge to social-cognitive theorists is to relate the development of social-cognitive structures to inherited biological qualities that contribute to individual differences.

14

Personality In Context: Interpersonal Relations, Culture, and Development Across The Course of Life

Chapter Focus

"I wish I was like you. You're always so optimistic about everything."

"Yeah, right. I just broke up with Pete."

"Oh no! What happened?"

"Well, I thought for sure that he was going to break up with me, so I challenged him on it, and we had a big fight."

"What made you think you'd break up?"

"That's what always happens, isn't it?"

"No. I mean, I've been with Sam for two years, and I'm sure we're going to stick together."

"Well, then you're the optimist, I guess. Except for how weird you get about exams."

"I'm telling you, I'm going to fail the final in this personality class."

"That's ridiculous. You said the same thing before the midterm, and then you got an A!"

Are both of these people optimists? Or are both pessimists? Or might there be a deeper lesson to be learned from this dialogue?

To many contemporary personality psychologists, the lesson is that personality must be understood "in context." We learn about someone's personality as we observe them interact with the social situations—the "contexts"—of their life. Even if the two people in the dialogue above are both "moderately optimistic" on average, this characterization perhaps does not tell you much about the differences in their personalities. In agreement with social-cognitive psychologists, there are those who suggest that a deeper understanding is obtained only if one explores how they cope with the different situations of their lives. The nature of their uniqueness and of the differences between them cannot be discovered by yanking their personality out of the life contexts in which they live. Instead, we can only understand *who* they are by asking *where* they are when they display the distinctive patterns of experience and action that are the hallmarks of their personality.

This chapter, then, considers the question of personality in context. Although the topics will vary, as you read the chapter, you will detect a consistent theme. In each case, scientific progress in understanding persons is made through a careful study of both persons and the contexts of their lives. Although drawing significantly on the social-cognitive approaches of Bandura, Mischel, and related investigators that were discussed in Chapters 12 and 13, we take an even broader view by capitalizing on a variety of research traditions in contemporary personality psychology that address the ways in which people make sense of their social world.

Questions to be Addressed in this chapter

1. In what ways does social context influence the development and expression of personality, and in what ways does personality influence the nature of different social contexts?

2. How are personality development and personality functioning influenced by socioeconomic conditions?

3. Through what personality processes are older adults able to maintain a strong sense of psychological well-being in the later years of life?

4. What is the nature of the relation between personality and culture?

Two of the chapters of this textbook—9 and the present chapter, 14—differ from the others. The other chapters (after our introductory ones, Chapters 1 and 2) introduced you to a given personality theory. We presented a theoretical view and then reviewed research and applications related to that theory. However, in this book, our goal is not only to introduce you to the theories of personality but also to research findings in the contemporary field of personality science. Many of these findings are associated with one versus another theoretical framework and thus were presented in association with their most relevant theory in the previous chapters. Yet, some research findings stand apart from any one theory in that they provide information that is important to *all* personality psychologists, no matter what their theoretical views.

One such set of these findings was reviewed in Chapter 9: research exploring the biological foundations of personality. The work reviewed here is the "flip side of the coin": research exploring cultural, social, and interpersonal foundations of personality.

Readers with a biological bent may be inclined to think that biological foundations are basic elements of personality, with sociocultural factors being more peripheral to questions of human nature. Anyone inclined to such a view should consider the sage advice of philosophers of psychology, who have admonished that a science of personality "should treat people, for scientific purposes, as if they were human beings" (Harré & Secord, 1972, p. 87). Yes, humans are lumps of biomass whose evolutionary ancestry can be traced to nonhuman origins. But they also are self-reflective beings who live in social and cultural settings. Without sociocultural experiences, no person would be fully human. Thus, understanding how persons develop in interaction with the sociocultural settings of their lives is no less basic to a science of personality than is a study of personality's biological foundations. This chapter, then, reviews recent research in personality psychology that illustrates how personality develops and functions in interpersonal and sociocultural contexts.

Interpersonal Relationships

The most significant contexts in most people's lives are those that involve other people. Although individuals face many financial, professional, and academic demands, challenges that involve relationships with others—friends, family, romantic partners, ex romantic partners, and prospective romantics partners—have a particular power. They capture our attention. They bring us joy and make us heartsick. "Close relationships provide the most central context for our daily lives" (Cooper, 2002, p. 758). In exploring personality in context, then, the first context we consider is that of interpersonal relationships—an aspect of life that has received increasing attention from personality scientists in recent years (Baldwin, 2005; Chen, Boucher, and Parker-Tapias, 2006).

Relationships are two-way streets; there are two people who influence one another. The role of personality factors thus must be considered from each of two directions. On the one hand, personality characteristics may lead a person to do things that are helpful or harmful to a relationship. One might, for example, insult his partner's appearance, start an argument, or start a relationship with a different partner—or, more happily, do things that support and strengthen the relationship. On the other hand, personality qualities may influence someone's *interpretation of* the partner's behavior *irrespective of* what the partner actually does. People's perceptions of their partner may not be accurate. Biases in perception may cause a person erroneously to think that his or her partner said something insulting, or was trying to start an argument, or was interested in a different relationship partner.

Research shows how this two-way impact of personality on relationships can work. When investigators study the interactions of relationship partners in detail (Gable, Reis, & Downey, 2003), they find that positive behaviors (e.g., being affectionate) and negative behaviors (e.g., being critical or inattentive) have positive and negative effects, respectively, on a partner's satisfaction and happiness with the relationship. This much is obvious. However, they also find that influences run in the opposite direction; specifically, inaccurate perceptions of one's partner affect relationship outcomes. People are less satisfied with their relationship when they infer that their partner has engaged in a negative behavior toward them—even in circumstances in which the partner reports that he or she never did engage in the behavior in the first place (Gable et al., 2003). The importance of people's subjective perceptions of their relationship partners is vividly illustrated in research on a personality quality known as rejection sensitivity.

Rejection Sensitivity

Consider again the dialogue that opened this chapter. One of the speakers—the one who broke up with Pete—displayed a style of personality in context known as **rejection sensitivity**.

As studied by the psychologist Geraldine Downey and her colleagues (Ayduk, Mischel, & Downey, 2002; Downey, Mougios, Ayduk, London, & Shoda, 2004; Pietrzak, Downey, & Ayduk, 2005), rejection sensitivity refers to a particular style of thinking. It is characterized by anxious expectations of rejection in interpersonal relationships. Some people seem particularly prone to expect that a relationship—even a relationship that is going quite well—will break up. Such persons dwell on, and become anxious about, the possibility that they will be rejected.

This thinking style is particularly important because it can harm a good relationship. Even if they are not grounded in fact, anxious expectations create interpersonal tension that can make a strong relationship less strong. Expectations of rejection, then, can be a self-fulfilling prophecy.

Downey and Feldman (1996) assess individual differences in rejection sensitivity through the *Rejection Sensitivity Questionnaire (RSQ)*. Respondents are presented with a list of interpersonal requests (e.g., asking a boyfriend/girlfriend to move in with you, asking someone out on a date). For each circumstance, they indicate their subjective sense of the likelihood that their relationship partner would accept versus reject their request (i.e., the request of moving in, going out on a date, etc.). They also indicate how concerned or anxious they would be regarding the other person's response in each circumstance. People who frequently say that there is a high likelihood of their being rejected, and also that they would be very anxious about being rejected, are classified as high in rejection sensitivity.

The potential impact of rejection sensitivity on interpersonal relationships has been documented in research involving first-year college students (Downey & Feldman, 1996). This was a longitudinal study, with key measures taken at two different points in time. First, participants completed the RSQ early in an academic year. Four months later, the researchers identified a subset of people who had begun a romantic relationship only *after* completing the RSQ. These individuals were asked to report on their new, current relationship; specifically, they completed a measure tapping attributions of hurtful intent in the new relationship. People were presented with hypothetical acts that could have a number of different causes (e.g., your boyfriend/girlfriend begins spending less time with you) and were asked whether each act was an indication that the relationship partner was being intentionally hurtful. By designing the research in this manner, with the relationship occurring only after the RSQ was completed, the researchers could be sure that RSQ responses were not themselves a reaction to the specific relationship that people reported on four months into the academic year. Thus, this research design enabled Downey and Feldman to determine whether rejection sensitivity would *contribute to* thoughts about the subsequent relationship.

Findings revealed that rejection sensitivity indeed did predict beliefs about the new relationship. People who were higher in rejection sensitivity before their relationship began were more likely to infer hostile intent on the part of their partner after the relationship was underway. Since the thought that "My partner is intentionally being hostile to me" obviously can be bad for the health of a relationship, this implies that the personality characteristic of rejection sensitivity can be consequential to the quality and longevity of relationships.

A second feature of the results speaks to the overall theme of this chapter: the importance of studying personality in context. Note that the researchers treated the personality variable, rejection sensitivity, as a *contextual* personality variable—that is, as a pattern of thinking (anxious expectations) that occurs in a specific context: interpersonal settings in which there is some possibility

Mixmike / Getty Images

Research on rejection sensitivity indicates that even in relationships that had been going well, people's subjective beliefs about the relationship can create problems in the long run.

of not being socially accepted by someone you care about. This is in contrast to *decontextual* or "global" personality variables such as neuroticism. The question then was whether the contextualized variable of rejection sensitivity better related to attributions of negative intent than did dispositional variables. Downey and Feldman (1996) related their contextualized variable, rejection sensitivity, to global trait variables in the following way. They determined whether rejection sensitivity predicted thoughts about hostility *after accounting for* the relation between these thoughts and a variety of global personality constructs. They found that the contextualized variable, rejection sensitivity, did predict thoughts about hostility after controlling for the effects of global trait variables. In contrast, none of the global trait variables uniquely predicted people's thoughts about their relationships. This result clearly highlights the value of studying personality in context.

Subsequent findings indicate that individual differences in rejection sensitivity are related not only to attributions of hostility but also to long-term relationship outcomes. Both rejection-sensitive individuals and their romantic partners have been found to experience less satisfaction with their relationships, as compared to persons low in rejection sensitivity (Downey & Feldman, 1996). As one might suspect, the relationships of people who are high in rejection sensitivity also are more likely to break up than are the relationships of people who are not prone to anxious expectations of rejection (Downey, Freitas, Michaelis, & Khouri, 1998).

"Hot" and "Cool" Focus

Ideally, personality psychologists would not only describe the fact that people high and low in rejection sensitivity have different experiences in relationships, they also would identify psychological processes through which people can gain control over their relationship experiences.

Researchers have taken up this challenge by exploring people's cognitive strategies—that is, strategic ways of thinking that, when executed properly, can give people control over their behavior and emotional life. Particularly important cognitive strategies involve attention. In any complex social situation, one might pay attention to lots of different things. Some of these things are emotionally neutral, whereas others stir one's emotions; psychologists describe this by saying that different aspects of a situation are "cool" versus "hot" (Metcalfe & Mischel, 1999).

Ayduk, Mischel, and Downey (2002) have explored the influence of **hot versus cool attentional focus** on emotions associated with interpersonal rejection. In their research, participants were asked to recall an experience from their past that had made them feel rejected by another person. Then, depending on the experimental condition to which they were assigned, participants were asked to think about this rejection experience in different ways. In a hot-focus condition, they thought about their emotions during the rejection experience (e.g., "How did your heart beat? How did your face feel?"). In a cool-focus condition, participants' attention was directed to features of the situation that did not involve emotional experience, such as the physical setting in which the experience occurred (e.g., "Where were you standing with respect to the people and the objects around you?").

Focusing attention on "hot" versus "cool" aspects of the past experience had a variety of effects. When asked to describe their mood after thinking about the rejection experience, people who focused on "cool" aspects of the experience described themselves as being less angry than people in the hot-focus condition or people in a control condition in which there were no "hot" or "cool" instructions. When participants wrote an essay describing their thoughts and feelings while thinking about the experience, cool-focus participants composed essays featuring less angry, emotional content. Other measures indicated that focusing attention on one's emotional reactions ("hot focus") activated thoughts about hostility. In summary, then, people who thought about the same type of interpersonal encounter but who focused their attention on *different aspects of* the encounter had substantially different psychological experiences.

Transference in Interpersonal Relationships

Have you ever met a person who vaguely reminded you of someone from your past? Have you ever had the intuition that your reactions toward someone were identical to your reactions toward someone else who you have known? In Chapter 4, we learned that this possibility was of much interest to psychoanalysts. They felt that patients repeat, in therapy, attitudes and styles of interaction they first experienced with significant figures from their past. This experience of attitudes toward the analyst that are based in attitudes toward such figures was called transference.

Contemporary experimental research suggests that transference processes may not be limited to the therapeutic setting. Many of our everyday reactions to people we meet may be influenced by a key contextual factor: the degree to which the new person we meet happens to resemble significant people in our past.

Highly informative research on this topic has been done by Susan Andersen and her colleagues. They have developed a social-cognitive analysis of transference in interpersonal relationships (Andersen & Chen, 2002). In other words, although Andersen is interested in the same phenomenon as Freud had been, she tries to explain the phenomenon using contemporary social-cognitive theory and methods, rather than Freud's theoretical model.

Andersen and Chen (2002) suggest that basic processes of social cognition might explain the phenomenon that Freud had recognized as transference. Suppose you meet a new person who happens to have qualities that resemble those of someone you have known well in your past. For example, the person might have a similar hairstyle or manner of speaking or a similar set of interests and hobbies. This informational overlap between the new person and your past acquaintance may activate knowledge about the individual in your past. This activated knowledge about the past acquaintance may then influence your thoughts and feelings toward the new individual. You may assume—even without realizing that you are doing so—that the new individual possesses the same qualities as those of your past acquaintance. In other words, you will "transfer" your beliefs from your past acquaintance to the new person.

Anderson and colleagues have developed strategies for studying transference experimentally. In an initial experimental session, participants write a description of a person with whom they have had a personally significant relationship. In a subsequent session, participants are asked to read descriptions of various target persons. Some of these descriptions include information that overlaps with their earlier description of their significant other. Later, participants are asked to try to recall information from the descriptions. The key dependent measure is "false positives," that is,

Personality and the Brain
Oxytocin in Context

We usually think of interpersonal relationships in terms of their psychology. But many researchers also investigate their biochemistry. Biochemical processes in the brain can create emotional responses that influence our relations with others.

A biochemical known as oxytocin has attracted particular attention. As we'll now see, research on oxytocin reinforces the theme of this chapter: the interactions among personality processes and social contexts.

Oxytocin is a biochemical that travels throughout the body. Among its various functions, oxytocin helps to bring about bodily changes that facilitate childbirth and breastfeeding. These biological functions have been known for decades. But recently, researchers noticed that the biochemical had a psychological effect as well.

In research on the psychological effects of oxytocin, researchers gave some people oxytocin (which can be administered in a nasal spray) before they played a financial game that provided a measure of their degree of trust in a second player. In a second experimental condition, participants did not receive oxytocin. People who received oxytocin made financial decisions that indicated higher levels of trust in the other player (Kosfeld, Heinrichs, Zak, Fischbacher, & Fehr, 2005). The researchers suggested that oxytocin may have this effect by activating neural circuits in the brain that trigger positive emotion and motivation toward others.

This story about oxytocin is simple: Oxytocin increases trust. But recent research suggests that the story is more complicated than that. Instead of having a consistent effect, oxytocin's effects are found to vary. Oxytocin increases trust in some social contexts and among some people, but not others.

A literature review reveals, for example, that whether oxytocin increases trust during the financial game depends on contextual factors. These factors include

whether the other player in the game is familiar or unknown, appears trustworthy or untrustworthy, and is a member of one's own social group or some other group (Bartz, Zaki, Bolger, & Ochsner, 2011). Other contextual factors that shape the effects of oxytocin include the facial expression displayed in tasks in which participants must detect facial expressions and the outcome (winning or losing) of a game in studies in which researchers examine people's tendency to gloat or to display envy of others (reviewed in Bartz et al., 2011).

Oxytocin's effects also vary for different people in the same context. Bartz and colleagues (2010) administered oxytocin to research participants who varied in social competencies, that is, abilities, in social interactions, to attend carefully to the flow of interpersonal events, detect meaningful social information, and participate in the events in a constructive manner. After receiving oxytocin, participants performed a task that required them to identify emotions being expressed by a person shown on film. Among people with low levels of social skill, oxytocin increased performance: It enhanced people's accuracy on the emotion-detection task. Among people high in social skills, oxytocin had no effect (as compared to a no-oxytocin control group).

Oxytocin, then, does not always increase trust. So what does it do? One possibility is that higher levels of oxytocin increase people's tendency to notice social cues (e.g., other people's statements, gestures, and facial expressions; Bartz et al., 2010, 2011). This possibility explains the results described above. Socially competent people already are good at picking up on social cues and thus are little affected by a dose of oxytocin. But less socially competent people, who commonly overlook such cues, are greatly affected. This hypothesis also would explain why oxytocin could have different effects in different social contexts, which naturally contain different social cues.

the "remembering" of information about the target person that was not actually in the description of the target person but was a characteristic of the significant other; these false-positive memories are evidence of the transference of information from the past relationships to the new person.

What do they find? People indeed are more likely to exhibit false-positive memories when target persons resemble significant others from their past (Andersen & Cole, 1990; Andersen, Glassman, Chen, & Cole, 1995). Transference processes influence not only memory but also emotional reactions and desires to establish a close relationship with a new acquaintance (Andersen & Baum, 1994; Andersen, Reznik, & Manzella, 1996). People are found to react differently to a new acquaintance when the new person has qualities that overlap with someone from their past.

Like the work on rejection sensitivity reviewed earlier, research on social-cognitive processes in transference also illustrates this chapter's theme. In this case, the key contextual variable in understanding "personality in context" is the relation between the attributes of an old and a new acquaintance. When these attributes overlap, a person's experiences and actions cannot be explained in terms of their general, average behavioral tendencies. Instead, they must be understood in terms of context-specific thoughts that link an old and a new acquaintance. Thanks to these transference processes, then, even after you break up with a person, that person may "live on in your head" and influence your future relationships.

Meeting Academic and Social Challenges: Optimistic Strategies and Defensive Pessimism

Research on rejection sensitivity sounds a theme that one hears often: People who have negative thoughts about an upcoming situation may "shoot themselves in the foot"; their negative expectations may cause them to do less well. But is this always the case? One important line of research suggests that the answer is no. The psychologists Nancy Cantor, Julie Norem, and their colleagues find that, for some people, thinking "bad" is a good thing. For some, there is "positive power" in "negative thinking" (Norem, 2001). These people are called defensive pessimists.

Defensive pessimism is a cognitive personality variable, that is, a personality variable that involves styles of thinking. Defensive pessimists think about life challenges in a different manner than do others; specifically, they differ from people referred to as "optimists." Optimists cope by having relatively realistic expectations about their capabilities (**optimism**). If they have the skills to handle a challenge, they generally will say so. Defensive pessimists, in contrast, often think negatively. Even when it seems like they might have the skills to succeed, they express doubts and expect the worst.

A key idea in research on defensive pessimism is that, for people who typically think in this way, pessimism may not be all that bad a thing. For some people, negative thinking may be an effective coping strategy that enables them to motivate themselves to attain high levels of performance.

Research on strategic optimism and defensive pessimism (Cantor et al., 1987) has examined a life transition that is of relevance to many readers of this text: the transition from high school to college. In the senior year of high school, students often settle into comfortable routines. They have well-established friendship patterns, know many of the school's teachers and administrators, and have figured out how to achieve decent grades. Moving on to college presents novel challenges: meeting new friends, staying in touch with old friends, keeping up with academics, becoming involved in social activities on campus. These hectic life transitions are of much interest to the personality psychologist. Because they are challenging, they are revealing of individual differences in coping skills and strategies. Just as challenging IQ test items are more revealing of differences in analytic intelligence than the question "What is 2 1 2?" challenging social situations are more revealing of individual differences in "social intelligence" (Cantor & Kihlstrom, 1987).

In this research, investigators studied college students throughout their freshman year (Cantor et al., 1987). At the beginning of the year, students completed a questionnaire measuring their optimism versus defensive pessimism when thinking about various life challenges. During the year, they assessed other variables of potential importance to academic performance, including expectations about one's GPA and "self-discrepancies," that is, discrepancies between one's actual self and one's ideal self-image in the domain of academics (Higgins, 1987; see Chapter 13). Finally, students' GPA at the end of the year was recorded.

Academic optimists and defensive pessimists did equally well at school. Yet they differed in one important way. They appeared to travel along different psychological paths to academic success. This difference is revealed by the way personality variables predicted GPA in the two groups. Among academic optimists, academic success was predicted by positive thinking; people who expected to do well and who experienced relatively few self-discrepancies at the beginning of the academic year earned higher grades. But among defensive pessimists, expectations about academic performance at the beginning of the year were *un*related to end-of-year grades. If the defensive pessimist said, "I'm going to get a low GPA," this did *not* predict low levels of subsequent performance. Furthermore, among defensive pessimists, large actual–ideal self-discrepancies predicted *higher*, not lower, academic attainment. Negative thinking was good, not bad.

Another feature of these results highlights the importance of studying personality in context. Optimism versus pessimism did not turn out to be a generalized variable that was evident in all aspects of a given student's life. Instead, many students who were pessimists with regard to getting good grades were optimists in other life contexts. Cantor and colleagues (1987) studied academic optimists' and pessimists' cognitions in two contexts: grade attainment and making new friends. In the domain of grade attainment, the groups differed enormously on cognitive factors such as their perceptions of the difficulty, controllability, and stress associated with academics. But when contemplating the challenge of making friends, they did not differ at all! When asked about the difficulty, controllability, and stress associated with the challenge of establishing new friendships, academic optimists and pessimists did not differ.

Personality Development in Socioeconomic Context

It is a fundamental fact of life that citizens of the world experience widely different socioeconomic conditions (Economist, 2005). Even within the world's industrialized and relatively rich nations, one finds great disparities in income and associated social opportunities. In many parts of the world, economic gaps between rich and poor have only widened in recent years.

Of what relevance are socioeconomic circumstances to the development of personality? Based on what you have learned about personality psychology so far, you might think that the answer is "little relevance." Historically, personality theorists have devoted relatively little attention to the socioeconomic conditions of the persons about whom they are theorizing. Theorists working in psychoanalytic, behavioral, and trait-theory traditions explicitly have sought to identify general principles of personality functioning that would transcend particular social circumstances (in the same way that, for example, a biologist might try to identify basic principles of human anatomy and physiology that transcend social circumstances). Recent work, however, suggests that this traditional approach to the study of personality might be inadequate. Specifically, different personality attributes appear to have different implications for the individual in different socioeconomic settings. Important advances on this topic come from the work of Caspi, Elder, and their colleagues (Caspi, 2002; Caspi, Bem, & Elder, 1989).

Consider a seemingly simple question: What are the implications of individual differences in impulsivity for social development? For example, if we identify adolescents who differ in the degree to which they are impulsive, will we find that more impulsive individuals experience more problems of social development, such as delinquency? One possibility is that adolescents who are less able to control their emotional impulses (i.e., "high impulsivity" adolescents) inevitably will experience more social difficulties in their teenage years; this might occur because the avoidance of such problems (e.g., drug and alcohol use, physical aggression, vandalism) requires that one control one's impulses. However, another possibility is that the effects of impulsivity are not inevitable. Instead, the implications of high versus low impulsivity perhaps can only be understood by examining personality in its socioeconomic context. In poor neighborhoods, adolescents may experience a relatively large number of circumstances that have the potential to trigger antisocial acts while having few opportunities to benefit community structures that might help them to develop self-control skills. In contrast, in affluent neighborhoods, there are fewer opportunities for delinquency and there are more social supports.

Findings indicate that these differences between affluent and poor neighborhoods are highly consequential. The relation between impulsivity and delinquency is found to vary in the different socioeconomic contexts. Lynam and colleagues (2000) studied a large sample of 13-year-olds in Pittsburgh, Pennsylvania. These individuals lived in widely varying socioeconomic circumstances that ranged from neighborhoods high in socioeconomic status (SES) to neighborhoods that were poverty stricken, including ones in which people lived in public housing that featured many factors that might foster delinquency. Using various laboratory measures that were administered when research participants were 13 years of age, the researchers determined whether each participant was high or low in impulsivity. With measures of both impulsivity and socioeconomic circumstances, Lynam and colleagues could determine whether the personality factor had different implications in different circumstances. It did. Among adolescents living in poor neighborhoods, high-impulsive individuals were more likely than low-impulsive individuals to become involved in delinquent behaviors. In contrast, in the affluent neighborhoods, adolescents who were either high or low in impulsivity did not differ in delinquency. Community resources in affluent neighborhoods appeared to buffer the potentially negative effects of the personality characteristic.

Personality Functioning Across the Life Span

Research in psychology has focused to a very large degree on the young. Critics of psychological research commonly have complained that a disproportionately large amount of the field's research involves young adults in college. In many respects, a focus on childhood, adolescence, and young adulthood is quite reasonable, for these are critical periods of personal development. However, this focus conflicts with a basic fact of 21st-century life: The world contains ever-larger percentages of older adults. Thanks to advances in medicine, people are living much longer than in the past. The changes in life span are quite dramatic. Today, large numbers of people in the industrialized world live into their 70s, 80s, and beyond. This is a circumstance unknown in prior human history.

Psychological Resilience in the Later Years

The growth of older-adult populations suggests a new research agenda for psychology: the study of personality functioning later in life. In the past decade, psychologists have responded to this agenda. Extensive research programs have examined psychological functioning in the later years of life (Baltes & Mayer, 1999).

One repeated finding in this area of research is somewhat surprising. Since old age is accompanied by many difficulties and challenges—retirement, physical declines, the death of peers and same-generation family members—one might expect that the psychological experience of older adults would be primarily negative. However, this is not the case. On objective measures of self-esteem, a sense of personal control, and psychological well-being versus depression, researchers commonly find that older adults are *not* worse off than middle-aged and younger adults (Baltes & Graf, 1996; Brändtstadter & Wentura, 1995). Rather than being characterized by despondency, in the later years of life, individuals commonly report deeply satisfying, rich, positive emotional experiences (Carstensen & Charles, 2003).

Older adults, then, exhibit much psychological resilience. They commonly are able to withstand the difficulties that accompany the later years and to maintain a remarkably strong sense of self and personal well-being. A challenge for the personality scientist, then, is to understand the processes through which many older adults maintain a positive sense of self.

A core insight into this issue has come from the work of the German psychologist Paul Baltes and his associates (Baltes, 1997; Baltes & Baltes, 1990; Baltes & Staudinger, 2000). These researchers recognized that development inherently involves trade-offs. When moving from one stage of life to another, people lose some psychological qualities but gain others. For example, early in life, children gain logical reasoning capacities but may lose some capacities for fantasy life. In the later years, older adults may experience a decline in some basic cognitive functions yet may gain in personal wisdom (Baltes & Staudinger, 2000). The gains in knowledge and wisdom that people acquire with age often enable them to compensate for any losses in cognitive capacities.

Baltes's analysis suggests a general model of psychological development and resilience in one's later years. In the Baltes model, people can maintain psychological well-being by selecting particular domains of life on which they focus their energies and knowledge. Although it may be difficult for the older adult to maintain a diverse array of life activities—work, clubs, athletic pursuits, hobbies, the development of new social networks, and so forth—he or she may be extremely capable of maintaining high levels of functioning and well-being within selected life domains. By focusing their energies on a few important aspects of life, older adults may be able to compensate for physical or cognitive declines and maintain a high sense of well-being.

Evidence of the beneficial impact of wise selection processes comes from a very large-scale study of adults conducted in Berlin (Freund & Baltes, 1998). Participants completed a self-report questionnaire that assessed the degree to which they engaged in selection processes to optimize their functioning in the face of physical declines in old age. This questionnaire measured people's tendency to select a small number of significant life goals on which to concentrate their energies, as well as their capacity to draw on family and social-network resources to cope with life challenges. Even after controlling for other personality variables, people who more frequently employed these strategies for social living were found to have a higher sense of personal well-being and to experience more positive emotions in their daily life.

Emotional Life in Older Adulthood: Socioemotional Selectivity

One illustration of selection processes comes from the research of Laura Carstensen and her colleagues (Carstensen, 1995, 1998; Carstensen, Isaacowitz, & Charles, 1999). Carstensen's **socioemotional selectivity theory** examines the ways in which social motivations shift across the course of life. The basic idea is that people are aware of the opportunities and constraints associated with different points in the life course. For example, a 20-year-old likely recognizes that many decades of family and professional life lie ahead, whereas an 85-year-old recognizes that he or she is likely entering, or already in, the last decade of life. This awareness of time influences one's life goals. For the younger adult, it makes sense to focus on the future, investing energy in long-term goals that involve the acquisition of information and skills that will prove useful in the decades ahead (e.g., skills of the sort acquired in college) or the development of one's self and sense of identity. In contrast, if one sees oneself as being near the end of life, focusing on long-term goals makes little sense. Instead, it is more reasonable to select one or two goals that have an immediate positive impact on one's life and to focus one's energies on them. Thus, socioemotional selectivity theory predicts that goals involving meaningful emotional experiences become relatively more important in older adulthood. The older adult is predicted to be relatively less motivated to gain information about the world and to start new social networks and is relatively more motivated to have positive emotional experiences, which may be achieved by maintaining personally meaningful relationships with family and long-term friends. In sum, Carstensen's theory predicts that the older adult will be more likely than the younger adult to invest energy into a small, select set of social relationships that enhance emotional experience.

Research supports this hypothesis. For example, Carstensen and Fredrickson (1998) tested socioemotional selectivity theory in a study involving a large and ethnically diverse sample of adults ranging in age from 18 to 88 years. Their goal was to test the hypothesis that older adults would focus their attention on the enhancement of current emotional experiences, whereas younger adults would focus on possibilities for the future, such as meeting new people from whom they could learn new things about the world. To test this idea, they gave younger- and older-adult research participants a long list of different types of people (e.g., a long-time close friend, the author of a book just read). They asked the participants to make ratings that would reveal the dimensions (i.e., the features that differentiated the individuals in the list) that were most important to them as they thought about the different people on the list.

Research on socioemotional selectivity theory reveals that, in older adulthood, people are particularly motivated to have emotionally meaningful experiences with family and long-term friends.

As predicted, older adults seemed to focus their thoughts on the emotional qualities of the people on the list and to pay less attention to whether a meeting with a given person might provide information that would be valuable in the future. In contrast, younger adults focused less on people's emotional qualities and more on the possibility of informative meetings with new people—whether or not those meetings involved experiences that were emotionally positive. Older adults, recognizing that they are in the latter years of life, thus seemed to be far more attentive to social experiences that would bring immediate emotional rewards. Interestingly, a subsequent study found similar results among HIV-positive men with symptoms of AIDS. Though not elderly, these men faced the possibility of a limited life span and, in a manner similar to older adults, focused largely on the immediate emotional qualities of social relationships (Carstensen & Fredricksen, 1998).

In previous sections of this chapter, the contexts we have examined have primarily been social settings. The work of Baltes, Carstensen, and colleagues indicates that age, and especially the number of years that one feels one has remaining in life, is another critical context for personality functioning.

Persons in Cultures

There is no such thing as a human nature independent of culture. Men without culture would not be clever savages . . . . They would be unworkable monstrosities with very few useful instincts, fewer recognizable sentiments, and no intellect: mental basket cases.

Source: Geertz, 1973, p. 49.

Two Strategies for Thinking About Personality and Culture

Strategy #1: Personality . . . and Culture?

There are two strategies for thinking about personality and culture. The first is one that you already have seen a number of times in this text. It is a strategy that begins with a particular theoretical conception or theory-driven hypothesis and then asks whether the idea happens to apply across cultures. Since so much of 20th-century psychological science was a product of the Western world (the United States and Europe), in practice, this strategy is one in which (1) a personality scientist starts with an idea about human nature that is based in Western culture and that reflects research findings or clinical experiences involving U.S. or European citizens and then (2) asks whether this conception of personality receives support when research is conducted in non-Western cultures. You saw this strategy back in Chapter 6, when learning about the phenomenological theory of personality and self developed by the American psychologist Carl Rogers. After reviewing his theory, we summarized contemporary research on the question of whether Rogerian self-processes occur in Asian cultures. You saw this strategy again in Chapter 8, where we asked whether the Big Five model of personality traits (another product of Western personality psychology) replicates cross-culturally.

In this strategy for thinking about personality and culture, questions of culture and personality boil down to what the research psychologist calls questions of "generalizability." The issue is whether a given psychological finding holds, or generalizes, from one setting to another. Just as one can ask whether a given research result generalizes across genders, socioeconomic circumstances, or age groups, one can ask whether it generalizes across cultures.

It is important to determine whether research findings generalize across cultures. This first strategy, then, is a good one, but it is not good enough. It has two significant limitations. First, it may fail to identify aspects of personality that are important in other cultures but not in one's own. If researchers simply import a Western conception of personality into a non-Western culture, they may completely overlook aspects of personhood that are key features in the non-Western culture but are relatively unimportant in their own.

As an example, consider the efforts of researchers studying the Big Five model of personality (Chapter 8) to characterize the basic units of language that individuals use to describe themselves and other persons. When researchers import the five-factor structure into non-Western cultures, they indeed do obtain evidence that members of these cultures recognize these personality dimensions as significant ways in which individuals differ (McCrae & Costa, 2008). It should be noted, however, that significant culture variations in the language of individual differences are also found (Saucier & Goldberg, 2001).

So this research could be overlooking important aspects of other cultures' language of human nature. For example, consider Buddhist cultures. In this cultural context, a primary term for thinking about persons and their actions is *karma*, which refers to the positive and negative effects of actions on one's stream of consciousness, where that consciousness can extend from one physical lifetime to another through reincarnation (Chodron, 1990). This conception of karma is not prevalent in the Western cultures in which the Big Five were first studied. Thus, questionnaires designed to measure the five personality dimensions do not contain many (if any) items that are directly relevant to the conception of karma. As a result, if these Western-world, English-language questionnaires are imported into a Buddhist culture, researchers probably will fail to "find karma." The notion of karma will be overlooked, despite the fact that it is important to the non-Western culture, because it is not a component of the Western-world research instrument.

There is a second limitation to the strategy of asking merely whether a given research finding generalizes from one cultural context to another: Notably, it treats culture as peripheral to the study of human nature. It implies that the personality theorist first can develop a culture-free model of core aspects of personality and individual differences and then—as a kind of afterthought—can ask whether the model has to be "tweaked" here or there to account for cultural variation. Such an approach treats issues of culture as an optional supplement to personality psychology's core concern with basic human nature.

The section-opening quote from the anthropologist Clifford Geertz suggests that this way of thinking is backward. For Geertz, there is no culture-free personality in the first place. Instead, psychological functioning is inherently cultural. People think about the world using languages and related communication systems that they acquire from their culture and that are themselves the products of generations of cultural experience. The things that people think about—other people, social settings, future possibilities, themselves—take on personal significance within meaning systems that are based on cultural and social practices, where those practices might vary from one cultural context to another.

Strategy #2: Culture and Personality

In this alternative approach, culture is not on the periphery of personality psychology—it is at the core. Persons are seen as acquiring their sense of personhood through interactions with their culture.

This way of thinking about personality–culture relations has important implications for how one thinks not only about personality but culture as well. Cultures consist of those very same persons who acquired their sense of personhood from that culture. Culture and personality, in other words, "make each other up" (Shweder & Sullivan, 1990, p. 399).

In this view, then, there is no culture-free personality on the one hand and no person-free culture on the other. Instead, there are persons who function psychologically by using cultural tools, including language and related meaning systems. And there are cultures whose practices are maintained by those very same people who inhibit them. For more than a decade, this way of thinking has been advanced within a field known as cultural psychology (Shweder & Sullivan, 1993). Cultural psychology is concerned with whether research findings generalize from one culture to another (the main question of what we have called Strategy #1). Yet it asks deeper questions about human nature.

The argument that one should view human experience through a cultural lens is made compelling by examples in which people of a given culture seem to lead lives that differ deeply from one's own. Consider, first, your own experiences and actions in a setting in which you meet a new acquaintance, for example, at a party. If you are a member of the Western world, you are likely to introduce yourself by stating your name, and if the conversation continues and the two of you want to get to know each other better, you are likely to talk about your own interests, hobbies, personal background, or goals in life. If, the next day, you describe your new acquaintance to an old friend, you are likely to use personality trait terms that describe personal qualities that differentiate the individual from others (you might see your new acquaintance as "somewhat extraverted," "very open-minded," etc.). This probably strikes you as obvious. Isn't it always like this? Don't people present themselves and talk about each other in this manner no matter where in the world you go? Apparently not.

Balinese family. The study of social practices in Bali suggests that Balinese culture emphasizes the relations among a person and the generations of his or her family, rather than highlighting the distinctive, unique features of the isolated individual, as is more common in Western cultures.

Detailed analyses of personhood within traditional culture on the island of Bali (Geertz, 1973) indicate that our own ways of being a person are not universal. In Bali, the label that people use to describe themselves is not a unique, personal name. Personal names are treated as very private; they are "treated as though they are military secrets" (Geertz, 1973, p. 375). Instead, people are differentiated using labels that make reference to the individual's place within family and community systems. Terms for referring to people make reference to family members (a person is "mother-of-"), social status (which strongly defines how the person should be treated), or social roles (e.g., village chief). This system reflects a broader cultural conception in which persons are not primarily thought of as unique, idiosyncratic individuals but as elements of a larger, eternal social order. Their cultural practices "[mute] the more idiosyncratic, merely biographical, and, consequently, transient aspects of . . . existence as a human being (what, in our more egoistic framework, we call 'personality') in favor of some rather more typical, highly conventionalized, and, consequently, enduring ones" (Geertz, 1973, p. 370).

Personality and Self as Socially Constructed Within Culture

The implications of cultural psychology for the study of personality are vividly illustrated by research on conceptions of self in American and Japanese culture conducted by Shinobu Kitayama and Hazel Markus (Cross & Markus, 1999; Kitayama & Markus, 1999; Markus et al., 2006). A central idea in this work is that there may be variations from culture to culture in people's implicit conceptions of self (Markus & Kitayama, 1991; Triandis, 1995). People's beliefs about what it is to be a "self" or a person may not be the same throughout the world. Different cultures may feature different beliefs about the rights, duties, possibilities, and most central features associated with personhood. Note that such beliefs are not necessarily explicit; in other words, it might be that many members of a culture do not explicitly put into words these culturally shared beliefs about the nature of personality. Yet, even if they do not stop to think about it explicitly, everyone does have conceptions about the most basic aspects of personality. It is these conceptions that appear to differ across cultures.

Independent and Interdependent Views of Self

Specifically, differences are found when contrasting European-American and East Asian cultures. In European-American culture, the self is primarily construed as being **independent**. An independent view conceives the self as containing a set of psychological qualities (personality traits, goals, etc.) that are distinct from, or independent of, those of other people. The person is a kind of "container" within which are stored a collection of psychological traits that cause the person's actions. Individuals also are construed as having independent rights, such as the right to pursue personal happiness.

By contrast, East Asian cultures feature an **interdependent** conception of self (Markus & Kitayama, 1991; Triandis, 1995). The interdependent conception highlights the individual's roles within family and social relationships and emphasizes responsibilities that accompany these roles, rather than the individual's self-centered pursuit of happiness. In interdependent cultures, behavior is not explained in terms of autonomous mental traits that reside in the person's head. Instead, people explain behavior in terms of networks of social obligations. It is the person's location within such social systems that is seen as the cause of behavior. For example, a person's chronic expression of "conscientious" behavior might be explained in terms of social obligations that compel the person to act conscientiously, rather than by saying that the person possesses a trait of conscientiousness.

A range of findings support the idea that Eastern and Western cultures foster differences in conceptions of self. As we reviewed in Chapter 6, psychological processes involving self-esteem differ from one culture to another. East Asians are less likely than Westerners to try to maintain a high sense of personal esteem (Heine et al., 1999). Instead, self-criticism functions as a salient motive (Kitayama et al., 1997). Unlike findings in the Western world, in East Asia, people are not more intrinsically motivated to engage in tasks when they choose them personally; instead, they experience greater intrinsic motivation when choices are made by authority figures or trusted peers (Iyengar & Lepper, 1999). Consistent with the notion that Western conceptions of the self draw attention to internal personal qualities that function as causes of behavior, Americans are found to overattribute the causes of action to personal rather than situational factors. People in Japan, India, and China are less likely to exhibit this attributional bias (Kitayama & Masuda, 1997; Miller, 1984; Morris & Peng, 1994). Studies of subjective well-being also reveal interesting cross-cultural variations. When predicting people's ratings of satisfaction with their life, the pleasantness of everyday emotional experiences is a stronger predictor in Western than in Eastern cultures (Suh, Diener, Oishi, & Triandis, 1998). Each of these findings, then, is consistent with the contention that people in Eastern versus Western cultures have different, interdependent versus independent, construals of self.

The interplay of culture and personality also is revealed in studies of people who move from one cultural context to another. For example, consider what happens when people move from an Eastern culture to the West. Western social practices, more than Eastern ones, emphasize the asserting of one's personal attributes. Becoming engaged in these new social practices should cause people to become more extraverted, as they learn to fit in with their new culture. There is evidence that this does indeed occur. McCrae, Yik, Trapnell, Bond, and Paulhus (1998) studied Chinese students enrolled in a Canadian university. Some of these students had been in North America for many years, whereas others had immigrated only a few years before the study was conducted. People who had longer exposure to Canadian culture tended to have higher extraversion scores (McCrae et al., 1998).

Research reveals that social cues—such as Chinese symbols and imagery in an American city—can cause bicultural individuals to adopt different cognitive frameworks for viewing the world.

The role of cognitive processes in these cultural differences is further revealed by studies of bicultural individuals. These are persons who have lived long enough in each of two different cultures that they have internalized the belief systems of both (Hong, Morris, Chiu, & Martinez, 2000). Such people are capable of "frame switching": They can change the culturally grounded framework through which they interpret any given event. Interestingly, stimuli that cognitively prime one versus another cultural frame can thereby influence the bicultural individual's subsequent thinking processes. Cultural frameworks have been primed by exposing people to symbols representative of Chinese versus American culture (e.g., an American flag, a picture of a Chinese dragon). Compared to when they view Chinese symbols, bicultural individuals are more likely to attribute the causes of actions to internal causes after viewing symbols of American culture. At its extreme, the argument is made that no cognition is free of culture; that is, it is not just the content of our knowledge that is influenced by culture but our entire way of thinking (Nisbett, 2003).

Putting Personality in Context into Practice

Our focus in this chapter has primarily been theoretical. We have explored ways in which personality theory, and theory-inspired research, can and must include an analysis of the social contexts in which people live.

Let's conclude the chapter by being more practical. What implications does the study of personality in context have for practical concerns? We'll consider two concerns: (1) clinical assessment, explored through a case study and (2) social change, as addressed in a large-scale effort to improve health.

Assessing Personality in Context: A Case Study

Basic research on personality in context has significant implications for personality assessment, including the assessment of individuals seeking psychotherapy. A case study illustrates the point.[1]

The case study involves a client called S. L., a 55-year-old, European-American, divorced woman with a high school education. When she arrived at a psychology clinic, S. L. stated that she was "depressed," reported losing interest in the "few things that [she] used to enjoy doing," and said she needed to "get her life back on track." She described feeling "extremely stressed" due to "unsatisfying" social relationships, stating that she "longs for time spent with adults doing something social."

Standard assessments of psychological distress indicated that S. L. was suffering from both depression and anxiety. On a measure of depression, she scored in the severely depressed range. On a measure of anxiety, she fell into the moderately anxious range of scores.

To learn more about S. L.'s personality functioning in context, her therapist devised novel assessment procedures. The procedures targeted three assessment goals suggested by basic research on personality in context (Cervone, 2004), including the KAPA model of personality discussed in Chapter 13. The goals are:

1. *Identifying contexts:* Pinpointing types of situations, or social contexts, of particular relevance to the given individual's psychological life.

2. *Identifying personality structures:* Assessing enduring personal qualities, including beliefs about the self, and others, that are particularly central to the given individual.

3. *Mapping personality to context:* Identifying the particular personality structures that most strongly bear upon each social context and that may directly influence behavior and emotional experience in that context.

Let's see how, exactly, the therapist executed these goals in the case of S. L.

Identifying Contexts. As the first step in identifying social contexts of particular importance to S.L., her therapist instructed her to pay attention to situations from her daily life that evoked strong emotions in her. S. L. reported these circumstances to her therapist, and using this report, the therapist created a list of about 20 situations that seemed particularly relevant to her.

S. L. then took part in the following mental exercise. Her therapist asked her, for each situation, to imagine the last time the situation occurred. Once S.L. envisioned it, the therapist asked her to report her cognitive appraisals (i.e., her thoughts about her relation to the situation and the people in it) and the feelings she experienced in that situation.

S. L. then was asked to reflect on the list of 20 situations, and their associated thoughts and feelings, and to identify any that were "functionally equivalent." Specifically, she was to group

---

[1] The therapist in the case reported here is Professor Walter D. Scott of the University of Wyoming. Professor Scott devised the novel personality-in-context assessment procedures, in collaboration with one of the present authors (D.C.), with whom the written case report was prepared.

together situations that were similar in that they triggered similar patterns of thinking and emotion. S. L. did so, identifying nine different types of situations—that is, nine social contexts—that
were particularly meaningful for her. The nine contexts included, for example:

— *When I am reflecting on my life*

— *When I worry "what if some bad thing happens?"*

— *When I try to appear better/more perfect than I am*

— *When people approach me, treat me well, or go out of their way to be with me*

Note that, although she was depressed, S. L.'s relevant contexts included some that were primarily positive for her.

Identifying Personality Structures. In addition to this assessment of social contexts, S. L. participated in tasks designed to assess her personality structures. One, which was designed to identify structural features of her self-concept that were particularly pertinent to her social life, had
two main steps.

The first step began with S.L. completing a "self-with-other" task. She listed about a dozen
individuals who play a prominent role in her life. Then, for each individual, she was asked to
envision a typical interaction with that individual, to describe thoughts about herself that came to
mind during that interaction, and to provide three to five adjectives that described her during that
interaction. Let's consider some results of this process:

— When describing a female friend who played a prominent role in her life and thinking about
  a recent negative interaction with that friend, S. L.'s thoughts included, "It's [my] own fault.
  I'm stupid, an idiot." The adjectives she used to describe herself were "frustrated, stupid, idiot,
  not important."

— When describing herself interacting with other people while she was shopping, her thoughts
  included, "I look hard, ruined; they can see it in my face." The adjectives she used to describe
  herself were "hard, ugly, bad, scarred."

— When describing herself interacting with customers at her job, her thoughts were entirely different. They included, "I am really good at this. They respect me." She described herself using
  the adjectives "competent, respected, good."

By attending to social context, then, the therapist was able to assess both negative and positive
thoughts held by this depressed individual.

In the second step of this procedure for identifying self-with-other personality structures, S. L.
showed her self-with-other descriptions to her therapist. After they discussed them, S. L. grouped
together the various descriptions into six categories, which constituted six general sets of beliefs
about herself, or self-schemas. The self-schemas included, for example:

— *Self as ruined, defective*

— *Self as inferior, incompetent*

— *Self as competent worker*

Another task designed to assess personality structures targeted S. L.'s personal goals. She
completed an assessment task (see Cox & Klinger, 2011) in which she listed her most important
goals in a number of different life domains (e.g., job, household, intimate relationships). When
completing this task, S. L. at first identified eight main life goals. She then grouped these goals
into categories. Three of these goals were so central to S. L.'s life that her therapist considered

her thoughts about the goals to be significant personality structures. This goal-related knowledge centered on S. L.'s aims of:

– *Attaining strong relationships with children and grandchildren*

– *Establishing friendships and having a life partner*

– *Becoming financially secure*

Mapping Personality to Context. The assessments, to this point, tell us something about the social contexts that make up S. L.'s daily life and the mental contents that make up her cognitive structures of personality. But how do the two go together? Ideally, the therapist (and the personality assessor, in general) would be able to map social contexts to personality structures, in order to understand the client's experiences from both a social and a cognitive-processing perspective (Cervone et al., 2001). This understanding, in turn, could benefit the formulation of therapy strategies. Note that this mapping was not achieved in many of the assessment strategies you read about earlier in this book. Kelly's Rep test (Chapter 11), for example, shed light on cognitive personality structures (constructs) but did not identify the social contexts that cause one versus another construct to come to mind for the given individual. Mischel and colleagues' *if–then* profile analysis (Chapter 12) charted situational contexts that are associated with variation in an individual's behavior, but did not identify the personality structures that are activated, for the given individual, in those contexts.

The therapist mapped personality to context in the following manner (cf. Cervone, 2004). S. L. was shown the nine different social contexts that were identified previously (see above). For each one, she was asked to rate the relevance of various personality structures to the given context. Specifically, she was asked, "to what extent did [e.g., your self-schema of X, or your goal of Y] influence what you thought, felt, and/or did in this situation?" For example, S. L. would be asked, "To what extent did your belief that you are inferior or incompetent influence what you thought, felt, and/or did in situations in which people approach you, treat you well, or go out of their way to be with you?" This procedure gave S. L. a mapping of personality qualities to social contexts.

The mapping revealed social contexts that were particularly problematic for S. L. and provided insight into the psychological source of the problems. For example, one of the most problematic settings was when S.L. is alone and reflecting on her life, a setting that recurred on a nearly daily basis for her. S. L. judged that her self-schemas involving notions of self as "ruined" and "neglected" were particularly relevant to this setting. These self-schemas may have contributed to her negative thoughts and feelings in this context. When reflecting on her life, S. L. became self-critical, blaming herself for being "off-track" in life—not where she should be in terms of her occupation, finances, and romantic life. During these self-reflections, she felt she was unable to change her life circumstances or mood, and she doubted that her life would improve in the future.

A review of these contextualized assessments also indicated to S. L.'s therapist that her "ruined" self-schema (that is, her cognitive personality structure that depicted her as a ruined individual) was affecting her experiences in multiple situations. S. L. rated her self-as-ruined schema as having a "great deal" of influence on three of her four most problematic situations and as having some influence in all but one problematic situation. Her self-as-inferior schema was also influential across a range of circumstances.

The point of these assessments was not merely to learn about S. L.'s current personality functioning, but to design a treatment to improve her well-being. Here, the contextualized nature of the assessments was a big advantage. To see this, first imagine a simpler assessment that neglected the role of social context. Her therapist might, for example, merely have assessed S. L.'s overall mood and self-esteem, irrespective of the contexts in which her feelings and thoughts occur. Such assessments would have revealed that S. L.—in general, on average—experiences negative mood states and has a low sense of self-esteem. And it's true, she does. But such assessments would have provided scant information to guide treatment. Ideally, assessment provides information about a client that can serve as a resource in formulating therapy. That's what the contextualized assessments provided. Critically, they revealed both "bad and good": circumstances that were difficult for S. L. but other circumstances in which she performed well, personality structures that contributed to her depression and other personality structures that were potentially useful in combatting her depression. Consider the therapist's strategy when discussing with S. L. the possibility of her getting a new job, at a grocery store, for which she lacked confidence.

Therapist: You say that you don't think you could do the job at the grocery store if you were to apply. Where do you think this thought is coming from? (S. L. traces these thoughts to her self-as-inferior schema.)

Therapist: Right, from your self-as-inferior schema—the schema that was based on the negative messages about yourself that you picked up from experiences with your stepfather, your mom, your ex. But what about your experiences at the job where you work now? Mightn't some of these experiences—positive, competent experiences—bear on your ability to operate the register at the grocery store? Tell me about those experiences at your current job. (S. L. discusses her current job experiences.)

Therapist: Ok, let's put it all on the table; let's look at all the evidence; what do you think? How confident are you that you could really operate the register?

After this discussion, S. L. reported higher confidence (e.g., a higher sense of self-efficacy; Chapter 12) in performing the grocery store job; that is, she "drew stronger connections" between her self-as-competent-worker schema and this prospective new situation, the grocery store job.

The person-in-context assessments, then, enabled the therapist to pinpoint both weaknesses and strengths in S. L.'s personality structure and social experiences. The assessed strengths served as a therapeutic resource in helping her to cope effectively with more difficult elements in her life.

Personality Processes in Context: Fostering Social Change

Let's consider a second example in which concepts from the study of personality in context are put into practice. This example is broader in scope than the first. Rather than focusing on an individual client in psychotherapy, it targets psychological chance on a society-wide basis.

Not long ago, researchers in the East African nation of Tanzania faced the following challenge. The nation's rates of HIV/AIDS were devastatingly high. Many citizens were poorly informed about the causes of HIV infection, not knowing how to prevent the disease and suffering from misinformation as a result of rumors such as that the young could not contract the disease, that condoms were ineffective, and that it was possible by casual observation to determine whether a potential sexual partner had the virus (Vaughn et al., 2000). The society also suffered from a gender imbalance, with women being less likely to receive HIV/AIDS counseling and testing than men (United Nations Population Fund, 2002).

Researchers needed a method for bringing about society-wide changes in behavior to combat the health epidemic. They drew upon a personality process originally studied in social-cognitive theory: the principle of learning through observation, or modeling (Chapter 12). They delivered a modeling intervention in a manner that fit the social context of the lives of the people of Tanzania, namely, a radio soap opera (Mohammed, 2001; Vaughn et al., 2000).

For more than five years, from 1993 to 1999, citizens of Tanzania were able to hear a radio soap opera entitled *Twende na Wakati* (Let's Go with the Times). In some ways, it was typical entertainment, with multiple characters whose lives unfolded gradually across broadcast episodes. Yet the program had a unique element. It was designed by the Tanzanian government, working in collaboration with the nonprofit Population Communications International (PCI) to provide both entertainment and education about HIV/AIDS risk behaviors that would reduce the prevalence of HIV/AIDS.

Twende na Wakati's characters modeled the full range of positive and negative possibilities regarding HIV/AIDS, so that listeners would be aware not only of the benefits of taking HIV-preventive steps but the costs of not doing so. Negative models (e.g., a promiscuous truck driver who failed to use condoms and acquired HIV) exemplified the costs of high-risk behavior. Positive models provided medically accurate information and counseling to other characters. Perhaps most important, the show featured "transitional" models. These were characters who, at first, were not engaging in safe-sex behaviors but who gradually adopted those behaviors as a result of the interventions of other characters. Research (Bandura, 1986, 1997) indicates that transitional models powerfully increase people's self-efficacy, since listeners can first identify with the character's struggles and then, after this sense of identification, can observe the person succeeding. Thanks to their knowledge of the life contexts and everyday challenges faced by people in Tanzania, the program's writers could design transitional models to which listeners could relate.

Remarkably, the Tanzanian government conducted an experiment of enormous scope to evaluate the program's effectiveness. From 1993 to 1995, the program was broadcast in some regions of the country but not in others; it subsequently was broadcast nationwide. The different regions could then be compared to gauge the effectiveness of the program. This experiment was done through interview/surveys that asked people about their practice of specific behaviors that prevent HIV infection (Vaughn et al., 2000).

The broadcasting of *Twende na Wakati* had a number of beneficial effects. Based on a survey of listener self-reports, it was found that listening to the program led people to engage in more interpersonal communication about HIV risks (Vaughn et al., 2000). Analyses indicate that the overall effect of the program was due in part to its role in encouraging people to discuss the problem of HIV/AIDS prevention more openly (Mohammed, 2001). The program also affected attitudes and beliefs about HIV/AIDS. As part of this study, the researchers examined the percentage of people who reported having one or more HIV/AIDS risk factors (e.g., multiple sexual partners, unprotected sex) and yet who felt that they personally were not at risk for getting the infection. During the 1993 to 1995 period, the percentage of such people in the region in which *Twende na Wakati* was broadcast fell from 21% to 10%. In contrast, in the region in which the show was not broadcast, the percentage of people who believed they were not at risk increased during the same period (Vaughn et al., 2000). Most importantly, the modeling of safe-sex practices on the radio show significantly affected people's actual sexual practices. In the broadcast region, both men and women reported declines in the number of their sexual partners during the years 1993–1995. (People in the region in which the show initially was not broadcast showed such declines after the show was beamed to their area.) Further, condom use increased in the broadcast regions more rapidly than it did in the regions that were not exposed to the radio soap opera (Vaughn et al., 2000).

In summary, the broadcast had its intended effect. By applying personality–psychology principles in a manner that was sensitive to the social contexts of people's lives, the researchers were able to bring about society-wide changes in HIV/AIDS risk behaviors. To anyone asking whether psychologists can do something socially useful with the theories of personality, the work in Tanzania provides a resounding yes.

SUMMARY

In this chapter, you have learned about a series of research programs in contemporary personality psychology. The research topics, though diverse, illustrated a common theme. Each concerned the interaction between persons and the social contexts in which they live. Questions about interpersonal relations, cross-situational coherence in experience and action, personality development in its socioeconomic context, development across the life span, personality and culture, and personality processes and social change were answered by research strategies that attended carefully both to personality and to social context.

At a very general level, this chapter's tour of contemporary research on personality in context conveys a message about the scientific field. It illustrates advances that have been made in the scientific study of personality. A generation ago, many investigators construed persons and situations as two separate, independent forces. Each presumably exerted a separate effect—a person effect and a situation effect—on behavior. As you saw in our coverage of the person–situation controversy, investigators debated the relative size of person and situation effects (Chapter 8), sometimes computing statistical indices of the size of each separate factor (Funder & Ozer, 1983).

The research reviewed in this chapter shows how much the science of personality has changed since that earlier era. Current research findings suggest that "person" and "context" are not independent forces; instead, persons and contexts interact dynamically. They "make each other up" (Shweder & Sullivan, 1990, p. 399). Contexts are comprised primarily of persons, and the meaning of a social situation is construed by the people who are in it. This may seem like an abstract theoretical point. Yet, as we have seen, recognizing it has practical advantages. It opens the door to a psychology of personality that can shed light on how people try to cope with the everyday challenges of their lives—and that can help them to do so.

MAJOR CONCEPTS

Defensive pessimism
Hot versus cool attentional focus

Independent
Independent versus interdependent

Interdependent
Optimism
Rejection sensitivity

Socioemotional selectivity theory

REVIEW

1. Contemporary research shows how personality can be understood by examining interactions between persons and the contexts in which they live. The first example of this general point involved interpersonal relations, which in the context of romantic relationships was seen to elicit negative, pessimistic, and ultimately self-defeating thoughts among a group of people with the personality characteristic of rejection sensitivity. Other research showed how people may transfer thoughts and feelings from a past relationship onto a new relationship partner.

2. Research on the coping strategies of optimism and defensive pessimism showed how people may address the same social stressor with very different yet sometimes equally effective strategies that involve optimistic versus pessimistic styles of thinking.

3. Research on knowledge, appraisal, and cross-situational coherence illustrated how a given aspect of knowledge may come into play across seemingly diverse contexts and, thus, produce consistent self-appraisals in the different settings.

4. Work on personality development in context illustrated how socioeconomic circumstances can affect personality development.

5. Research on personality and culture shows how the meaning of personality and of the self may vary from one culture to another; major differences involve self-construals that are **independent versus interdependent**.

GLOSSARY

ABA research design A Skinnerian variant of the experimental method consisting of exposing one subject to three experimental phases: (A) a baseline period, (B) introduction of reinforcers to change the frequency of specific behaviors, and (A) withdrawal of reinforcement and observation of whether the behaviors return to their earlier frequency (baseline period).

ABC assessment In behavioral assessment, an emphasis on the identification of antecedent (A) events and the consequences (C) of behavior and (B) a functional analysis of behavior involving identification of the environmental conditions that regulate specific behaviors.

Ability, temperament, and dynamic traits In Cattell's trait theory, these categories of traits capture the major aspects of personality.

Acquisition The learning of new behaviors viewed by Bandura as independent of reward and contrasted with performance—which is seen as dependent on reward.

Adoption studies An approach to establishing genetic–behavior relationships through the comparison of biological siblings reared together with biological siblings reared apart through adoption. Generally combined with twin studies.

Anal personality Freud's concept of a personality type that expresses a fixation at the anal stage of development and related to the world in terms of the wish for control or power.

Anal stage Freud's concept for that period of life during which the major center of bodily excitation or tension is the anus.

Anxiety In psychoanalytic theory, a painful emotional experience that signals or alerts the ego to danger.

Attachment behavioral system (ABS) Bowlby's concept emphasizing the early formation of a bond between infant and caregiver, generally the mother.

Attributions Beliefs about the causes of events.

Authenticity The extent to which the person behaves in accord with his or her self as opposed to behaving in terms of roles that foster false self-presentations.

Behavioral assessment The emphasis in assessment on specific behaviors that are tied to defined situational characteristics (e.g., ABC approach).

Behavioral genetics The study of genetic contributions to behaviors of interest to psychologists, mainly through the comparison of degrees of similarity among individuals of varying degrees of biological-genetic similarity.

Behavioral signatures Individually distinctive profiles of situation–behavior relationships.

Behaviorism An approach within psychology, developed by Watson, that restricts investigation to overt, observable behavior.

Big Five In trait factor theory, the five major trait categories including emotionality, activity, and sociability factors.

Cardinal trait Allport's concept for a disposition that is so pervasive and outstanding in a person's life that virtually every act is traceable to its influence.

Case studies An approach to research in which one studies an individual person in great detail. This strategy commonly is associated with clinical research, that is, research conducted by a therapist in the course of in-depth experiences with a client.

Catharsis The release and freeing of emotion through talking about one's problems.

Castration anxiety Freud's concept of the boy's fear, experienced during the phallic stage, that the father will cut off the son's penis because of their sexual rivalry for the mother.

Central trait Allport's concept for a disposition to behave in a particular way in a range of situations.

Classical conditioning A process, emphasized by Pavlov, in which a previously neutral stimulus becomes capable of eliciting a response because of its association with a stimulus that automatically produces the same or a similar response.

Client-centered therapy Rogers's term for his earlier approach to therapy in which the counselor's attitude is one of interest in the ways in which the client experiences the self and the world.

Cognitive-affective processing system (CAPS) A theoretical framework developed by Mischel and colleagues in which personality is understood as containing a large set of highly interconnected cognitive and emotional processes; the interconnections cause personality to function in an integrated, coherent way or as a system.

Cognitive complexity/simplicity An aspect of a person's cognitive functioning that is defined at one end by the use of many constructs with many relationships to one another (complexity) and at the other end by the use of few constructs with limited relationships to one another (simplicity).

Collective unconscious Carl Jung's term for inherited, universal unconscious features of mental life that reflect the evolutionary experiences of the human species.

Competencies A structural unit in social-cognitive theory reflecting the individual's ability to solve problems or perform tasks necessary to achieve goals.

Computerized text analysis methods Software tools that take, as their input, words and sentences and analyze linguistic features that may, in the context of personality research, by revealing of personality and individual differences.

Conditioned emotional reaction Watson and Rayner's term for the development of an emotional reaction to a previously neutral stimulus, as in Little Albert's fear of rats.

Conditions of worth Standards of evaluation that are not based on one's own feelings, preferences, and inclinations but instead on others' judgments about what constitutes desirable forms of action.

Congruence Rogers's concept expressing an absence of conflict between the perceived self and experience. Also one of three conditions suggested as essential for growth and therapeutic progress.

Conscious Those thoughts, experiences, and feelings of which we are aware.

Construct In Kelly's theory, a way of perceiving, construing, or interpreting events.

Constructive alternativism Kelly's view that there is no objective reality or absolute truth, only alternative ways of construing events.

Context specificity The idea that a given personality variable may come into play in some life settings or contexts but not others, with the result that a person's behavior may vary systematically across contexts.

Contingencies of self-worth The positive and negative events on which one's feelings of self-esteem depend.

Contrast pole In Kelly's personal construct theory, the contrast pole of a construct is defined by the way in which a third element is perceived as different from two other elements that are used to form a similarity pole.

Core construct In Kelly's personal construct theory, a construct that is basic to the person's construct system and cannot be altered without serious consequences for the rest of the system.

Correlational coefficient A numerical index that summarizes the degree to which two variables are related linearly.

Correlational research An approach to research in which existing individual differences are measured and related to one another, rather than being manipulated as in experimental research.

Counterconditioning The learning (or conditioning) of a new response that is incompatible with an existing response to a stimulus.

Death instinct Freud's concept for drives or sources of energy directed toward death or a return to an inorganic state.

Defense mechanisms Freud's concept for those mental strategies used by the person to reduce anxiety. They function to exclude from awareness some thought, wish, or feeling.

Defensive pessimism A coping strategy in which people use negative thinking as a way of coping with stress.

Delay of gratification The postponement of pleasure until the optimum or proper time, a concept particularly emphasized in social-cognitive theory in relation to self-regulation.

Demand characteristics Cues that are implicit (hidden) in the experimental setting and influence the subject's behavior.

Denial A defense mechanism, emphasized by both Freud and Rogers, in which threatening feelings are not allowed into awareness.

Determinism The belief that people's behavior is caused in a lawful scientific manner; determinism opposes a belief in free will.

Discrimination In conditioning, the differential response to stimuli depending on whether they have been associated with pleasure, pain, or neutral events.

Distortion According to Rogers, a defensive process in which experience is changed so as to be brought into awareness in a form that is consistent with the self.

Dysfunctional expectancies In social-cognitive theory, maladaptive expectations concerning the consequences of specific behaviors.

Dysfunctional self-evaluations In social-cognitive theory, maladaptive standards for self-reward that have important implications for psychopathology.

Ego Freud's structural concept for the part of the personality that attempts to satisfy drives (instincts) in accordance with reality and the person's moral values.

Emotion-focused coping Coping in which an individual stresses to improve his or her internal emotional state, for example, by emotional distancing or the seeking of social support.

Empathic understanding Rogers's term for the ability to perceive experiences and feelings and their meanings from the standpoint of another person. One of three therapist conditions essential for therapeutic progress.

Energy system Freud's view of personality as involving the interplay among various forces (e.g., drives, instincts) or sources of energy.

Erogenous zones According to Freud, those parts of the body that are the sources of tension or excitation.

Evaluative standards Criteria for evaluating the goodness or worth of a person or thing. In social-cognitive theory, people's standards for evaluating their own actions are seen as being involved in the regulation of behavior and the experience of emotions such as pride, shame, and feelings of satisfaction or dissatisfaction with oneself.

Evolved psychological mechanisms In evolutionary psychology, psychological mechanisms that are the result of evolution by selection, that is, they exist and have endured because they have been adaptive to survival and reproductive success.

Existentialism An approach to understanding people and conducting therapy, associated with the human potential movement, that emphasizes phenomenology and concerns inherent in existing as a person. Derived from a more general movement in philosophy.

Expectancies In social-cognitive theory, what the individual anticipates or predicts will occur as the result of specific behaviors in specific situations (anticipated consequences).

Experimental research An approach to research in which the experimenter manipulates a variable of interest, usually by assigning different research participants, at random, to different experimental conditions.

Experimenter expectancy effects Unintended experimenter effects involving behaviors that lead subjects to respond in accordance with the experimenter's hypothesis.

Extinction In conditioning, the progressive weakening of the association between a stimulus and a response: in classical conditioning because the conditioned stimulus is no longer followed by the unconditioned stimulus, and in operant conditioning because the response is no longer followed by reinforcement.

Extraversion In Eysenck's theory, one end of the introversion–extraversion dimension of personality characterized by a disposition to be sociable, friendly, impulsive, and risk taking.

Facets The more specific traits (or components) that make up each of the broad Big Five factors. For example, facets of extraversion are activity level, assertiveness, excitement seeking, positive emotions, gregariousness, and warmth.

Factor analysis A statistical method for analyzing correlations among a set of personality tests or test items in order to determine those variables or test responses that increase or decrease together. Used in the development of personality tests and of some trait theories (e.g., Cattell, Eysenck).

Fear In Kelly's personal construct theory, fear occurs when a new construct is about to enter the person's construct system.

Five-factor theory Costa and McCrae's theory that the basic structure of personality consists of five biologically based traits: neuroticism, extraversion, openness, agreeableness, and conscientiousness (NEOAC or CANOE).

Fixation Freud's concept expressing a developmental arrest or stoppage at some point in the person's psychosexual development.

Fixed (schedules of reinforcement) Schedules of reinforcement in which the relation of behaviors to reinforcers remains constant.

Fixed-role therapy Kelly's therapeutic technique that makes use of scripts or roles for people to try out, thereby encouraging people to behave in new ways and to perceive themselves in new ways.

Functional magnetic resonance imaging (fMRI) A brain imaging technique that identifies specific regions of the brain that are involved in the processing of a given stimulus or the performance of a given task; the technique relies on recordings of changes in blood flow in the brain.

Focus of convenience In Kelly's personal construct theory, those events or phenomena that are best covered by a construct or by the construct system.

Free association In psychoanalysis, the patient's reporting to the analyst of every thought that comes to mind.

Functional analysis In behavioral approaches, particularly Skinnerian, the identification of the environmental stimuli that control behavior.

Functional autonomy Allport's concept that a motive may become independent of its origins; in particular, motives in adults may become independent of their earlier basis in tension reduction.

Fundamental lexical hypothesis The hypothesis that over time the most important individual differences in human interaction have been encoded as single terms in language.

Fundamental postulate (of Kelly's personal construct theory) The postulate that all psychological processes of interest to the personality psychologist are shaped, or channeled, by the individual's anticipation of events.

Generalization In conditioning, the association of a response with stimuli similar to the stimulus to which the response was originally conditioned or attached.

Generalized reinforcer In Skinner's operant conditioning theory, a reinforcer that provides access to many other reinforcers (e.g., money).

General principles approach Higgins's term for an analysis of personal and situational influences on thought and action in which a common set of causal principles is used to explain both cross-situational consistency in thought and action that results from personal influences and variability in thought and action that results from situational influences.

Genital stage In psychoanalytic theory, the stage of development associated with the onset of puberty.

Goals In social-cognitive theory, desired future events that motivate the person over extended periods of time and enable the person to go beyond momentary influences.

Guided mastery A treatment approach emphasized in social-cognitive theory in which a person is assisted in performing modeled behaviors.

Heritability coefficient The proportion of observed variance in scores in a specific population that can be attributed to genetic factors.

Hierarchy A relation between entities in which one of them is an example of, or serves the purpose of, the other. In any given personality theory, different variables often are related hierarchically.

Hot versus cool attentional focus The focusing of one thought on emotionally arousing (hot) versus less arousing (cool) aspects of a situation or stimulus.

Human potential movement A group of psychologists, represented by Rogers and Maslow, who emphasize the actualization or fulfillment of individual potential, including an openness to experience.

Id Freud's structural concept for the source of the instincts or all of the drive energy in people.

Ideal self The self-concept the individual would most like to possess. A key concept in Rogers's theory.

Identification The acquisition, as characteristics of the self, of personality characteristics perceived to be part of others (e.g., parents).

Idiographic (strategies) Strategies of assessment and research in which the primary goal is to obtain a portrait of the potentially unique, idiosyncratic individual.

Implicit theories Broad, generalized beliefs that we may not be able to state explicitly in words, yet that influence our thinking.

Incongruence Rogers's concept of the existence of a discrepancy or conflict between the perceived self and experience.

Independent versus interdependent views of self Alternative implicit beliefs about self-concept in which the self is viewed either as possessing a set of psychological qualities that are distinct from other people (independent self) or is viewed in terms of roles in family, social, and community relationships (interdependent self).

Inhibited–uninhibited temperaments Relative to the uninhibited child, the inhibited child reacts to unfamiliar persons or events with restraint, avoidance, and distress, takes a longer time to relax in new situations, and has more unusual fears and phobias. The uninhibited child seems to enjoy these very same situations that seem so stressful to the inhibited child. The uninhibited child responds with spontaneity in novel situations, laughing and smiling easily.

Internal working model Bowlby's concept for the mental representation (images) of the self and others that develop during the early years of development, in particular in interaction with the primary caretaker.

Introversion In Eysenck's theory, one end of the introversion–extraversion dimension of personality characterized by a disposition to be quiet, reserved, reflective, and risk avoiding.

Isolation The defense mechanism in which emotion is isolated from the content of a painful impulse or memory.

Knowledge-and-Appraisal Personality Architecture (KAPA) Theoretical analysis of personality architecture that distinguishes two aspects of cognition in personality functioning: enduring knowledge and dynamic appraisals of the meaning of encounters for the self.

Latency stage In psychoanalytic theory, the stage following the phallic stage in which there is a decrease in sexual urges and interest.

Learning goals In Dweck's social-cognitive analysis of personality and motivation, a goal of trying to enhance one's knowledge and personal mastery of a task.

L-data Life record data or information concerning the person that can be obtained from his or her life history or life record.

Libido The psychoanalytic term for the energy associated first with the sexual instincts and later with the life instincts.

Life instinct Freud's concept for drives or sources of energy (libido) directed toward the preservation of life and sexual gratification.

Maladaptive response In the Skinnerian view of psychopathology, the learning of a response that is maladaptive or not considered acceptable by people in the environment.

Mechanism An intellectual movement of the 19th century that argued that basic principles of natural science could explain not only the behavior of physical objects but also human thought and action.

Microanalytic research Bandura's suggested research strategy concerning the concept of self-efficacy in which specific rather than global self-efficacy judgments are recorded.

Need for positive regard Rogers's concept expressing the need for warmth, liking, respect, and acceptance from others.

NEO-PI-R A personality questionnaire designed to measure people's standing on each of the factors of the five-factor model, as well as on facets of each factor.

Neuropsychoanalysis A scientific movement in which investigators try to identify brain systems that correspond to psychological structures and functions identified in Freud's psychoanalytic theory of personality.

Neuroticism In Eysenck's theory, a dimension of personality defined by stability and low anxiety at one end and by instability and high anxiety at the other end.

Neurotransmitters Chemical substances that transmit information from one neuron to another (e.g., dopamine and serotonin).

Nomothetic (strategies) Strategies of assessment and research in which the primary goal is to identify a common set of principles or laws that apply to all members of a population of persons.

Observational learning (modeling) Bandura's concept for the process through which people learn merely by observing the behavior of others, called models.

OCEAN The acronym for the five basic traits: openness, conscientiousness, extraversion, agreeableness, and neuroticism.

O-data Observer data or information provided by knowledgeable observers such as parents, friends, or teachers.

Oedipus complex Freud's concept expressing a boy's sexual attraction to the mother and fear of castration by the father, who is seen as a rival.

Operant conditioning Skinner's term for the process through which the characteristics of a response are determined by its consequences.

Operants In Skinner's theory, behaviors that appear (are emitted) without being specifically associated with any prior (eliciting) stimuli and are studied in relation to the reinforcing events that follow them.

Optimism A coping strategy that features relatively realistic expectations about one's capabilities.

Oral personality Freud's concept of a personality type that expresses a fixation at the oral stage of development and relates to the world in terms of the wish to be fed or to swallow.

Oral stage Freud's concept for that period of life during which the major center of bodily excitation or tension is the mouth.

OT-data In Cattell's theory, objective test data or information about personality obtained from observing behavior in miniature situations.

Parental investment theory The view that women have a greater parental investment in offspring than do men because women pass their genes on to fewer offspring.

Penis envy In psychoanalytic theory, the female's envy of the male's possession of a penis.

Perceived self-efficacy In social-cognitive theory, the perceived ability to cope with specific situations.

Perception without awareness Unconscious perception or perception of a stimulus without conscious awareness of such perception.

Perceptual defense The process by which an individual defends (unconsciously) against awareness of a threatening stimulus.

Performance The production of learned behaviors, viewed by Bandura as dependent on rewards, in contrast with the acquisition of new behaviors, which is seen as independent of reward.

Performance goals In Dweck's social-cognitive analysis of personality and motivation, a goal of trying to make a good impression on other people who may evaluate you.

Peripheral construct In Kelly's personal construct theory, a construct that is not basic to the construct system and can be altered without serious consequences for the rest of the system.

Personality Those characteristics of the person that account for consistent patterns of experience and action.

Personality architecture A term to describe the overall design and operating characteristics of those psychological systems that underlie personality functioning.

Person-as-scientist Kelly's metaphor for conceptualizing persons; the metaphor emphasizes that a central feature of everyday personality functioning is analogous to a central feature of science, namely, using constructs to understand and predict events.

Person-situation controversy A controversy between psychologists who emphasize the importance of personal (internal) variables in determining behavior and those who emphasize the importance of situational (external) influences.

Phallic personality Freud's concept of a personality type that expresses a fixation at the phallic stage of development and strives for success in competition with others.

Phallic stage Freud's concept for that period of life during which excitation or tension begins to be centered in the genitals and during which there is an attraction to the parent of the opposite sex.

Phenomenal field The individual's way of perceiving and experiencing his or her world.

Phenomenology The study of human experience; in personality psychology, an approach to personality theory that focuses on how the person perceives and experiences the self and the world.

Phrenology The early 19th-century attempt to locate areas of the brain responsible for various aspects of emotional and behavioral functioning. Developed by Gall, it was discredited as quackery and superstition.

Plasticity The ability of parts of the neurobiological system to change, temporarily and for extended periods of time, within limits set by genes, to meet current adaptive demands and as a result of experience.

Pleasure principle According to Freud, psychological functioning based on the pursuit of pleasure and the avoidance of pain.

Preconscious Freud's thoughts for those thoughts, experiences, and feelings of which we are momentarily unaware but can readily bring into awareness.

Preverbal construct In Kelly's personal construct theory, a construct that is used but cannot be expressed in words.

Primary process In psychoanalytic theory, a form of thinking that is governed not by logic or reality testing and that is seen in dreams and other expressions of the unconscious.

Problem-focused coping Attempts to cope by altering features of a stressful situation.

Process In personality theory, the concept that refers to the motivational aspects of personality.

Projection The defense mechanism in which one attributes to (projects onto) others one's own expressions of the unconscious.

Projective test A test that generally involves vague, ambiguous stimuli and allows subjects to reveal their personalities in terms of their distinctive responses (e.g., Rorschach Inkblot Test, Thematic Apperception Test).

Proximate causes Explanations for behavior associated with current biological processes in the organism.

Psychoticism In Eysenck's theory, a dimension of personality defined by a tendency to be solitary and insensitive at one end and to accept social custom and care about others at the other end.

Punishment An aversive stimulus that follows a response.

Q-data In Cattell's theory, personality data obtained from questionnaires.

Q-sort technique An assessment device in which the subject sorts statements into categories following a normal distribution. Used by Rogers as a measure of statements regarding the self and the ideal self.

Range of convenience In Kelly's personal construct theory, those events or phenomena that are covered by a construct or by the construct system.

Rationalization The defense mechanism in which an acceptable reason is given for an unacceptable motive or act.

Reaction formation The defense mechanism in which the opposite of an unacceptable impulse is expressed.

Reality principle According to Freud, psychological functioning based on reality in which pleasure is delayed until an optimum time.

Reciprocal determinism The mutual, back-and-forth effects of variables on one another; in social-cognitive theory, a fundamental causal principle in which personal, environmental, and behavioral factors are viewed as causally influencing one another.

Regression Freud's concept expressing a person's return to ways of relating to the world and the self that were part of an earlier stage of development.

Reinforcer An event (stimulus) that follows a response and increases the probability of its occurrence.

Rejection sensitivity A thinking style that is characterized by anxious expectations of rejection in interpersonal relationships.

Reliability The extent to which observations are stable, dependable, and can be replicated.

Repression The primary defense mechanism in which a thought, idea, or wish is dismissed from consciousness.

Response style The tendency of some subjects to respond to test items in a consistent, patterned way that has to do with the form of the questions or answers rather than with their content.

Role Behavior considered to be appropriate for a person's place or status in society. Emphasized by Cattell as one of a number of variables that limit the influence of personality variables on behavior relative to situational variables.

Role Construct Repertory Test (Rep test) Kelly's test to determine the constructs used by a person, the relationships among constructs, and how the constructs are applied to specific people.

Sample approach Mischel's description of assessment approaches in which there is an interest in the behavior itself and its relation to environmental conditions, in contrast to sign approaches that infer personality from test behavior.

Schedule of reinforcement In Skinner's operant conditioning theory, the rate and interval of reinforcement of responses (e.g., response ratio schedule and time intervals).

Schemas Complex cognitive structures that guide information processing.

S-data Self-report data or information provided by the subject.

Secondary disposition Allport's concept for a disposition to behave in a particular way that is relevant to few situations.

Secondary process In psychoanalytic theory, a form of thinking that is governed by reality and associated with the development of the ego.

Selective breeding An approach to establishing genetic-behavior relationships through the breeding of successive generations with a particular characteristic.

Self-actualization The fundamental tendency of the organism to actualize, maintain, enhance itself, and fulfill its potential. A concept emphasized by Rogers and other members of the human potential movement.

Self-concept (or the "Self") The perceptions and meaning associated with the self, me, or I.

Self-consistency Rogers's concept expressing an absence of conflict among perceptions of the self.

Self-determination theory Deci and Ryan's theory that the basic human psychological needs are for competence, autonomy, and relatedness (CAR).

Self-discrepancies In theoretical analyses of Higgins, incongruities between beliefs about one's current psychological attributes (the actual self) and desired attributes that represent valued standards or guides.

Self-enhancement A motive to maintain or enhance positive views of the self.

Self-esteem The person's overall evaluative regard for the self or personal judgment of worthiness.

Self-evaluative reactions Feelings of dissatisfaction versus satisfaction (pride) in oneself that occur as people reflect on their actions.

Self-experience discrepancy Rogers's emphasis on the potential for conflict between the concept of self and experience—the basis for psychopathology.

Self-produced consequences In social-cognitive theory, the consequences of behavior that are produced personally (internally) by the individual and that play a vital role in self-regulation and self-control.

Self-regulation Psychological processes through which persons motivate their own behavior.

Self-schemas Cognitive generalizations about the self that guide a person's information processing.

Self-verification A motive to obtain information that is consistent with one's self-concept.

Shaping In Skinner's operant conditioning theory, the process through which organisms learn complex behavior through a step-by-step process in which behavior increasingly approximates a full, target response.

Shared and nonshared environments The comparison in behavior genetics research of the effects of siblings growing up in the same or different environments. Particular attention is given to whether siblings reared in the same family share the same family environment.

Sign approach Mischel's description of assessment approaches that infer personality from test behavior, in contrast to sample approaches to assessment.

Similarity pole In Kelly's personal construct theory, the similarity pole of a construct is defined by the way in which two elements are perceived to be similar.

Situational specificity The emphasis on behavior as varying according to the situation, as opposed to the emphasis by trait theorists on consistency in behavior across situations.

Socioemotional selectivity theory Theoretical analysis by Carstensen that examines the ways in which social motivations shift across the course of life.

Source trait In Cattell's theory, behaviors that vary together to form an independent dimension of personality, which is discovered through the use of factor analysis.

State Emotional and mood changes (e.g., anxiety, depression, fatigue) that Cattell suggested may influence the behavior of a person at a given time. The assessment of both traits and states is suggested to predict behavior.

Stress inoculation training A procedure to reduce stress developed by Meichenbaum in which clients are taught to become aware of such negative, stress-inducing cognitions.

Structure In personality theory, the concept that refers to the more enduring and stable aspects of personality.

Subception A process emphasized by Rogers in which a stimulus is experienced without being brought into awareness.

Sublimation The defense mechanism in which the original expression of the instinct is replaced by a higher cultural goal.

Subliminal psychodynamic activation The research procedure associated with psychoanalytic theory in which stimuli are presented below the perceptual threshold (subliminally) to stimulate unconscious wishes and fears.

Submerged construct In Kelly's personal construct theory, a construct that once could be expressed in words but now either one or both poles of the construct cannot be verbalized.

Subordinate construct In Kelly's personal construct theory, a construct that is lower in the construct system and is thereby included in the context of another (superordinate) construct.

Successive approximation In Skinner's operant conditioning theory, the development of complex behaviors through the reinforcement of behaviors that increasingly resemble the final form of behavior to be produced.

Superego Freud's structural concept for the part of personality that expresses our ideals and moral values.

Superfactor A higher-order or secondary factor representing a higher level of organization of traits than the initial factors derived from factor analysis.

Superordinate construct In Kelly's personal construct theory, a construct that is higher in the construct system and thereby includes other constructs within its context.

Surface trait In Cattell's theory, behaviors that appear to be linked to one another but do not in fact increase and decrease together.

Symptom In psychopathology, the expression of psychological conflict or disordered psychological functioning. For Freud, a disguised expression of a repressed impulse.

System A collection of highly interconnected parts that function together; in the study of personality, distinct psychological mechanisms may function together as a system that produces the psychological phenomena of personality.

Systematic desensitization A technique in behavior therapy in which a competing response (relaxation) is conditioned to stimuli that previously aroused anxiety.

Target behaviors (target responses) In behavioral assessment, the identification of specific behaviors to be observed and measured in relation to changes in environmental events.

T-data Test data or information obtained from experimental procedures or standardized tests.

Temperament Biologically based emotional and behavioral tendencies that are evident in early childhood.

Threat In Kelly's personal construct theory, threat occurs when the person is aware of an imminent, comprehensive change in his or her construct system.

Three-dimensional temperament model The three superfactors describing individual differences in temperament: positive emotionality (PE), negative emotionality (NE), and disinhibition versus constraint (DvC).

Token economy Following Skinner's operant conditioning theory, an environment in which individuals are rewarded with tokens for desirable behaviors.

Trait An enduring psychological characteristic of an individual; or a type of psychological construct (a "trait construct") that refers to such characteristics.

Transference In psychoanalysis, the patient's development toward the analyst of attitudes and feelings rooted in past experiences with parental figures.

Twin studies An approach to establishing genetic–behavior relationships through the comparison of degree of similarity among identical twins, fraternal twins, and nontwin siblings. Generally combined with adoption studies.

Type A cluster of personality traits that may constitute a qualitatively distinct category of persons (i.e., a personality type).

Ultimate causes Explanations for behavior associated with evolution.

Unconditional positive regard Rogers's term for the acceptance of a person in a total, unconditional way. One of three therapist conditions suggested as essential for growth and therapeutic progress.

Unconscious Those thoughts, experiences, and feelings of which we are unaware. According to Freud, this unawareness is the result of repression.

Undoing The defense mechanism in which one magically undoes an act or wish associated with anxiety.

Units of analysis A concept that refers to the basic variables of a theory; different personality theories invoke different types of variables, or different basic units of analysis, in conceptualizing personality structure.

Validity The extent to which observations reflect the phenomena or constructs of interest to us (also "construct validity").

Variable (schedules of reinforcement) Schedules of reinforcement in which the relation of behaviors to reinforcers changes unpredictably.

Verbal construct In Kelly's personal construct theory, a construct that can be expressed in words.

Vicarious conditioning Bandura's concept for the process through which emotional responses are learned through the observation of emotional responses in others.

Vicarious experiencing of consequences In social-cognitive theory, the observed consequences to the behavior of others that influence future performance.

Working self-concept The subset of the self-concept that is in working memory at any time; the theoretical idea that different social circumstances may activate different aspects of self-concept.

REFERENCES

Adams, N. (2012). Skinner's *Walden Two*: An anticipation of positive psychology? *Review of General Psychology*, *16*, 1–9.

Adams-Webber, J. R. (1979). *Personal construct theory: Concepts and applications*. New York: Wiley.

Adams-Webber, J. R. (1982). Assimilation and contrast in personal judgment: The dichotomy corollary. In J. C. Mancuso & J. R. Adams-Webber (Eds.), *The construing person* (pp. 96–112). New York: Praeger.

Adams-Webber, J. R. (1998). Differentiation and sociality in terms of elicited and provided constructs. *American Psychological Society*, *9*, 499–501.

Adler, A. (1927). *Understanding human nature*. New York: Garden City Publishing.

Ainsworth, M., Bleher, M., Waters, E., & Wall, S. (1978). *Patterns of attachment: A psychological study of the strange situation*. Hillsdale, NJ: Erlbaum.

Ainsworth, M., & Bowlby, J. (1991). An ethological approach to personality development. *American Psychologist*, *46*, 333–341.

Alexander, F., & French, T. M. (1946). *Psychoanalytic therapy*. New York: Ronald.

Allen, J. J., Iacono, W. G., Depue, R. A., & Arbisi, P. (1993). Regional electroencephalographic asymmetries in bipolar seasonal affective disorder before and after exposure to bright light. *Biological Psychiatry*, *33*, 642–646.

Allik, J, Realo, A., Mottus, R., Borkenau, P., Kuppens, P., & Hrebickova, H. (2010). How people see others is different from how people see themselves: A replicable pattern across cultures. *Journal of Personality and Social Psychology*, *99*, 870–882.

Alloy, L. B., Abramson, L. Y., & Francis, E. L. (1999). Do negative cognitive styles confer vulnerability to depression? *Current Directions in Psychological Science*, *8*, 128–132.

Allport, F. H., & Allport, G. W. (1921). Personality traits: Their classification and measurement. *Journal of Abnormal and Social Psychology*, *16*, 1–40.

Allport, G. W. (1937). *Personality: A psychological interpretation*. New York: Holt, Rinehart & Winston.

Allport, G. W. (1961). *Pattern and growth in personality*. New York: Holt, Rinehart & Winston.

Allport, G. W. (1967). Autobiography. In E. G. Boring & G. Lindzey (Eds.), *A history of psychology in autobiography* (pp. 1–26). New York: Appleton-Century-Crofts.

Allport, G. W., & Odbert, H. S. (1936). Trait-names: A psycholexical study. *Psychological Monographs*, *47*(Whole No. 211).

American College Health Association. (2016). *College Health Association-National College Health Assessment II: Reference Group Executive Summary Fall 2015*. Hanover, MD: American College Health Association.

American Psychological Association. (1981). Ethical Principles of Psychologists. *American Psychologist*, *36*, 633–638.

Andersen, B. L., & Cyranowski, J. M. (1994). Women's sexual self-schema. *Journal of Personality and Social Psychology*, *67*, 1079–1100.

Andersen, S. M., & Baum, A. (1994). Transference in interpersonal relations: Inferences and affect based on significant-other representations. *Journal of Personality*, *67*, 459–498.

Andersen, S. M., & Chen, S. (2002). The relational self: An interpersonal social-cognitive theory. *Psychological Review*, *109*, 619–645.

Andersen, S. M., & Cole, S. W. (1990). "Do I know you?": The role of significant others in general social perception. *Journal of Personality and Social Psychology*, *59*, 384–399.

Andersen, S. M., Glassman, N. S., Chen, S., & Cole, S. W. (1995). Transference in social perception: The role of chronic accessibility in significant-other representations. *Journal of Personality and Social Psychology, 69*, 41–57.

Andersen, S. M., Reznik, I., & Manzella, L. M. (1996). Eliciting facial affect, motivation, and expectancies in transference: Significant-other representations in social relations. *Journal of Personality and Social Psychology, 71*, 1108–1129.

Anderson, A. K., & Phelps, E. A. (2002). Is the human amygdala critical for the subjective experience of emotion? Evidence of intact dispositional affect in patients with amygdala lesions. *Journal of Cognitive Neuroscience, 14*, 709–720.

Anderson, C. A., & Bushman, B. J. (2001). Effects of violent video games on aggressive behavior, aggressive cognition, aggressive affect, physiological arousal, and prosocial behavior: A meta-analytic review of the scientific literature. *Psychological Science, 12*, 353–359.

Anderson, C. A., Lindsay, J. J., & Bushman, B. J. (1999). Research in the psychological laboratory: Truth or triviality? *Current Directions in Psychological Science, 8*, 3–9.

Anderson, M. C., Ochsner, K. N., Kuhl, B., Cooper, J., Robertson, E., Gabrieli, S., ..., Gabrieli, D. E. (2004). Neural systems underlying the suppression of memories. *Science, 303*, 232–235.

Anderson, N., & Ones, D. S. (2003). The construct validity of three entry level personality inventories used in the UK: Cautionary findings from a multiple inventory investigation. *European Journal of Personality, 17*, S39–S66.

Antonuccio, D. O., Thomas, M., & Danton, W. G. (1997). A cost-effectiveness analysis of cognitive behavior therapy and fluoxetine (Prozac) in the treatment of depression. *Behavior Therapy, 28*, 187–210.

APA Monitor. (1982). The spreading case of fraud, *13*, 1.

Ariely, D. (2012). *The (honest) truth about dishonesty*. New York: Harper.

Aronson, E., & Mettee, D. R. (1968). Dishonest behavior as a function of differential levels of induced self-esteem. *Journal of Personality and Social Psychology, 9*, 121–127.

Artistico, D., Berry, J. M., Black, J., Cervone, D., Lee, C., & Orom, H. (2011). Psychological functioning in adulthood: A self-efficacy analysis. In C. H. Hoare (Ed.), *The Oxford handbook of adult development and learning* (2nd ed., pp. 215–247). New York: Oxford University Press.

Artistico, D., Cervone, D., Orom, H., Montes, C., & King, S. (2018). *Understanding individuals' everyday problem solving abilities: The advantages of idiographic methods and a knowledge-and-appraisal model of personality architecture*. Under editorial review.

Asendorpf, J. B., Banse, R., & Mucke, D. (2002). Double dissociation between implicit and explicit personality self-concept: The case of shy behavior. *Journal of Personality and Social Psychology, 83*, 380–393.

Asendorpf, J. B., Caspi, A., & Hofstee, W. K. B. (Eds.). (2002). The puzzle of personality types. *European Journal of Personality, 16*, S1–S5.

Asendorpf, J. B., & Van Aken, M. A. G. (1999). Resilient overcontrolled, and undercontrolled personality prototypes in childhood: Replicability, predictive power, and the trait-type issue. *Journal of Personality and Social Psychology, 77*, 815–832.

Ashton, M. C., Lee, K., & Paunonen, S. V. (2002). What is the central feature of extraversion? Social attention versus reward sensitivity. *Journal of Personality and Social Psychology, 83*, 245–252.

Ashton, M. C., Lee, K., Perugini, M., Szarota, P., DeVries, R. E., DiBlas, L., ..., & DeRaaad, B. (2004). A six-factor structure of personality descriptive adjectives: Solutions from psycholexical studies in seven languages. *Journal of Personality and Social Psychology, 86*, 356–366.

Aspinwall, L. G., & Staudinger, U. M. (Eds.). (2002). *A psychology of human strengths: Perspectives on an emerging field*. Washington, DC: American Psychological Association.

Associated Press. (November 14, 2002). Teen says game inspired crime spree.

Ayduk, O., Mischel, W., & Downey, G. (2002). Attentional mechanisms linking rejection to hostile reactivity: The role of "hot" versus "cool" focus. *Psychological Science, 13*, 443–448.

Ayllon, T., & Azrin, H. H. (1965). The measurement and reinforcement of behavior of psychotics. *Journal of the Experimental Analysis of Behavior, 8*, 357–383.

Baccus, J. R., Baldwin, M. W., & Packer, D. J. (2004). Increasing implicit self-esteem through classical conditioning. *Psychological Science, 15*, 498–502.

Balay, J., & Shevrin, H. (1988). The subliminal psychodynamic activation method. *American Psychologist, 43*, 161–174.

Balay, J., & Shevrin, H. (1989). SPA is subliminal, but is it psychodynamically activating? *American Psychologist, 44*, 1423–1426.

Baldwin, A. L. (1949). The effect of home environment on nursery school behavior. *Child Development, 20*, 49–61.

Baldwin, M. W. (1999). Relational schemas: Research into social-cognitive aspects of interpersonal experience. In D. Cervone & Y. Shoda (Eds.), *The coherence of personality: Social-cognitive bases of consistency, variability, and organization* (pp. 127–154). New York: Guilford Press.

Baldwin, M. W. (Ed.). (2005). *Interpersonal cognition*. New York: Guilford Press.

Baltes, P. B. (1997). On the incomplete architecture of human ontogeny: Selection, optimization, and, compensation as foundation of developmental theory. *American Psychologist, 52*, 366–380.

Baltes, P. B., & Baltes, M. M. (1990). *Successful aging: Perspective from the behavioral sciences*. Cambridge, UK: Cambridge University Press.

Baltes, P. B., & Graf, P. (1996). Psychological aspects of aging: Facts and frontiers. In D. Magnusson (Ed.), *The lifespan development of individuals: Behavioral, neurobiological, and psychosocial perspectives* (pp. 427–460). Cambridge, UK: Cambridge University Press.

Baltes, P. B., & Mayer, K. U. (1999). *The Berlin aging study: Aging from 70 to 100*. Cambridge, UK: Cambridge University Press.

Baltes, P. B., & Staudinger, U. M. (2000). Wisdom: A methateuristic (pragmatic) to orchestrate mind and virtue toward excellence. *American Psychologist, 55*, 122–136.

Baltes, P. B., Staudinger, U. M., & Lindenberger, U. (1999). Lifespan psychology: Theory and application to intellectual functioning. *Annual Review of Psychology, 50*, 471–507.

Bandura, A. (1965). Influence of models' reinforcement contingencies on the acquisition of imitative responses. *Journal of Personality and Social Psychology, 1*, 589–595.

Bandura, A. (1969). *Principles of behavior modification*. New York: Holt, Rinehart and Winston.

Bandura, A. (1977). Self-efficacy: Toward a unifying theory of behavioral change. *Psychological Review, 84*, 191–215.

Bandura, A. (1986). *Social foundations of thought and action: A social cognitive theory*. Englewood Cliffs, NJ: Prentice Hall.

Bandura, A. (1989a). Social cognitive theory. *Annals of Child Development, 6*, 1–60.

Bandura, A. (1989b). Self-regulation of motivation and action through internal standards and goal systems. In L. A. Pervin (Ed.), *Goal concepts in personality and social psychology* (pp. 19–85). Hillsdale, NJ: Erlbaum.

Bandura, A. (1990). Self-regulation of motivation through anticipatory and self-reactive mechanisms. *Nebraska Symposium on Motivation, 38*, 69–164.

Bandura, A. (1992). Self-efficacy mechanism in psychobiologic functioning. In R. Schwarzer (Ed.), *Self-efficacy: Thought control of action* (pp. 335–394). Washington, DC: Hemisphere.

Bandura, A. (1997). *Self-efficacy: The exercise of control*. New York: Freeman.

Bandura, A. (1999). Social cognitive theory of personality. In L. A. Pervin & O. P. John (Eds.), *Handbook of personality: Theory and research* (pp. 154–196). New York: Guilford Press.

Bandura, A. (2001). Social cognitive theory: An agentic perspective. *Annual Review of Psychology, 52*, 1–26.

Bandura, A. (2004). Health promotion by social cognitive means. *Health Education and Behavior, 31*, 143–164.

Bandura, A. (2006). Toward a psychology of human agency. *Perspectives on Psychological Science, 1*, 164–180.

Bandura, A. (2012). Social cognitive theory. In P. A. M. van Langer, A. Kruglanski, & E. T. Higgins (Eds.), *Handbook of theories of social psychology* (Vol. 1, pp. 349–375). Washington, DC: Sage.

Bandura, A., & Adams, N. E. (1977). Analysis of self efficacy theory of behavioral change. *Cognitive Therapy and Research, 1*, 287–310.

Bandura, A., Adams, N. E., & Beyer, J. (1977). Cognitive processes mediating behavioral change. *Journal of Personality and Social Psychology*, *35*, 125–139.

Bandura, A., Barbaranelli, C., Caprara, G. V., & Pastorelli, C. (1996). Mechanisms of moral disengagement in the exercise of moral agency. *Journal of Personality and Social Psychology*, *71*, 364–374.

Bandura, A., & Cervone, D. (1983). Self-evaluative and self-efficacy mechanisms governing the motivational effect of goal systems. *Journal of Personality and Social Psychology*, *45*, 1017–1028.

Bandura, A., Grusec, J. E., & Menlove, F. L. (1967). Some social determinants of self-monitoring reinforcement systems. *Journal of Personality and Social Psychology*, *5*, 449–455.

Bandura, A., & Kupers, C. J. (1964). Transmission of patterns of self-reinforcement through modeling. *Journal of Abnormal and Social Psychology*, *69*, 1–9.

Bandura, A., & Mischel, W. (1965). Modification of self-imposed delay of reward through exposure to live and symbolic models. *Journal of Personality and Social Psychology*, *2*, 698–705.

Bandura, A., Pastorelli, C., Barbaranelli, C., & Caprara, G. V. (1999). Self-efficacy pathways to childhood depression. *Journal of Personality and Social Psychology*, *76*, 258–269.

Bandura, A., Reese, L., & Adams, N. E. (1982). Micro-analysis of action and fear arousal as a function of differential levels of perceived self-efficacy. *Journal of Personality and Social Psychology*, *43*, 5–21.

Bandura, A., & Rosenthal, T. L. (1966). Vicarious classical conditioning as a function of arousal level. *Journal of Personality and Social Psychology*, *3*, 54–62.

Bandura, A., Ross, D., & Ross, S. (1963). Imitation of film-mediated aggressive models. *Journal of Abnormal and Social Psychology*, *66*, 3–11.

Bandura, A., & Schunk, D. H. (1981). Cultivating competence, self-efficacy, and intrinsic interest. *Journal of Personality and Social Psychology*, *41*, 586–598.

Bandura, A., & Walters, R. H. (1959). *Adolescent aggression*. New York: Ronald.

Bandura, A., & Walters, R. H. (1963). *Social learning and personality development*. New York: Holt, Rinehart & Winston.

Bandura, A. (2015). *Moral disengagement: How people do harm and live with themselves*. New York: Worth Publishers.

Barenbaum, N. B., & Winter, D. G. (2008). History of modern personality theory and research. In O. P. John, R. R. W. Robins, & L. A. Pervin (Eds.), *Handbook of personality: Theory and research* (pp. 29–60). New York: Guilford Press.

Bargh, J. A., & Ferguson, M. J. (2000). Beyond behaviorism: On the automaticity of higher mental processes. *Psychological Bulletin*, *126*, 925–945.

Bargh, J. A., & Gollwitzer, P. M. (1994). Environmental control of goal-directed action: Automatic and strategic contingencies between situations and behavior. In W. D. Spaulding (Ed.), *Nebraska symposium on motivation: Vol. 41. Integrative views of motivation, cognition, and emotion* (pp. 71–124). Lincoln: University of Nebraska Press.

Bargh, J. A., & Tota, M. E. (1988). Context-dependent automatic processing in depression: Accessibility of negative constructs with regard to self but not others. *Journal of Personality and Social Psychology*, *54*, 925–939.

Barlow, D. H. (1991). Disorders of emotion. *Psychological Inquiry*, *2*, 58–71.

Barrick, M. R., & Mount, M. K. (1991). The Big Five personality dimensions and job performance: A meta-analysis. *Personnel Psychology*, *44*, 1–26.

Bartholomew, K., & Horowitz, L. K. (1991). Attachment styles among young adults: A test of a four-category model. *Journal of Personality and Social Psychology*, *61*, 226–244.

Bartz, J. A., Zaki, J., Bolger, N., Hollander, E., Ludwig, N. N., Kolevzon, A., & Ochsner, K. N. (2010). Oxytocin selectively improves empathic accuracy. *Psychological Science*, *21*, 1426–428.

Bartz, J., Zaki, J., Bolger, N., & Ochsner, K. (2011). Social effects of oxytocin in humans: Context and person matter. *Trends in Cognitive Sciences*, *15*, 301–309.

Bartoszek, G., & Cervone, D. (2017). Toward an implicit measure of emotions: Ratings of abstract images reveal distinct emotional states. *Cognition and Emotion*, *31*, 1377–1391.

Baumeister, R. F. (1999). On the interface between personality and social psychology. In L. A. Pervin & O. P. John (Eds.), *Handbook of personality: Theory and research* (pp. 367–377). New York: Guilford Press.

Baumeister, R. F., Campbell, J. D., Krueger, J. I., & Vohs, K. D. (2003). Does high self-esteem cause better performance, interpersonal success, happiness, or healthier lifestyles? *Psychological Science in the Public Interest*, *4*, Whole Issue (Supplement to Psychological Science).

Baumeister, R. F., & Vohs, K. D. (Eds.). (2004). *Handbook of self-regulation: Research, theory, and applications*. New York: Guilford Press.

Baumert, A., Schmitt, M., Perugini, M., Johnson, W., Blum, G., ... Wrzus, C. (2017). Integrating personality structure, personality process, and personality development. *European Journal of Personality*, *31*(5), 503–528.

Beck, A. T. (1987). Cognitive models of depression. *Journal of Cognitive Psychotherapy*, *1*, 2–27.

Beck, A. T. (1991). Cognitive therapy: A 30-year retrospective. *American Psychologist*, *46*, 368–375.

Beck, A. T. (1993). Cognitive therapy: Past, present, and future. *Journal of Consulting and Clinical Psychology*, *61*, 194–198.

Beck, A. T., Rush, A. J., Shaw, B. F., & Emery, G. (1979). *Cognitive therapy of depression*. New York: Guilford.

Beilock, S. L., Lyons, I. M., Mattarella-Micke, A., Nusbaum, H. C., & Small, S. L. (2008). Sports expertise changes the neural processing of language. *Proceedings of the National Academy of Sciences USA*, *105*, 13269–13273.

Benet-Martinez, V., & John, O. P. (1998). Los Cinco Grandes across cultures and ethnic groups: Multi-trait multimethod analyses of the Big Five in Spanish and English. *Journal of Personality and Social Psychology*, *75*, 729–750.

Benet-Martinez, V., & Oishi, S. (2008). Culture and personality. In O. P. John, R. W. Robins, & L. A. Pervin (Eds.), *Handbook of personality: Theory and research* (pp. 542–567). New York: Guilford Press.

Benjamin, J., Lin, L., Patterson, C., Greenberg, B. D., Murphy, D. L., & Hamer, D. H. (1996). Population and familial association between the D4 dopamine receptor gene and measures of novelty seeking. *Nature Genetics*, *12*, 81–84.

Benight, C. C., & Bandura, A. (2004). Social cognitive theory of posttraumatic recovery: The role of perceived self-efficacy. *Behaviour Research and Therapy*, *42*, 1129–1148.

Benson, E. S. (2004). Behavioral genetics: Meet molecular biology. *Monitor on Psychology*, *35*, 42–45.

Benware, C., & Deci, E. L. (1984). Quality of learning with an active versus passive motivational set. *American Educational Research Journal*, *21*, 755–765.

Berkowitz, L., & Donnerstein, E. (1982). External validity is more than skin deep. *American Psychologist*, *37*, 245–257.

Bernard, J. D., Baddeley, J. L., Rodriguez, B. F., & Burke, P. A. (2016). Depression, language, and affect: An examination of the influence of baseline depression and affect induction on language. *Journal of Language and Social Psychology*, *35*, 317–326.

Berndt, T. J. (2002). Friendship quality and social development. *Current Directions in Psychological Science*, *11*, 7–10.

Bieri, J. (1955). Cognitive complexity-simplicity and predictive behavior. *Journal of Abnormal and Social Psychology*, *51*, 263–268.

Bieri, J. (1986). Beyond the grid principle. *Contemporary Psychology*, *31*, 672–673.

Blackwell, L. A., Trzesniewski, K. H., & Dweck, C. S. (2007). Theories of intelligence and achievement across the junior high school transition: A longitudinal study and an intervention. *Child Development*, *78*, 246–263.

Bleidorn, W., Hopwood, C. J., & Wright, A. G. C. (2017). Using big data to advance personality theory. *Current Opinion in Behavioral Sciences*, *18*, 79–82.

Block, J. (1971). *Lives through time*. Berkeley, CA: Bancroft Books.

Block, J. (1993). Studying personality the long way. In D. C. Funder, R. D. Parke, C. Tomlinson-Keasey, & K. Widaman (Eds.), *Studying lives through time* (pp. 9–41). Washington, DC: American Psychological Association.

Block, J. (2002). *Personality as an affect-processing system: Toward an integrative theory*. Mahwah, NJ: Erlbaum.

Block, J., & Robins, R. W. (1993). A longitudinal study of consistency and change in self-esteem from early adolescence to early childhood. *Child Development*, *64*, 909–923.

Boag, S. (2011). Explanation in personality psychology: "Verbal magic" and the five-factor model. *Philosophical Psychology*, *24*, 223–243.

Bogaert, A. F. (2006). Biological versus non-biological older brothers and men's sexual orientation. *Proceedings of the National Academy of Sciences*, *103*, 10771–10774.

Boldero, J., & Francis, J. (2002). Goals, standards, and the self: Reference values serving different functions. *Personality and Social Psychology Review, 6*, 232–241.

Borkenau, P., & Ostendorf, F. (1998). The Big Five as states: How useful is the five-factor model to describe intraindividual variations over time? *Journal of Research in Personality, 32*, 202–221.

Bornstein, R. F., & Masling, J. M. (1998). *Empirical perspectives on the psychoanalytic unconscious.* Washington, DC: American Psychological Association.

Borsboom, D., Mellenbergh, G. J., & Van Heerden, J. (2003). The theoretical status of latent variables. *Psychological Review, 110*, 203–219.

Botvinick, M. M., Braver, T. S., Barch, D. M., Carter, C. S., & Cohen, J. D. (2001). Conflict monitoring and cognitive control. *Psychological Review, 108*, 624–652.

Bouchard, T. J., Jr., Lykken, D. T., McGue, M., Segal, N. L., & Tellegen, A. (1990). Sources of human psychological differences: The Minnesota study of twins reared apart. *Science, 250*, 223–228.

Bourne, M. (2014, January 12). We didn't eat the marshmallow: The marshmallow ate us. *The New York Times Magazine*, 44–45.

Bozarth, J. D. (1992, October). Coterminous intermingling of doing and being in person-centered therapy. *The Person-Centered Journal: An International Journal Published by the Association for the Development of The Person-Centered Approach.* Retrieved October 9, 2004 http://www.adpca.org/ Journal/vol1 1/indexpage.htm.

Bradley, R. H., & Corwyn, R. F. (2002). Socioeconomic status and child development. *Annual Review of Psychology, 53*, 371–399.

Brandtstadter, J., & Wentura, D. (1995). Adjustment to shifting possibility frontiers in later life: Complementary adaptive modes. In R. A. Dixon & L. Bäckman (Eds.), *Compensating for psychological deficits and declines: Managing losses and promoting gains.* Mahwah, NJ: Erlbaum.

Bressler, S. L. (2002). Understanding cognition through large-scale cortical networks. *Current Directions in Psychological Science, 11*, 58–61.

Bretherton, I. (1992). The origins of attachment theory: John Bowlby and Mary Ainsworth. *Developmental Psychology, 28*, 759–775.

Brewin, C. R. (1996). Theoretical foundations of cognitive-behavior therapy for anxiety and depression. *Annual Review of Psychology, 47*, 33–57.

Brooks, D. (2011). *The social animal.* New York: Random House.

Brown, J. D. (1998). *The self.* New York: McGraw-Hill.

Bruner, J. S. (1956). You are your constructs. *Contemporary Psychology, 1*, 355–356.

Buchheim, A., Heinrichs, M., George, C., Pokorny, D., Koops, E., Henningsen, P., O'Connor, M., & Gundel, H. (2009). Oxytocin enhances the experience of attachment security. *Psychoneuroendocrinology, 34*, 1417–1422.

Bullmore, E., & Sporns, O. (2009). Complex brain networks: Graph theoretical analysis of structural and functional systems. *Nature Reviews: Neuroscience, 10*, 186–198.

Burns, M. J., & Dillon, F. R. (2005). AIDS health locus of control, self-efficacy for safer sexual practices, and future time orientation as predictors of condom use in African American college students. *Journal of Black Psychology, 31*, 172–188.

Bushman, B. J., & Anderson, C. A. (2002). Violent video games and hostile expectations: A test of the general aggression model. *Personality and Social Psychology Bulletin, 28*, 1679–1686.

Buss, A. H. (1989). Personality as traits. *American Psychologist, 44*, 1378–1388.

Buss, A. H., & Plomin, R. (1975). *A temperament theory of personality development.* New York: Wiley Interscience.

Buss, A. H., & Plomin, R. (1984). *Temperament: Early-developing personality traits.* Hillsdale, NJ: Erlbaum.

Buss, D. M. (1989). Sex differences in human mate preferences: Evolutionary hypotheses tested in 37 cultures. *Behavioral and Brain Sciences, 12*, 1–14.

Buss, D. M. (1999). Human nature and individual differences: The evolution of human personality. In L. A. Pervin & O. P. John (Eds.), *Handbook of personality: Theory and research* (pp. 31–56). New York: Guilford Press.

Buss, D. M. (Ed.). (2005). *The handbook of evolutionary psychology.* Hoboken, NJ: Wiley.

Buss, D. M. (2008). Human nature and individual differences: Evolution of human personality. In O. P. John, R. W. Robins, & L. A. Pervin (Eds.), *Handbook of personality: Theory and research* (pp. 29–60). New York: Guilford Press.

Buss, D. M. (2012). *Evolutionary psychology: The new science of the mind* (4th ed.). Boston: Allyn & Bacon.

Buss, D. M., & Hawley, P. H. (Eds.). (2011). *The evolution of personality and individual differences*. New York: Oxford University Press.

Buss, D. M., Larsen, R., Westen, D., & Semmelroth, J. (1992). Sex differences in jealousy: Evolution, physiology and psychology. *Psychological Science, 3*, 251–255.

Bussey, K., & Bandura, A. (1999). Social cognitive theory of gender development and differentiation. *Psychological Bulletin, 106*, 676–713.

Butler, J. M., & Haigh, G. V. (1954). Changes in the relation between self-concepts and ideal concepts consequent upon client centered counseling. In C. R. Rogers & R. F. Dymond (Eds.), *Psychotherapy and personality change* (pp. 55–75). Chicago: University of Chicago Press.

Butler, R. (2009). Coming to terms with personal construct theory. In R. Butler (Ed.), *Reflections in personal construct theory* (pp. 3–20). West Sussex, UK: Wiley-Blackwell.

Cacioppo, J. T. (1999). The case for social psychology in the era of molecular biology. Keynote address at the Society for Personality and Social Psychology Preconference, June 3, 1999, Denver, CO.

Cain, S. (2012). *Quiet: The power of introverts in a world that can't stop talking*. New York: Crown.

Caldwell, T. L., Cervone, D., & Rubin, L. H. (2008). Explaining intra-individual variability in social behavior through idiographic assessment: The case of humor. *Journal of Research in Personality, 42*, 1229–1242.

Campbell, J. B., & Hawley, C. W. (1982). Study habits and Eysenck's theory of extroversion-introversion. *Journal of Research in Personality, 16*, 139–146.

Campbell, W. K. (1999). Narcissism and romantic attraction. *Journal of Personality and Social Psychology, 77*, 1254–1270.

Canli, T. (2008). Toward a "molecular psychology" of personality. In O. P. John, R. W. Robins, & L. A. Pervin (Eds.), *Handbook of personality: Theory and research* (pp. 311–327). New York: Guilford Press.

Cantor, N. (1990). From thought to behavior: "Having" and "doing" in the study of personality and cognition. *American Psychologist, 45*, 735–750.

Cantor, N., & Kihlstrom, J. F. (1987). *Personality and social intelligence*. Englewood Cliffs, NJ: Prentice Hall.

Cantor, N., Norem, J. K., Neidenthal, P. M., Langston, C. A., & Brower, A. M. (1987). Life tasks, self-concept ideals, and cognitive strategies in a life transition. *Journal of Personality and Social Psychology, 53*, 1178–1191.

Caporael, L. R. (2001). Evolutionary psychology: Toward a unifying theory and a hybrid science. *Annual Review of Psychology, 52*, 706–628.

Caprara, G. V., & Perugini, M. (1994). Personality described by adjective: The generalizability of the Big Five to the Italian lexical context. *European Journal of Personality, 8*, 351–369.

Caprara G. V., Vecchione M., Alessandri G., Gerbino M., Barbaranelli C. (2011). The contribution of personality traits and self-efficacy beliefs to academic achievement: A longitudinal study. *British Journal of Educational Psychology, 81*, 78–96.

Carnelley, K. B., Pietromonaco, P. R., & Jaffe, K. (1994). Depression, working models of others, and relationships functioning. *Journal of Personality and Social Psychology, 66*, 127–140.

Carstensen, L. L. (1995). Evidence for a life-span theory of socioemotional selectivity. *Current Directions in Psychological Science, 4*, 151–156.

Carstensen, L. L. (1998). A life-span approach to social motivation. In J. Heckhausen & C. Dweck (Eds.), *Motivation and self-regulation across the life span* (pp. 341–364). New York: Cambridge University Press.

Carstensen, L. L., & Charles, S. T. (2003). Human aging: Why is even good news taken as bad? In L. G. Aspinwall & U. M. Staudinger (Eds.), *A psychology of human strengths: Perspectives on an emerging field* (pp. 75–86). Washington, DC: American Psychological Association.

Carstensen, L. L., & Fredrickson, B. L. (1998). Influence of HIV status and age on cognitive representations of others. *Health Psychology, 17*, 494–503.

Carstensen, L. L., Isaacowitz, D. M., & Charles, S. T. (1999). Taking time seriously: A theory of socioemotional selectivity. *American Psychologist, 54*, 165–181.

Cartwright, D. S. (1956). Self-consistency as a factor affecting immediate recall. *Journal of Abnormal and Social Psychology, 52*, 212–218.

Carver, C. S., Scheier, M. F., & Fulford, D. (2008). Self-regulatory processes, stress, and coping. In O. P. John, R. W. Robins, & L. A. Pervin (Eds.), *Handbook of personality: Theory and research* (pp. 725–742). New York: Guilford Press.

Casey, B. J., Somerville, L. H., Gotlib, I. H., Ayduk, O., Franklin, N. T., Askrend, M. K., ... Shoda, Y. (2011). Behavioral and neural correlates of delay of gratification 40 years later. *Proceedings of the National Academy of Sciences, 108*, 14998–15003.

Caspi, A. (2000). The child is father of the man: Personality correlates from childhood to adulthood. *Journal of Personality and Social Psychology, 78*, 158–172.

Caspi, A. (2002). Social selection, social causation, and developmental pathways: Empirical strategies for better understanding how individuals and environments are linked across the life course. In L. Pulkkinen and A. Caspi (Eds.), *Paths to successful development: Personality in the life course* (pp. 281–301). Cambridge, UK: Cambridge University Press.

Caspi, A., Bem, D. J., & Elder, G. H. (1989). Continuities and consequences of interactional styles across the life course. *Journal of Personality, 57*, 375–406.

Caspi, A., & Roberts, B. (1999). Personality continuity and change across the life course. In L. A. Pervin & O. P. John (Eds.), *Handbook of personality: Theory and research* (pp. 300–326). New York: Guilford Press.

Caspi, A., Sugden, K., Moffitt, T. E., Taylor, A., Craig, I. W., Harrington, H., ..., Poulton, R. (2003). Influence of life stress on depression: Moderation by a polymorphism in the 5-HTT gene. *Science, 301*, 386–389.

Casson, A. J., Smith, S., Duncan, J. S., & Rodriguez-Villegas, E. (2010). Wearable EEG: What is it, why is it needed and what does it entail? *IEEE Engineering in Medicine and Biology Magazine* (May/June Issue), 44–56.

Cattell, R. B. (1965). *The scientific analysis of personality*. Baltimore: Penguin.

Cattell, R. B. (1979). *Personality and learning theory*. New York: Springer.

Cattell, R. B., & Gruen, W. (1955). The primary personality factors in 11-year-old children, by Objective Tests. *Journal of Personality, 23*, 460–478.

Cavalli-Sforza, L. L., & Cavalli-Sforza, F. (1995). *The great human diasporas: The history of diversity and evolution*. Reading, MA: Addison-Wesley.

Centonze, D., Siracusano, A., Calabresi, P., & Bernardi, G. (2004). The project for a scientific psychology (1895): A Freudian anticipation of LTP-memory connection theory. *Brain Research Reviews, 46*, 310–314.

Cervone, D. (1991). The two disciplines of personality psychology. *Psychological Science, 6*, 371–377.

Cervone, D. (1997). Social-cognitive mechanisms and personality coherence: Self-knowledge, situational beliefs, and cross-situational coherence in perceived self-efficacy. *Psychological Science, 8*, 43–50.

Cervone, D. (1999). Bottom-up explanation in personality psychology: The case of cross-situational coherence. In D. Cervone & Y. Shoda (Eds.), *The coherence of personality: Social-cognitive bases of personality consistency, variability, and organization* (pp. 303–341). New York: Guilford Press.

Cervone, D. (2004). The architecture of personality. *Psychological Review, 111*, 183–204.

Cervone, D. (2008). Explanatory models of personality: Social-cognitive theories and the knowledge-and-appraisal model of personality architecture. In Boyle, G. J., Matthews, G., & Saklofske, D. H. (Eds.), *The Sage handbook of personality theory and assessment* (pp. 80–100). London: Sage Publications.

Cervone, D. (2008). Explanatory models of personality: Social-cognitive theories and the knowledge-and-appraisal model of personality architecture. In G. Boyle, G. Matthews, & D. Saklofske (Eds.), *Handbook of personality and testing* (pp. 80–100). London: Sage Publications.

Cervone, D., Caldwell, T. L., & Orom, H. (2008). Beyond person and situation effects: Intraindividual personality architecture and its implications for the study of personality and social behavior. In A. Kruglanski & J. Forgas (Series Eds.) & F. Rhodewalt (Volume Ed.), *Frontiers of social psychology: Personality and social behavior* (pp. 9–48). New York: Psychology Press.

Cervone, D., & Caprara, G. V. (2001). Personality assessment. In N. J. Smelser & P. B. Baltes (Eds.), *International encyclopedia of the social and behavioral sciences* (pp. 11281–11287). Oxford, UK: Elsevier.

Cervone, D., Kopp, D. A., Schaumann, L., & Scott, W. D. (1994). Mood, self-efficacy, and performance standards: Lower moods induce higher standards for performance. *Journal of Personality and Social Psychology, 67*, 499–512.

Cervone, D., & Mischel, W. (2002). Personality science. In D. Cervone & W. Mischel (Eds.), *Advances in personality science* (pp. 1–26). New York: Guilford Press.

Cervone, D., Orom, H., Artistico, D., Shadel, W. G., & Kassel, J. (2007). Using a knowledge-and-appraisal model of personality architecture to understand consistency and variability in smokers' self-efficacy appraisals in high-risk situations. *Psychology of Addictive Behaviors, 21*, 44–54.

Cervone, D., & Peake, P. K. (1986). Anchoring, efficacy, and action: The influence of judgmental heuristics on self-efficacy judgments and behavior. *Journal of Personality and Social Psychology, 50*, 492–501.

Cervone, D., & Scott, W. D. (1995). Self-efficacy theory of behavioral change: Foundations, conceptual issues, and therapeutic implications. In W. O'Donohue & L. Krasner (Eds.), *Theories in behavior therapy.* Washington, DC: American Psychological Association.

Cervone, D., & Shadel, W. G. (2003). Idiographic methods. In R. Ferdandez-Ballasteros (Ed.), *Encyclopedia of psychological assessment* (pp. 456–461). London: Sage.

Cervone, D., Shadel, W. G., & Jencius, S. (2001). Social-cognitive theory of personality assessment. *Personality and Social Psychology Review, 5*, 33–51.

Cervone, D., Shadel, W. G., Smith, R. E., & Fiori, M. (2006). Self-regulation: Reminders and suggestions from personality science. *Applied Psychology: An International Review, 55*, 333–385.

Cervone, D., & Shoda, Y. (Eds.). (1999b). *The coherence of personality: Social-cognitive bases of consistency, variability, and organization.* New York: Guilford Press.

Cervone, D., & Little, B. R. (in press). Personality architecture and dynamics: The new agenda, and what's new about it. Special issue, *Personality and Individual Differences: Dynamic Personality Psychology.*

Cervone, D., & Williams, S. L. (1992). Social cognitive theory and personality. In G. Caprara & G. L. Van Heck (Eds.), *Modern personality psychology* (pp. 200–252). New York: Harvester Wheatsheaf.

Champagne, F. A. (2018). Social and behavioral epigenetics: Evolving perspectives on nature-nurture interplay, plasticity, and inheritance. In M. Meloni, J. Cromby, D. Fitzgerald, & S. Lloyd (Eds.), *The Palgrave Handbook of Biology and Society* (pp. 227–250). London: Palgrave Macmillan.

Chan, W., McCrae, R. R., De Fruyt, F., Jussim, L., Lockenhoff, C. E., De Bolle, M., ..., Terracciano, A. (2012). Stereotypes of age differences in personality traits Universal and accurate? *Journal of Personality and Social Psychology, 103*, 1050–1066.

Chaplin, W. F., John, O. P., & Goldberg, L. R. (1988). Conceptions of states and traits: Dimensional attributes with ideals as prototypes. *Journal of Personality and Social Psychology, 54*, 541–557.

Chase, M. A., Magyar, M. T., & Drake, B. M. (2005). Fear of injury in gymnastics: Self-efficacy and psychological strategies to keep on tumbling. *Journal of Sports Sciences, 23*, 465–475.

Chen, S., Boucher, H. C., & Parker-Tapias, M. (2006). The relational self revealed: Integrative conceptualization and implications for interpersonal life. *Psychological Bulletin, 132*, 151–179.

Cheng, C., Wang, F., & Golden, D. L. (2011). Unpacking cultural differences in interpersonal flexibility: Role of culture-related personality and situational factors. *Journal of Cross-Cultural Psychology, 42*, 425–444.

Cheung, F. M., Leung, K., Fan, R. M., Song, W. Z., Zhang, J. X., & Zhang, J. P. (1996). Development of the Chinese Personality Assessment Inventory. *Journal of Cross-Cultural Psychology, 27*, 181–199.

Chiao, J. Y., Harada, T., Komeda, H., Li, Z., Mano, Y., Saito, D., ..., Iidaka, T. (2009). Neural basis of individualistic and collectivistic views of self. *Human Brain Mapping, 30*, 2813–2820.

Chodorkoff, B. (1954). Self perception, perceptual defense, and adjustment. *Journal of Abnormal and Social Psychology, 49*, 508–512.

Chodron, T. (1990). *Open heart, clear mind.* Ithaca, NY: Snow Lion.

Chomsky, N. (1959). A review of B. F. Skinner's *Verbal Behavior. Language, 35*, 26–58.

Church, A. T. (2016). Personality traits across cultures. *Current Opinion in Psychology*, *8*, 22–30.

Churchland, P. S. (2002). *Brain-wise: Studies in neurophilosophy*. Cambridge, MA: MIT Press.

Clark, L. A., & Watson, D. (1999). Temperament: A new paradigm for trait psychology. In L. A. Pervin & O. P. John (Eds.), *Handbook of personality: Theory and research* (pp. 399–423). New York: Guilford Press.

Clark, L. A., & Watson, D. (2008). Temperament: An organizing paradigm for trait psychology. In O. P. John, R. W. Robins, & L. A. Pervin (Eds.), *Handbook of personality: Theory and research* (pp. 265–286). New York: Guilford Press.

Cloninger, C. R., Svrakic, D. M., & Przbeck, T. R. (1993). A psychobiological model of temperament and character. *Archives of General Psychiatry*, *50*, 975–990.

Collins, M. D., Jackson, C. J., Walker, B. R., O'Connor, P. J., & Gardiner, E. (2017). Integrating the context-appropriate balanced attention model and reinforcement sensitivity theory: Towards a domain-general personality process model. *Psychological Bulletin*, *143*, 91–106.

Colvin, C. R. (1993). "Judgable" people: Personality, behavior, and competing explanations. *Journal of Personality and Social Psychology*, *64*, 861–873.

Coan, J. A. (2010). Adult attachment and the brain. *Journal of Social and Personal Relationships*, *27*, 210–217.

Colvin, C. R. (1993). Judgable people: Personality, behavior, and competing explanations. *Journal of Personality and Social Psychology*, *64*, 861–873.

Colvin, C. R., & Block, J. (1994). Do positive illusions foster mental health? An examination of the Taylor and Brown formulation. *Psychological Bulletin*, *116*, 3–20.

Colzato, L. S., Slagter, H. A., Van Den Wildenberg, W. P. M., & Hommel, B. (2009). Closing one's eyes to reality: Evidence for a dopaminergic basis of psychoticism from spontaneous eye blink rates. *Personality and Individual Differences*, *46*, 377–380.

Connelly, B. S., & Ones, D. S. (2010). Another perspective on personality: Meta-analytic integration of observers' accuracy and predictive validity. *Psychological Bulletin*, *136*, 1092–1122.

Contrada, R. J., Czarnecki, E. M., & Pan, R. L. (1997). Health-damaging personality traits and verbal-autonomic dissociation: The role of self-control and environmental control. *Health Psychology*, *16*, 451–457.

Contrada, R. J., Leventhal, H., & O'leary, A. (1990). Personality and health. In L. A. Pervin (Ed.), *Handbook of personality: Theory and research* (pp. 638–669). New York: Guilford Press.

Conway, M. A., & Pleydell-Pearce, C. W. (2000). The construction of autobiographical memories in the self memory system. *Psychological Review*, *107*, 261–288.

Cooper, M. L. (2002). Personality and close relationships: Embedding people in important social contexts. *Journal of Personality*, *70*, 757–782.

Cooper, R. M., & Zubek, J. P. (1958). Effects of enriched and restricted early environments on the learning ability of bright and dull rats. *Canadian Journal of Psychology*, *12*, 159–164.

Coopersmith, S. (1967). *The antecedents of self-esteem*. San Francisco: Freeman.

Cosmides, L. (1989). The logic of social exchange: Has natural selection shaped how humans reason? Studies with the Wason selection task. *Cognition*, *31*, 187–276.

Costa, P. T., Jr., & McCrae, R. R. (1985). *The NEO personality inventory manual*. Odessa, FL: Psychological Assessment Resources.

Costa, P. T., Jr., & McCrae, R. R. (1989). *The NEOPI/ NEO-FFI manual supplement*. Odessa, FL: Psychological Assessment Resources.

Costa, P. T., Jr., & McCrae, R. R. (1992). *NEO-PI-R: Professional manual*. Odessa, FL: Psychological Assessment Resources.

Costa, P. T., Jr., & McCrae, R. R. (1994). Stability and change in personality from adolescence through adulthood. In C. F. Halverson Jr., G. A. Kohnstamm, & Roy P. Martin (Eds.), *The developing structure of temperament and personality from infancy to adulthood* (pp. 139–155). Hillsdale, NJ: Erlbaum.

Costa, P. T., Jr., & McCrae, R. R. (1995). Primary traits of Eysenck's PEN system: Three- and five-factor solutions. *Journal of Personality and Social Psychology*, *69*, 308–317.

Costa, P. T. Jr., & McCrae, R. R. (2002). Looking backward: Changes in the mean levels of personality traits from 80 to 12. In D. Cervone & W. Mischel (Eds.), *Advances in personality science* (pp. 219–237). New York: Guilford Press.

Costa, P. T., & Widiger, T. A. (Eds.). (1994). *Personality disorders and the five factor model of personality*. Washington, DC: American Psychological Association.

Costa, P. T. Jr., & Widiger, T. A. (2001). *Personality disorders and the five-factor model of personality* (2nd ed.). Washington, DC: American Psychological Association.

Cox, T., & Mackay, C. (1982). Psychosocial factors and psychophysiological mechanisms in the etiology and development of cancer. *Social Science and Medicine, 16,* 381–396.

Cox, W. M., & Klinger, E. (2011). *Handbook of motivational counseling: Goal-based approaches to assessment and intervention with addiction and other problems*. West Sussex, UK: John Wiley & Sons.

Cozzarelli, C. (1993). Personality and self-efficacy as predictors of coping with abortion. *Journal of Personality and Social Psychology, 65,* 1224–1236.

Crews, F. (1993, November 18). The unknown Freud. *The New York Review of Books,* 55–66.

Crews, F. (1998). (Ed.). *Unauthorized Freud: Doubters confront a legend*. New York: Penguin Books.

Crocker, J., & Knight, K. M. (2005). Contingencies of self-worth. *Current Directions in Psychological Science, 14,* 200–203.

Crocker, J., Sommers, S. R., & Luhtanen, R. K. (2002). Hopes dashed and dreams fulfilled: Contingencies of self-worth and graduate school admissions. *Personality and Social Psychology Bulletin, 28,* 1275–1286.

Crocker, J., & Wolfe, C. T. (2001). Contingencies of self-worth. *Psychological Review, 108,* 593–623.

Crockett, W. H. (1982). The organization of construct systems: The organization corollary. In J. C. Mancuso & J. R. Adams-Webber (Eds.), *The construing person* (pp. 62–95). New York: Praeger.

Cronbach, L. J., & Meehl, P. E. (1955). Construct validity in psychological tests. *Psychological Bulletin, 52,* 281–302.

Cross, H. J. (1966). The relationship of parental training conditions to conceptual level in adolescent boys. *Journal of Personality, 34,* 348–365.

Cross, S. E., & Markus, H. R. (1999). The cultural constitution of personality. In L. A. Pervin & O. P. John (Eds.), *Handbook of personality: Theory and research* (2nd ed., pp. 378–396). New York: Guilford Press.

Csikszentmihalyi, M. (1990). *Flow: The psychology of optimal experience*. New York: Harper & Row.

Curtis, R. C., & Miller, K. (1986). Believing another likes or dislikes you: Behaviors making the beliefs come true. *Journal of Personality and Social Psychology, 51,* 284–290.

Cyranowski, J. M., & Andersen, B. L. (1998). Schemas, sexuality, and romantic attachment. *Journal of Personality and Social Psychology, 74,* 1364–1379.

Dabbs, J. M., Jr. (2000). *Heroes, rogues and lovers: Out-croppings of testosterone*. New York: McGraw-Hill.

Damasio, A. R. (1994). *Descartes' error*. New York: Avon.

Danner, D. D., Snowdon, D. A., & Friesen, W. V. (2001). Positive emotions in early life and longevity: Findings from the nun study. *Journal of Personality and Social Psychology, 80,* 804–813.

D'Argembeau, A., Feyers, D., Majerus, S., Collette, F., Van Der Linden, M., Maquet, P., & Salmon, E. (2008). Self-reflection across time: Cortical midline structures differentiate between present and past selves. *Social Cognitive and Affective Neuroscience, 3,* 244–252.

D'Argembeau, A., Stawarczyk, D., Majerus, S., Collette, F., Van Der Linden, M., Feyers, D., Maquet, P., Salmon, E. (2010). The neural basis of personal goal processing when envisioning future events. *Journal of Cognitive Neuroscience, 22,* 1701–1713.

D'Argembeau, A., Stawarczyk, D., Majerus, S., Collette, F., Van Der Linden, M., & Salmon, E. (2010). Modulation of medial prefrontal and inferior parietal cortices when thinking about past, present, and future selves. *Social Neuroscience, 5,* 187–200.

Darley, J. M., & Fazio, R. (1980). Expectancy confirmation processes arising in the social interaction sequence. *American Psychologist, 35,* 867–881.

Darwin, C. (1859). *The origin of the species*. London: Murray.

Darwin, C. (1872). *The expression of the emotions in man and animals*. London: Murray.

Davidson, R. J. (1994). Asymmetric brain function, affective style, and psychopathology. *Development and Psychopathology, 66*, 486–498.

Davidson, R. J. (1995). Cerebral asymmetry, emotion, and affective style. In R. J. Davidson & K. Hugdahl (Eds.), *Brain asymmetry* (pp. 361–387). Cambridge, MA: Massachusetts Institute of Technology.

Davidson, R. J. (1998). Affective style and affective disorders: Perspectives from affective neuroscience. *Cognition and Emotion, 12*, 307–330.

Davidson, R. J., & Fox, N. A. (1989). Frontal brain asymmetry predicts infants' response to maternal separation. *Journal of Abnormal Psychology, 98*, 127–131.

Dawes, R. M. (1994). *House of cards: Psychology and psychotherapy built on myth*. New York: The Free Press.

Deci, E. L., & Ryan, R. M. (2012a). Motivation, personality, and development within embedded social contexts: An overview of self-determination theory. In R. M. Ryan (Ed.), *The Oxford handbook of motivation* (pp. 85–107). New York: Oxford.

Deci, E. L., & Ryan, R. M. (2012b). Self-determination theory. In P. A. M. van Lange, A. Kruglanski, & E. T. Higgins (Eds.), *Handbook of theories of social psychology* (Vol. 1, pp. 416–437). Thousand Oaks, CA: Sage.

De Fruyt, F., & Salgado, J. F. (Eds.). (2003). Personality and industrial, work and organizational applications. *European Journal of Personality, 17* (whole issue).

De Fruyt, F., Wiele, L. V., & Van Heeringen, C. (2000). Cloninger's psychobiological model of temperament and character and the five-factor model of personality. *Personality and Individual Differences, 29*, 441–452.

De La Ronde, C., & Swann, W. B., Jr. (1998). Partner verification: Restoring shattered images of our intimates. *Journal of Personality and Social Psychology, 75*, 374–382.

Denes-Raj, V., & Epstein, S. (1994). Conflict between intuitive and rational processing: When people behave against their better judgment. *Journal of Personality and Social Psychology, 66*, 819–829.

Denollet, J., Martens, E. J., Nyklíček, I., Conraads, V. M., & De Gelder, B. (2008). Clinical events in coronary patients who report low distress: Adverse effect of repressive coping. *Health Psychology, 27*, 302–308.

Depue, R. A. (1995). Neurobiological factors in personality and depression. *European Journal of Personality, 9*, 413–439.

Depue, R. A. (1996). A neurobiological framework for the structure of personality and emotion: Implications for personality disorders. In J. Clarkin & M. Lenzenweger (Eds.), *Major theories of personality disorders* (pp. 347–390). New York: Guilford Press.

Depue, R. A., & Collins, P. F. (1999). Neurobiology of the structure of personality: Dopamine, facilitation of incentive motivation, and extraversion. *Behavioral and Brain Sciences, 22*, 491–517.

De Raad, B. (2005). Situations that matter to personality. In A. Eliasz, S. E. Hampson, & B. de Raad (Eds.), *Advances in personality psychology* (Vol. 2, pp. 179–204). Philadelphia, PA: Psychology Press.

De Raad, B., & Peabody, D. (2005). Cross-culturally recurrent personality factors: Analyses of three factors. *European Journal of Personality, 19*, 451–474.

de Raad, B., & Mlačić, B. (2017). The lexical foundation of the Big Five model. In T. W. Widiger (Ed.), *The Oxford Handbook of the Five Factor Model* (pp. 191–216). New York: Oxford University Press.

Derakshan, N., & Eysenck, M. W. (1997). Interpretive biases for one's own behavior and physiology in high-trait-anxious individuals and repressors. *Journal of Personality and Social Psychology, 73*, 816–825.

Desteno, D., Bartlett, M. Y., Braverman, J., & Sa-Lovey, P. (2002). Sex differences in jealousy: Evolutionary mechanism or artifact of measurement? *Journal of Personality and Social Psychology, 83*, 1103–1116.

Dewsbury, D. A. (1997). In celebration of the centennial of Ivan P. Pavlov's (1897/1902). *The Work of the Digestive Glands. American Psychologist, 52*, 933–935.

Deyoung, C. G., Hirsh, J. B., Shane, M. S., Papademetris, X., Rajeevan, N., Gray, J. R. (2010). Testing predictions from personality neuroscience: Brain structure and the Big Five. *Psychological Science, 21*, 820–828.

Di Blas, L., & Forzi, M. (1999). Refining a descriptive structure of personality attributes in the Italian language: The abridged big three circumplex structure. *Journal of Personality and Social Psychology, 76*, 451–481.

Di Blas, L., Grassi, M., Carnaghi, A., Ferrante, D., & Calarco, D. (2017). Within-person and between-people variability in personality dynamics: Knowledge structures, self-efficacy, pleasure appraisals, and the Big Five. *Journal of Research in Personality, 70*, 84–92.

Dobson, K. S., & Shaw, B. F. (1995). Cognitive therapies in practice. In B. Bongar & L. E. Bentler (Eds.), *Comprehensive textbook of psychotherapy* (pp. 159–172). New York: Oxford University Press.

Dolnick, E. (1998). *Madness on the couch: Blaming the victim in the heyday of psychoanalysis.* New York: Simon & Schuster.

Domjan, M. (2005). Pavlovian conditioning: A functional perspective. *Annual Review of Psychology, 56*, 179–206.

Donahue, E. M. (1994). Do children use the Big Five, too? Content and structural form in personality descriptions. *Journal of Personality, 62*, 45–66.

Downey, G., & Feldman, S. I. (1996). Implications of rejection sensitivity for intimate relationships. *Journal of Personality and Social Psychology, 70*, 1327–1343.

Downey, G., Freitas, A. L., Michaelis, B., & Khouri, H. (1998). The self-fulfilling prophecy in close relationships: Rejection sensitivity and rejection by romantic partners. *Journal of Personality and Social Psychology, 75*, 545–560.

Downey, G., Mougios, V., Ayduk, O., London, B. E., & Shoda, Y. (2004). Rejection sensitivity and the defensive motivational system: Insights from the startle response to rejection cues. *Psychological Science, 15*, 668–673.

Draganski, B., Gaser, C., Busch, V., Schuierer, G., Bogdahn, I., & May, A. (2004). Changes in grey matter induced by training. *Nature, 427*, 311–312.

Dunning, D., Heath, C., & Suls, J. M. (2004). Flawed self-assessment: Implications for health, education, and the workplace. *Psychological Science in the Public Interest, 5*, 69–106.

Duck, S. (1982). Two individuals in search of agreement: The commonality corollary. In J. C. Mancuso & J. R. Adams-Webber (Eds.), *The construing person* (pp. 222–234). New York: Praeger.

Duckworth, A. L. (2011). The significance of self-control. *Proceedings of the National Academy of Sciences, 108*, 2639–2640.

Duckworth, A. L., & Carlson, S. M. (in press). Self-regulation and school success. In .W. Sokol, F. M. E. Grouzet, & U. Miller (Eds.), *Self-regulation and autonomy.* New York: Cambridge University Press.

Duckworth, A. L., & Kern, M. L. (2011). A meta-analysis of the convergent validity of self-control measures. *Journal of Research in Personality, 45*, 259–268.

Duckworth, A. L., Tsukayama, E., & Kirby, T. A. (2013). Is it really self-control? Examining the predictive power of the delay of gratification task. *Personality and Social Psychology Bulletin, 39*, 843–855.

Dunn, J., & Plomin, R. (1990). *Separate lives: Why siblings are so different.* New York: Basic Books.

Dutton, K. A., & Brown, J. D. (1997). Global self esteem and specific self-views as determinants of people's reactions to success and failure. *Journal of Personality and Social Psychology, 73*, 139–148.

Dweck, C. S. (1991). Self-theories and goals: Their role in motivation, personality, and development. In R. D. Dienstbier (Ed.), *Nebraska Symposium on Motivation* (pp. 199–235). Lincoln: University of Nebraska Press.

Dweck, C. S. (1999). *Self-theories: Their role in motivation, personality, and development.* Philadelphia: Psychology Press/Taylor & Francis.

Dweck, C. S. (2008). Can personality be changed? *Current Directions in Psychological Science, 17*, 391–394.

Dweck, C. S. (2012). Implicit theories. Implicit theories. In P. A. M. van Lange, A. Kruglanski, & E. T. Higgins (Eds.), *Handbook of theories of social psychology* (Vol. 2, pp. 43–62). Washington, DC: Sage.

Dweck, C. (2017). From needs to goals and representations: Foundations for a unified theory of motivation, personality, and development. *Psychological Review, 124*, 689–719.

Dweck, C. S., Chiu, C., & Hong, Y. (1995). Implicit theories and their role in judgments and reactions: A world from two perspectives. *Psychological Inquiry, 6*, 267–285.

Dweck, C. S., Higgins, E. T., & Grant-Pillow, H. (2003). Self-systems give unique meaning to self variables. In M. R. Leary & J. P. Tangney (Eds.), *Handbook of self and identity* (pp. 239–252). New York: Guilford Press.

Dweck, C. S., & Leggett, E. (1988). A social-cognitive approach to motivation in personality. *Psychological Review*, *95*, 256–273.

Dykman, B. M. (1998). Integrating cognitive and motivational factors in depression: Initial tests of a goal orientation approach. *Journal of Personality and Social Psychology*, *74*, 139–158.

Eagle, M., Wolitzky, D. L., & Klein, G. S. (1966). Imagery: Effect of a concealed figure in a stimulus. *Science*, *18*, 837–839.

Eagly, A. H., & Wood, W. (1999). The origins of sex differences in human behavior. *American Psychologist*, *54*, 408–423.

Ebstein, R. P., Novick, O., Umansky, R., Priel, B., Os-Her, Y., Blaine, D., ... Belmaker, R. H. (1996). Dopamine D4 receptor (D4DR) exon III polymorphism associated with the human personality trait of novelty seeking. *Nature Genetics*, *12*, 78–80.

The Economist. (2005). *Pocket world in figures* (2005 Ed.). London: Profile Books.

Edelman, G. M., & Tononi, G. (2000). *A universe of consciousness: How matter becomes imagination*. New York: Basic Books.

Edelson, M. (1984). *Hypothesis and evidence in psychoanalysis*. Chicago: University of Chicago Press.

Ekman, P. (1993). Facial expression and emotion. *American Psychologist*, *48*, 384–392.

Ekman, P. (1994). Strong evidence for universals in facial expressions: A reply to Russell's mistaken critique. *Psychological Bulletin*, *115*, 268–287.

Ekman, P. (Ed.). (1998). *Third edition of Charles Darwin: The expression of emotions in man and animals*. New York: Oxford University Press.

Elfenbein, H. A., Barsade, S. G., & Eisenkraft, N. (2015). The social perception of emotional abilities: Expanding what we know about observer ratings of emotional intelligence. *Emotion*, *15*(1), 17–34.

Elliot, A. J., & Dweck, C. S. (1988). Goals: An approach to motivation and achievement. *Journal of Personality and Social Psychology*, *54*, 5–12.

Elliot, A. J., & Sheldon, K. M. (1998). Avoidance personal goals and the personality-illness relationship. *Journal of Personality and Social Psychology*, *75*, 1282–1299.

Elliot, A. J., Sheldon, K. M., & Church, M. A. (1997). Avoidance personal goals and subjective well-being. *Personality and Social Psychology Bulletin*, *9*, 915–927.

Ellis, A. (1962). *Reason and emotion in psychotherapy*. Secaucus, NJ: Lyle Stuart.

Ellis, A. (1987). The impossibility of achieving consistently good mental health. *American Psychologist*, *42*, 364–375.

Ellis, A., & Harper, R. A. (1975). *A new guide to rational living*. North Hollywood, CA: Wilshire.

Ellis, A., & Tafrate, R. C. (1997). *How to control your anger before it controls you*. New York: Citadel Press.

Epstein, S. (1983). A research paradigm for the study of personality and emotions. In M. M. Page (Ed.), *Personality: Current theory and research* (pp. 91–154). Lincoln: University of Nebraska Press.

Epstein, S. (1992). The cognitive self, the psychoanalytic self, and the forgotten selves. *Psychological Inquiry*, *3*, 34–37.

Epstein, S. (1994). Integration of the cognitive and the psychodynamic unconscious. *American Psychologist*, *49*, 709–724.

Epting, F. R., & Eliot, M. (2006). A constructive understanding of the person: George Kelly and humanistic psychology. *The Humanistic Psychologist*, *34*, 21–37.

Erdelyi, M. (1985). *Psychoanalysis: Freud's cognitive psychology*. New York: Freeman.

Ericsson, K. A., & Simon, H. A. (1993). *Protocol analysis: Verbal reports as data*. Cambridge, MA: MIT Press.

Erikson, E. (1950). *Childhood and society*. New York: Norton.

Erikson, E. H. (1982). *The life cycle completed: A review*. New York: Norton.

Esterson, A. (1993). *Seductive mirage: An exploration of the work of Sigmund Freud*. New York: Open Court.

Evans, R. I. (1976). *The making of psychology*. New York: Knopf.

Ewart, C. K. (1992). The role of physical self-efficacy in recovery from heart attack. In R. Schwarzer (Ed.), *Self-efficacy: Thought control of action* (pp. 287–304). Washington, DC: Hemisphere.

Exner, J. E. (1986). *The Rorschach: A comprehensive system: Basic foundations* (Vol. 1, 2nd ed.). New York: Wiley.

Eysenck, H. J. (1970). *The structure of personality* (3rd ed.). London: Methuen

Eysenck, H. J. (1982). *Personality genetics and behavior*. New York: Praeger.

Eysenck, H. J. (1990). Biological dimensions of personality. In L. A. Pervin (Ed.), *Handbook of personality: Theory and research* (pp. 244–276). New York: Guilford Press.

Eysenck, H. J. (1998). *Intelligence: A new look*. London: Transaction Publishers.

Farber, I. E. (1964). A framework for the study of personality as a behavioral science. In P. Worchel & D. Byrne (Eds.), *Personality change* (pp. 3–37). New York: Wiley.

Ferster, C. B. (1973). A functional analysis of depression. *American Psychologist, 28*, 857–870.

Ferster, C. B., & Skinner, B. F. (1957). *Schedules of reinforcement*. New York: Appleton-Century-Crofts.

Fiske, S. T., & Taylor, S. E. (1991). *Social Cognition*. New York: McGraw-Hill.

Fleeson, W. (2001). Toward a structure- and process-integrated view of personality: Traits as density distributions of states. *Journal of Personality and Social Psychology, 80*, 1011–1027.

Fleeson, W., & Leicht, C. (2006). On delineating and integrating the study of variability and stability in personality psychology: Interpersonal trust as illustration. *Journal of Research in Personality, 40*, 5–20.

Fodor, J. A. (1983). *The modularity of mind: An essay on faculty psychology*. Cambridge, MA: MIT Press.

Forgas, J. (1995). Mood and judgment: The affect Infusion model. *Psychological Bulletin, 117*, 39–66.

Folkman, S., Lazarus, R. S., Gruen, R. J., & DeLongis, A. (1986). Appraisal, coping, health status, and psychological symptoms. *Journal of Personality and Social Psychology, 50*, 571–579.

Folkman, S., & Moskowitz, J. T. (2004). Coping: Pitfalls and promises. *Annual Review of Psychology, 55*, 745–774.

Fox, N. A., Henderson, H. A., Marshall, P. J., Nichols, K. E., & Ghera, M. A. (2005). Behavioral inhibition: Linking biology and behavior within a developmental framework. *Annual Review of Psychology, 56*, 235–262.

Fox, N. A., & Reeb-Sutherland, B. C. (2010). Biological moderators of infant temperament and its relation to social withdrawal. In K. H. Rubin & R. J. Coplan (Eds.), *The development of shyness and social withdrawal* (pp. 84–103). New York: Guilford Press.

Fraley, R. C. (2002). Attachment stability from infancy to adulthood: Meta-analysis and dynamic modeling of developmental mechanisms. *Personality and Social Psychology Review, 6*, 123–151.

Fraley, R. C. (2007). Using the Internet for personality research: What can be done, how to do it, and some concerns. In R. W. Robins, R. C. Fraley, & R. F. Krueger (Eds.), *Handbook of research methods in personality psychology* (pp. 130–148). New York: Guilford Press.

Fraley, R. C., & Roberts, B. W. (2005). Patterns of continuity: A dynamic model for conceptualizing the stability of individual differences in psychological constructs across the life course. *Psychological Review, 112*, 60–74.

Fraley, R. C., & Shaver, P. R. (1998). Airport separations: A naturalistic study of adult attachment dynamics in separating couples. *Journal of Personality and Social Psychology, 75*, 1198–1212.

Fraley, R. C., & Shaver, P. R. (2008). Attachment theory and its place in contemporary personality theory and research. In O. P. John, R. W. Robins, & L. A. Pervin (Eds.), *Handbook of personality: Theory and research* (pp. 518–541). New York: Guilford Press.

Fraley, R. C, & Spieker, S. J. (2003). Are infant attachment patterns continuously or categorically distributed? A taxometric analysis of strange situation behavior. *Developmental Psychology, 39*, 387–404.

Frankl, V. E. (1955). *The doctor and the soul*. New York: Knopf.

Frankl, V. E. (1958). On logotherapy and existential analysis. *American Journal of Psychoanalysis, 18*, 28–37.

Fredrickson, B. L. (2001). The role of positive emotions in positive psychology: The broaden-and-build theory of positive emotions. *American Psychologist, 56*, 218–226.

Fredrickson, B. L. (2009). *Positivity*. New York: Crown.

Freud, A. (1936). *The ego and the mechanisms of defense*. New York: International Universities Press.

Freud, S. (1915/1970). Instincts and their vicissitudes. In W. A. Russell (Ed.), *Milestones in motivation: Contributions to the psychology of drive and purpose* (pp. 324–331). New York: Appleton-Century-Crofts.

Freud, S. (1930/1949). *Civilization and its discontents*. London: Hogarth.

Freud, S. (1949). *Civilization and its discontents*. London: Hogarth Press. (Original Edition, 1930.)

Freund, A. M., & Baltes, P. B. (1998). Selection, optimization, and compensation as strategies of life management: Correlations with subjective indicators of successful aging. *Psychology and Aging, 13*, 531–543.

Friedman, H. S., & Kern, M. L. (2014). Personality, well-being, and health. *Annual Review of Psychology, 65*, 719–742.

Friedman, H. S., Tucker, J. S., Schwartz, J. E., Martin, L. R., Tomlinson-Keasy, C., Wingard, D. L., & Criqui, M. H. (1995b). Childhood conscientiousness and longevity: Health behaviors and cause of death. *Journal of Personality and Social Psychology, 68*, 696–703.

Friedman, H. S., Tucker, J. S., Schwartz, J. E., Tomlinson-Keasy, C., Martin, L. R., Wingard, D. L., & Criqui, M. H. (1995a). Psychosocial and behavioral predictors of longevity: The aging and death of the "Termites." *American Psychologist, 50*, 69–78.

Fromm, E. (1959). *Sigmund Freud's mission*. New York: Harper.

Fulton, A. (1999). *Apostles of Sartre: Existentialism in American 1945-1963*. Evanston, IL: Northwestern University Press.

Funder, D. C. (1995). On the accuracy of personality judgment: A realistic approach. *Psychological Review, 102*, 652–670.

Funder, D. C. (2008). Persons, situations, and person-situation interactions. In O. P. John, R. W. Robins, & L. A. Pervin (Eds.), *Handbook of personality: Theory and research* (pp. 568–582). New York: Guilford Press.

Funder, D. C., Kolar, D. C., & Blackman, M. C. (1995). Agreement among judges of personality: Interpersonal relations, similarity, and acquaintanceship. *Journal of Personality and Social Psychology, 69*, 656–672.

Funder, D. C., & Ozer, D. J. (1983). Behavior as a function of the situation. *Journal of Personality and Social Psychology, 44*, 107–112.

Gable, S. L., & Haidt, J. (2005). What (and why) is positive psychology? *Review of General Psychology, 9*, 103–110.

Gable, S. L., Reis, H. T., & Downey, G. (2003). He said, she said: A quasi-signal detection analysis of daily interactions between close relationship partners. *Psychological Science, 14*, 100–105.

Gaensbauer, T. J. (1982). The differentiation of discrete affects. *Psychoanalytic Study of the Child, 37*, 29–66.

Gailliot, M. T., Mead, N. L., & Baumeister, R. F. (2008). Self-regulation. In O. P. John, R. W. Robins, & L. A. Pervin (Eds.), *Handbook of personality: Theory and research* (pp. 472–491). New York: Guilford Press.

Galatzer-Levy, R. M., Bachrach, H., Skolnikoff, A., & Waldron, S., Jr. (2000). *Does psychoanalysis work?* New Haven: Yale University Press.

Gawronski, B., & De Houwer, J. (2014). Implicit measures in social and personality psychology. In H. T. Reis & C. M. Judd (Eds.), *Handbook of research methods in social and personality psychology* (2nd ed., 283–310). New York, NY: Cambridge University Press.

Gay, P. (1998). *Freud: A life for our time*. New York: Norton.

Geen, R. G. (1984). Preferred stimulation levels in introverts and extroverts: Effects on arousal and performance. *Journal of Personality and Social Psychology, 46*, 1303–1312.

Geen, R. G. (1997). Psychophysiological approaches to personality. In R. Hogan, J. A. Johnson, & S. R. Briggs (Eds.), *Handbook of personality psychology* (pp. 387–414). San Diego: Academic Press.

Geertz, C. (1973). *The interpretation of cultures*. New York: Basic Books.

Geertz, C. (2000). *Available light: Anthropological reflections on philosophical topics*. Princeton, NJ: Princeton University Press.

Geisler, C. (1986). The use of subliminal psychodynamic activation in the study of repression. *Journal of Personality and Social Psychology, 51*, 844–851.

Gerard, H. B., Kupper, D. A., & Nguyen, L. (1993). The causal link between depression and bulimia. In J. M. Masling & R. F. Bornstein (Eds.), *Psychoanalytic perspectives in psychopathology* (pp. 225–252). Washington, DC: American Psychological Association.

Giesler, R. B., Josephs, R. A., & Swann , W. B., Jr. (1996). Self-verification in clinical depression: The desire for negative evaluation. *Journal of Abnormal Psychology, 105*, 358–368.

Gladue, B. A., Boechler, M., & McCaul, D. D. (1989). Hormonal response to competition in human males. *Aggressive Behavior*, *15*, 409–422.

Goble, F. (1970). *The third force: The psychology of Abraham Maslow*. New York: Grossman.

Goldberg, L. R. (1990). An alternative "description of personality": The Big-Five factor structure. *Journal of Personality and Social Psychology*, *59*, 1216–1229.

Goldberg, L. (1992). The development of markers for the Big-Five factor structure. *Psychological Assessment*, *4*, 26–42.

Goldberg, L. R., & Rosolack, T. K. (1994). The Big Five factor structure as an integrative framework: An empirical comparison with Eysenck's P-E-N model. In C. F. Halverson Jr., G. A. Kohnstamm, & R. P. Martin (Eds.), *The developing structure of temperament and personality from infancy to adulthood* (pp. 7–35). New York: Erlbaum.

Goldsmith, H. H., & Campos, J. J. (1982). Toward a theory of infant temperament. In R. M. Emde & R. J. Harmon (Eds.), *The development of attachment and affiliative systems* (pp. 161–193). New York: Plenum.

Goldstein, K. (1939). *The organism*. New York: American Book.

González, R. J. (2017). Hacking the citizenry? Personality profiling, 'big data' and the election of Donald Trump. *Anthropology Today*, *33*, 9–12.

Gosling, S. D., & John, O. P. (1998, May). Personality dimensions in dogs, cats, and hyenas. Paper presented at the annual meeting of the American Psychological Society, Washington, DC.

Gosling, S. D., & John, O. P. (1999). Personality dimensions in nonhuman animals: A cross-species review. *Contemporary Directions in Psychological Science*, *8*, 69–75.

Gosling, S. D., John, O. P., Craik, K. H., & Robins, R. W. (1998). Do people know how they behave? Self reported act frequencies compared with online codings by observers. *Journal of Personality and Social Psychology*, *74*, 1337–1349.

Gosling, S. D., Ko, S. J., Mannarelli, T., & Morris, M. E. (2002). A room with a cue: Judgments of personality based on offices and bedrooms. *Journal of Personality and Social Psychology*, *82*, 379–398.

Gottlieb, G. (1998). Normally occurring environmental and behavioral influences on gene activity: From central dogma to probabilistic epigenesis. *Psychological Review*, *105*, 792–802.

Gould, E., Reeves, A. J., Graziano, M. S. A., & Gross, C. G. (1999). Neurogenesis in the neocortex of adult primates. *Science*, *286*, 548–552.

Grant, H., & Dweck, C. (1999). A goal analysis of personality and personality coherence. In D. Cervone & Y. Shoda (Eds.), *The coherence of personality: Social cognitive bases of consistency, variability, and organization* (pp. 345–371). New York: Guilford Press.

Gray, J. A. (1987). *The psychology of fear and stress*. Cambridge, UK: Cambridge University Press.

Gray, J. A. (1990). A critique of Eysenck's theory of personality. In H. J. Eysenck (Ed.), *A model for personality* (2nd ed.). Berlin: Springer-Verlag.

Gray, J. A. (1991). Neural systems, emotion and personality. In J. Madden IV (Ed.), *Neurobiology of learning, emotion and affect*. New York: Raven Press.

Gray, J. A. (1990). Brain systems that mediate both emotion and cognition. *Cognition & Emotion*, *4*, 269–288.

Gray, J. A. (1991). Neural systems, emotion and personality. In J. Madden IV (Ed.), *Neurobiology of learning, emotion, and affect* (pp. 273–306). New York: Raven Press.

Gray, J. A., & McNaughton, N. (2000). *The neuropsychology of anxiety: An enquiry into the functions of the septo-hipocampal system* (2nd ed.). Oxford, United Kingdom: Oxford University Press.

Greenberg, J., Solomon, S., & Arndt, J. (2008). A basic but uniquely human motivation: Terror management. In J. Shah (Ed.), *Handbook of motivation science* (pp. 114–134). New York: Guilford Press.

Greenberg, J. R., & Mitchell, S. A. (1983). *Object relations in psychoanalytic theory*. Cambridge, MA: Harvard University Press.

Greenwald, A. G., Banaji, M. R., Rudman, L. A., Farn-ham, S. D., Nosek, B. A., & Mellot, D. S. (2002). A unified theory of implicit attitudes, stereotypes, self-esteem, and self-concept. *Psychological Review*, *109*, 3–25.

Grice, J. W. (2004). Bridging the idiographic-nomothetic divide in ratings of self and others on the Big Five. *Journal of Personality*, *72*, 203–241.

Grice, J. W., Jackson, B. J., & McDaniel, B. L. (2006). Bridging the idiographic-nomothetic divide: A follow-up study. *Journal of Personality, 74*, 1191–1218.

Griffin, D., & Bartholomew, K. (1994). Models of the self and other: Fundamental dimensions underlying measures of adult attachment. *Journal of Personality and Social Psychology, 67*, 430–445.

Grigorenko, E. L. (2002). In search of the genetic engram of personality. In D. Cervone & W. Mischel (Eds.), *Advances in personality science* (pp. 29–82). New York: Guilford Press.

Groddeck, G. (1961). *The book of the it*. New York: Vintage. (Original Edition, 1923).

Grunbaum, A. (1984). *Foundations of psychoanalysis: A philosophical critique*. Berkeley: University of California Press.

Grunbaum, A. (1993). *Validation in the clinical theory of psychoanalysis: A study in the philosophy of psychoanalysis*. Madison, CT: International Universities Press.

Gurven, M., von Rueden, C., Massenkoff, M., & Kaplan, H. (2013). How universal is the Big Five? Testing the five-factor model of personality variation among forager-farmers in the Bolivian Andes. *Journal of Personality and Social Psychology, 104*, 354–370.

Haggbloom, S. J., Warnick, R., Warnick, J. E., Jones, V. K., Yarbrough, G. L., Russell, T. M., ... Monte, E. (2002). The 100 most eminent psychologists of the 20th century. *Review of General Psychology, 6*, 139–152.

Hall, C. S. (1954). *A primer of Freudian psychology*. New York: Mentor.

Halpern, J. (1977). Projection: A test of the psychoanalytic hypothesis. *Journal of Abnormal Psychology, 86*, 536–542.

Hamer, D. (1997). The search for personality genes: Adventures of a molecular biologist. *Current Directions in Psychological Science, 6*, 111–114.

Hamer, D., & Copeland, P. (1998). *Living with our genes*. New York: Doubleday.

Hampson, S. E., & Friedman, H. S. (2008). Personality and health: A lifespan perspective. In O. P. John, R. W. Robins, & L. A. Pervin (Eds.), *Handbook of personality: Theory and research* (pp. 770–794). New York: Guilford Press.

Hampson, S. E., Goldberg, S. E., Vogt, T. M., & Dubanoski, J. P. (2007). Mechanisms by which childhood personality traits influence adult health status: Educational attainment and healthy behaviors. *Health Psychology, 26*, 121–125.

Hankin, B. L., Fraley, R. C., & Abela, J. R. Z. (2005). Daily depression and cognitions about stress: Evidence for a trait like depressogenic cognitive style and the prediction of depressive symptoms in a prospective daily diary study. *Journal of Personality and Social Psychology, 88*, 673–685.

Harkness, A. R., & Lilienfeld, S. O. (1997). Individual differences science for treatment planning: Personality traits. *Psychological Assessment, 9*, 349–360.

Harmon-Jones, E. (2003). Clarifying the emotive functions of asymmetrical frontal cortical activity. *Psychophysiology, 40*, 838–848.

Harré, R. (1998). *The singular self: An introduction to the psychology of personhood*. London: Sage.

Harré, R., & Secord, P. F. (1972). *The explanation of social behaviour*. Oxford, UK: Blackwell.

Harrington, D. M., Block, J. H., & Block, J. (1987). Testing aspects of Carl Rogers's theory of creative environments: Child-rearing antecedents of creative potential in young adolescents. *Journal of Personality and Social Psychology, 52*, 851–856.

Harris, B. (1979). Whatever happened to Little Albert? *American Psychologist, 34*, 151–160.

Harris, C. R. (2000). Psychophysiological responses to imagined infidelity: The specific innate modular view of jealousy reconsidered. *Journal of Personality and Social Psychology, 78*, 1082–1091.

Harris, C. R. (2002). Sexual and romantic jealousy in heterosexual and homosexual adults. *Psychological Science, 13*, 7–12.

Harris, J. R. (1995). Where is the child's environment? A group socialization theory of development. *Psychological Review, 102*, 458–489.

Harris, J. R. (2000). Context-specific learning, personality, and birth order. *Current Directions in Psychological Science, 9*, 174–177.

Harter, S. (2012). *The construction of the self* (2nd ed.), *Developmental and sociocultural foundations*. New York: Guilford Press.

Hartshorne, H., & May, M. A. (1928). *Studies in the nature of character. Vol. 1: Studies in deceit*. New York: Macmillan.

Hawkins , R. P., Peterson, R. F., Schweid, E., & Bijou, S. W. (1966). Behavior therapy in the home: Amelioration of problem parent-child relations with the parent in a therapeutic role. *Journal of Experimental Child Psychology*, *4*, 99–107.

Hayden, B. C. (1982). Experience—A case for possible change: The modulation corollary. In J. C. Mancuso & J. R. Adams-Webber (Eds.), *The construing person* (pp. 170–197). New York: Praeger.

Hazan, C., & Shaver, P. (1987). Romantic love conceptualized as an attachment process. *Journal of Personality and Social Psychology*, *52*, 511–524.

Hazan, C., & Shaver, P. (1990). Love and work: An attachment-theoretical perspective. *Journal of Personality and Social Psychology*, *59*, 270–280.

Heilbroner, R. L. (1986). *The worldly philosophers: The lives, times and ideas of the great economic thinkers*. New York: Simon and Schuster.

Heimpel, S. A., Wood, J. V., Marshall, M. A., & Brown, J. D. (2002). Do people with low self-esteem really want to feel better? Self-esteem differences in motivation to repair negative moods. *Journal of Personality and Social Psychology*, *82*, 128–147.

Heine, S. J., Lehman, D. R., Markus, H. R., & Kitayama, S. (1999). Is there a universal need for positive self-regard? *Psychological Review*, *106*, 766–794.

Heller, W., Schmidtke, J. I., Nitschke, J. B., Koven, N. S., & Miller, G. A. (2002). States, traits, and symptoms: Investigating the neural correlates of emotion, personality, and psychopathology. In D. Cervone & W. Mischel (Eds.), *Advances in personality science* (pp. 106–126). New York: Guilford Press.

Helson, R., & Kwan, V. S. Y. (2000). Personality change in adulthood: The broad picture and processes in one longitudinal study. In S. Hampson (Ed.), *Advances in personality psychology* (Vol. 1, pp. 77–106). East Sussex, UK: Psychology Press, Ltd.

Helson, R., Kwan, V. S. Y., John, O. P., & Jones, C. (2002). The growth of evidence for personality change in adulthood: Findings from research with personality inventories. *Journal of Research in Personality*, *36*, 287–306.

Hermans, H. J. M. (2001). The construction of a personal position repertoire: Method and practice. *Culture and Psychology*, *7*, 323–365.

Hesse, B. W. (2018). Can psychology walk the walk of open science? *American Psychologist*, *73*, 126–137.

Hesse, H. (1951). *Siddhartha*. New York: New Directions.

Higgins, E. T. (1987). Self-discrepancy: A theory relating self and affect. *Psychological Review*, *94*, 319–340.

Higgins, E. T. (1996). Knowledge activation: Accessibility, applicability, and salience. In E. T. Higgins & A. W. Kruglanski (Eds.), *Social psychology: Handbook of basic principles* (pp. 133–168). New York: Guilford Press.

Higgins, E. T. (1999). Persons and situations: Unique explanatory principles or variability in general principles? In D. Cervone & Y. Shoda (Eds.), *The coherence of personality* (pp. 61–93). New York: Guilford Press.

Higgins, E. T. (2006). Value from regulatory fit. *Current Directions in Psychological Science*, *14*, 209–213.

Higgins, E. T. (2012). Regulatory focus theory. In P. A. M. van Lane, A. Kruglanski, & E. T. Higgins (Eds.), *Handbook of theories of social psychology* (Vol. 1, pp. 483–505). Los Angeles, CA: Sage.

Higgins, E. T. (2014). Promotion and prevention: How "O" can create dual motivational forces. In J. W. Sherman, B. Gawronski, & Y. Trope (Eds.), *Dual process theories of the social mind* (pp. 325–348). New York: Guilford.

Higgins, E. T., Bond, R. N., Klein, R., & Strauman, T. (1986). Self-discrepancies and emotional vulnerability: How magnitude, accessibility, and type of discrepancy influence affect. *Journal of Personality and Social Psychology*, *51*, 5–15.

Higgins, E. T., & King, G. A. (1981). Accessibility of social constructs: Information processing consequences of individual and contextual variability. In N. Cantor & J. F. Kihlstrom (Eds.), *Personality, cognition, and social interaction* (pp. 69–121). Hillsdale, NJ: Erlbaum.

Higgins, E. T., King, G. A., & Mavin, G. H. (1982). Individual construct accessibility and subjective impressions and recall. *Journal of Personality and Social Psychology*, *43*, 35–47.

Higgins, E. T., & Scholer, A. A. (2008). When is personality revealed?: A motivated cognition approach. In O. P. John, R. W. Robins, & L. A. Pervin (Eds.), *Handbook of personality: Theory and research* (pp. 182–207). New York: Guilford Press.

Hilimire, M. R., Mayberg, H. S., Holtzheimer, P. E., Broadway, J. M., Parks, N. A., DeVylder, J. E., & Corballis, P. M. (2015). Effects of subcallosal cingulate deep brain stimulation on negative self-bias in patients with treatment-resistant depression. *Brain Stimulation, 8,* 185–91.

Hofmann, S. G., Moscovitch, D. A., Litz, B. T., Kim, H. J., Davis, L. L., & Pizzagalli, D. A. (2005). The worried mind: Autonomic and prefrontal activation during worrying. *Emotion, 5,* 464–475.

Hofstee, W. K. B. (1994). Who should own the definition of personality? *European Journal of Personality, 8,* 149–162.

Hogan, J., & Ones, D. S. (1997). Conscientiousness and integrity at work. In R. Hogan, J. Johnson, & S. Briggs (Eds.), *Handbook of personality psychology* (pp. 849–870). San Diego, CA: Academic Press.

Holender, D. (1986). Semantic activation without conscious identification in dichotic listening, paraforeal vision, and visual masking: A survey and appraisal. *Behavioral and Brain Sciences, 9,* 1–66.

Holland, J. H. (2014). *Complexity: A very short introduction.* Oxford: Oxford University Press.

Hollon, S. D., & Kendall, P. C. (1980). Cognitive self statements in depression: Development of an automatic thoughts questionnaire. *Cognitive Therapy and Research, 4,* 383–395.

Holmes, D. S. (1981). The evidence for repression: An examination of sixty years of research. In J. L. Singer (Ed.), *Regression and dissociation: Implications for personality theory, psychopathology, and health* (pp. 85–102). Chicago: University of Chicago Press.

Hong, Y., Morris, M. W., Chiu, C., & Martinez, V. (2000). Multicultural minds: A dynamic constructivist approach to culture and cognition. *American Psychologist, 55,* 709–720.

Hough, L. M., & Oswald, F. L. (2000). Personal selection: Looking toward the future—Remembering the past. *Annual Review of Psychology, 51,* 631–664.

Huesmann, L. R., Eron, L. D., & Dubow, E. F. (2002). Childhood predictors of adult criminality: Are all risk factors reflected in childhood aggressiveness? *Criminal Behaviour and Mental Health, 12,* 185–208.

Huesmann, L. R., Moise-Titus, J., Podolski, C., & Eron, L. D. (2003). Longitudinal relations between children's exposure to TV violence and their aggressive and violent behavior in young adulthood: 1977–1992. *Developmental Psychology, 39,* 201–221.

Huprich, S. K., & Meyer, G. J. (2011). Introduction to the JPA Special Issue: Can the Psychodynamic Diagnostic Manual put the complex person back at the center-stage of personality assessment? *Journal of Personality Assessment, 93,* 109–111.

Hyman, S. (1999). Susceptibility and "second hits." In R. Conlan (Ed.), *States of mind* (pp. 24–28). New York: Wiley.

Iyengar, S. S., & Lepper, M. R. (1999). Rethinking the value of choice: A cultural perspective on intrinsic motivation. *Journal of Personality and Social Psychology, 76,* 349–366.

Izard, C. E. (1994). Innate and universal facial expressions: Evidence from developmental and cross-cultural research. *Psychological Bulletin, 115,* 288–299.

Jackson, D. N., & Paunonen, S. V. (1985). Construct validity and the predictability of behavior. *Journal of Personality and Social Psychology, 49,* 554–570.

Jacoby, L. L., Lindsay, D. S., & Toth, J. P. (1992). Unconscious influences revealed. *American Psychologist, 47,* 802–809.

James, W. (1890). *Principles of psychology.* New York: Holt.

Jankowicz, A. D. (1987). Whatever became of George Kelly? *American Psychologist, 42,* 481–487.

Jin, M. K., Jacobvitz, D., Hazan, N., & Hoon, S. (2012). Maternal sensitivity and infant attachment security in Korea: Cross-cultural validation of the Strange Situation. *Attachment and Human Development, 14,* 33–44.

John, O. P. (1990). The "Big Five" factor taxonomy: Dimensions of personality in the natural language and in questionnaires. In L. A. Pervin (Ed.), *Handbook of personality: Theory and research* (pp. 66–100). New York: Guilford Press.

John, O. P., Naumann, L. P., & Soto, C. J. (2008). Paradigm shift to the Big Five trait taxonomy: History, measurement, and conceptual issues. In O. P. John, R. W. Robins, & L. A. Pervin (Eds.), *Handbook of personality: Theory and research* (pp. 114–158). New York: Guilford Press.

John, O. P., & Robins, R. W. (1993). Gordon Allport: Father and critic of the five-factor model. In K. H. Craik, R. T. Hogan, & R. N. Wolfe (Eds.), *Fifty years of personality psychology* (pp. 215–236). New York: Plenum.

John, O. P., & Robins, R. W. (1994). Accuracy and bias in self-perception: Individual differences in self enhancement and the role of narcissism. *Journal of Personality and Social Psychology, 66*, 206–219.

John, O. P., & Srivastava, S. (1999). The Big Five: History, measurement, and development. In L. A. Pervin & O. P. John (Eds.), *Handbook of personality: Theory and research* (pp. 102–138). New York: Guilford Press.

Johnson, B., & Flores Mosri, D. (2016). The neuropsychoanalytic approach: Using neuroscience as the basic science of psychoanalysis. *Frontiers in Psychology, 7*, 1459.

Jones, A., & Crandall, R. (1986). Validation of a short index of self-actualization. *Personality and Social Psychology Bulletin, 12*, 63–73.

Jones, M. C. (1924). A laboratory study of fear. The case of Peter. *Pedagogical Seminar, 31*, 308–315.

Jourard, S. M., & Remy, R. M. (1955). Perceived parental attitudes, the self, and security. *Journal of Consulting Psychology, 19*, 364–366.

Jung, C. G. (1939). *The integration of the personality*. New York: Farrar & Rinehart.

Jung, C. G., & Collaborators. (1964). *Man and his symbols*. New York: Doubleday & Company.

Kagan, J. (1994). *Galen's prophecy: Temperament in human nature*. New York: Basic Books.

Kagan, J. (1998). *Three seductive ideas*. Cambridge, MA: Harvard University Press.

Kagan, J. (1999). Born to be shy? In R. Conlan (Ed.), *States of mind* (pp. 29–51). New York: Wiley.

Kagan, J. (2002). *Surprise, uncertainty, and mental structures*. Cambridge, MA: Harvard University Press.

Kagan, J. (2003). Biology, context, and developmental inquiry. *Annual Review of Psychology, 54*, 1–23.

Kagan, J. (2011). Three lessons learned. *Perspectives on Psychological Science, 6*, 107–113.

Kagan, J., Arcus, D., & Snidman, N. (1993). The idea of temperament: Where do we go from here? In R. Plomin & G. E. McClearn (Eds.), *Nature, nurture and psychology* (pp. 197–210). Washington, DC: American Psychological Association.

Kamin, L. J. (1974). *The science and politics of IQ*. Hillsdale, NJ: Erlbaum.

Kammrath, L. K., Mendoza-Denton, R., & Mischel, W. (2005). Incorporating if then ... personality signatures in person perception: Beyond the person-situation dichotomy. *Journal of Personality and Social Psychology, 88*, 605–618.

Kandel, E. R. (2000). Autobiography. Retrieved from http://www.nobel.se/medicine/laureates/2000/kandel-autobio.html. Accessed August 28, 2002.

Kanfer, F. H., & Saslow, G. (1965). Behavioral analysis: An alternative to diagnostic classification. *Archives of General Psychiatry, 12*, 519–538.

Kasser, T., & Ryan, R. M. (1996). Further examining the American dream: Differential correlates of intrinsic and extrinsic goals. *Personality and Social Psychology Bulletin, 22*, 280–287.

Kavanagh, D. (1992). Self-efficacy as a resource factor in stress appraisal processes. In R. Schwarzer (Ed.), *Self-efficacy: Thought control of action* (pp. 177–194). Washington, DC: Hemisphere.

Kazdin, A. E. (1977). *The token economy: A review and evaluation*. New York: Plenum.

Kehoe, E. G., Toomey, J. M., Balsters, J. H., & Bokde, A. L. W. (in press). Personality modulates the effects of emotional arousal and valence on brain activation. *Social Cognitive and Affective Neuroscience*.

Keller, H., & Zach, U. (2002). Gender and birth order as determinants of parental behaviour. *International Journal of Behavioral Development, 26*, 177–184.

Kelley, W. M., Macrae, C. N., Wyland, C. L., Caglar, S., Inati, S., & Heatherton, T. F. (2002). Finding the self? An event-related fMRI study. *Journal of Cognitive Neuroscience, 14*, 785–794.

Kelly, G. A. (1955). *The psychology of personal constructs*. New York: Norton.

Kelly, G. A. (1964). The language of hypothesis: Man's psychological instrument. *Journal of Individual Psychology, 20*, 137–152.

Keltner, D., Gruenfeld, D. H., & Anderson, C. (2003). Power, approach, and inhibition. *Psychological Review, 110*, 265–284.

Kenny, D. A. (1994). *Interpersonal perception.* New York: Guilford Press.

Kenny, D. A., Albright, L., Malloy, T. E., & Kashy, D. A. (1994). Consensus in interpersonal perception: Acquaintance and the Big Five. *Psychological Bulletin, 116,* 245–258.

Khorsandi, M., Vakilian, K., Salehi, B., Goudarzi, M. T., & Abdi, M. (2015). The effects of stress inoculation training on perceived stress in pregnant women. *Journal of Health Psychology, 21,* 2977–2982.

Kihlstrom, J. F. (2002). No need for repression. *Trends in Cognitive Science, 6,* 502.

Kihlstrom, J. F. (2008). The psychological unconscious. In O. P. John, R. W. Robins, & L. A. Pervin (Eds.), *Handbook of personality: Theory and research* (pp. 583–602). New York: Guilford Press.

Kihlstrom, J. F., Barnhardt, T. M., & Tataryn, D. J. (1992). The cognitive perspective. In R. F. Bornstein & T. S. Pittman (Eds.), *Perception without awareness* (pp. 17–54). New York: Guilford Press.

Kim, Y. (Ed.). (2009). *Handbook of behavior genetics.* New York: Springer.

King, J. E., & Figueredo, A. J. (1997). The five-factor model plus dominance in chimpanzee personality. *Journal of Research in Personality, 31,* 257–271.

Kirkpatrick, L. A. (1998). God as a substitute attachment figure: A longitudinal study of adult attachment style and religious change in college students. *Personality and Social Psychology Bulletin, 9,* 961–973.

Kirkpatrick, L. A., & Davis, K. E. (1994). Attachment style, gender, and relationship stability: A longitudinal analysis. *Journal of Personality and Social Psychology, 66,* 502–512.

Kirschenbaum, H. (1979). *On becoming Carl Rogers.* New York: Delacorte.

Kirschenbaum, H., & Jourdan, A. (2005). The current status of Carl Rogers and the person-centered approach. *Psychotherapy: Theory, Research, Practice, Training, 42,* 37–51.

Kitayama, S., & Markus, H. R. (1999). Yin and Yang of the Japanese self: The cultural psychology of personality coherence. In D. Cervone & Y. Shoda (Eds.), *The coherence of personality: Social-cognitive bases of consistency, variability, and organization* (pp. 242–302). New York: Guilford Press.

Kitayama, S., Markus, H. R., Matsumoto, H., & Norasakkunit, V. (1997). Individual and collective processes of self-esteem management: Self-enhancement in the United States and self-depreciation in Japan. *Journal of Personality and Social Psychology, 72,* 1245–1267.

Kitayama, S., & Masuda, T. (1997). [A cultural mediation model of social inference: Correspondence bias in Japan.] In K. Kashiwagi, S. Kitayama. & H. Azuma (Eds.), [*Cultural psychology: Theory and research*] (pp.109–127). Tokyo: University of Tokyo Press. (In Japanese; Cited in Kitayama & Markus, 1999.)

Klinger, E., Marchetti, I., & Koster, E. H. W. (2016). Spontaneous thought and goal pursuit: From functions such as planning to dysfunctions such as rumination. In K. C. R. Fox & K. Christoff (Eds.), *The Oxford handbook of spontaneous thought.* Oxford, UK: Oxford University Press.

Klinger, M. R., & Greenwald, A. G. (1995). Unconscious priming of association judgments. *Journal of Experimental Psychology: Learning, Memory, and Cognition, 21,* 569–581.

Knutson, B., Wolkowitz, O. M., Cole, S. W., Chan, T., Moore, E. A., Johnson, R. C., ..., Reus, V. I. (1998). Selective alteration of personality and social behavior by serotonergic intervention. *American Journal of Psychiatry, 155,* 373–378.

Kober, H., Barrett, L., Joseph, J., Bliss-Moreau, E., Lindquist, K., & Wager, T. D. (2008). Functional grouping and cortical–subcortical interactions in emotion: A meta-analysis of neuroimaging studies. *Neuroimage, 42,* 998–1031.

Koestner, R., Lekes, N., Powers, T. A., & Chicoine, E. (2002). Attaining personal goals: Concordance plus implementation intentions equals success. *Journal of Personality and Social Psychology, 83,* 231–244.

Konnikova, M. (2013). You're so self-controlling. *The New York Times, November 17, lp. 1R.*

Kosfeld, M., Heinrichs, M., Zak, P. J., Fischbacher, U., & Fehr, E. (2005). Oxytocin increases trust in humans. *Nature, 435,* 673–676.

Krantz, D. S., & Manuck, S. B. (1984). Acute psychophysiologic reactivity and risk of cardiovascular disease: A review and methodologic critique. *Psychological Bulletin, 96,* 435–464.

Krasner, L. (1971). The operant approach in behavior therapy. In A. E. Bergin & S. L. Garfield (Eds.), *Handbook of psychotherapy and behavior change* (pp. 612–652). New York: Wiley.

Kretschmer, E. (1925). *Physique and character*. London: Routledge & Kegan Paul.

Krosnick, J. A., Betz, A. L., Jussim, L. J., Lynn, A. R., & Kirschenbaum, D. (1992). Subliminal conditioning of attitudes. *Journal of Personality and Social Psychology*, *18*, 152–162.

Krueger, R. F., & Johnson, W. (2008). Behavioral genetics and personality: A new look at the integration of nature and nurture. In O. P. John, R. W. Robins, & L. A. Pervin (Eds.), *Handbook of personality: Theory and research* (pp. 287–310). New York: Guilford Press.

Kuhl, J. (2000). A functional-design approach to motivation and self-regulation: The dynamics of personality systems and interactions. In M. Boekaerts & P. R. Pintrich (Eds.), *Handbook of self-regulation* (pp. 111–169). San Diego, United States: Academic Press.

Kuhl, J. (2010). *Lehrbuch der Persönlichkeitspsychologie: Motivation, Emotion, Selbststeuerung* [Personality: Motivation, Emotion, Self-regulation]. Göttingen: Hogrefe.

Kuhl, J., & Koole, S. L. (2004). Workings of the will: A functional approach. In J. Greenberg, S. L. Koole, & T. Pyszczynski (Eds.), *Handbook of experimental existential psychology* (pp. 411–430). New York: Guilford.

Kuhl, J., Quirin, M., & Koole, S. L. (2015). Being someone: The integrated self as a neuropsychological system. *Social and Personality Psychology Compass*, *3*, 115–132.

Kwan, V. S. Y., John, O. P., Kenny, D. A., Bond, M. H., & Robins, R. W. (2004). Reconceptualizing individual differences in self-enhancement bias: An interpersonal approach. *Psychological Review*, *111*, 94–110.

Lakoff, G., & Johnson, M. (1999). *Philosophy in the flesh: The embodied mind and its challenge to Western thought*. New York: Basic Books.

Lamiell, J. T. (2013). Statisticism in personality psychologists' use of trait constructs: What is it? How was it contracted? Is there a cure? *New Ideas in Psychology*, *31*, 65–1.

Landfield, A. W. (1971). *Personal construct systems in psychotherapy*. Chicago: Rand McNally.

Landfield, A. W. (1982). A construction of fragmentation and unity. In J. CMancuso & J. R. Adams-Webber (Eds.), *The construing person* (pp. 198–221). New York: Praeger.

Lazarus, A. A. (1965). Behavior therapy, incomplete treatment and symptom substitution. *Journal of Nervous and Mental Disease*, *140*, 80–86.

Lazarus, R. S. (1990). Theory-based stress measurement. *Psychological Inquiry*, *1*, 3–13.

Lazarus, R. S. (1991). *Emotion and adaptation*. New York: Oxford University Press.

Lazarus, R. S. (1993). From psychological stress to the emotions: A history of changing outlooks. *Annual Review of Psychology*, *44*, 1–21.

Leary, M. R. (2007). Motivational and emotional aspects of the self. *Annual Review of Psychology*, *58*, 317–344.

Lecky, P. (1945). *Self-consistency: A theory of personality*. New York: Island.

Ledoux, J. L. (1995). Emotion: Clues from the brain. *Annual Review of Psychology*, *46*, 209–235.

Ledoux, J. (1999). The power of emotions. In R. Conlan (Ed.), *States of mind* (pp. 123–149). New York: Wiley.

Levy, S. (1991). Personality as a host risk factor: Enthusiasm, evidence, and their interaction. *Psychological Inquiry*, *2*, 254–257.

Lewis, M. (2002). Models of development. In D. Cervone, & W. Mischel (Eds.), *Advances in personality science* (pp. 153–176). New York: Guilford Press.

Lewis, M., Feiring, C., Mcguffog, C., & Jaskir, J. (1984). Predicting psychopathology in six year olds from early social relations. *Child Development*, *55*, 123–136.

Lewontin, R. (2000). *The triple helix: Gene, organism, and environment*. Cambridge, MA: Harvard University Press.

Lieberman, M. D., Jarcho, J. M., & Satpute, A. B. (2004). Evidence-based and intuition-based self-knowledge: An fMRI study. *Journal of Personality and Social Psychology*, *87*, 421–435.

Lilienfeld, S. O., Wood, J. M., & Garb, H. N. (2000). The scientific status of projective techniques. *Psychological Science in the Public Interest*, *1* (whole issue).

Linville, P. (1985). Self-complexity and affective extremity: Don't put all your eggs in one basket. *Social Cognition*, *3*, 94–120.

Linville, P. (1987). Self-complexity as a cognitive buffer against stress-related illness and depression. *Journal of Personality and Social Psychology, 52*, 663–676.

Little, B. R., Lecci, L., & Watkinson, B. (1992). Personality and personal projects: Linking Big Five and PAC units of analysis. *Journal of Personality, 60*, 502–525.

Little, B. R. (1999). Personality and motivation: Personal action and the conative revolution. In L. A. Pervin & O. P. John (Eds.), *Handbook of personality: Theory and research* (pp. 501–524). New York: Guilford Press.

Locke, E. A., & Latham, G. P. (1990). *A theory of goal setting and task performance.* Englewood Cliffs, NJ: Prentice-Hall.

Locke, E. A., & Latham, G. P. (2002). Building a practically useful theory of goal setting and task motivation: A 35-year odyssey. *American Psychologist, 57*, 705–717.

Loehlin, J. C. (1982). *Rhapsody in G. Contemporary Psychology, 27*, 623.

Loehlin, J. C. (1992). *Genes and environment in personality development.* Newbury Park, CA: Sage.

Loehlin, J.C, McCrae, R. R., Costa, P. T., & John, O. P. (1998). Heritabilities of common and measure specific components of the Big Five personality factors. *Journal of Research in Personality, 32*, 431–453.

Loevinger, J. (1993). Measurement in personality: True or false. *Psychological Inquiry, 4*, 1–16.

Loftus, E. F. (1997). Creating childhood memories. *Applied Cognitive Psychology, 11*, 75–86.

Lombardo, G. P., & Foschi, R. (2003). The concept of personality in 19th French and 20th century American psychology. *History of Psychology, 6*, 123–142.

Lucas, R. E., & Diener, E. (2008). Personality and subjective well-being. In O. P. John, R. W. Robins, & L. A. Pervin (Eds.), *Handbook of personality: Theory and research* (pp. 795–814). New York: Guilford Press.

Lucas, R. E., Diener, E., Grob, A., Suh, E. M., & Shao, L. (2000). Cross-cultural evidence for the fundamental features of extraversion. *Journal of Personality and Social Psychology, 79*, 452–468.

Lykken, D. T., Bouchard, T. J., Jr., McGue, M., & Tel-legen, A. (1993). Heritability of interests: A twin study. *Journal of Applied Psychology, 78*, 649–661.

Lynam, D. R., Caspi, A., Moffit, T. E., Wikstroem, P., Loeber, & Novak, S. (2000). The interaction between impulsivity and neighborhood context on offending: The effects of impulsivity are stronger in poorer neighborhoods. *Journal of Abnormal Psychology, 109*, 563–574.

Lyons, I. M., Mattarella-Micke, A., Cieslak, M., Nusbaum, H. C., Small, S. L., & Beilock, S. L. (2010). The role of personal experience in the neural processing of action-related language. *Brain and Language, 112*, 214–222.

MacKoon, D. G., Wallace, J. F., & Newman, J. P. (2004). Self-regulation: Context-appropriate balanced attention. In R. F. Baumeister & K. D. Vohs (Eds.), *Handbook of self-regulation: Research, theory, and applications* (pp. 422–444). New York: Guilford Press.

Magnusson, D. (2012). The human being in society: Psychology as a scientific discipline. *European Psychologist, 17*, 21–27.

Mancuso, J. C., & Adams-Webber, J. R. (Eds.). (1982). *The construing person.* New York: Praeger.

Manuck, S. B., & Mccaffery, J. M. (2014). Gene-environment interaction. *Annual Review of Psychology, 65*, 41–70.

Marcia, J. (1994). Ego identity and object relations. In J. M. Masling & R. F. Bornstein (Eds.), *Empirical perspectives on object relations theory* (pp. 59–104). Washington, DC: American Psychological Association.

Marino, G. (Ed.). (2004). *Basic writings of existentialism.* New York: Modern Library.

Markus, H. (1977). Self-schemata and processing information about the self. *Journal of Personality and Social Psychology, 35*, 63–78.

Markus, H. R., & Stephens, N. M. (2017). Editorial overview: The psychological and behavioral consequences of inequality and social class: A theoretical integration. *Current Opinion in Psychology, 18*.

Markus, H. (1983). Self-knowledge: An expanded view. *Journal of Personality, 51*, 543–565.

Markus, H., & Cross, S. (1990). The interpersonal self. In L. A. Pervin (Ed.), *Handbook of personality: Theory and research* (pp. 576–608). New York: Guilford Press.

Markus, H., & Kitayama, S. (1991). Culture and the self: Implications for cognition, emotion, and motivation. *Psychological Review, 98*, 224–253.

Markus, H., & Kitayama, S. (2011). Cultures and selves: A cycle of mutual constitution. *Perspectives on Psychological Science*, *5*, 420–430.

Markus, H. R., Uchida, Y., Omoregie, H., Townsend, S. S. M., & Kitayama, S. (2006). Going for the gold: Models of agency in Japanese and American contexts. *Psychological Science*, *17*, 103–112.

Markus, H., & Wurf, E. (1987). The dynamic self-concept: A social psychological perspective. *Annual Review of Psychology*, *38*, 299–337.

Maslow, A. H. (1954). *Motivation and personality*. New York: Harper.

Maslow, A. H. (1968). *Toward a psychology of being*. Princeton, NJ: Van Nostrand.

Maslow, A. H. (1971). *The farther reaches of human nature*. New York: Viking.

Matthews, G. (1997). The Big Five as a framework for personality assessment In N. Anderson & P. Herriot (Eds.), *International handbook of selection and assessment* (pp. 475–492). Chichester, UK: Wiley.

Matthews, G. (2016). Traits, cognitive processes and adaptation: An elegy for Hans Eysenck's personality theory. *Personality and Individual Differences*, *103*, 61–67.

Matthews, G. (2018). Cognitive-adaptive trait theory: A shift in perspective on personality. *Journal of Personality*, *86*, 69–82.

May, E. R., & Zelikow, P. D. (1997). (Eds.). *The Kennedy tapes: Inside the White House during the Cuban missile crisis*. Cambridge, MA: Harvard University Press.

Mayberg, H. S., Lozano, A. M., McNeely, H. E., Seminowicz, D., Hamani, C., ..., Kennedy, S. H. (2005). Deep brain stimulation for treatment-resistant depression. *Neuron*, *45*, 651–660.

Mayer, J. D. (2015). The personality system framework: Current theory and development. *Journal of Research in Personality*, *56*, 4–14.

Mayo, C. W., & Crockett, W. H. (1964). Cognitive complexity and primacy; recency effects in impression formation. *Journal of Abnormal and Social Psychology*, *68*, 335–338.

Mazzoni, G., & Memon, A. (2003). Imagination can create false childhood memories. *Psychological Science*, *14*, 186–188.

McAdams, D. P. (1994). A psychology of the stranger. *Psychological Inquiry*, *5*, 145–148.

McAdams, D. P. (2006). *The redemptive self: Stories Americans live by*. New York: Oxford University Press.

McAdams, D. P., & Pals, J. L. (2006). A new Big Five: Fundamental principles for an integrative science of personality. *American Psychologist*, *61*, 204–217.

McAdams, D. P. (2011). Exploring psychological themes through life-narrative accounts. In J. A. Holstein & J. F. Gubrium (Eds.), *Varieties of narrative analysis* (pp. 15–32). Los Angeles: Sage.

McCaul, K. D., Gladue, B. A., & Joppe, M. (1992). Winning, losing, mood, and testosterone. *Hormones and Behavior*, *26*, 486–504.

McClelland, D., Koestner, R., & Weinberger, J. (1989). How do self-attributed and implicit motives differ? *Psychological Review*, *96*, 690–702.

McCoy, M. M. (1981). Positive and negative emotion: A personal construct theory interpretation. In H. Bonarius, R. Holland, & S. Rosenberg (Eds.), *Personal construct psychology: Recent advances in theory and practice* (pp. 96–104). London: Macmillan.

McCrae, R. R. (1996). Social consequences of experiential openness. *Psychological Bulletin*, *120*, 323–337.

McCrae, R. R., & Costa, P. T. (1987). Validation of the five-factor model of personality across instruments and observers. *Journal of Personality and Social Psychology*, *52*, 81–90.

McCrae, R. R., & Costa, P. T., Jr. (1990). *Personality in adulthood*. New York: Guilford Press.

McCrae, R. R., & Costa, P. T. (1996). Toward a new generation of personality theories: Theoretical contexts for the five-factor model. In J. S. Wiggins (Ed.), *The five-factor model of personality. Theoretical perspectives* (pp. 51–37). New York: Guilford Press.

McCrae, R. R., & Costa, P. T. (1997). Personality trait structure as a human universal. *American Psychologist*, *52*, 509–516.

McCrae, R. R., & Costa, P. T., Jr., (1999). A five-factor theory of personality. In L. A. Pervin & O. P. John (Eds.)., *Handbook of personality: Theory and research* (pp. 139–153). New York: Guilford Press.

McCrae, R. R., & Costa, P. T., Jr. (2008). The five-factor theory of personality. In O. P. John, R. W. Robins, & L. A. Pervin (Eds.), *Handbook of personality: Theory and research* (pp. 159–181). New York: Guilford Press.

Mccrae, R. R., & Costa, P. T., Jr. (2010). *NEO Inventories* (Professional Manual). Lutz, FL: PAR.

Mccrae, R. R., & Costa, P. T., Jr. (2013). Introduction to the empirical and theoretical status of the Five-Factor model of personality traits. In T. A. Widiger & P. T. Costa Jr. (Eds.), *Personality disorders and the five-factor model of personality* (3rd ed., pp. 15–27). Washington, DC: American Psychological Association.

McCrae, R. R., Costa, P. T., Ostendorf, F., Angleitner, A., Hrebickova, M., Avia, M. D., ..., Smith, P. B. (2000). Nature over nurture: Temperament, personality, and lifespan development. *Journal of Personality and Social Psychology, 78*, 173–186.

Mccrae, R. R., Gaines, J. F., & Wellington, M. A. (2013). The five-factor model in fact and fiction. In K. H. Tennen & J. Suls (Eds.), *Handbook of psychology* (Vol. 5, pp. 65–91). Hoboken, NJ: Wiley.

McCrae, R. R., Yik, S. M., Trapnell, P. D., Bond, M. H., & Paulhus, D. L. (1998). Interpreting personality profiles across cultures: Bilingual, acculturation, and peer rating studies of Chinese undergraduates. *Journal of Personality and Social Psychology, 74*, 1041–1055.

McGee Ng, S., Bagby, R. M., Goodwin, B. E., Sellbom, M., Ayearst, L. E., Dhillon, S., ..., Burchett, D. (2016). The effect of response bias on the Personality Inventory for DSM-5 (PID-5). *Journal of Personality Assessment, 98*, 51–61.

McGinnies, E. (1949). Emotionality and perceptual defense. *Psychological Review, 56*, 244–251.

McGregor, I., & Little, B. R. (1998). Personal projects, happiness, and meaning: On doing well and being yourself. *Journal of Personality and Social Psychology, 74*, 494–512.

McGue, M., Boucharad, T. J., Jr., Iacono, W. G., & Lykken, D. T. (1993). Behavioral genetics of cognitive ability: A life-span perspective. In R. Plomin & G. E. McClearn (Eds.), *Nature, nurture, and psychology* (pp. 59–76). Washington, DC: American Psychological Association.

McMillan, M. (2004). *The person-centred approach to therapeutic change*. London: Sage.

Meaney, M. J. (2010). Epigenetics and the biological definition of gene x environment interactions. *Child Development, 81*, 41–79.

Medinnus, G. R., & Curtis, F. J. (1963). The relation between maternal self-acceptance and child acceptance. *Journal of Consulting Psychology, 27*, 542–544.

Meichenbaum, D. (1995). Cognitive-behavioral therapy in historical perspective. In B. Bongar & L. E. Bentler (Eds.), *Comprehensive textbook of psychotherapy* (pp. 140–158). New York: Oxford University Press.

Menand, L. (2002). *The metaphysical club: A story of ideas in America*. New York: Farrar, Straus, & Giroux.

Menand, L. (November 25, 2002). What comes naturally: Does evolution explain who we are? *The New Yorker.*

Mendel, G. (1865/1966). Experiments on plant hybrids. In C. Stern & E. R. Sherwood (Eds.), *The origin of genetics: A Mendel source book*. San Francisco: Freeman.

Mendoza-Denton, R., & Ayduk, O. (2012). Personality and social interaction: Interpenetrating processes. In K. Deaux & M. Snyder (Eds.), *The Oxford handbook of personality and social psychology* (pp. 446–466). New York: Oxford University Press.

Meston, C. M., & Buss, D. (2007). Why humans have sex. *Archives of Sexual Behavior, 36*, 477–507.

Metcalfe, J., & Mischel, W. (1999). A hot/cool-system analysis of delay of gratification: Dynamics of willpower. *Psychological Review, 106*, 3–19.

Mikulciner, M., Florain, V., & Weller, A. (1993). Attachment styles, coping strategies, and post-traumatic psychological distress: The impact of the Gulf War in Israel. *Journal of Personality and Social Psychology, 64*, 817–826.

Mikulincer, M., & Shaver, P. (2012). An attachment perspective on psychopathology. *World Psychiatry, 11*, 11–15.

Milgram, S. (1965). Some conditions of obedience and disobedience to authority. *Human Relations, 18*, 57–76.

Miller, L.C, Putcha-Bhagavatula, A., & Pedersen, W. C. (2002). Men's and women's mating preferences: Distinct evolutionary mechanisms? *Current Directions in Psychological Science, 11*, 88–93.

Miller, S. M., Shoda, Y., & Hurley, K. (1996). Applying cognitive-social theory to health-protective behavior: Breast self-examination in cancer screening. *Psychological Bulletin, 119*, 70–94.

Miller, T. R. (1991). Personality: A clinician's experience. *Journal of Personality Assessment, 57*, 415–433.

Mineka, S., Davidson, M., Cook, M., & Kleir, R. (1984). Observational conditioning of snake fear in rhesus monkeys. *Journal of Abnormal Psychology, 93*, 355–372.

Mischel, W. (1968). *Personality and assessment.* New York: Wiley.

Mischel, W. (1971). *Introduction to personality.* New York: Holt, Rinehart & Winston.

Mischel, W. (1973). Toward a cognitive social learning reconceptualization of personality. *Psychological Review, 80*, 252–283.

Mischel, W. (1974). Processes in delay of gratification. In L. Berkowitz (Ed.), *Advances in experimental social psychology* (Vol. 7, pp. 249–292). San Diego, CA: Academic Press.

Mischel, W. (1976). *Introduction to personality.* New York: Holt, Rinehart & Winston.

Mischel, W. (1990). Personality dispositions revisited and revised: A view after three decades. In L. A. Pervin (Ed.), *Handbook of personality: Theory and research* (pp. 111–134). New York: Guilford Press.

Mischel, W. (1999). Personality coherence and dispositions in a cognitive-affective processing system (CAPS) approach. In D. Cervone and Y. Shoda (Eds.), *The coherence of personality: Social-cognitive bases of consistency, variability, and organization* (pp. 37–60). New York: Guilford Press.

Mischel, W. (2004). Toward an integrative science of the person. *Annual Review of Psychology, 55*, 1–22.

Mischel, W. (2012). Self-control theory. In P. A. M. van Lange, A. Kruglanski, & E. T. Higgins (Eds.), *Handbook of theories of social psychology* (Vol. 2, pp. 1–22). Washington, DC: Sage.

Mischel, W. (2014). *The marshmallow test: Mastering self-control.* NY: Little, Brown & Co.

Mischel, W., & Baker, N. (1975). Cognitive transformations of reward objects through instructions. *Journal of Personality and Social Psychology, 31*, 254–261.

Mischel, W., & Liebert, R. M. (1966). Effects of discrepancies between observed and imposed reward criteria on their acquisition and transmission. *Journal of Personality and Social Psychology, 3*, 45–53.

Mischel, W., & Moore, B. (1973). Effects of attention to symbolically-presented rewards on self-control. *Journal of Personality and Social Psychology, 28*, 172–197.

Mischel, W., & Peake, P. K. (1983). Analyzing the construction of consistency in personality. In M. M. Page (Ed.), *Personality: Current theory and research* (pp. 233–262). Lincoln: University of Nebraska Press.

Mischel, W., & Shoda, Y. (1999). Integrating dispositions and processing dynamics within a unified theory of personality: The cognitive-affective personality system. In L. A. Pervin & O. P. John (Eds.), *Handbook of personality: Theory and research* (pp.197–218). New York: Guilford Press.

Mischel, W., & Shoda, Y. (2008). Toward a unified theory of personality: Integrating dispositions and processing dynamics within the cognitive-affective processing system. In O. P. John, R. W. Robins, & L. A. Pervin (Eds.), *Handbook of personality: Theory and research* (pp. 208–241). New York: Guilford Press.

Moffitt, T. E., Arseneault, L., Belsky, D., Dickson, N., Hancox, R. J., Harrington, H., ..., Caspi, A. (2011). A gradient of childhood self-control predicts health, wealth, and public safety. *Proceedings of the National Academy of Sciences, 108*, 2693–2698.

Mohammed, S. (2001). Personal communication networks and the effects of an entertainment-education radio soap opera in Tanzania. *Journal of Health Communication, 6*, 137–154.

Molenaar, P. C. M., & Campbell, C. G. (2009). The new person-specific paradigm in psychology. *Current Directions in Psychological Science, 18*, 112–117.

Moore, B., Mischel, W., & Zeiss, A. R. (1976). Comparative effects of the reward stimulus and its cognitive representation in voluntary delay. *Journal of Personality and Social Psychology, 34*, 419–424.

Moors, A., Ellsworth, P. C., Scherer, K. R., & Fridja, N. H. (2013). Appraisal theories of emotion: State of the art and future development. *Emotion Review, 5*, 119–124.

Morf, C. C., & Rhodewalt, F. (2001). Unraveling the paradoxes of narcissism: A dynamic self-regulatory processing model. *Psychological Inquiry, 12*, 177–196.

Morokoff, P. J. (1985). Effects of sex, guilt, repression, sexual "arousability," and sexual experience on female sexual arousal during erotica and fantasy. *Journal of Personality and Social Psychology, 49*, 177–187.

Morris, M. W., & Peng, K. (1994). Culture and cause: American and Chinese attributions for social and physical events. *Journal of Personality and Social Psychology, 67*, 949–971.

Morrison, J. K., & Cometa, M. C. (1982). Variations in developing construct systems: The experience corollary. In J. C. Mancusco & J. R. Adams-Webber (Eds.), *The construing person* (pp. 152–169). New York: Praeger.

Moskowitz, D. S., & Herschberger, S. L. (Eds.). (2002). *Modeling intraindividual variability with repeated measures data: Methods and applications.* Mahwah, NJ: Lawrence Erlbaum Associates.

Moskowitz, D. S., & Zuroff, D. C. (2005). Robust predictors of flux, pulse, and spin. *Journal of Research in Personality, 39*, 130–147.

Moss, P. D., & McEvedy, C. P. (1966). An epidemic of over-breathing among school-girls. *British Medical Journal, 2*, 1295–1300.

Mroczek, D. K., & Little, T. (2006). (Eds.). *Handbook of personality development*, Mahwah, NJ: Erlbaum.

Murphy, G. (1958). *Human potentialities.* New York: Basic Books.

Murray, H. A. (1938). *Explorations in personality.* New York: Oxford University Press.

Nadel, L. (2005). *Why we can't remember when.* Monitor on Psychology, November, 36–37.

Nagy, M. (1991). *Philosophical issues in the psychology of C. G. Jung.* Albany: State University of New York Press.

Nakamura, J., & Csikszentmihalyi, M. (2009). Flow theory and research. In S. J. Lopez and C. R. Snyder (Eds.), *Handbook of Positive Psychology* (195–206). New York: Oxford University Press.

Nash, M. (1999). The psychological unconscious. In V. J. Derlega, B. A. Winstead, & W. H. Jones (Eds.), *Personality: Contemporary theory and research* (pp. 197–228). Chicago: Nelson-Hall.

Neimeyer, G. J. (1992). Back to the future with the psychology of personal constructs. *Contemporary Psychology, 37*, 994–997.

Neimeyer, R. A. (1994). *Death anxiety handbook: Research, instrumentation, and application.* Washington, DC: Taylor & Francis.

Neimeyer, R. A., & Neimeyer, G. J. (Eds.). (1992). *Advances in personal construct psychology* (Vol. 2). Greenwich, CT: JAI Press.

Nesselroade, J. R., & Delhees, K. H. (1966). Methods and findings in experimentally based personality theory. In R. B. Cattell (Ed.), *Handbook of multivariate experimental psychology* (pp. 563–610). Chicago: Rand McNally.

Newsweek Magazine (March 27, 2006). Freud is not dead. (Cover story headline.)

New York Times (August 20, 1990). *B.F. Skinner, the champion of behaviorism, is dead at 86.* Retrieved from http://www.nytimes.com/1990/08/20/obituaries/b-f-skinner-the-champion-of-behaviorism-is-dead-at-86.html?pagewanted5all&src5pm.

New York Times (November 2, 2011). *Fraud case seen as red flag for psychology research.*

Newman, L. S., Duff, K. J., & Baumeister, R. F. (1997). A new look at defensive projection: Thought suppression, accessibility, and biased person perception. *Journal of Personality and Social Psychology, 72*, 980–1001.

Nicholson, I. A. M. (2002). *Inventing personality: Gordon Allport and the science of selfhood.* Washington, DC: American Psychological Society.

Niedenthal, P. M., Barsalou, L., Winkielman, P., Krauth-Gruber, S., & Ric, F. (2005). Embodiment in attitudes, social perception, and emotion. *Personality and Social Psychology Review, 9*, 184–211.

Nilsson, A. (2014). Personality psychology as the integrative study of traits and worldviews. *New Ideas in Psychology, 32*, 18–32.

Nisbett, R. (2003). *The geography of thought: How Asians and Westerners think differently.* New York: Free Press.

Nisbett, R. E., Peng, K., Choi, I., & Norenzayan, A. (2001). Culture and systems of thought: Holistic versus analytic cognition. *Psychological Review, 108*, 291–310.

Nisbett, R., & Ross, L. (1980). *Human inference: Strategies and shortcomings of social judgment.* Englewood Cliffs, NJ: Prentice Hall.

Nisbett, R. E., & Wilson, T. D. (1977). Telling more than we know: Verbal reports on mental processes. *Psychological Review, 84*, 231–279.

Norem, J. K. (2001). *The positive power of negative thinking: Using defensive pessimism to manage anxiety and perform at your peak.* New York: Basic Books.

Norman, W. T. (1963). Toward an adequate taxonomy of personality attributes. *Journal of Abnormal and Social Psychology, 66*, 574–583.

Northoff, G. (2012). Psychoanalysis and the brain—why did Freud abandon neuroscience? *Frontiers in Psycholology,* Retrieved from https://doi.org/10.3389/fpsyg.2012.00071.

Nowak, A., Vallacher, R. R., & Zochowski, M. (2002). The emergence of personality: Personality stability through interpersonal synchronization. In D. Cervone & W. Mischel (Eds.), *Advances in personality science* (pp. 292–331). New York: Guilford Press.

Nowak, A., Vallacher, R. R., & Zochowski, M. (2005). The emergence of personality: Dynamic foundations of individual variation. *Developmental Review, 25*, 351–385.

Oh, I., Wang, G., & Mount, M. K. (2011). Validity of observer ratings of the five-factor model of personality traits: A meta-analysis. *Journal of Applied Psychology, 96*, 762–773.

Ohman, A., & Soares, J. F. (1993). On the automaticity of phobic fear: Conditional skin conductance responses to masked phobic stimuli. *Journal of Abnormal Psychology, 102*, 121–132.

O'leary, A. (1990). Stress, emotion, and human immune function. *Psychological Bulletin, 108*, 363–382.

O'leary, A. (1992). Self-efficacy and health: Behavioral and stress-physiological mediation. *Cognitive Therapy and Research, 16*, 229–245.

O'leary, K. D. (1972). The assessment of psychopathology in children. In H. C. Quay & J. S. Werry (Eds.), *Psychopathological disorders of childhood* (pp. 234–272). New York: Wiley.

Olson, K. R., & Dweck, C. S. (2008). A blueprint for social cognitive development. *Perspectives on Psychological Science, 3*, 193–202.

Orne, M. T. (1962). On the social psychology of the psychological experiment: With particular reference to demand characteristics and their implications. *American Psychologist, 17*, 776–783.

Orom, H., & Cervone, D. (2009). Personality dynamics, meaning, and idiosyncrasy: Identifying cross-situational coherence by assessing personality architecture. *Journal of Research in Personality, 43*, 228–240.

Osgood, C. E., & Luria, Z. (1954). A blind analysis of a case of multiple personality using the semantic differential. *Journal of Abnormal and Social Psychology, 49*, 579–591.

Osgood, C. E., Suci, G. J., & Tannenbaum, P. H. (1957). *The measurement of meaning.* Urbana: University of Illinois Press.

Osofsky, M. J., Bandura, A., & Zimbardo, P. (2005). The role of moral disengagement in the execution process. *Law and Human Behavior, 29*, 371–393.

Owens, C., & Dein, S. (2006). Conversion disorder: The modern hysteria. *Advances in Psychiatric Treatment, 12*, 152–157.

Oyserman, D. (2017). Culture three ways: Culture and subcultures within countries. *Annual Review of Psychology, 68*, 435–463.

Ozer, D. J. (1999). Four principles for personality assessment. In L. A. Pervin & O. P. John (Eds.), *Handbook of personality: Theory and research* (pp. 671–686). New York: Guilford Press.

Ozer, E., & Bandura, A. (1990). Mechanisms governing empowerment effects: A self-efficacy analysis. *Journal of Personality and Social Psychology, 58*, 472–486.

Panksepp, J. (2011). Cross-species affective neuroscience decoding of the primal affective experiences of humans and related animals. *PLoS ONE 6*, e21236.

Panksepp, J., & Solms, M. (2012). What is neuropsychoanalysis? Clinically relevant studies of the minded brain. *Trends in Cognitive Science, 16*, 6–8.

Panksepp, J., Wright, J. S., Döbrössy, M. D., Schlaepfer, T. E., & Coenen, V. A. (2014). Affective neuroscience strategies for understanding and treating depression: From preclinical models to three novel therapeutics. *Clinical Psychological Science, 2*, 472–494.

Park, G., Schwartz, H. A., Eichstaedt, J. C., Kern, M. L., Kosinski, M., Stillwell, D. J., & Seligman, M. E. P. (2015). Automatic personality assessment through social media language. *Journal of Personality and Social Psychology*, *108*, 934–952.

Park, R. (2004). Development in the family. *Annual Review of Psychology*, *55*, 365–399.

Patton, C. J. (1992). Fear of abandonment and binge eating. *Journal of Nervous and Mental Disease*, *180*, 484–490.

Paulhus, D. L., Fridhandler, B., & Hayes, S. (1997). Psychological defense: Contemporary theory and research. In R. Hogan, J. Johnson, & S. Briggs (Eds.), *Handbook of personality psychology* (pp. 543–579). San Diego, CA: Academic Press.

Paulhus, D. L., Trapnell, P. D., & Chen, D. (1999). Birth order effects on personality and achievement within families. *Psychological Science*, *10*, 482–488.

Pavlov, I. P. (1927). *Conditioned reflexes*. London: Oxford University Press.

Pavot, W., Fujita, F., & Diener, E. (1997). The relation between self-aspect congruence, personality and subjective well-being. *Personality and Individual Differences*, *22*, 183–191.

Pedersen, N. L., Plomin, R., McClearn, G. E., & Friberg, L. (1998). Neuroticism, extraversion, and related traits in adult twins reared apart and reared together. *Journal of Personality and Social Psychology*, *55*, 950–957.

Pervin, L. A. (1964). Predictive strategies and the need to confirm them: Some notes on pathological types of decisions. *Psychological Reports*, *15*, 99–105.

Pervin, L. A. (1967a). A twenty-college study of student/college interaction using TAPE (Transactional Analysis of Personality and Environment): Rationale, reliability, and validity. *Journal of Educational Psychology*, *58*, 290–302.

Pervin, L. A. (1967b). Satisfaction and perceived self environment similarity: A semantic differential study of student-college interaction. *Journal of Personality*, *35*, 623–634.

Pervin, L. A. (1983). Idiographic approaches to personality. In J. Mc V. Hunt & N. Endler (Eds.), *Personality and the behavior disorders* (pp. 261–282). New York: Wiley.

Pervin, L. A. (1994). A critical analysis of current trait theory. *Psychological Inquiry*, *5*, 103–113.

Pervin, L. A. (1996). *The science of personality*. New York: Wiley.

Pervin, L. A. (1999). Epilogue: Constancy and change in personality theory and research. In L. A. Pervin & O. P. John (Eds.), *Handbook of personality: Theory and research* (pp. 689–704). New York: Guilford Press.

Pervin, L. A. (2003). *The science of personality* (2nd ed.). London: Oxford University Press.

Petrie, K. J., Booth, R. J., & Pennebaker, J. W. (1998). The immunological effects of thought suppression. *Journal of Personality and Social Psychology*, *75*, 1264–1272.

Pfungst, O. (1911). *Clever Hans: A contribution to experimental, animal, and human psychology*. New York: Holt, Rinehart & Winston.

Phillips, A. G., & Silvia, P. J. (2005). Self-awareness and the emotional consequences of self-discrepancies. *Personality and Social Psychology Bulletin*, *31*, 703–713.

Pickering, A. D., & Gray, J. A. (1999). The neuroscience of personality. In L. A. Pervin & O. P. John (Eds.), *Handbook of personality: Theory and research* (pp. 277–299). New York: Guilford Press.

Pickering, A. D., & Corr, P. J. (2008). J. A. Gray's reinforcement sensitivity theory (RST) of personality. In G. J. Boyle, G. Matthews, & D. H. Saklofske (Eds.), *The Sage handbook of personality theory and assessment: Volume 1, personality theories and models* (pp. 33–55). Los Angeles: Sage.

Pietrzak, J., Downey, G., & Ayduk, O. (2005). Rejection sensitivity as an interpersonal vulnerability. In M. W. Baldwin (Ed.), *Interpersonal cognition* (pp. 62–84). New York: Guilford Press.

Pinker, S. (1997). *How the mind works*. New York: Norton.

Plomin, R. (1990). *Nature and nurture*. Pacific Grove, CA: Brooks/Cole.

Plomin, R., & Caspi, A. (1999). Behavioral genetics and personality. In L. A. Pervin & O. P. John (Eds.), *Handbook of personality: Theory and research* (pp. 251–276). New York: Guilford Press.

Plomin, R., Chipuer, H. M., & Loehlin, J. C. (1990). Behavioral genetics and personality. In L. A. Pervin (Ed.), *Handbook of personality: Theory and research* (pp. 225–243). New York: Guilford Press.

Plomin, R., & Daniels, D. (1987). Why are children in the same family so different from each other? *Behavioral and Brain Sciences*, *10*, 1–16.

Plomin, R., & Neiderhiser, J. M. (1992). Genetics and experience. *Current Directions in Psychological Science*, *1*, 160–163.

Plomin, R., & Rende, R. (1991). Human behavioral genetics. *Annual Review of Psychology*, *42*, 161–190.

Pomerantz, E. M., & Thompson, R. A. (2008). Parents role in children's personality development: The psychological resource principle. In O. P. John, R. W. Robins, & L. A. Pervin (Eds.), *Handbook of personality: Theory and research* (pp. 351–374). New York: Guilford Press.

Ponomarev, I., & Crabbe, J. C. (1999). Genetic association between chronic ethanol withdrawal severity and acoustic startle parameters in WSP and WSR mice. *Alcoholism: Clinical and Experimental Research*, *23*, 1730–1735.

Powell, R. A., & Boer, D. P. (1994). Did Freud mislead patients to confabulate memories of abuse? *Psychological Reports*, *74*, 1283–1298.

Pribram, K. (2005). Freud's project for a scientific psychology in the 21st century. In Giampieri-Deutsch P. (a cura di), *Psychoanalysis as an empirical, interdisciplinary science*. Vienna, Verlag der Österreichen Akademie der Wissenschaften.

Proctor, R. W., & Capaldi, E. J. (2001). Empirical evaluation and justification of methodologies in psychological science. *Psychological Bulletin*, *127*, 759–772.

Puterman, E., Gemmill, A., Karasek, D., Weir, D., Adler, N. E., Prather, A. A., & Epel, E. S.(2016). Lifespan adversity and later adulthood telomere length in the nationally representative US Health and Retirement Study. *Proceedings of the National Academy of Sciences*, *113*, (42), E6335–E6342.

Quirin, M., Kazén, M., & Kuhl, J. (2009). When nonsense sounds happy or helpless: The Implicit Positive and Negative Affect Test (IPANAT). *Journal of Personality and Social Psychology*, *97*, 500–516.

Rafaeli-Mor, E., & Steinberg, J. (2002). Self-complexity and well-being: A review and research synthesis. *Personality and Social Psychology Review*, *6*, 31–58.

Raghanti, M. A., Edler, M. K., Stephenson, A. R., Munger, E. L., Jacobs, B., Hof, P. R., ..., Lovejoy, C. O. (2018). A neurochemical hypothesis for the origin of hominids. *Proceedings of the National Academy of Sciences of the United States of America*, *115*, E1108–E1116.

Raleigh, M. J., & Mcguire, M. T. (1991). Bidirectional relationships between tryptophan and social behavior in vervet monkeys. *Advances in Experimental Medicine and Biology*, *294*, 289–298.

Rammstedt, B., & John, O. P. (2007). Measuring personality in one minute or less: A 10-item short version of the Big Five Inventory in English and German. *Journal of Research in Personality*, *41*, 203–12.

Raskin, R., & Hall, C. S. (1979). A narcissistic personality inventory. *Psychological Reports*, *45*, 590.

Raskin, R., & Hall, C. S. (1981). The Narcissistic Personality Inventory: Alternate form reliability and further evidence of construct validity. *Journal of Personality Assessment*, *45*, 159–162.

Raskin, R., & Shaw, R. (1987). *Narcissism and the use of personal pronouns*. Unpublished manuscript.

Raskin, R., & Terry, H. (1987). *A factor-analytic study of the Narcissistic Personality Inventory and further evidence of its construct validity*. Unpublished manuscript.

Rauthmann, J. (Ed.) *Handbook of personality dynamics and processes*. San Diego, CA: Elsevier.

Reiss, D. (1997). Mechanisms linking genetic and social influences in adolescent development: Beginning a collaborative search. *Current Directions in Psychological Science*, *6*, 100–105.

Reiss, D., Neiderhiser, J., Hetherington, E. M., & Plomin, R. (1999). *The relationship code: Deciphering genetic and social patterns in adolescent development*. Cambridge, MA: Harvard University Press.

Reitz, A. K., Zimmermann, J., Hutteman, R., Specht, J., & Neyer, F. J. (2014). How peers make a difference: The role of peer groups and peer relationships in personality development. *European Journal of Personality*, *28*, 279–288.

Reynolds, G. S. (1968). *A primer of operant conditioning*. Glenview, IL: Scott, Foresman.

Rhodewalt, F., & Morf, C. C. (1995). Self and interpersonal correlates of the Narcissistic Personality Inventory: A review and new findings. *Journal of Research in Personality*, *29*, 1–23.

Rhodewalt, F., & Sorrow, D. L. (2002). Interpersonal self-regulation: Lessons from the study of narcissism. In M. R. Leary & J. P. Tangney (Eds.), *Handbook of self and identity* (pp. 519–535). New York: Guilford Press.

Ricoeur, P. (1970). *Freud and philosophy.* (D. Savage, trans.). New Haven, CT: Yale University Press.

Ridley, M. (2003). *Nature via nurture: Genes, experience, and what makes us human.* New York: HarperCollins.

Riemann, R., Angleitner, A., & Strelau, J. (1997). Genetic and environmental influences on personality: A study of twins reared together using the self and peer report NEO-FFI scales. *Journal of Personality, 65,* 449–476.

Roberts, B. W. (1997). Plaster or plasticity: Are adult work experiences associated with personality change in women? *Journal of Personality, 65,* 205–232.

Roberts, B. W., & Chapman, C. N. (2000). Change in dispositional well-being and its relation to role quality: A 30-year longitudinal study. *Journal of Research in Personality, 34,* 26–41.

Roberts, B. W., & Del Vecchio, W. F. (2000). The rank-order consistency of personality traits from childhood to old age: A quantitative review of longitudinal studies. *Psychological Bulletin, 126,* 3–25.

Roberts, B. W., & Hogan, R. (Eds.). (2001). *Personality in the workplace.* Washington, DC: American Psychological Association.

Roberts, J. A., Gotlib, I. H., & Kassel, I. D. (1996). Adult attachment security and symptoms of depression: The mediating roles of dysfunctional attitudes and low self-esteem. *Journal of Personality and Social Psychology, 70,* 310–320.

Robins, R. W., & John, O. P. (1996). Self-perception, visual perspective, and narcissism: Is seeing believing? *Psychological Science, 8,* 37–42.

Robins, R. W., Norem, J. K., & Cheek, J. M. (1999). Naturalizing the self. In L. A. Pervin & O. P. John (Eds.), *Handbook of personality: Theory and research* (pp. 443–477). New York: Guilford Press.

Robins, R. W., Tracy, J. L., & Trzesniewski, K. H. (2008). Naturalizing the self. In O. P. John, R. W. Robins, & L. A. Pervin (Eds.), *Handbook of personality: Theory and research* (pp. 421–447). New York: Guilford Press.

Robinson, R. G., & Downhill, J. E. (1995). Lateralization of psychopathology in response to focal brain injury. In R. J. Davidson & K. Hugdahl (Eds.), *Brain asymmetry* (pp. 693–711). Cambridge, MA: MIT Press.

Roccas, S., & Brewer, M. (2002). Social identity complexity. *Personality and Social Psychology Review, 6,* 88–106.

Rogers, C. R. (1951). *Client-centered therapy.* Boston: Houghton Mifflin.

Rogers, C. R. (1956). Some issues concerning the control of human behavior. *Science, 124,* 1057–1066.

Rogers, C. R. (1959). A theory of therapy, personality, and interpersonal relationships as developed in the client-centered framework. In S. Koch (Ed.), *Psychology: A study of science* (pp. 184–256). New York: McGraw-Hill.

Rogers, C. R. (1961). *On becoming a person.* Boston: Houghton Mifflin.

Rogers, C. R. (1963). The actualizing tendency in relation to "motives" and to consciousness. In M. R. Jones (Ed.), *Nebraska symposium on motivation* (pp. 1–24). Lincoln: University of Nebraska Press.

Rogers, C. R. (1964). Toward a science of the person. In T. W. Wann (Ed.), *Behaviorism and phenomenology* (pp. 109–133). Chicago: University of Chicago Press.

Rogers, C. R. (1966). Client-centered therapy. In S. Arieti (Ed.), *American handbook of psychiatry* (pp. 183–200). New York: Basic Books.

Rogers, C. R. (1977). *Carl Rogers on personal power.* New York: Delacorte Press.

Rogers, C. R. (1980). *A way of being.* Boston: Houghton Mifflin.

Rogers, T. B., Kuiper, N. A., & Kirker, W. S. (1977). Self-reference and the encoding of personal information. *Journal of Personality and Social Psychology, 35,* 677–688.

Rorer, L. G. (1990). Personality assessment: A conceptual survey. In L. A. Pervin (Ed.), *Handbook of Personality: Theory and Research* (pp. 693–720). New York: Guilford Press.

Rosenberg, S. (1980). A theory in search of its zeitgeist. *Contemporary Psychology, 25,* 898–900.

Rosenthal, R. (1994). Interpersonal expectancy effects: A 30-year perspective. *Current Directions in Psychological Science, 3,* 176–179.

Rosenthal, R., & Rubin, D. (1978). Interpersonal expectancy effects: The first 345 studies. *Behavioral and Brain Sciences, 3*, 377–415.

Rosenzweig, S. (1941). Need-persistive and ego-defensive reactions to frustration as demonstrated by an experiment on repression. *Psychological Review, 48*, 347–349.

Rothbard, J. C., & Shaver, P. R. (1994). Continuity of attachment across the life-span. In M. B. Sperling & W. H. Berman (Eds.), *Attachment in adults: Clinical and developmental perspectives* (pp. 31–71). New York: Guilford Press.

Rothbart, M. K. (2011). *Becoming who we are: Temperament and personality development*. New York: Guilford Press.

Rothbart, M. K., & Bates, J. E. (1998). Temperament. In W. Damon (Ed.), *Handbook of child psychology: Vol. 3. Social, emotional, and personality development* (5th ed., pp. 105–176). New York: Wiley.

Rozin, P., & Zellner, D. (1985). The role of Pavlovian conditioning in the acquisition of food likes and dislikes. *Annals of the New York Academy of Sciences, 443*, 189–202.

Ruggiero, K. M., & Marx, D. M. (2001). Less pain and more to gain: Why high-status group members blame their failure on discrimination: Retraction. *Journal of Personality and Social Psychology, 81*, 178.

Rutter, M. (2012). Gene–environment interdependence. *European Journal of Developmental Psychology, 9*, 391–412.

Ryan, R. M. (1993). Agency and organization: Intrinsic motivation, autonomy, and the self in psychological development. In J. Jacobs (Ed.), *Nebraska symposium on motivation*. (Vol. 40, pp. 1–56). Lincoln: University of Nebraska Press.

Ryan, R. M., & Deci, E. L. (2008). Self-determination theory and the role of basic psychological needs in personality and the organization of behavior. In O. P. John, R. W. Robins, & L. A. Pervin (Eds.), *Handbook of personality: Theory and research* (pp. 654–678). New York: Guilford Press.

Ryff, C. D. (1995). Psychological well-being in adult life. *Current Directions in Psychological Science, 4*, 99–104.

Ryff, C. D., & Singer, B. (1998). The contours of positive human health. *Psychological Inquiry, 9*, 1–28.

Ryff, C. D., & Singer, B. (2000). Interpersonal flourishing: A positive health agenda for the new millennium. *Personality and Social Psychology Review, 4*, 30–44.

Salmon, W. C. (1989). Four decades of scientific explanation. In P. Kitcher & W. C. Salmon (Eds.), *Minnesota studies in the philosophy of science, Vol. XIII. Scientific Explanation* (pp. 3–219). Minneapolis: University of Minnesota Press.

Samson, A., Simpson, D., Kamphoff, C., & Langlier, A. (2017). Think aloud: An examination of distance runners' thought processes. *International Journal of Sport and Exercise Psychology, 15*, 176–189.

Sapolsky, R. M. (1994). *Why zebras don't get ulcers*. New York: W.H. Freeman.

Saucier, G. (1997). Effects of variable selection on the factor structure of person descriptors. *Journal of Personality and Social Psychology, 73*, 1296–1312.

Saucier, G., & Goldberg, L. R. (1996). Evidence for the Big Five in analyses of familiar English personality adjectives. *European Journal of Personality, 10*, 61–77.

Saucier, G., & Goldberg, L. R. (2001). Lexical studies of undigenous personality factors: Premises, products, and prospects. *Journal of Personality, 69*, 847–880.

Saucier, G., Hampson, S. E., & Goldberg, L. R. (2000). Cross-language studies of lexical personality factors. In S. E. Hampson (Ed.), *Advances in personality psychology* (Vol. 1, pp. 1–36). East Sussex, UK: Psychology Press, Ltd.

Saudino, K. (1997). Moving beyond the heritability question: New directions in behavioral genetic studies of personality. *Current Directions in Psychological Science, 6*, 86–90.

Saunders, T., Driskell, J. E., Johnston, J. H., & Salas, E. (1996). The effect of stress inoculation training on anxiety and performance. *Journal of Occupational Health Psychology, 1*, 170–186.

Schafer, R. (1954). *Psychoanalytic interpretation in Rorschach testing*. New York: Grune & Stratton.

Schlam, T. R., Wilson, N. L., Shoda, I. Y., Mischel, W., & Ayduk, O. (2013). Preschoolers' delay of gratification predicts their body mass 30 years later. *The Journal of Pediatrics, 162*, 90–93.

Schmidt, L. A., & Fox, N. A. (2002). Individual differences in childhood shyness: Origins, malleability, and developmental course. In D. Cervone & W. Mischel (Eds.), *Advances in personality science* (pp. 83–105). New York: Guilford Press.

Schmitt, D. P., Allik, J., McCrae, R. R., & Benet-Martinez, V. (2007). The geographic distribution of Big Five personality traits: Patterns and profiles of human self-description across 56 nations. *Journal of Cross-Cultural Psychology*, *38*, 173–212.

Schneider, D. J. (1982). Personal construct psychology: An international menu. *Contemporary Psychology*, *27*, 712–713.

Schultheiss, O. C. (2008). Implicit motives. In O. P. John, R. W. Robins, & L. A. Pervin (Eds.), *Handbook of personality: Theory and research* (pp. 603–633). New York: Guilford Press.

Schunk, D. H., & Cox, P. D. (1986). Strategy training and attributional feedback with learning disabled students. *Journal of Educational Psychology*, *1986*, 78, 201–209.

Schutter, D., & van Honk, J. (2009). The cerebellum in emotion regulation: A repetitive transcranial magnetic stimulation study. *Cerebellum*, *8*, 28–34.

Schwartz, C. E., Wright, C. I., Shin, L. M., Kagan, J., & Rauch, S. L. (2003). Inhibited and uninhibited children "grown up": Amygdalar response to novelty. *Science*, *300*, 1952–1953.

Schwarz, N. (1999). Self-reports: How the questions shape the answers. *American Psychologist*, *54*, 93–105.

Schwarzer, R. (Ed.). (1992). *Self-efficacy: Thought control of action.* Washington, DC: Hemisphere.

Scott, J. P., & Fuller, J. L. (1965). *Genetics and the social behavior of the dog.* Chicago: University of Chicago Press.

Scott, W. D., & Cervone, D. (2002). The impact of negative affect on performance standards: Evidence for an affect-as-information mechanism. *Cognitive Therapy and Research*, *26*, 19–37.

Sechrest, L. (1963). The psychology of personal constructs. In J. M. Wepman & R. W. Heine (Eds.), *Concepts of personality* (pp. 206–233). Chicago: Aldine.

Sechrest, L. (1977). The psychology of personal constructs. In J. M. Wepman & R. W. Heine (Eds.), *Concepts of personality* (pp. 206–233). Chicago: Jossey-Bass.

Sechrest, L., & Jackson, D. N. (1961). Social intelligence and accuracy of interpersonal predictions. *Journal of Personality*, *29*, 167–182.

Seeyave, D. M., Coleman, S., Appugliese, D., Corwyn, R. F., Bradley, R. H., Davidson, N. S., ..., Lumeng, J. C. (2009). Ability to delay gratification at age 4 years and risk of overweight at age 11 years. *Archives of Pediatrics and Adolescent Medicine*, *163*, 303–308.

Segal, N. (2014). The closest of strangers. *The New York Times*, May 25, p. SR 12.

Segal, Z. V., & Dobson, K. S. (1992). Cognitive models of depression: Report from a consensus development conference. *Psychological Inquiry*, *3*, 219–224.

Seligman, M. E. P., & Csikszentmihalyi, M. (2000). Positive psychology. *American Psychologist*, *55*, 5–14.

Seligman, M. E. P., & Peterson, C. (2003). Positive clinical psychology. In L. G. Aspinwall & U. M. Staudinger (Eds.), *A psychology of human strengths: Fundamental questions and future directions for a positive psychology* (pp. 305–317). Washington, DC: American Psychological Association.

Seligman, M. E. P., Rashid, T., & Parks, A. C. (2006). Positive psychotherapy. *American Psychologist*, *61*, 774–788.

Shah, J., & Higgins, E. T. (1997). Expectancy × value effects: Regulatory focus as a determinant of magnitude and direction. *Journal of Personality and Social Psychology*, *73*, 447–458.

Shapiro, L. (2011). *Embodied cognition.* New York: Routledge.

Sharot, T. (2011). *The optimism bias.* New York: Pantheon.

Shaver, P. R., & Mikulincer, M. (2005). Attachment theory and research: Resurrection of the psychodynamic approach to personality. *Journal of Research in Personality*, *39*, 22–45.

Shaver, P. R., & Mikulincer, M. (2012). Attachment theory. In P. A. M. van Lange, A. Kruglanski, & E. T. Higgins (Eds.), *Handbook of theories of social psychology* (Vol. 2, pp. 160–180). Washington, DC: Sage.

Shedler, J. (2010). The efficacy of psychodynamic psychotherapy. *American Psychologist*, *65*, 98–109.

Shedler, J., Mayman, M., & Manis, M. (1993). The illusion of mental health. *American Psychologist*, *48*, 1117–1131.

Sheldon, K. M., & Elliot, A. J. (1999). Goal striving, need satisfaction, and longitudinal well-being: The self-concordance model. *Journal of Personality and Social Psychology*, *76*, 482–497.

Sheldon, K. M., Ryan, R. M., Rawsthorne, L. J., & Ilardi, B. (1997). Trait self and true self: Cross-role variation in the Big-Five personality traits and its relations with psychological authenticity and subjective well-being. *Journal of Personality and Social Psychology*, *73*, 1380–1393.

Sheldon, W. H. (1940). *The varieties of human physique*. New York: Harper.

Sheldon, W. H. (1942). *Varieties of temperament*. New York: Harper.

Shiner, R. L. (1998). How shall we speak of children's personalities in middle childhood? A preliminary taxonomy. *Psychological Review*, *124*, 308–332.

Shoda, Y., Mischel, W., & Peake, P. K. (1990). Predicting adolescent cognitive and self-regulatory competencies from preschool delay of gratification: Identifying diagnostic conditions. *Developmental Psychology*, *26*, 978–986.

Shoda, Y., Mischel, W., & Wright, J. C. (1994). Intraindividual stability in the organization and patterning of behavior: Incorporating psychological situations into the idiographic analysis of personality. *Journal of Personality and Social Psychology*, *67*, 674–687.

Shoda, Y., Wilson, N. L., Chen, J., Gilmore, A. K., & Smith, R. E. (2013). Cognitive-affective processing system analysis of intra-individual dynamics in collaborative therapeutic assessment: Translating basic theory and research into clinical applications. *Journal of Personality*, *81*, 554–568.

Shrout, P. E., & Rodgers, J. L. (2018). Psychology, science, and knowledge construction: Broadening perspectives from the replication crisis. *Annual Review of Psychology*, *69*, 487–451.

Shumyatsky, G. P., Malleret, G., Shin, R., Takizawa, S., Tully, K., Tsvetkov, E., ..., Bolshakov, V. Y. (2005). Stathmin, a gene enriched in the amygdala, controls both learned and innate fear. *Cell*, *123*, 697–709.

Shweder, R. A., & Sullivan, M. A. (1990). The semiotic subject of cultural psychology. In L. A. Pervin (Ed.), *Handbook of Personality* (pp. 399–416). New York: Guilford Press.

Shweder, R. A., & Sullivan, M. A. (1993). Cultural psychology: Who needs it? *Annual Review of Psychology*, *44*, 497–523.

Siegel, P., & Weinberger, J. (2009). Very brief exposure: The effects of unreportable stimuli fearful behavior. *Consciousness and Cognition*, *18*, 939–951.

Sigel, I. E. (1981). Social experience in the development of representational thought: Distancing theory. In I. E. Sigel, D. Brodzinsky, & R. Golinkoff (Eds.), *New directions in Piagetian theory and practice* (pp. 203–217). Hillsdale, NJ: Erlbaum.

Silverman, L. H. (1976). Psychoanalytic theory: The reports of its death are greatly exaggerated. *American Psychologist*, *31*, 621–637.

Silverman, L. H. (1982). A comment on two subliminal psychodynamic activation studies. *Journal of Abnormal Psychology*, *91*, 126–130.

Silverman, L. H., Ross, D. L., Adler, J. M., & Lustig, D. A. (1978). Simple research paradigm for demonstrating subliminal psychodynamic activation: Effects of Oedipal stimuli on dart-throwing accuracy in college men. *Journal of Abnormal Psychology*, *87*, 341–357.

Simpson, B., Large, B., & O'brien, M. (2004). Bridging difference through dialogue: A constructivist perspective. *Journal of Constructivist Psychology*, *17*, 45–59.

Singh, J. K., Misra, G., & De Raad, B. (2013). Personality structure in the trait lexicon of Hindi, a major language spoken in India. *European Journal of Personality*, *27*, 605–620.

Skinner, B. F. (1948). *Walden two*. New York: Macmillan.

Skinner, B. F. (1953). *Science and human behavior*. New York: Macmillan.

Skinner, B. F. (1959). *Cumulative record*. New York: Appleton-Century-Crofts.

Skinner, B. F. (1967). Autobiography. In E. G. Boring & G. Lindzey (Eds.), *A history of psychology in autobiography* (pp. 385–414).

Skinner, B. F. (1971). *Beyond freedom and dignity*. New York: Knopf.

Skinner, B. F. (1974). *About behaviorism*. New York: Knopf.

Smith, C. A., & Lazarus, R. S. (1990). Emotion and adaptation. In L. A. Pervin (Ed.), *Handbook of personality: Theory and research* (pp. 609–637). New York: Guilford Press.

Smith, D. (October, 2002). The theory heard 'round the world: Albert Bandura's social cognitive theory is the foundation of television and radio shows that have changed the lives of millions. *APA Monitor on Psychology, 33.*

Smith, D. (January, 2003). Five principles for research ethics: Cover your bases with these ethical strategies. *Monitor on Psychology, 34,* 56.

Smith, E. R. (1998). Mental representations and memory. In D. T. Gilbert, S. T. Fiske, & G. Lindzey (Eds.), *The handbook of social psychology* (4th ed., Vol. 1, pp. 391–445). Boston: McGraw-Hill.

Smith, R. E. (1989). Effects of coping skills training on generalized self-efficacy and locus of control. *Journal of Personality and Social Psychology, 56,* 228–233.

Solms M. (2000). Dreaming and REM sleep are controlled by different brain mechanisms. *Behavioral and Brain Sciences, 23,* 843–850.

Solms, M. (2013). The conscious id. *Neuropsychoanalysis, 15,* 5–19.

Solms, M. Retrieved from https://www.futurelearn.com/courses/what-is-a-mind/0/steps/9266.

Solomon, S., Greenberg, J., & Pyszczynski, T. (2004). The cultural animal: Twenty years of terror management theory and research. In J. Greenberg, S. L. Koole & T. Psyzczynski (Eds.), *Handbook of experimental existential psychology* (pp. 13–34). New York: Guilford Press.

Sotomayor, S. (2013). *My beloved world.* New York: Knopf.

Specht, J. (2017) (Ed.). *Personality development across the lifespan.* London: Academic Press.

Spencer, S. J., Steele, C. M., & Quinn, D. M. (1999). Stereotype threat and women's math performance. *Journal of Experimental Social Psychology, 35,* 4–28.

Sperling, M. B., & Berman, W. H. (Eds.). (1994). *Attachment in adults: Clinical and developmental perspectives.* New York: Guilford Press.

Sporns, O. (2011). *Networks of the brain.* Cambridge, MA: MIT Press.

Srivastava, S., John, O. P., Gosling, S. D., & Potter, J. (2003). Development of personality in early and middle adulthood: Set like plaster or persistent change? *Journal of Personality and Social Psychology, 84,* 1041–1053.

Staddon, J. E. R., & Cerutti, D. T. (2003). Operant conditioning. *Annual Review of Psychology, 54,* 115–144.

Stajkovic, A. D., & Luthans, F. (1998). Self-efficacy and work-related performance: A meta-analysis. *Psychological Bulletin, 124,* 240–261.

ST. Clair, M. (1986). *Object relations and self psychology: An introduction.* Monterey, CA: Brooks Cole.

Steele, C. M. (1997). A threat in the air: How stereotypes shape intellectual identity and performance. *American Psychologist, 52,* 613–629.

Steiner. J. F. (1966). *Treblinka.* New York: Simon & Schuster.

Stephens, N. M., Markus, H. R., & Phillips, L. T. (2014). Social class culture cycles: How three gateway contexts shape selves and fuel inequality. *Annual Review of Psychology, 65,* 611–634.

Stephenson, W. (1953). *The study of behavior.* Chicago: University of Chicago Press.

Stock, J., & Cervone, D. (1990). Proximal goal-setting and self-regulatory processes. *Cognitive Therapy and Research, 14,* 483–498.

Stone, V. E., Cosmides, L., Tooby, J., Kroll, N., & Knight, R. T. (2002). Selective impairment of reasoning about social exchange in a patient with bilateral limbic system damage. *Processing of the National Academy of Sciences, 99,* 11531–11536.

Strauman, T. J. (1989). Self-discrepancies in clinical depression and social phobia: Cognitive structures that underlie emotional disorders? *Journal of Abnormal Psychology, 98,* 14–22.

Strauman, T. J. (1990). Self-guides and emotionally significant childhood memories: A study of retrieval efficiency and incidental negative emotional content. *Journal of Personality and Social Psychology, 59,* 869–880.

Strauman, T. J., Kolden, G. G., Stromquist, V., Davis, N., Kwapil, L., Heerey, E., & Schneider, K. (2001). The effects of treatments for depression on perceived failure in self-regulation. *Cognitive Therapy and Research, 25,* 693–712.

Strauman, T. J., Lemieux, A. M., & Coe, C. L. (1993). Self-discrepancy and natural killer cell activity: Immunological consequences of negative self-evaluation. *Journal of Personality and Social Psychology, 64*, 1042–1052.

Strelau, J. (1997). The contribution of Pavlov's typology of CNS properties to personality research. *European Psychologist, 2*, 125–138.

Strelau, J. (1998). *Temperament: A psychological perspective*. New York: Plenum Press.

Suedfeld, P., & Tetlock, P. E. (Eds.). (1991). *Psychology and social policy*. New York: Hemisphere.

Sugiyama, L. S., Tooby, J., & Cosmides, L. (2002). Cross-cultural evidence of cognitive adaptations for social exchange among the Shiwiar of Ecuadorian Amazonia. *Processing of the National Academy of Sciences, 99*, 11537–11542.

Suh, E., Diener, E., Oishi, S., & Triandis, H. C. (1998). The shifting basis of life satisfaction judgments across cultures: Emotions versus norms. *Journal of Personality and Social Psychology, 74*, 482–493.

Sullivan, H. S. (1953). *The interpersonal theory of psychiatry*. New York: Norton.

Sulloway, F. J. (1979). *Freud: Biologist of the mind*. New York: Basic Books.

Sulloway, F. J. (1991). Reassessing Freud's case histories. *ISIS, 82*, 245–275.

Sulloway, F. J. (1996). *Born to rebel: Birth order, family dynamics, and creative lives*. New York: Pantheon.

Suomi, S. (1999, June). Jumpy monkeys. Address presented at the annual meeting of the American Psychological Association, Denver, CO.

Swann, W. B., Jr. (1991). To be adored or to be known? The interplay of self-enhancement and self-verification. In E. T. Higgins & R. M. Sorrentino (Eds.), *Handbook of motivation and cognition* (pp. 408–450). New York: Guilford Press.

Swann, W. B., Jr. (1992). Seeking "truth," finding despair: Some unhappy consequences of a negative self-concept. *Current Directions in Psychological Science, 1*, 15–18.

Swann, W. B., Jr. (2012). Self-verification theory. In P. A. M. van Lange, A. Kruglanski, & E. T. Higgins (Eds.), *Handbook of theories of social psychology* (Vol. 2, pp. 23–43). Washington, DC: Sage.

Swann, W. B., Jr., & Bosson, J. K. (2008). Identity negotiation: A theory of self and social interaction. In O. P. John, R. W. Robins, & L. A. Pervin (Eds.), *Handbook of personality: Theory and research* (pp. 448–471). New York: Guilford Press.

Swann, W. B., Jr., De La Ronde, C., & Hixon, J. G. (1994). Authenticity and positivity strivings in marriage and courtship. *Journal of Personality and Social Psychology, 66*, 857–869.

Swann, W. B., Jr., Griffin, J. J., Jr., Predmore, S. C., & Gaines, B. (1987). The cognitive-affective crossfire: When self-consistency confronts self-enhancement. *Journal of Personality and Social Psychology, 52*, 881–889.

Swann, W. B., Jr., Rentfrow, P. J., & Guinn, J. S. (2003). Self-verification: The search for coherence. In M. R. Leary & J. P. Tangney (Eds.), *Handbook of self and identity* (pp. 367–383). New York: Guilford Press.

Tamir, M., John, O. P., Srivastava, S., & Gross, J. J. (2007). Implicit theories of emotion: Affective and social outcomes across a major life transition. *Journal of Personality and Social Psychology, 92*, 731–744.

Tang, T. Z., & De Rubeis, R. J. (1999a). Reconsidering rapid early response in cognitive behavioral therapy for depression. *Clinical Psychology: Science and Practice, 6*, 283–288.

Tang, T. Z., & De Rubeis, R. J. (1999b). Sudden gains and critical sessions in cognitive-behavioral therapy for depression. *Journal of Consulting and Clinical Psychology, 67*, 894–904.

Tauber, A. I. (2010). *Freud: The reluctant philosopher*. Princeton, NJ: Princeton University Press.

Tausczik, Y. R., & Pennebaker, J. W. (2010). The psychological meaning of words: LIWC and computerized text analysis methods. *Journal of Language and Social Psychology, 29*, 24–54.

Taylor, S. E., & Brown, J. D. (1994). Positive illusions and well-being revisited: Separating fact from fiction. *Psychological Bulletin, 116*, 21–27.

Taylor, S. E., Kemeny, M. E., Reed, G. M., Bower, J. E., & Gruenwald, T. L. (2000). Psychological resources, positive illusions, and health. *American Psychologist, 55*, 99–109.

Tellegen, A. (1985). Structures of mood and personality and their relevance to assessing anxiety, with an emphasis on self-report. In A. H. Tuma & J. D. Maser (Eds.), *Anxiety and the anxiety disorders* (pp. 681–706). Mahwah, NJ: Erlbaum.

Tellegen, A., & Waller, N. G. (2008). Exploring personality through test construction: Development of the Multidimensional Personality Questionnaire. In G. J. Boyle, G. Matthews, & D. H. Saklofske (Eds.), *The Sage handbook of personality theory and assessment: Vol. II. Personality measurement and testing* (pp. 261–292). London: Sage.

Temoshok, L. (1985). The relationship of psychosocial factors to prognostic indicators in cutaneous malignant melanoma. *Journal of Psychosomatic Research, 29*, 139–153.

Temoshok, L. (1991). Assessing the assessment of psychosocial factors. *Psychological Inquiry, 2*, 276–280.

Tesser, A. (1993). The importance of heritability in psychological research: The case of attitudes. *Psychological Review, 100*, 129–142.

Tesser, A., Pilkington, C. J., & Mcintosh, W. D. (1989). Self-evaluation maintenance and the mediational role of emotion: The perception of friends and strangers. *Journal of Personality and Social Psychology, 57*, 442–456.

Tetlock, P. E., Peterson, R. S., & Berry, J. M. (1993). Flattering and unflattering personality portraits of integratively simple and complex managers. *Journal of Personality and Social Psychology, 64*, 500–511.

Thomas, A., & Chess, S. (1977). *Temperament and development*. New York: Brunner/Mazel.

Tillema, J., Cervone, D., & Scott, W. D. (2001). Dysphoric mood, perceived self-efficacy, and personal standards for performance: The effects of attributional cues on self-defeating patterns of cognition. *Cognitive Therapy and Research, 25*, 535–549.

Times Higher Education. Retrieved from http://www.timeshighereducation.co.uk/story.asp?storyCode5405956&sectioncode526

Tobacyk, J. J., & Downs, A. (1986). Personal construct threat and irrational beliefs as cognitive predictors of increases in musical performance anxiety. *Journal of Personality and Social Psychology, 51*, 779–782.

Tononi, G., & Edelman, G. M. (1998). Consciousness and complexity. *Science, 282*, 1846–1851.

Tooby, J., & Cosmides, L. (1992). The psychological foundations of culture. In J. H. Barkow, L. Cosmides, & J. Tooby (Eds.), *The adapted mind: Evolutionary psychology and the generation of culture*. New York: Oxford University Press.

Toulmin, S. E. (1961). *Foresight and understanding: An inquiry into the aims of science*. Bloomington: Indiana University Press/London.

Triandis, H. (1995). *Individualism and collectivism*. Boulder, CO: Westview Press.

Trivers, R. (1972). Parental investment and sexual selection. In B. Campbell (Ed.), *Sexual selection and the descent of man: 1871–1971* (pp. 136–179). Chicago: Aldine.

Tugade, M. M., & Fredrickson, B. L. (2004). Resilient individuals use positive emotions to bounce back from negative emotional experiences. *Journal of Personality and Social Psychology, 86*, 320–333.

Tupes, E. C., & Christal, R. C. (1992). Recurrent personality factors based on trait ratings. *Journal of Personality, 60*, 225–251.

Turkheimer, E. (2006). Using genetics to understand human behavior: Promises and risks. In E. Parens, A. R. Chapman, & N. Press (Eds.), *Wrestling with behavior genetics: Science, ethics, and public conversation* (pp. 242–250). Baltimore: Johns Hopkins University Press.

Turner, M. S., Cipolotti, L., Yousry, T. A., & Shallice, T. (2008). Confabulation: Damage to a specific inferior medial prefrontal system. *Cortex, 44*, 637–648.

Tversky, A., & Kahneman, D. (1974). Judgment under uncertainty: Heuristics and biases. *Science, 185*, 1124–1131.

Twenge, J. (2002). Birth cohort, social change, and personality: The interplay of dysphoria and individualism in the 20th century. In D. Cervone & W. Mischel (Eds.), *Advances in personality science* (pp. 196–218). New York: Guilford Press.

Uher, J. (2013). Personality psychology: Lexical approaches, assessment methods, and trait concepts reveal only half of the story—why it is time for a paradigm shift. *Integrative Psychological and Behavioral Science, 47*, 1–55.

Ulmer, S., & Jansen, O. (Eds.). (2010). *fMRI: Basics and clinical applications*. Berlin: Springer-Verlag.

United Nations Population Fund (2002). *State of World Population 2002: People, Poverty, and Possibilities*. New York: United Nations.

Valchev, V. H., Nel, J. A., Van de Vijver, F. J. R., Meiring, D., De Bruin, G. P., & Rothmann, S. (2013). Similarities and differences in implicit personality concepts across ethnocultural groups in South Africa. *Journal of Cross-Cultural Psychology*, *44*, 3, 365–388.

van de Vijver, F. J. R., & He, J. (2017). Equivalence in research on positive development of minority children: Methodological approaches. *Handbook on Positive Development of Minority Children and Youth* (pp. 53–66).

Van Der Linden, D., Tsaousis, I., & Petrides, K. V. (2012). Overlap between general factors of personality in the Big Five, Giant Three, and trait emotional intelligence. *Personality and Individual Differences*, *53*, 175–179.

Van Ijzendoorn, M. H., & Kroonenberg, P. (1988). Cross-cultural patterns of attachment: A meta analysis of the strange situation. *Child Development*, *59*, 147–156.

Vaughn, P. W., Rogers, E. M., Singhal, A., & Swalehe, R. M. (2000). Entertainment-education and HIV/ AIDS prevention: A field study in Tanzania. *Journal of Health Communication*, *5* (Suppl.), 81–200.

Vazire, S. (2010). Who knows what about a person? The self–other knowledge asymmetry (SOKA) model. *Journal of Personality and Social Psychology*, *98*, 281–300.

Voon, V., Brezing, C., Gallea, C., Amerlii, R., Roelofs, K., LaFrance, W. C., Jr., & Hallett, M. (2010). Emotional stimuli and motor conversion disorder. *Brain*, *133*, 1526–1536.

Voon, V., Brezing, C., Gallea, C., & Hallett, M. (2011). Aberrant supplementary motor complex and limbic activity during motor preparation in motor conversion disorder. *Movement Disorders*, *26*, 2396–2403.

Walker, B. M., & Winter, D. A. (2007). The elaboration of personal construct psychology. *Annual Review of Psychology*, *58*, 453–477.

Waller, N. G., & Shaver, P. R. (1994). The importance of nongenetic influences on romantic love styles. *Psychological Science*, *5*, 268–274.

Walters, R. H., & Parke, R. D. (1964). Influence of the response consequences to a social model on resistance to deviation. *Journal of Experimental Child Psychology*, *1*, 269–280.

Watson, D. (2000). *Mood and temperament*. New York: Guilford Press.

Watson, D., & Clark, L. A. (1997). Extraversion and its positive emotional core. In R. Hogan, J. Johnson, & S. Briggs (Eds.), *Handbook of personality psychology* (pp. 681–710). San Diego, CA: Academic Press.

Watson, D., & Tellegen, A. (1999). Issues in the dimensional structure of affect-effects of descriptors, measurement error, and response formats: Comment on Russell and Carroll. *Psychological Bulletin*, *125*, 601–610.

Watson, D., Wiese, D., Vaidya, J., & Tellegen, A. (1999). The two general activation systems of affect: Structural findings, evolutionary considerations, and psychobiological evidence. *Journal of Personality and Social Psychology*, *76*, 820–838.

Watson, J. B. (1913). Psychology as the behaviorist views it. *Psychological Review*, *20*, 158–177.

Watson, J. B. (1914). *Behavior*. New York: Holt, Rinehart, & Winston.

Watson, J. B. (1919). *Psychology from the standpoint of a behaviorist*. Philadelphia: Lippincott.

Watson, J. B. (1924). *Behaviorism*. New York: People's Institute Publishing.

Watson, J. B. (1936). Autobiography. In C. Murchison (Ed.), *A history of psychology in autobiography* (pp. 271–282). Worcester, MA: Clark University Press.

Watson, J. B., & Rayner, R. (1920). Conditioned emotional reactions. *Journal of Experimental Psychology*, *3*, 1–14.

Watson, M. W., & Getz, K. (1990). The relationship between Oedipal behaviors and children's family role concepts. *Merrill-Palmer Quarterly*, *36*, 487–506.

Watson, R. I. (1963). *The great psychologists: From Aristotle to Freud*. Philadelphia: Lippincott.

Weber, S. J., & Cook, T. D. (1972). Subject effects in laboratory research: An examination of subject roles, demand characteristics, and valid inference. *Psychological Bulletin*, *77*, 273–295.

Wegner, D. M. (1992). You can't always think what you want: Problems in the suppression of unwanted thoughts. *Advances in Experimental Social Psychology*, *25*, 193–225.

Wegner, D. M. (1994). Ironic processes of mental control. *Psychological Review*, *101*, 34–52.

Wegner, D. (2003). The mind's best trick: How we experience conscious will. *Trends in Cognitive Science*, *7*, 65–69.

Wegner, D. M., Shortt, G. W., Blake, A. W., & Page, M. S. (1990). The suppression of exciting thoughts. *Journal of Personality and Social Psychology, 58*, 409–418.

Weinberger, D. A. (1990). The construct reality of the repressive coping style. In J. L. Singer (Ed.), *Repression and dissociation: Implications for personality, psychopathology, and health* (pp. 337–386). Chicago: University of Chicago Press.

Weinberger, J. (1992). Validating and demystifying subliminal psychodynamic activation. In R. F. Bornstein & T. S. Pittman (Eds.), *Perception without awareness* (pp. 170–188). New York: Guilford Press.

Weinberger, J., & Westen, D. (2008). RATS, we should have used Clinton: Subliminal priming in political campaigns. *Political Psychology, 29*, 631–651.

Weinstein, T. A. R., Capitanio, J. P., & Gosling, S. D. (2008). Personality in animals. In O. P. John, R. W. Robins, & L. A. Pervin (Eds.), *Handbook of personality: Theory and research* (pp. 328–348). New York: Guilford Press.

Weitlauf, J., Cervone, D., & Smith, R. E. (2001). Assessing generalization in perceived self-efficacy: Multidomain and global assessments of the effects of self-defense training for women. *Personality and Social Psychology Bulletin, 27*, 1683–1691.

West, S. G., & Finch, J. F. (1997). Personality measurement: Reliability and validity issues. In R. Hogan, J. Johnson, & S. Briggs (Eds.), *Handbook of personality psychology* (pp. 143–165). San Diego, CA: Academic Press.

Westen, D. (1990). Psychoanalytic approaches to personality. In L. A. Pervin (Ed.), *Handbook of personality: Theory and research* (pp. 21–65). New York: Guilford Press.

Westen, D. (1991). Clinical assessment of object relations using the TAT. *Journal of Personality Assessment, 56*, 56–74.

Westen, D., Blagov, P. S., Harenski, K., Kilts, C., & Hamann, S. (2006). Neural bases of motivated reasoning: An fMRI study of emotional constraints on partisan political judgments in the 2004 U.S. presidential election. *Journal of Cognitive Neuroscience, 18*, 1947–1958.

Westen, D., & Gabbard, G. O. (1999). Psychoanalytic approaches to personality. In L. A. Pervin & O. P. John (Eds.), *Handbook of personality: Theory and research* (pp. 57–101). New York: Guilford Press.

Westen, D., Gabbard, G. O., & Ortigo, K. M. (2008). Psychoanalytic approaches to personality. In O. P. John, R. W. Robins, & L. A. Pervin (Eds.), *Handbook of personality: Theory and research* (pp. 61–113). New York: Guilford Press.

White, P. (1980). Limitations of verbal reports of internal events: A refutation of Nisbett and Wilson and of Bem. *Psychological Review, 87*, 105–112.

Widiger, T. A., & Costa, P. T., Jr. (2013). *Personality disorders and the five-factor model of personality* (3rd ed.). Washington, DC: American Psychological Association.

Widiger, T. A., & Smith, G. T. (2008). Personality and psychopathology. In O. P. John, R. W. Robins, & L. A. Pervin (Eds.), *Handbook of personality: Theory and research* (pp. 743–769). New York: Guilford Press.

Wiedenfeld, S. A., Bandura, A., Levine, S., O'Leary, A., Brown, S., & Raska, K. (1990). Impact of perceived self-efficacy in coping with stressors in components of the immune system. *Journal of Personality and Social Psychology, 59*, 1082–1094.

Wiggins, J. S. (1984). Cattell's system from the perspective of mainstream personality theory. *Multi-variate Behavioral Research, 19*, 176–190.

Williams, L. (1994). Recall of childhood trauma: A prospective study of women's memories of child sexual abuse. *Journal of Consulting and Clinical Psychology, 62*, 1167–1176.

Williams, S. L. (1992). Perceived self-efficacy and phobic disability. In R. Schwarzer (Ed.), *Self-efficacy: Thought control of action* (pp. 149–176). Washington, DC: Hemisphere.

Wilson, T. D. (1994). The proper protocol: Validity and completeness of verbal reports. *Psychological Science, 5*, 249–252.

Wilson, T. D., Hull, J. G., & Johnson, J. (1981). Awareness and self-perception: Verbal reports on internal states. *Journal of Personality and Social Psychology, 40*, 53–71.

Winter, D. A., & Viney, L. L. (2005). *Personal construct psychotherapy: Advances in theory, practice, and research.* London: Whurr.

Winter, D. G. (1992). Content analysis of archival productions, personal documents, and everyday verbal productions. In C. P. Smith (Ed.), *Motivation and personality: Handbook of thematic content analysis* (pp. 110–125). Cambridge, UK: Cambridge University Press.

Wise, J. B. (2007). Testing a theory that explains how self-efficacy beliefs are formed: Predicting self-efficacy appraisals across recreation activities. *Journal of Social and Clinical Psychology, 26,* 829–836.

Wise, J. B. (2009). Using the knowledge-and-appraisal personality architecture to predict physically active leisure self-efficacy in university students. *Journal of Applied Social Psychology, 39,* 1913–1927.

Wise, R. A. (1996). Addictive drugs and brain stimulation reward. *Annual Review of Neuroscience, 19,* 319–340.

Wittgenstein, L. (1980). *Remarks on the philosophy of psychology.* (Vol. 1). Chicago: The University of Chicago Press.

Woike, B., & Polo, M. (2001). Motive-related memories: Content, structure, and affect. *Journal of Personality, 69,* 391–415.

Wolpe, J. (1961). The systematic desensitization treatment of neuroses. *Journal of Nervous and Mental Disorders, 132,* 189–203.

Wolpe, J., & Rachman, S. (1960). Psychoanalytic "evidence." A critique based on Freud's case of Little Hans. *Journal of Nervous and Mental Disease, 130,* 135–148.

Wood, J. V. (1989). Theory and research concerning social comparison of personal attributes. *Psychological Bulletin, 106,* 231–248.

Wood, J. V., Saltzberg, J. A., & Goldsamt, L. A. (1990). Does affect induce self-focused attention? *Journal of Personality and Social Psychology, 58,* 899–908.

Wood, W., & Eagly, A. H. (2002). A cross-cultural analysis of the behavior of women and men: Implications for the origins of sex differences. *Psychological Bulletin, 128,* 699–727.

Woodward, S. A., Lenzenweger, M. F., Kagan, J., Snidman, N., & Arcus, D. (2000). Taxonic structure of infant reactivity: Evidence from a taxometric perspective. *Psychological Science. 11,* 296–301.

Woodworth, R. S. (1917). *Personal data sheet.* Chicago, IL: Stoelting.

Wrzesniewski, A., & Schwartz, B. (2014). The secret of effective motivation. *The New York Times,* July 6, p. SR9.

Wrzesniewski, A., Schwartz, B., Cong, X., Kane, M., Omar, A., & Kolditz, T. (2014). Multiple types of motives don't multiply the motivation of West Point cadets. *Proceedings of the National Academy of Sciences,* in press.

Zhu, Y., Zhang, L., Fan, J., & Han, S. (2007): Neural basis of cultural influence on self-representation. *Neuroimage, 34,* 1310–1316.

Zimbardo, P. G. (1973). On the ethics of intervention in human psychological research: With special reference to the Stanford prison experiment. *Cognition, 2,* 243–256.

Zuckerman, M. (1991). *Psychobiology of personality.* New York: Cambridge University Press.

Zuckerman, M. (1995). Good and bad humors: Biochemical bases of personality and its disorders. *Psychological Science, 6,* 325–332.

Zuckerman, M. (1996). The psychobiological model for impulsive unsocialized sensation seeking: A comparative approach. *Neuropsychobiology, 34,* 125–129.

Zuroff, D. C. (1986). Was Gordon Allport a trait theorist? *Journal of Personality and Social Psychology, 51,* 993–1000.

AUTHOR INDEX

SUBJECT INDEX